International Handbook on Privatization

Edited by

David Parker

Chair of Business Economics and Strategy, Aston Business School, Aston University, UK and Co-Director of the Regulation Research Programme, Centre on Regulation and Competition, University of Manchester, UK

and

David Saal

Lecturer in Industrial Economics, Aston Business School, Aston University, UK

Edward Elgar
Cheltenham, UK • Northampton, MA, USA

Published by
Edward Elgar Publishing Limited
Glensanda House
Montpellier Parade
Cheltenham
Glos GL50 1UA
UK

Edward Elgar Publishing, Inc.
136 West Street
Suite 202
Northampton
Massachusetts 01060
USA

A catalogue record for this book
is available from the British Library

Library of Congress Cataloguing in Publication Data

Parker, David, 1949 Sept. 28–
    International handbook on privatization / David Parker, David Saal.
        p. cm.
    Includes bibliographical references.
    1. Privatization. I. Saal, David S. II. Title.

HD3845.6.P37 2003
338.9′25–dc21

2003046363

ISBN 1 84064 613 6 (cased)

Printed and Bound in Great Britain by MPG Books Ltd, Bodmin, Cornwall

Contents

Tables

Figures

Preface

Privatization as public policy and industrial restructuring is now well established in many parts of the world. This handbook is intended to provide a comprehensive source for policy makers, managers and students keen to understand privatization theory, the privatization process and its content, and to learn lessons from the privatization experiences of countries in the developed and developing worlds and the transition economies of Central and Eastern Europe.

In putting together this book we have been assisted by a number of people, including the editorial and publication staff at Edward Elgar, the staff of the library at Aston University, and especially Liz Blackford who has, always cheerfully and with great patience, typed and retyped the various drafts. We thank them all. We also thank our families for their support over a number of months. We dedicate the book to all those who share with us an interest in the subject of privatization.

David Parker
David Saal
Aston University, August 2002

Contributors

Werner Baer is Professor of Economics at the University of Illinois at Urbana-Champaign, USA. He has written extensively on Latin American Economic Development. The fifth edition of his book *The Brazilian Economy* was published by Praeger in 2002.

Maciej Baltowski is Professor of Economics and Chair of the Department of Industrial Organisation at the Technical University, Lublin, Poland. He is author and co-author of four books on privatization in Poland.

Paul Bennell is an independent consultant specializing in human resources development in sub-Saharan Africa. He has also undertaken extensive research on foreign investment, industrial policy and privatization in Africa.

Anthony E. Boardman is Van Dusen Professor of Business Management in the Strategy and Business Economics Division at the University of British Columbia, Canada, and an expert on the comparative performance of public and private enterprise.

Dieter Bös is Professor of Economics at the University of Bonn. He has been managing editor of the *Journal of Economics* (Zeitschrift für Nationalökonomie) since 1973. He has published many books and papers in refereed journals, mainly on regulation and privatization, on taxation and on public procurement.

Joseph C.H. Chai is Associate Professor at the University of Queensland, Australia. He has published extensively on the Chinese economy. His latest books include *China: Transition To a Market Economy*, *Industrial Reform and Macroeconomic Instability in China* (Clarendon Press, 1998, 1999) and *The Economic Development of Modern China* (Edward Elgar, 2000).

Paul Cook is Professor of Economics and Development Policy in the Institute for Development Policy and Management (IDPM) at the University of Manchester, UK. He is the Director of the Department for International Development (DFID) funded Centre on Regulation and Competition in the Institute. He has previously held teaching positions in universities in Canada and the United States, and has published widely in the areas of privatization and public enterprise reform and development policy.

Michael A. Crew is Professor of Economics and Director of the Center for Research in Regulated Industries, Rutgers University in the USA and editor of the *Journal of Regulatory Economics*. He has published five books, 20 edited books and numerous articles in journals.

Saul Estrin is a Professor of Economics at the London Business School and the Research Director of its Centre for New and Emerging Markets. He researches on privatization in transition economies.

Igor Filatotchev received his PhD in Economics from the Institute of World Economy and International Relations, Moscow, in 1985. Since 2002 he has been Professor of Strategic Management at the University of Bradford School of Management. He has published extensively in the fields of corporate governance and strategy, as well as in various international business areas.

Cosmo Graham is a Professor of Law at the University of Leicester, UK. He is a public lawyer who specializes in the law relating to the regulation of public utilities. His other main specialism is in competition law and he has teaching interests in company law. He is the Director of the Centre for Utility Consumer Law and a member of the UK's Competition Commission.

Paul Hare is Professor of Economics in the School of Management, Heriot-Watt University, Edinburgh. Professor Hare founded the research centre, CERT (Centre for Economic Reform and Transformation) at Heriot-Watt University and directed it from 1990 to 1997. Since then he has been Head of School before becoming Director of Research in the School. His research concentrates on transition economies, with recent work including studies of institutional change, trade policy and industrial restructuring.

Graeme A. Hodge is Professor of Law and Director of the Privatization and Public Accountability Centre at Monash University in Australia. He is an advisor to Australasian governments and has written books and articles on privatization, contracting out and management.

Colin Kirkpatrick is Professor of Development Economics and Director of the Institute for Development Policy and Management (IDPM) at the University of Manchester, UK. He has published extensively in the field of impact assessment of public policy and decision making. His earlier research work focused on the impact of privatization on economic performance in the context of developing countries. He is currently researching on issues of regulatory impact assessment and the utilities sector in lower-income countries. Professor Kirkpatrick is Co-Director of the Regulation Programme at the IDPM's Centre on Regulation and Competition.

Paul R. Kleindorfer is the Universal Furniture Professor of Decision Sciences and Economics and Professor of Business and Public Policy at the Wharton School of the University of Pennsylvania, USA.

Claude Laurin is Associate Professor at l'Ecole des HEC in Montreal, Canada. His research interests and publications lie primarily in the areas of privatization, performance measurement and corporate governance.

Iván Major chairs the Department of Economics at the University of Veszprém and is Senior Fellow at the Institute of Economics of the Hungarian Academy of Sciences.

William L. Megginson is Professor and Rainbolt Chair in Finance at the University of Oklahoma, USA. He is also a member of the Global Advisory Committee on Privatization in Italy and has published privatization-related articles in several top academic journals.

Michal Mejstřík is Professor of Corporate Finance and Banking at Charles University, Prague. He has published over 50 contributions on privatization and corporate governance in Central and Eastern Europe, including the co-authored book, *The Privatization Process in East–Central Europe: Evolutionary Process of Czech Privatization* (Kluwer, 1997).

Tomasz Mickiewicz works at University College, London, School of Slavonic and East European Studies, UK, and is Director of the Centre for the Study of Economic and Social Change in Europe. He publishes on privatization, corporate governance and employment.

Alexander Muravyev is Lecturer in Economics at the School of Management, St Petersburg State University, Russia. He also works for the Russian–European Centre for Economic Policy based in Moscow, a policy research and advice centre funded by the EU-TACIS Programme. His main research area is privatization and corporate governance in transition economies, a field in which he has already carried out empirical studies and published a number of papers.

Jeffry M. Netter is Professor of Finance at the University of Georgia. His research and teaching is in corporate governance and government regulation. He has published in leading finance, law and economics journals.

Anthony Ogus is Professor of Law at the University of Manchester, UK, and Research Fellow at the University's Centre on Regulation and Competition. He is also Research Professor at Maastricht University and has written books and articles on regulation and the economic analysis of law.

David Parker is Professor of Business Economics and Strategy at Aston Business School, Aston University, UK, and Co-Director of the Regulation Programme at the Centre on Regulation and Competition in the Institute for Development Policy and Management (IDPM) at the University of Manchester, UK. He has written extensively on privatization and economic regulation and is a member of the UK's Competition Commission and an Economic Advisor to the Office of Utilities Regulation in Jamaica.

Miguel D. Ramírez is Professor of Economics at Trinity College in Hartford, CT, USA. His research is primarily dedicated to analysing the challenges and opportunities that Latin American nations face as they attempt to stabilize and reform their economies.

Colin Robinson is Professor of Economics at the University of Surrey and Editorial Director of the Institute of Economic Affairs. His research is mainly in energy economics and regulation.

Adam Rosevear graduated from London Business School with a doctorate on enterprise restructuring in Ukraine. Adam has also been involved in a number of consultancy projects in the former Soviet Union and Eastern Europe.

David Saal is Lecturer in Industrial Economics at Aston Business School, Aston University, UK. His research focuses on the impact of public policy on industrial performance, including work on the impact of utility privatization and regulation on productivity growth, as well as analysis of the impact of defence procurement policies on manufacturing performance.

Erwin Schwella is Professor and Director of the School of Public Management at the University of Stellenbosch in South Africa. He is a senior consultant to governments in and outside South Africa. He has published widely in academic journals and is co-author of a number of well-known academic textbooks. Currently his main academic and professional interests are in the fields of leadership and change management in the context of transformation. He is listed in *Who's Who in the World* as an international leader in his fields of endeavour.

Aidan R. Vining is the CNABS Professor of Business and Government Relations in the Faculty of Business Administration, Simon Fraser University, Vancouver, BC, Canada. He has published extensively in public policy and policy analysis. Recent articles have appeared in the *Journal of Policy Analysis and Management*, the *Journal of Risk and Insurance*, *Public Administration Review* and *Social Science and Medicine*, among others. He is the co-author of *Policy Analysis: Concepts and Practice* (Prentice-Hall, 1999) and *Cost–Benefit Analysis: Concepts and Practice* (Prentice-Hall, 2001).

Thomas Weyman-Jones is Professor of Industrial Economics, Loughborough University, UK. He researches incentive regulation and productivity analysis, and is a specialist advisor on network utility price controls to several European regulatory authorities.

Johan Willner has been Professor of Economics at Åbo Akademi University, Turku/Åbo, Finland since 1988. His published or forthcoming papers deal with imperfect competition, privatization and public ownership, and taxation and equality.

Acknowledgements

The publishers wish to thank the following who have kindly given permission for the use of copyright material:

Blackwell Publishers for material from I. Filatotchev, M. Wright and M. Bleaney (1999) 'Privatisation, insider control and managerial entrenchment in Russia' in *Economics of Transition*, 7, (2) 481–504.

Department of Treasury and Finance (Australia) for material from 'Victoria's Electricity Supply Industry Toward 2000' (1997), *Department of Treasury and Finance*, June.

Elsevier Science for material from Miguel Ramirez (2001) 'The Mexican Regulatory Experience in the Airline, Banking and Telecommunications Sectors' in *Quarterly Review of Economics and Finance*, 41 (5).

Oxford University Press for material from Joseph C.H. Chai (1997) *China: Transition to a Market Economy*, pp. 15–20, 169–70, 173 and 176–8.

Reserve Bank of Australia for material from 'Privatisation in Australia' (1997) *Reserve Bank of Australia Bulletin*, December.

Routledge Publishers for material from 'Privatization in the EU: An Overview', in D. Parker (ed) *Privatisation in the European Union: Theory and Policy Perspectives*, London: Routledge.

Sage Publications for material from David Parker (1999) 'Privatisation in the European Union: A Critical Assessment of its Development, Rationale and Consequences' in *Economic and Industrial Democracy, An International Journal*, 20, 9–38.

Taylor and Francis (Carfax Publishing) for article Maciej Bałtowski and Tomasz Mickiewicz (2000) 'Privatisation in Poland: Ten years after' in *Communist Economies*, 12, (4) December 425–44.

John Wiley and Sons for material from I. Filatotchev, R. Kapelyushnikov, N. Dyomina and S. Aukusionek (2001) 'The effects of ownership concentration on investment and performance in privatized firms' in Russia in *Managerial and Decision Economics*, 22, 299–313.

Every effort has been made to trace all the copyright holders but if any have been inadvertently overlooked the publishers will be pleased to make the necessary arrangements at the first opportunity.

1 Introduction
David Parker and David Saal

This handbook presents a comprehensive study of privatization and should be of interest to scholars and practitioners of the subject in the public and private sectors. In developing this book, we have attracted leading writers on privatization from across the globe. The result is a thorough summary of the rationale, methods, processes and outcomes of privatization at both the theoretical and empirical levels and for the full range of economies. The book consists of chapters on general privatization issues complemented by detailed country case studies. While it is impracticable to summarize the progress of privatization as policy in each and every nation, the country studies do provide valuable pointers to the reasons for privatization successes and failures. These studies cover the developed economies of the European Union, North America and Australia, the transition economies of Poland, Hungary, the Czech Republic, Ukraine and Russia, and the developing countries of Chile, Mexico and Brazil in Latin America and the sub-Saharan region of Africa and South Africa. China, the outstanding development success of the last 20 years, is also included.

Privatization has caught the imagination of both scholars and policy makers. The study of privatization and related subjects, such as market liberalization and the economics of regulation, are now an integral part of most undergraduate and postgraduate studies in economics and related disciplines. At the policy level governments around the world have introduced privatization programmes since the 1980s, although the results in some countries have been much more successful than in others, as a number of the chapters in this book emphasize. In the 1990s, total global privatization receipts are estimated by the OECD to have exceeded US$936.6 billion (OECD, 2001), making the planning and implementation of privatization a very profitable activity for international banks and consultancy firms. Privatizations have taken a number of forms, from outright sales of state assets, through initial public offering (IPOs) of shares, to sales to domestic and foreign companies and to various forms of operating concessions such as build–operate–transfer schemes (BOTs) and the like. The extent of continuing state involvement in the management of assets varies, with some governments more or less abdicating complete responsibility to the private sector and others retaining considerable residual control rights to protect the public interest.

1

The largest privatizations have occurred in the utilities sectors, namely in telecommunications, power, water and transport. In these sectors privatization (whether through asset disposals or concessions) has involved the transfer to the private sector of enterprises with considerable market power. Private monopoly is not attractive for all the usual reasons associated with the abuse of market power, namely high prices, lax cost control, a lack of innovation and poor customer service. For this reason, utility privatizations create the need for both the active encouragement of new competition, perhaps involving the development and maintenance of an effective competition policy regime, and continuing state regulation of the monopolist until such time as effective competition is fully developed. Where 'natural monopoly' exists, normally in the operation of distribution networks and the like with high fixed costs, competition would be uneconomic and therefore regulation will need to be permanent. This regulation can be centred in government departments but increasingly the establishment of dedicated regulatory offices or commissions at arm's length from direct political control has been favoured, to prevent continuing political intervention in the management of enterprises by the back door. Chapters 22 to 26 look specifically at the theoretical and practical issues surrounding the regulation of privatized enterprises.

Economists argue that competition in the product market is an important driver of cost reduction and product innovation. Therefore, in the absence of effective competition, or in the case of natural monopoly effective economic regulation as a surrogate for competition, ownership change may have limited benefits for economic performance (Vickers and Yarrow, 1988; de Fraja, 1993). This will be particularly true where the capital market or the market for ownership rights is underdeveloped and does not provide an effective constraint on managerial discretionary behaviour. The *principal–agent* model in economics has drawn attention to the importance for achieving economic efficiency of principals monitoring and controlling agent behaviour effectively (Jensen and Meckling, 1976; Vickers and Yarrow, 1988; Hart, 1995; Martin and Parker, 1997, ch.1). In corporate activities in both the private and state sectors it is to be expected that, in the absence of effective incentives and controls, management will pursue its own interests rather than that of its agents (owners), including the pursuit of high managerial salaries, an expense preference and a quiet life. This will be true of the private sector, where owners can be expected instead to want maximum profits or return on their investments, but equally of the state sector, where the principals (the public) desire some wider and perhaps more nebulous goal of the 'public interest' or 'social welfare'. In the latter case, the issue is complicated by the intervention of a further tier or tiers of agency between the public (voters) and agents (state enterprise managers) in the form of politicians and layers of the state bureaucracy. *Public choice theory* provides a powerful critique of the incentives and information asymmetries within the state sector (Niskanen, 1971 Mitchell, 1988; Boycko *et al.*, 1996). It points to both self-interest as a driver of decision making within government and inadequate information to pursue public interest goals efficiently, even where the pursuit of self-interest does not dominate.

Principal–agent theory, especially when coupled with the arguments from public choice theory, provides a very powerful theoretical rationale for privatization to increase economic efficiency (Parker, 2000), but arguably only where private capital markets operate efficiently to constrain agent behaviour. A discussion and critique of principal–agent theory is provided in the early chapters of this volume. For example, whereas Megginson and Netter (chapter 2) provide a generally favourable review, Willner (chapter 4) is far more critical. The country studies later in the book provide supporting evidence that effective capital markets cannot be taken for granted. This is particularly so in the transition economies where enterprises suffer from 'insider' control. The chapter by Filatotchev (chapter 16) is particularly educational in this respect. In the developing economies of Latin America, Africa and Asia, capital markets are usually thin and cannot be relied upon to police agent behaviour effectively.

While some of the contributions to this book provide differing accounts of the theoretical merits of privatization, a number of the other contributions provide more empirically oriented studies, looking at the actual impacts of privatization on both enterprises and the whole economy. Again the results are mixed: hence at both the theoretical and empirical levels the net benefits of privatization are not clear cut. Nevertheless, privatization as 'policy transfer' (Dolowitz and Marsh, 1996; Parker, 1999) continues internationally, supported by a range of international donor agencies and notably the IMF and World Bank (although in the case of the latter especially recently there have been signs of a greater recognition of the need for appropriate supporting 'institutions' than was the case earlier; see, for example, World Bank, 2001). As many of the studies in this volume indicate, successful private ownership requires supporting institutions including protected property rights, effective contract laws, supportive and efficient banks and financial markets, effective and stable government, effective pro-competition legislation, as well as developed capital markets. In a number of the economies of Central and Eastern Europe and the developing world these institutions cannot be taken for granted. Hence privatization can lead to forms of private enterprise very different to those found in the developed economies of Western Europe and North America. In particular, cronyism and corruption are rampant in some countries and mutually advantageous contracting for resources is therefore replaced by favouritism and fear (Saha and Parker, 2002).

Table 1.1 provides a country breakdown of the global amounts raised from privatization in the OECD in the 1990s alongside estimates of global privatization receipts. It is clear that the 30 largest economies which make up the OECD membership have accounted for the vast bulk of the privatizations since 1990, with 70 per cent of global receipts in value terms. Of these countries, Australia, France, Germany, Italy, Japan, Mexico, Portugal, Spain and the UK have been responsible for 50 per cent of the global total. However, value figures can be misleading as an indicator of privatization activity because they reflect only sales receipts and not necessarily the volume of production transferred. Also they can be biased by a small number of very large sales; for example, Germany's figures are heavily weighted by the sale of shares in Deutsche Telekom in 1996. In addition, the extent of privatization should be considered in relation to the size of an economy: a given figure for the total value of privatization receipts will be more economically significant the smaller the economy. In the transition countries, in particular, privatizations have accounted for a much larger share of GDP than elsewhere, involving large-scale sell-offs of tens of thousands of small and medium-sized enterprises as well as large state firms. Moreover, value figures tell us nothing about the *true* scale of privatization in the sense of removing government control or influence over industries' strategies. In some countries governments have retained influence over enterprises that nominally, at least, have been 'privatized'. This has occurred through formal 'golden shares' or the retention of a strategic minority (and sometimes majority) shareholding, government board-level appointees, sales of assets to political cronies and leading families in the country, and through 'moral suasion' and the threat of renationalization. Even in the EU, with its protected private property rights, the enthusiasm for private sector autonomy and the reliance on private enterprise has varied. As the London *Economist* concluded in a special report on privatization in Europe:

> Arguably only Britain has accepted the true retreat of the state from its biggest industries. Even there, this was done initially with caution. Golden shares were widely used, for example, to block the threat of rapid takeovers in the utilities sectors. In continental Europe, privatization has too often been a phrase that has disguised economic reality. Governments have raised money, either for their own coffers or to boost the balance sheets of state-owned companies. But they have rarely forfeited control and have remained inclined to meddle. (*Economist*, 2002: 73.)

The *Economist* report documents a number of cases where 'privatized' businesses have been subject to continued government interference. For example, it cites a study from Italy's federation of industrialists, Confindustria, which found that only around a third of the assets involved in state sell-offs were fully freed from government control, and Franco Reviglio, then chairman of

*Table 1.1   Total privatization receipts for the OECD countries in the
1990s*

	Total amount raised US$mn	Percentage of global total
OECD Countries		
Australia	69627	7.43
Austria	10436	1.11
Belgium	9611	1.03
Canada	10583	1.13
Czech Rep.	5438	0.58
Denmark	6048	0.65
Finland	11000	1.17
France	75488	8.06
Germany	22451	2.40
Greece	12329	1.32
Hungary	11530	1.23
Iceland	400	0.04
Ireland	7613	0.81
Italy	108586	11.59
Japan	37670	4.02
South Korea	14275	1.52
Luxemburg	0	0.00
Mexico	28628	3.06
Netherlands	13641	1.46
New Zealand	9413	1.00
Norway	2900	0.31
Poland	17805	1.90
Portugal	25292	2.70
Slovak Republic	1979	0.21
Spain	37645	4.02
Sweden	17295	1.85
Switzerland	10869	1.16
Turkey	7231	0.77
UK	63129	6.74
USA	6750	0.72
Total OECD	655662	70.00
Of which, EU 15	420564	44.90
Non-OECD countries	280962	30.00
Global total	936624	100.00

Source: OECD (2001: 44, Table 1).

ENI and a former finance minister, in the mid-1980s describing privatization as 'a good way to raise cash without losing control' (ibid.). Thus, while economists might concentrate upon the efficiency arguments for privatization, privatization as policy is rooted in *realpolitik* resulting in objectives from financing more public spending without unpopular tax increases, to satisfying special interest groups and paying off campaign supporters. In particular, during the 1980s and 1990s, governments around the world, and not least the Thatcher governments in the UK, found privatization a tempting means of raising cash to fund tax cuts. Nevertheless, maximizing the receipts from asset sales may not always be compatible with privatizing state industries to maximize economic efficiency because firms with market power, and therefore with the ability to earn economic rents, attract a premium price for their shares. Firms facing an effective regulatory regime or a competitive market after privatization may be much less attractive to investors.

Privatization, both in theory and in practice, is therefore complicated by a set of conditions relating to: (a) the motivation for sale – *why* is privatization favoured? (b) which industries to sell and in what order – *what* is to be privatized and *when*? (c) to whom should assets be sold – *how* should privatization be conducted? Alongside these 'why', 'what', 'when' and 'how' questions lie a series of complementary ones relating to the following:

- The institutional environment: do the institutions exist to support a thriving and efficient private sector? If not, can they be quickly created?
- The degree of competition: will the privatized firms face real competition and in what forms (for example, do tariff barriers need to be reduced or restrictive licensing conditions removed)?
- The role and nature of current state intervention in the economy: to what extent will state involvement continue and what forms will it take? This will be particularly an issue for the utilities sectors where monopoly activities need continued state regulation. But the argument could extend to defence and other 'strategic' sectors such as agriculture, as well as liberalized utility markets where regulation to preserve competition may remain a permanent necessity.

Peter Evans has written that 'exogenous inspirations . . . build on indigenous institutional foundations' (Evans, 1995: 243). Privatization programmes reflect a transfer of policy around the world reflecting mimetic influences tempered by normative interpretations based on local conditions. It should not be anticipated, therefore, that privatization transfers policy simply and neatly from country to country, leading to the same predicable improvements in economic efficiency.

Although this is not a comforting conclusion for policy makers looking for clear guidance, the chapters in this book do provide assistance in addressing the above issues. An understanding of privatization theory and practice is critical to establishing a sound appreciation of both the potential and the limitations of privatization and the need to achieve a complementary institutional context. In sum, a thorough understanding of both theory and practice is necessary if privatizations are to be appropriately designed and implemented and are not to disappoint.

A summary of the contents
It is not possible to do justice to the detailed contents of each of the chapters in this book. Each provides a rich source on the theory and/or the practice of privatization. Nevertheless, to assist the reader we provide here a brief summary of each chapter.

The first contribution, in chapter 2, is by William L. Megginson and Jeffry M. Netter, who look at both the history of privatization and its rationale and the different methods of privatization that have been adopted. They demonstrate that the trend to privatization worldwide is a reflection of the failures of the nationalization introduced after the Great Depression and the Second World War. State ownership led to inefficiencies that a range of both developed and developing economies felt the need to tackle by the 1980s. In the view of Megginson and Netter, privatization as government policy developed because of a new and more favourable attitude to markets at around this time, but also because government ownership 'did not work'. The Thatcher governments in the UK are seen as a model. On methods of privatization, Megginson and Netter summarize a number of studies that identify the circumstances under which either direct assets sales or share issues are most likely to occur. This chapter provides a solid foundation for the more specialized studies of privatization at both the theoretical and empirical levels found later in the book.

Chapter 3, by Colin Robinson, argues that privatization is not a matter of the political 'right' versus the political 'left', as often portrayed. Instead he points out that governments of all political persuasions have introduced privatization programmes and discusses why. His study complements that of Megginson and Netter by arguing that the benefits of private over state ownership lie in an acute failure at the heart of state ownership, which can be summed up in terms of the statement, 'what is owned by everyone is perceived to be owned by no one'. He also looks at the relationship between privatization and market liberalization, concluding that 'a move from state to private ownership is usually a necessary condition for significant market liberalization'. At the same time, he recognizes that not all privatizations have gone smoothly. He attributes some of the failures of privatization to the political process and conflicting policy objectives. Using the UK as the exemplar, he describes a number of problems that were left to be sorted out by the competition authorities and industry regulators. He concludes that achieving the full potential benefits from privatization requires market liberalization.

Johan Willner in chapter 4 is far more sceptical about the benefits of privatization than the authors of the two previous chapters. He criticizes the international trend to privatization for undervaluing the benefits of state ownership and argues that, both on theoretical and empirical grounds, the policy is open to challenge. He also holds some dissenting views on the benefits of market liberalization. Concentrating upon the claimed gains from privatization in terms of cost efficiency, he concludes that neither excessive costs nor biased objectives in state firms are sufficient grounds for advocating privatization. This is because state ownership may achieve superior allocative efficiency, especially when the pay-offs to different stakeholders are taken into account. Using a simple model with linear demand, he outlines the circumstances under which privatization would lead to a deterioration in allocative efficiency that could more than outweigh any cost efficiency gains. He also explains that the social welfare consequences of privatization are sensitive to the weights placed on the rents to consumers, employees and owners. Willner also cites both theoretical and empirical studies that question the possible benefits from privatization.

The various methods of privatization used internationally are discussed by Cosmo Graham in chapter 5. The chapter's aim is to provide an overview of the different methods of privatization, with some observations on the success or failure of the techniques. Countries have used varying methods reflecting in part the differing aims and speeds of privatization. These techniques, including sales to the public, voucher distribution and private sales and buy-outs, are reviewed. Graham demonstrates that there is no one ideal method of privatization and that each method has trade-offs. These trade-offs significantly affect the likely outcome, or success or failure, of a privatization programme. This chapter, read alongside the chapters by Megginson and Netter, Robinson and Willner, provides an excellent analytical foundation for the country studies that follow.

The first 'country' study is a regional survey. David Parker, in chapter 6, studies the privatization experiences of the countries that make up the EU. After a brief history of public and private ownership in each of the countries, he goes on to explain how, while there is some similarity across the various privatization programmes, the similarity is potentially misleading. EU countries have their own motives for privatization and have conducted it with differing degrees of enthusiasm. In particular, it is not the case that the motive of promoting greater economic efficiency has dominated.

Indeed, budgetary pressures, especially ahead of the introduction of the Euro, have been important in a number of instances, while the various EU market liberalization initiatives have also made it less desirable to retain industries in state hands. Parker also considers some of the potential consequences of privatization in Europe in terms not only of economic efficiency but of social welfare. He stresses that the UK's 'outsider' model of corporate governance contrasts with the 'insider' model still prevalent in much of the rest of the EU and that, in terms of social welfare, privatization is leading to possible changes in the distribution of economic power that have yet to be properly explored.

Chapter 7 deals with privatization in North America. Anthony E. Boardman, Claude Laurin and Aidan R. Vining concentrate particularly on Canada, where most of the interesting privatization activity has taken place. The United States has a much less extensive state-owned sector and this has necessarily limited the scope for privatization activity. Nevertheless, the chapter does review some of the limited privatization activity that has taken place. In Canada, important privatizations have occurred at both the federal and provincial levels. Turning to the effects, Boardman, Laurin and Vining provide evidence that the privatizations have led to performance improvements, using a range of financial and economic measures and stock market data. For example, they show that profitability, efficiency and dividends increased in the three years after privatization. They also comment that there is still considerable room for further privatizations. However, the more straightforward privatizations have already taken place and they conclude that the remaining state assets in Canada will prove more difficult and controversial to sell because of plausible market failure concerns.

In chapter 8, Graeme A. Hodge provides a review of privatization activity in Australia, where the state of Victoria has been especially active. He explains the rationale for privatization in a country with a long history of state-owned industry. He details the privatizations of electricity and telecommunications and comments that the resulting economic effects of privatization still await full consideration. Nevertheless, on the basis of the available evidence, he concludes that 'the divestitures have been generally well implemented, resulting in reasonable value for money for taxpayers and modest public welfare gains in some cases. . . . although Australia's divestitures have not been perfect, the performance has probably been better than for many earlier privatizations around the globe'. This chapter provides useful case study material relevant to an understanding of the basis for successful privatization, including the need for appropriate reforms in competition and regulatory policies.

Chapter 9 by Michael A. Crew and Paul R. Kleindorfer, returns to privatization in North America, concentrating upon the scope for privatization of the United States postal service (USPS). This study provides a useful complement to the previous chapters by focusing on the arguments surrounding privatization of an activity almost universally provided by the state sector. Comparisons are made with the management of postal services elsewhere and notably in Germany and the Netherlands where, unusually, privatization has occurred or is occurring. While they argue that privatization of USPS appears at first glance to be attractive, given the organization's obvious inefficiencies, they emphasize the practical difficulties of bringing about a successful privatization. They provide a possible scenario for the future of a privatized postal service but recognize significant problems in establishing an effective regulatory regime. The USPS, like incumbent postal services in other countries, faces serious challenges in terms of the impact of technological change, financing, institutional constraints and, especially, the power of organized labour. Adding to these problems is the recent enhanced awareness of the vulnerability of the mail service to terrorism following well-publicized anthrax incidents in the USA. Hence, although they believe that privatization of the postal service could lead to significant static and dynamic efficiency gains, they are pessimistic that it will come about, especially in the short term. This chapter provides a useful illustration of the public policy tensions that lie at the heart of privatization policy.

Paul Cook and Colin Kirkpatrick turn our attention from privatization in the industrialized economies to privatization in the developing world. In chapter 10, they first assess the impact of privatization in terms of its objectives in the context of development needs and constraints. They then review the various empirical studies of the impact of privatization in developing countries on economic performance, at both the macroeconomic and microeconomic levels. They conclude that the results 'reveal a complex and sometimes contradictory picture . . . The experience with policy and performance has been diverse, making it difficult to identify common patterns of experience or to draw general lessons for policy'. Like a number of the other authors in this book, they warn that simply changing the ownership from public to private is unlikely to be sufficient to bring about economic gains. Privatization is effective in terms of promoting economic development only where appropriate 'corporate governance, institutional capacity, market competition, and political economy' conditions exist. These are commonly absent or at least immature in the developing world and need to be created and nurtured if a privatization programme is to be successful.

This set of conclusions is borne out in the subsequent chapters by Werner Baer, Joseph C.H. Chai, Erwin Schwella and Paul Bennell on the privatization experiences of Brazil, China, South Africa and sub-Saharan Africa, respectively. Werner Baer's study of Brazil in chapter 11 draws attention to the importance of state enterprise in the country's economic development and the fact that for a long time the active role of government was considered both necessary and beneficial. Benefits extended to 'crowding in' private investment by providing crucial physical inputs and cheap official financing. However, by the 1970s and 1980s, weaknesses in the management of state enterprises were becoming increasingly evident, exacerbated by governments using state firms as instruments of macroeconomic policy. Brazil's privatization programme began in the late 1970s in the face of declining economic growth but developed only slowly during the 1980s owing to political and other constraints. From 1990, the privatization programme of the Collor administration led to a larger scale of privatization, which was continued from September 1992 by the two subsequent presidents, Itamar Franco and Fernanco Henrique Cardoso. Amongst other things, this led to the spread of privatization into the utilities sectors. In the decade from 1991 to 2001, 121 state-owned enterprises were sold, raising US$103bn. Baer stresses, however, that the privatization programme of the 1990s was largely driven by the need of government for revenue and that this led to the sale of state assets to the highest bidder, normally large domestic private firms and foreign enterprises. The result was a worsening of a traditional problem in Brazil, that of income and wealth inequality.

Joseph Chai's account of privatization in China describes a number of the most important changes that have occurred in the Chinese economy since the late 1970s and are associated with an opening up to international trade and investment. In chapter 12 he catalogues how state enterprises have been subject to a series of reforms aimed at incentivizing management to pursue efficiency improvements, and highlights the results of these reforms. While paying tribute to the contribution of state-owned enterprises to the maintenance of political, social and economic stability in China, through employment preservation and the continuing provision of social welfare services, he concludes that China's continued fast economic growth requires their privatization. He dismisses the argument that in China privatization is unnecessary, pointing to the scale of productivity improvements possible in the state-owned sector. However, he stresses that privatization of the state-owned sector will need the provision of an efficient capital market, legal protection of private property rights and effective forms of corporate governance to prevent principal–agent abuses. Chai's account confirms that, while China has gone far down the road of economic development in recent years, the state-owned enterprises remain a real economic burden owing to their inefficiencies.

Chapter 13 is concerned with privatization in Mexico and Chile. Here Miguel D. Ramirez provides a critical account of policy in the two countries. In particular, he points to the resulting concentration of economic power in a small number of firms and business groupings (*grupos*). As he comments: 'There is a general presumption that the transfer of state-owned enterprises to the private sector takes place in a competitive environment that is devoid of major market failures. However . . . product market competition under optimal conditions rarely exists, if at all, in most Latin American countries, including Chile and Mexico.' He also stresses that in Latin America a major reason for state asset sales has been financial. Cash-strapped governments have seen privatization as a convenient way of balancing the state's books, irrespective of the longer-term economic consequences. Using case studies of the banking, telecommunications and power sectors, Ramirez's chapter confirms that, in the absence of adequate antitrust laws and regulatory structures, the results of privatization can be contrary to expectation.

By contrast, chapter 14 is concerned with South Africa, where privatization policy is less well developed. Here Erwin Schwella discusses the continuing tensions within the post-apartheid government about the future of state ownership. Historically the ANC and its alliance partners favoured state enterprise to help transfer income and wealth to the newly franchised black community. Also, under the apartheid regime, state enterprises had been created across the South African economy as part of the effort to stave off the effects of international sanctions. This resulted in extremely inefficient firms, such as the arms maker, ARMSCOR, and SASOL, which produces oil from coal. Tracing policy developments in the 1990s, Schwella identifies a gradual shift in favour of liberalized markets and private ownership, but at the same time he identifies institutional constraints revolving around the black empowerment agenda and the role of the powerful Congress of South African Trade Unions (COSATU). He emphasizes that, although the country is not immune to the international tide in favour of privatization, historical baggage and the current political balance continue to limit the degree of progress that can be expected. Even the term 'privatization', he notes, is still avoided within government circles, in favour of the less politically contentious description of 'restructuring' state enterprises.

Chapter 15, by Paul Bennell, turns to privatization in sub-Saharan Africa generally. In spite of political and economic failures, privatization has occurred, although sometimes hesitatingly. Bennell emphasizes the role of changing attitudes to state ownership in the major donor agencies during the 1980s, notably the IMF and the World Bank, as a catalyst of privatization in this part of the world. The most far-reaching privatization programmes have been in Côte d'Ivoire, Mozambique and Zambia, with the latter two countries very heavily aid-dependent. While he concludes that 'most governments are genuinely committed to completing their privatization programmes as quickly as possible', the lack of developed domestic capital markets, a lack of transparency in government and outright corruption continue to dog the privatization process in sub-Saharan Africa.

Chapters 16 to 21 turn our attention from the problems in developing countries to those in the transition economies of Central and Eastern Europe. These economies are generally more developed than those found in much of Latin America, Africa and Asia, but are heavily distorted because of the years of misallocation of resources during the communist era. Following the turbulent events of 1989, these countries have chosen to destroy socialist planning and to introduce capitalist principles. This is particularly true of the countries studied here, although the progress, form and success of privatization have varied, for the reasons discussed.

Igor Filatotchev initiates the discussion with a study of the theory and concepts relating to privatization and corporate governance in the transition economies. The starting point for these countries, and the stresses they have faced in reorienting their economies to survive in the international market place, has inevitably meant numerous failures as well as successes. The transition economies have had to learn not only about how to operate competitive private sector businesses but also about what institutional structures are necessary if these business are to thrive, and have subsequently needed to implement them. Some have gone about this more successfully than others. Using a mixture of privatization methods including voucher schemes, the economies have transferred very large numbers of both small-scale and large-scale enterprises from the state to the private sector and over a remarkably short period of time: the scale of privatization in Central and Eastern Europe as a share of national production far outweighs that in the rest of Europe and North America combined. The result, however, as Filatotchev stresses, has too often been 'insider' privatization and managerial entrenchment, with 'the extent of managerial equity ownership . . . identified as a crucial aspect of managerial willingness and capacity to implement change'. Weighing the relative merits of 'insider' and 'outsider' control in the context of economic transition, he argues that effective restructuring requires outsider ownership, but also that 'Diffused share ownership among individual, inexperienced shareholders is unlikely to provide an effective constraint on self-serving behaviour by former "Red Directors"'. Externally imposed change may be the only way to bring about the changes needed and this is probably best facilitated by large block shareholdings held by dominant, strategic investors. However, such a shareholding pattern can bring with it other problems, not least the protection of the interests of the minority shareholders. Using a simple theoretical model, Filatotchev is able to show that the impact of privatization on a firm's performance 'depends on an interaction between the entrenchment and incentive effects of concentrated ownership'. In other words, on the basis of the specific experiences of the transition economies, he confirms that good corporate governance, supported by institutions such as sound regulation and an efficient capital market, are crucial to the success of any privatization.

This conclusion also applies to Russia. In chapter 17, Paul Hare and Alexander Muravyev study the difficulties Russia has faced in introducing efficient and effective forms of private ownership. Barriers to reform have included traditional networks for commerce that were inherited from the Soviet period and are based on barter and similar forms of trading, the banking system and the financial markets more generally, and the labour market. The task facing reformers has been enormous. In the late 1980s, state enterprises with more than 200 employees accounted for 95 per cent of industrial employment and production in Russia. Large firms with more than 1000 employees accounted for 75 per cent of employment and output. Compared to a market economy, the Russian economy was dominated by relatively few large firms. Private enterprise was effectively discouraged and enterprise management followed plans determined by government. The 1990s saw a mass privatization programme, including a voucher scheme, alongside programmes of small-scale privatizations. This resulted in substantial ownership in the hands of managers and employees or 'insiders'. Following the loans-for-shares scheme in 1995, under which banks lent funds to government in return for blocks of shares in state enterprises as collateral, the privatization programme became even more deeply mired in controversy. Hare and Muravyev argue that 'the outcome of the process has been disappointing, characterized by weak and often poorly directed restructuring efforts, and the survival of many enterprises that should have disappeared long ago'. Using the examples of the power sector, the railways and telecommunications, they underline the degree of reform that still needs to be implemented if the reputation of the Russian privatization programme is to be rescued.

Chapter 18, by Michal Mejstrík, again picks up the theme of the importance of institutional structures and corporate governance in the transition economies. Mejstrík argues that the success of Czech privatization, which in the early reform period had relied on both enterprise sales and voucher or coupon privatizations, was at first severely hampered by an inadequate legal framework that could not support the functioning of a market economy. As a result, incomplete contracts led to the unenforceability of contract obligations, and an unassailable position of debtors vis-à-vis creditors and of majority shareholders vis-à-vis minority shareholders. This had detrimental effects, with the most significant being that those in control of the large investment funds in which many citizens had invested their coupons were allowed to employ the incomplete contracts for their own individual benefit at the expense of their minority shareholders. This seriously biased corporate governance structure resulted in the departure of many portfolio investors and the poor performance of the Czech capital market. It also substantially limited the possibility of restructuring state-owned enterprises through coupon privatization, and meant that the most stable ownership structures were dominated by foreign, strategic shareholders. Subsequently, bank privatization, the creation of an independent regulatory Securities Exchange Commission, and the current plethora of necessary reforms and legislation to facilitate accession to the EU, have all contributed significantly to improvements in the Czech Republic's corporate governance structure. However, Mejstrík also believes that substantial improvements in the Czech institutional structure will still need to be made before the transition to a market economy will be complete.

The privatization process seems to have been much more successful in Poland. In chapter 19, Tomasz Mickiewicz and Maciej Baltowski review this country's privatization programme since 1989. Again various forms of sell-off were adopted, including a voucher scheme, but with employee buy-outs common. Although the process was pursued more slowly than privatization in Russia, the results appear more immediately encouraging. The results of research, reported in the chapter, suggest that privatization has had a positive impact on economic performance and that the ownership structure in privatized companies has undergone changes with both the emergence of dominant ownership groups inside companies and major outsider investments. These changes have come about following privatization as a result of market competition and the resulting financial pressures on undercapitalized businesses.

In chapter, 20 Iván Major provides an appraisal of Hungary's privatization experience since the political changes of 1989–90. While finding much to celebrate in terms of Hungary's economic transformation, his study cautions against any simple interpretation of the link between private ownership and economic performance. While he concludes that privatization and the associated company restructuring led to a considerable improvement in productive efficiency and profitability, 'the improvement was not without setbacks ... [and] ... profitability and economic efficiency did not always improve with the expansion of private ownership'. Using his own detailed analysis of data on ownership and performance in Hungary since 1988, he is able to identify the significant role of foreign ownership in raising performance after privatization, especially through a 'core group of foreign companies'. At the same time, the method by which performance is assessed – using profitability indices and value added to total cost ratios – raises a challenge to Central and Eastern European economists to develop more robust measures of enterprise performance in the transition economies.

The privatization process in Ukraine is the subject of chapter 21. Here Saul Estrin and Adam Rosevear explain how the opportunities that opened up when independence from the former Soviet Union was achieved in 1991 were squandered. Although the private sector had grown from 10 per cent of GDP in 1991 to 60 per cent by 2000, privatization had faced significant political and social obstacles. The result has been enterprises transferred into private hands in forms unlikely to lead to productivity improvements. Corruption and 'capture' by powerful groups have occurred and the supporting institutions necessary for a sound private enterprise economy are still underdeveloped. State ownership has commonly been replaced by 'insider' ownership by managers and employees because of entrenched interests who would otherwise have opposed the ownership change. Even where 'outsider' ownership exists it tends to be widely dispersed and not conducive to effective corporate governance. The shift from insider to outsider ownership which has occurred, for example, in Poland, and the important role of foreign investment in Hungary discussed in the previous chapter, appear to have been largely absent in most Ukrainian firms. In their survey work, Estrin and Rosevear find that there has been disappointingly little restructuring of Ukraine firms following privatization. They also find no obvious relationship between ownership and performance: privatized firms were not found to be significantly more profitable or productive than state-owned ones. A key factor in the economic growth of neighbouring Poland has been the development of new privately owned firms. Again, there has been the absence of a similar development in Ukraine, suggesting that the institutional context still remains insufficiently supportive of private enterprise.

The last five chapters of the book turn in detail to the subject of economic regulation. As part of an effective institutional structure for private enterprise to flourish and to protect the public interest from market failure, governments need to develop and maintain efficient and effective regulatory systems. This is particularly so where public utilities are transferred to the private sector retaining considerable market power, as has been the case in a number of the countries covered in the earlier chapters. When these enterprises are sold, and even if broken up or 'unbundled' at sale, they have tended to retain important monopoly power, leading to the real threat of market failure. To counter this effect and protect consumers from resulting high prices and poor services, normally state regulatory regimes have either had to be created from scratch or improved.

In chapter 22, Dieter Bös models the regulatory process, taking as the starting point a two-person game with information asymmetries. The regulator is a welfare maximizer (or a politician wanting to maximize votes or a bureaucrat wanting to maximize power) and the enterprise manager is an agent interested in his/her personal income and the disutility of effort. A regulatory constraint exists in the form of regulation failing if the enterprise is forced into bankruptcy or, alternatively, the manager quits. Bös then explores simple regulatory rules, developed first using an iterative process of regulatory adjustment of prices based on costs and then using 'yardstick competition'. He finds both approaches wanting; in particular, regulating prices according to costs provides disincentives for the manager to minimize supply costs, while yardstick competition is open to collusion and difficulty of operation where firms' cost and demand functions differ. Dieter Bös then explores the economic implications of information asymmetry with regulation under different forms of contracting or incentives. The implications for price cap regulation and quality regulation are then discussed. This theoretical chapter highlights the behaviour of the manager of a privatized enterprise if the regulator lacks information and the role of an appropriate incentive mechanism. It also highlights how difficult it is to design an effective regulatory mechanism.

The theme of regulatory information asymmetries and incentive mechanisms is also pursued in Thomas Weyman-Jones's chapter, chapter 23. Thomas Weyman-Jones provides a detailed study of the price cap regime for setting prices, now widely adopted internationally. After summarizing the principles of price cap setting (using an RPI-X formulation), he identifies two major issues of principle and one of practice. The first issue of principle concerns the difficulty of achieving incentive-compatible and individually rational forecasts for demand and costs. The second concerns the explicit financial modelling used and whether this 'adequately represents the decision making behaviour of a firm maximizing the present value of future cash flows and operating through agency relationships with the firm's managers'. The practical issue relates to the incentives for cost savings in terms of the timing of regulatory price reviews. As the length of the control period declines so the incentive power of the RPI-X mechanism also falls because of the resulting decline in the net present value of the cost savings passed through to profits. Weyman-Jones then develops his critique by considering how to establish the benchmarking of operating and capital expenditures and thereby derive the extent of reasonable efficiency gains that can be built into the X factor. He explores some of the various methods used by regulators to benchmark costs and the difficulties faced. Other subjects covered are the valuation of depreciation allowances and the regulatory asset base and deriving the cost of capital. Whereas Dieter Bös considers information asymmetries and incentives very much at the theoretical level, Thomas Weyman-Jones's chapter illustrates the practical difficulties of implementing optimal state regulation for privatized companies. Both chapters underline why privatizing enterprises is particularly problematic where competition cannot be assured.

Anthony Ogus continues on the same theme in a comparison of regulatory systems. Whereas Bös and Weyman-Jones take a strictly economic approach to the subject of state regulation, in chapter 24 Anthony Ogus takes a wider perspective, beginning with an attempt to identify how regulation fits into the constitutional and cultural environment of a country. He shows that economic regulation will take on varying forms reflecting each country's constitutional and cultural environment and hence its laws and norms. This in turn leads to different regulatory styles and differing degrees of autonomy for regulatory agencies. However, 'One reason for the observed world-wide trend towards consensual, decentralised regulatory rule-making, is the growing recognition that governments cannot always be relied on to possess or properly process the information necessary to meet the regulatory goals at low cost'. The degree to which discretionary power should be devolved to quasi-independent governmental bodies continues to remain a source of disagreement. Ogus's study helps in ascertaining under what environments such devolution is most likely to be favoured. Similarly, differences between countries in regulatory accountability, procedures and management are to be expected. He concludes that, while ideas about regulation have been evolving across jurisdictional boundaries and there may have been some convergence of view (no doubt influenced by developments in the economics of regulation discussed by Bös and Weyman-Jones in their chapters), 'the character of national regulatory institutions is still best to be understood within each jurisdiction's culture'.

This conclusion is pertinent to the discussion of privatization and regulation of public utilities in developing economies, as discussed by David Parker in chapter 25. This chapter considers the problems faced in developing countries when monopoly public utilities are transferred to the private sector through direct sell-offs or operating concessions. Around one-third of all the privatizations that have taken place in the developing world have involved the public utilities and they dominate in terms of revenues raised from privatization. Parker argues that privatization in these economies cannot be separated from the need to develop appropriate institutions by improving both the regulatory and the competitive environments for enterprise and investment. Like Anthony Ogus, Parker embeds his discussion of regulation (and privatization) within the institutional and cultural environment of the countries. After setting out the usual arguments for regulation, and a price cap regime in particular, he points especially to costs that can arise in terms of reduced efficiency incentives, the costs of administration and compliance, information asymmetries, regulatory risk and regulatory capture. It is to be expected that all of these costs will be prevalent and perhaps appreciable in developing economies, given their institutional weaknesses. Parker particularly singles out the concept of 'trust' and its

relationship to regulatory risk. He also stresses that in developing economies poverty reduction is a high priority, which further complicates the task
of regulating privatized companies. Parker's chapter is exploratory and
conceptual and is based on study and practical experience of working on
privatization and economic regulation in a range of developing countries.
His main conclusion is that, while much privatization and regulation
research has been concerned with the developed economies, 'it is not self-
evident that the lessons from these economies are readily transferable to
developing nations'. The conclusions of this chapter seem also relevant to
the transition economies.

Lastly, in chapter 26, David Saal reviews the liberalization and restructuring of the UK's telecommunications, gas and electricity industries, which
had originally been nationalized on natural monopoly grounds. The chapter
reveals that, despite high hopes that privatization would rapidly result in
effectively competitive markets, with only the rump natural monopoly essential facility of these industries being subject to regulation, the necessary
restructuring to promote competition has subsequently proved to be much
more difficult to accomplish than was initially anticipated. Saal argues that
creating and sustaining competitive markets has required much more regulation than the early UK proponents of utility privatization had believed,
because of both the failure properly to separate essential network facilities
from potentially competitive activities at privatization, and inherent difficulties in creating and sustaining competition that had not been anticipated.
Thus, even though some of the UK's utilities have achieved substantial levels
of competition, the creation of functioning markets required constant regulatory pressure over many years, including forced vertical and horizontal
divestiture, just to break down the dominant market position that incumbent
firms held in the potentially competitive parts of the industry. Likewise, as
competition in formerly vertically integrated natural monopolies is dependent on access to the pipe or wire network, there can be no competition
without regulation to define the terms and cost of network access and to
ensure a level playing field for all potential competitors. Similarly, detailed
regulation for competition will be permanently required because such
network access rules will require continuous policing and are industry-
specific, thereby making general competition law insufficient to maintain
competition. It has therefore been necessary for UK policy makers to refocus
their objectives, leading to a system with both regulation of the non-
competitive network as a natural monopoly and the establishment and regulation of appropriate structures to maintain competition in potentially
competitive sectors. Industry-specific regulation of the former state-owned
natural monopoly industries has therefore remained a fundamental necessity
to both promote and sustain competition and also to prevent monopoly

abuse. Thus Saal's review of UK experience suggests that utility privatization has not resulted in the withering away of the regulatory state, as early advocates of utility privatization had once believed would occur.

Conclusions

Both the theory of privatization and practical experience of implementing privatization schemes continue to develop. This book provides a comprehensive coverage of the issues in theory and policy that surround the current privatization debate. It is intended to foster critical analysis with a view to improving understanding of the appropriate form of economic restructuring of industries internationally. The contents suggest that many challenges remain, related to an understanding of when privatizations are most likely to succeed in improving economic performance and what forms the institutional context must take to increase the chances of success. Controversy continues about the appropriate speed of privatization and the form it should best take. Controversy also continues about the extent to which the transfer of privatization policy around the globe involves some form of Anglo-American hegemony that is not appropriate in many economies. Moreover, the degree to which ownership and market liberalization can be usefully separated, and whether privatization without either competition or effective regulation is worthwhile, continue to be discussed.

Privatization has been a dominant feature of industrial restructuring since the 1980s and continues to be so. The studies in this volume provide evidence of its scope and effects and therefore provide the basis for improving both policy formulation and implementation. However, they also emphasize that privatization is not an end in itself. Moreover, they demonstrate that, for privatization to be worthwhile and for lasting economic efficiency gains to be achieved, supporting reforms in the arenas of corporate governance and capital markets, product market competition and state regulatory processes must accompany most privatization programmes.

References

Boycko, M., A. Shleifer and R.W. Vishny (1996) 'A Theory of Privatization', *Economic Journal*, 106, March, 309–19.

de Fraja, G. (1993) 'Productive efficiency in public and private firms', *Journal of Public Economics*, 30, 15–30.

Dolowitz, D.P. and D. Marsh (1996) 'Who Learns from Whom: a Review of the Policy Transfer Literature', *Political Studies*, 44(2), 343–57.

Economist (2002) 'Coming home to roost: Special report, Privatization in Europe', 29 June, pp. 71–3.

Evans, P. (1995) *Embedded Autonomy: States and Industrial Transformation*, Princeton, NJ: Princeton University Press.

Hart, O.D. (1995) *Firms, Contracts and Financial Structure*, Oxford: Oxford University Press.

Jensen, M.C. and W.H. Meckling (1976) 'Theory of the Firm: Managerial Behaviour, Agency Costs and Ownership Structure', *Journal of Financial Economics*, 3(4), 305–60.

Martin, S. and D. Parker (1997) *The Impact of Privatization: Ownership and corporate performance in the UK*, London: Routledge.

Mitchell, W.C. (1988) *Government As It Is*, Hobart Paper 109, London: Institute of Economic Affairs.

Niskanen, W.A. Jr. (1971) *Bureaucracy and Representative Government*, Chicago: Aldine.

OECD (2001) 'Privatisation: Recent Trends', in *Financial Market Trends*, no. 79, June, OECD Paris.

Parker, D. (1999) 'Policy Transfer and Policy Inertia: Privatization in Taiwan', *Asia Pacific Business Review*, 6(2), 1–20.

Parker, D. (2000) 'Introduction', in Parker, D., (ed.) *Privatization and Corporate Performance*, The International Library of Critical Writings in Economics, series editor Mark Blaug, Cheltenham, UK and Northampton, MA, USA: Edward Elgar.

Saha, S.K. and D. Parker (eds) (2002) *Globalisation and Sustainable Development in Latin America: Perspectives on the New Economic Order*, Cheltenham, UK and Northampton, MA, USA: Edward Elgar.

Vickers, J. and G. Yarrow (1988) *Privatization: An Economic Analysis*, Cambridge, MA: MIT Press.

World Bank (2001) 'Private Sector Development Strategy – Directions for the World Bank Group', mimeo, World Bank, Washington, DC.

PART I

PRIVATIZATION IN THEORY AND PRACTICE

2 History and methods of privatization
William L. Megginson and Jeffry M. Netter

Historical background

One truth dominates economics: resources are scarce. Because resources are scarce, individuals and societies must make choices. The choices include what to produce, how to produce and for whom to produce. And it must be determined what is the appropriate role of markets versus state mandates in answering all the above questions. As Edmund Burke said in 1795, 'one of the finest problems in legislation [is namely to determine] what the State ought to take upon itself to direct by the public wisdom, and what it ought to leave, with as little interference as possible, to individual discretion' (Middelton, 1996:41).

Intrinsic to answering the above questions is who should own the means of production and direct commerce. Throughout history, there has been a mixture of public (often including religious institutions) and private ownership of production and commerce. Sobel (1999) writes that state ownership of the means of production, including mills and metal working, was common in the ancient Near East, while private ownership was more common in trading and money lending. The Bible mentions money lenders, who were essentially bankers (Means, 2001:3). In ancient Greece, the government owned the land, forests and mines, but contracted out the work to individuals and firms. The rise of state owned-banks also occurred in Greece at essentially the same time. In the Ch'in dynasty of China, the government had monopolies on salt and iron but by the 1500s had developed sophisticated markets where private parties transacted in luxury goods such as silk and tortoise shells (ibid.). Ancient Egypt had state monopolies on the manufacture of various products including papyrus, beer, honey, salt and vegetable oils. The state controlled the entire production process – planting, retailing, prices and wages. In addition, the state severely restricted foreign imports.

Ancient Rome provides examples of both private and state ownership (Sobel, 1999:19). Sobel notes that in the Roman Republic the '*publicani* (private individuals and companies) fulfilled virtually all the of the state's economic requirements' (ibid.:21). He writes that the state contracted out for 'tax collection, supplying the army, providing for religious sacrifices and . . . construction'. In the Roman Republic almost all goods, whether contracted for by the state or by private parties, were produced by the private sector. Some very large firms even arose: one mining firm employed 40 000 people. Sobel goes on to discuss the fact that the replacement of the Roman Republic by the Roman Empire led to a greatly increased role for the state in producing and distributing goods. For example, much of the grain for the Empire was grown on large estates belonging to the Emperor and worked by tenant farmers. Private enterprise remained, especially in the manufacturing and trading of textiles. Sobel also suggests that the great cost of the government bureaucracy was one of the reasons for the fall of Rome.

In the thousand years between the fall of Rome and the beginning of the Industrial Revolution, Europe's economic system evolved in various ways. Throughout this time the Catholic Church exerted a large influence on how commerce developed and for whom goods were produced (often for the Church). As in Imperial Rome, there were wealthy landowners and tenant farmers, a mixture of state and private ownership. However, as time went on markets and private entrepreneurs began to arise in many different contexts. Sobel reports that, by the year 1000, local knights would organize fairs that often lasted several weeks, where merchants, who had paid a fee to the knight, would sell goods they had bought from other private producers (or made themselves). At the same time, money lenders would lend to many people, including the rulers. Many of the loans had large default risks with no enforceable collateral (especially the loans to the rulers). Thus the money lenders charged high interest rates and as a result were often despised, an example of how people do not like the distribution of wealth that arises with the use of markets. Sobel notes that Dante reserved a special place for money lenders in Hell. However, the finance industry developed and by the 1300s the Italian city-states became major centres for monetary commerce. Markets and private ownership developed in other settings and Rondinelli and Iacono (1996) note that, by the time of the Industrial Revolution in the western industrialized societies and their colonies, the private sector was the most important producer of commercial goods and was also important in providing public goods and services. This pattern, with more government involvement in some countries and less in others, continued into the twentieth century in both Western Europe and its colonies and former colonies. However, in the United States, for a host of reasons, there was less government involvement in the economy than in many other countries.

The point of the above discussion is to demonstrate that the organization of economic activity and the ownership of the means of production and trade have moved throughout history from the state sector to the private sector and back at many times and in many ways. However, our discussion of privatization as the term is used today really begins with the Great

Depression of the 1930s and the two world wars. Put simply, the Great Depression was widely seen as evidence of the failure of capitalism, and the devastation of the two world wars, especially the second, seemed to most people to require massive government action. Yergin and Stanislaw (1998) provide an excellent overview of the history of this time (and of the later privatizations) and the power of ideas in influencing policy. They write:

> At the end of the war, in Europe and throughout much of the world, capitalism was discredited in a way that is not easily imagined today. It seemed infirm, inept and incapable. It could not be counted on to deliver economic growth and a decent life. 'Nobody in Europe believes in the American way of life – that is private enterprise,' the British historian A.J.P. Taylor wrote at the time. (Ibid.:22)

Yergin and Stanislaw suggest that there was a defining moment in the rise of state power in economic matters and government. It was July 1945, when British voters voted the Conservatives (and Winston Churchill) out of power and replaced them with the Labour Party headed by Clement Attlee. Labour had as its goal the nationalization of major industries and taking control of the 'Commanding Heights' of the economy (the title of Yergin and Stanislaw's book and a phrase coined by Lenin). They quickly nationalized coal, iron and steel, railroads, utilities and some other major firms (ibid:25). Note that the motivation for these nationalizations was largely that these firms under private ownership had not operated well and had underinvested. Thus the assumption was that nationalization would lead to better operation of the firms, full employment and growth. Additionally, it was hoped that government ownership would lead to a 'fairer' allocation of resources. Yergin and Stanislaw note that, by 1946, 20 per cent of Britain's workforce was in state-owned firms (ibid.:26). Labour's policies between 1945 and 1951, including nationalization, transformed the United Kingdom into a 'welfare state'.[1]

While the path to government ownership varied from country to country around the world, it occurred in most countries. In essentially all European countries, the tremendous devastation of the Second World War, in addition to the lack of faith in capitalism, led to increased government involvement in the economy in comparison to the pre-war era. Government planning was viewed as necessary to rebuild economies. An additional factor was that US aid was dependent on a government developing a viable plan for recovery. Finally, the growth of government in world economies was stimulated by the World Bank, created at the Bretton Woods conference in 1944 (ibid.:79). It began with a mission to help rebuild Europe but expanded its role to the economies of developing countries. The World Bank primarily dealt with governments and motivated additional government intervention.

In Western Europe, governments debated how deeply involved the national government should be in regulating the national economy and which industrial sectors should be reserved exclusively for state ownership. In general, the answer to this debate (as in the UK) was that the government should at least own the telecommunications and postal services, electric and gas utilities, and most forms of non-road transport, especially airlines and railroads. Many politicians also believed that the state should control certain 'strategic' manufacturing industries, such as steel and defence production. In many countries, state-owned banks were also given either monopoly or protected positions, as discussed in La Porta *et al.* (2000a). In most countries what arose were state-owned enterprises (SOEs).

Rondinelli and Iacono (1996) and Yergin and Stanislaw (1998) argue that government ownership grew in the developing world for slightly different reasons, primarily that government ownership was perceived as necessary to promote growth, build a nation and eliminate the influence of the colonial powers. In the post-colonial countries of Asia, Africa and Latin America, governments sought rapid growth through heavy investment in physical facilities. Another reason for nationalization was the resentment of the foreigners who owned many of the largest firms in these countries (see also Noll, 2000).

The outcome was different in the United States. First, much of the movement to government involvement in the economy occurred in response to the Great Depression and before the Second World War. Before the Great Depression, the USA was an industrial nation with a great reliance on laissez-faire capitalism. However, the Great Depression in the USA, as elsewhere, eroded people's faith in markets and capitalism. Franklin Roosevelt came to the presidency in 1933 with the will and the mandate to involve the government much more in the economy. The resulting New Deal led to a particularly American response to the alleged failures of capitalism – state regulation rather than state ownership. Investment banking and commercial banking were separated. Security markets were regulated with a two-pronged approach of mandated disclosure and government enforcement of the rules. The Federal Power Commission regulated power, the Federal Communications Commission (FCC) regulated communications, and so on. With rare exceptions the federal government did not take over ownership of firms but instead regulated them. Governments provided and produced goods and services in the USA but mainly at the local level (except for national defence).

Theory of ownership, government involvement and privatization
Megginson and Netter (2001) argue that the theoretical arguments for the advantages of private ownership of the means of production are based on

a fundamental theorem of welfare economics: a competitive equilibrium is pareto optimal, under certain assumptions. These assumptions include that there are no externalities in production or consumption, that the product is not a public good, that the market is not monopolistic in structure, and that information costs are low. Thus a theoretical argument for government intervention based on efficiency grounds rests on an argument that markets have failed in some way, in that one or more of these assumptions do not hold, and that the government can resolve the market failure.

Intellectual arguments for government intervention based on efficiency considerations have been made in many areas. Some argue that governments need to regulate (or own) natural monopolies or other monopolies, intervene in the case of externalities (such as regulating pollution) and help provide public goods (such as providing national defence and education or, in areas where there is a public good aspect to it, providing information). Additionally, as discussed above, the post-Second World War movement by governments into firm ownership began with the perception that private ownership of firms had not worked well. Private firms did not provide goods adequately at reasonable prices. Even more importantly, private markets could lead to high unemployment.

There are non-efficiency arguments for government ownership, generally based on a redistribution of resources. That is, government ownership will change the distribution of wealth and income. In some cases, this is based on some broad concepts of fairness. In others, it is a blatant attempt by one group to take resources from others (such as foreigners or different ethnic groups).

Privatization, in turn, is a response to the failings of state ownership. Megginson and Netter (2001) outline some of the theoretical arguments on the advantages of private versus state ownership. First, contracting ability affects the efficiency of state ownership. There is an advantage to the goal of shareholder wealth maximization. It provides a well-defined goal that can guide firm policy. Governments have many objectives other than profit or shareholder wealth maximization. Further, government objectives can change from one administration to the next. Thus the inability of the government to commit itself credibly to a policy can significantly reduce the efficiency of a firm's operations and governance. Even if the government does attempt to maximize social welfare, for example, welfare is a difficult thing to measure and use in guiding policy. In addition, the government's goals can be inconsistent with efficiency, inconsistent with maximizing social welfare, or even malevolent. Even if the government and the nation's citizens agree that profit maximizing is the goal of the firm, it is difficult to write complete contracts that adequately tie managers' incentives to that goal.

The state is also unlikely to allow a large SOE to face bankruptcy. Thus the discipline enforced on private firms by the capital markets and the threat of financial distress is less important for state-owned firms, thereby resulting in the so-called 'soft budget' constraint. Numerous authors have noted that soft budget constraints were a major source of inefficiency in communist firms, and supposedly 'hard' budget constraints imposed by a government on SOEs are not very effective either.

There is another set of reasons for privatization. These motivations arise from the use of revenues from privatization to improve governments' finances. Governments have raised huge amounts of money by selling SOEs. Such sales have helped reduce the fiscal deficit in many countries. Davis *et al.* (2000) review the evidence on the macroeconomic effects of privatization, discuss the difficulties of using macroeconomic privatization data, and report some evidence on the effects from 18 developing countries. They find evidence that the proceeds from privatization are saved by governments and not used to increase government spending.

Another theoretical reason for privatization is to develop factor markets, product markets and security markets. Welfare economics argues that efficiency is achieved through competitive markets. If privatization promotes competition, privatization can have important efficiency effects. Inevitably, the effectiveness of privatization programmes and markets themselves are simultaneously determined. It has been clear in the transition economies that the success of the privatization programme depends on the strength of the markets within the same country, and vice versa. Thus the impact of privatization will differ across countries, depending on the strength of the existing private sector. Similarly, the evidence suggests that the effectiveness of privatization depends on institutional factors, such as the protection of investors. However, privatization can also stimulate the development of institutions that improve the operations of markets.

In sum, theoretical work that examines privatization offers many reasons why, even in the case of market failure, state ownership has important weaknesses. Shleifer (1998) sums up much of the literature with, 'a good government that wants to further "social goals" would rarely own producers to meet its objectives'. A question for the post-privatization world is the role of the public sector in the economy and in the regulation of firms. The alternative to state ownership is rarely purely private, unregulated firms. State ownership is only one form of the continuum of governance structures that reflect the level of state regulation of public and privately owned firms (Laffont and Tirole, 1993). Many of the theoretical arguments for privatization are based on the premise that the harmful effects of state intervention have a greater impact under state ownership than under state regulation, not that the harmful effects can be eliminated through privatization.

The rise of privatization

Most people associate modern privatization programmes with Margaret Thatcher's Conservative government, which came to power in the United Kingdom in 1979. Using a broader definition of privatization – one that encompassed reactively changing the policies of an immediate predecessor government – the Churchill government's denationalization of the British steel industry during the early 1950s could well be labelled the first 'privatization'. Additionally, the Adenauer government in the Federal Republic of Germany launched the first large-scale, ideologically motivated 'denationalization' programme of the post-war era. In 1961, the German government sold a majority stake in Volkswagen in a public share offering heavily weighted in favour of small investors. Four years later, the government launched an even larger offering for shares in VEBA. Both offerings were initially received favourably, but the appeal of share ownership did not survive the first cyclical downturn in stock prices, and the government was forced to bail out many small shareholders.

It was almost 20 years before another major western nation chose to pursue privatization as a core economic or political policy. Yotopoulos (1989) describes and assesses the Chilean programmes which began, under the Pinochet government, before the programme in the UK. Although the Thatcher government may not have been the first to launch a large privatization programme, its programme is without question the most important historically. Privatization was not a major campaign theme for the Tories in 1979, but the new Conservative government embraced the policy. Margaret Thatcher adopted the label 'privatization', which was originally coined by Peter Drucker and which replaced the name 'denationalization' (Yergin and Stanislaw, 1998:114). The time was ripe for a movement to the market. Britain had won the Falklands War with Argentina in 1982 and the following election gave Thatcher tremendous political capital. At the same time, the state-owned enterprises in the UK had become inefficient inflexible 'employment agencies' (ibid.:115). There was little market discipline in management or the product markets and, basically, the state owned firms were not run well. Given the inflation and slow growth of the UK in the 1970s, privatizations were part of the move towards markets that was needed to change economic conditions. However, early sales were strenuously attacked by the Labour opposition, which promised that, if it were re-elected, it would renationalize divested firms such as British Aerospace and Cable and Wireless.[2]

Of course, the Thatcher government had to learn how to privatize SOEs. Yergin and Stanislaw (1998:117) quote a government official as saying of the difficulty of privatization, 'to all extents and purposes it had never been done before . . . there was no departmental dossier to dust down'. We discuss the factors that influence the design of privatization programmes in the next section. It was not until the successful British Telecom initial public offering in November 1984 that privatization became established as a basic economic policy in the UK. A series of increasingly massive share issue privatizations (SIPs) during the last half of the 1980s and early 1990s reduced the role of SOEs in the British economy to nearly nothing after the Tories left office in 1997, from more than 10 per cent of GDP 18 years earlier. The remaining major state enterprise is the Post Office.

We note that the objectives set for the British privatization programme by the Conservatives were virtually the same as those listed by the Adenauer government 20 years before – and almost every government in the years since. These goals, as described in Price Waterhouse (1989a; 1989b) were to (1) raise revenue for the state, (2) promote economic efficiency, (3) reduce government interference in the economy, (4) promote wider share ownership, (5) provide the opportunity to introduce competition, and (6) subject SOEs to market discipline. The other major objective mentioned by the Thatcher and subsequent governments was to develop the national capital market (see also Menyah and Paudyal, 1996, for a more detailed discussion of the goals of the British privatization programme).

The perceived success of the British privatization programme helped to persuade many other industrialized countries to begin divesting SOEs through public share offerings. Jacques Chirac's government, which came to power in France in 1986, privatized 22 companies (worth US$12bn) before being ousted in 1988. The returning Socialist government did not execute any further sales, but neither did it renationalize the divested firms. Beginning in 1993, the Balladur government launched a new and even larger French privatization programme, which has continued under the Jospin administration. The Socialists in the 1990s in fact carried out the two largest French privatization sales ever, the US$7.1bn France Telecom initial public offering (IPO) in October 1997 and the subsequent US$10.5bn France Telecom issue in November 1998.

Numerous other European governments, including Italy, Germany and Spain, also launched large privatization programmes during the 1990s (Parker, 1998). These programmes typically relied on public share offerings, and were launched by governments that varied across the political spectrum. Megginson *et al.* (2001) report that, from 1977 to 2000, there were 736 privatizations in Western Europe with an average (median) value of US$894mn ($177.5mn). The total value of these privatizations was 55 per cent of the value of all privatizations worldwide at this time.

The European privatizations were also related closely to the Maastricht Treaty. This treaty, which set out the way to a single currency and a common monetary policy, put significant fiscal requirements on the nations that signed. There was a requirement to reduce deficits, and the sale of

SOEs was a way to raise cash. Further, in the economic integration of Europe, there was a movement against protecting national markets, especially in the case of public monopolies.

Yergin and Stanislaw (1998:150) also note the influence of the World Bank, as exemplified by the 1991 edition of the World Bank's *World Development Report*. The report, written under the direction of the renowned economist Larry Summers (who went on to be Secretary of the Treasury and President of Harvard), argued against government intervention. Instead the report suggested that governments pursue 'market-friendly' policies.

Another factor, that is implicit in the above discussion, was the changing view of markets that began in the 1970s and continued through the 1990s (see Yergin and Stanislaw, 1998, especially chapter 5, for a more complete discussion). Just as the rise of nationalization in the 1940s and 1950s was fuelled by intellectual and popular dissatisfaction with the operation of private firms, the movement towards markets (of which privatization was a part) was fuelled by powerful intellectual arguments. Margaret Thatcher and her followers were guided by the writings of Nobel Laureate Friedrich von Hayek. In his books, including *The Road to Serfdom* and the *Constitution of Liberty*, Hayek argued against government planning. At the same time, economists, especially from the University of Chicago, presented stinging critiques of government intervention in almost all aspects of the economy. Much of the work included a critical component, which was that government should not be viewed as acting in the 'public interest'. Instead, government and the individuals in government responded to incentives, as do all people, which had the result that much government intervention was inconsistent with the efficient allocation of resources. Note, however, that, as Milton Friedman, Nobel prize winner from the University of Chicago and a leading intellectual voice for the use of markets to determine the allocation of resources, said:

> People are not influential in arguing for different courses in the economy . . . The role of people is to keep ideas alive until a crisis occurs. It wasn't my talking that caused people to embrace these ideas, just as the rooster doesn't make the sun rise. Collectivism was an impossible way to run an economy. What has brought the change is reality, fact – and what Marx called the inevitable forces of history. (Yergin and Stanislaw, 1998:149)

In other words, privatization arose not because of ideas but because government ownership and management of firms did not work.

Privatization techniques
Governments usually choose one of three techniques to privatize: asset sales, share issue privatizations (SIPs) or voucher privatizations. With an

asset sale, the government sells ownership of the state-owned enterprise to an existing private firm or to a small group of investors. This is similar to the traditional use of the private capital market in non-SOE transactions. The government may sell a fraction or all of the SOE through an asset sale. Typically, these asset sales are implemented through an auction, although governments sometimes sell SOEs directly to private investors. López-de-Silanes (1997) and LaPorta and López-de-Silanes (1999) describe a very important national privatization programme, in Mexico, that relied almost exclusively on asset sales.

In share issue privatizations (SIPs), the privatizing government sells equity shares through the public capital market to both retail and institutional investors. SIPs are the largest and most economically significant of all privatizations, and account for the preponderance of assets privatized in terms of value. Jones *et al.* (1999) report that, up to 1997, governments in 59 countries raised over US$446bn through 630 SIP transactions.

Formerly Communist Eastern European nations, such as Russia, Poland and the Czech Republic, have used voucher privatizations. Voucher privatizations are similar to SIPs in that shares of ownership are distributed broadly. However, in this method of privatization the government distributes vouchers (paper claims that are exchanged for ownership in previously state-owned firms) to each citizen. These vouchers are usually free or very low cost and are available to most citizens. Thus voucher privatizations result in assets being virtually given away to citizens. In a sense, they are SIPs offered at a very low price.

Voucher privatizations arose in different circumstances from other privatizations. Boycko *et al.* (1994), for example, discuss the fundamental differences between the communist (and formerly communist) countries and the rest of the world. Low income levels characterize the communist countries, and income is also distributed very unequally. In addition, the communist countries had huge amounts of assets to be privatized quickly. SIPs were often politically unacceptable in Eastern Europe because the only individuals with the wealth to acquire shares were 'communists, criminals and foreigners'. Thus the only viable way to privatize and maintain significant domestic ownership was perceived to be through voucher distributions. Note also that no voucher privatizations have been used outside former communist countries.

Gibbon (1997) provides a discussion of the decisions facing a government that wants to privatize through cash sales, and discusses the steps such a government must take in developing a divestment programme. These include setting up a structure for privatization (including legislation), providing adequate performance records for SOEs being sold (generating believable accounting data), developing any necessary new regulatory structures and determining the appropriate post-sale relationship between the firm and the government. Other authors who examine non-pricing issues relating to the divestment contracts involved in privatization include Baldwin and Bhattacharyya (1991), Rondinelli and Iacono (1996), Schmidt (1996) and Cornelli and Li (1997).

Another set of choices is whether to sell the SOE in the public capital market or in the private capital market. As noted above, there are two primary ways in which a government may sell an SOE to raise revenue for a country: either by an asset sale of the SOE to a small group of investors or another firm (that is, through the private capital market) or as a share-issue privatization (that is, through the public capital market). Megginson, *et al.* (2001) study the factors that influence the choice between using public capital markets (SIP) or private capital markets (asset sale) for the sale of an SOE. They find that the nature of the capital market in the privatizing country affects the privatization decision: SIPs may be used in countries with less developed capital markets, perhaps resulting from the government's need and desire to use SIPs to develop the national market's liquidity and absorptive capacity. In addition, SIPs are more likely when income is more equal throughout the country, providing for more potential investors and avoiding the need for extensive underpricing of offerings.

Megginson *et al.*'s (2001) results also support the importance of a country's political and legal environment in the privatization decision. They find that governments that have a greater ability to commit themselves credibly to property rights are more likely to privatize SOEs via asset sales. Investors should be more willing to make the substantial investments required for acquiring SOEs through asset sales when there is a stronger commitment that they will be able to maintain ownership of those assets without fear of renationalization.

Firm-specific characteristics, such as the size of the offering or sale and the profitability of the SOE, also have an impact on the method of privatization. Larger offerings and more profitable SOEs are more likely to be privatized through SIPs and the public capital markets. Asymmetric information problems are less for larger and more profitable offerings, attracting more potential investors. In addition, some have argued that governments are more likely to choose to privatize profitable firms via SIPs in order to gain more political support for their privatization policies.

Selling shares to individual shareholders is the most important privatization technique in terms of the value of assets divested. The largest SOEs can usually only be sold by a SIP. Further, there are several advantages to selling SOEs in a share offering to individual shareholders. SIPs are a transparent way of selling assets and can be very important to a government trying to show it is selling the firm fairly. Perhaps most importantly, governments are able to modify the share allocation, pricing and other terms of a SIP to achieve political and economic objectives.

Jones *et al.* (1999) provide a comprehensive study of sales of SOEs through SIPs. They test empirically whether government issuers are attempting to maximize SIP offering proceeds or are instead trying to achieve multiple political and economic objectives, even at the cost of revenue maximization. They analyse a large sample of 630 SIPs from 59 countries made over the period June 1977 to July 1997. One result that Jones *et al.* document is the sheer size of SIP offers: the mean (median) size of initial SIPs is US$555.7mn (US$104.0 mn) and the mean size of subsequent, seasoned issues is US$1.069bn (median US$311.0mn), much larger than typical stock offerings. Their evidence on the allocation of control in SIPs supports a political interpretation of the divesting governments' motives. They find that nearly all SIPs are purely secondary offerings, in which only the government sells its shares and no money flows to the firm itself. Since the divesting government sells an average (median) of 43.9 per cent (35.0 per cent) of the SOE's capital in initial offers and 22.7 per cent (18.1 per cent) in other issues, the offers cited in the Jones *et al.* study represent significant reductions in direct government stock ownership. The authors find that, although governments typically surrender day-to-day operating control of the SOE to private owners in the initial SIP, they retain effective veto power through a variety of techniques. The most common technique is government retention of a 'golden share', which gives it the power to veto certain actions, such as foreign takeovers. These golden shares have been used infrequently, however.

Jones *et al.* (1999) also test the underpricing models of Perotti (1995) and Biais and Perotti (2002). Both models predict that governments that are ideologically committed to privatization and economic reform will deliberately underprice SIPs and will privatize in stages, to signal their commitment to protecting investor property rights. 'Populist' governments that are pursuing privatization strictly as a means of raising revenue will be unwilling to underprice as much as will committed governments. Populist governments will also try to sell larger stakes in SOEs. Jones *et al.* find that SIPs are significantly underpriced by government sellers. The mean level of underpricing for initial SIPs is 34.1 per cent (median 12.4 per cent). Even seasoned SIP offers are underpriced by an average of 9.4 per cent (median 3.3 per cent).

They also find that initial returns (reflecting underpricing on flotation) are significantly positively related to the fraction of the firm's capital sold and to the degree of income inequality (measured by the Gini coefficient) in a country, and that initial returns are negatively related to the level of government spending as a fraction of GDP (a proxy for how socialist a society is) and to a dummy variable indicating that more than 50 per cent of a company's stock is being sold. Collectively, these findings strongly support the predictions of Perotti (1995) and Biais and Perotti (2002).

The above studies generally examine privatizations performed everywhere but the United States. This is because there were few state-owned enterprises of the type that had developed in the rest of the world to privatize in the USA (one exception was the Conrail privatization included by Jones *et al.*, 1999, in their study). In the USA, privatization refers more to

> government's contracting out of local public services to private providers. A city or county government may contract with a private company to pick up the garbage, to keep city parks clean, to manage its hospitals, to provide ambulance services, to run schools and airports, or even to provide police and fire protection. (López-de-Silanes *et al.*, 1997)

In the USA, since about 1970, local governments' contracting out for the provision of services has become more popular. The basic reason is saving money, owing to the generally greater efficiencies of privately run firms. López-de-Silanes *et al.* use data from the 1987 and 1992 Census of Government to examine factors that lead county government to privatize public services. They suggest that politicians benefit from in-house provision of public services through patronage and support from public employee unions. The trade-off is that government provision is more expensive, which means higher taxes, which voters do not like. Their evidence suggests that the parameters of this trade-off affect the decision to privatize.

Privatization and corporate governance
There has been a significant amount of academic research on corporate governance, which has flourished just as governments have begun reaching for policy guidance on governance. Shleifer and Vishny (1997), provide a survey of corporate governance as of about 1997, and since then much research has developed. One line of research examines how a country's legal system (especially whether the system is based on English common law) influences the size, efficiency and productivity of that nation's capital markets. This stream is complemented by the second line of inquiry, which studies whether the size and efficiency of a nation's capital markets influences the rate of economic growth the country can achieve.

The work of LaPorta *et al.* (1997, 1998, 1999, 2000a, 2000b; hereafter LLSV) has had an unprecedented impact owing to its volume and the fact that the papers have been published in very prestigious academic journals. Using a sample of 49 countries, LLSV (1997) show that countries with poorer investor protection – measured both by the character of legal rules and by the quality of law enforcement – have smaller and less liquid capital markets. This is true for both debt and equity markets, suggesting that stock and bond markets are complements rather than substitutes, and both require the proper legal infrastructure to reach maturity. LLSV (1997) also show that French civil law countries offer much poorer investor protection than do common law countries, and LLSV (1998) show why this is so. They examine the investor protection characteristics of the world's four basic legal systems (English common law, French civil law and German and Scandinavian law) and find that the common law countries offer by far the greatest protection to non-controlling investors. Further, LLSV (1998) document and provide a rationale for the fact that ownership concentration is highest in countries offering poor investor protection, which is consistent with the idea that small, diversified shareholders are unlikely to be important in countries that fail to protect outside investors. In a specific investigation of the ownership structures of the largest publicly traded companies in the world's developed economies, LLSV (1999) show that dispersed ownership structures are common only in the USA, Japan and Britain. Effective family control over even the largest companies – often exercised through pyramidal share ownership structures – is the norm everywhere else. LLSV (2000a) also find that dividend policies in different nations are related to ownership structure-related agency costs.

Empirical studies by LLSV and others support their proposition that a nation's legal system influences the optimal ownership structures of publicly listed companies, and that ownership structure 'matters'. LLSV (1999) find that the size of a nation's government is related to its efficiency, honesty (the legal system again) and the demographic make-up of its citizenry. LLSV (2000b) document that countries with the greatest legal protection for investors also assign the highest valuation to publicly traded shares. The clear implication of this finding is that individual investors are more willing to entrust their savings to capital market investments when they are confident that insiders will not expropriate their wealth. Demirgüç-Kunt and Maksimovic (1998) show that, in countries whose legal systems score high on an efficiency index, a greater proportion of firms use long-term external financing. Since their measure of efficiency is different from LLSV's, the results are not a direct test of the LLSV hypothesis that common law countries offer better investor protection than civil law countries (especially since France receives higher efficiency scores than Britain). Nonetheless, Demirgüç-Kunt and Maksimovic document that an active stock market and large banking sector are associated with externally financed firm growth, and that companies in countries with weak financial sectors are unable to fund maximum achievable growth. Finally, though Coffee (1999) takes issue with LLSV's focus on the transcending importance of a nation's system of corporate law, he agrees that the commercial legal system is a vitally important part of an effective corporate governance system, notwithstanding his emphasis on differences in national securities laws and regulations.

Conclusions

This chapter has provided an introduction to the history of privatization, the theory of privatization, the techniques of privatization and the relationship between privatization and corporate governance. Privatization represents a movement away from state allocation of resources towards decisions on resource allocation being made by private parties and the actions of markets. The debate on the role of the state and markets has occurred many times throughout history. Whether the movement represented by privatization will continue will be determined to a large extent by how well markets work.

Notes

1. Gough (1989) notes that Briggs (1961) claimed that Archbishop Temple first used the term 'welfare state' in wartime Britain to differentiate Britain from the 'warfare' state of Nazi Germany.
2. Ironically, a Labour government partially privatized an SOE just before Thatcher came to power. In 1977, the Labour government sold a relatively small fraction of the government's shares in British Petroleum as a means of raising cash.

References

Baldwin, C.Y. and S. Bhattacharyya (1991) 'Choosing the Method of Sale: A Clinical Study of Conrail', *Journal of Financial Economics*, 30, 69–98.

Biais, B. and E. Perotti (2002) 'Machiavellian Privatization', *American Economic Review*, 92, 240–58.

Boycko, M., A. Shleifer and R.W. Vishny (1994) 'Voucher Privatization', *Journal of Financial Economics*, 35, 249–66.

Briggs, A. (1961) 'The Welfare State in Historical Perspective', *Archives Européennes de Sociologie*, 2(2), 221–59.

Coffee, J.C., Jr. (1999) 'Privatization and Corporate Governance: The Lessons From Securities Market Failure', *Journal of Corporate Law*, 25, 1–39.

Cornelli, F. and D.D. Li (1997) 'Large Shareholders, Private Benefits of Control, and Optimal Schemes of Privatization', *Rand Journal of Econmics*, 28, 585–604.

Davis, J., R. Ossowski, T. Richardson and S. Barnett (2000) 'Fiscal and Macroeconomic Aspects of Privatization', IMF Occasional Paper No. 194, International Monetary Fund, Washington, DC.

Demirgüç-Kunt, A. and V. Maksimovic (1998) 'Law, Finance, and Firm Growth', *Journal of Finance*, 53, 2107–39.

Gibbon, H. (1997) 'A Seller's Manual: Guidelines for Selling State-Owned Enterprises', *Privatisation Yearbook*, London: Privatisation International.

Gough, I. (1989) 'The Welfare State', in *The New Palgrave Social Economics*, New York: W.W. Norton, pp. 276–81.

Jones, S.L., W.L. Megginson, R.C. Nash and J.M. Netter (1999) 'Share Issue Privatizations as Financial Means to Political and Economic Ends', *Journal of Financial Economics*, 53, 217–53.

Laffont, J.J. and J. Tirole (1993) *A Theory of Incentives in Procurement and Regulation*, Cambridge, MA: MIT Press.

La Porta, R. and F. López-de-Silanes (1999) 'Benefits of Privatization – Evidence From Mexico', *Quarterly Journal of Economics*, 114(4), 1193–242.

La Porta, R., F. López-de-Silanes and A. Shleifer (2000a) 'Government Ownership of Banks', NBER Working Paper 7620, National Bureau of Economic Research, Cambridge, MA.

La Porta, R., F. López-de-Silanes and A. Shleifer (2000b) 'Investor Protection and Corporate Governance', *Journal of Financial Economics*, 58, 3–27.

La Porta, R., F. López-de-Silanes, A. Shleifer and R. Vishny (1997) 'Legal Determinants of External Finance', *Journal of Finance*, 52, 1131–50.

La Porta, R., F. López-de-Silanes, A., Shleifer and R. Vishny (1998) 'Law and Finance', *Journal of Political Economy*, 106, 1113–55.

La Porta, R., F. López-de-Silanes, A., Shleifer and R. Vishny (1999) 'The Quality of Government', *Journal of Law and Economic Organization*, 15, 222–79.

López-de-Silanes, F. (1997) 'Determinants of Privatization Prices', *Quarterly Journal of Economics*, 112, 965–1025.

López-de-Silanes, F., A. Shleifer and R.W. Vishny (1997) 'Privatization in the United States', *Rand Journal of Economics*, 28, 447–71.

Means, H. (2001) *Money and Power*, New York: John Wiley and Sons.

Megginson, W., R. Nash, J. Netter and A. Poulsen (2001) 'The Choice Between Private and Public Markets: Evidence From Privatizations', Working Paper, University of Georgia, Athens.

Megginson, W. and J. Netter (2001) 'From State to Market: A Survey of Empirical Studies on Privatization', *Journal of Economic Literature*, 39, 321–89.

Menya, K. and K. Paudyal (1996) 'Share Issue Privatisations: The UK Experience', in M. Levis (ed.), *Empirical Issues in Raising Equity Capital*, Amsterdam: Elsevier Science.

Middelton, R. (1996) *Government versus the Market*, Cheltenham, UK and Brookfield, US: Edward Elgar.

Noll, R.G. (2000) 'Telecommunications Reform in Developing Countries', in A.O. Kreuger (ed.), *Economic Policy Reform: The Second Stage*, Chicago: University of Chicago Press.

Parker, D. (ed.) (1998) *Privatization in the European Union: Theory and Policy Perspectives*, London: Routledge.

Perotti, E. (1995) 'Credible Privatization', *American Economic Review*, 85, 847–59.

Price Waterhouse (1989a) *Privatization: Learning the Lessons from the U.K. Experience*, London: Price Waterhouse.

Price Waterhouse (1989b), *Privatization: The Facts*, London: Price Waterhouse.

Rondinelli, D. and M. Iacono (1996) *Policies and Institutions for Managing Privatization*, Turin: International Training Centre, International Labor Office.

Schmidt, K. (1996) 'The Costs and Benefits of Privatization: An Incomplete Contracts Approach', *Journal of Law and Economic Organization*, 12, 1–24.

Shleifer, A. (1998) 'State Versus Private Ownership', *Journal of Economic Perspectives*, 12, 133–50.

Shleifer, A. and R.W. Vishny (1997) 'A Survey of Corporate Governance', *Journal of Finance*, 52, 737–83.

Sobel, R. (1999) *The Pursuit of Wealth*, New York: McGraw-Hill.

Yergin, D. and J. Stanislaw (1998) *The Commanding Heights: The Battle Between Government and the Marketplace that is Remaking the Modern World*, New York: Simon & Schuster.

Yotopoulos, P.A. (1989) 'The (Rip)tide of Privatization: Lessons From Chile', *World Development*, 17, 683–702.

3 Privatization: analysing the benefits
Colin Robinson

Introduction

The purpose of this chapter is to discuss the concept and theory of privatization. It does not examine in any detail the empirical evidence about the effects of privatization on efficiency, costs, prices, service standards and other indicators of performance: these effects are considered in subsequent chapters.[1] This chapter concentrates on the reasons which lie behind privatization, the potential benefits and the way in which privatization is, in practice, affected by the political calculus.

The privatization movement, which began towards the end of the twentieth century and which is now under way in many parts of the world, had its origins primarily in Britain. According to the OECD:

> The United Kingdom by its persistent action over a decade created a framework for the planning and execution of privatisation programs in an advanced industrial economy with well-developed capital markets, which would serve as a model for other countries at later times. (OECD, 1997)

Forty years earlier, a British government had carried out a major change in industrial policy by nationalizing what were then regarded as the 'commanding heights' of the economy. Influenced by the apparent failings of capitalist economies in the 1930s, the perceived success of the planned wartime economy in Britain and the prevailing view that detailed government control of industry was both possible and desirable, Clement Attlee's post-war Labour government took industries such as coal, electricity, gas, long-distance road transport, the railways, inland waterways, the airlines and, later, steel into state ownership.[2] By the 1980s, the prevailing view had changed as the 'counter revolution' in economics had revived interest in using market forces rather than relying on planning (Robinson, 2000). A new 'semi-consensus' had emerged (Henderson, 2001). The recently-elected Conservative government under Margaret (now Lady) Thatcher, began the second major shift in industrial policy of the post-war period by denationalizing the industries which had been placed in state ownership 40 years earlier.

Privatization UK-style was, appropriately enough, from the 1980s onwards spread around the world by private initiatives. The army of management consultants, lawyers and other experts which had participated in the UK privatizations had a powerful incentive to employ elsewhere the expertise that had been developed. As other countries began to contemplate emulating the UK, a demand for privatization advice emerged which these experts satisfied, thus exporting British experience to the rest of the world.

One indication of the scale of privatization programmes in recent years is given by the annual OECD survey of gross revenues raised from privatizations (Table 3.1). In the early 1990s, these revenues were running at US$30–50 bn a year: by the late 1990s, worldwide revenues had risen to US$130–160 bn, before subsiding to US$100 bn in 2000 in the face of weak equity markets. At one time the bulk of privatization was taking place in the UK (in the early 1990s, UK privatization revenues were about 40 per cent of the world total) but since 1997 there has been very little privatization in the UK. The centres of privatization activity within the OECD area have shifted to other EU countries, especially France, Germany, Italy, Portugal and Spain and to Japan and Australia. Some smaller European countries in 'transition', such as the Czech Republic, Poland and Hungary, have also had active privatization programmes (see Chapters 18, 19 and 20 below). Favoured sectors for privatization have been telecommunications, electricity, gas, water, airlines, airports and those manufacturing activities which were in state hands.

The value of revenues raised is not a particularly good indicator of the impact of privatization: using it implies that the prime objective of privatization is to raise revenues for government which, as explained in the section, 'Privatization in practice', below, may be the main political objective but is not the aim most economists would emphasize. However, the trend of worldwide revenues and the distribution of the proceeds among countries (Table 3.1), imperfect indicators as they are, do help to show how privatization has spread. It is now no longer a phenomenon of the more economically advanced countries but, partly because of the influence of the international financial institutions, extends to less developed countries. In recent years the share of OECD countries in worldwide privatization revenues has been around two-thirds.

Reasons for privatization

Privatization is sometimes regarded as either a purely 'ideological' phenomenon or as a response to the perceived poor performance of state-owned industries. As for ideology, there is no doubt that, in the home of privatization, the Thatcher administrations had a strong commitment to freeing markets that were then state-controlled and so they were inclined to privatize. Before the Thatcher administrations were first elected, and in their early years, there was a great deal of preparation for privatization in the sense that liberal market economists argued the case for privatization in general and

Table 3.1　*International privatization by gross value, 1990–2000*
　　　　　(US$ mn)

	1990	1995	1997	1998	1999	2000*
Australia	19	8089	16815	7146	15220	6239
Austria	32	1035	2438	2537	70	2083
Belgium		2745	1842	2288	10	
Canada	1504	3998		11		
Czech Rep.		1205	442	469	707	544
Denmark	644	10	45	4502	19	111
Finland		363	835	1999	3716	1827
France		4136	10105	13596	9478	17438
Germany			1125	364	6734	
Greece		44	1395	3960	4880	1384
Hungary	38	3813	1966	353	88	66
Iceland		6	4	128	228	1
Ireland		157			4846	1458
Italy		10131	24536	14497	25594	9728
Japan				6641	15115	
Korea		480	539	599	6249	1307
Luxemburg						
Mexico	3124	170	2670	988	279	406
Netherlands	716	3993	842	335	1481	310
New Zealand	3895	264		441	1331	
Norway	73	521	35		454	1039
Poland	23	1101	2043	2079	3422	5993
Portugal	1092	2362	4909	4299	1620	3256
Slovak Republic		1004	11			
Spain	172	2940	12529	11618	1129	1079
Sweden		852	2390	172	2071	8082
Switzerland				10869		
Turkey	486	572	466	1020	38	2712
UK	12906	6691	4544			
US			3650	3100		
Total OECD	24724	56684	96175	94011	104780	65063
Of which, EU 15	15562	35460	67535	60167	61649	46756
Other countries	8494	13546	57099	45153	37107	35000
Global total	33218	70230	153273	139164	141886	100063

Note:　* provisional.

Source:　OECD (2001).

made proposals for particular schemes – though on economic grounds rather than in terms of political ideology.[3] In other countries, there have been equally strong commitments to privatize. However, if the claim is that privatization is a policy of the 'right', it does not stand up to examination.

First, it is naive, if not meaningless, to label parties as 'left' 'right' or 'centre' as though the complexities of people's views on economic, social and other matters could be adequately captured by so simplified a political spectrum. The 'median voter theorem', for example, which assumes that political views can be described by a distribution shown on a two dimensional diagram, though a useful pedagogic device, is a gross simplification of reality (Rowley, 1984). Moreover, the evidence shows that privatization is a policy which has been embraced by governments of many different political complexions (Henderson, 2001), including New Labour in Britain. Whereas the Conservative Party in Britain denationalized industries that Clement Attlee's Labour government had nationalized in the 1940s, New Labour is venturing into the new territories of health and education because it evidently believes that 'what works' is what matters and that private enterprise has a role, even if as yet that role is not clearly defined, in health and education. It is also undertaking a variety of public–private partnership (PPP) initiatives. In other countries – for example, China, Mexico, Argentina and New Zealand – governments of the 'left' have undertaken liberalizing economic reform programmes, including privatization.

The argument that privatization was undertaken for negative reasons has more substance. Many governments have felt the urge to privatize, partly because they were concerned that state-owned industries were becoming a burden: subsidies were mounting, managements were not responsive to consumers and unions were over-powerful. The state monopolies which employed their members could pass on to consumers the costs of wage settlements.[4] Consequently, governments which were being blamed for the shortcomings of these industries wanted to try something new in the hope of relieving the burden.

In Britain, it is certainly true that in the 1980s the Thatcher privatizations were undertaken partly because the performance of the then nationalized industries was generally agreed to be so poor. Consumers were dissatisfied and there were constant tensions between governments of both major parties and the managements of the state corporations, which a succession of White Paper proposals from 1961 onwards[5] (many of which were not put into practice) did nothing to ease (Heald, 1980). Public disquiet about the nationalized industries and about the public sector unions which were so powerful in those industries (as demonstrated in the 'winter of discontent' in 1978/9) was such that Mrs Thatcher could proceed to privatize with some support from the electorate. It is true too that New Labour's enthusiasm today for introducing private enterprise into health and education is driven partly by the perceived failures of state ownership and control in those sectors.

But there is more to privatization than political ideology or negative arguments. There are sound economic reasons to expect private companies to perform better than their state-owned counterparts. They are examined in the rest of this chapter, which begins by making some relevant distinctions and then considers reasons of principle why private enterprise is likely to be superior to state ownership. It also discusses the extent to which real-world privatizations may differ from those that economists might recommend, principally because of government failure.

Some distinctions

Privatization can have many different meanings.[6] Clearly, there must be state ownership in the pre-existing state or there is nothing to privatize, but 'privatization' is a term applied to a great variety of arrangements. For instance, state ownership may be superseded by 'public–private partnerships' which come in various forms. The private sector's role may be no more than providing capital for projects, which are devised and operated by government bodies; or the private sector may manage the assets as well as provide finance; or it may build, own and operate some assets for a period before they revert to government ownership; or there may be a more permanent arrangement for joint ownership and operation.

Going beyond these partnerships, more radical forms of privatization involve the sale of government-owned assets, creating private property rights, either to the public through a share flotation as in most privatizations in OECD countries with well-developed capital markets, or to existing companies ('trade sales'), as has been the dominant method outside the OECD area, where countries not only lack capital markets but also seek access to product markets, capital and technology.[7] The new organizations resulting from privatization may be entirely in private hands or government may retain a share, as through a 'golden share', which provides a veto over ownership changes.

Privatization in all its forms should also be distinguished from other policies with which it is often linked – liberalization (the establishment of competitive product markets) and deregulation (the removal of government rules that hinder competition). Liberalization and deregulation tend to be complements: competitive product markets cannot exist unless they have been substantially deregulated. But privatization can proceed independently of either. Because, under state ownership, state monopolies are often established – so producing insurmountable barriers to entry – privatization of state-owned companies is often a necessary condition for liberalization. But it is not sufficient. Some privatizations transfer monopolies whole into the private sector and so, initially at least, do not liberalize markets (though the new private companies will find it difficult to retain their monopoly power unless some government-imposed barrier to entry remains). The markets in which the privatized companies operate may also remain heavily regulated by government.

Moreover, liberalization and deregulation can proceed independently of privatization. For example, there may be a degree of liberalization if restrictions on imports are lifted and regulations are removed that had previously hindered competition, even if a state-owned corporation remains in the market (for example, see the description of the US postal system in Chapter 9). As a further example, the controls which had kept imported coal out of the British market from the late 1950s onwards were relaxed almost 10 years before the British coal industry was privatized, so that the coal market became significantly more competitive well in advance of privatization (Robinson and Marshall, 1985).

Potential benefits of privatization
A number of economic benefits can be expected from privatization though, as explained below, they will not necessarily be realized in any particular privatization programme.

Change of ownership
Privatization *per se* produces a change of ownership which, in principle, can yield efficiency gains. An inherent problem in markets where there are state-owned corporations is the absence of transferable property rights. The problem is neatly captured in the well-known phrase, 'what is owned by everyone is perceived to be owned by no-one'. That is, citizens of a country may be told that a corporation is in 'public ownership', but in practice that 'ownership' is valueless since they have no property rights and it is virtually impossible for them to influence what the corporation does. The agency problem, which always exists when there is a divorce between the ownership and the management of an organization, is maximized.[8] The corporation is not in the market for corporate control (Chiplin and Wright, 1987); it has no shareholders other than government; and it is immune to the pressures normally exerted by shareholders on managements.

The owners of a company require means of monitoring and controlling the actions of managers, who are their agents: they do not want managers to pursue their own interests but those of the owners. Incentive structures that align the interests of owners and managers, such as performance-related rewards, are notoriously difficult to devise. Nevertheless, shareholders have the power of exit as well as of voice (Hirschman, 1970). Complaints to managers or protests at Annual General Meetings may not be very effective, but the prospect of a plunging share price, as disgruntled shareholders sell their holdings in protest at underperforming managers, is a wonderful way of concentrating managers' minds. Not only will the wealth of managers who are also shareholders be reduced but, more important, the decline in the company's stock market value may well put it into play as a target for a potential bidder.

Efficiency pressures on state-owned corporations are, by contrast, extremely weak. They are subject to monitoring by finance ministries or sponsoring departments of government, which, in the absence of a capital market, have no way of establishing a relevant standard of comparison to determine how efficient the corporations are. The problem is particularly serious if, as is often the case, the state corporation has a monopoly of the domestic market. If, for example, there is only one electricity generator in a country, the government has no standard of comparison by which to determine what an efficient generator would look like. It can only fall back on international comparisons – which are unsatisfactory because it is hard to control for the many likely differences in circumstances across countries and because of possible exchange rate distortions – or turn to management consultants who can carry out 'efficiency audits', but who also have no appropriate benchmarks for comparison. In summary, where there are monopoly state corporations, the absence of information from either capital markets or product markets means that virtually all the information required for useful efficiency comparisons is missing.

Citizens, as principals of a state-owned company, lack the power of exit enjoyed by private shareholders. They have to rely on making their voices heard, primarily through the politicians and civil servants who are the immediate principals of the state corporation managements. But this very indirect influence is highly unsatisfactory. Not only do politicians and civil servants lack relevant information, as explained above; they may have all kinds of objectives in mind for the corporations other than their being efficient and responsive to the wishes of citizens. Unless one makes the heroic assumption that politicians and civil servants are altruistic, wise individuals devoted to the interests of the community as a whole, and the further assumption that those interests are discoverable and can be pursued other than through market processes, much more serious principal–agent problems seem inevitable in markets where there are state corporations than where there is private ownership.

Depoliticization
Another issue in markets where there are state-owned corporations is politicization, which has implications for efficiency. The presence of a state corporation inevitably means that governments will be held responsible for its

major (and possibly minor) decisions. The corporation's management will therefore constantly be second-guessed by members of the government, who have an incentive to know in some detail what the corporation is doing and to influence its decisions. One consequence is that lobbying is rife. The managements of the corporations realize that their activities are affected at least as much by the actions of politicians and civil servants as by their own efforts to innovate and to cut costs. Lobbying therefore appears to be a relatively high return activity into which corporate resources will inevitably flow, diverting scarce productive factors away from efficiency improvements.

Of course, markets where there are private corporations are not immune to lobbying activity, so the difference between private and state ownership should not be exaggerated. But the returns to lobbying tend to be relatively high in state-owned corporations, so lobbying is innate. The predictable result is less attention to cost reduction than in private corporations.

Liberalization
The case for liberalization needs some brief explanation. It is not, as might appear from mainstream economics textbooks, that the economy can and should be transformed into a series of perfectly competitive markets so that the well-known Pareto optimal results will appear, or that some individual market can be moved closer to a perfectly competitive state.[9] There are numerous problems with this mainstream view. First, the textbook model of perfect competition describes an end-state but is silent about the process ('competition') by which this state is reached (Kirzner, 1997). Second, it is difficult to see how a perfectly competitive market can ever exist because it requires perfect knowledge and, by definition, that is not a realizable condition: knowledge of the future, which is what is required for decision making (Robinson, 1971) must, so far as we know, remain forever imperfect. Moreover, it is not obvious that a state of atomistic competition would be particularly desirable even if it could exist. It is therefore unhelpful to regard perfectly competitive markets as an ideal at which one should aim. Targets which can never be reached and which, even if they could be reached, are not clearly desirable are of little value.[10]

The case for market liberalization is that competitive processes can be set in train which will have efficiency advantages and bring benefits to consumers. In essence, the argument is that competitive markets give consumers the power of exit – they can move from suppliers they do not like to others – and so there is constant pressure on producers to set higher standards, which their competitors must then try to emulate: in other words, there is a race to the top. This kind of market process is what the classical economists meant by competition (Blaug, 1987) and it is also what neo-Austrian economists mean (Littlechild, 1978; Kirzner, 1997; Robinson, 1997). At the heart of the competitive market process is entrepreneurship – the constant search by alert entrepreneurs for better ways of doing things.

On this view, the market is not a state (like the long-run equilibrium of perfect competition) but a *process* of dynamic change, in which the status quo is constantly being disturbed. Market disequilibrium, not equilibrium, is the norm as rivals constantly seek new opportunities. The benefits of the process are to be measured not in terms of the static efficiency gains, which are supposed to result from a perfectly competitive market, but by dynamic gains produced by constant innovation, which is itself a consequence of market rivalry. Gains are passed on to consumers because companies in the market are competing. The key to a market of this sort is that there should be free entry. There do not have to be many producers in a market at any one time for there to be a competitive process: provided there is a credible threat of entry, incumbents will behave as though they were in competitive conditions. Seen in these terms, market liberalization means stimulating a competitive market process.

As explained above, product market liberalization is not necessarily associated with privatization. A programme of privatization may merely transform state monopolies into private monopolies, in the short run at least. And, even while state ownership exists, there can be limited liberalization moves. However, a move from state to private ownership is usually a necessary condition for significant market liberalization. So long as there is a state corporation that enjoys a monopoly of some activity, or tax and other privileges, entry to that corporation's market will range from the impossible (where there is a monopoly granted by the state) to the very difficult. Privatization of the state corporation will therefore free entry to the market, opening the way for the greater product market competition, which most economists would probably regard as the biggest source of benefit from privatization.[11]

As recently as 20 years ago, liberalization of industries such as gas, electricity, water, telecommunications and the railways – which were in state ownership in many countries – would have been regarded as unfeasible or, if feasible, undesirable, because they were thought to be 'natural monopolies'. Natural monopolies are industries that would naturally gravitate to single ownership, even if the starting point were multiple ownership, for example because of significant economies of scale. So structural issues were thought to rule out market liberalization, even if the industries were privatized.

However, one of the principal insights of those who devised Britain's privatization programme, which has been carried over to privatizations elsewhere, was that it is only the network at the heart of such industries – the wires, pipes or rails – which constitutes the natural monopoly element. Production is potentially competitive and so is supply to consumers.

Indeed, in the electricity and gas industries in Britain, the natural monopoly element has now been pared to a minimum: production is competitive, so is supply of electricity and gas to consumers, and so are other activities such as storage, meter provision and meter reading. Competition thus takes place in large parts of the two industries over a common network, which is regulated as a natural monopoly. The realization that these 'network utilities' could be opened up to competition, with regulation eventually confined to the natural monopoly network, was a genuine intellectual advance. In principle, the other network industries – water, telecommunications and the railways – can be similarly treated.[12]

Market liberalization and privatization are best seen as complementary policies. Both are liberalizing measures in the sense that both bring market forces to bear, either in product markets or in capital markets. Market liberalization opens up product markets at the same time that the change of ownership consequent on privatization exposes companies to the market for corporate control. Moreover, as already explained, product market liberalization eases agency problems: the more competitive the market, the less discretion managers have to veer away from the pursuit of shareholder objectives.

Privatization in practice
The potential benefits of privatization, especially when coupled with market liberalization, are clear. However, that does not mean that any given privatization programme will realize all (or indeed any) of the potential benefits. Students of public choice theory (Tullock *et al.*, 2000) and those who understand the tendency for economists to relapse into 'Nirvana economics' (Demsetz, 1969; 1989) will recognize the problem. An ideal privatization programme is potentially highly beneficial in efficiency terms. A programme carried out by a real-world government will be subject to government failure and its results are uncertain.

A paradox of privatization plans is that a policy which is intended to reduce government involvement and to depoliticize will invariably be designed and executed by government. It follows that the policy will be subject to political calculation and marred by the problems inherent in government action. As an example, take Britain's privatization programme under the Conservative governments of the 1980s and 1990s (Robinson, 1992; 1998). It holds many lessons for countries which wish to privatize in ways that will yield economic benefits.

Conflicting objectives in Britain's privatization programme
Among various myths surrounding the privatizations carried out by British Conservative governments, between the early 1980s and the mid-1990s, is

the view that this was a carefully planned and executed programme carried out by governments devoted to the introduction of market forces. In practice, it is probably incorrect to call the process a 'programme' (which implies careful planning and execution): there was more than a hint of accident about it and it seems doubtful whether its main objective was to liberalize capital and product markets, as the rhetoric of the time suggested (Robinson, 1992; 1998). Privatization in Britain turns out to be a good example of the interplay between government and pressure groups as policy is implemented, with relatively little regard for the interests of consumers. To point this out is not to criticize the implementation of policy so much as to make it clear that political objectives are bound to dominate government actions.

One of the main insights of public choice theory is that, between elections, government policies are heavily influenced by producer and other organized pressure groups: hence the observed tendency for policies to be swayed by organized groups rather than by unorganized consumers (Tullock *et al.*, 2000). Interest groups expect high returns from lobbying because any resultant favours from government will be concentrated on their members, whereas the costs will be spread thinly over the community as a whole (so thinly that the marginal cost of resisting the policy change will appear high to potential opponents compared with the marginal benefits). Consequently, in any politicized market, organized groups have a powerful incentive to invest in lobbying. An event such as privatization, where major political decisions are being made, provides such groups, both in the industry concerned and in associated industries, with a one-off opportunity to make gains for their members. If they can influence policy significantly, big benefits are in prospect.

Inferring the objectives
The objectives of Britain's privatization programme have to be inferred, because they were never clearly stated.[13] They seem to fall into four categories: widening share ownership, raising revenue, depoliticizing decisions and liberalizing markets. There are potential conflicts among these objectives, particularly in the sense that actions designed to spread share ownership and to raise large revenues may be inimical to the liberalization of markets. The evidence of how the programme was carried out suggests that the first two objectives were pursued most vigorously and that market liberalization was lowest on the list of government priorities.

There clearly was a major effort by the government to widen share ownership. Shares in the privatized corporations were generally offered at a substantial discount to initial market valuations. In addition, employees and customers were given special deals and applicants for small numbers of shares were favoured: the aim was evidently to spread the available shares over a large part of the population. An opportunity appeared which was irresistible to many – either of buying shares and then selling quickly to realize a cash transfer from the state or of holding the shares and feeling wealthier. Not surprisingly, share ownership soared[14] and the government seemed to reap a return in terms of increased votes: certainly, this was one of the Conservative Party's most visible policies and the party remained in the ascendant throughout the 1980s and early 1990s.

As well as seeking to widen share ownership, British governments were plainly trying to raise substantial revenues. In the 1980s, there were fears that governments of many countries were running up against the limits of taxable capacity. Cutting state expenditures was proving difficult, state bor- rowing was mounting and the search was on for policies that would provide extra revenues without there being a taxpayers' revolt. From that viewpoint, privatization seemed a heaven-sent opportunity. It promised an apparently painless means of raising large revenues, applying the proceeds to the reduc- tion of state borrowing and consequent lowering of interest rates, which seemed very desirable objectives, especially in the early and mid-1980s.

Depoliticization was another aim of Britain's privatization programme. Indeed, it is inherent in all privatization programmes, if not as a specific objective, then as a consequence of reducing state involvement in the markets concerned.

But it was the fourth possible objective which was most obviously in con- flict with the others. Market liberalization, which would rank high in the priorities of most economists involved in privatization, was much stressed in the government's rhetoric about privatization. But it seems that much of this was lip-service because the way in which most privatizations were carried out did little to liberalize product markets (Robinson, 1989; 1992; 1998). It is not difficult to see why.

Liberalization versus other objectives
The first reason is that the prime conflict among the objectives of privatiza- tion is between schemes which, on the one hand, raise large revenues and spread share ownership widely and, on the other, liberalize the markets concerned. The government evidently believed in the 1980s that privatizing state corporations, whole or with only weak competitors, was best because monopoly privatizations would raise substantial revenues and be very attractive to potential shareholders. Breaking up state corporations at the time of privatization was generally not favoured (Robinson, 1988).

To see why in more detail, the matter has to be considered from the politi- cian's point of view. From his or her viewpoint, the social benefits of compe- tition will appear intangible and probably not realizable within the normal short political timescale. Before embarking on a policy, politicians must perceive that winners are likely considerably to exceed losers. Moreover, winners must perceive that they *are* winners so that they will repay their gains with votes. Consequently, there tends to be an inherent bias against competition-promoting policies because it is difficult for people to recognize that they have won. Benefits may be thinly spread, even if large in the aggregate, and not easily identifiable with the originating action, which may well precede gains by a period of many years.

Pressure group influences
Then the influence of pressure groups must be considered. Briefly, the problem is that most of the organized pressure groups likely to be active in any privatization programme will probably have little interest in promoting competition and may indeed be downright antagonistic towards it. In Britain's case, the incumbent managements of the nationalized corporations in all cases opposed market-liberalizing measures. For obvious reasons they wanted to retain their market power after privatization: their prime interest was in raising their salaries and other benefits of office to private sector levels without facing significant competition in product markets. They were supported by the trade unions in the industries concerned, presumably because they expected to be able to conclude cosier arrangements with a private monopoly than with a number of competing firms, and by civil servants in the 'sponsoring' government departments, which had become used to pleading on behalf of 'their' industries.

Managements and unions also favoured 'golden shares', which restricted the operation of the market for corporate control, hindering potential bidders if, post-privatization, company managements were not performing well. The government's financial advisers in the City, though not favouring restrictions on takeovers, also had a preference for floating companies with product market monopolies rather than firms in a competitive industry: they perceived it to be easier and (because of the expected higher revenues) more lucrative.

In other words, Britain's privatization programme did little initially to liberalize markets because there was no influential constituency in favour of liberalization. A privatization programme that had emphasized liberalization would have clearly separated 'natural monopoly' activities, such as the networks of wires and pipes at the heart of the electricity, gas, water and telecommunications industries, from the potentially competitive activities of those industries and regulated only the former. Instead, in some cases (gas, water and telecoms) there was no separation at all and in others (such as electricity) the separation was only partial (Robinson, 1992). Regulators were therefore left to supervise whole industries rather than just their naturally monopolistic elements, making the task of regulation, always extremely difficult, even more so (Blundell and Robinson, 2000). The result was that the area in which competition was permitted was much narrower than it could have been.

Consumers, who stood to benefit significantly from an injection of competition into markets long monopolized, were not sufficiently organized to exert effective pressure. Establishing competitive markets appeared contrary to the interests, not only of politicians, but of all the major interest groups – state corporation managements, unions, civil servants and the City of London.

It was not until well after privatization that significant liberalization took place, mainly because of the efforts of industry regulators and the Monopolies and Mergers Commission (now the Competition Commission). By then the influence of the previously active pressure groups had faded somewhat, mainly because they had achieved their immediate objectives. The nationalized industry managements had, on the whole, achieved their aims of avoiding serious competition immediately after privatization; the unions were relieved that they were bargaining with organizations with substantial market power; the civil servants had avoided radical break-up of the nationalized corporations and, in any case, had less influence after privatization; and the City institutions had realized the proceeds of British privatizations and had moved on to promoting privatization elsewhere.

Just as these groups waned in influence, counter pressure groups emerged in the form of industrial and commercial consumers of the products of the privatized companies, who were, by and large, disappointed with the results of privatization, especially its failure to reduce prices and improve service significantly in the early years. Unlike small consumers, these companies, acting in their roles as consumers of the products of the privatized companies, were organized and could put effective pressure on regulators and government (Robinson, 1998). They combined with the industry regulators – most of whom had duties to promote competition – to bring about a second wave of action, this time specifically designed to liberalize product markets at a time when potential entrants were in any case beginning to find ways in. Some of the regulators, notably in the energy (electricity and gas) industries, worked assiduously at this task and have been very successful, particularly in bringing down prices (Littlechild, 2000). Others were less successful, especially in water and the railways, the two privatized industries in which the privatization schemes assumed there was virtually no scope for competition and in which the regulators have been faced with the virtually impossible task of attempting to regulate the industries as a whole (Robinson, 1997).

Conclusions

There are various ways to characterize the process just described. One is that it was just a muddle. The British government, which was a pioneer in privatization, had little relevant experience on which to draw, its objectives were confused and it was buffeted by pressure groups: the result was rather messy schemes that initially did little to benefit consumers. In the early and mid-1980s, in particular, government was operating in the 'fog' which surrounds political decision making, when the views of the electorate are unclear and probably unformed (Downs, 1957). Nevertheless it was, in the end, baled out by the industry regulators and the competition authorities, whose objectives (set by government) were much clearer. Another, more charitable, view is that, considering the pioneering nature of the privatization programme, politicians in the UK were quite far-sighted, realizing that, provided they freed entry by privatizing, in the end competitive markets would emerge, no matter what the short-term obstacles.

A third view, which is perhaps the most plausible, is that, in terms of the political calculus, politicians behaved entirely rationally in Britain's privatization programme, as politicians in other countries have subsequently done. At the time of privatization they pursued the objectives (raising revenues and widening share ownership) which would bring them short-run political gains, enhancing their chances of re-election. They left the industry regulatory bodies they had established and the (then) Monopolies and Mergers Commission (MMC) to carry forward the task of liberalization. A major problem with liberalizing monopolized markets, from the politicians' point of view, is that it is likely to involve measures which, for a time, will cause public concern and may lose votes. There will be transitional costs before consumers begin to see benefits in terms of lower prices and improved service standards. Markets may, for instance, be disrupted temporarily in the transition; for example, in electricity, the fear is 'the lights might go out'. Furthermore, politicians are reluctant to preside over the unwinding of the cross subsidies that often exist in markets where there are state-owned enterprises because the losers are likely to complain vociferously. Government can therefore hope to sidestep some of the political costs of privatization, while reaping the political gains, by leaving the detailed work of introducing competition to the industry regulators and the competition authorities.

None of the above is intended to belittle the effects of privatization in the UK as a major policy change and an important enabling step – one which has, in many countries, removed the prohibition on entry to the markets concerned even if, in many cases, entry remained for a time extremely difficult – rather than as a liberalizing measure in itself. One should also beware of judging past privatization schemes in the light of present-day circumstances.

At the time, they were often bold moves, made by governments unclear about the electoral consequences.

However, on the view presented here, privatization is always likely to be incomplete as a policy. The British example has been used as an illustration, but the hypothesis that privatization schemes will always and everywhere be dominated by political objectives (since they are carried out by governments) is a perfectly general theory of privatization. A possible conclusion is that privatization schemes should always be expected to be illiberal, because the organized groups influential at the time of privatization will not generally favour competition. If that is so, as in Britain, the liberalized markets which are likely to produce the bulk of the gains from privatization will appear not at the time of privatization but only in a second wave of reform some years later. This second wave could appear because of efforts by regulators and the competition authorities, because of pressure from larger consumers, because privatization stimulated significant entry or because of some combination of the three.

But, in some cases, the forces which would produce a second wave may be weak so that it does not occur and consequent disappointment at the results of privatization brings about a reversion to state control (with or without state ownership). Something of the sort has already happened with the railways in Britain and may also occur in the water industry in England and Wales. In neither case has there been any serious attempt at liberalization: tight regulation has been substituted for state ownership, with little benefit to consumers.

To summarize, a move from state ownership – which has numerous inherent disadvantages – to private ownership is potentially very beneficial to consumers. But, to ensure that these gains are realized, market liberalization is required as a complementary policy. In theory, privatization even if unaccompanied by initial liberalization could in the long run result in the emergence of competitive markets if it frees market entry. But before the long run arrives, political control may be reasserted as impatience and disappointment at the early results of privatization stimulate a reversion to state control and heavy-handed regulation. Ownership would then be nominally private but it is unlikely there would be any noticeable improvement over the results of state ownership.

Notes

1. There is a useful summary of the literature on privatization effects up to 1998 in Europe Economics (1998).
2. For a discussion of the ideas leading up to nationalization and experience in the early years of the nationalized industries, see Kelf-Cohen (1969).
3. Richard Cockett (1994) shows how the 'counter revolution' in economics evolved and how it was translated into practical ideas about the greater use of markets. See also Littlechild (1982) and Robinson and Marshall (1985).

4. In a telling phrase, the late Jack Wiseman said that the 'commanding heights' had, by the late 1970s, become the 'abysmal depths' of the economy (Wiseman, 1978).
5. There were White Papers on the nationalized industries in 1961, 1967 and 1978.
6. For some of the early discussion of privatization, see Beesley and Littlechild (1983), Peacock (1984), Shackleton (1984), Rees (1985). A general review of privatization in theory and in practice is in Vickers and Yarrow (1988).
7. Also see Chapter 2. The sale of state or local authority-owned housing or of other assets owned by government departments is also privatization (Peacock, 1984), but this chapter concentrates on the dominant form of privatization – the sale to the public of organizations previously in the hands of the state.
8. The problem was recognized many years ago (Berle and Means, 1932).
9. Attempting to move one market towards perfect competition while the rest of the markets in an economy remain imperfectly competitive raises the problem of 'second best'. There can be no general presumption that such a move will improve social welfare (Lipsey and Lancaster, 1956).
10. A brief discussion of the problems of the perfectly competitive model and how it compares with classical and neo-Austrian competition models can be found in Robinson (1997).
11. For example, in an article which helped define the intellectual principles underlying privatization, Michael Beesley and Stephen Littlechild argued that 'The promotion of competition . . . is the most effective means of maximising consumer benefits and curbing monopoly power' (Beesley and Littlechild, 1983).
12. It is sometimes argued that both water and the railways are industries where consumers will not benefit from market liberalization. Similar claims were made in the 1980s about gas and electricity liberalization, although, in the case of the railways, there certainly are some practical problems in implementing liberalization, as evidenced by the UK's recent experience. A discussion of how to apply liberalization principles to the water industry is in Robinson (2002).
13. One of the few discussions of the privatization programme by a government minister is in a speech by Mr (now Lord) Moore (Moore, 1985). There were also discussions by academic economists of what the objectives *should* be (notably Beesley and Littlechild, 1983). Much of the intellectual basis for privatization was laid by the late Professor Michael Beesley (see Beesley, 1992, for a collection of his articles).
14. In the three years after the first major privatization (50 per cent of British Telecom in 1984), the proportion of the adult population which owned shares increased from 7 per cent to 21 per cent (though not all the increase was due to privatization) and rose slightly higher to 22 per cent by the early 1980s (*Financial Times*, 1989; 1991). However, share ownership was not deepening in this period. The proportion of UK company equity held directly by individuals declined from 28 per cent in 1981 to 21 per cent in 1992 (*The Economist*, 1993).

References

Beesley, M.E. (1992) *Privatization, Regulation and Deregulation*, 2nd edn 1997, London and New York: Routledge.

Beesley, M. and S.C. Littlechild (1983) 'Privatization: principles, problems and priorities', *Lloyds Bank Review*, July, reprinted in Beesley (1992).

Berle, A. and G.C. Means (1932) *The Modern Corporation and Private Property*, New York: The Commerce Clearing House.

Blaug, M. (1987) 'Classical Economics', in J. Eatwell, M. Milgate and P. Newman, (eds) *The New Palgrave – A Dictionary of Economics*, vol. 1, London: Macmillan – now Palgrave.

Blundell, J. and C. Robinson (2000) 'Regulation Without the State . . . The Debate Continues', Readings 52, Institute of Economic Affairs, London.

Chiplin, B. and M. Wright (1987) 'The Logic of Mergers', Hobart Paper 107, Institute of Economic Affairs, London.

Cockett, R. (1994) *Thinking the Unthinkable: think tanks and the economic counter-revolution*, London: HarperCollins.

Demsetz, H. (1969) 'Information and Efficiency: Another Viewpoint', *Journal of Law and Economics*, 12(1), 1–22.
Demsetz, H. (1989) *Efficiency, Competition and Policy*, Oxford: Blackwell.
Downs, A. (1957) *An Economic Theory of Democracy*, New York: Harper & Row.
Economist (1993) 'Share ownership: risk aversion', 6 November.
Europe Economics (1998) *Water and Sewerage Industries General Efficiency and Potential for Improvement* (with Nick Crafts), London: Europe Economics for Ofwat.
Financial Times (1989) 'Biggest expansion in share ownership since 1987', 13 December.
Financial Times (1991) 'Lamont seeks share ownership in depth', 15 May.
Heald, D. (1980) 'The Economic and Financial Control of UK Nationalised Industries', *The Economic Journal*, June, 243–65.
Henderson, D. ([1998] 2001) 'The Changing Fortunes of Economic Liberalism', Occasional Paper 105, Institute of Economic Affairs, London.
Hirschman, A.O. (1970) *Exit, Voice and Loyalty: Responses to Decline in Firms, Organizations and States*, Cambridge, MA: Harvard University Press.
Kelf-Cohen, R. (1969) *Twenty Years of Nationalisation: The British Experience*, London: Macmillan and New York: St Martin's Press.
Kirzner, I.M. (1997) 'How Markets Work: Disequilibrium, Entrepreneurship and Discovery', Hobart Paper 133, Institute of Economic Affairs, London.
Lipsey, R. and K. Lancaster (1956) 'General theory of second best', *Review of Economic Studies*, 24(63), 11–32.
Littlechild, S.C. (1978) 'The Fallacy of the Mixed Economy', Hobart Paper 80, 2nd edn 1986, Institute of Economic Affairs, London.
Littlechild, S.C. (1982) 'Ten Steps to Denationalisation', *Economic Affairs*, 2 (1), 11–19.
Littlechild, S.C. (2000) 'Privatisation, Competition and Regulation', Occasional Paper 110, Institute of Economic Affairs, London.
Moore, J. (1985) 'The Success of Privatisation', HM Treasury Press Release, 107/85.
OECD (1997) 'Privatisation: Recent Trends', in *Financial Market Trends*, no. 66, March, OECD, Paris.
OECD (2001) 'Privatisation: Recent Trends', in *Financial Market Trends*, no. 79, June, OECD, Paris.
Peacock, A. (1984) 'Privatisation in Perspective', *Three Banks Review*, December.
Rees, R. (1985) 'Is There an Economic Case for Privatisation?', *Public Money*, March.
Robinson, C. (1971) *Business Forecasting: An Economic Approach*, London: Nelson.
Robinson, C. (1988) 'Liberalising the Energy Industries', *Proceedings of the Manchester Statistical Society*.
Robinson, C. (1992) 'Privatising the British Energy Industries: The Lessons to be Learned', *Metroeconomica*, 43(1–2), 103–29.
Robinson, C. (1997) 'Introducing Competition into Water' in M.E. Beesley (ed.), *Regulating Utilities: Broadening the Debate*, Readings 46, Institute of Economic Affairs, London.
Robinson, C. (1998) 'Pressure Groups and Political Forces in Britain's Privatisation Programme', Surrey Energy Economics Discussion Papers no. 91, Department of Economics, University of Surrey, Guildford.
Robinson, C. (2000) 'Energy Economists and Economic Liberalism', *The Energy Journal*, 2(2), 1–22.
Robinson, C. (2002) 'Moving to a Competitive Market in Water', in Colin Robinson (ed.), *Utility Regulation and Competition Policy*, Cheltenham, UK and Northampton, MA, USA: Edward Elgar.
Robinson, Colin (1989) 'Privatising the Energy Industries', in C. Veljanovski (ed.), *Privatisation and Competition: A Market Prospectus*, Institution of Economic Affairs, London.
Robinson, C. and E. Marshall (1985) 'Can Coal be Saved?', Hobart Paper 105, Institute of Economic Affairs, London.
Rowley, C.K. (1984) 'The Relevance of the Median Voter Theorem', *Zeitschrift für die Gesamte Staatswissenschaft*, 140(1), 104–35.
Shackleton, J.R. (1984) 'Privatisation: The Case Examined', *National Westminster Bank Review*, May, 59–73.

Tullock, G., A. Seldon and G. Brady (2000) 'Government: Whose Obedient Servant?', Readings 51, Institute of Economic Affairs, London.

Vickers, J. and G. Yarrow (1988) *Privatisation: An Economic Analysis*, Cambridge, MA: MIT Press.

Wiseman, J. (1978) 'The Political Economy of Nationalised Industry', in A. Seldon (ed.), *The Economics of Politics*, Readings 18, Institute of Economic Affairs, London.

4 Privatization: a sceptical analysis
Johan Willner

Introduction

This contribution criticizes the present international trend to minimize the extent of public ownership. Public ownership is associated with potential benefits, for example if there are externalities or if it is not possible to achieve a sufficient degree of competitiveness. Even if privatization leads to lower production costs (which is not certain), it is not beneficial unless the cost reductions overshadow the lost benefits of public ownership. This sceptical view does not, however, rule out public enterprises being sold, because the state or the local authority might want to transfer its activities from one sector to another. This underlines the role of proper procedures for privatization, which is the topic of other chapters in this volume.

The first section of this chapter deals with the rationale for public ownership and privatization. The following section compares the costs and benefits of public and private ownership. Later sections show that the empirical comparisons of cost efficiency tend to go either way, and offer some explanations of why this is the case. It is sometimes argued that competition, and therefore deregulation, might be more important than the privatization of the incumbent, but some dissenting views on market structure are provided in the argument below. The chapter also addresses the need to transcend the traditional and simplistic behavioural assumptions, and ends with some concluding remarks. Theoretical points will be illustrated throughout the chapter by a simple model of a market with linear demand. While the analysis can often be generalized, its purpose is mainly to provide counter-examples to the belief that it is always economically rational to privatize.

Motives for public ownership

Democracy means that decisions are derived from individual judgments, in general through majority voting. While most decisions on what and how to produce are made in markets where customers vote with their money, some services but also goods are produced by the public sector and hence are subject to direct or indirect political governance.

At best, markets can be efficient in the sense that no individual can be made better off without hurting someone else. But economic decisions, like privatization, typically create winners and losers. A change in social welfare can therefore be defined only in terms of an (imperfect) aggregation of individual preferences or values, as when a political decision is based on individual votes.

Political intervention can help when markets fail, provided that the cure does not cost more than the disease. Intervention can mean public ownership, for example in the case of pure public goods, natural monopolies and externalities, or when there is a lack of private venture capital. There is also a grey zone in which there will always be disagreement on the need for public sector activity. Few would question public ownership of natural monopolies (see, however, Bradburd, 1995), but private oligopolies might also merit intervention, in particular where there is open or tacit collusion between them. Instead of regulating, the public sector can then own a firm with a mixed oligopoly strategy that forces its competitors to keep prices low (Cremér *et al.*, 1989; De Fraja and Delbono, 1990). Public ownership can also be used for other good or bad reasons, such as regional or macro-economic policy.

However, an allocation is not necessary desirable just because it is Pareto-efficient. The more general concept of a strategic failure means that the policy of a (public or private) firm does not benefit society as a whole, but only its strategic decision makers (Cowling and Sugden, 1998). Pareto-optimality does not rule out, for example, low growth or extreme inequality (see, for example, Hammond, 1990). Even a successful market may work like an election with an uneven distribution of votes, which may reinforce the inequalities.

Right- and left-wing ideologies used to emphasize ownership of the means of production, but practical policy is often based on disagreement on facts rather than values (Ng, 1972). The motives for public ownership have often been pragmatic, with exceptions in France, Portugal and the UK (De Bandt, 1998; Parris, *et al.*, 1987; Willner, 1998; Cook, 1998), and it has sometimes been implemented by non-socialists. The real reasons behind nationalization and privatization can, therefore, often be difficult to establish with certainty.

State enterprises have been part of a policy to benefit consumers through lower prices in Italy and the UK, and have been used for anti-inflationary and/or expansionary purposes in, for example, France, Germany and the UK (Marrelli and Stroffolini, 1998; De Bandt, 1998; Esser, 1998; Cook, 1998). But more often they were established because of a lack of private venture capital, or as a way to accelerate post-war restructuring, as in Austria, Finland, Germany, Italy, Ireland and Sweden (Aiginger, 1998; Willner, 1998; Esser, 1998; Marrelli and Stroffolini, 1998). In the USA, islands of public ownership such as the Tennessee Valley Authority were established, as private investors were not interested in investing, because of riskiness and high costs (Monsen and Walters, 1983; Hausman and Neufeld, 1999).

It is not straightforward to define the boundaries of the state enterprise sector and there are conflicting definitions. However, Austria, Finland, Greece and Portugal had comparatively large state enterprise sectors among the OECD countries (12–26 per cent in terms of value added) before the privatization wave. This should be compared to 4–6 per cent in, for example, Denmark, Italy and the Netherlands, and 1–2 per cent in the USA. Other OECD countries are situated between these extremes (Parker, 1998; World Bank, 1995:263–4).

Why privatization?

The present privatization wave in Europe started with Margaret Thatcher's second government in Britain between 1983 and 1987, despite some early and later abandoned attempts in West Germany in the 1950s and 1960s. The British government was then strongly influenced by think-tanks such as the Adam Smith Institute. While privatization is now often motivated by economic arguments, the policy was not inspired by professional economists, whose comments were in the beginning often cautious or even sceptical.[1] Privatization was not seen as beneficial without competition, which was not always seen as feasible (Vickers and Yarrow, 1988).

The most cited motive for privatization is the belief that state enterprises are inefficient (Ikenberry, 1990), as expressed in the Adam Smith Institute's writings (Pirie, 1988). But the view that the public sector is inherently inefficient and in need of trimming is difficult to distinguish from a purely ideological mistrust, as for example in the following quotation from Thatcher's memoirs:

> Just as nationalization was at the heart of the collectivist programme by which Labour sought to remodel British society, so privatization is at the centre of any programme of reclaiming territory for freedom. [. . .] But, of course, the narrower economic arguments for privatization were also overwhelming. The state should not be in business. State ownership effectively removes – or at least radically reduces – the threat of bankruptcy which is a discipline on privately owned firms. (Thatcher, 1993:676–7)

The authorities have referred to private sector cost efficiency in some other countries as well, such as in Austria (Aiginger, 1998; Parker, 1998; Parris *et al.*, 1987), but to a lesser extent than usually believed. As in Britain, privatization partly appeared as a right-wing reaction to previous nationalization in Portugal and France: private ownership and commercial values became ends in themselves (see Parker, 1998). Ideological views were also influential in Sweden, but the crisis in the 1990s prevented large-scale privatization until the Social Democrats returned to power (Willner, 1998).[2]

A number of other justifications for privatization have been used, but they are consistent with the economy remaining mixed or can be addressed through other means than divestiture. One such reason has been to reduce the influence of politics in enterprise decision making (Boycko *et al.*, 1996), but Scandinavian experiences suggest that public ownership does not rule out managerial independence. Moreover, independent central banks are not privatized, and state universities are often autonomous. Privatized utilities may on the other hand require so much regulation that they become less independent than some state-owned firms. Also the related motive to fund investments requires privatization only if specific funding constraints have been imposed on the public sector.[3]

Raising funds for the state, as in Denmark, Finland, France and Germany, is another motive for privatization (Willner, 1998; De Bandt, 1998; Esser; 1998). But some divestiture may even be consistent with an increase in ownership in other industries, and successful state companies can yield dividends, as in Finland (Willner, 1998). Popular capitalism is another motive that does not rule out some state ownership. Moreover, experiences from Austria and Germany in the 1950s and 1960s suggest that privatization can be an inefficient method to expand share ownership (Parris *et al.*, 1987; Aiginger, 1998). Privatizations meant undervalued shares in Britain (where work motivation and Tory support were to be strengthened through a concern about share prices rather than public services), but ownership became less widespread as the new owners sold their shares after subsequent share price increases (Vickers and Yarrow, 1988; Bös, 1993; Lashmar, 1994).

But as privatization became widespread, countries like Denmark and Finland jumped on the bandwagon (Willner, 1998). Public enterprises were few and fairly efficient in the Netherlands, but also the Dutch decision makers chose a conformist approach (Ikenberry, 1990; Hulsink and Schenk, 1998).[4]

If economists favour privatization, they usually refer to cost efficiency. Profit-maximizing owners subject to threats of bankruptcy and takeover are believed to have stronger incentives to reduce costs than politicians or bureaucrats, and will therefore monitor and/or motivate appointed managers more effectively. Wider objectives and complicated chains of command in state-owned activities are also believed to have adverse effects (World Bank, 1995). Public sector inefficiency is often presented as a stylized fact, without empirical discussion (see, for example, Boycko *et al.*, 1996; Bradburd, 1995; Beesley and Littlechild, 1994; Holmström and Honkapohja, 1994).

It has also been argued that dynamic efficiency can be more important than cost reductions. An often cited model by Bös and Peters (1991) predicts that state enterprises will spend less on cost-saving R&D investments; but this happens because the public sector is for some reason assumed to be unable to hire a competent manager and pay her according to performance.

Moreover, there are counter-examples, like the highly innovative former state-owned telecommunications monopoly in Finland (now called Sonera). In addition, there seems to be evidence of a positive rather than negative relationship between economic growth and the size of the public enterprise sector (see Fowler and Richards, 1995).

However, even when production is technically efficient, political failure can cause distortions such as excessive output and/or overmanning for opportunistic reasons (Boycko *et al.*, 1996).[5] But this is not necessarily a criticism of public ownership as such, because subsidies and other distortions can occur after privatization as well.[6] Also a criticism of public ownership which emphasizes the need to please voters identifies democracy (the occurrence of elections) as the main culprit, leading to the somewhat controversial prediction that state-owned firms would be more efficient under dictatorship, such as in the Soviet Union, than in a Western democracy.

If privatization leads to imperfect competition in markets, such political failures would imply that private ownership is biased towards too high a price and public ownership towards too low a price, with ambiguous consequences for social welfare. Moreover, a political failure means decisions that are not just mistaken but selfish, and this can be assessed empirically (see below). Only a very strong belief in opportunism among decision makers can make it meaningless to find out how enlightened politicians should intervene.

Extreme critics accuse state enterprises of distorting competition and free trade even without political failures and high costs, because of better access to credit so they cannot go bankrupt. Like Soviet-style socialism, they become a threat to the private sector if their objectives are in addition non-commercial. Investments with sub-normal returns are, for example, seen as inefficient and should be treated as subsidized even when they lead to reduced costs (Monsen and Walters, 1983). In similar way, Ferguson (1988) argues that excessive quality, better working conditions and price systems that are too easy to use and administer are typical distortions caused by public sector managers who want to avoid conflict. But to argue that private firms are superior because public firms do not conform to their quality, rates of return and working conditions comes close to being an ideological statement.

While Monsen and Walters (1983) see public ownership as a danger to US business interests, others doubt its ability to survive. As they argue, non-commercial objectives lead to losses that violate regulations against subsidies (see, for example, Bös, 1993). This happens in some wage bargaining models (see Haskel and Szymanski, 1992),[7] but other models give opposite or ambiguous results, in particular if there is central bargaining as in Scandinavia (De Fraja, 1993b; Willner, 1999b; Gravelle 1984). Wider objectives may even, under some conditions, become more viable under international competition (Willner, 1998).

Of the many motives for privatization, we shall focus on cost inefficiency and to some extent distorted objectives because there is an economic case for privatization if these overshadow all benefits from public ownership. Other reasons may have been equally prominent in practice, but they are focused on problems that can be solved without a complete abolition of the public enterprise sector, and may even be consistent with an increased public sector presence in some areas of the economy.

Allocative efficiency, excessive costs and political failure

This section makes the point that excessive costs or biased objectives among public firms are not sufficient reasons for privatization, because allocative efficiency is defined in terms of the pay-off of different stakeholders, such as the consumers, and of the weights that are given to them in the definition of social welfare. Privatization often leads to an oligopoly, and this section analyses by how much costs then have to be reduced before private ownership becomes superior. Later sections of the chapter suggest that such cost reductions cannot be taken for granted.

Privatization means in this section replacing a public monopoly with private oligopolists with different variable or fixed costs. Cost reductions would normally increase welfare, but monopolies have usually been in public ownership because they are required not to maximize profits. Privatization can, under such conditions, improve allocative efficiency only if the post-privatization market failure matters less for social welfare than the cost reduction.

A simple model with linear demand will be used to illustrate a number of points throughout this chapter. The analysis can in many cases be generalized, but linear demand is familiar to most readers and offers the simplest way to show by counter-example that privatization is not always beneficial. Suppose that the inverse demand function is $p = a - x$, where p denotes price, x industry output and a a positive parameter. Marginal costs are c before privatization; their weighted average is $(1 - \mu)c$ afterwards. Public ownership means welfare maximization, which is defined in terms of profits (produce surplus) and consumer surplus. We ignore the employee's pay-off in the definition of welfare until the discussion of internal rent capture.

The usual way to evaluate either imperfect competition or privatization is to analyse the change in the total surplus (consumer surplus + profits); (Harberger, 1954; Cowling and Mueller, 1978; Willner and Ståhl, 1992; Bradburd, 1995; Willner, 1996). This approach is not innocuous, because a given reduction in consumer and employee welfare can be offset by an equal increase in profits.[8] We shall, therefore, introduce weights for profits and the consumer surplus. These may affect the sign of the welfare change, which means that our analysis is not restricted to those value judgments that are implied by equal weights.

It is also convenient to define social welfare in terms of a geometric rather than an arithmetic average. This allows for a wider choice of weights for different stakeholders, and requires more compensation if some group becomes worse off. Note that the consumer surplus is $x^2/2$, and let the weights be ρ and $1 - \rho$. Ignore fixed costs and distortions in the objectives of the public firm, because these will be analysed below. The public firm then maximizes:[9]

$$W = \left(\frac{1}{2}x^2\right)^\rho [(a - x - c)x]^{1-\rho}. \tag{4.1}$$

This yields the following output:

$$x_G = \frac{(1 + \rho)(a - c)}{2}. \tag{4.2}$$

If the public monopoly is replaced by an n-firm Cournot oligopoly, each firm i maximizes:

$$\pi_i = ax_i - xx_i - c_i. \tag{4.3}$$

The first-order conditions for the oligopolists can now be manipulated so as to yield an industry output in terms of the Herfindahl index of concentration,[10] H, and the weighted average of the marginal costs, as for example in Cowling and Waterson (1976):

$$x_P = \frac{a - (1 - \mu)c}{1 + H}. \tag{4.4}$$

Inserting (4.2) and (4.4) into (4.1) yields expressions for the social welfare as defined above before and after privatization, W_G and W_P. Note that the intercept a can be eliminated using the absolute value of the often known pre-privatization price elasticity of demand (η):

$$\eta = \frac{(1 - \rho)a + (1 + \rho)c}{(1 + \rho)(a - c)}. \tag{4.5}$$

Set $W_P > W_G$, use (4.5) and solve for μ to see by how much marginal costs must decrease if privatization is to improve welfare:

$$\mu > \frac{(1 + H)[(1 + \rho)^{1+\rho}(1 - \rho)^{1-\rho} H^{\rho-1}]^{1/2} - 2}{\eta(1 + \rho) - (1 - \rho)}. \tag{4.6}$$

It follows that the necessary cost increase depends on post-privatization concentration demand elasticity, but also social values as reflected in ρ.

The fact that social welfare is defined in terms of a product means that a zero-profit solution can be optimal only if profits are given no weight. The lowest value of μ is zero, and is reached for $H = (1-\rho)/(1+\rho)$, because any value of ρ lower than 1.0 means that there exists a concentration level which would give the same distribution between profits and the consumer surplus as in the public monopoly for a given marginal cost. Thus, $\rho = 0.5$ makes a public monopoly equivalent to a symmetric three-firm oligopoly, but $\rho = 0.75$ would correspond to $H = 0.14$.

If η is, for example, 1.0, equal weights for profits and the consumer surplus would then mean that the condition for privatization to increase welfare is:

$$\mu > 1.140(1+H)H^{-1/4} - 2. \tag{4.7}$$

If H is 0.2, 0.6 and 0.8, marginal costs would have to be reduced by 23.00 per cent, 7.20 per cent and 16.93 per cent. But if the consumer surplus is given the weight 0.75, the same values of H would require cost reductions of 0.86 per cent, 22.69 per cent and 35.99 per cent, respectively. We would get higher values for low values of η, as is often the case in public utilities.[11] Note also that any $\rho < 1$ means that post-privatization concentration may also be too low.

On the other hand, it can be argued that pure profits are always a symptom of market failure in a model like this. Let ρ therefore approach 1.0, and suppose that the price elasticity of demand is 1.0.[12] It then turns out that (4.6) tends to the simple expression $\mu > H$. In other words, if social values emphasize consumers rather than profits, market concentration after privatization requires very large cost reductions, in particular under price-inelastic demand.

However, cost differences may also reflect internal rent capture under public ownership, in the form of, for example, 'excessive' wages, salaries and fringe benefits. Some arguments in favour of privatization emphasize this reason for lower costs (see, for example, Bradburd, 1995). Higher wage costs under public ownership would, of course, imply a social cost in the same way as profits under imperfect competition. But profits themselves are not part of the social cost, because they represent a redistribution, and excess wages should be excluded for the same reason. Higher costs are a redistribution which causes a deadweight loss, but, like profits, excess wages are not in themselves wasteful. To measure social welfare in terms of the sum of the profits and the consumer surplus is then a flawed procedure.[13]

To illustrate the paradoxical significance of internal rent capture when the total surplus includes excess wages, suppose that public ownership means marginal cost pricing at c. Private owners would be able to lower marginal costs by μc because of lower direct or indirect labour costs. Total surplus before privatization is then

$$W_G = \frac{(a-c)^2}{2} + \mu c(a-c), \tag{4.8}$$

because profits are zero, whereas the post-privatization value is

$$W_P = \frac{(1+2H)[a-(1-\mu)c]^2}{2(1+H)^2}. \tag{4.9}$$

Take the difference between (4.8) and (4.9), express a in terms of the pre-privatization price elasticity of demand $\eta = c/(a-c)$ and rearrange. It then follows that privatization improves allocative efficiency if, and only if, $\mu > H/\eta$. Privatization cannot then increase welfare even if marginal costs are reduced to zero if the pre-privatization elasticity is lower than the post-privatization Herfindahl index, which may be the case in industries like electricity and water.

It may, on the other hand, be misleading to focus on differences in marginal costs in industries where these are very low, while there are fixed costs as a barrier to fragmentation. Suppose therefore that state ownership means that fixed costs are F and that prices are set so that the firm breaks even. This yields the following output:

$$X_G = \frac{a - c + [(a-c)^2 - 4F]^{1/2}}{2}. \tag{4.10}$$

An n-firm oligopoly means $x_G = n(a-c)/(n+1)$. Suppose that n^* firms can break even and that privatization lowers fixed costs by γF in each firm. The fact that we have (approximately) zero profits after privatization as well means that the conventional total surplus changes from $(x_g^2/2) - F$ to $(x_p^2/2) - n^*(1-\gamma)F$ and that we can replace F in (4.10) with

$$F \approx \frac{(a-c)^2}{(1-\gamma)(n^*+1)^2}. \tag{4.11}$$

Comparing total surplus using (4.11) shows that privatization increases welfare only if

$$\gamma > 1 - 1/n^*. \tag{4.12}$$

Note also that privatization reduces welfare if more than $1/(1-\gamma)$ firms can break even, because of the costs of duplication.

Thus, if privatization means a five-firm oligopoly with approximately zero profits, a welfare increase would require fixed costs to be reduced to a fifth of their previous size. The necessary cost reduction approaches 100 per cent as the number of firms that can break even becomes very large.

The public sector decision makers have been benevolent in the examples above, but the model can be generalized to political failure as well. The public firm would then be given a different set of weights than in the true social welfare function. Privatization means a change from one set of distorted objectives to another. Ownership cannot then be evaluated a priori; we would get conditions for privatization to be beneficial in terms of weights and post-privatization concentration. For example, to favour consumers and employees by more than in the true social welfare function may nevertheless provide higher allocative efficiency than an oligopoly (Willner, 2001). The analysis can be extended to different types of strategic failure.

Empirical evidence
Many studies, such as Boardman and Vining (1989) and Dewenter and Malatesta (1997) suggest lower profitability under public ownership, but to compare profitability is unfair because higher profit margins can also reflect market failure. Moreover, excessive labour intensity under public ownership may have to be compared with excessive capital intensity after privatization (Pint, 1991). This section therefore focuses on cost efficiency and total factor productivity, arguing that it is far from certain that privatization improves performance.

Part of the empirical literature compares performance before and after privatization. This research requires a sufficiently long period of private ownership after privatization, as in Britain, so as not to confuse the effects of business cycles and changes in ownership. Other problems of establishing causality arise because of productivity changes in organizations that have remained public or private. In the electricity industry in Britain, costs are lower, but this might have happened without privatization (Newbery and Pollitt, 1997). A comprehensive study of privatized companies in Britain provides examples of both improved and reduced performance, and suggests that ownership as such may not matter. Many of those firms that improved their performance actually became more efficient while still under public ownership (Martin and Parker, 1997).[14]

A study of 39 medium-sized firms in Italy by Fraquelli and Erbetta (2000), covering a 10-year period, suggests privatization led to improved labour productivity but no significant increase in total factor productivity. Similar results have been reached in Austria, where profitability increased without any significant improvement in overall efficiency (Schaffhauser-Linzatti and Dockner, 2001). Dewenter and Malatesta (1997), who are cited by Megginson and Netter (2001) as favouring privatization, report improved profitability but otherwise mixed results on performance from a comparison of 500 public and private firms from different countries. Moreover, in a subsequent contribution they emphasize that most of the accounting measures of profitability were actually lower after privatization than during the last years under public ownership, as often in Britain (Dewenter and Malatesta, 2001). A conclusion that privatization generally improves performance seems, therefore, at best premature.

Another line of research compares similar firms under different ownership. This and earlier overviews, such as Millward (1982), Boyd (1986) and Willner (2001), report conflicting results but overall do not support a negative view of public ownership.[15]

It may be helpful to distinguish between services, which are in general labour intensive, and industrial production. For example, seven out of 13 of a series of studies on refuse collection from the 1960s and 1970s in the USA, Canada and Switzerland suggest that private ownership is cheaper (Bennett and Johnson, 1979; Collins and Downes, 1977; Hirsch, 1965; Kemper and Quigley, 1976; Kitchen, 1976; Pier et al., 1974; Pommerehne and Frey, 1977; Savas, 1977; Spann, 1977; Stevens, 1978). But, partly for reasons discussed below, insurance appears as better organized under public ownership (and often under monopoly) (see Epple and Schäfer, 1996; Felder, 1996; Finsinger, 1984; von Ungern-Sternberg, 1996). Comparisons of cost efficiency in transport,[16] hospitals, health and social care provide mixed results. Private ownership is sometimes cheaper than public ownership, which is, on the other hand, better or no worse in more than half of the cases (Willner, 2001).

However, the comparison becomes difficult if higher quality means higher costs, in which case cheap public sector healthcare would not necessarily mean superior performance. Ownership may affect the nature of public transport, broadcasting, hospitals or refuse collection, in particular when public ownership is associated with wider objectives. Moreover, cost differences may reflect differences in wages and working conditions, and the threshold for beneficial privatization is then higher (see the discussion in the previous section of this chapter).

A focus on industrial production of homogeneous goods makes a comparison somewhat easier. For example, studies by Çakmak and Zaim (1992) and Tyler (1979) do not find significant differences in efficiency in cement and plastics. A number of British state enterprises seemed to have faster productivity growth than in manufacturing in general during the 1980s (Molyneux and Thompson, 1987). Public ownership appears as superior in comparative studies on electricity and water (where demand elasticity is in addition low; see above). The willingness to privatize these industries is therefore somewhat surprising. With the exception of Bagdadioglu et al. (1996), most studies, such as Atkinson and Halvorsen (1986), De Alessi (1974), Färe *et al.* (1985), Foreman-Peck and Waterson (1985), Hausman and Neufeld (1991), Hayashi *et al.* (1987),[17] Hjalmarsson and Veiderpass (1992), Meyer (1975), Moore (1970), Nelson and Primeaux (1988), Neuberg (1977), Pescatrice and Trapani (1980), Peters (1993), Spann (1977) and Yunker (1975), suggest that cost efficiency in electricity is better or no worse under public ownership in the UK, the USA or Sweden.[18] Crain and Zardkoohi (1978) find public ownership to be less efficient in the US water industry, but Bhattacharyya *et al.* (1994), Bruggink (1982), Byrnes *et al.* (1986), Feigenbaum and Teeples (1983), Lynk (1993), Mann and Mikesell (1976)[19] and Teeples and Glyer (1987) reach the opposite conclusion for the USA and the UK. Saal and Parker (2000) suggest privatization of water in England and Wales had little if any immediate beneficial effect on costs of production.

An analysis of the production function can reveal whether a company is technically inefficient, and provides potentially a less ambiguous criterion than costs. Geographical and cultural factors cause large variations between countries, but public monopolies like the postal system or the railways in 19 and 22 mainly European countries did not appear as inherently inefficient in Deprins *et al.* (1984) and Perelman and Pestieau (1988), respectively.

However, quality can matter in this kind of industry. For example, anecdotal evidence suggests that some of the privatized monopolies in Britain have reduced their spending on infrastructure maintenance to an extent that has reduced safety. The number of workers employed by Railtrack for track maintenance was reduced from 31 000 to 15–19 000 during the period 1992–7, while Transco made 1000 engineers responsible for maintaining gas pipes redundant in 1997 (*Guardian*, 3 April 2001 and 18 June 2001). As pointed out below, such problems may even be compounded by the presence of competition after privatization.

The studies above mainly cover a subset of the developed countries, and cannot necessarily be generalized.[20] They stand in striking contrast to the overview of efficiency in mixed industries or after privatization by Megginson and Netter (2001), who focus on third-world and transition economies, with very few references to the studies surveyed here.[21] Insofar as differences in development are about the capabilities of firms (see Sutton, 2001), privatization without foreign ownership would not necessarily help (see also World Bank, 1995). But it might then be better to introduce the necessary know-how by other means than a nearly irreversible sell-out of the industrial sector as a whole.

We can hardly conclude from the studies surveyed here that privatization is likely to achieve a significant improvement in technical efficiency. They rather suggest that there is no robust relationship between ownership and efficiency. Moreover, it seems appropriate to conclude that static cost efficiency alone is not a relevant criterion for the choice between private and public ownership.

The theoretical significance of ownership

An entrepreneur who is exposed to competition has strong incentives to cut costs, but large public or private firms are, in general, run by a manager, whose efforts may or may not be in the owner's interest. If ownership affects performance, it must affect either the manager's intrinsic motivation (see below) or the structure of rewards and punishments. According to property rights theory, managers are better monitored if there is a profit motive, because the owner can keep the money that is thereby saved.

There is no detailed analysis of mechanisms that cause changes in efficiency in Vickers and Yarrow (1988), where incentives towards cost reductions may or may not be weaker under public ownership, or they are exogenous, such as in Bös and Peters (1991), where the presence of experienced private sector managers ensures higher cost-reducing R&D investments after privatization. Models where efficiency is genuinely endogenous are usually based on the assumption that managers are motivated by rewards and punishments only. If there is asymmetric information on the true state of nature, managers can reduce their efforts and pretend that costs are high because of unfavourable conditions. Employers must therefore ensure that managers do not quit and that they have an incentive not to misrepresent the true state of nature. In general, this implies performance-related pay, which causes managers to bear some of the entrepreneurial risk.

When there is no built-in public sector inferiority, principal–agent models of managerial discretion do not necessarily predict that public ownership is less cost-efficient. For example, Pint (1991) predicts that state and private ownership are biased in opposite directions with respect to factor intensity, with ambiguous consequences for total factor productivity. Public ownership is even associated with lower managerial slack in De Fraja (1993b). Moreover, as privatization usually leads to a private monopoly or oligopoly, there must be regulation, and this means that the manager has to adapt to principals with conflicting interests (Laffont and Tirole, 1991).

The following model is inspired by De Fraja (1993b), but includes a more explicit model of the market. The demand function is the same as set out earlier and is known by both owner and manager. One part of the marginal costs c depends on the state of nature, which will be indexed by L ('low-cost') and H ('high-cost'), and cannot be affected by the manager's efforts. The owner knows c_L, c_H, and the probability for low marginal costs, q, but only the manager knows the state of nature. The other part of the marginal costs depends on the manager's efforts to increase efficiency by reducing managerial slack, s. The manager's quasi-linear utility function is $u = y + v(s)$, where $v(s)$ is an increasing concave function. There are no other fixed costs than y_L and y_H.

Suppose that the firm is a monopoly that may or may not give some weight to consumer surplus (later the discussion will be extended to the analysis of competition). The objective function is the sum of profits and the consumer surplus, with a weight $\rho \geq 0$ attached to the latter. As ρ approaches infinity, profits get less and less important, but we shall assume a low enough value for the firm to be able to break even. Privatization makes ρ equal to zero. Thus a firm maximizes:

$$W = q\left\{\frac{\rho x_L^2}{2} + [(a - x_L - c_L - s_L)x_L - y_L]\right\}$$

$$+ (1 - q)\left\{\frac{\rho x_H^2}{2} + [(a - x_H - c_H - s_H)x_H - y_H]\right\}. \qquad (4.13)$$

Note that this objective function is not necessarily a definition of social welfare. All it says is that a public firm gives some weight to consumer welfare, maybe partly for opportunistic reasons.

The manager's utility must be sufficiently high to prevent her from leaving the firm and achieving an outside option utility $\bar{u}$. The *participation constraints* are then $y_L + v(s_L) \geq \bar{u}$ and $y_H + v(s_H) \geq \bar{u}$. She must also have an incentive to reveal truthfully that (the non-avoidable) marginal costs are c_L in the good state of nature and not c_H. In other words, truthful revelation must be more rewarding than cheating by pretending that circumstances have been unfortunate, which would make additional slack of the size $c_L - c_H$ possible. The *incentive compatibility constraint* therefore requires $y_L + v(s_L) \geq y_H + v(s_H + c_H - c_L)$. Truthful revelation can be achieved through a sufficiently high salary, but it may turn out to be cheaper to allow for some slack. Therefore the firm maximizes its objective function with respect to the permitted slack levels s_L or s_H as well.

The participation constraint is satisfied in the good state of nature, because $u(y_H, s_H + c_H - c_L)$ is larger than $u(y_H, s_H)$. The other constraints are binding, because the objective function is decreasing in y and s. We can therefore substitute $y_L = \bar{u}(s_L) + v(s_H + c_H - c_L) - v(s_H)$ and $y_H = \bar{u}(s_H)$ into W. Using the abbreviations $a_L = a - c_L$, $a_H = a - c_H$, and $\Delta c = c_L - c_H$:

$$EW = q\left\{\frac{\rho x_L^2}{2} + (a_L - x_L - s_L)x_L - [\bar{u} - v(s_L) + v(s_H + \Delta c) - v(s_H)]\right\} - (1 - q)$$

$$\left\{\frac{\rho x_H^2}{2} + (a_H - x_H - s_H)x_H - [\bar{u} - v(s_H)]\right\}. \qquad (4.14)$$

Like De Fraja (1993b), we focus on the good state of nature. Rearrange the first-order conditions with respect to x_L and x_H:

$$q[a_L - (2-\rho)x_L - s_L] = 0, \tag{4.15}$$

$$-qx_L + qv'(s_L) = 0 \tag{4.16}$$

Output is therefore:

$$x_L^* = \frac{a_L - s_L}{2-\rho}. \tag{4.17}$$

Substitute this into (4.16) and rearrange:

$$\frac{a_L - s_L}{2-\rho} = v'(s_L). \tag{4.18}$$

We can now analyse the effect of, for example, a decrease in ρ on managerial slack by differentiating (4.18) and rearranging:

$$\frac{ds_L}{d\rho} = \frac{(a_L - s_L)/(2-\rho)^2}{v''(s_L) + 1/(2-\rho)}. \tag{4.19}$$

It is obvious that the numerator of (4.19) is positive. At first sight it seems as if the sign of the denominator and hence the effect of ownership depends on whether the manager's marginal utility function is steep or flat. But it can be shown that the objective function is not concave unless v'' is below $-1/(2-\rho)$, in which case a reduction of ρ would increase managerial slack in the good state.[22] The objective function is decreasing in s_L everywhere in the opposite case, which means that managerial slack is zero whoever owns the firm.[23]

The explanation for the fact that public ownership may actually lead to higher efficiency is paradoxically the manager's greed and laziness, because a non-zero ρ means a stronger incentive to pay for good management. A decision maker for whom consumer welfare matters would be prepared to buy and bribe the manager to reduce costs because this benefits society as whole. Private shareholders are not prepared to pay as much because they will buy cost reductions only to the extent that this benefits themselves.

This model is useful because it shows that a conventional principal–agent analysis can turn popular views on their head, but is not necessarily robust to alterations. This sensitivity to details in the model specification just emphasizes the point that there may be no general and simple rules about ownership and cost efficiency.

In practice, private ownership is often dispersed and the largest shareholders may be institutional investors which focus on shareholder value only. Willner and Parker (2002) distinguish between passive and active ownership, depending on who makes the output decision. Active ownership means that the principal decides on output and observes costs, but not their composition in terms of necessary costs and slack because of asymmetric information on the state of nature. In both cases, the manager is fired if observed performance falls below a threshold and the probability for this is endogenous. Public ownership is associated with equal or lower managerial slack under active ownership, while results can go either way in the opposite case, depending on the manager's reward schedule. This suggests that governance is more important than ownership.

Privatization and competition
Many economists, such as Vickers and Yarrow (1988), have suggested that privatization may not increase efficiency without competition. But industries with privatized companies, like energy or telecommunications, are usually now oligopolistic. As argued earlier, the cost reduction may be too small to outweigh the benefits of public ownership. Moreover, it also follows from Martin and Parker (1997) and Fraquelli and Erbetta (2000) that being exposed to competition did not necessarily make privatization in Britain and Italy more successful, the British car industry being a case in point.

Theory can explain why competition does not always reduce cost. While the effects on the profit margin are well understood, less is known about the impact of competition on cost efficiency. Some studies suggest, however, that competition can occasionally have adverse effects. The following model reformulates the principal–agent model from above so as to include competition. The analysis then becomes very similar to that of Martin (1993).

There is the same kind of asymmetric information as featured in the previous section of the chapter and there are n private profit-maximizing Cournot oligopolists that are run by managers. The non-avoidable marginal costs are the same everywhere, as are the managers' utility functions and outside options and the probabilities for each outcome. The salaries in each state of nature are derived in the same way as earlier and substituted into the expected profits for firm i; $i = 1, 2, ...n$:

$$E\pi_i = q\{(a_L - x_L - s_{Li})x_{Li} - [\bar{u} - v(s_{Li}) + v(s_{Hi}) - v(s_{Hi} + \Delta c)]\}$$

$$+ (1 - q)\{(a_H - x_H - s_{Hi})x_{Hi} - [\bar{u} - v(s_{Hi})]\}. \tag{4.20}$$

Rearrange to get the solution for the low-cost situation:

$$q[a_L - x_L - x_{Li} - s_{Li}] = 0, \tag{4.21}$$

$$-qx_{Li} + qv'(s_{Li}) = 0. \tag{4.22}$$

The equation represented by (4.21) now yields output levels $x^c_{Li}(s_{L1}, s_{L2},...s_{Ln},n)$ as functions of managerial slack and market structure. Combining (4.21) and (4.22) yields the following condition:

$$x^c_{Li}(s_{L1}, s_{L2},...s_{Ln},n) = v'(s^c_{Li}). \tag{4.23}$$

There are n such equations, which can be used to determine the level of slack in each firm. However, as the equilibrium is symmetric, we can add the conditions and divide by n to get the following condition for the equation for slack in the good state of nature:

$$\frac{a_L - s_L}{n+1} = v'(s^c_L). \tag{4.24}$$

Differentiating yields:[24]

$$\frac{ds^c_L}{dn} = \frac{(a_L - s_L)/(n+1)^2}{n[v''(s_L) + 1/(n+1)]}. \tag{4.25}$$

In a similar way as in the discussion above, it can be shown that concavity requires $|\bar{v}''(s_L)| > 1/2$ (see Willner, 1999a). The denominator of (4.24) is negative, because $1/2 \geq 1/(n+1)$. This implies that an increase in the number of firms will increase the amount of managerial slack. If (4.23) has no positive solution while production is still feasible or if the second-order conditions are not satisfied, slack is zero and not dependent on the number of firms.

Thus, to privatize a public monopoly would reduce cost efficiency if (4.14) is concave in slack, but to split the privatized monopoly or to induce entry then leads to even higher marginal costs. The combination of privatization and deregulation is not then beneficial, unless competition means a sufficiently large number of entrepreneurial rather than managerial firms. Note also that the possible increase in slack means that the effect of entry on price and industry output is ambiguous.

This model is very specific and Willner and Parker (2002) provide conditions for both improved and reduced performance after entry. But the well-known multitude of solutions that industrial organization can sometimes generate must be taken seriously; in particular, we should avoid dogmatism. Thus, while competition may be beneficial in general, those cases where things can go wrong should be identified.

Natural monopoly is sometimes understood as an industry where only one firm can break even. But the above discussion has highlighted the social costs of duplication. In a wider sense, a natural monopoly means that even a commercial monopoly would be more beneficial than competition (see Vogelsang, 1988). As Salvanes and Tjøtta (1998) point out, insufficient tests have been made before deregulation. They find that electricity distribution in Norway is a natural monopoly in this sense.

Monopoly may be preferable also if competition affects quality adversely, as when new entrants free-ride on the investments made by an incumbent. An interconnected system of power plants in different ownership may then break down because of failures in one particular plant (Auriol, 1998). Moreover, the Californian electricity crisis in 2001 has highlighted the difficulties of organizing a deregulated system efficiently (Martinek and Orlando, 2001; Lijesen, *et al.*, 2001).[25]

Telecommunications have usually been seen as the flagship industry of deregulation. Long-distance calls have become cheaper following the introduction of competition in the USA (Blank *et al.*, 1998; Hausman *et al.*, 1993), but some authors have pointed out that the market is now oligopolistic, possibly with tacit collusion, and that improvements in physical and human capital and intervention from the Federal Communications Commission have been more important for the industry's development than deregulation (MacAvoy, 1998; Taylor and Taylor, 1993; Sung, 1998). In Europe, there has been considerable variation and no conclusive evidence of necessarily higher labour or total factor productivity growth associated with the EU's liberalization directives – though it is early days (Daßler *et al.*, 2002). Moreover, doubts have been raised about service quality and the industry has been accused of 'confusion marketing' (van Dam and Went, 2001; Stephen, 2001; *Guardian*, 14 October 2000).

The merits of competition have been questioned also in road transport. Deregulation can reduce industry performance in bus transport because individual operators have insufficient incentives to attract customers away from cars by offering low prices (Ireland, 1991). Competition and free entry and exit may affect welfare adversely because of a lack of coordination, instability and confusing changes in schedules and network, and reduced through- and inter-ticketing (Tyson, 1990; White, 1990; Oldale, 1997). Competition without regulation might be dysfunctional in the taxi industry too (Cairns and Liston-Heyes, 1996).

Thus the merits of competition are questionable in industries like energy, telecommunications and road and rail transport. As privatization without competition produces no benefits in general, public ownership has to be reconsidered as a serious alternative.

Intrinsic motivation and not-for-profit organizations
Economists typically focus on the self-interested behaviour of the economic man (*homo economicus*). This is a useful simplification that may be

innocuous when analysing demand or portfolio choice. But the assumption of economic self-interest cannot sensibly be extended to all our social roles. In particular, to assume such behaviour when comparing different types of organizations implies a potential bias, although not always in favour of free market solutions (see our earlier discussion, and Bowles and Gintis, 1993).

As Fehr and Fischbacher (2002) point out, experimental economics overwhelmingly suggests that a significant proportion of individuals are reciprocal in their behaviour rather than self-interested, with profound consequences for issues such as joint ownership. While the consequences for privatization are not obvious, such findings strengthen the point that governance issues, such as the ability to encourage cooperation, may be more important than ownership in improving economic performance.

Cooperation as part of reciprocal behaviour is not necessarily the same as intrinsic work motivation, which means that high performance yields benefits and not only costs for an individual (Frey, 1997).[26] But the issues are related, in the sense that the way in which individuals are motivated can be changed. An excessive focus on rewards and punishment (extrinsic work motivation) may be less productive than an encouragement of intrinsic motivation. Threatening leadership may be counter-productive (Fehr and Fishbacher, 2002) and extrinsic motivation may reduce or crowd out intrinsic motivation (Frey, 1997). A suspicion of low work morale and opportunism may therefore be self-fulfilling, and may explain why performance-related pay is less widespread than is usually believed (Frey, 1993; Jensen and Murphy, 1990).

Labour-managed firms and organizations, which are strictly speaking outside our scope, are indirectly relevant in the sense that the emphasis on profit maximization, which is typical of property rights theory, puts state enterprises in the same category as not-for-profit firms in the private sector (Furubotn and Pejovich, 1972). But the property rights theory predictions are contradicted by the experience of successful cooperative firms (see Bartlett *et al.*, 1992), which again suggests that public, private and cooperative enterprises can be efficient with the right kind of organization. For example, the Israeli *Kibbutz* system tended to be more efficient than the Soviet *Kolkhoz* system, despite or because of the fact that economic incentives were more prominent in the latter (Guttman and Schnytzer, 1989).

Conclusions

Those who favour a mixed economy are now perceived as old-fashioned and orthodox, although it is reasonable that the burden of proof should rest on those who argue that only one form of ownership can work. But a general privatization policy can only be justified by showing that it causes cost reductions that overshadow any benefits from public ownership. Neither theory nor evidence suggest that this is *always* the case. Moreover, competition in the product market may not be desirable or even possible, which strengthens the case against privatization.

There are motives for privatization other than cost efficiency, but while they might justify some divestiture, they do not require abolishing the public enterprise sector completely. It is therefore reasonable to be sceptical about general privatization, particularly because the policy is costly to reverse if it turns out to be wrong. Traditional and now often dismissed arguments for public ownership consequently should be reconsidered.

Notes

1. Typically, one early contribution was titled 'Privatization: A Policy in Search of a Rationale' (Kay and Thompson, 1986). Few of the otherwise influential and free market-oriented Chicago economists have dealt with privatization, probably because of the limited extent of public ownership in the USA (see, for example, Friedman, 1962).
2. Despite the ideological significance of ownership, the extent of privatization is not explained by the dividing lines between political parties. Left-of-centre parties have been responsible for sometimes radical privatization policies, in Australia, Austria, Belgium, Britain, Denmark, Finland, France, Germany, Greece, Italy, Luxemburg, Netherlands, New Zealand, Portugal and Sweden, while (West) Germany under the Christian Democrats adopted a cautious policy.
3. State enterprises in Britain were typically more integrated into the public sector than those in Scandinavia, where they had access to the banking system (Willner, 1998).
4. 'Certainly, for a small and open economy such as the Netherlands it would be difficult to ignore developments elsewhere in Europe. Thus, the Dutch privatization programme can be described as a "curtsy to the times" rather than the result of a positive, grand design to revitalise the economy' (Hulsink and Schenk, 1998:255).
5. There is limited evidence of political failures of this kind, because their scope is restricted by competition from other political parties and by the media (Bohm, 1986; Besley and Case, 1995). Moreover, political failures can matter only when there are significant transaction costs, which also cause markets to fail because smart agents would otherwise offset both public sector distortions and market failures (Hammond, 1990).
6. Privatization cannot be successful if politicians are always selfish. Firms must be restructured so as to become attractive for investors, voters should not be manipulated by too cheap share prices, as in Britain (see Vickers and Yarrow, 1988), and there should be no distortionary regulation, taxes or subsidies afterwards.
7. Their model of 'vested interests' actually gives employees a lower weight than under pure welfare maximization, where employees, consumers and companies' owners get the same weight.
8. For example, privatization and deregulation in electricity and bus transport in Britain have increased profits but made consumers worse off (Newbery and Pollitt, 1997; White, 1990).
9. This objective function can also be interpreted in terms of Nash-bargaining between groups with different objectives.
10. The (Hirschman-)Herfindahl index of concentration is the sum of the squared market shares of each firm.
11. Willner (1996) includes a short survey of findings related to the price elasticity of demand in the electricity industry.
12. Note that the multiplicative form of the objective function means that the profits implied by the socially optimal solution are always non-negative.
13. However, higher wages are not necessarily just a harmful side-effect of public ownership but may be part of the welfare-maximizing solution (De Fraja, 1993a; Willner, 1999b). There are other reasons why private sector conditions should not always set the

norm. Privatization might increase inequality because the public–private wage difference is higher among low wage workers (Gunderson, 1979). The wage disadvantages of females within the public sector did increase in Sweden in the 1980s because of a convergence to private sector conditions in the public sector (Zetterberg, 1992).

14. Martin and Parker conclude that their investigation: 'provides little evidence that privatization has caused a significant improvement in performance. Generally the great expectations for privatization evident in ministerial speeches have not been borne out. Certainly, privatization has been associated with improvements in some of the eleven firms studied, especially in terms of profitability and value added per employee, although what performance improvement there was often pre-dated privatization' (Martin and Parker, 1997: 217).

15. Borcherding *et al.* (1982) are often cited as supporting the superiority of private ownership, but a large proportion of their sources consist of reports by municipal authorities and other non-academic contributions. They suggest that competition may explain more of the performance variations than ownership.

16. Private ownership of airlines appeared as more efficient in Davies (1971; 1977), Ehrlich *et al.* (1994) and Liu (2001), but not in Forsyth and Hocking (1980) and Gillen *et al.* (1990). Private sector cost advantages in the bus industry are reported by Heseltine and Silcock (1990), McGuire and Van Gott (1984) and White (1990), but not by Kennedy (1995), and not in railways (Caves and Christensen, 1980; Caves *et al.*, 1982).

17. Public ownership tended to be more efficient in the 1960s and less efficient in the 1970s.

18. In a comparison of public and private electricity generation in Spain, Arocena and Waddams Price (2002) find that the former is more efficient under cost of service regulation, while the reverse is true under price cap regulation.

19. This source is misquoted in Borcherding *et al.* (1982).

20. The islands of public ownership in the USA have usually meant municipal utilities or ownership by the (regional) states, with benchmarking within the public sector. The 50 per cent federal state ownership in hydroelectric power in 1990 has been an exception (Hausman and Neufeld, 1999). Also see Chapter 7.

21. It is often believed that overmanning in the public sector or in state enterprises in developing economies is a symptom of rent-seeking behaviour, but evidence suggests that it is usually a response to undiversifiable external risk, in the absence of other social safety nets (Rodrik, 2000).

22. Note that it would be optimal with lower slack under public ownership without asymmetric information as well; the model shows that this holds true also when it is difficult for the owner to monitor the manager. The result can easily be generalized to a downward-sloping demand function of the form $p = P(x)$. Willner (1999a) provides the full solution, including the so-called 'Hessian determinant'.

23. It is of course possible that (4.14) is downward-sloping in s_L for some given value of ρ, but concave if ρ is zero. Privatization would then introduce slack in the firm.

24. The number of firms can, of course, take only integer values, but we can treat (4.21) as including a variable n which can take any value. The sign of the derivative would then tell whether managerial slack would increase or decrease as n changed from, say, n_0 to n_1.

25. A more amusing example is reported by *Helsingin Sanomat* (30 November 1997) in Finland. The state-owned cleaning service Engel is not privatized but is subject to competitive tender. In the beginning it always lost the tender, until it discovered that the key to success was to leave more dust in the customers' corridors.

26. More precisely, benefits B and costs C are then described as functions of work performance P and external interventions E. The agent then maximizes $B - C$, which means that $B_P = C_P$.

References

Aiginger, K. (1998) 'The Privatisation Experiment in Austria', in D. Parker (ed.), *Privatization in the European Union: Theory and Policy Perspectives*, London and New York: Routledge.

Arocena, P. and C. Waddams Price (2002) 'Generating Efficiency: Economic and Environmental Regulation of Public and Private Electricity Generators in Spain', *International Journal of Industrial Organization*, 20(1), 41–69.

Atkinson, S. and R. Halvorsen (1986) 'The Relative Efficiency of Public and Private Firms in a Regulated Environment: The case of U.S. Electric Utilities', *Journal of Public Economics*, 29, 281–94.

Auriol, E. (1998) 'Deregulation and Quality', *International Journal of Industrial Organization*, 16(2), 169–94.

Bagdadioglu, N., C.M.W. Price and T.G. Weyman-Jones (1996) 'Efficiency and Ownership in Electricity Distribution: A Non-parametric Model of the Turkish Experience', *Energy Economics*, 18(1), 1–23.

Bartlett, W., J. Cable, S. Estrin, D.C. Jones and S.C. Smith (1992) 'Labour Managed Firms and Private Firms in North-Central Italy: An Empirical Comparison', *Industrial and Labour Relations Review*, 46(1), 103–18.

Beesley, M. and S. Littlechild (1994) 'Privatization: Principles, problems and priorities', in M. Bishop, J. Kay, and C. Mayer (eds), *Privatization and Economic Performance*, Oxford: Oxford University Press.

Bennett, J.T. and M.H. Johnson (1979) 'Public vs. Private Provision of Collective Goods and Services: Garbage Collection Revisited', *Public Choice*, 34, 55–63.

Besley, T. and A. Case (1995) 'Does Electoral Accountability Affect Economic Policy Choices?', *Quarterly Journal of Economics*, 110, 769–98.

Bhattacharyya, A., E. Parker and K. Raffiee (1994) 'An Examination of the Effect of Ownership on the Relative Efficiency of Public and Private Water Utilities', *Land Economics*, 70(2), 197–209.

Blank, L., D.L. Kaserman and J.W. Mayo (1998) 'Dominant Firm Pricing with Competitive Entry and Regulation: The Case of IntraLATA Toll', *Journal of Regulatory Economics*, 14(1), 5–53.

Boardman, A. and A. Vining (1989) 'Ownership and Performance in Competitive Environments: A Comparison of the Performance of Private, Mixed and Share-Owned Enterprises', *Journal of Law and Economics*, 32, 1–33.

Bohm, P. (1986) *Samhällsekonomisk effektivitet*, Uddevalla: SNS förlag.

Borcherding, T.E., W.W. Pommerehne and F. Schneider (1982) 'Comparing the Efficiency of Private and Public Production: The Evidence from Five Countries', *Zeitschrift für Nationalökonomie*, Suppl. 2, 127–56.

Bös, D. (1993) 'Privatization in Europe: A Comparison of Approaches', *Oxford Review of Economic Policy*, 9(1), 94–111.

Bös, D. and W. Peters (1991) 'Privatization of Public Enterprises. A Principal–Agent Approach Comparing Efficiency in Private and Public Sectors', *Empirica*, 18(1), 5–16.

Bowles, S. and H. Gintis (1993) 'The Revenge of Homo Economicus: Contested Exchange and the Revival of Political Economy', *Journal of Economic Perspectives*, 7(1), 83–102.

Boycko, M., A. Schleifer and R.W. Vishny (1996) 'A Theory of Privatisation', *Economic Journal*, 106, 309–19.

Boyd, C.W. (1986) 'The Comparative Efficiency of State Owned Enterprises', in A.R. Negandhi (ed.), *Multinational Corporations and State-Owned Enterprises: A New Challenge in International Business*, Greenwich, CT and London: Research in International Business and International Relations, JAI Press.

Bradburd, R. (1995) 'Privatization of Natural Monopoly Public Enterprises: The Regulation Issue', *Review of Industrial Organization*, 19(3), 247–67.

Bruggink, T.M. (1982) 'Public versus Regulated Private Enterprise in the Municipal Water Industry: A Comparison of Water Costs', *Quarterly Review of Economics and Business*, 22(1), 111–25.

Byrnes, P., S. Grosskopf and K. Hayes (1986) 'Efficiency and Ownership: Further Evidence', *Review of Economics and Statistics*, 68(2), 337–41.

Cairns, R.D. and C. Liston-Heyes (1996) 'Competition and Regulation in the Taxi Industry', *Journal of Public Economics*, 59(1), 1–16.

Çakmak, E.H. and O. Zaim (1992) 'Privatization and Comparative Efficiency of Public and

Private Enterprise in Turkey. The Cement Industry', *Annals of Public and Cooperative Economics*, 63(2), 271–84.

Caves, D.W. and L.R. Christensen (1980) 'The Relative Efficiency of Public and Private Firms in a Competitive Environment: The Case of Canadian Railroads', *Journal of Political Economy*, 88(5), 958–76.

Caves, D.W., L.R. Christensen, J.A. Swanson and M.W. Thretheway (1982) 'Economic Performance of U.S. and Canadian Railroads: The Significance of Ownership and the Regulatory Environment', in T. Stanbury and F. Thompson (eds.), *Managing Public Enterprises*, New York: Praeger.

Collins, J.N. and B.T. Downes (1977) 'The Effect of Size on the Provision of Public Services: The Case of Solid Waste Collection in Smaller Cities', *Urban Affairs Quarterly*, 12, 223–6.

Cook, P. (1998) 'Privatization in the UK: Policy and Performance', in D. Parker (ed.), *Privatisation in the European Union: Theory and Policy Perspectives*, London and New York: Routledge.

Cowling, K. and D. Mueller (1978) 'The Social Costs of Monopoly Power', *Economic Journal*, 88, 727–48.

Cowling, K. and R. Sugden (1998) 'Strategic Trade Policy Reconsidered: National Rivalry vs Free Trade vs International Cooperation', *Kyklos*, 51(3), 339–58.

Cowling, K. and M. Waterson (1976) 'Price cost margins and market structure', *Economica*, 43, 267–74.

Crain, W.M. and A. Zardkoohi (1978) 'A Test of the Property Rights Theory of the Firm: Water Utilities in the United States', *Journal of Law and Economics*, 21(2), 395–408.

Cremér, H., M. Marchand and J.F. Thisse (1989) 'The Public Firm as an Instrument for Regulating an Oligopolistic Market', *Oxford Economic Papers*, 41, 283–301.

Daßler, T., D. Parker and D. Saal (2002) 'Economic Performance in European Telecommunications, 1978–98: A Comparative Study', *European Business Review*, 14(36), 194–209.

Davies, D.G. (1971) 'The Efficiency of Public Versus Private Firms: The Case of Australia's Two Airlines', *Journal of Law and Economics*, 14, 149–65.

Davies, D.G. (1977) 'Property Rights and Economic Efficiency: The Australian Airlines Revisited', *Journal of Law and Economics*, 20, 223–6.

De Alessi, T. (1974) 'An Economic Analysis of Government Ownership and Regulation: Theory and Evidence From Electric Power Industry', *Public Choice*, 19(1), 1–42.

de Bandt, J. (1998) 'Privatisation in an Industrial Policy Perspective: The Case of France', in D. Parker (ed.), *Privatisation in the European Union: Theory and Policy Perspectives*, London and New York: Routledge.

De Fraja, G. (1993a) 'Unions and Wages in Public and Private Firms: A Game Theoretic Analysis', *Oxford Economic Papers*, 45(3), 457–69.

De Fraja, G. (1993b) 'Productive Efficiency in Public and Private Firms', *Journal of Public Economics*, 50(1), 15–30.

De Fraja, G. and F. Delbono (1990) 'Game Theoretic Models of Mixed Oligopoly', *Journal of Economic Surveys*, 4,(1), 1–18.

Deprins, D., L. Simar and H. Tulkens (1984) 'Measuring Labor-Efficiency in Post Offices', in M. Marchand, P. Pestieau and H. Tulkens (eds), *The Performance of Public Enterprises. Concepts and Measurement*, Amsterdam: North-Holland.

Dewenter, K. and P.H. Malatestra (1997) 'Public Offerings of State-Owned and Privately-Owned Enterprises: An International Comparison', *Journal of Finance*, 52, 1659–79.

Dewenter, K. and P.H. Malatestra (2001) 'State-Owned and Privately Owned Firms: An Empirical Analysis of Profitability, Leverage, and Labor Intensity', *American Economic Review*, 91, 320–34.

Ehrlich, I., G. Gallais-Hamonno, Z. Liu and R. Lutter (1994) 'Productivity Growth and Firm Ownership', *Journal of Political Economy*, 102, 283–306.

Epple, K. and R. Schäfer (1996) 'The Transition from Monopoly to Competition: The Case of Housing Insurance in Baden-Württemberg', *European Economic Review*, 40(3–5), 1123–31.

Esser, J. (1998) 'Privatisation in Germany. Symbolism in the Social Market Economy', in D. Parker (ed.), *Privatisation in the European Union: Theory and Policy Perspectives*, London and New York: Routledge.

Färe, R., S. Grosskopf and J. Logan (1985) 'The Relative Performance of Publicly Owned and Privately Owned Electric Utilities', *Journal of Public Economics*, 26(1), 89–106.

Fehr, E. and U. Fishbacher (2002) 'Why Social Preferences Matter – The Impact of Non-Selfish Motives on Competition, Cooperation and Incentives', *Economic Journal*, 112, C1–C33.

Feigenbaum, S. and R. Teeples (1983) 'Public versus Private Water Delivery: A Hedonic Cost Approach', *Review of Economics and Statistics*, 65(4), 672–8.

Felder, S. (1996) 'Fire Insurance in Germany: A Comparison of Price-performance Between State Monopolies and Competitive Regions', *European Economic Review*, 40(3–5), 1133–41.

Ferguson, P. (1988) *Industrial Economics: Issues and Perspectives*, Houndmills and London: Macmillan.

Finsinger, J. (1984) 'The Performance of Public Enterprises in Insurance Markets', in M. Marchand, P. Pestieau and H. Tulkens (eds), *The Performance of Public Enterprises: Concepts and Measurement*, Amsterdam: North-Holland.

Foreman-Peck, J.O. and M. Waterson (1985) 'The Comparative Efficiency of Public and Private Enterprise in Britain: Electricity Generation Between the World Wars', *Economic Journal*, 95, 83–95.

Forsyth, P.J. and R.D. Hocking (1980) 'Property Rights and Efficiency in a Regulated Environment: The Case of Australian Airlines', *Economic Record*, 56, 182–5.

Fowler, P.C. and D.F. Richards (1995) 'Test Evidence for the OECD-Countries, 1965–85: The Relationship Between the Size of the Public Enterprise Sector and Economic Growth', *International Journal of Social Economics*, 22(3), 11–23.

Fraquelli, G. and F. Erbetta (2000) ' Privatisation in Italy: An Analysis of Factor Productivity and Technical Efficiency', in D. Parker (ed.), *Privatisation and Corporate Performance*, Cheltenham, UK and Northampton, MA, USA: Edward Elgar.

Frey, B.S. (1993) 'Shirking or Work Morale?: The Impact of Regulating', *European Economic Review*, 37(8), 1523–32.

Frey, B.S. (1997) 'On the Relationship Between Intrinsic and Extrinsic Work Motivation', *International Journal of Industrial Organization*, 15(4), 427–40.

Friedman, M. (1962) *Capitalism and Freedom*, Chicago: University of Chicago Press.

Furubotn, E. and S. Pejovich (1972) 'Property Rights and Economic Theory: A Survey of Recent Literature', *Journal of Economic Literature*, 10(4), 1137–62.

Gillen, D.W., T.H. Oum and M.W. Tretheway (1990) 'Airline Cost Structure and Policy Implications', *Journal of Transport Economics and Policy*, 24(1), 9–34.

Gravelle, H.S.E. (1984) 'Bargaining and Efficiency in Public and Private Sector Firms', in M. Marchand, P. Pestieau and H. Tulkens (eds), *The Performance of Public Enterprises: Concepts and Measurement*, Amsterdam: North-Holland.

Guardian (2000) 'Ringing up the Right Numbers', 14 October, Jobs and Money section, pp. 2.

Guardian (2001) 'The Breaking Point', 3 April, pp.4–5.

Guardian (2001) 'Shockwave for Transco', 18 June, pp.10.

Gunderson, M. (1979) 'Earning Differentials Between the Public and the Private Sectors', *Canadian Journal of Economics*, 12(2), 228–42.

Guttman, J.M. and A. Schnytzer (1989) 'Strategic Work Interaction and the *Kibbuz–Kolkhoz* paradox', *Economic Journal*, 99, 689–99.

Hammond, P. (1990) 'Theoretical Progress in Public Economics: A Provocative Assessment', *Oxford Economic Papers*, 42(1), 6–33.

Harberger, A. (1954) 'Monopoly and Resource Allocation', *American Economic Review*, 44, 77–87.

Haskel, J. and S. Szymanski (1992) 'A Bargaining Theory of Privatization', *Annals of Public and Cooperative Economics*, 63, 207–28.

Hausman, J., T. Tardiff and A. Belifante (1993) 'The Effects of the Breakup of AT&T on Telephone Penetration in the United States', *American Economic Review*, 83, 178–84.

Hausman, W.J. and J.L. Neufeld (1991) 'Property Rights versus Public Spirit: Ownership and Efficiency of U.S. Electric Utilities Prior to Rate or Return Regulation', *Review of Economic Statistics*, 73(3), 414–23.

Hausman, W. J. and J.L. Neufeld (1999) 'Falling water: The origins of direct federal participation in the U.S. electric utility industry 1902–1933', *Annals of Public and Cooperative Economics*, 76(1), 49–74.

Hayashi, P.M., M. Sevier and J.M. Trapani (1987) 'An analysis of Pricing and Production Efficiency of Electric Utilities by Mode of Ownership', in M.A. Crew (ed.), *Regulating Utilities in an Era of Deregulation*, Houndmills and London: Macmillan Press.

Helsingin Sanomat (1997) 'Palkka patosi ja työt lisääntyivät', Talous & Työ, pp. E2, 30 November.

Heseltine, P. and D. Silcock (1990) 'The Effects of Bus Deregulation on Costs', *Journal of Transport Economics and Policy*, 24(3), 239–54.

Hirsch, W.Z. (1965) 'Cost Functions of Urban Government Services: Refuse Collection', *Review of Economics and Statistics*, 47(1), 87–92.

Hjalmarsson, L. and A. Veiderpass (1992) 'Efficiency and Ownership in Swedish Electricity Retail Distribution', *Journal of Productivity Analysis*, 3(1), 7–23.

Holmström, B. and S. Honkapohja (1994) 'Yksityistäminen kansantaloudellisena kysymyksenä', in *Uudistuva teollisuus, valtionyhtiöt ja yksityistäminen*. Helsinki: Kauppa-ja Teollisuusministeriö (Ministry of Trade and Industry, Finland).

Hulsink, W. and H. Schen (1998) 'Privatisation and Deregulation in the Netherlands', in D. Parker (ed.), *Privatisation in the European Union: Theory and Policy Perspectives*, London and New York: Routledge.

Ikenberry, G.J. (1990) 'The International Spread of Privatization Policies: Inducements, Learning and "policy bandwagoning"', in E.N. Suleiman and J. Waterbury (eds), *The Political Economy of Public Sector Reform and Privatization*, Boulder: Westview Press.

Ireland, N.J. (1991) 'A Product Differentiation Model of Bus Deregulation', *Journal of Transport Economics and Policy*, 25, 153–62.

Jensen, M.C. and K.J. Murphy (1990) 'Performance Pay and Top-management Incentives', *Journal of Political Economy*, 98, 225–64.

Kay, J.A. and D.J. Thompson (1986) 'Privatisation: A Policy in Search of a Rationale', *Economic Journal*, 96(1), 18–32.

Kemper, P. and J.M. Quigley (1976) *The Economics of Refuse Collection*, Cambridge, MA: Ballinger.

Kennedy, D. (1995) 'London bus tendering: the impact of costs', *International Journal of Applied Economics*, 9(3), 305–317.

Kitchen, H. (1976) 'A Statistical Estimation of an Operating Cost Function for Municipal Refuse Collection', *Public Finance Quaterly*, 4(1), 56–76.

Laffont, J.J. and J. Tirole (1991) 'Privatization and Incentives', *Journal of Law, Economics and Organization*, 7, 84–105.

Lashmar, P. (1994) 'Going for Brokers?', *New Statesman*, 10 June, pp. 24–5.

Lijesen, M., H. Mannaerts and M. Mulder (2001) 'Will California Come to Europe?', mimeo, CPB, Netherlands Bureau for Economic Policy Research.

Liu, Z. (2001) 'Efficiency and Firm Ownership: Some New Evidence', *Review of Industrial Organization*, 19(4), 483–98.

Lynk, E.L. (1993) 'Privatisation, Joint Production and the Comparative Efficiencies of Private and Public Ownership: The UK Water Industry Case', *Fiscal Studies*, 14(2), 98–116.

MacAvoy, P.W. (1998) 'Testing for Competitiveness of Markets for Long Distance Telephone Services: Competition Finally?', *Review of Industrial Organization*, 13(3), 295–319.

Mann, P.C. and J.L. Mikesell (1976) 'Ownership and Water Systems Operation', *Water Resources Bulletin*, 12(5), 995–1004.

Marrelli, M. and F. Stroffolini (1998) 'Privatisation in Italy: a tale of "capture"', in D. Parker (ed.), *Privatisation in the European Union: Theory and Policy Perspectives*, London and New York: Routledge.

Martin, S. (1993) 'Endogenous Firm Efficiency in a Cournot Principal–Agent Model', *Journal of Economic Theory*, 59(2), 445–50.

Martin, S. and D. Parker (1997) *The Impact of Privatization. Ownership and Corporate Performance in the UK*, London and New York: Routledge.

Martinek, J.P. and M.J. Orlando (2001) 'Neither Lucky Nor Good: The Case of Electricity Deregulation in California', mimeo, Federal Reserve Bank of Kansas City.

McGuire, R.A. and N.T. Van Gott (1984) 'Public Versus Private Economic Activity: A New Look at School Bus Transportation', *Public Choice*, 43, 23–43.

Megginson, W.L. and J.M. Netter (2001) 'From State to Market: A Survey of Empirical Studies on Privatization', *Journal of Economic Literature*, 39(2), 321–89.

Meyer, R.A. (1975) 'Publicly Owned versus Privately Owned Utilities: A Policy Choice', *Review of Economics and Statistics*, 57(4), 391–9.

Millward, R. (1982) ' The Comparative Performance of Public and Private Ownership', in L.E. Roll (ed.), *The Mixed Economy*, London: Macmillan.

Molyneux, R. and D. Thompson (1987) 'Nationalised Industry Performance: Still Third-Rate?', *Fiscal Studies*, 8(1), 48–82.

Monsen, R.J. and K.D. Walters (1983) *Nationalized Companies: A Threat to American Business*, New York: McGraw-Hill.

Moore, T.G. (1970) 'The Effectiveness of Regulation of Electric Utility Prices', *Southern Economic Journal*, 37, 365–75.

Nelson, R.A. and. W.J. Primeaux, Jr (1988) 'The Effects of Competition on Transmission and Distribution Costs in the Municipal Electric Industry', *Land Economics*, 64(4), 338–46.

Neuberg, L.G. (1977) 'Two Issues in the Municipal Ownership of Electric Power Distribution Systems', *Bell Journal of Economics*, 8, 303–23.

Newbery, D.M. and M.G. Pollitt (1997) 'The Restructuring and Privatisation of Britain's GEGB – Was it Worth it?', *Journal of Industrial Economics*, 45(3), 269–304.

Ng, Y.K. (1972) 'Value Judgements and Economists' Role in Policy Recommendation', *Economic Journal*, 82, 1014–18.

Oldale, A. (1997) 'Local Bus Deregulation and Timetable Instability', working paper, The Economics of Industry Group, London School of Economics.

Parker, D. (1998) 'Privatisation in the European Union: An Overview', in D. Parker (ed.), *Privatisation in the European Union: Theory and Policy Perspectives*, London and New York: Routledge.

Parris, H., P. Pestieau and P. Saynor (1987) *Public Enterprise in Western Europe*, London: Croom Helm.

Perelman, S. and P. Pestieau (1988) 'Technical Performance in Public Enterprises. A Comparative Study of Railways and Postal Services', *European Economic Review*, 32(2–3), 432–41.

Pescatrice, D.R. and J.M. Trapani (1980) 'The Performance of Public and Private Utilities Operating in the United States', *Journal of Public Economics*, 13(3), 259–76.

Peters, L.L. (1993) 'For-Profit and Non-Profit Firms: Limits of the Simple Theory of Attenuated Property Rights', *Review of Industrial Organization*, 8(5), 623–34.

Pier, W.J., R.B. Vernon and J.H. Wicks (1974) 'An Empirical Comparison of Government and Private Production Efficiency', *National Tax Journal*, 27, 653–6.

Pint, E.M. (1991) 'Nationalization vs. Regulation of Monopolies: The Effects of Ownership on Efficiency', *Journal of Public Economics*, 44(2), 131–64.

Pirie, M. (1988) *Privatization. Theory, Practice and Choice*, Aldershot: Wildwood House.

Pommerehne, W.W. and B.S. Frey (1977) 'Public versus Private Production in Switzerland: A Theoretical and Empirical Comparison', *Urban Affairs Annual Review*, 221–42.

Rodrik, D. (2000) 'What Drives Public Emploment in Developing Countries?', *Review of Development Economics*, 4(3), 229–43.

Saal, D. and D. Parker (2000) 'The Impact of Privatization and Regulation on the Water and Sewerage Industry in England and Wales: A Translog Cost Function Model', *Managerial and Decision Economics*, 21, 253–68.

Salvanes, K.G. and S. Tjøtta (1998) 'A Test for Natural Monopoly with Application to Norwegian Electricity Distribution', *Review of Industrial Organization*, 13(6), 669–85.

Savas, E.S. (1977) 'Policy Analysis for Local Government: Public vs. Private Refuse Collection', *Policy Analysis*, 3(1), 49–74.

Schaffhauser-Linzatti, M.M. and E.J. Dockner (2001) 'The Financial and Operating Performance of Privatized Firms in Austria', mimeo, University of Vienna.

Spann, R.M. (1977) 'Public versus Private Provision of Public Services', in T.E. Borcherding (ed.), *Budgets and Bureaucrats*, Durham NC: Duke University Press.

Stephen, A. (2001) 'Coast to Coast with the Baby Bells', *New Statesman*, 27 August, pp. 20.

Stevens, B.J. (1978) 'Scale, Market Structure, and the Cost of Refuse Collection', *Review of Economics and Statistics*, 60(3), 438–48.

Sung, N. (1998) 'The Embodiment Hypothesis Revisited: Evidence From the Local U.S. Local Exchange Carriers', *Information Economics and Policy*, 10(2), 219–36.

Sutton, J. (2001) 'Rich Trades, Scarce Capabilities: Industrial Development Revisited', STICERD, Discussion Paper no. EI/28.

Taylor, W.E. and L.D. Taylor (1993) 'Postdivestiture Long-Distance Competition in the United States', *American Economic Review*, 83, 185–90.

Teeples, R. and D. Glyer (1987) 'Cost of Water Delivery Systems: Specification and Ownership Effects', *Review of Economics and Statistics*, 69, 399–408.

Thatcher, M. (1993) *The Downing Street Years*, Glasgow: Harper Collins Publishers.

Tyler, W.G. (1979) 'Technical efficiency in production in a developing country: an empirical examination of the Brazilian plastics and steel industries', *Oxford Economics Papers*, 31, 477–95.

Tyson, W.J. (1990) 'Effects of Deregulation on Service Co-ordination in the Metropolitan Areas', *Journal of Transport Economics and Policy*, 24(3), 283–95.

van Dam, J. and R. Went (2001) 'Liberalizing Network Utilities: What's in it for the Citizen?', mimeo, The Netherlands Court of Audit.

Vickers, J. and G. Yarrow (1988) *Privatization: An Economic Analysis*, Cambridge, MA: MIT Press.

Vogelsang, I. (1988) 'Regulation of Public Utilities and Nationalised Industries', in P. G. Hare (ed.), *Surveys in Public Sector Economics*, Oxford: Basil Blackwell.

von Ungern-Sternberg, T. (1996) 'The Limits of Competition: Housing Insurance in Switzerland', *European Economic Review*, 40(3–5), 1111–21.

White, P.J. (1990) 'Bus Deregulation: A Welfare Balance Sheet', *Journal of Transport Economics and Policy*, 24(3), 311–32.

Willner, J. (1996) 'A Comment on Bradburd: Privatisation of Natural Monopolies', *Review of Industrial Organization*, 11(6), 869–82.

Willner, J. (1998) 'Privatisation in the Nordic EU-countries – Fashion or Necessity?', in D. Parker (ed.), *Privatisation in the European Union: An Industrial Policy Perspective*, London and New York: Routledge.

Willner, J. (1999a) 'Market Structure, Corporate Objectives and Cost Efficiency', in K. Cowling (ed.), *Practical Proposals for Industrial Policy in Europe*, London and New York: Routledge.

Willner, J. (1999b) 'Policy objectives and performance in a mixed market with bargaining', *International Journal of Industrial Organization*, 17(1), 137–45.

Willner, J. (2001) 'Ownership, Efficiency, and Political Interference', *European Journal of Political Economy*, 17(6), 723–48.

Willner, J. and D. Parker (2002) 'The Relative Performance of Public and Private Enterprise under Conditions of Active and Passive Ownership', Working Paper No. 22, Centre on Regulation and Competition, Institute for Development Policy and Management, University of Manchester.

Willner, J. and L. Ståhl (1992) 'Where are the Welfare Losses of Imperfect Competition Large?', *European Journal of Political Economy*, 8, 477–91.

World Bank (1995) *Bureaucrats in Business*, Washington, DC: World Bank.

Yunker, J.A. (1975) 'Economic Performance of Public and Private Enterprise', *Journal of Economics and Business*, 28(1), 60–75.

Zetterberg, J. (1992) 'Effects of Changed Wage Setting Conditions on Male–Female Wage Differentials in the Swedish Public Sector', Working Paper 1992:8, Department of Economics, Uppsala University.

5 Methods of privatization
Cosmo Graham

Introduction

The aim of this chapter is to present an overview of the different methods of privatization, with some observations on the success or failure of certain techniques.[1] For the purposes of this chapter, 'privatization' is taken to mean the transfer of assets from the public or state sector into the private sector. Issues such as contracting out are thus not examined, although an increasing use of such devices may go along with privatization in the sense of transfer of assets.

Assessing the success or otherwise of particular methods of privatization cannot be divorced from the aims and objectives of those behind a privatization programme. This does, however, raise a difficult issue. As a policy, privatization has been used in a wide range of states with dramatically different socioeconomic contexts ranging from developed countries, such as the United Kingdom, France and Germany to the transition economies of Central and Eastern Europe, to the developing nations of Africa and Asia. Moreover, the enterprises to which privatization are applied vary greatly, from one-person retail shops to large network industries such as electricity. Finally, there are different types of privatization programmes. In their research on the dynamics of privatization, Feigenbaum and Henig (1994) distinguish, in ideal–typical terms, between pragmatic, tactical and systemic privatizations. A further problem is that the sponsors, in a broad sense, of a privatization programme may have a number of conflicting objectives. To use Feigenbaum and Henig's language, some may be interested in the pragmatic benefits, others in short-term political gains, hence tactical privatization, and others in more systemic change. Thus, to take the UK as an example which is discussed in more detail in Chapters 3 and 6, although it is easy to assume that there was a coherent privatization programme between 1979 and 1997, this was, in fact, not the case. Vickers and Yarrow (1988:157; see also Swann, 1988:228–38, and Veljanovski, 1987:7–11) list seven aims: reducing government involvement in industry, improving efficiency in the privatized industries, reducing the public sector borrowing requirement (PSBR), easing problems in public sector pay determination, widening share ownership, encouraging employee share ownership, and gaining political advantage. Abromeit (1988:72) has commented:

> [the system of aims] was not formulated at the beginning of the policy of privatisation: we search in vain for official Government pronouncements – e.g. a White Paper – from the early years which comprehensively presents and adequately clarifies the aims and scope of the proposed measures. Only in recent times, after this policy has steadily expanded by a dynamic of its own, have Government members . . . made it their business in various speeches to equip the *de facto* policy, after the event, with a more or less consistent philosophy.

This is not a problem unique to the UK (Guislain, 1992:4). On a less elevated level, there is some evidence that in certain countries those who argue for privatization can see it as a means of entrenching market mechanisms and private ownership; whereas those in charge of implementing it may see it as an opportunity to gain valuable assets at a low price or even for nothing.

One issue that does require emphasizing is the need for speed in a privatization programme. This is an important and somewhat underestimated requirement for privatization programmes that does seem to cut across different contexts. Thus a speedy privatization programme was important in, for example, the Russian Federation and Czechoslovakia, because of worries about the stability of the new, non-communist regime (see Chapters 17 and 18; also Nellis, 2002), just as much as it was important to keep the momentum of the privatization programme going in the United Kingdom. On the other hand, privatization in Poland and Hungary has taken place at a slower pace, although not without success (see Chapters 19 and 20). The necessity for speed does cut across a number of other possible objectives of privatization programmes.

Having said this, there are three main issues that have to be considered in relation to any privatization. The first issue is the value accruing to the state from the sale of the enterprises either directly or in long-term savings or revenue. The second issue is the relationship between reward and competition. Often state-owned enterprises benefit from a monopoly, usually legally protected, in relation to their activities and one question to be asked is whether or not this monopoly should be removed on sale, or shortly thereafter. It may be that more than just removing the legal monopoly is needed; restructuring may be necessary in, for example, network industries, where potentially competitive elements of previously integrated industries have been separated from these elements such as transmission that have natural monopoly characteristics. Good examples would be the way that the electricity industry in England and Wales and Argentina's railways were restructured before privatization. The issue of competition clearly affects the sale price of an enterprise, so any privatizing authority must balance the immediate costs with the long-term benefits of introducing competition. A third issue is that of ownership: is part of the objective of the privatization process to create a wider class of shareowners, to benefit the employees or to encourage foreign investment or keep the enterprises in domestic hands? The thesis of this chapter is that there is no one ideal method of privatization. The trade-off between these issues will, if not addressed, lead to the failure of a programme, but there are different ways of approaching them, depending on the desired outcomes.

The chapter has a simple structure. After discussion of some introductory issues relating to privatization, sales to the public are discussed, including voucher sales. This is followed by discussion of private sales, including small privatizations, management and employee buy-outs, and sales of assets. There are then some brief overall conclusions.

Introduction to the methods of privatization
Although for presentational purposes the various methods of privatization will be dealt with separately, all countries have used a mixture of methods and, to a greater or lesser extent, concentrated on those methods which seemed appropriate or successful in their own context. Given the wide variety of enterprises being privatized, from single shops in the Czech Republic to British Telecommunications in the UK, this is a sensible strategy.

A second introductory point is that privatization often requires the creation of new institutions to manage the process. Although this was not the case with the UK, and there was criticism from the country's National Audit Office[2] for failing to learn from experience, in almost all other countries specialist institutions have been created to manage and oversee the process. The institutional arrangements have varied widely. At one extreme, Russia created a State Committee for the Management of State Property, which, among other things, prepared the annual privatization programme, supervised its implementation, established commissions responsible for preparing privatization plans for individual enterprises and promoted investment funds involved in voucher privatization (see Chapter 17, and Frydman *et al.*, 1993, for details). Other countries have not given such a wide range of powers to bodies responsible for privatization. By comparison, in France, the remit of the Privatization Commission was restricted to ensuring that the enterprises chosen for privatization had not been undervalued. It has been reported that fragmented institutional arrangements for privatization have been common in Africa (Campbell White and Bhatia, 1998:60). Regardless of the institutional structure adopted, it seems clear from the studies that there needs to be a central political commitment to the programme in order to ensure that it is successful. Certainly, clear institutional arrangements will help: Campbell White and Bhatia (ibid.:111) cite the institutional arrangements for Zambia as one of the reasons why, in their opinion, its privatization programme has been the most successful in Africa.[3] Conversely, even though the

Russian Committee for the Management of State Property had wide-ranging powers, the use of them in the second phase of privatization in Russia has been criticized for being notably ineffective.

Guislain (1992:47) makes the point that there is no perfect institutional arrangement, but that five things need to be clear. First, the responsibilities of each agency involved in the process must be clearly identified. Secondly, conflicts of interest should be avoided, for example, between agencies responsible for restructuring state-owned enterprises (SOEs) and those responsible for privatizing them. Thirdly, the agencies responsible for divestiture should have a broad mandate and corresponding powers to implement the programme. Fourthly, the process should be streamlined as much as possible. Finally, the controls should be a posteriori rather than a priori. As regards Africa, it was commented that none of the case study countries had a mechanism for monitoring the impact of the process or the performance of the privatized enterprises (see Chapter, 15 and Campbell White and Bhatia, 1998:46).

Corporatization

I have used the word 'corporatization' to refer to the process by which an SOE is transformed into a private corporate form prior to its sale to the private sector. Changing the legal form is not always necessary; in some countries, such as Spain, the SOEs take the legal form of commercial companies with their shares held entirely by the government. It is noticeable that in almost all countries the period before privatization is devoted to trying to ensure that the SOE runs along more 'business-like' lines in preparation for privatization. In New Zealand, the State-Owned Enterprises Act 1986 was entirely devoted to this issue.

Assuming that an SOE can be transformed into an at least plausible going concern, there are a number of issues that need to be decided. First, and perhaps foremost, is the question of the company's balance sheet. Transformation requires the state authorities to value the company's assets and liabilities, something which is by no means straightforward even with the assistance of outside experts. The difficulties of valuing an enterprise operating in a communist economy are particularly formidable as there are few, or limited, market mechanisms that allow an accurate valuation of the assets. Similar problems may occur in other countries either because the monitoring systems are ineffective or because the information needed for control of SOEs is very different from that required by prospective purchasers. Cramer (2001:86) commented that there was 'no remotely accurate information basis on which to reach precise valuation estimates' for many SOEs in Mozambique. Because, almost inevitably, incumbent managements have greater knowledge of their enterprise's assets, liabilities and trading positions, this puts them in a stronger position compared to the government that is attempting to sell the enterprises.

A major issue in relation to the privatization of any SOE is the extent of debt and liabilities that the enterprise is going to start life with in the private sector. A government's ability to deal with debt is constrained by its own overall financial position, but it is worth noting that in the UK experience for instance, the government restructured the balance sheets of most companies that it was selling. For example, a cash injection of £283 million was made into Rolls-Royce, against the advice of the government's advisers, after it had been demanded by the company chairman as a condition of agreeing to privatization. In the case of the water authorities, a total of £6.5 billion in debts were written off and cash was injected (Graham and Prosser, 1991:91).

As well as writing off any debt, there is also the issue in each privatization as to whether any subsidy or other financial aid should be given to encourage the sale. This can be explicit, as was the case with Rolls-Royce, or implicit, as, for example, with the deferred purchase terms that have often been used in African privatizations, where the domestic purchasers have often later defaulted on the payment agreement. This is, in effect, a hidden subsidy to the purchasers (Cramer, 2001).

A further issue to be considered is what continuing influence the state may wish to retain over the privatized enterprise, outside more general means of influence such as taxation, the regulatory system, if any, and the power to pass legislation or to make grants. Leaving aside regulation for the moment, there are two main methods that have been adopted: the appointment of government directors and the use of 'golden shares' or equivalent devices. Dealing with government directors first, the British experience has been that these are not an effective means of government retaining influence over companies. This is in part because the legal regime relating to directors in the UK clearly states that their primary duties are to the company and also because governments in Britain never seem to have had a coherent view of the purposes of government directors (Graham and Prosser, 1987:34–6). This may be to an extent a peculiarity of the British system. It has been argued in relation to East German privatization that the *Treuhandanstalt* strengthened the supervisory boards in large firms and that these boards took a more active role in enterprise restructuring than was common in Germany (Dininio, 1999:53–4).

The next device is 'golden shares' or, put more generally, restrictions on shareholding. These were pioneered in the UK (see Graham and Prosser, 1988; McHarg, 1998) where they took the form of provisions in the company's articles, which allotted one special share to the government and then provided for weighted voting rights on certain matters. In later forms of the 'golden share', restrictions were placed on shareholding and the disposal of assets was made subject to the approval of the golden shareholder. Any change in the articles of association was expressed to be subject to the approval of the golden shareholder. It is notable that these provisions did not require legislation. Quite what the purpose of these devices was has never been entirely clear. They offered the government the possibility of vetoing any particular takeover bid, although when the government became involved in the Britoil and Jaguar takeovers (Graham and Prosser, 1991:144–9) there was substantial political fuss. More generally, the golden shares have served to give the privatized companies a breathing space before they became fully subject to the disciplines of the capital market. This is most noticeable in relation to the electricity industry, where the regional electricity companies were privatized in 1990 and had the protection of a golden share until 1995. When that protection was lifted, almost all of them were subject to successful bids from other, mainly foreign, companies.

The issue of using golden shares to restrict foreign investment has been highly controversial, particularly within the European Union, where one of the basic rules is that there should be free movement of capital and no discrimination on the grounds of nationality, although there are limited exceptions to this. The Commission of the European Communities investigated the British golden share schemes and negotiated some changes. More importantly, the Commission challenged the schemes in place in Portugal, Belgium and France, and the case has recently been decided by the European Court of Justice (Cases C-367/98, C483/99 and C-503/99 *Commission v. Portugal*, 4 June 2002). This decision said such schemes could only be justified if they fulfilled two requirements: (1) they were founded on overriding requirements of the general interest, and (2) they were proportionate to the objective pursued. On these grounds, the court held that the Belgian scheme, which was aimed at maintaining minimum supplies of gas in the event of a real and serious threat, was compatible with Community law. By contrast the French scheme with a similar aim was deemed unlawful because the potential measures went beyond what the court felt was necessary in order to obtain the objective. In particular, the powers were too wide and imprecise. The Portuguese scheme, which required prior authorization for foreign shareholdings and holdings above 10 per cent in certain companies, did not meet an overriding requirement of the general interest. For our purposes, the consequence of this case is that there are now distinct limitations on the use of golden shares within the EU. This may become even more relevant following enlargement of the EU in the next few years.

The French government has not used golden shares as much as the British. Instead, in the privatizations of the 1980s, they used the concept of 'hard cores' or *noyaux durs* (see Chapter 6). What happened here is that a proportion of the capital was allocated on privatization to a group of investors. Although the allocation was done ostensibly because of a lack of large institutional shareholders in France, and there were some legal procedures to be followed to prevent arbitrary ceding of interests, this technique has been criticized as rewarding government supporters and creating a highly incestuous group of investors (Graham and Prosser, 1991:154–60). One can perhaps see a similar pattern in Russia with the sales of controlling interests to the so-called 'outsiders'. It is interesting that this attempt to create a controlling block has been highly criticized, whereas, in the context of Czech voucher privatization, the lack of sufficiently concentrated shareholders has equally been criticized (see Chapters 17 and 18 below). Indeed, it is common for governments to seek strategic investors in large SOEs before a public flotation of the remainder of the shares.

The issue of regulation after privatization needs to be addressed, although the evidence is that this issue is often of secondary concern to those engaged in a privatization programme.[4] The presence of economic regulation after privatization will affect the sale price of an enterprise, depending on the perception of what impact such regulation will have on the profitability of the enterprise and how stable the regulatory arrangements will be. So, in the context of British privatization, there were promises of 'light touch' regulation initially and much controversy was generated in the mid-1990s when the privatized companies, notably British Gas, thought that the 'regulatory contract' they had signed up to had been broken (Veljanovski, 1993; Prosser, 1999). The type of regulation will vary from natural monopolies, where permanent price control is appropriate, to those where regulation is seen as temporary until suitable competition develops, although the temporary phase may be quite lengthy, as in telecommunications in the UK. Transfer into the private sector means that the enterprises will be subject to the ordinary rules of the country in relation to contracts, consumer protection and competition law, which may require changes both in the enterprise's practice and in the law.

Sales to the public
According to OECD statistics (OECD, 2002), privatization through public offering of shares has been the predominant method of privatization since 1990, although in the last year or so other methods have seen an increasing use. The OECD also makes the point that a combination of methods is often used. So there may be the sale of a controlling stake to a strategic buyer, followed by a public offering. In many cases, a portion of the stake is also allocated to employees. The World Bank (1988) specifies four conditions that must be met before a public offering is feasible. First, the enterprise must be a sizeable going concern with a reasonable earnings record or potential or

can be reconstituted to meet these requirements. Secondly, there must be a full body of financial management or other information available for disclosure. Thirdly, there must be discernible liquidity in the local market. Finally, either the equity markets are developed or some structural mechanism must be used to attract the investing public. These conditions cannot always be met. For example, the World Bank's report on Africa suggests that African countries have been constrained by a thin capital market and that mobilization of investors has remained weak (Campbell White and Bhatia, 1998:50).

The procedure followed in the UK can be given in outline as an exemplar of the methods used in a developed Western country. The normal procedure in Britain was to employ merchant banks to act as financial advisers and to give advice on the price to be set; sometimes another independent adviser was appointed to give a second opinion. The sale would be underwritten and, prior to the British Steel sale in 1988, the financial advisers would have been the underwriters, although after this sale the roles were given to two different institutions to avoid conflicts of interest. A prospectus would be published and the public would be invited to subscribe on the basis of the information contained in the prospectus – typically a certain percentage of the shares would have been placed with investment institutions, as well as offering a percentage to individual members of the public.[5] In most cases, all the shares in the company were to be sold, although British Telecom was a notable exception to this policy, as just over 50 per cent of the shares were sold initially. In the case of BT, the then Conservative government made renationalization through share purchase more difficult by imposing a target investment limit in the legislation. This set a maximum government shareholding of around 49 per cent. In theory, future legislation could have repealed this limit, but it could have been politically embarrassing. In any event, the remainder of the government's stake in BT was sold off in separate transactions in 1991 and 1993.

A critical element of this process is that it required the financial advisers to specify a price for the company. The difficulty for the financial advisers was that if the price was too high the offer would be undersubscribed, whereas if it was too low the government faced the charge of selling off the assets too cheaply. This has proved to be the most controversial part of the programme within the UK, with the accusation made that the companies were sold off too cheaply and that alternative methods would have led to a better return to the government. In earlier work (Graham and Prosser, 1991) a contrast with the position in France was drawn, where share issues were not underwritten and the Privatization Commission did the valuation. The result was that premiums for investors at the end of the first day of stock market trading were significantly less than those that were obtained in the UK. When alternative tender offers were used in the UK, the premiums for investors were significantly less but the vast majority of sales were still at a fixed price.

Voucher privatization

An important variant of large-scale privatization has been developed in some of the transition economies of Central and Eastern Europe, namely voucher or 'mass' privatization.[6] One of the perceived problems here was the need to privatize large enterprises quickly but, at the same time, not to sell them exclusively either to foreign investors or to the incumbent management. Because of the lack of functioning capital markets and the lack of individual savings or money, this could not be accomplished through a public offering of shares, as was done in Western European countries. Instead, the idea was developed of issuing vouchers to adult citizens, which would give them the opportunity to invest in the privatized companies either directly through share purchases or indirectly through investment funds. There were two main variants to this method, depending on the amount of freedom given to individuals and the status of investment funds, which can be illustrated by looking at the Czech and Polish experiences (see Chapters 18 and 19).

In what was then Czechoslovakia, the basic process was that adult citizens were offered a book of vouchers, which entitled them to invest in the companies that were to be privatized. A list of companies to be privatized was drawn up, with very basic financial information being provided, and a sophisticated auctioning procedure was devised. At around the same time, a number of investment funds were created, which offered to purchase these books of vouchers for a premium. These investment funds, dominated largely by the Czech and Slovak banks, became the major holders of shares in the privatized enterprises. The auction process took around seven months and the transfer of shares a further six months, at the end of which over 90 per cent of the shares in those companies being sold had been transferred to private hands (Mladek and Hashi, 1993).

By contrast, in Poland, the vouchers issued to citizens did not entitle them to invest directly in the privatized enterprises, but instead allowed them to invest in National Investment Funds, which were to be managed by foreign experts. These Funds were then assigned certain enterprises in which they were to be the leading fund and have some 27 per cent of the shareholding, as well as having a number of companies in which they would have a small stake, say 2–3 per cent of the shares. In addition, in any enterprise, employees would have a 15 per cent stake and the state Treasury a 25 per cent stake (Thieme, 1995).

However, a standard criticism of Czech, and indeed other, voucher privatizations is that it led to a dispersed ownership structure without long-term commitment and did not become a source for necessary capital investments. As a result firms with domestic investment have not been able to enhance productivity to the same extent as firms with foreign ownership (Zempinerova, 2000:9; Nellis, 2002). By comparison, Nellis (2002) claims that the Estonian programme has been more successful because Estonia welcomed foreign investment, partly as a counterweight to the Russians, and limited the exchange of vouchers to minority stakes in firms with a controlling majority sold to a core investor. In Poland, it has been reported that the investment funds have delegated their voting powers, in enterprises in which they have under 2 per cent of the votes, to the leading fund, thus perhaps overcoming the problems of dispersed ownership (Schollmann, 2001). Overall, Nellis (2002) concludes that the World Bank placed too much faith in voucher schemes and should have paid more attention to prudential regulation in capital and financial markets and to other institutional developments.

Private sales
Under this heading are included all methods of sale that are not offerings to the general public. So included here are sales to one buyer, as well as sales conducted through any form of auction or tender process. It also includes the sale of subsidiaries by state-owned enterprises, which has been a significant part of privatization activity in a number of countries, notably France and Italy. Perhaps one of the most startling things about the entire UK privatization process is that no general legislation authorizing the programme needed to be passed, although there was a proposal for such legislation, which was shelved in part owing to lack of parliamentary time. Instead, the government proceeded in a piecemeal fashion, deciding on a case-by-case basis which enterprises should be privatized. This is in marked contrast to almost all other countries that have engaged in privatization, where some general law or executive order has been promulgated in order to give the authority to privatize. This is true both of Central and Eastern European countries but also in regard to Western European countries, such as Spain and France, as well as African countries.

In organizing private sales, the key issue to be considered is the transparency and objectivity of the sale method. It is, however, easier to state this as a principle as opposed to finding satisfactory solutions in practice. One possibility is to have an auction process, but as Guislain (1997:125) points out, this only works when the key aspects of the transaction can be identified and defined. So this is most appropriate for simple transactions in competitive sectors. It is also the case that the auction process needs to be designed carefully in order to ensure the optimum results (Maskin, 1996; Klemperer, 2002).

Even if a straightforward auction cannot be held, it is better to inject more competition into the process of sale. It is suggested in the literature that relying on expert valuations is not sufficient because valuation commissions have an inbuilt bias to be conservative in their valuation, that is, on the high side, which can cause problems with the process, as apparently happened in Morocco (Guislain, 1997:120). The worst possible procedure is when there is a sale without an independent, expert valuation and without competition. The difficulty with such private sales is that there is substantial discretion open to the selling body to tailor the terms of the sale in a way that is not objective. Thus, although it is recommended that there be a pre-qualification stage where potential buyers are evaluated, the terms for qualification may be set so as to exclude certain purchasers (ibid.:252, 254). There is also the question as to whether the whole of the framework, bar price, is specified or whether it should be left to the bidders to specify how they will reach the objectives.

Small privatizations
In Central and Eastern European countries the state sector extended right down to very small enterprises, down indeed to the retail kiosk. There has been a need, therefore, to move small businesses out of the state sector and into private hands. Generally, this has been done through straightforward auctioning or sale, largely to those people who were engaged in running the enterprises and not necessarily at market value. Nellis (2002:8) has commented that such transfers have been relatively non-contentious and have been judged to be a great success in terms of improving the quality and quantity of services and goods provided and creating a large number of jobs for those shifting out of restructured SOEs.

Management or employee buy-outs
This section is concerned with the privatization of larger firms, with over 250 workers, and their sale to the management or employees. This is a technique which has been used occasionally in western countries, although it has been more common in Central and Eastern Europe. It has been particularly popular in Russia, where the rules allowing workers and management to purchase shares were such that they received a large discount on the true value (see Chapter 17, and Guislain, 1997:134). In Britain, the most high-profile example was the employee buy-out of the National Freight Corporation, which was heralded as a success because the worth of the employees' investment rose dramatically in the seven years after privatization, when the company became listed on the Stock Exchange. There were other examples of employee and management buy-outs (Graham and Prosser, 1991:130–1; Wright and Petrin, 1987), notably in the bus industry.

In the British context, these deals have been relatively small and the companies have not enjoyed any long-term success. Although in transition countries these types of sales are politically popular and relatively easy to implement, Havrylyshyn and McGettigan (1999:8) concluded:

> experience shows that these buyouts suffer serious disadvantages. Yielding to insider interests often entails large costs in inefficiency and poor management. The process may be inequitable, handing employees, rather than the population at large, most of the benefits. The record of labor-managed firms suggests that they may grant excessive wage increases, maintain excessively high employment, and undertake insufficient investment.

Insolvency and sale of assets

It may be that it is impossible to restructure an enterprise as a going concern. In that case, a distinction needs to be drawn between selling off the assets of the enterprise or selling the enterprise itself in its insolvent or bankrupt state.[7] The critical difference between the two processes is that, when the insolvent company is sold, the purchaser will usually take not only the assets but also any liabilities. This is a much less attractive proposition, particularly where there are large contingent liabilities, for example relating to claims over environmental damage. The literature suggests that asset sales are much easier than disposal of an insolvent company, although there are examples, such as in Mexico, where this has been done.

Conclusions

Although some of the literature suggests that there is an ideal way of disposing of SOEs, this depends on making an assumption about the aims behind such a programme. In reality, there is often a mixture of aims and objectives that will pull in different directions and require trade-offs to be made, implicitly at least. The techniques to be used for privatization can only be assessed against the objectives. For example, as Guislain (1992:3) points out, if the aim is revenue maximization, free vouchers would not be the appropriate instrument. Nevertheless, there are certain pitfalls or concerns that need to be addressed when choosing the technique.

Perhaps the first thing to notice is that privatization is a relatively long-term programme, even in countries like the UK that have a mixed economy. Even here the core of the privatization programme ran from about 1982 to around 1993, somewhat over 10 years. When a privatization programme is introduced into a non-market economy, as in Central and Eastern Europe, it is likely to take even longer and be tied into the reform of other matters, such as contract and competition law. The timing issue suggests that there is a virtue in developing specialized, independent institutions, whose job is to implement divestiture as well as having analytical capacity to look back on the programme and learn from events. This also suggests that there needs to be a long-term political will to implement such a programme, although that is perhaps more elusive.

The second thing is that, for both political and economic reasons, whichever methods are chosen have to be implemented in as transparent a way as possible with the maximum amount of competition. In political terms, one of the standard criticisms of privatization programmes is that they involve selling off assets to favoured parties. A transparent process, using as objective criteria as possible, where private sales are concerned or using a public flotation where that is possible, can rebut this criticism. One of the big economic problems is that of valuing the enterprises to be sold, although it is also a political issue. Even in developed countries this is a difficult issue, whereas in developing and transition countries it can be a nightmare. Competitive processes help to solve this problem because they introduce an element of market discipline into the valuation process, as well as rebutting political claims that the enterprises are being sold for far less than their true value.

It seems to be necessary as well to open up the privatization process to foreign enterprises. There is some evidence that attempting to restrict foreign involvement in the long run is detrimental to the economy, particularly where there is not sufficient capital or expertise in the indigenous economy. This ties in with the issue of corporate governance; a reform programme has to address what corporate governance will look like after the privatization of SOEs, particularly in countries where there is little or no history of private investment in companies (see Chapter 12, for the example of China).

Just as importantly, successful privatization also involves thinking about the conditions for the regulation, in the broadest sense, of market structures after divestiture. On a relatively small scale, this can be seen as the problem with privatizing British Gas as, in effect, a private sector monopoly in 1986. The following nine years were spent reconsidering this decision until it was effectively reversed in 1995; on a larger canvas it is the issue of regulation after privatization, which faces Russia currently.

In conclusion, there is a great irony about privatization programmes that are aimed at cutting the link between politics and economics and introducing greater market forces into a society. The irony is that the design and implementation of the process is a matter of political decision within the society engaged on it.

Notes

1. For further discussion, see World Bank (1988), Guislain (1997) and Welch and Fremond (1998).
2. For a list of NAO reports, see *http://www.nao.gov.uk/publications/vfmsublist/vfm_pas.htm.*

3.　Although see Craig (2000) for a different view of Zambia.
4.　The subject of regulation of privatized firms is discussed in detail in Chapters 22 to 26.
5.　In some instances there were preferential schemes for employee share purchases.
6.　Its first use appears to have been in British Columbia, in Canada: see Ohashi (1987).
7.　Insolvency is the term used for companies in the UK, whereas bankruptcy is the term used in the USA for both companies and individuals.

References

Abromeit, H. (1988) 'British Privatisation Policy', *Parliamentary Affairs*, 41, 68–85.

Campbell White, O. and A. Bhatia (1998) *Privatization in Africa*, Washington, DC: World Bank.

Craig, J. (2000) 'Evaluating Privatisation in Zambia: a tale of two processes', *Review of African Political Economy*, 27(85), 357–66.

Cramer, C. (2001) 'Privatisation and Adjustment in Mozambique: a hospital pass?', *Journal of Southern African Studies*, 27(1), 79–104.

Dininio, P. (1999), *The Political Economy of East German Privatization*, Westport, CT: Praeger.

Feigenbaum, H. and J. Henig (1994) 'The Political Underpinnings of Privatization – a typology', *World Politics*, 46(2), 185–208.

Frydman, R. *et al.* (1993) *The Privatization Process in Russia, Ukraine and the Baltic States*, London: Central European University Press.

Graham, C. and T. Prosser (1987) 'Privatising Nationalised Industries: Constitutional Issues and New Legal Techniques', *Modern Law Review*, 50(1), 16–51.

Graham, C. and Prosser, T. (1988) 'Golden Shares: Industrial Policy by Stealth?', *Public Law* pp. 413–31

Graham, C. and T. Prosser (1991) *Privatizing Public Enterprises*, Oxford: Clarendon Press.

Guislain, P. (1992), 'Divestiture of State Enterprises: An Overview of the Legal Framework', World Bank Technical Paper 186, Washington, DC.

Guislain, P. (1997) *The Privatization Challenge: A Strategic, Legal, and Institutional Analysis of International Experience*, Washington, DC: World Bank.

Havrylyshyn, O. and D McGettigan (1999) *Privatization in transition countries: lessons of the first decade*, Washington, DC: International Monetary Fund.

Klemperer, P. (2002) 'What Really Matters in Auction Design', *Journal of Economic Perspectives*, 16(1), 169–89.

McHarg, A. (1998) 'Government Intervention in Privatised Industries: The Potential and Limitations of the Golden Share', *Utilities Law Review*, 9(4), 198–201.

Maskin, E. (1996) 'Auctions and Privatization' in G. Yarrow and P. Jasinski (eds), *Privatization: Critical Perspectives in the World Economy*, vol. II, London: Routledge.

Mladek, J. and I. Hashi (1993) 'Voucher Privatisation, Investment Funds and Corporate Governance in Czechoslovakia', *British Review of Economic Issues*, 15(37), 67–95.

Nellis, J. (2002) *The World Bank, Privatization and Enterprise Reform in Transition Economies: A Retrospective Analysis*, Washington, DC: World Bank.

OECD (2002), *Financial Market Trends*, 82, June.

Ohashi, T. (1987) 'Privatisation: The case of British Columbia' in S. Hanke (ed.), *Privatization and Development*, San Francisco: Institute For Contemporary Studies.

Prosser, T. (1999) 'Theorising Utility Regulation', *Modern Law Review*, 62, 196–217.

Schollmann, W. (2001) 'Foreign Participation in Privatisation: What Does it Mean?', *Post-communist Economies*, 13(3), 373–88.

Swann, D. (1988), *The Retreat of the State*, Brighton: Wheatsheaf.

Thieme, J. (1995) 'The Polish Mass Privatisation Programme', in OECD (ed.), *Mass Privatisation: An Initial Assessment*, Paris: OECD.

Veljanovski, C. (1987), *Selling the State*, London: Weidenfeld and Nicolson.

Veljanovski, C. (1993) *The Future of Industry Regulation in the UK*, London: European Policy Forum.

Vickers, J. and G. Yarrow (1988) *Privatisation: An Economic Analysis*, London: MIT Press.

Welch, J. and O. Fremond (1998) *The Case-by-Case Approach to Privatization: Techniques and Examples*, Washington, DC: World Bank.

World Bank (1988) *Techniques of Privatization of State Owned Enterprises*, Washington, DC: World Bank.

Wright, M. and T. Petrin (1987) 'Privatisation through Employee Buy-Outs in the UK: The experience of five formerly state owned enterprises', Centre for Management Buy-out Research, University of Nottingham.

Zempinerova, A. (2000) 'Privatisation of Network Industries: the Case of the Czech Energy Sector', Paper prepared for the plenary session 'Managing Commercial Assets under State ownership' of Advisory Group on Privatisation, OECD, Budapest, 19–20 September.

PART II

PRIVATIZATION IN DEVELOPED ECONOMIES

6 Privatization in the European Union
David Parker

Introduction[1]

Europe has a history of state ownership with a major expansion of state ownership of industry occurring in the inter-war years and more especially after 1945 (Monsen and Walters, 1983:1; Anastassopolou et al., 1987). Until the 1980s, state intervention was generally accepted in Europe, particularly where there was a suggestion of market failure, such as in the network industries (telecommunications, gas, electricity, water and the railways) with their natural monopoly characteristics.

Although major privatization activity in Europe is associated with the UK since 1979, there are examples of earlier sales of state assets, such as in West Germany after 1959, in the UK in the early 1950s and early 1970s, Ireland in the 1960s and 1970s and Italy in the 1950s and 1960s. These sales were not, however, part of a systematic programme aimed at slimming down the state sector (with the partial exception of the UK in the early 1950s). This is what marks out the current privatizations in Europe compared to earlier programmes.

This chapter considers the development of privatization in the European Union. It provides an overview of privatization activity in each of the EU states before turning to consider why privatization is fashionable at the present time. The consequences of privatization are then assessed. There are four main reasons for the privatization activity with expected efficiency gains seemingly not the main driving force in a number of EU states. Even where economic efficiency gains are the main goal, they are not guaranteed because of the forms privatization is taking, while privatization implies a redistribution of income and economic power in Europe which has not been widely discussed and researched.

An overview of privatization in the EU

The first major privatizations in the EU occurred in the UK following the election in 1979 of a Conservative government. By 1997, the total value of UK privatization sales had risen to around £65 billion and the share of nationalized industries in GDP had fallen from 9 per cent in 1979 to under 2 per cent. In May 1997, a Labour government was elected for the first time since 1979. During the 1980s and early 1990s the Labour Party strongly opposed the Conservatives' privatization programme. In office, however, the New Labour administration has continued with some state asset sales, such as the air traffic control system, and has agreed the introduction of private capital into the London Underground, though this falls short of full privatization. Similar 'private finance initiatives' (PFIs) have been announced for other areas of the public sector, such as education and the health service.

Throughout much of the rest of the EU privatization activity was on a much smaller scale in the 1980s. The main exception is France where a right-of-centre government between November 1986 and January 1988 privatized 14 large industrial, banking and financial trusts (Andreff, 1992: 135). Notable sales included Elf Aquitaine in September 1986, Saint Gobain in November 1986, Paribas in January 1987 and Alcatel-Alsthom in May 1987. Most of the firms affected had been nationalized in the early 1980s, although a few, such as the bank, Société Générale, could trace their state ownership back to just after the Second World War. This extensive privatization activity was brought to a halt by the re-election of a socialist administration in 1988.

The 1990s saw far more privatization activity in Europe. This was associated with two principal economic pressures, namely liberalization of markets at the EU level and government budgetary difficulties. These two motives are discussed in more detail later. Also relevant has been the election of governments sympathetic to privatization. For example, March 1993 saw the re-election of a right-of-centre government in France and a renewal of the privatization activity halted by the socialist administration in 1988. The Privatization Law of 1993 slated 21 enterprises for privatization and since then shares have been sold in a number of French state enterprises, including Elf Aquitaine, the insurance group UAP, Renault, Rhône Poulenc, the Banque Nationale de Paris (BNP), Usinor Sacilor and the aluminium business Pechiney. Initially, France chose to concentrate on privatizing industrial and commercial firms operating in competitive markets rather than monopoly public utilities, but in 1997 and 1998 a partial sale of France Télécom occurred. The election of a socialist government in June of 1997 only slowed the pace of privatization. For example, although the new government rejected the wholesale privatization of Thomson CSF, the electronics group, it agreed to reduce the state's shareholding from 58 to 43 per cent and in June 1999 an initial public offering in Aérospatiale Matra occurred (*Financial Times*, 1999a:30).

Italy began its current privatization programme in 1993 in the face of mounting debts in the state sector. By 1994 the losses of the state-holding corporation the IRI (*Istituto per la Ricostruzione Industriale*) alone were equivalent to 5 per cent of Italy's GDP. In January 1992, after delay arising from political opposition and disagreement between government and the state-holding companies over who should benefit from the privatization revenues, legislation to clear the way for the corporatization, restructuring and sale of state industries was passed. The first important privatization involved 67 per cent of the shares in the bank, Credito Italiano in 1993 and this sale was followed by the sale of shares in two other large banks, the Istituto Mobiliare Italiano and Banca Commerciale Italiana, and the state-owned insurance group, Istituto Nazionale della Assicurazioni (INA). By 1996, some 300 state companies had been involved in corporatization and share sales and the total privatization receipts exceeded L18000bn. Nevertheless, continuing argument and frequent changes of government hampered the privatization programme.

Portugal is another 1990s convert to privatization. Until June 1989, the majority sale of state firms was prohibited under the Portuguese constitution and it was not until 1990 that a privatization programme was launched, under a centre–right Social Democrat (PSD) government. Afterwards the programme developed quickly and became more extensive than anywhere else on the continent. By mid-1997, sales had raised over ES.3 tn (over £5 bn), representing about 10 per cent of Portugal's GDP and reducing the state's share of the economy from around 20 per cent in 1989 to 11 per cent. When Portugal elected a socialist government, the new government immediately announced that it intended not only to continue the privatization programme but to accelerate it.

In Spain, state enterprises were an integral part of industrial policy from the Franco era and were organized around holding companies, similar to those in Italy. By the early 1980s, these holding companies accounted for two-thirds of the value added of state industry. Between 1984 and 1986, the government dissolved or sold off over 30 mainly smaller state concerns, but including the state car firm, Seat, sold to Volkswagen (Garcia Delgado, 1989:496) and since then, with continuing losses in a number of state industries and budgetary pressures, further sales have occurred. The years 1989, 1991 and 1997 saw particularly heavy privatization activity. Sales of shares occurred in SKF Española (tyre manufacturer), Endesa (the largest electricity enterprise in Spain), Repsol (formed out of the oil interests of the state-holding company, Instituto Nacional de Hidrocarburos, INH), Telefónica (telephones), Argentaria (banking group) and holdings in the textile and cellulose industries. In 2001, the privatization of the airline, Iberia, was completed.

In Finland, state-owned enterprises developed as a response to a failure on the part of private investors to invest in the fledgling state, threatened by the Soviet Union to its east. The result was a comparatively large state sector by the 1980s, totalling as much as 20 per cent of domestic valued added and 15 per cent of the industrial labour force. Since 1987, successive governments have been committed to a privatization programme. In February 1988, there was a first share issue in the state airline, Finnair, and some share sales occurred around the same time involving the paper machinery, mining and steel sectors. The economic difficulties of the early 1990s halted the programme, however, and indeed a commercial bank was, temporarily, nationalized. After 1993, the pace of privatization accelerated again in the face of more buoyant stock market prices. For example, stakes were sold in Outokumpu, involved in mining and metals, Rautaruukki, the steel producer, and Kemira Oy, a major chemicals group.

In 1985, the West German Federal Minister of Finance outlined a general privatization programme affecting 13 firms, but with the government intending to retain a substantial shareholding and in some cases a majority holding. Also the government ruled out a sale of shares in the loss-making steel, coal and shipbuilding industries and state banks, the railways, posts and telecommunications and research institutes. However, even these limited privatization proposals met with protests from the trade unions, and in March 1985 the government reduced the number of firms selected from 13 to five.

In the following years a cautious privatization programme evolved in Germany (Hawkins, 1991), until the absorption of the former communist East Germany and the introduction of extensive privatization for that region. Between 1990 and 1994, nine former West German enterprises were sold entirely and three partially, thereby almost ending the Federal government's shareholdings in the industrial sector. However, the *Länder* (regional government) continued to have major shareholdings in public credit institutions, insurance companies, power supplies, transport, construction and property, and some manufacturing firms. The flotation of Deutsche Telecom in late 1996 at a stroke more than doubled the total value of (West) Germany's privatization sales. In 1990, Germany joined the Netherlands in introducing private ownership of its postal service.

Turning to the Netherlands, this country was one of the most laissez-faire in Europe after the Second World War in terms of economic policy, resulting in fewer state enterprises than elsewhere in the EU (Parris *et al.*, 1987). Nevertheless, by the 1980s, the state participated directly in 41 companies and indirectly in many others, for example through the National Investment Bank and the Industrial Guarantee Fund. The result, according to one observer, was 'a motley collection, each individual holding to be explained by accident rather than by any grand design or strategy' (Andeweg, 1994:205). A privatization programme was announced in 1982, but the approach has since been pragmatic. Shares have been sold in state enterprises whenever it seemed to make economic and administrative sense and when it was profitable to do so. Noteworthy sales have involved the Royal Dutch Airlines (KLM),

Koninklijke PTT Nederland, NMB-Postbank Groep (renamed ING Bank), the chemical firm DSM and the state's holding in the aircraft firm Fokker. The total value of privatization sales was inflated by the disposal of Koninklijke PTT Nederlands, the country's largest privatization. In general, the scale of privatization has been limited.[2]

Sweden developed one of the largest welfare states in Europe after 1945, but like the Netherlands saw little need for extensive state ownership of industry. The private sector was viewed as the primary generator of wealth on which large taxes could be levied to pay for welfare services. In the 1970s, however, a number of failing companies were rescued by the state, notably in shipbuilding and steel, and by the mid-1980s the state sector included steel plants, mines, a bank, food and pharmaceutical companies and timber enterprises. In total there were around 70 state-owned joint stock companies and nearly 1400 local government enterprises.

The defeat of the Social Democrats in the September 1991 election led to a major change in policy. In December 1992, a privatization bill was passed by parliament and early in 1992 a privatization commission was set up within the government. The result was a plan to sell 34 state firms, including the electricity company Vattenfall, Nordbanken, Procordia in biomedicine and food products, Celsius in shipping and ASSI and Doman in forestry. However, progress in privatizing companies proved slow, at first because of a crisis in the Swedish economy and the wider European economic recession. More recent years have seen some build-up of privatization activity, including sales of shares in Procordia, Nordbanken, Stadshypotek AB, AssiDoman and Celsius. In addition, state organizations such as Vattenfall have been turned into joint stock companies and given commercial objectives (Lane, 1994:183). In total, between 1991 and 1994, the government sold shares in 20 companies, involving assets worth Skr 24 bn. However, the re-election of a Social Democrat government in 1994 brought about a reassessment of the privatization programme. The new government agreed to go ahead with the privatization of Nordbanken but shelved the other planned sales.

In the case of Denmark, in the main what state industrial holdings existed have already been sold. In the early 1990s, the government began to change the legal status of public enterprises to limited liability companies and later sold shares in some of these companies. The sale of a 51 per cent holding in the post office's banking business, GiroBank, in 1993 was the country's first privatization sale. Other sales have involved the state life assurance company, Statsangstalten for Livforsikring, and the telecom business, Tele Danmark. In 1994, a restructuring of the share capital of Tele Danmark had the effect of reducing the state's holding from 89 per cent to 51 per cent. The government also sold 25 per cent of its shareholding in Copenhagen airport.

In a number of other EU member states there has been less privatization activity. The economy of Luxemburg is small and the scope for privatization is limited. In Belgium, there exists a long-established tradition of mixed ownership or public and private joint ventures. As a consequence the Belgian government, particularly through the Societé Nationale d'Investissement, owns shares in many companies. Policy towards the sale of these shares has been pragmatic rather than ideological. In large part this results from the federal structure in Belgium and the existence of two linguistic communities. This in turn results in complex, unstable coalition governments and an emphasis on governing by consensus. In 1992, a new coalition government drew up a programme to sell state assets, motivated by budgetary pressures, and a government commission was established to review assets for possible sale. One result was the sale of 49.9 per cent of the shares in the banking and insurance company ASLK-CGER in 1994, another was the sale of shares in NIM-SNI, an industrial holding company. The government has also looked for foreign telecom partners to invest in the state telephone company. However, the approach to privatization in Belgium has been cautious and there have been no mass state asset sales comparable to those in the UK, France and Portugal, for example.

A similar trend is evident in Ireland. Here the government has undertaken only modest privatizations, including sales of shares in state-owned insurance firms, sugar production and telecommunications (Barrett, 1998). State ownership played a key role in economic policy from the 1920s and, although by the 1980s financial losses in state industries produced pressure for a transfer of some industrial and commercial assets to the private sector, this did not develop into a total programme of privatization. Irish policy remains pragmatic with still some leaning towards continued state ownership. Similarly, privatization has remained at a low level in Greece, in this case reflecting political differences over continued state ownership. The election defeat of a right-wing government in 1993 led to the scrapping of earlier privatization plans, including a 35 per cent stake in OTE, the state telecommunications company. However, within a year the new socialist government shelved its ideological objections to privatization and decided to float minority stakes in some state-controlled companies; small privatizations occurred, such as the sale of Neorian shipyards by the state-owned development bank, ETVA, to a consortium of Greek shipowners and other business interests. Notwithstanding these sales, political disagreements, union opposition, a statutory limit on equity sales and constraints on the pricing of share issues imposed by the conservative political opposition all combined to block a number of further privatizations.

In the postwar period, Austria had one of the largest state sectors in the EU, and the largest on some counts. This dated back to 1946 when industry and commerce seized from the Nazis were nationalized. In 1987, of the nine largest enterprises in Austria, five were totally state-owned, one was under majority state ownership and two others were state-controlled through large nationalized banks. Only one was privately owned. Following a financial crisis in Voest-Alpine (the steel and engineering group) in November 1985, exacerbated by losses incurred speculating in the oil market, and difficulties in the major state-holding company, ÖIAG, the government announced that it would introduce private funding into some of the state-owned companies. Progress occurred with the ÖIAG's holdings in Siemens Austria and the organization OMV significantly reduced and minority sales of shares in the Landerbank, Creditanstalt and Austrian Airlines. The state also reduced its holdings in certain other companies. However, adverse economic conditions and a subdued stock market in the early 1990s led to a postponement of further privatizations.

In November 1993, the coalition government parties agreed to renewed privatization and in the following months the state holding company, Austrian Industries, was merged with the ÖIAG, which became responsible for selling assets. Also plans were announced to privatize all of Austria's state industries by the end of the decade. Nevertheless, sales have been slow and hesitant. The speed of sale has been slowed by a desire to protect 'Austrian interests': for example, the privatization of the state bank, Creditanstalt, dragged on for over five years, as the government tried to put together a consortium of predominantly Austrian buyers.

It is clear from the above review of privatization activity in the EU that enthusiasm for privatization and the economic significance of privatization have varied considerably from country to country since the 1980s. This is borne out by the figures in Table 6.1, which provides estimates of the amounts raised by privatization in a number of the EU member states between 1990 and 2000, the latest date for which reasonably complete figures existed at the time of writing. It is also worth noting that, in 2001 and 2002, the pace of privatization slackened in Europe, with planned sales of infrastructure – such as airports, railways and postal services – postponed. This decline in privatization activity has been attributed to (a) some privatization failures in the UK, which had been a model for state sell-offs, such as the effective renationalization of Railtrack and the financial difficulties quickly faced by the privatized air traffic control system; (b) weak stock markets, which means that privatization issues are less lucrative for governments and more difficult to off-load; (c) poor returns to investors from some privatization issues, such as France Télécom and Deutsche Telecom; and (d) reluctance of some governments to contemplate the transfer of a majority share ownership of 'strategic' industries to the private sector, such as French opposition to the privatization of Electricité de France. Only a minority of privatization deals

Table 6.1 Privatization receipts in the EU countries, 1990–2000 (US$ mn)

	1990	1991	1992	1993	1994	1995	1996	1997	1998	1999	2000*
Austria	32	48	49	142	700	1035	1302	2438	2537	70	2083
Belgium	644				956	548	2745	1222	1842	2288	10
Denmark				122	229	10	366	45	4502	19	111
Finland				229	1120	363	911	835	1999	3716	1827
France				12160	5479	4136	3096	10105	13596	9478	17438
Germany			325		435	240		13228	1125	364	6734
Greece				35	73	44	558	1395	3960	4880	1384
Ireland		515	70	274		157	293			4846	1458
Italy			759	3039	9077	10131	11225	24536	14497	25594	9728
Luxemburg											
Netherlands	716	179		780	3766	3993	1239	842	335	1481	310
Portugal	1092	1002	2206	422	1123	2362	3001	4909	4299	1620	3256
Spain	172		820	3222	1458	2940	2678	12529	11618	1129	1079
Sweden			378	252	2313	852	785	2390	172	2071	8082
UK	12906	21825	604	8523	1341	6691	6695	4544			
Total EU	15562	23894	4886	30590	27469	35460	46599	67535	60167	61649	46756

Note: * provisional figure.

Source: OECD (2001).

in the EU outside the UK have involved the complete transfer of a business from government to the private sector (*Economist*, 2002).

Arguments for privatization

To assess properly privatization in the EU and the forms it is taking, it is important to understand its rationale. Across the EU four arguments dominate: (1) that state industries are inefficient and that privatization will lead to improved economic efficiency; (2) that privatizations can make a useful contribution to developing domestic capital markets; (3) that selling state assets is a legitimate way of reducing government debt, also removing the risk of future public capital injections into loss-making enterprises; and (4) that privatization is a necessary response to measures within the EU aimed at liberalizing markets. In general, it seems that privatization policies in much of the EU have been more pragmatic and less ideologically based than in the UK and, at times since the mid-1980s, in France.

Promoting efficiency

The usual argument for privatization over state ownership in the economics literature centres on the comparative economic efficiency of the public and private sectors (for a recent statement, see Boycko *et al.*, 1996). In general, inefficiency is traced back to the ideological and political motives for government ownership of firms and continuing political involvement in their management (Aharoni, 1986; Shapiro and Willig, 1990). Enhanced management accountability in the private sector results from a combination of the transfer from public to private sector funding and the introduction of competitive product markets following privatization (see Chapter 2 and 3; also Vickers and Yarrow, 1988; Jensen, 1989; Zeckhauser and Horn, 1989). Insofar as state provision is associated with monopoly provision, the expectation is that privatization, combined with opening up markets to competition (liberalization), will lead to higher operating efficiency.

In the UK, the supposed superior efficiency of private ownership was a main driving force of privatization policy for the Conservative governments of 1979 to 1997. But for some European governments this has not been so, particularly where state enterprises are considered to have performed well. For example, in Finland, where state enterprises were initially set up to offset a lack of interest by private investors in industrial investment, 'Efficiency has not been an issue, because the state-owned companies' commercial performance was in general the same as in private firms' (Willner, 1994:2). The same is to some extent true in the Netherlands, where the managements of state firms have been expected to run them efficiently, as if they were private companies. In (West) Germany public enterprises have generally operated commercially with private business interests represented on their supervisory boards. Even where efficiency is an important issue, the post-privatization structure of industry has often been poorly articulated; for example, in the case of Austria it has been argued that

> Privatization began . . . as a political programme, designed to take advantage of the electorate's increasing dissatisfaction with the nationalized industries. In the 1986 elections both parties referred to privatization as a way of increasing their electoral fortunes, but neither had developed a clear idea of what role privatization would realistically play in future economic strategy. (Meth-Cohn and Muller, 1994: 175–6)

Although in recent years French governments may have argued that privatization promotes economic efficiency, this view is not necessarily widely held in France: '*the case of France demonstrates that the status of a firm (private/public) is not the only or even the most powerful factor determining its behaviour*. The dynamic of the environment plays a fundamental role' (Redor, 1992: 163; in the original).

Certainly, there are plenty of examples of political intervention leading to loss-making activities in state industries in Europe. However, the exact extent to which these interventions have been social welfare reducing as against profit reducing is less certain. For example, from time to time in the UK and France state industries have been used to control prices and to preserve jobs, both of which are generally incompatible with maximizing short-term profit but can be compatible with a wider social welfare goal. Employment preservation and good working conditions have also been objectives in EU economies, notably Sweden, Austria and Ireland. In Finland and Italy, state firms have made an important contribution to regional policy, while, particularly in Sweden, Finland and France, state ownership has been associated with industrial policies to build and preserve international competitiveness though 'national' champions. In Finland, state industries were supposed to forgo profits and supply private firms with cheap supplies (Willner, 1998). By contrast, in Germany in the 1960s, the Social Democrats expected state firms to compete aggressively with private enterprises to raise the general level of operating efficiency in oligopolistic markets. Moreover, as many so-called privatizations in the EU have left the state with sizeable shareholdings, governments 'have rarely forfeited control and have remained inclined to meddle' (*Economist*, 2002: 73).

In other words, the usual economists' case for privatization – higher economic efficiency – is not necessarily the chief motivation for privatization in the member states of the EU, while any resulting efficiency gains may incur a cost in terms of reducing the ability of governments to intervene in their economies to promote economic growth, preserve employment and pursue other welfare enhancing objectives.

Promoting the capital market

The UK has a large and well-developed capital market and to a lesser degree so have countries such as France and Germany. But this was not so across the whole of the EU in the 1980s. Hence there was a desire on the part of governments and business interests alike to promote the national capital market, particularly in Spain, Portugal and Austria and to a slightly lesser extent in Italy. In these countries, privatization flotations were seen as a way of increasing the stock market capitalization and of providing a means to encourage investment and international activity by domestic banks. Privatization was also viewed as a useful vehicle to attract small investors to own shares, as against the fixed interest securities (bonds) traditionally preferred by investors on the continent. In the UK, Conservative governments in the 1980s made a point of emphasizing the role of privatization in spreading share ownership more widely (also see Chapter 3).

The extent to which the new small shareholders invested for the long term rather than for short-term speculative gain is, however, very questionable. For example, of the two million Germans who bought Deutsche Telecom shares in 1996, about one-half had sold their shares within one year. A similar pattern of 'stagging' gains was recorded in UK privatizations.

Reducing government debt

Government financing through asset sales became more important as the prospect of monetary union in Europe loomed. Indeed, meeting the Maastricht criteria for eligibility to join a single currency became a very important consideration driving privatizations in a number of EU countries.[3] Although the European Commission ruled that privatization receipts could not be taken into account when calculating budget deficits under the Maastricht criteria, privatization receipts could be used to reduce the public debt – another of the treaty criteria – and a lower debt reduced interest payments made by government and therefore, indirectly, the budget deficit. Privatization receipts were seen as a less politically painful way of reducing state debt than either spending cuts or tax increases.

Indeed, so close did the link between privatization and the public finances become in member states that governments announced targets for annual sales as part of their budget forecasts. In Austria, privatization share issues were not priced low (as occurred in the UK, especially in the 1980s) specifically because the government wanted to raise the maximum revenue possible for the budget and industry restructuring. In France and Italy, legislation was passed to limit the use to which privatization receipts could be put. Under French legislation of 1986, privatization proceeds had to go to repay public debt or recapitalize the remaining state enterprises. This was amended in 1993, after which receipts were paid into the general budget. In

Italy, a law of October 1993 required that revenues from privatization be set aside in a special fund to be used for the sole purpose of buying back outstanding public debt. In Portugal, revenue generation was a prime objective behind the privatization programme from 1990. Until July 1993, 80 per cent of privatization funds were to be used for state debt reduction (*Privatisation Yearbooks*, various editions). In Spain, later privatization proceeds went through a state-holding company, Sepi, and were used to offset the costs of running loss-making shipyards, arms factories and mines and meeting redundancy costs in the state steel industry. These are costs that would otherwise have fallen on the government's budget.

EU liberalization directives
Traditionally, EU policy has been neutral on the subject of the appropriate ownership of industry, accepting the existing mix of state and private sector industry across Europe. This approach arose from the need to accommodate within the EU from the time of the Treaty of Rome in 1957 countries with differing levels of state ownership. It also arose from the belief that state monopolies were necessary in the public utility sectors to ensure a universal service and network economies. In post-war Europe, postal services, telecommunications, railways, scheduled air and bus transport, electricity and gas industries and water and sewerage services were typically owned by central government or local municipal or regional bodies, although there were some important exceptions, such as water supply in France.[4]

Throughout the Treaty of Rome ran the principle of free trade in Europe. Articles 9–37 set out the aim of free circulation of goods, while Articles 48–73 were concerned with the freedom to provide services and the freedom of establishment. Article 37 stated: 'Member states shall progressively adjust any State monopolies of a commercial character so as to ensure that when the transitional period has ended no discrimination regarding the conditions under which goods are procured and marketed exists between nationals or Member states'.

Article 222 confirmed neutrality on ownership by stating that the commitment to a market economy 'shall in no way prejudice the rules in Member states governing the system of property ownership'. In other words, competitive markets are favoured in the EU but this is not taken to prejudge the form of ownership that should be adopted in member states. EU policy intervenes only when government policies are seen to be in conflict with free and fair trade within the EU. In particular, Article 92 forbids state aid that distorts competition between member countries, although in practice derogations have been granted under Commission guidelines that allow for the influence of other policy objectives, such as regional development, protection of the environment, industrial policy and R&D. At

Maastricht in 1991, Article 130 was inserted into the Treaty confirming that industrial policy measures must comply 'with a system of open and competitive markets'.

Until the 1980s the Commission stressed coordination and network economies when discussing the public utilities and to a degree still continues to do so, in part 'to reduce tensions between the Member states and the Community institutions' (Scott, 1995:35). The attitudes of member states now vary on the proper role of the state in the ownership and control of public utilities, with some members, notably France, more cautious about privatization than, most obviously, the UK, where all the utilities have already been privatized. Nevertheless, an interest in market liberalization exists in all parts of the EU.

Particularly significant in changing attitudes was the passage of the Single European Act in 1986. This aimed to remove the remaining non-tariff barriers to free trade within the EU by the end of 1992 and had implications for the public utilities, which were generally protected from competition in terms of both outputs and procurement policies. Utilities remain governed by national legislation and regulatory rules, but, following the Single Market Agreement, the European Commission has applied pressure on member states for utility markets to be opened up to competition.

However, European Union-level intervention in utility markets was, and remains, controversial. Member states are reluctant to see national sovereignty over their public utilities transferred to Brussels. In response the European Commission has fought shy of proposing EU-wide regulation. Instead, the Commission has endeavoured to convince member states of the case for opening up their utility markets to competition and of the need to develop their own national regulatory systems to promote competition and protect the consumer. To minimize opposition and to ensure a more speedy liberalization, the Commission has adopted a 'vertical' or sectoral approach to policy making, rather than attempting to force through a 'horizontal' or across-the-board programme. This has meant developing separate market liberalization policies for each utility sector.

Each policy has progressed at different speeds reflecting practical opportunities for liberalization in the member states and the strength of national opposition. For example, the Commission has suggested that rail links between member states should be opened up to competition and that operators should pay for track use (Hitiris, 1994:273). Under a 1991 EU directive railways should separate infrastructure charges from operating costs for book-keeping purposes. Separate accounting is a step towards enabling new train operating companies to provide services on the rail network. This liberalization, however, has met with fierce resistance from the railway unions, especially in France. In addition, governments are suspicious of the impact on railway finances and the viability of their current rail networks. In 1995, the Commission proposed opening up rail freight to cross-border competition, but, following a serious rail strike in France, the proposals were scaled back to cover only the busiest freight routes.

There has been similar slow progress in the liberalization of the gas market and postal services, but there has been more progress in deregulating European air routes, the electricity power market and telecommunications. In response, a number of governments have sold some or all of their stakes in national airlines and power and telecommunications companies (for full details, see Parker, 1998). Although at the EU level no explicit stance has been taken on ownership, from time to time there has been recognition that privatization may be beneficial where markets are liberalized. For example, in 1994, the Commission stated that 'attention should be devoted to improving the competitive environment in which firms operated' and that 'privatization, to the extent that Member states judge it compatible with their objectives, could further the progress already made in this direction' (European Commission, 1994:11). In a 1995 White Paper the Commission repeated the point:

> progress is required . . . in the areas of insurance, intellectual and industrial property, public procurement, new technologies and services and freedom of movement. Moreover, progress has been slow in the extension of the single market to telecommunications and energy, while the internal market in transport remains incomplete. Furthermore, additional progress is necessary in reinforcing competition rules, reducing State aid and reducing the role of the public sector. Privatization, to the extent that Member states judge it compatible with their objectives, could further the progress already made in this direction. (European Commission, 1995:15)

Summary of the arguments
In summary, across the EU there has been no single, common rationale for privatization. Some countries have promoted privatization to achieve efficiency gains; but important in other member states has been the potential of privatization sales to expand the capital market and meet the Maastricht criteria for monetary union. Some governments have seemingly pursued all of these objectives, even though they may not be compatible. For example, to achieve efficiency gains an industry may benefit from restructuring ahead of sale to promote competition, but when the opportunity for monopoly profits is removed sale receipts are reduced and therefore so is their contribution to the state budget. Promoting a domestic capital market may mean restricting foreign shareholdings, but foreign investors may help promote a more effective capital market constraint on managerial behaviour, as discussed later.

As the EU has worked towards removing restraints on trade resulting from regulation, this has had implications for the nature of ownership in industries previously protected from competition. Deregulation policy implies a change in the relationship between government and state-owned utilities, most notably in terms of ruling out state subsidies and introducing private sector competition. In turn, this creates a policy environment which leads member states to review the benefits of retaining state ownership. State-owned firms may be handicapped when facing competition from large private sector companies with ready access to capital markets. At the very least, competition can be expected to worsen the finances of the incumbent state-owned utilities, perhaps necessitating large capital injections. Privatization is therefore a means by which governments can avoid financial risk when markets previously dominated by state-owned companies are liberalized.

Consequences for economic efficiency and social welfare
Privatization has changed the ownership of major industries and services across the EU. Exploring the precise economic and social consequences is, however, complex. Here two issues are discussed, economic efficiency and social welfare.

Economic efficiency
Where privatization does lead to higher economic efficiency, this is most likely to occur in the early years after a disposal through cost reductions, for example through reduced staff levels. This leads to what economists call *static* efficiency gains. Static gains involve moving the firm to its production possibility frontier (removing 'waste') and are inherently 'one off'. Longer-term competitiveness depends rather more on improved products and production processes. In other words, it requires a movement outwards in the firm's production possibility frontier, which in turn requires technological change, including continuous restructuring, appropriate capital investment, innovation, marketing, human resource policies to improve productivity and improved supply chain management. Whether these *dynamic* gains result from privatization is, however, particularly unclear at the present time. So far the empirical evidence from the economy with the largest and longest-standing privatization programme, the UK, is mixed. There is evidence of initial cost cutting in privatized companies (static gains) but less evidence of continuing performance improvements (see Martin and Parker, 1997), though it will only be possible to reach a final decision on the results of the UK's privatizations over a much longer time frame. Industrial policy involving state investment and encouragement to markets to redirect resources, as practised within the EU in the past, particularly by the French,

is based on the notion that private markets fail to provide adequate invest-ment, especially in new technologies. Privatization involves a reliance on private markets.

The economic case for privatization is predicated on arguments from the public choice, property rights and agency literatures in economics (for example, Niskanen, 1971; Mitchell, 1988; Shapiro and Willig, 1990; Boycko *et al.*, 1996). This literature needs to be viewed carefully, however. In par-ticular, the notion that the private capital is a more effective monitor of management discretionary behaviour than state control needs to be dem-onstrated. It is usually argued that shareholder pressure, trading in shares and ultimately the threat of a hostile takeover bid reduce managerial non-profit behaviour in the private sector, leading to higher economic efficiency. But, where privatizations are associated with dispersed shareholdings, it is not clear that any shareholding group will be able to bring sufficient influ-ence to bear on management to ensure that companies are efficiently run, while the corporate governance debate in the UK has raised questions about the lack of involvement of even large institutional investors in the oversight of firms (Stapledon, 1996). Also the takeover market is expensive and disruptive and there is little evidence that it is necessarily the poorly performing firms, in terms either of earnings, dividends or share price, that are the prime takeover targets in modern stock markets, or that improve-ments in performance necessarily result after a takeover (Jenkinson and Mayer, 1994; Mayer, 1997:294). Cosh and Hughes (1995) have concluded that 'acquisition has an insignificant impact on profitability'. Moreover, empirical studies of the comparative efficiency of public versus private sector firms (usually measured in terms of either productivity or costs of production) suggest that, while private enterprises are sometimes more effi-cient than their state-owned counterparts, state enterprises can be as effi-cient, especially in markets where there is little or no product competition (for an early summary of this research, see Millward and Parker, 1983; for a more recent review, and one more favourable to privatization, see Megginson and Netter, 2001).

The economics literature emphasizes the role of a competitive capital market in raising economic efficiency, but with respect to privatizations in a number of member states a competitive capital market is not the inevita-ble result. In continental Europe, the term 'equity' in financial markets implies a right to the residual income. The long delay in Austria in the sale of Creditanstalt was the result of opposition in Austrian business circles to the country's second biggest bank falling into foreign hands (Hall, 1996). In Sweden, the government has either favoured large and friendly investors or retained a controlling stake in companies, now placed under one minis-try, the Ministry of Industry (*Financial Times*, 1999b). But it is in France and Italy that a traditional hostility to foreign ownership of industry has developed into the most obvious policies to retain national ownership.

Some foreign investor participation in French privatizations has been permitted, but in general policy has discriminated against foreign capital. Legislation of August 1986 prevented the state transferring more than a 20 per cent stake in privatized firms to foreign investors, though the limit was removed in 1993. However, French policy has continued to favour established, mainly French, core shareholders, or *noyaux durs.* The objective of a *noyau dur* or favoured shareholder is to facilitate a smooth privatization and to limit any post-privatization takeover threat. For instance, in the 'first phase' of denationalizations, in 1986–8, the hard core were 12 industrial firms, 12 banks, 11 insurance companies and 10 other corporations in France (Andreff, 1992:148); included were the banks Crédit Lyonnais, Société Génerale and BNP and the insurance business AGF. Since 1993, the core shareholders in France have been widened to include some foreigners, but still on the basis that these shareholders will not sell quickly for speculative gains. Similarly, Italy has its own *noyau dur* policy; for instance, the preferred purchasers of shares in Istituto Mobiliare Italiano were banks owned by the government, while the sale of Credito Italiano was structured around the Milanese merchant bank Mediobanca.[5]

Although such policy conflicts with the notion of a Europe-wide competitive capital market, it reflects a deep-seated fear among some EU governments that privatization will lead to a loss of national control over important industries. Even the UK has placed limits on foreign shareholdings in some privatized companies. A further argument relates to the size of the domestic capital market. The UK has a large and international market, but capital markets are much smaller in a number of other EU countries, necessitating more effort to attract specific investors to privatization issues.

Improvements in economic performance are less likely the smaller the pressures on management to restructure their organizations and assets of a company, following privatization. In some countries companies are subject to a much wider stakeholder (for example, workforce) influence than in the UK. Also the stock markets in countries such as Germany are less open to the mounting of hostile takeover bids than is the case in the UK and the USA, from which much of the economics literature on principal–agent relationships originates. In other words, the so-called 'outsider' model of corporate governance, relevant to the UK and USA with arm's-length shareholders and active stock markets, and on which the notion of the takeover as a discipline on management behaviour is based, may not be so relevant (Albert, 1993). On the continent an 'insider' model is more common, in which shareholders sit on boards and have a longer-term relationship with the firm, although this model is being challenged by larger and more competitive capital markets, for example in Germany. Where the insider model continues, action to change management decisions occurs through internal channels, such as participation on boards and committees, and not through share trading and takeovers. This form of corporate governance is much closer to that found under state ownership, which also involves a long-term investor and influence on management through internal, 'political' channels, in which case, while the objectives of the 'stakeholders' may differ between the private and public sectors, the mechanism of corporate governance may not be so very different.

Improvements in efficiency are also less likely where constraints on restructuring exist. For example, in Italy, legal restrictions on job cuts in banking and finance, where early privatizations were concentrated, meant formidable difficulties in rationalizing staff levels. In the Netherlands, employees made redundant because of privatization were offered jobs elsewhere in the public sector and workers retained a right to preferential civil service unemployment benefits (Andeweg, 1994: 204–5). A similar situation existed in Germany, where many railway, telecommunications and postal service employees had civil service status. When a new state-owned telecommunications company replaced the former state enterprise in Italy, all of the employees were guaranteed their jobs. In the Netherlands, incomes of the low-paid were guaranteed by the state during the first years after privatization (ibid.).

In other words, at least in some parts of Europe, privatization does not appear to have offered the same scope for early (static) efficiency gains through reduced staffing costs as existed in the UK. Also the extent to which efficiency improves depends upon management responses to the new private sector environment. State ownership has been associated with civil service procedures, caution and bureaucracy (Mitchell, 1988). However, the extent to which management behaviour differs following privatization is unclear. Capital market pressures may not alter much; there may be restrictions on altering working practices; and often the same management remains. Moreover, the social and educational background of public sector and private sector management in big businesses tends to be the same, which may reinforce similar behaviour. For example, in France, typically both have studied at state-financed *grandes écoles*, of which the most famous are the National Schools of Administration (Redor, 1992: 158). Also managers have moved between public and private firms much more frequently than is the case in the UK. All of these considerations may help to explain why, on the continent, there is often a lower expectation of large efficiency gains when enterprises are privatized than has existed in UK policy-making circles.

Finally, it is important to emphasize that 'privatization' is not necessarily associated with the ending of state involvement in industries. In particular, 'corporatization' is not the same as privatization. This needs stressing since a number of countries have transferred state activities from departmental control to quasi-independent corporations and insisted on describing the policy as 'privatization', even when the state retains majority voting rights. In other cases, restrictions have been placed on the rights of private shareholders. If the term 'privatization' is to be meaningful it should be limited to those cases where the state agrees to sell all or a majority of its (voting) shares, places no special restrictions on voting rights and share trading, and ceases to interfere in the management of the enterprises. Defined in these terms, privatization has been much less extensive in the EU than the bare figures for share sales might suggest.

Social welfare

Even where higher economic efficiency results from privatization, it is important to recognize that economic efficiency is only one part of social welfare. In particular, social welfare also requires attention to the *distribution* of income and wealth. To assess the full effects of privatization on social welfare requires a cost–benefit analysis with identification of gainers and losers and measurement of the precise gains and losses. It also requires some form of social weighting of the gains and losses so as to be able to aggregate them.

At this stage economists usually retreat, commenting that income distribution issues are beyond their competence. However, a proper study of the consequences of privatization cannot avoid attention to gainers and losers. To date there have been some studies of the impact of privatization on consumers (in terms of prices and services), shareholders (in terms of profits and share prices) and workers (in terms of wages, conditions of service and unemployment) suggesting income effects (see Martin and Parker, 1997, for a review). A number of the studies have viewed lower wages and other input costs as desirable outcomes, as they reduce costs and prices and raise consumer surplus and profit. In particular, higher payments to labour under state ownership are interpreted as 'inefficient' rents.

Arguably, such discussion side-steps the importance of income effects. Across the EU privatization implies a shift in economic power from the state to private capital markets with an associated redistribution of income – in just the same way as nationalization after the Second World War implied income transfers, though to a different set of interests. More specifically, there is evidence that privatization is leading to a shift in economic power and income to large business groupings. For example, and as already observed, French privatization has directly benefited the *noyaux durs*, made up of large banks and companies. In Italy, privatization has strengthened the position of already powerful business groups, such as those connected with the Agnelli and De Benedetti families (Wright, 1994:33). In general, privatization in the EU has been driven from the top, at government/industry/banker level; very little has occurred as a result of action from below, in terms of worker/manager-initiated ownership restructuring. McAllister and Studler (1989) claim that the UK's privatization policy was primarily instigated by Conservative governments to favour an 'elite interest'.

The result is that some groups in society are benefiting much more than others. In addition to those business interests that now own shares in privatized concerns, other obvious gainers have been the bankers, financial advisers and management consultants, who have received commissions and fees for arranging the sales, certain politicians who have been rewarded by jobs, and senior management in the privatized companies where, as in the UK, remuneration has rocketed. In the UK, there are close ties between the City of London, which has gained from privatization through consultancy and flotation fees, and the Conservative Party, which governed from 1979 to May 1997. A number of government ministers involved in privatization have subsequently obtained highly paid board-level appointments in privatized companies and City firms.

The losers are those interests now less favoured by government, usually the trade unions and those vulnerable to unemployment and wage cuts post-privatization. In particular, those workers most likely to lose are the lower skilled, less well educated workers who were likely to be more highly unionized under state ownership. New investment along with new manning agreements aimed at boosting profitability are likely to have adverse impacts on this group of workers, and at a time when global economic trends are already removing lower skilled jobs across Europe. An increased interest in 'outsourcing', to reduce headcount and cut costs, has been associated with privatization in the UK (Harris *et al.*, 1998). By contrast, more highly skilled and educated workers are often less vulnerable to post-privatization restructuring including outsourcing (for a detailed discussion, see Pendleton and Winterton, 1993; Parker, 1995).

Privatization suggests a more favourable view of the role of private (sometimes multinational) investment in promoting social well-being and a less favourable view of employment, employment rights, wages and trade union collective bargaining than existed for much of the post-war period in Europe. Whereas such 'rights' were once part of a post-war political consensus based on the notion of a 'welfare state', they are now viewed as 'inefficiencies' that threaten European competitiveness. As Shapiro and Willig (1990:65) note in their study of privatization, 'The key distinction between public and private-sector enterprise . . . is that privatization gives informational autonomy to a party who is not under direct public control'.

Nationalization resulted from a belief that state ownership could counter the adverse effects on economic welfare of large-scale private enterprise, much of which today is transnational (Holland, 1975). Privatization is removing this means of state influence in the economy. In this sense it is substituting private markets for earlier social welfare and industrial policy objectives in Europe. Where a penetration of international capital into industries previously controlled by government leads to a transfer of economic power out of EU countries, a decline in state control over the economy results. Moreover, this is occurring at a time of other economic changes, resulting in greater capital mobility and reduced state control over factor and product markets.

In sum, privatization across the EU raises important questions about 'power' and 'control': where is economic power centred in terms of individuals, corporations and geographic head offices, and who controls in terms of making strategic decisions, for example relating to industrial expansion and contraction? There is a large literature on income distribution, social justice and state/class power on which to draw to assess the impact of privatization in terms of power and control. However, the privatization literature tends to be dominated by concern with economic efficiency. Issues to do with power and control in social welfare terms either are secondary issues in this literature or, much more frequently, are ignored altogether.

Conclusions
This chapter has reviewed privatization activity since the 1980s in the different member states of the EU and has revealed some marked differences in both the pace and the content of privatization programmes. It has also reviewed the reasons for the interest in privatization in Europe. Whereas in the UK and France privatization has been justified in terms of inefficiency in state industries, this has been less true in a number of other EU states, especially those with more efficient state enterprises or where state firms were created to overcome inefficiencies in private capital markets. Across Europe, privatization was a response to increased market liberalization required by development of the European Single Market and supporting Commission directives. It was also a response to budget deficits as member states endeavoured to meet the Maastricht criteria to join the single currency. In addition, some countries with less developed capital markets have pursued the flotation of state firms to expand trading in their stock markets.

The study has also looked at the consequences of privatization for economic efficiency and social welfare. The economic case for privatization raising economic efficiency relies heavily on a competitive private sector capital market being a superior monitor of management behaviour to the state. However, the use of preferred, long-term investors at the time of privatization coupled with the 'insider' model of corporate governance, still found on the continent though under strain, suggests that efficiency incentives may be blunted. The result may not be the active trading in shares and hostile takeover bids that many economists have argued are essential if enterprises are to be managed efficiently in the private sector. Management in the newly privatized firms may face long-term and sometimes passive investors, investors not very dissimilar to those management faced when firms were state-owned.

Turning to social welfare, judging the outcome is complex but it is clear nevertheless that privatization is leading to important changes in income and wealth distribution. As Eisner (1993) has pointed out, the last 20 years have witnessed the end of the *societal regime* of the 1960s and 1970s, with the goal of raising social conditions in Europe, and the arrival of the *efficiency regime*, involving market liberalization and reducing the state's role. This change, in turn, has implications for social welfare and particularly the distribution of income and economic power in Europe.

These conclusions should not be viewed as necessarily implying that in the EU privatization is the wrong policy. There is evidence that privatization has introduced a new competitive spirit into sleepy state enterprises, though not necessarily all (Martin and Parker, 1997). What the conclusions do suggest is that the subject of privatization in the EU deserves far more critical attention from European economists and others than it has so far received, centring on the longer-term effects on the competitiveness of European industry and the implications for social welfare.

Notes

1.   Earlier versions of this chapter appeared in Parker (1998: 10–48; 1999: 9–38). I would like to thank Routledge, Sage and the editor of *Economic and Industrial Democracy* for permission to reproduce text from these publications.
2.   In addition to central government asset sales, in common with a number of other countries the municipalities in the Netherlands have developed policies to contract out municipal functions. Space precludes a discussion of the contracting out of government services.
3.   The Maastricht criteria for 'sustainable economic convergence' and eligibility to join the European Monetary Union are (1) an inflation rate in the previous year of 1.5 per cent, at most, above the three member states with the lowest inflation; (2) long-term nominal interest rates in the previous year not exceeding by more than 2 per cent the average rate in the three member states with the lowest rates; (3) general government net borrowing and nominal gross debt below 3 per cent and 60 per cent of GDP, respectively (known as the *fiscal convergence* requirement); and (4) a stable currency within the narrow band of the European Monetary System without realignments or 'severe tensions' for at least two years.
4.   The French water sector is a hybrid of public and private management with about 70 per cent of French water supply consumers and 35 per cent of sewerage service customers served by private companies under contracts with municipalities (communes) (Burns and Parker, 1997).
5.   In Italy, the Privatization Law of February 1994 allows for a stable nucleus of sharehold-

ers (*nocciolo duro*) in privatization issues. It also includes powers for the government to restrict individual investors' and associated parties' voting rights to no more than 5 per cent of a company's shares. 'So far Italy's treasury has sold only two businesses completely – INA, an insurer, and IMI, a financial-services group. But neither was a true privatisation. In both cases, control passed to "core" share-holder groups of public-sector banks' (*Economist*, 2 November 1996:102).

References

Aharoni, Y. (1986) *The Evolution and Management of State-Owned Enterprises*, Cambridge, MA: Ballinger.

Albert, M. (1993) *Capitalism against Capitalism*, London: Whurr.

Anastassopolous, J.P., G. Blanc and P. Dussauge (1987) *State-Owned Multinationals*, New York: John Wiley.

Andeweg, R.B. (1994) 'Privatization in the Netherlands: The Result of a Decade', in V. Wright (ed.), *Privatization in Western Europe*, London: Pinter.

Andreff, W. (1992) 'French Privatization Techniques and Experience: A Model for Central–Eastern Europe?', in F. Targetti (ed.), *Privatization in Europe: West and East Experiences*, Aldershot: Dartmouth.

Barrett, S. (1998) 'The Importance of State Enterprises in the Irish Economy and the Future', in D. Parker (ed.), *Privatisation in the European Union: Theory and Policy Perspectives*, London: Routledge.

Boycko, M., A. Shleifer and R.W. Vishny (1996) 'A Theory of Privatisation', *Economic Journal*, 106 (March), 309–19.

Burns, P. and D. Parker (1997) 'France', in I. Lewington (ed.), *Utility Regulation*, London: Privatisation International/Centre for the Study of Regulated Industries.

Cosh, A. and A. Hughes (1995) 'Failures, Acquisitions and Post-Merger Success: The Comparative Financial Characteristics of Large and Small Companies', Working Paper 18, Centre for Business Research, University of Cambridge.

Economist (1996) 'Italian Privatisation: Pianissimo', 2 November: 101–2.

Economist (2002) 'Coming home to roost', 29 June, 71–3.

Eisner, M.A. (1993) *Regulatory Politics in Transition*, Baltimore, MD: Johns Hopkins University Press.

European Commission (1994) 'Broad Economic Policy Guidelines', *European Economic Policy*, 58, 11.

European Commission (1995) 'Broad Economic Policy Guidelines', *European Economic Policy*, 60, 15.

Financial Times (1996) 'Welcome to the ways of the market', 12 November, 14.

Financial Times (1998) 'Thomson Suitor Prepares for Rematch', 20 February, 34.

Financial Times (1999a) 'French aerospace IPO on the runway for take-off', 4 June, 30.

Garcia Delgado, J.L. (1989) *España-Economia*, Madrid: Espasa-Calpe.

Hall, W. (1996) 'First Austrian Leaves Creditanstalt Bidding Group', *Financial Times*, 7 September, 9.

Harris, L., D. Parker and A. Cox (1998) 'UK Privatisation: Its Impact on Procurement', *British Journal of Management* (special issue), 9: S13–S26.

Hawkins, R.A. (1991) 'Privatisation in Western Germany, 1957 to 1990', *National Westminster Bank Quarterly Review*, November, 14–22.

Hitiris, T. (1994) *European Community Economics*, 3rd edn, London: Harvester Wheatsheaf.

Holland, S. (1975) *The Socialist Challenge*, London: Quartet Books.

Jenkinson, T. and C. Mayer (1994) *Hostile Takeovers*. London: McGraw-Hill.

Jensen, M.C. (1989) 'Eclipse of the Public Corporation', *Harvard Business Review*, 67(5), 61–74.

Lane, J.E. (1994) 'Sweden: Privatization and Deregulation', in V. Wright (ed.), *Privatization in Western Europe*, London: Pinter.

McAllister, I. and D.T. Studler (1989) 'Popular versus Elite Views of Privatization: The Case of Britain', *Journal of Public Policy*, 9(2), 157–78.

Martin, S. and D. Parker (1997) *The Impact of Privatisation: Ownership and Corporate Performance in the UK*, London: Routledge.

Mayer, C. (1997) 'The City and Corporate Performance: Condemned or Exonerated?', *Cambridge Journal of Economics*, 21(2), 291–302.

Megginson, W.L. and J.M. Netter (2001) 'From State to Market: A Survey of Empirical Studies on Privatization', *Journal of Economic Literature*, 39 (June), 321–89.

Meth-Cohn, D. and W.C. Muller (1994) 'Looking Reality in the Eye: The Politics of Privatization in Austria', in V. Wright (ed.), *Privatization in Western Europe*, London: Pinter.

Millward, R. and D. Parker (1983) 'Public and Private Enterprise: Comparative Behaviour and Relative Efficiency', in R. Millward, D. Parker, L. Rosenthal, M.T. Sumner and N. Topham (eds), *Public Sector Economics*. London: Longman.

Mitchell, W.C. (1988) 'Government as It Is', Hobart Paper 109, Institute of Economic Affairs, London.

Monsen, R.J. and K.D. Walters (1983) *Nationalized Companies: A Threat to American Business*, New York: McGraw-Hill.

Niskanen, W.A., Jr (1971) *Bureaucracy and Representative Government*, Chicago: Aldine.

Parker, D. (1995) 'Privatization and Agency Status: Identifying the Critical Factors for Performance Improvement', *British Journal of Management*, 6(1), 29–43.

Parker, D. (1998) 'Privatisation in the EU: An Overview', in D. Parker (ed.), *Privatisation in the European Union: Theory and Policy Perspectives*, London: Routledge.

Parker, D. (1999) 'Privatization in the European Union: A Critical Assessment of its Development, Rationale and Consequences', *Economic and Industrial Democracy*, 20, 9–38.

Parris, H., P. Pestieau and P. Saynor (1987) *Public Enterprise in Western Europe*, London: Croom Helm.

Pendleton, A. and J. Winterton (eds) (1993) *Public Enterprise in Transition: Industrial Relations in State and Privatized Corporations*, London: Routledge.

Privatisation Yearbooks, various edns, London: Privatisation International.

Redor, D. (1992) 'The State Ownership Sector: Lessons from the French Experience', in F. Targetti (ed.), *Privatization in Europe: West and East Experiences*, Aldershot: Dartmouth.

Scott, C. (1995) *Competition and Coordination: Their Role in the Future of European Community Utilities Regulation*, International Series 3, London: Centre for the Study of Regulated Industries.

Shapiro, C. and R.D. Willig (1990) 'Economic Rationales for the Scope of Privatization', in E.N. Suleiman and J. Waterbury (eds), *The Political Economy of Public Sector Reform and Privatization*, London: Westview Press.

Stapledon, G. (1996) *Institutional Shareholders and Corporate Governance*, Oxford: Clarendon Press.

Vickers, J. and G. Yarrow (1988) *Privatization: An Economic Analysis*, Cambridge, MA: MIT Press.

Willner, J. (1994) 'Efficiency under Public and Private Ownership: A Survey', Department of Economics paper, Ser. A:422, Abo Akademi University, Turku.

Willner, J. (1998) 'Privatisation in Finland, Sweden and Denmark – Fashion or Necessity?', in D. Parker (ed.), *Privatisation in the European Union: Theory and Policy Perspectives*, London: Routledge.

Wright, V. (ed.) (1994) *Privatization in Western Europe*, London: Pinter.

Zeckhauser, R.J. and M. Horn (1989) 'The Control and Performance of State Owned Enterprises', in P.W. MacAvoy, W.T. Stanbury, G. Yarrow and R.J. Zeckhauser (eds), *Privatization and State Owned Enterprises: Lessons from the United States, Great Britain and Canada*, Boston, MA: Kluwer.

7   Privatization in North America
Anthony E. Boardman, Claude Laurin and Aidan R. Vining

Introduction[1]

At the beginning of the 1980s, Canada and the United States represented the extremes of state ownership in developed, industrial countries. Canada, like many Western European nations and Japan, had developed an extensive panoply of state-owned enterprises (SOEs). These organizations, which were called Crown Corporations in Canada, permeated the economy, most prominently in transport, natural resource development, and energy production and development, but also in many other sectors (Trebilcock, 1999). Indeed, state ownership was more extensive in Canada than in many other countries, taking into consideration Provincial Crown Corporations in addition to Federal Crown Corporations (Vining and Botterell, 1983).

The USA, in contrast, had a much less extensive state-owned sector than other developed industrial nations. In spite of this, there has been, and still is, a degree of government ownership in the economy (see Chapter 9 for an example). Much of this ownership centred on government involvement in hydroelectric power development during the 'New Deal', as exemplified by the Tennessee Valley Authority (TVA) and the Bonneville Power Administration. In addition, government expropriations of enemy-controlled corporations during and following the Second World War resulted in the (short-run) creation of a number of SOEs and mixed enterprises.

Over the last 20 years, there has been extensive privatization in Canada and some in the USA. A major purpose of this chapter is to provide summary information about the major privatizations in both countries. Many Canadian privatizations have been controversial (Jörgensen *et al.*, 1993), as have privatizations elsewhere (Clarke and Pitelis, 1993; Peters, 1993). There are many interesting questions relating to the causes and the effects of these privatizations. While the politics of privatization in both countries and around the world is fascinating from a political economy perspective (for a sample of this literature, see Campos and Esfahani, 1996; Feigenbaum and Henig, 1997; Dudley, 1999; Vergas, 2001), we focus on the efficiency implications of privatization in North America. A central question is whether privatization has improved the efficiency and performance of the firms and thus contributed to aggregate welfare improvements (Vining and Boardman, 1992; Kikeri *et al.*, 1992). The chapter reviews the evidence on privatization in both countries over approximately the last 20 years. It also considers the prospects for further privatization in both countries and their potential efficiency implications.

The chapter proceeds as follows. The next section lists and describes the Canadian privatization experience at both the federal and provincial levels over the last 20 years, while the following section reviews the evidence on the efficiency impacts of these privatizations. A subsequent section describes the US privatization experience over the same period. Later sections of the chapter assess the potential for further privatization in Canada and the USA, respectively, recognizing that, from an efficiency perspective, most of the relatively straightforward privatizations have already taken place. Finally, some conclusions and generalizable lessons from privatization in North America are presented. In places, we provide monetary measures. The figures for Canadian firms are in Canadian dollars (C$), while the figures for US firms are in US dollars (US$).[2]

Privatization in Canada
Canada has undergone an extensive programme of privatizations at both the federal and provincial levels over the last 20 years. The federal government has also engaged in a series of asset divestitures that can best be described as quasi-privatization.

There were some early privatizations in Canada. In the 1970s, some SOEs were given away and some were transferred to private ownership by direct sale (Economic Council of Canada, 1986). The province of British Columbia experienced an early wave of privatization, including the giving away of the British Columbia Resources Investment Corporation, in which each BC resident received five free shares (Ohashi *et al.*, 1980).

Most Canadian privatizations lagged behind the global privatization wave and privatization did not really get started in Canada until the mid-1980s. At that time, federal SOEs had almost 200 000 employees and assets worth more than C$55 bn, and received approximately C$4.4 bn in annual subsidies from the federal treasury (Stanbury, 1992; Trebilcock, 1999). Provincial ownership was also extensive, with over 200 Provincial Crown Corporations (Vining and Botterell, 1983), including almost total ownership of electricity supply and distribution (Vining, 1981). In addition, a number of federal and provincial SOEs had partial ownership positions in many other corporations, generally in industrial sectors.[3] Examples of these partially government-owned firms, or mixed enterprises, included Canada Development Corporation, Domtar, Suncor, B.C. Forest Products, Interprovincial Steel and Pipe, Alberta Energy, Agra Industries, Asbestos Corporation, Telesat Canada and Massey-Ferguson (Boardman *et al.*, 1983). Prior to the Mulroney government, which was elected in 1984, there was some degree of political consensus that share ownership in a broad range of industrial sectors was good industrial policy and would provide a way for Canadians to profit directly from growth in the Canadian economy. However, in practice, many government share acquisitions were bail-outs and attempts to save threatened jobs.

Federal privatizations

Table 7.1 contains information describing the major federal privatizations since 1985. These privatizations are listed chronologically by date of sale. The table includes the name of the privatized company, the year of privatization, the percentage sold, the name of the purchaser if not sold through a public offering, the proceeds from the sale and relevant details on corporate sales, assets and employment near the time of privatization. For companies that were privatized in stages ('tranches'), information is included about each tranche.

The largest federal privatizations were effected through initial public offerings (IPOs). Several of these IPOs were very large: indeed, the IPO of Canadian National Railway (CN) in 1995 was the largest stock flotation in Canadian history as of that date. Many smaller federal privatizations were implemented through private sales as the government expected to realize higher prices by offering control to purchasers (Levac and Wooldridge, 1997).

Privatization was a significant source of revenue to the federal government for a number of years. The total value of the privatizations listed in Table 7.1 amounts to over C$10 bn.[4] However, most of the proceeds were realized from a few privatizations. Petro-Canada and CN accounted for about 45 per cent of the proceeds and the five largest privatizations provided over 70 per cent of the proceeds. As importantly from a budgetary perspective, the government also removed itself from the contingent liability to cover any future losses of these corporations. As mentioned above, the federal government had previously provided large subsidies to many of these SOEs.

Over the last decade, the federal government has also engaged in a form of assest divestiture that might best be described as 'quasi-privatization'. The sale and subsequent organizational restructuring of the air navigation system is illustrative of this general process, although specific details vary by institutional setting. In this case, the federal government established Nav Canada as the sole provider of civilian air traffic control in Canada. Nav Canada is a not-for-profit, non-share company. It is governed by four voting members that are nominated by the government, the air navigation labour unions, the general aviation community and Canadian airlines. These four members appoint the 15-member board of directors. The federal government sold the navigation system to Nav Canada for approximately C$1.5 bn,

Table 7.1 Major Canadian federal privatizations

Company	Sale information					Company information		
	Date	Sold (%)	Retained (%)	Buyer	Sale price ($mn)	Sales ($mn)	Assets ($mn)	Employment
Northern Transportation Company Ltd.	15/7/1985	100	0	Inuvialuit/Nunasi Consortium (negotiated sale)	53	41	75	389
Canada Development Corp.	16/9/1985 5/6/87 8/10/1987	47	0	First public offering Second public offering Private placement	246 15.8 99	2625	6324	17808
The de Havilland Aircraft Canada Ltd.	31/1/1986	100	0	Boeing	98.5	300	346	4405
Pêcheries Canada Inc.	18/4/1986	100	0	La Coopérative Agro-Alimentaire Purdel (negotiated sale)	5	16	16	575
Canadian Arsenals Ltd.	9/5/1986	100	0	The SNC group	92.2	103	126	879
Nanisivik Mines	28/10/1986	18	0	Mineral Resources Int'l Ltd. (qualified auction)	6	26	65	195
CN Route (CN subsidiary)	5/12/1986	100	0	Route Canada Holdings Inc. (negotiated sale)	29	145	40	2227
Canadair Ltd.	23/12/1986	100	0	Bombardier Inc.	143	451	478	5431
Northern Canada Power Commission (Yukon)	31/3/1987	100	0	Yukon Power Corp. (negotiated sale)	75.5	89	269	320

Company	Date	%		Buyer				
Teleglobe Canada	31/3/1987	100	0	Memotec Data Inc. (qualified auction)	611.5	274	502	1180
Fishery Products Int. Ltd	15/4/1987	62.6	0	Public offering	104.4	387	224	8650
Varity Corp.	31/12/1987	n.a.		Private placement and sale on the TSE (8mn warrants)	3.2	n.a.	n.a.	n.a.
	Dec. 1991	n.a.	0	Private placement and sale on the TSE (450000 shares)	6	n.a.	n.a.	n.a.
CN Hotels (CN subsidiary)	31/3/1988	100	0	Canadian Pacific Ltd. (negotiated sale)	265	135	136	3309
Northern Canada Power Commission (NWT)	5/5/1988	100	0	The Government of the NWT (negotiated sale)	53.7	99	143	322
Air Canada	13/10/1988	43	57	First public offering (30.8 mn shares)	233.8	3426	3437	22640
	18/7/1989	57	0	Second public offering (41.1 mn shares)	473.8	3650	4121	23247
Northwest Tel Inc. (CN subsidiary)	1/12/1988	100	0	BCE Inc. (qualified auction)	200	69	152	467
Terra Nova Telecommunications Inc. (CN subsidiary)	1/1/1988	100	0	Newfoundland Telephone Company Ltd. (negotiated sale)	170	46	112	412
CNCP Telecommunications and Telecommunications Terminal Systems	16/12/1988	50	0	Canadian Pacific Ltd. (negotiated sale)	235	317	352	3371

Table 7.1 (continued)

Company	Date	Sold (%)	Retained (%)	Buyer	Sale price ($mn)	Sales ($mn)	Assets ($mn)	Employment
				Sale information		Company information		
Petro-Canada	June 1991	19.5	81	First public offering (42.0 mn shares)	520.4	4961	6039	6213
	1992	15	66	Second public offering (30.4 mn shares)	240.4	4718	5350	5329
	1995	63	20	Third public offering (123.9 mn shares)	1746.3	4820	6488	4567
Nordion Int'l Inc	Nov. 1991	100	0	MDS Health Group Ltd. (qualified auction)	165	107	n.a.	450
Cameco (formerly Eldorado Nuclear Ltd.)	July 1991	20	31.1	First public offering (10.4 mn shares)	123.5	284.3	1374	1200
	Jan. 1992	11.8	19.3	Public offering (6 mn shares)	83.9	305	1376	1078
	1993	9.8	9.5	Public offering (5 mn shares)	98.4	306	1353	1133
	1994	3.7	5.8	Public offering (2 mn shares)	50.0	348	1427	1191
	1995	5.8	0	Public offering (3 mn shares)	88.6	395	1667	1237
Telesat Canada	March 1992	53.7	0	Alouette Telecom. Inc. (3.2 mn shares), now a subsidiary of BCE Inc. (qualified auction)	154.8	178	n.a.	850

Company	Year	% sold	% retained	Purchaser / offering	Proceeds	Sales	Assets	Employment
CN short line in Nova Scotia	Sept. 1992	100	0	RailTex Inc.	20	n.a.	n.a.	110
Co-enerco Resources Ltd.	1992	62	38	First public offering (8.5 mn shares)	45.5	n.a.	n.a.	n.a.
	1993	38	0	Second public offering (5.3 mn shares)	29.1	n.a.	n.a.	n.a.
CN Exploration (CN's oil and gas assets)	1995	100	0	Smart on Resources Ltd.	97	36	54	n.a.
Canadian National Railway	1995	100	0	Public offering (80 mn shares)	2079	4098	6198	26951
Canarctic Shipping Company	1996	51	0	Fednav Ltd. (qualified auction)	0.3			
Air Navigation System (Transport Canada)	1996	100	0	Nav Canada	1500	n.a.	n.a.	6100
Canada Communication Group Printing, Warehousing and Distribution Services	March 1997	100	0	St. Joseph Corp.	7	120	n.a.	1254
National Sea Products Ltd.	1997	10.5	0	Scotia Investments Ltd.	5.8	278	144	1492
Theratronics International Ltd.	1998	100	0	MDS Inc.	15.5	40	n.a.	n.a.

135

Note: Starting in 1997, Cameco reports number of employees of the parent company as well as subsidiaries. The above includes the name of the privatized company, year (or date) of privatization, percentage sold, percentage retained, name of the purchaser if not sold through a public offering, proceeds from the sale and corporate sales, assets and employment around the time of privatization. Information is included about each tranche where relevant.

Sources: Various, including communication from Pat Murray at Finance Canada, Annual Reports and Stanbury (1992).

which is being paid over time out of revenues. Estimating the present value of the sale is difficult to compute and, of course, it does not represent an 'arm's-length' valuation. The federal government explicitly mandated that it would not guarantee Nav Canada's debt (Whiteman *et al.*, 1998).

Federal devolution of major airports and seaports has followed a somewhat similar pattern to that of Nav Canada, although payment methods vary, representation on the board of directors tends to be regional rather than national, and formal ownership remains with the federal government. Following the National Airports Policy (1994), the 26 major airports have been leased to local, not-for-profit, 'non-shareholder equity' corporations.[5] These organizations typically lease the assets for 60 years and make specified annual lease payments to the federal government. Given the length of the leases and the formalism of these contracts, it would be virtually impossible for the government to move to for-profit corporate privatization in the foreseeable future.

The divestiture of the seaports is less clear and less formalized. Management responsibility for the 18 major ports has also been transferred to independent local port authorities. Typically, there are no formal leases, there is no specified time frame and payments to the federal government are not stipulated and are often nominal. Some of these port authorities own and manage their own facilities in addition to managing federal assets. Although these legal arrangements suggest that complete privatization is more feasible than for airports, local politicians and managers are already acting as if they have de facto property rights.

The reluctance of the federal government to engage in outright privatization to for-profit entities is understandable as many major seaports and airports have some degree of local monopoly power. Because of geographic factors, this power may be somewhat greater than in other countries, although it is constrained by intranational and international competition (Richards and Vining, 2001). For example, the port of Vancouver faces some competition from west coast ports in the USA. As yet, there have been no efficiency studies of these quasi-privatizations, but some critics are not optimistic about this form of privatization. Richards and Vining (ibid.: 7), for example, argue that 'transforming these entities from line agencies of the Federal government into nonprofit local organizations does not deal with the fundamental problem of generating strong responsiveness or accountability to users, who are the relevant principals' (similarly, see Lovink, 2001).

Recently, the Canadian government has formed some public–private partnerships (PPPs). As these projects do not involve the sale of assets, they are not included in Table 7.1. However, they are worth noting briefly as they considerably reduce 'up-front' expenditures on assets by governments. In

Canada, the Confederation Bridge, which links Price Edward Island to the mainlaind, is one of the most famous PPP projects. This bridge was completed at a cost of more than C$1 bn in 1997. Straight Crossing Development Inc., which receives an annual subsidy of C$41.9 mn in real 1997 dollars, will operate the bridge for 35 years, after which it will become federal government property.

Provincial privatizations
Table 7.2 provides information about the major provincial privatizations.[6] This table includes the name of the privatized company, the provincial owner, the sector, the year of privatization, the initial provincial stake, the percentage sold, the percentage retained, the name of the purchaser if it was not sold through a public offering, the proceeds from the sale, and corporate sales, assets and employment at the time of privatization. The provincial privatizations are in sectors that do not raise serious market failure concerns. Telecommunications markets have become contestable. There are some resource rent appropriation issues, but these can be handled by taxation or regulation.

The total value of the provincial privatizations in this table amounts to over C$13 bn, indicating that these privatization raised large sums for provincial treasuries. Alberta and Saskatchewan were the most active provinces. In Alberta, the right-of-centre government of Ralph Klein realized C$1.7 bn from Alberta Government Telephones, now Telus, which was the largest provincial prviatization. However, Saskatchewan realized more money in aggregrate, largely because they had more SOEs to privatize.

As at the federal level, provincial privatizations have reduced governments' subsequent liabilities. Consider, for example, the privatization of Skeena Cellulose. Since 1997, this company has built up total debts owed to the province in excess of C$400 mn (*http://los 8150.pb.gov.bc.ca/4dcgi/nritem?4998*). While the government and minority bank owners will receive only C$6 million from the sale, future government bail-outs will be reduced considerably and possibly eliminated.

The C$3.1 bn sale of Highway 407 was unusual (see Mendoza *et al.*, 1999). Initially, the Ontario government wanted to develop the highway through a build-operate-transfer (BOT) concession. Normally, BOT contracts are not considered as privatization and we do not include them in Tables 7.1 or 7.2. In this instance, the BOT bidders demanded significant provincial financial support and the government concluded that it would be less expensive to finance the project itself. The province financed a design–build construction programme and then sold the asset after it had been operating for 18 months. The proceeds were more than double the province's estimated investment. The operator sets tolls based on time of

Table 7.2 *Major Canadian provincial privatizations*

Company	Owner	Sector	Date	Initial provincial stake (%)	Sold (%)	Retained (%)	Buyer	Sale proceeds ($mn)	Sales ($mn)	Assets ($mn)	Employ-ment
									Company information		
					Sale information						
Alberta Energy Company	Alberta	Oil and gas	1975	100	50	50	Public offering	75	0	196	43
			1994	n.a.	n.a.	0	Final public offering	485	922	2357	n.a.
Prince Albert Pulp Co.	Saskatchewan	Pulp	1986	100	100	0	Weyerhauser	300			
Saskatchewan Oil and Gas Corp.	Saskatchewan	Oil and gas	1986	100	41.7	59.3	Public offering	110	115	371	
			1987	41.7	12	29.7	Public offering	50	222	1143	
			1989	29.7	15	14.7	Public offering	96.8			
			1990	14.7	14.7	0	Public offering	145			
Fishery Products International	New Foundland (+ federal govt)	Fish harvesting and processing	1987	37.4	37.4	0	Public offering	62.4	224	387	8600
Donohue Inc	Quebec	Forest products	Feb. 1987	56	56	0	Single buyer	320	522	864	
SOQUIP Alberta	Quebec	Oil and gas	Oct. 1987	100	100	0	Sceptre Resources	195 (est.)			

Entity	Province	Sector	Date	%	%	%	Purchaser				
BC Hydro's mainland natural gas division	B.C.	Natural gas distribution	July 1988	100	100	0	B.C. Gas	741	370	506	
Saskatchewan Power's oil and gas assets	Saskatchewan	Oil and gas	April 1988	100	100	0	Saskatchewan Oil and Gas	325			
Potash Corporation of Saskatchewan	Saskatchewan	Mining	1989	100	37	63	Public offering	388	322	1282	1256
			1991	63	n.a.	n.a.	Public offering	849	307	1260	1227
Manitoba Forestry Manitoba Resources Ltd.	Manitoba	Forest products	March 1989	100	100	0	Repap	132			
Alberta Government Telephones (now Telus)	Alberta	Telecom	1990	100	58	42	Public offering	896	1188	3122	10201
			1991	42	42	0	Public offering	870	1237	3034	10201
Cameco[a] (formerly Saskatchewan Mining Development Corporation)	Saskatchewan (+ federal govt)	Mining	1991	48.9	10	38.9	Public offering	75	284	1374	1200
			1994	38.9	9.2	29.7	Public offering	49	348	1427	1191
			1996	29.7	19.5	10.2	Public offering	731	590	1778	1350
			Feb. 2002	10.2	10.2	0	Public offering	226.4	642	2270	2469
Novatel's systems business	Alberta	Telecom	May 1992	100	100	0	Northern Telecom Ltd	38			
Novatel's cellular telephone business	Alberta	Cellular phones	May 1992	100	100	0	Telexel Holding Ltd	3			

Table 7.2 (continued)

Company	Owner	Sector	Date	Initial provincial stake (%)	Sold (%)	Retained (%)	Buyer	Sale proceeds ($mn)	Sales ($mn)	Assets ($mn)	Employment
Nova Scotia Power Corp. (now a subsidiary of Emera)	Nova Scotia	Electricity generation	1992	100	100	0	Public offering	816	638	2323	2435
Suncor	Ontario	Oil and gas	1992	25	18	7	Public offering	299	1539	1947	3292
Alberta Liquor Control Board Stores	Alberta	Retail (liquor)	1993	100	100	0	Owner-licensees	51.2	718	47	2073
Syncrude Canada	Alberta	Oil and gas	1993	16.7	5	11.7		502	1410		
Vencap Equities Alberta	Alberta	Financial Services	1995	31	31	0	Onex	174	9	282	
Manitoba Telephone Systems	Manitoba	Telecom	1997	100	100	0	Public offering	860	589	1608	3688
Highway 407	Ontario	Highway	May 1999	100	100	0	Highway 407 International Inc	3100			

| Ontario Power Generation-4 hydroelectric stations | Ontario | Electricity generation | Feb. 2002 | 100 | 100 | 0 | Brascan | 340 |
| Skeena Cellulose[b] | B.C. | Pulp and lumber | 2002 | Majority | Majority | 0 | NWBC Timber and Pulp Ltd | 6 |

Notes:

[a] Starting in 1997, Cameco reports the number of employees of the parent company and subsidiaries. The above includes the name of the privatized company, provincial owner, sector, date or year of privatization, initial provincial stake, percentage sold, percentage retained, name of the purchaser if not sold through a public offering, proceeds from the sale and corporate sales, assets and employment at the time of privatization. Information is included about each tranche where relevant.

[b] Subject to approval; Toronto Dominion Bank is a minority shareholder.

Sources: Various, including Stanbury (1992), Levac and Wooldridge (1997) and annual reports.

day and vehicle size and collects tolls electronically. The term of the concession was finally set at 99 years, after which ownership of the asset will
revert to the government.

Municipal and regional district privatizations
Most municipal and regional services, including health, sanitation and
transport, have been provided by government for many years and their
assets continue to be government-owned. However, there have been some
privatizations at these levels.[7] For example, Edmonton Telephones, which
was owned by the municipality of Edmonton, was sold to Telus for
C$468 mn in 1995. This was unusual as most telephone companies were not
municipally owned. In addition, there has been some contracting out of
highway maintenance.

The efficiency effects of privatization in Canada
This section reviews the empirical evidence relating to the efficiency effects
of privatization in Canada. First, it examines the accounting, productivity
and related performance evidence. Second, it looks at the stock price performance of share-issue privatizations following privatization. Using both
accounting measures and stock price measures is useful because the former
provides evidence of current performance, whereas the latter incorporates
market expectations concerning future performance. Also profitability evidence alone, while a useful welfare measure in competitive environments, is
less useful in sectors with natural monopoly characteristics or extensive
market power (Boardman and Vining, 1989; Foster, 1992; Martin and
Parker, 1995; Newbery and Pollitt, 1997). Third, this section briefly discusses the pricing of Canadian share issue privatizations.

Accounting and productivity measures of the impact of privatization
Prior to the global privatization wave, the bulk of the evidence concerning the
relative efficiency of SOEs versus private shareholder-owned corporations
was based on cross-sectional comparisons. For example, using Canadian
data, Vining and Boardman (1992: 218) compared private corporations,
SOEs and mixed enterprises and concluded that 'ownership does matter and
there is strong evidence of superior private corporation performance'. More
recently, the main empirical evaluation strategy has shifted to 'before–after'
(times-series) comparisons. This section summarizes Boardman *et al.* (2002),
henceforth BLV, who used before–after comparisons to examine the efficiency impacts of the major Canadian share-issue privatizations, Laurin and
Bozec (2001), who compared productivity improvements at CN and
Canadian Pacific (CP), and West (1997, 2000), who examined the short-run
effects of retail liquor privatization in Alberta.

BLV examine all of the federal share-issue privatizations, including Air Canada, CN and Petro-Canada, and all of the provincial share-issue privatizations, between 1985 and 1996, including Nova Scotia Power (NS Power, now a subsidiary of Emera), Potash Corporation of Saskatchewan (Potash Corp.), Suncor and Telus. In addition, they include Cameco and Fishery Products International (FPI), which, prior to privatization, were partially owned by both a provincial government and the federal government.

BLV examine accounting-based performance measures for each firm from three years prior to privatization to three years after. They focus on profit (net income), profitability, total product (sales), efficiency/productivity, employees, capital investment, leverage and dividend payments. They also compute the average of these variables across all firms in the sample during the three years prior to privatization and during the three years following. These results are shown in Table 7.3, columns 1 and 2. The year of privatization is omitted because part of the year was prior to privatization and part of it was afterwards. BLV also compute the mean change in each variable from the three-year period prior to privatization and the three-year period following (c.f. Megginson *et al.*, 1994; Boubakri and Cosset, 1998; D'Souza and Megginson, 1999). The mean change appears in column 3 and the Wilcoxon signed-rank test of the difference between the *medians* appears in column 4. For comparison purposes, Table 7.3 also presents the aggregate performance evidence on privatizations in industrialized countries from D'Souza and Megginson (1999). They conducted a comprehensive evaluation of privatization impacts using a large international sample of privatizations that occurred during approximately the same period as the Canadian privatizations.

We now discuss each of the variables in turn, beginning with real net income. On average, the real net income of Canadian privatized firms improved during the three years prior to privatization. Most firms then recorded a large drop in net income during the year of privatization. CN was most conspicuous in this respect, posting a loss of more than a billion dollars in the year it was privatized. Comparing the three years prior to privatization to the three years after shows that, on average, Canadian firms significantly increased their real net income following privatization. Petro-Canada enjoyed the most dramatic increase, while FPI, Potash Corp, Telus, NS Power and CN all showed increases. Suncor was little changed; only Air Canada's real net income declined.

Profitability, which is measured by return on sales (ROS) and return on assets (ROA), is a more useful measure of performance. On average, profitability was substantially higher in the three years following privatization than in the three years prior (7.7 and 3.3 percentage points higher for ROS and ROA, respectively). The change was statistically significant for ROA,

Table 7.3   The pre- and post-privatization performance of Canadian privatizations and other privatizations

	Canadian privatizations				Industrial country privatizations			
	Mean 3 years before (1)	Mean 3 years after (2)	Mean change (3)	z (4)	Mean 3 years before (5)	Mean 3 years after (6)	Mean change (7)	z (8)
Real net income	5371	121775	116404	1.73*	8	11	3	4.20**
Return on sales (%)	1.6	9.3	7.7	1.64				
Return on assets (%)	0.9	4.2	3.3	1.73*				
Real sales (adjusted)	1.02	1.00	−0.02	−0.77	0.98	2.75	1.77	6.18**
Real sales per employee (adjusted)	0.93	1.12	0.19	2.82**	1.06	2.90	1.84	5.69**
Real net income per employee	14.70	27.98	13.28	2.31*				
Number of employees	10328	8188	−2139	−3.59**	16914	16159	−755	−2.19*
Capital expenditures to sales (%)	19.6	20.0	0.4	1.04	11.0	12.0	1.0	1.35
Capital expenditures to assets (%)	8.4	10.1	1.7	1.20				
Debt to total assets (%)	60.8	45.7	−15.1	−3.30**	29.0	23.0	−6.0	−2.79**
Dividends to sales (%)	0.5	4.8	4.3	3.68**	0.7	4.4	3.7	5.09**

Notes: This is a summary of accounting-based performance measures averaged across all firms in the sample during the three years prior to privatization and during the three years following privatization. Also reported are the mean changes in each variable from the three-year period prior to privatization to the three-year period following privatization. The variables are real net income (net income adjusted for changes in the CPI), return on sales (net income divided by sales), return on assets (net income divided by total assets), real adjusted sales (= 1.0 in year 0; = real sales in year t divided by real sales in year 0 for the other years), real adjusted sales per employee (= 1.0 in year 0; = real sales per employee in year t divided by real sales per employee in year 0 for the other years), real net income per employee (real net income divided by the total number of employees), number of employees, capital expenditures to sales (total amount of capital expenditures divided by sales), capital expenditures to assets (total amount of capital expenditures divided by total assets), debt to total assets (total debt divided by total assets) and dividends to sales (dividends divided by sales). For comparison purposes, summary statistics are also reported on privatizations in industrialized countries from D'Souza and Megginson (1999). Wilcoxon signed-rank (z score) tests the difference between the *medians* before and after privatization: * denotes significantly different from zero at the 5% level with a one-tailed alternative;** denotes significantly different from zero at the 1% level with a one-tailed alternative.

Source: Boardman, Laurin and Vining (2002).

but not for ROS. The average increase in the ROS of Canadian firms was larger than for firms in other countries, although the post-privatization profitability level of Canadian firms lagged that in other countries.

Table 7.3 provides measures of average adjusted real sales for the three-year periods before and after privatization. The adjusted real sales of a firm in year *t* equals the ratio of real sales in year *t* to the real sales of that firm in year 0. The advantage of this measure is that it weights firms equally, irrespective of sales. The average adjusted real sales of Canadian firms do not change significantly after privatization. This result is quite different to that for privatizations in other industrialized countries, which have substantial increases in adjusted real sales following privatization.

Productivity, as measured by real sales per employee and real net income per employee, improves in each year prior to privatization, it declines in the year of privatization and improves each year following privatization. On average, both measures of productivity were better in the three-year period following privatization than in the three-year period before. These improvements, which are broadly consistent with changes in other countries, are economically and statistically significant. Suncor, NS Power and CN experienced the largest productivity increases.[8]

Privatized Canadian firms significantly reduced their employment levels. Much of the efficiency improvements can be attributed to lowering employment without significantly reducing output. All privatized firms had fewer employees three years after privatization than three years before privatization, except Cameco, which had a small increase. Although Canadian firms were generally smaller than privatized firms in other countries, the decrease in employment was greater, possibly indicating more job padding in Canadian SOEs prior to privatization than in SOEs in other countries.

Capital investment was measured by the ratio of capital expenditures to sales and the ratio of capital expenditures to assets. BLV found that capital investment increased in Canadian firms following privatization, but not by a statistically significant amount. This experience was similar to that in other industrialized countries.

Canadian firms significantly reduced their debt levels following privatization. This decrease was larger than in other privatizations, which is not surprising given the higher levels of debt in Canadian firms prior to privatization. Potash Corp, Cameco, Telus and NS Power had the largest reductions in their debt ratios. However, Air Canada, which was already highly levered prior to privatization, increased its leverage afterwards, which has contributed to its subsequent financial problems.

BLV also found that Canadian firms significantly increased their dividend payments (as a percentage of sales) following privatization. This increase was slightly higher than in other countries. Prior to privatization only

Petro-Canada and Suncor paid dividends. Following privatization, all companies paid dividends except Air Canada, the most highly levered company.

Laurin and Bozec (2001) analysed productivity changes at CN, one of the largest privatizations in Canada. They found that the total factor productivity of CN started to improve three years prior to privatization. In the post-privatization period, productivity improvements are reflected in financial ratios and stock price performance that surpasses its competitors, including CP and the market.

West (1997, 2000) found that, following privatization of the Alberta real retail liquor stores, the number of stores increased and product selection increased, but prices rose slightly. The potential for efficiency gains was limited by a number of factors. For example, the (government-owned) wholesaler maintained uniform prices and transport charges, reducing the incentive for the formation of retail chains. For these and other reasons, West (2000) does not draw a conclusion regarding the welfare effects of this privatization.

Stock price performance

An alternative measure of privatization performance is to examine long-run returns and long-run abnormal returns during some period following privatization. Because these measures of performance are based directly on stock prices, and therefore on firm market value, they are useful measures of investors' assessment of firm performance and future prospects.

The finance literature uses two main approaches to compute long-run returns following privatization (Boardman and Laurin, 2000). The cumulative return method consists of adding periodic returns over a given time horizon. Another method calculates returns based on a buy-and-hold strategy. Although both approaches have been used in the literature, the cumulative return approach has been widely used in event studies (Spiers and Affleck-Graves, 1999; Brav *et al.*, 2000). Here we focus on the long-run cumulative returns.[9]

The abnormal (or market-adjusted) return is calculated by subtracting the daily return on the Canadian market index from each firm's daily return. We begin the return horizon four days after the first trading day to exclude the underpricing effect, which we discuss below, and continue for five years. Let r_{it} denote the return to the stock of privatized company i on day t of trading following privatization, and let r_{mt} denote the return to the market index on day t; then the (daily) abnormal return (AR_{it}) is

$$AR_{it} = r_{it} - r_{mt}. \tag{7.1}$$

The (unadjusted) cumulative returns (CR) and the market-adjusted cumulative returns or cumulative abnormal returns (CAR) on day t are given by:

$$CR_{it} = \sum_{t=4}^{t} r_{it} \qquad (7.2)$$

and

$$CAR_{it} = \sum_{t=4}^{t} AR_{it}. \qquad (7.3)$$

Table 7.4 contains the average CRs and the average CARs for the Canadian firms in BLV's sample. Results are presented at the end of each month for the first 12 months and thereafter at the end of each subsequent six-month period, up to five years. For comparison purposes, the tables also contain comparable figures for a global sample of 118 privatizations, expanding on Boardman and Laurin (2000).

Both the average CRs and the average CARs are positive in all periods except at the end of the first month. The average CARs of Canadian privatizations are just over 9 per cent after the first 12 months, which is very similar to the CARs obtained by privatized firms in other countries. The CARs for Canadian privatizations are similar to other privatizations until towards the end of the third year, when many Canadian firms had negative returns, most conspicuously Air Canada. After five years, at the end of the sample period, Canadian firms have average CARs of 20 per cent. Although this is four percentage points lower than for other privatized firms, it is still a large abnormal return. The main conclusions are that there were major unexpected efficiency improvements in Canadian firms following privatization and that these improvements continued to be realized over a five-year period.

Underpricing Canadian share issue privatizations
While not directly related to efficiency, it is interesting to discuss the evidence on the underpricing of privatization shares, which is given in the final row of Table 7.4. On average, Canadian firms were underpriced by just over 7 per cent. This is considerably lower than the average for all privatizations, which is about 16 per cent. However, it is very similar to the average underpricing of firms in large developed markets (excluding the UK), which equals 8 per cent (Laurin *et al.*, 2001). Also it is similar to the underpricing of private sector firm IPOs in Canada, which averages about 6.4 per cent (Clarkson and Merckley, 1994). As in the IPO market, some underpricing is necessary but, given the characteristics of Canadian privatized firms, one would not expect as much underpricing to be necessary. This suggests that the Canadian government, like governments in other developed markets, was both risk-averse and politically motivated in price setting, but at the same time did not want to leave 'too much money on the table'.

Table 7.4　Cumulative unadjusted and market-adjusted stock price returns
for a portfolio of privatized Canadian corporations

Month following privatization	Unadjusted cumulative returns		Market adjusted cumulative returns	
	Canadian firms (n = 9)	Global sample (n = 118)	Canadian firms (n = 9)	Global sample (n = 118)
1	−0.0055	0.0278[***]	−0.0074	0.0204[**]
2	0.0220	0.0664[***]	0.0174	0.0439[***]
3	0.0518	0.0926[***]	0.0289	0.0563[***]
4	0.0933	0.0983[***]	0.0588	0.0439[**]
5	0.1028	0.1060[***]	0.0642	0.0491[**]
6	0.0745[*]	0.1131[***]	0.0353	0.0482[**]
7	0.1138[*]	0.1250[***]	0.0798	0.0582[**]
8	0.1296	0.1386[***]	0.0859	0.0755[***]
9	0.1058[*]	0.1396[***]	0.0609	0.0808[***]
10	0.1413	0.1461[***]	0.0858	0.0841[***]
11	0.1642[*]	0.1484[***]	0.1047[*]	0.0896[***]
12	0.1644[*]	0.1609[***]	0.0936	0.0905[***]
18	0.1948	0.2441[***]	0.1014	0.1058[***]
24	0.2746[*]	0.3266[***]	0.1527	0.1350[***]
30	0.3704[*]	0.4053[***]	0.1527	0.1402[***]
36	0.3188[*]	0.4461[***]	0.1103	0.1563[***]
42	0.3483	0.5296[***]	0.0859	0.1784[***]
48	0.4399[*]	0.6274[***]	0.0924	0.2010[***]
54	0.5618[**]	0.6953[***]	0.1379	0.2059[***]
60	0.7169[**]	0.7765[***]	0.1983	0.2417[***]
Day 1 to 3	0.0725[**]	0.1640[***]	0.0713[**]	0.1630[***]

Notes: [*] denotes significantly different from zero at the 10% level; [**] denotes significantly different from zero at the 5% level; [***] denotes significantly different from zero at the 1% level. The above is a summary of the average CRs and the average CARs for Canadian share-issue privatizations. Results are presented at the end of each month for the first 12 months and thereafter at the end of each subsequent six-month period, up to five years. For comparison purposes, the table also summarizes comparable figures for a global sample of 118 privatizations taken from Boardman and Laurin (2000).

Privatization in the USA

At the outset it is important to emphasize that the nomenclature in the USA is different from that in most other parts of the world. In the USA, the word 'privatization' typically includes contracting out and outsourcing, where government retains the responsibility for selecting the contractor and financing the service. Elsewhere, the word 'privatization' is usually restricted to asset divestitures of commercial enterprises, where governments normally renounce any commitment to financial support or control, although they may provide specified subsidies. Here we focus primarily on asset divestitures, but also briefly discuss contracting out developments.

Asset divestitures

As mentioned in the introduction, US government ownership of enterprises, especially at the federal level, has been quite limited. It is noteworthy that Megginson and Netter (2001) hardly mention the USA in a recent exhaustive review of empirical studies of privatization. However, there have been some privatizations in the USA. The largest public offering was the sale of the government's 85 per cent stake in Consolidated Rail Corporation (Conrail) in 1987. This public offering, which was then the largest stock offering on Wall Street, raised about US$1.9bn, although this was less than expected. Conrail was subsequently bought by CSX Corporation and Norfolk Southern Corporation in 1997. We are not aware of any academic study of the efficiency effects of this privatization. However, the stock price rose from a split-adjusted equivalent of US$13 per share at the time of privatization to US$115 per share after approximately 10 years in the private sector (*www.conrail.com/history.htm*).

During the Second World War, the federal government seized the shares of German and Japanese-owned firms. Kole and Mulhern (1997) examined the seizure and subsequent privatization of 17 of these firms. The government seized most of the firms in 1942 and maintained their share ownership for between one and 23 years, with a median ownership period of seven years. The federal government clearly stated its intention to privatize. Not surprisingly, given these special circumstances, Kole and Mulhern find no evidence of efficiency impacts following privatization.

The two most recent important privatizations in the USA at the federal level have been the Internet backbone network and the Internet domain name system (DNS). Kesan and Shah (2001) conclude that the government's privatization strategy for DNS was flawed and led to reduced competition, high domain name prices and restricted choice. It is unclear why these problems occurred and why they have attracted relatively little policy attention. Part of the problem appears to have simply been that the government grossly underestimated the economic importance of the Internet. DNS was sold to Network Solutions Inc. for US$3.9mn in 1995 and subsequently grew to a market capitalization of around US$2bn! Since privatization, the government has tried to mitigate and rectify some of these mistakes with some, but not complete, success (Borowski, 1999; Mueller, 1999; Niccolai and Briody, 1999).

Contracting out

Contracting out government services has increased slowly over the last decade (GAO, 1997; Hirsch and Osborne, 2000). It has grown somewhat more rapidly at the state than at the county or municipal level. The most common areas for contracting out at the municipal level are solid waste disposal, street construction, facilities operations, building repair, ambulance services, vehicle maintenance and engineering and architectural services (Hirsch and Osborne, 2000). Contracting out information technology services is now also common at all levels of government (Globerman and Vining, 1996).

When governments contract out the provision of services or activities, they usually select a for-profit firm from among a set of bidders. Bidders are selected on the basis of price and competency. In 'managed competition', an internal government agency competes against private sector suppliers to provide the service. More recently, and especially at the state level, contracting out includes the delivery of a wide array of social services by not-for-profit providers (Bachman, 1996; Ryan, 1999).

It is, as yet, difficult to assess comprehensively the efficiency impacts of contracting out in the USA. Almost all the state agencies reviewed by the GAO (1997: Appendix III) claimed significant budgetary savings *and* service improvements from their contracting out of a wide variety of services. These findings are consistent with most other empirical evidence that contracting out lowers production costs (Pack, 1987; 1989). However, the costs of providing these contracted out services also include the bargaining costs associated with the contracting out process and the opportunism costs associated with a contractual relationship (Globerman and Vining, 1996). These 'governance costs' of contracting out have not been widely studied. But given that the case study evidence suggests that these costs are significant (Sclar, 1997), it is not possible to be definitive on the efficiency impacts of contracting out.

Future prospects for privatization in Canada

At the federal level the most obvious candidates for privatization have now been privatized. However, the federal government still owns many organizations where the whole entity or specific businesses could be privatized. Some of the major privatization candidates are Canada Post, Purolator Courier, Canada Mortgage and Housing Corporation, Atomic Energy of Canada, the Business Development Bank of Canada, and Canada Development Investment Corporation. Also the federal government has still to sell its remaining 21.5 per cent stake in Petro-Canada.

In the medium term, most of the privatization activity in Canada is likely to be at the provincial level. Provincial governments still own many major

enterprises. The largest provincially owned enterprises are the electric utilities (except in Alberta and Nova Scotia). The Province of Ontario has gone
the furthest in preparing for, and committing itself to, privatization of its
electricity production and distribution system. In 2000, Ontario Hydro –
until that time North America's largest electric utility – was broken up into
three entities: Ontario Power Generation, Ontario Hydro Services (which
owns the electricity distribution grid) and Ontario Hydro Financial (which
retains Ontario Hydro's stranded debt). The stated plan is to privatize both
Ontario Power Generation and Ontario Hydro Services (Hydro One), while
at the same time opening power generation to competition. Recently, after
legal issues surrounding the Ontario government's plan to privatize Ontario
Hydro by an IPO and disputes about executive compensation, the Ontario
government replaced the CEO, forced the resignation of the board and
announced that it intends to partially privatize Hydro One (the distribution
system).

British Columbia may also be moving towards privatization of some or
all facets of its publicly owned electricity supplier (BC Hydro). Recently,
the provincially appointed Task Force on Energy Policy (2001) released its
interim report, which recommended that 'the province establish an independent transmission entity clearly separate from all generators, distribution utilities and utilities' and that 'in addition to a separate transmission
entity, the province needs to establish two separate corporations; a generation entity and a distribution utility' (Task Force, 2001:54). While the
interim report stopped short of recommending privatization, these recommendations, if implemented, would clearly make privatization of one or all
of these entities more feasible. Recently, BC Hydro privatized a number of
its smaller service units.

Most of the planned and potential provincial privatizations, especially
those in electricity supply, will raise complex regulatory issues (see Chapters
22 and 23, and Weyman-Jones, 2001). There is considerable disagreement on
the potential for efficiency-enhancing privatization in these circumstances
(for example, Vickers and Yarrow, 1988; Bradburd, 1995; Pollitt, 1995;
Kwoka, 1996; Willner, 1996; VanDoren, 1998; Newbery, 2000; Trebing,
2001). Although the global evidence on privatization in areas with natural
monopoly characteristics, such as the electricity, gas, water and sewer
sectors, has generally shown large efficiency gains, realization of these gains
appears to depend on effective post-privatization regulatory structures
(Burns and Weyman-Jones, 1996; Newbery and Pollitt, 1997; Green and
McDaniel, 1998; Rudnick, 1998; Saal and Parker, 2000; Domah and Pollitt,
2001; Rossi, 2001; Wallsten, 2001).

In addition to the electric utilities there is a range of other provincial
prospects. These include liquor distribution and retailing in most provinces,

motor insurance firms in several provinces and a railroad and some ferry service routes in British Columbia. The recently elected Liberal government in British Columbia has also expressed a desire for more public–private partnerships for constructing new facilities in such areas as roads, hospitals and a convention centre.

Finally, it is important to mention the potential for some privatization in healthcare delivery. Currently, almost every aspect of Canadian health care is provided and financed by provincial governments. There is a greater degree of legislated public monopoly than in almost any other developed country (Globerman and Vining, 1998). There is some evidence that the quality of healthcare services has declined on certain dimensions over the past few years, while government costs have increased substantially. In 2001, Canada's total expenditures on health exceeded C$100 bn. An aging population, more costly drugs and higher labour costs are increasing the fiscal pressure on the public system. Several recent reports, including the Commission on the Future of Health Care in Canada, chaired by Roy Romanow, have discussed the potential for some degree of privatization (*www.healthcoalition.calinterim.pdf*). However, any reduction in publicly funded, universal, free health services will be controversial (Globerman and Vining, 1998).

Future prospects for privatization in the USA
The current major assets of the US federal government that might be privatized include electricity production and distribution (MacAvoy and McIsaac, 1995; Kwoka, 1996; VanDoren, 1998; Hausman and Neufeld, 1999; Gordon, 2001), Amtrak (Vranich and Hudgins, 2001), government 'sponsorship' of mortgages through the Federal National Mortgage Association (Fannie Mae) and the Federal Home Loan Mortgage Corporation (Freddie Mac), and the US postal service. All were considered for privatization by the federal government during the 1990s (CBO, 1996, 1997; also see Chapter 9 below).

At the state and sub-state level, the major potential for privatization probably lies in electrical power generation and distribution and transport, including urban transport (Gomez-Ibanez and Meyer, 1993; Winston and Shirley, 1998; Oster and Strong, 2000; Winston, 2000) and airports (GAO, 1996).

The exact extent of government ownership of the electrical power and distribution system is hard to determine as the definition of 'public' ownership in this sector is complex (Hollas *et al.*, 1994). Using one definition, publicly owned utilities currently provide about 20 per cent of all electricity. Federally owned utilities are few in number but have relatively large generating capacity. State-owned, municipally owned and hybrid entities with some degree of public ownership are much more numerous, but produce and distribute much less electrical power (Gordon, 2001).

The Congressional Budget Office (CBO) estimates that the private sector would be willing to pay between US$45 bn and US$62 bn for all of the power assets of the federal government (1997 dollars). The TVA is one of the largest electric power companies in North America (Cordaro, 1997). Despite the fact that it has over US$27 bn of debt, the CBO estimates that it might sell for between US$22 bn and US$30 bn. However, Logue and MacAvoy (2001) argue that the TVA is close to insolvency. The CBO (1997) estimates that the Bonneville Power Administration (and related government-owned power generating assets) may be worth between US$15 bn and US$20 bn and the assets of the smaller federal power marketing authorities – such as the Southwestern and the Southeastern – could be sold for between US$8 bn and US$11 bn.

The CBO argues that government production of electricity has resulted in high costs that could be reduced under private ownership. Other authors have identified some of the allocative efficiency costs of the inherently political nature of public ownership (Kwoka, 1996; VanDoren, 1998). The CBO (1997: section 2, 3) also identifies some of the X-inefficiency problems (Leibenstein, 1976; Frantz, 1988) associated with government production:

> At the heart of the problems with the high costs of Federal production are government failures: behavioral impediments to socially efficient power operations. The managerial structure of the Federal power program, for example, makes it hard to operate efficiently. Sources of problems include the divided responsibilities of different agencies and branches of government, the constraints of the Congressional budgeting process, and the lack of independent financial oversight or significant financial constraints on pricing and investment decisions.

The CBO makes the case that, while government production may have had a historical rationale, 'growing competition weakens one argument for direct government ownership of production and transmission facilities: it reduces any market power that nonfederal utilities may hold' (CBO, 1997: section 2, 3). The CBO concludes, 'privatization may offer the greatest opportunity for enhancing the efficiency of power production' (ibid., section 2, 4).

Amtrak is a rail passenger corporation created in 1970. It is technically incorporated as a private company and, therefore, it is not an official federal entity. However, its board of directors is appointed by the President and the US Department of Transportation is the only holder of the firm's preferred stock (the only voting stock of the corporation). Given this, it is de facto a government corporation. It has received approximately US$25 bn in subsidies since its inception (Vranich and Hudgins, 2001).

The expectation was that Amtrak would eventually become profitable and survive with minimal government financing, but Amtrak's record of repeated losses (US$1.2bn in 2001) and seeming inability to control costs suggests that this is unlikely in the foreseeable future. The Amtrak Reform and Accountability Act of 1997 currently mandates that, if Amtrak does not become financially self-sufficient by December 2002, it must be restructured and liquidated (ibid.). Although this date was approaching fast at the time of writing, and there is some pressure to privatize Amtrak, there was no indication that Congress was willing to sell off or liquidate Amtrak.

Fannie Mae and Freddie Mac are both owned by shareholders and their shares are publicly traded on the New York Stock Exchange. However, they are unusual hybrids. They were established by federal law and have operating benefits not available to for-profit firms, including exemption from state and local income taxes and registration requirements of the Securities and Exchange Commission. The CBO, a non-partisan organization with highly-regarded analytic skills, has conducted a comprehensive review of both organizations. The CBO (1996:3) concluded that they are 'principally a vehicle for delivering a Federal subsidy' and that they are not efficient delivery vehicles because they retain nearly US$1 for every US$2 they pass through. The CBO (ibid.) noted that 'when the government initially turned to [Fannie Mae and Freddie Mac] as a means for improving housing finance . . . no fully private firms could create profitable, high-volume links between the bond and mortgage markets. Today, numerous private groups can perform that service.' The CBO's preferred policy option is some form of privatization.

Since the advent of firms such as Federal Express and UPS, the monopoly of the US postal service over mail delivery has been substantially eroded. New substitutes for postal delivery such as e-mails, faxes and other forms of on-line communication are further reducing the monopoly. As a result, the US postal service revenue is expected to decrease substantially over the next decade. Supporters of the postal service have proposed broader monopoly rights over communication, such as on-line security services, in order to compensate for this loss in revenue. Critics have argued that the rationale for a public entity no longer exists, given the array of competitive substitutes (Hudgins, 2000). There are currently no obvious indications as to the direction in which the US government or Congress will lean with respect to the partial or complete privatization of the postal service. The future of the US postal service is considered in more detail in Chapter 9.

Advani and Borins (2001:92) point out, 'while the United States has much less public ownership than most other countries, airports have been an exception'. In contrast, airports have been major targets of privatization in other parts of the world (Kapur, 1995; Parker, 1999; Hooper *et al.*, 2000).

Generally, US airports are owned by public sector, substate-level entities, such as counties and municipalities (Truitt and Esler, 1996). In some cases, however, they are under long-term management by private sector firms (ibid.). Based on a (self-report) survey of approximately 50 airports in the USA, Advani and Borins (2001) found that very few of these airports expected privatization in the foreseeable future.

Conclusions

There has been extensive privatization in Canada over the last 20 years. Major federal privatized Canadian firms include CN, Petro-Canada and Air Canada. Privatization revenues from the major privatizations have exceeded C$10bn in aggregate. There has also been extensive privatization of provincially owned firms, including Telus, NS Power and Manitoba Telephone Systems. In aggregate, the major provincial privatizations that we identified raised C$13bn.

Evidence from BLV and others suggests that privatization in Canada has resulted in significant efficiency improvements. BLV found that profits, profitability, efficiency and dividends increased in the three years prior to privatization and were still significantly higher after privatization than before. Employment and debt levels were significantly lower after privatization than before privatization. Real sales and capital expenditures did not change significantly. These findings are broadly consistent with those in other countries, with one exception – real sales declined slightly in Canadian privatizations but increased significantly elsewhere.

In the USA, there has been far less privatization activity largely because there was less government ownership, although there has been considerable contracting out of public services. There is very little evidence about the efficiency and welfare effects of privatization in the USA.

There remains considerable room for further privatization in both Canada and the USA. However, further privatization in both countries is likely to be incremental, for a number of reasons. First, with the exception of electricity generation and distribution in Canada, state-owned enterprises no longer dominate any of the 'commanding heights' of either economy. This reduces the vigour of pro-privatization advocates and interest groups, which are often most active when there are large external gains from any efficiency improvements flowing from privatization. Second, almost all potential privatizations now raise at least some plausible *prima facie* market failure concerns. This throws into greater doubt the size (and even sign) of potential welfare changes following privatization. This doubt tends both to weaken consensus among pro-privatization forces (for example, about the need for extensive regulatory requirements) and to reduce their numbers and political influence. Privatization is less saleable when it cannot be sold as the simple withdrawal of the state. When there is doubt about the degree of market failure, advocates of privatization may have serious disagreements about optimal post-privatization regulatory regimes. (The nature of regulatory regimes is discussed fully in Chapters 23 to 26 below.) Third, many of the remaining candidates for privatization, such as airports, are owned by an array of subnational entities. These entities, whether state, provincial, regional or municipal, appear to be relatively insulated from global intellectual influences that have fostered widespread privatization by national governments. Local politicians and civil servants are both less knowledgeable about and, perhaps, less interested in, the evidence on efficiency gains from other countries.

Notes

1. This research was supported by a grant from the Social Sciences and Humanities Research Council of Canada. The authors would like to thank Walid Ben-Amar and Aziz Sunderji for research assistance. We would also like to thank Pat Murray, Department of Finance Canada, and Eric Larson, Transport Canada, for providing information.
2. Most privatizations occurred in 1985 or later. At the beginning of 1985, one Canadian dollar was worth about 75 US cents (US$0.75). The Canadian dollar fell throughout 1985, but started to rise at the beginning of 1986. It peaked in October 1991 at almost 89 US cents but subsequently fell to a level of about 63 US cents at the time of writing (*http://pacific.commerce.ubc.ca/xr*). Over this 17-year period, C$1 was worth about US$0.75, on average.
3. These vehicles included La Caisse de Dépôt et Placement du Québec, Canada Development Investment Corporation, Crown Investments Corporation of Saskatchewan, Société Générale de Financement du Québec, Sidbec and Cape Breton Development Corporation.
4. The government did not receive all of the proceeds in all privatizations. For example, Cameco retained the C$130mn proceeds from the first privatization tranche and used the proceeds to reduce debt.
5. The 26 airports specified in the National Airports Policy (1994) are the largest airports in Canada (with over 200000 passengers per year) and the airports of the provincial and territorial capitals.
6. For details on smaller provincial privatizations during the period 1983 to 1992, see Stanbury (1992).
7. A regional district government usually covers a few municipalities.
8. For more information about the productivity gains at CN, see Laurin and Bozec (2001).
9. Returns based on a buy-and-hold strategy are available from the authors upon request.

References

Advani, A. and S. Borins (2001) 'Managing Airports: A Test of the New Public Management', *International Public Management Journal*, 4(1), 91–107.

Bachman, S. (1996) 'Why Do States Privatize Mental Health Services? Six State Experiences', *Journal of Health Politics, Policy and Law*, 21(4), 807–24.

Boardman, A.E. and C. Laurin (2000) 'Factors Affecting the Stock Price Performance of Share Issued Privatizations', *Applied Economics*, 32(1), 451–64.

Boardman, A.E. and A.R. Vining (1989) 'Ownership and Performance in Competitive Environments: A Comparison of the Performance of Private, Mixed, and State-Owned Enterprises', *Journal of Law and Economics*, 32(1), 1–33.

Boardman, A.E., C. Laurin and A.R. Vining (2002) 'Privatization in Canada: Operating and Stock Price Performance with International Comparisons', *Canadian Journal of Administrative Sciences*, 19(2), 137–54.

Boardman, A.E., C. Eckel, M-A. Linde and A. Vining (1983) 'An Overview of Mixed Enterprises in Canada', *Business Quarterly*, 48(2), 101–6.

Borowski, S. (1999) 'Whose "Net Is It Anyway?"', *Electronic Business*, 25(9), 44.

Boubakri, N. and J-C. Cosset (1998) 'The Financial and Operating Performance of Newly Privatized Firms: Evidence from Developing Countries', *Journal of Finance*, 53(1), 1081–10.

Bradburd, R. (1995) 'Privatization of Natural Monopoly Public Enterprises: The Regulation Issue', *Review of Industrial Organization*, 19(3), 247–67.

Brav, A., C. Geczy and P.A. Gompers (2000) 'Is the Abnormal Return Following Equity Issuance Anomalous?', *Journal of Financial Economics*, 56(2), 209–49.

Burns, P. and T. Weyman-Jones (1996) 'Cost Functions and Cost Efficiency in Electricity Distribution: A Stochastic Frontier Approach', *Bulletin of Economic Research*, 48(1), 41–64.

Campos, J. and H. Esfahani (1996) 'Why and When Do Governments Initiate Public Enterprise Reform?', *The World Bank Economic Review*, 10(1), 451–85.

Clarke, T. and C. Pitelis eds. (1993) *The Political Economy of Privatization*, New York: Routledge.

Clarkson, P. and J. Merckley (1994) 'Ex Ante Uncertainty and the Underpricing of Initial Public Offerings: Further Canadian Evidence', *Canadian Journal of Administrative Sciences*, 11(1), 54–67.

CBO (Congressional Budget Office) (1996) *Assessing the Public Costs and Benefits of Fannie Mae and Freddie Mac*, Washington, DC: CBO.

CBO (Congressional Budget Office) (1997) *Should the Federal Government Sell Electricity?*, Washington, DC: CBO.

Cordaro, M. (1997) 'What Future for Public Power?', *The Electricity Journal*, 10(9), 72–7.

Domah, P. and M. Pollitt (2001) 'The Restructuring and Privatisation of Electricity Distribution and Supply Businesses in England and Wales: A Social Cost–Benefit Analysis', *Fiscal Studies*, 22(1), 107–46.

D'Souza, J. and W.L. Megginson (1999) 'The Financial and Operating Performance of Privatized Firms During the 1990s', *Journal of Finance*, 54(4), 1397–438.

Dudley, G. (1999) 'British Steel and Government Since Privatization: Policy "Framing" and the Transformation of Policy Networks', *Public Administration*, 77(1), 51–71.

Economic Council of Canada (1986) *Minding the Public's Business*, Ottawa: Supply and Services.

Feigenbaum, H.B. and J.R. Henig (1997) 'Privatization and Political Theory', *Journal of International Affairs*, 50(2), 338–55.

Foster, C. (1992) *Privatization, Public Ownership and the Regulation of Natural Monopoly*, Oxford: Basil Blackwell.

Frantz, R.S. (1988) *X-Efficiency: Theory, Evidence and Applications*, Boston: Kluwer Academic Publishers.

GAO (General Accounting Office) (1996) *Airport Privatization: Issues Related to the Sale or Lease of U.S. Commercial Airports*, RCED-97-3, Washington, DC: GAO.

GAO (General Accounting Office) (1997) *Privatization: Lessons Learned by State and Local Governments*, GGD-97-48, Washington, DC: GAO.

Globerman, S. and A. Vining (1996) 'A Framework for Evaluating the Government Contracting-Out Decision with an Application to Information Technology', *Public Administration Review*, 56(6), 577–86.

Globerman, S. and A. Vining (1998) 'A Policy Perspective on "Mixed" Health Care Financing Systems', *Journal of Risk and Insurance*, 65(1), 57–80.

Gomez-Ibanez, J. and J. Meyer (1993) *Going Private: The International Experience with Transport Privatization*, Washington, DC: Brooking Institution.

Gordon, R. (2001) 'Don't Restructure Electricity; Deregulate', *Cato Journal*, 20(3), 327–58.

Green, R., and T. McDaniel (1998) 'Competition in Electricity Supply: Will "1998" Be Worth It?', *Fiscal Studies*, 19(3), 273–93.

Hausman, W. and J. Neufeld (1999) 'Falling Water: The Origins of Direct Federal Participation in the US Electric Utility Industry, 1902–1933', *Annals of Public and Cooperative Economics*, 70(1), 49–74.

Hirsch, W. and E. Osborne (2000) 'Privatization of Government Services: Pressure-Group Resistance and Service Transparency', *Journal of Labor Research*, 21(2), 315–26.

Hollas, D., S. Stansell and E.T. Claggett (1994) 'Ownership Form and Rate Structure: An Examination of Cooperative and Municipal Electric Distribution Utilities', *Southern Economic Journal*, 6(2), 519–30.

Hooper, P., R. Crain and S. White (2000) 'The Privatization of Australia's Airports', *Transportation Research Part E, Logistics and Transportation Review*, 36(3), 181–204.

Hudgins, E.L. (2000) *Mail @ the millennium: Will the Postal Service Go Private?*, Washington, DC: Cato Institute.

Jörgensen, J.J., T. Hafsi and C. Demers (1993) 'Context and Process in Privatization: Canada/Quebec', in T. Clarke and C. Piletis (eds), *The Political Economy of Privatization*, New York: Routledge, pp. 234–72.

Kapur, A. (1995) 'Airport Infrastructure: The Emerging Role of the Private Sector', World Bank Technical Report #313, World Bank, Washington, DC.

Kesan, J.P. and R.C. Shah (2001) 'Fool us Once Shame on You – Fool us Twice Shame on Us: What We Can Learn from the Privatizations of the Internet Backbone Network and the Domain Name System', working Paper No. 00–18, University of Illinois College of Law.

Kikeri, S., J. Nellis and M. Shirley (1992) *Privatization: The Lessons of Experience*, Washington, DC: World Bank.

Kole, S. and J.H. Mulhern (1997) 'The Government as a Shareholder: A Case from the United States', *Journal of Law and Economics*, 40(1), 1–22.

Kwoka, J., Jr. (1996) *Power Structure: Ownership, Integration, and Competition in the U.S. Electricity Industry*, Boston: Kluwer Academic Publishers.

Laurin, C. and Y. Bozec (2001) 'Privatization and Productivity Improvement: The Case of Canadian National', *Transportation Research Part E, Logistics and Transportation Review*, 37(5), 355–74.

Laurin, C., A.E. Boardman and A.R. Vining (2001) 'The Role of Government Revenue and Political Motivations for Underpricing Privatizations', UBC Working Paper, Vancouver.

Leibenstein, H. (1976) *Beyond Economic Man: A New Foundation for Microeconomics*, Cambridge, MA: Harvard University Press.

Levac, M. and P. Wooldridge (1997) 'The Fiscal Impact of Privatization in Canada', *Bank of Canada Review*, Summer, 25–40.

Logue, D.E. and P.W. MacAvoy (2001) 'The Tennessee Valley Authority: Competing in Markets for Capital and Electricity in Pursuit of Solvency', Working Paper Series OL #18, Yale School of Management.

Lovink, J.A.A. (2001) 'Improving the Governance of Airport Authorities', *Policy Options*, April, 50–56.

MacAvoy, P.W. and G.S. McIsaac (1995) 'The Current File on the Case for Privatization of the Federal Government Enterprises', *The Hume Papers on Public Policy*, 3(3), 121–47.

Martin, S. and D. Parker (1995) 'Privatization and Economic Performance Throughout the UK Business Cycle', *Managerial and Decision Economics*, 16(3), 225–37.

Megginson, W. and J. Netter (2001) 'From State to Market: A Survey of Empirical Studies on Privatization', *Journal of Economic Literature*, 39(2), 321–89.

Megginson, W., R. Nash and M.V. Randenborgh (1994) 'The Financial and Operating Performance of Newly Privatized Firms: An International Empirical Analysis', *The Journal of Finance*, 49(2), 403–52.

Mendoza, E., M. Gold, P. Cater and J. Parmar (1999) 'The Sale of Highway 407 Express Toll Route: A Case Study', *Journal of Project Finance*, 5(3), 5–14.

Mueller, M. (1999) 'Competition in the Domain Name Market', *Business Communications Review*, 29(8), 59–66.

Newbery, D. (2000) *Privatization, Restructuring, and Regulation of Network Utilities*, Cambridge, MA: MIT Press.

Newbery, D. and M. Pollitt (1997) 'The Restructuring and Privatization of Britain's CEGB – Was it Worth It?', *Journal of Industrial Economics*, 45(3), 269–303.

Niccolai, J. and D. Briody (1999) 'Government, NSI Reach Understanding on Domain Names', *InfoWorld*, 21(40), 28.

Ohashi, T.M., T.P. Roth, Z.A. Spindler, M.L. McMillan and K.H. Norrie (1980) *Privatization, Theory and Practice: Distributing Shares in Private and Public Enterprises*, Vancouver, BC: Fraser Institute.

Oster, C., Jr. and J. Strong (2000) 'Transport Restructuring and Reform in an International Context', *Transportation Journal*, 39(3), 18–32.

Pack, J. (1987) 'Privatization of Public Sector Services in Theory and Practice', *Journal of Policy Analysis and Management*, 6(4), 523–40.

Pack, J. (1989) 'Privatization and Cost Reduction', *Policy Sciences*, 22, 1–25.

Parker, D. (1999) 'The Performance of BAA Before and After Privatisation: A DEA Study', *Journal of Transport Economics and Policy*, 33(2), 133–45.

Peters, L. (1993) 'Non-Profit and For-Profit Electric Utilities in the United States: Pricing and Efficiency', *Annals of Public and Cooperative Economics*, 64, 575–604.

Pollitt, M. (1995) *Ownership and Performance in Electric Utilities: The International Evidence on Privatization and Efficiency*, New York: Oxford University Press.

Richards, J. and A. Vining (2001) 'Thinking about Infrastructure', in Aidan Vining and John Richards (eds), *Building the Future: Issues in Public Infrastructure in Canada*, Toronto: C.D. Howe Institute.

Rossi, M. (2001) 'Technical Change and Efficiency Measures: the Post-Privatization in the Gas Distribution Sector in Argentina', *Energy Economics*, 23(3), 295–304.

Rudnick, H. (1998) 'Competitive Markets in Electricity Supply: Assessment of the South American Experience', *Revista Abante*, 1(2), 189–211.

Ryan, W. (1999) 'The New Landscape for Nonprofits', *Harvard Business Review*, 77(1), 127–36.

Saal, D. and D. Parker (2000) 'The Impact of Privatization and Regulation on the Water and Sewerage Industry in England and Wales: A Translog Cost Function Model', *Managerial and Decision Economics*, 21(6), 253–68.

Sclar, E. (1997) *The Privatization of Public Service: Lessons from Case Studies*, Washington, DC: Economic Policy Institute.

Spiers, K.D. and J. Affleck-Graves (1999) 'The Long-run Performance of Stock Returns Following Debt Offerings', *Journal of Financial Economics*, 54, 45–73.

Stanbury, W. (1992) 'Privatization by Federal and Provincial Governments in Canada: An Empirical Analysis', paper delivered at 'The Down-Sized State' colloquium, 9–10 April, Montreal.

Task Force on Energy Policy (2001) 'Strategic Considerations for a New British Columbia Energy Policy', Interim Report of the Task Force, 30 November.

Trebilcock, M. (1999) 'Lurching Around Chicago: The Positive Challenge of Explaining the Recent Regulatory Reform Agenda', in Richard Bird, Michael Trebilcock and Thomas Wilson, 'Rationality in Public Policy: Retrospect and Prospect, A Tribute to Douglas G. Hartle', Canadian Tax Paper #104, Canadian Tax Foundation, Toronto.

Trebing, H. (2001) 'New Dimensions of Market Failure in Electricity and Natural Gas Supply', *Journal of Economic Issues*, 35(2), 395–403.

Truitt, L. and M. Esler (1996) 'Airport Privatization: Full Divestiture and Its Alternatives', *Policy Studies Journal*, 24(1), 100–10.

VanDoren, P. (1998) 'The Deregulation of the Electricity Industry: A Primer', Cato Institute, #320, 6 October.

Vergas, J. (2001) 'Why Governments Sell Public Firms: The Spanish Case', *International Advances in Economic Research*, 7(1), 114–32.

Vickers, J. and G. Yarrow (1988) *Privatization: An Economic Analysis*, Cambridge, MA: MIT Press.

Vining, A. (1981) 'The History, Nature, Role and Future of Provincial Hydro Utilities', in Bruce Doern and Alan Tupper (eds), *Crown Corporations and Public Policy in Canada*, Montreal: Institute for Research on Public Policy, pp.149–88.

Vining, A. and A. Boardman (1992) 'Ownership Versus Competition: Efficiency in Public Enterprise', *Public Choice*, 73(2), 205–39.

Vining, A.R. and R. Botterell (1983) 'An Overview of the Origins, Growth, Size and Functions of Provincial Crown Corporations' in Robert Pritchard (ed.), *Crown Corporations in Canada*, Toronto: Butterworths.

Vranich, J. and E.L. Hudgins (2001) 'Help Passenger Rail by Privatizing Amtrak', #419, 1 November, Cato Institute.

Wallsten, S. (2001) 'An Econometric Analysis of Telecom Competition, Privatization, and Regulation in Africa and Latin America', *The Journal of Industrial Economics*, 49(1), 1–19.

West, D. (1997) 'The Privatization of Liquor Retailing in Alberta', #5 in the Fraser Institute Series Public Policy Sources, The Fraser Institute, Vancouver.

West, D. (2000) 'Double Marginalization and Privatization in Liquor Retailing', *Review of Industrial Organization*, 16(4), 399–415.

Weyman-Jones, T. (2001) 'Yardstick and Incentive Issues in UK Electricity Distribution Price Controls', *Fiscal Studies*, 22(2), 233–47.

Whiteman, A., C.M. Hu, T. Marshella and S. Atkinson (1998) 'Implicit Government Pledges for Airport and Air Navigation System-Related Infrastructure Project Debt', *The Journal of Project Finance*, 4(1), 47–54.

Willner, J. (1996) 'A Comment on Bradburd: Privatisation of Natural Monopolies', *Review of Industrial Organization*, 11(6), 869–82.

Winston, C. (2000) 'Government Failure in Urban Transportation', *Fiscal Studies*, 21(4), 403–25.

Winston, C. and C. Shirley (1998) *Alternative Route: Toward Efficient Urban Transportation*, Washington, DC: Brookings Institution.

8 Privatization: the Australian experience

Graeme A. Hodge

Introduction

In this chapter some of the Australian experiences of privatization are reviewed. With a land mass a little below that of the United States of America, Australia has a population of around 20 million people concentrated mainly along the eastern coast. The national political system is based on the United Kingdom's Westminster tradition, but a federal system of government has been grafted onto it. Thus the federal government, based in Canberra, and several state governments and territories share power. This has left some privatization and regulation matters in the hands of the federal government, and some in the hands of the various states, each of which has adopted quite a different stance.

Australia has had an interesting record in the area of privatization from several perspectives. First, we might note that a wide range of ownership and regulatory structures have been employed in the past. The nation has enjoyed a large state-owned enterprise (SOE) sector, and while not ever forming part of any party platform for state socialism, public enterprise was largely created by deliberate action in the context of both market and private sector failures. Looking at the beginnings of several of the state-owned enterprises in Victoria is instructive. Being poorly run by private companies, the Melbourne Chamber of Commerce requested in the late nineteenth century that the government take over telephony services. Private coal mining operations also failed to provide the state's primary energy needs, with a Royal Commission in 1905 finding the cause to be the 'greed and short term horizons of its owners' (Russell, 1990:11). Likewise, statewide electricity provision failed under the early companies. The failure of market firms at this time is likely to have had several causes. The spread of markets over extensive geographical areas, the huge size of the task against the comparatively small firms operating, as well as poor management skills and thin availability of capital for much needed expansions, no doubt all contributed. Each of these would have provided a contrast to the strong community expectations for the provision of a comprehensive and effective infrastructure.

Historically, it is interesting to note that decisions to institute a widespread public enterprise sector were taken by conservative political parties in the main (Wettenhall, 1983). The result was that public ownership became a central feature of large portions of the energy and telecommunications sectors, some insurance and financial services, air, sea and land transport, as well as many other areas such as defence-related manufacturing.

Public enterprise in Australia was fortunately supported by charismatic managerial leaders such as Sir John Monash (who oversaw the creation of a vertically integrated coal mining and electricity generation and distribution system across Victoria) and 'the frequent application of great innovation and creativity', according to Russell (1990:3). Such developments were also aided by the statutory corporation as a preferred means of managing in preference to the Department of State, Board, Trust or Committee models in vogue elsewhere across the globe (Wettenhall, 1965; Russell, 1990).

Overall, it might be said that the Australian public enterprise machinery was large and well oiled, but that, rather than having ideology as a base, Australian public enterprise has been non-socialist in philosophy, being based primarily on pragmatism and a marriage of ideological reluctance and economic necessity, as Wettenhall (1983) puts it. It would also have to be added that both national and state governments throughout the twentieth century saw state-owned enterprise as a development stimulator and that this philosophy underpinned much public enterprise, ranging from traditional areas such as telecommunications and physical infrastructure through to examples such as the Commonwealth Oil Refinery and Amalgamated Wireless Australia (Wettenhall, 1965).

In terms of policy issues associated with the public–private divide, Australia's history is replete with debates throughout the twentieth century on the benefits and costs of using private contractors for public works, in comparison to a public labour force. One hundred years ago, Australia witnessed a well-developed practice of competitive contracting and tendering. Honed over several decades, this practice was interrupted by a Royal Commission in 1896 that found widespread malpractice in the contracting-out system, schedule rigging and inferior work. This led to the use by government of direct (in-house) labour forces. Subsequent decades saw periodic swings towards and away from the average in-house and external labour mix. In terms of history, therefore, we ought nowadays to regard Australia as simply being further along a path of 'well rehearsed argument' on the effectiveness, efficiency and probity of these two types of service production systems (McIntosh *et al.*, 1997:39).

A second point here is that Australian SOEs have, to a larger degree than appears to have been the case elsewhere, generally been both profitable and increasingly commercial in outlook.[1] Most of these SOEs had, throughout the 1970s and 1980s, gradually been subject to the disciplines and pressures of commercialization and the requirement to make business decisions through the establishment of corporate objectives and strategic planning.

Indeed, most Australian public enterprises had already moved away from the simple government department model, with, for example, the railways being established in government corporations almost one hundred years earlier (Wettenhall, 1965).

Throughout the past century many Australian public enterprises moved progressively along a path of greater independence and commercial viability. Federal government departments such as the postal service, for instance, were first restructured as a commission with an independent board, and then as a government corporation. Today, Australia Post continues its profitable operations in the midst of an increasingly competitive market, with the majority of its services now subject to competition. Delivering financial rates of return and reporting performance against corporate objectives and targets has generally produced significant improvements in productivity and financial viability in government enterprises. As well as the bulk of government utilities being profitable, they have also, in the main, been highly regarded by citizens.

Thus, while other countries such as the United Kingdom had swung between private ownership and nationalization of 'the commanding heights' of the economy, and back to private ownership, Australia appears to have taken a much more gradual line towards economic change.

By the mid-1980s to 1990s, though, Australia was increasingly turning to market solutions and private ownership ideas.[2] The Australian Federal Treasurer in the mid-1980s, Paul Keating, made one of the famous remarks of recent political history when he warned the country that if it did not adapt to global trends and reform its economy and its public sector, it risked becoming a 'banana republic'. From that time forward, state and federal governments in Australia took a more critical approach to existing public enterprise arrangements. The accepted paradigm for the past century of monopoly Australian public enterprise was challenged. The 1990s saw dramatic change, with Australia now amongst the OECD's most prolific privatizing countries. This is the third reason why Australia has had an interesting privatization record. Comparing enterprise sales in the OECD, the Reserve Bank of Australia (1997) put Australia's divestiture activities in the late 1990s as second on the basis of both gross sale proceeds (A\$61 bn at that time) and proceeds as a proportion of GDP. A more recent report by Mahboobi (2001) also ranked Australia third amongst OECD countries on the latter criterion, with estimated privatization sales for the decade at US\$62.39 bn.

There has also been considerable variation within Australia in terms of Commonwealth and state policies, with Victoria being by far the most willing privatizer. Indeed, accounting for the relative regional product against the state's revenues from divestitures probably awards the State of

Victoria top billing throughout the 1990s across the entire OECD. Added to Australia's divestitures have been some aggressive policies on the use of compulsory competitive tendering, contracting out and outsourcing for public sector services at both state and federal levels.

Australian governments at all levels, therefore, have been increasingly turning to a greater role for both market solutions and the private sector in delivering services. There has been an undeniable transformation from traditional administrative practices towards the contractualized state as part of the new public management ethos. Interestingly, Woodrow Wilson's early notion that politics (along with the development of policy) is separable from administration[3] (along with policy implementation) has underpinned these recent developments.

Divestiture experience
Australia's privatization revenues throughout the 1990s were around A$96.6bn, based on listings of divestitures from the Reserve Bank of Australia (1997) and Walker and Walker (2000), in addition to other recent information. These proceeds were derived almost equally from federal and state-level governments, with the primary sectors being electricity and gas, transport and communications, and financial services.

As confidence in privatization has grown, the more recent sales have also been larger than earlier sales. The largest single privatizations occurred at the federal level, with two initial public flotations of the telecommunications company, Telstra, raising A$30.33bn and taking private ownership of this company to 49.9 per cent, along with four progressive flotations of the now fully privatized Commonwealth Bank raising A$8.16bn. At the state level, Victoria's electricity sector sales raised A$22.55bn, whilst the sale of its gas distribution assets raised A$6.28bn.

In addition to the above mentioned sectors, it is also notable that divestitures included a large range of government business types. As well as traditional utilities and SOEs, divestitures also included businesses as diverse as the Commonwealth Serum Laboratories (providing anti-toxins, vaccines and blood products), business units from the Federal Department of Administrative Services (such as fleet cars and interior building services), entertainment ticket sales (Bass), timber plantations in Victoria and South Australia, a radio station (Radio 5AA) and healthcare linen services. A summary of these divestitures is shown in Table 8.1.

It is evident from this table that the bulk of divestitures around Australia have been undertaken through trade sales rather than public share flotations. Across the nation as a whole, trade sales outnumbered flotations by a factor of five to one, whilst in states such as South Australia, every divestiture transaction occurred through a trade sale. Australian governments

Table 8.1   *Summary of divestitures in Australia in the 1990s*

	Proceeds (A $mn)	Type of sale	Year(s) of sale
Commonwealth			
ADI	347	trade	99/00
Aerospace Technologies of Australia	40	trade	94/95
Airports (17)	4069	trades[1]	96/97–97/98
Auscript	1	staff buy-out	97/98
Aussat	504	trade	91/92
Australian Airlines	400	trade	92/93
Australian Industry Development Corp	225	trades	89/90, 97/98
Australian Multimedia Enterprises Ltd	29	trade	97/98
Australian National Railways Corp	95	trade	97/98
Commonwealth Bank	8157	flotations[2]	91/92–97/98
Commonwealth Funds Management	63	trade	96/97
Commonwealth Serum Laboratories (CSL)	299	flotation	93/94
Dept of Administrative Services (DAS) Business Units (7)	437	trade[3]	97/98
Housing Loans Insurance Corp	108	trade	97/98
Moomba–Sydney Pipeline System	534	trade	93/94
National Transmission Network (NTN)	650	trade	98/99
Qantas	2115	flotation	92/93
Removals Australia	10.4	trade	99/00
Shipping Businesses	21	trade	98/99
Snowy Mountains Engineering Corp	1.6	staff buy-outs	93/94–95/96
Telstra	30330	flotations[4]	97/98, 99/00
Total Commonwealth	*48436*		
New South Wales			
Axiom Funds Management	240	trade	96/97
Government Insurance Office	1260	floatation	92/93
NS Investment Corp	60	trade	89/90
NSW Grain Corp	96	trade	93/94
State Bank of NSW	527	trade	94/95
Tab Ltd	937	flotation	97/98
Total NSW	*3120*		
Victoria			
Aluvic	502	trade	98/99
Bass (Ticket Sales)	3	trade	94/95
Electricity Industry (14)	22546	trades[5]	92/93–98/99
Gas Distribution (4)	6277	trade[6]	98/99
GFE (Gas & Fuel Exploration) Resources	56	trade	95/96

Table 8.1 (continued)

	Proceeds (A $mn)	Type of sale	Year(s) of sale
Grain Elevators Board	52	trade	94/95
Heatane Division of Gas & Fuel Corp	130	trade	92/93
Portland Smelter Unit Trust	171	trade	92/93
Ports: Geelong, Portland	81	trades	95/96
State Insurance Office	125	trade	92/93
Tabcorp	609	flotation	94/95
Victorian Plantations Corp	550	trade	98/99
V/Line Freight Corp	163	trade	95/96
Total Victoria	*31265*		
Queensland			
Bank Of Queensland	129	flotation	99/00
Gladstone Power Station	750	trade	93/94
State Gas Pipieline	163	trade	96/97
Suncorp/Metway Ltd	1621	flotation	98/99
Suncorp/Qld Industry Development Corp	698	trade	96/97
TabQ	267	flotation	99/00
Total Queensland	*3628*		
South Australia			
Austrust Trustees	44	trade	94/95
Enterprise Investments	38	trade	94/95
ETSA Power and Power Utilities	3815	trade[7]	99/00
Forwood Products (Timber)	123	trade	95/96
Island Seaway	2	trade	94/95
Pipeline Authority of SA	304	trade	94/95
Port Bulk Handling Facilities	18	trade	97/98
Radio 5AA	8	trade	96/97
SA Financing Trust	5	trade	93/94
SAGASCO	446	trades	92/93, 93/94
Samcor (Meatworks)	5	trade	96/97
Sign Services	0.2	trade	95/96
State Bank of South Australia	730	trades	94/95, 95/96
State Chemistry Laboratories	0.3	trade	95/96
State Clothing Corp	1.4	trade	95/96
State Government Insurance Commission	175	trade	95/96
Total South Australia	*5715*		
Western Australia			
AlintaGas	971	flotation/trade	99/00, 00/01
Bankwest	900	trade	95/96

Table 8.1 (continued)

	Proceeds (A $mn)	Type of sale	Year(s) of sale
Dampier-Bunbury Natural Gas Pipeline	2303	trade	97/98
Healthcare Linen	9	trade	96/97
State Government Insurance Office	165	flotation	93/94
Total Western Australia	*4348*		
Tasmania			
State Insurance Office	42	trade	93/94
Total state governments	*48118*		
Total all governments	*96554*		

Notes:
1. Airports included Adelaide, Alice Springs, Archerfield, Avalon/Geelong, Brisbane, Canberra, Coolangatta, Darwin, Jandakot, Launceston, Melbourne, Moorabin, Mt Isa, Townsville, Perth.
2. Four Commonwealth Bank flotations occurred with proceeds ranging from A$1.31bn to A$3.39bn.
3. DAS Business Units included Asset Services, Australian Operational Support Services, Australian PropertyGroup, Centre for Environmental Management, DAS Distribution, DASFleet, Interiors Australia and Works Australia.
4. Two Telstra floatations occurred, with the first (33 per cent) raising A$14.33bn and the second (17 per cent) raising A$16.0bn.
5. Electricity Industry sales included Citipower, Eastern Energy, Hazelwood/Energy Brix, Hume, Loy Yang A, Loy Yang B, Powercor, PowerNet, Solaris, Southern Hydro, United Energy, Victorian Electricity Metering, Victorian Network Switching Centre and Yallourn Energy. The bulk of these divestitures occurred between 1995/96 and 1997/98.
6. Gas sales included Westar/Kinetic, Multinet/Ikon, Stratus/Energy 21 and Transmission Pipelines Australia.
7. ETSA and power utilities were not sold, but transferred to the private sector on a 200-year lease. Optima Energy (A$315mn) was also leased, for 100 years.

Source: Walker and Walker (2000: 20–24), Reserve Bank of Australia (1997), supplemented by additional information.

tended, therefore, to stay away from public share flotations as the major divestiture mechanism following the UK experience of these as a poor revenue-raising technique. Notable exceptions to this general trend, however, included the Commonwealth Bank and Telstra public flotations at the federal level, as well as public flotations for state gambling agencies and government insurance offices in some states. Interestingly, although the number of transactions undertaken by public flotations was small, these few public flotations were so large that they formed almost 80 per cent of the federal divestiture revenues. A small number of employee buy-outs were also adopted for a few federal agency divestitures.

A range of stated political aims were put forward for these privatizations. Desirable reductions of public debt, the potential for improved efficiency and the creation of shareholding citizenry were all nominated at various stages by different governments. In a few cases, including the state banks of Victoria and South Australia, government enterprises were sold in distress following spectacularly poor financial performance.[4] These however, were by far the exception rather than the rule. From a policy perspective, various analytical frameworks grounded in public choice economics and managerialism were also behind these sales, in common with international experience (Hodge, 2000).

The proceeds from the Australian privatizations have mostly been used by governments to reduce debt levels. The Reserve Bank of Australia (1997) reports that the net debt outstanding for state governments as a whole reduced by over one-third, from A$76 bn in 1993 to A$47 bn in 1997. States such as Victoria in particular made much political capital out of the rationale of debt reduction to justify the privatization programme, as well as claiming success following the restoration of the State's AAA credit rating as a consequence of reduced debt levels. Divestiture proceeds at the Commonwealth level have resulted in a capacity to contain debt growth in recent years.

The establishment by the federal government of a fund of about A$1 bn to finance environmental initiatives was a major exception to the trend of public debt reduction. The earmarking of these funds was agreed as part of the political manoeuvring behind the partial privatization decision for Telstra. In terms of share ownership, the proportion of adults directly owning shares has more than doubled over the decade, with around 25 per cent of adults directly holding shares by 1997.

Having said all this, it is important to reflect that large slices of state-owned enterprise sectors still remain in public hands in several Australian states. For instance, whilst electricity provision in Victoria is now effectively entirely privately based, the adjacent State of New South Wales continues to favour its electricity being provided by a wholly government-owned electricity sector. Likewise, whilst public transport in Victoria now operates under a series of private franchises, public transport across most other states has remained in public hands.

Privatization, regulation and competition landmarks
The divestitures noted above occurred within a broader context of strong competition and regulatory reforms. The biggest regulatory landmark in Australia through the 1980s was the deregulation of banking and financial services announced by the Hawke government in the middle of the decade. The opening up of the banking sector to foreign competition stood as a

clear warning to all industries, including SOEs, that protected environments with little real competition were increasingly becoming relics of the past. Even so, it is fair to say that early privatizations, such as the flotations of the public airlines Qantas and TAA (Australian Air), did not really take seriously the issues of competition and regulation, probably because of the domestic duopoly existing in this sector and strong competition in the international market. When it came, Qantas's privatization, as Walker (1998:2) put it, 'attracted a good price, created no substantial consumer benefit and had no marked political repercussions – other than to further blur the electorate's differentiation of the two major political parties'. For Qantas, as well as for other services which existed in competitive markets, 'government ownership some time ago ceased to make sense . . . they were simply sold into competitive markets by governments of both persuasions when political circumstances provided an opportunity' (ibid.). A quantum change in attitudes towards competition was about to occur, however, through the arrival of national competition policy in the 1990s.

The Commonwealth and all state and territory governments of Australia signed a National Competition Policy Agreement in 1995. This agreement[5] aimed to increase the competitiveness of government businesses by removing unnecessary restrictions to competition, and placed SOEs on the same financial footing as private sector businesses. Broadly, it aimed for 'competitive neutrality' between all providers within a market for services – whether public or private – and was a significant Federal Labor government initiative.

SOEs therefore became largely subject to the same regulatory regime as private sector entities, with the 'shield of the crown' being removed (Macmillan, 1998). The principal thrusts of this agreement related to pricing oversight, business practices, competitive neutrality and issues of market access. Under national competition policy, for instance, SOEs became subject to state-appointed regulators that could overview prices of essential services and the National Competition Council. SOEs were also included within the scope of the Trade Practices Act, with the consequence that they came under the surveillance of the Australian Competition and Consumer Commission. The philosophy of competitive neutrality specified that, where an SOE was in competition or had the potential to be in competition with a private sector business, it must be subject to the same regulation, pay equivalent taxes and pay for any debt guarantees provided by governments. Lastly, national competition policy specified that SOEs might be required to share their infrastructure where they enjoyed a monopoly in areas such as telecommunications or rail services, for instance.

The Australian Competition and Consumer Commission (ACCC) was formed in late 1995 out of the former Trade Practices Commission. An independent statutory authority, it administers the Trade Practices Act

1983, now applying to all businesses whether public or private. Thus anti-competitive and unfair market practices can now be penalized and product safety/liability and third party access to facilities of national significance can now be comprehensively enforced.[6] Both the powers of the ACCC and the authority's willingness to act to ensure that actions are not taken that could substantially lessen competition, even on the international stage, are well known in Australia.

In return for state governments progressively reviewing all legislation and opening up areas of government service provision to competition, a series of 'competition payments' were made by the federal government. Different states, as one might expect, took to these competition requirements with varying degrees of enthusiasm. Victoria pursued competition in public sector services more aggressively than other states. There, the response was wide-ranging, and varied from opening up a majority of local government services to external competition, as noted previously,[7] to reviewing the legislation underpinning the provision of ambulance and emergency services, as well as restructuring and putting out to competitive tender many of the services of the state's auditor general.[8]

Two Australian case studies
The divestiture of the electricity sector in Victoria provides a good example of privatization in Australia, and also indicates the manner in which government services are evolving in essential services. In this section, we look at this from both a national and a state-level perspective. A brief outline of the privatization of telecommunications is also provided.

National electricity market
Traditionally, the Australian electricity supply industry has developed on a state-by-state basis. This has typically resulted in each state being dominated by a vertically integrated, publicly owned monopoly utility. Some electricity trade between jurisdictions has occurred, but this has been at the margin, rather than being a central driver for reforms and economic efficiencies (OECD, 1997). Historically, the strongest influences on centrally controlled capital investment decisions in the industry have had a political basis, with ministers acting on the advice of engineering-dominated SOE bureaucracies. The culture of these decisions was steeped in years of political sensitivity to the possibility of energy blackouts and the longer-term historical need for complete self-reliance for each state jurisdiction. Independence, rather than notions of an interconnected electricity grid or of competitive markets, drove planning and operations. A 1991 study by the federal government's Industry Commission into Australia's electricity supply industry changed this, and a cooperative relationship between the

federal and state governments was subsequently formed. All governments agreed to work towards a national market for electricity covering southern and eastern Australia. The Industry Commission argued that competition should be promoted in the industry and that interconnections between states should be improved. They also recommended that transmission, generation and distribution be separated and that the separate utilities ought to be corporatized (Industry Commission, 1991).

The overall thrust of these recommendations, therefore, was to break up single vertically integrated monopolies into generation, transmission, distribution and retailing components, within a national electricity market. Each of the states tackled these recommendations in different ways. Nevertheless, the result today is that the Australian electricity industry has been dramatically restructured. Most state-owned vertically integrated organizations have been broken up. Competing generation and retailing entities have been formed, and regulated transmission and distribution entities have developed (Roarty, 1998). All entities have been corporatized and, in Victoria and South Australia, privatized. The national electricity market began operating in Australia in December 1998. At present, South Australia, Victoria, New South Wales, Queensland and the Australian Capital Territory are included.

The national market is governed by an Electricity Code of Conduct that operates under a mix of state and federal legislation. As Australia's submission in OECD (1997:11) puts it:

> market behaviour will be subject to the broader 'light handed' market conduct oversight of national competition law as administered by the ACCC, whilst customer franchise pricing, environment, and health and safety matters will remain state-based responsibilities. Market operations (network connection and access, market rules and operation, and systems security) will be covered by an enforceable Code of conduct which establishes the uniform rules, procedures and regulations which will underwrite the market. The Code also sets out network pricing principles for network owners, although jurisdictions will be responsible for regulation of network prices.

Under this arrangement there are two markets for competitive electricity – a wholesale market and a retail market. Large generators (over 30 MW) must trade through the wholesale market. Trading is undertaken through bilateral contracts, short-term forward trading and spot market trading. Further details of these types of contracts are available in OECD (1997). The introduction of the national electricity market was staged, with the early harmonization of state market rules and removal of artificial limitations across boundaries being followed by full operation of the Code under the auspices of the ACCC.

This national progression towards a combined electricity market reflected the increasingly important political acknowledgment that both structures and attitudes to coordinated and competitive production arrangements were overdue in electricity. It also established a supportive environment as the backdrop to Victoria's more radical industry restructuring.

Victoria's electricity industry restructuring
We noted above that the Victorian government was the most aggressive in restructuring its SOEs. How did the restructuring of electricity proceed? In 1993 the former State Electricity Commission of Victoria (SECV), a monopoly structure, was divided into three separate interim organizations for generation, transmission and distribution. Following this, further disaggregation occurred.

The interim generation business (Generation Victoria) was divided into five separate businesses in 1995 and generators commenced bidding independently into the Victorian wholesale electricity market for the right to supply electricity. A 'pool' arrangement provided the mechanism for this trading. The interim transmission organization (National Electricity) was further divided up into a wires business (Powernet Victoria) and a trading business (Victorian Power Exchange). The electricity pool for trading was managed by the Victorian Power Exchange when first introduced, but this function was later largely transferred to the National Electricity Market Management Company (NEMMCO). The interim distribution organization (Electricity Services Victoria) was disaggregated into five distribution businesses, including two rural businesses. Each of these businesses operates as a 'ring-fenced' distribution monopoly and a competitive energy retailer.[9] Distribution businesses must by law provide open access to their grid to any retailer and/or large non-franchise customer. These arrangements are shown in Figure 8.1.

Although the Victorian government has described the regulatory regime established as 'light handed', this is misleading. In reality, the regime introduced is quite sophisticated, rather than being simply a 'hands-off' approach to regulation. The legislative base for these reforms included national legislation such as National Electricity Law, Corporations Law and the Trade Practices Act. It also included a range of key Victorian state legislation and regulatory instruments, including the Office of the Regulator General Act, the Electricity Industry Act, regulations and orders in Council made pursuant to these Acts, as well as Licences, Codes and Pool Rules. Moreover, statements, determinations and guidelines have been issued by the Office of the Regulator General. The regulatory framework operating is shown in Figure 8.2.

Broadly, therefore, the industry operates under national and state law pertaining specifically to the electricity industry, and under the general Federal Corporations Law and the Trade Practices Act. Corporate misbe-

Generation

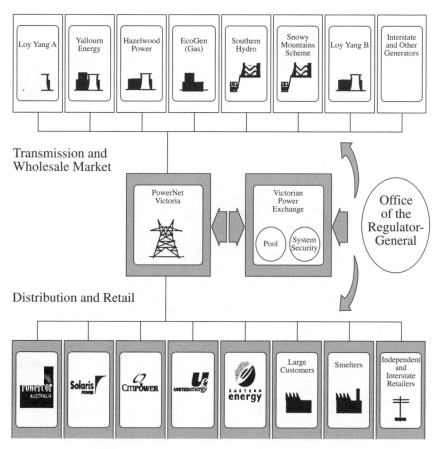

Source: Department of Treasury and Finance (1997:4).

Figure 8.1 Australia: the Victorian electricity supply industry following privatization

haviour such as misleading conduct or price fixing would therefore come under this umbrella. Moreover, the Office of the Regulator General (ORG) has been established as an independent regulator which issues licences for operations within the electricity industry, ensures that the code is maintained and publishes reports on service standards and performance (Department of Treasury and Finance, 1997). Cross-ownership restrictions also exist to limit common ownership of distributors and generators.

The Victorian government created a market for electricity generation

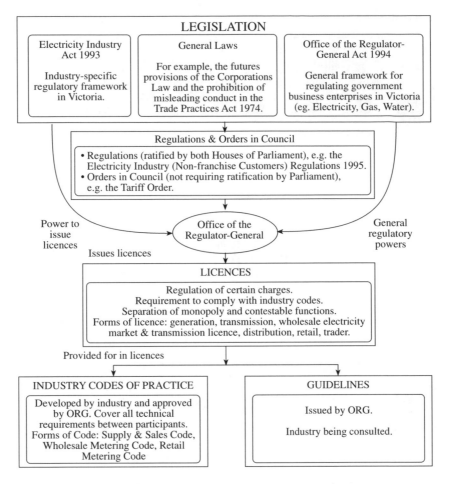

Source: Department of Treasury and Finance (1997:46).

*Figure 8.2   Australia: regulatory framework for the Victorian electricity
            supply industry*

and distribution but tariffs for the sale of electricity to customers are still
capped through the state's 'Tariff Order'. The Tariff Order regulates prices
according to a 'CPI – X' formula, with the Regulator General setting X at
around 1 per cent to 2 per cent for domestic users over the recent past, and
between 1 per cent and 10 per cent for businesses.

   The planning for these radical reforms was undertaken by the specialist
private consultants, Troughton Swier, whose earlier experience had been in
telecommunications in the UK and in the restructuring of the New Zealand

Electricity Industry. From a public policy perspective, one of the most interesting aspects of this reform was the multi-million dollar success fee negotiated between the government and the consultants, based on the sale price of the enterprises, and the intense secrecy which accompanied contractual and policy negotiations.

From a political perspective, as well, these reforms were interesting. Victoria was unique in that the treasurer, Alan Stockdale, had taken an unusually strong personal interest in the intricacies of establishing competitive markets in electricity, including personal visits to international schools of business and economics to research such matters. This personal interest in the analytical and financial economics of industry restructuring did not necessarily augur well for the dynamics of Australian politics. Earlier public figures had staked their political careers on such expertise but had subsequently lost ministerial positions rather than succeeded.[10] No doubt the strong political leadership and the ultimate trust put in the Victorian treasurer by Premier Kennett were instrumental here. So was the strong majority held by Kennett's party in both houses of the Victorian Parliament during the reform process.

This having been said, the complete restructuring and privatization of electricity in Victoria was a risky political gamble. 'In political terms, this was the highest risk strategy that could have been devised', according to Walker (1998: 3), who followed the intricacies of the government's privatization programme throughout the 1990s. As well as attracting the opposition of interest groups, the Churches and the Business Council, it even attracted the doubt of Professor Fred Hilmer, the noted architect of Australia's competition reforms.

Telecommunications in Australia
The privatization and regulation of Australia's major telecommunications company Telstra (previously Telecom), followed quite a different path to the restructuring and sales within the Victorian electricity supply industry. Dominated by what might be termed more traditional democratic policy dynamics, the policy decision to privatize Telstra rested on a parliamentary knife-edge. To begin with, Prime Minister Howard, who had been badly buffeted a decade earlier by his unpopular promise to sell off Telecom, offered a much more easy to digest option in 1996. He promised that no more than one-third of the telecommunications giant would be privatized in his first term. Furthermore, he anticipated the Opposition's easiest political line of attack, also promising that he would 'not break up Telstra the way Kennett and Stockdale had broken up the SECV' (ibid.: 5). This was perhaps a remarkable public admission of the political exposure that the federal members of Australia's conservative party, the Liberal Party, had

felt during the privatizations being undertaken by its Liberal Party brothers in Victoria. After months of negotiations, the Bill privatizing Telstra passed, by just one vote, in the Upper House of the Federal Parliament. With the Telstra sell-off announced, Prime Minister Howard said little about the shape of the telecommunications regulation to come.

The initial one-third Telstra share flotation was deemed by both investors and the government to be hugely successful when it occurred in 1997/98. In large part this was because share prices rose strongly in the period following the flotation, in much the same way as UK privatization shares often rose during the 1980s. No doubt Telstra's market dominance would also have played an influential role here. The second Telstra tranche, taking the private ownership of Telstra up to 49.9 per cent, was not so well regarded by investors, who saw their shares immediately decline in value. More importantly from a public policy perspective, a critical observation was that the Telstra regulatory challenge remained significant throughout both share flotations, with a lack of a clear response continuing up to the present time.

So how did Australia deal with the need to restructure the former monopoly to ensure efficiency and competition, resolve access pricing issues and develop market conduct rules to prevent anti-competitive behaviour?

The government had previously lifted restrictions on new entrants to the telecommunications market before Telstra's initial floatation. This resulted in gains for consumers in the form of price reductions for telephone services. Some services, such as local calls, were still subject to significant price regulation, whilst other services in more competitive arenas were not. Private ownership was now on the way, albeit progressively. It appeared that the government had applied the correct regulatory formulae – at least in traditional terms. In addition to this, the additional competitive safeguards taken in Australia were primarily based on the application of the Trade Practices Act. This was potentially a strong pressure, since it provided the threat of a A$10 mn dollar fine with an additional A$1 mn dollars per day for continuing breaches of the Act. In practice, though, its effectiveness appears to have been far from perfect. Disputes between the ex-monopolist and new entrants have been commonplace and have often involved litigation. It has proved to be a rather slow and arduous legal remedy, and one criticized by new competitors in the industry as being ineffectual (Suckling, 1999).

In essence, then, Telstra was not disaggregated from its previous vertically integrated structure, an approach quite different to the far stronger regulatory approaches adopted in the electricity and gas industries in Victoria. This may well have enabled Telstra to use its control over the local network to its own advantage.[11]

Performance after privatization

There has been no comprehensive evaluation of the performance of Australia's privatization programme thus far. Nevertheless, it is possible to get some clues on corporate performance and public benefits from those few that have been undertaken. In this section we briefly review the privatization evidence available to date and comment on the findings.

There has been the usual policy proselytizing and praise on the one hand and severe criticism on the other. This has been a feature of privatizations around the world. Examples of these include Victorian commentators Davidson (2001), who called the state's transport privatization a 'failed experiment' and Crosweller (2002), who quoted a newly elected minister describing privatized prisons[12] and hospitals as 'time bombs' and describing privatized electricity provision simply as 'dreadful planning, and dreadful structure'. At the other extreme have been influential reformers such as Porter (2002), who saw privatization as bringing substantial economic and financial benefits to Victoria and leaving a 'permanent and hugely beneficial legacy', and commentators such as Bartholomeusz (2002), who viewed the electricity reform programme as 'astonishingly successful privatization (in terms of the prices paid)', and Crosweller (2002), who quotes one Victorian advocate as saying that 'by any criteria, electricity is miles better under privatization'.

The research is less colourful. Despite showing mixed performance, it suggests that, although Australia has not experienced perfect divestitures, its performance has probably been better than earlier privatizations elsewhere around the globe. Given the importance of the Victorian electricity and federal telecommunications sell-offs, we will first look at the performance of these privatizations. Comments will then be made on some of the remaining research studies of Australian divestitures.

Victorian electricity reforms

Victoria's electricity privatizations have been a remarkable success, at least in terms of the political achievements which have been made in the name of consumers and taxpayers. This has been despite the criticisms, risks and concerns expressed throughout the reform period. The appointed Regulator General has provided professional and independent monitoring in support of the consumers' interests and has certainly acted, when appropriate, as a strong and fiercely independent force for consumers throughout occasional public debates.[13] Publicly available data from the Victorian Office of the Regulator General also continue to show good annual performance characteristics for electricity services in terms of reliability, affordability and customer service, as well as profitability for the distribution businesses. In political terms, the Kennett government also successfully defended its large majority in both houses of parliament in the state election of mid-1996 following the electricity sector privatizations. In addition, it achieved its stated aim of returning the state to its former 'AAA' rating with international credit rating agencies.

Research undertaken on service quality changes since privatization support these general contentions. Compared to the previous government monopoly operating in 1993/94, there was a general decline in the total length of time customers have spent 'off-supply' (from around 260 to 157 minutes per annum).[14] This result, though, needs to be qualified as, within this figure, there has also been an increase in the unplanned minutes off supply. Such unplanned outages probably have a greater impact on customers, since they are given notice of the planned interruption and can take mitigating action. Furthermore, knowing that the number of 'minutes off-supply' is made up of the product of both the interruption frequency and the interruption duration, these two variables also need examination. Here it is evident that the trend has been for more frequent interruptions but each of less duration since the transfer from government operation.

The affordability of electricity in Victoria generally improved compared to price levels prior to privatization, with a 14 per cent reduction in actual retail prices comparing 1994 'before' privatization prices to 1998 'after' prices. This was made up of a 7 per cent fall due to CPI-X regulatory price controls and a further 7 per cent reduction through government subsidy, termed a 'A$60 Winter Power Bonus'. We might note that this domestic price reduction was regulated, with domestic supply prices still being subject to legislation. Furthermore, this price reduction was measured against a point immediately after a price increase of 10 per cent was introduced by the government shortly after its election in 1992. Price reductions also occurred in the case of large industrial and business customers with an average saving of 10 per cent of costs[15] since 1994 being reported.

The number of residential customers disconnected for non-payment has fallen by around two-thirds since 1995, and business disconnections have halved over this time. Both of these performance results are impressive. These results are not without their complications, however, with Romeril (1997), for instance, arguing that disconnection figures for the state-owned monopoly as at 1994 are an inappropriate benchmark. Romeril points out that these 1994 figures were around 75 per cent higher than those of the state facility two years previously, and that, in the lead-up to 1994, credit management was tightened, electricity supply charges in Victoria were increased by 10 per cent and the state monopoly was broken up into three vertically disaggregated businesses. In other words, Romeril argues that disconnections post-restructuring and privatization are reducing, but from a base which was artificially high owing to the restructured supply arrangements. Additionally, these disconnection reductions since privatization have been largely due to regulation, not competition.

Surveys from the Electricity Supply Association of Australia discuss how Victoria's system compares with other state systems. Interestingly, government critics[16] argue that the price of power in Victoria relative to other Australian states has increased since restructuring. Furthermore, the number of supply interruptions per customer is claimed to be the highest of any Australian state. Clearly, there is a need for more independent research in this area to clarify the extent to which changes in service prices and quality have indeed occurred and the extent to which these can be directly linked back to the government's industry restructuring.

Since 1995, customer service levels have been of mixed quality, with 'customer appointment' service levels, 'supply connection timeliness' and 'street lights fixed on time' all being monitored for each of the retail businesses. Few data are published to compare such post-privatization service levels to previous performance under the state-owned utility. The greater effort now being put into monitoring a wide range of electricity services is, itself, one important indicator of the community's increased expectations of utility services following privatization.

Politically, earlier successes of the reformist Kennett government were not repeated at the 1999 state polls, with the government being defeated. The role of privatization *per se* was perhaps not a key reason for this loss, but the privatization policy was a symptom of the government's overall reform approach that was rejected. Its privatization reforms, along with a host of others, seemed to be 'city centric' and more oriented to business and commercial ends than to citizens. It is likely that the 1999 poll loss was due to the disenfranchisement of rural and regional voters. From this perspective, some of the criticisms of privatization take on a new and revealing light. Usher (1997) reports that 'ghost towns' were one regional outcome of privatizations, and that, where once thriving communities underpinned an electricity industry with 10000 workers having secure jobs, these had been replaced by only 1700 workers having jobs, and jobs that are no longer secure. Victoria's privatization programme had, to this critic, resulted in the decimation of regional towns and communities and had resulted in a resounding rebuff for privatization proponents in states such as New South Wales.

The future of the Australian electricity industry will continue to be interesting given that Victoria and South Australia have been the only two states to embrace privatization. Major differences in ownership of electricity systems now exist. Added to this is the incomplete nature of the national network for transmission and the need for significant improvements to enable an effective national network to function. Most interesting of all will be the effects of the recently introduced full retail competition in both

Victoria and New South Wales, which enables domestic customers to choose their electricity supplier. This has been introduced as a further step towards complete deregulation; but domestic electricity prices are still being regulated and full price deregulation is not expected for another year.

Although the Victorian electricity market is not perfect, it has certainly performed better to date than that of California because of the use of hedging contracts on future price movements and because of fewer environmental constraints on future generation growth. There is also no doubt at all that the biggest losers from Victoria's electricity restructuring were international investors, having bought the electricity assets at hugely inflated prices. In judging the absolute effectiveness of Victoria's electricity privatizations for citizens and consumers, though, the jury is still out.

Telstra

Telstra was not disaggregated from its vertically integrated structure, and this may well have provided the company with an important economic advantage. The legislation specified that Telstra must provide access to essential facilities on 'fair and reasonable terms', and that it must not abuse its market power. In practice, though, Telstra's relevant cost data have been slow in coming. Despite being aware of overseas lessons in regulation, Australian regulators appear to have struggled to put in place regulation strong enough to be fair to the incumbent (Telstra) and, importantly, regulation which is also seen to be fair by new competitors (Suckling, 1999). Telstra's control over the local telephone lines remains an important barrier to competition.

Even with Australia favouring improved competition in telecoms, regulators have had only partial success in dealing with the three central regulatory questions of vertical structure, interconnection prices and market conduct rules. These observations suggest that, whilst significant consumer benefits have certainly been achieved through the privatization of Telstra in terms of price reductions for calls,[17] the optimal regulatory prescription to promote has taken some time to evolve. In this regard, the recent announcement by government of its impatience with Telstra's tactics of delaying access to potential rivals in the high-speed internet or broadband market and the government's action to call in the ACCC for advice have been welcomed by most observers (for example, Henderson, 2002).

The completion of Telstra's privatization has remained a sensitive political issue, with the re-elected Liberal/National Party coalition having gone to the last polls amid claims of Telstra reducing service quality in the bush. As a result, the Howard government put forward a populist policy platform guaranteeing no further state sale of Telstra shares in the next government term. It was promptly re-elected.

The overall lesson from the Telstra privatization seems clear: there is a need for both care and caution when approaching the development of regulatory and competition infrastructure during the privatization process.

Other comments on the performance of privatization
In terms of the integrity of sales and the achievement of reasonable value for money, there is no doubt that Australia had been able to learn lessons from the earlier Thatcher sales programme in the UK. Kennett's Victorian divestiture programme opted for trade sales, and put in place a strong regulatory regime (Woodward, 1999). Importantly too, the international buyers paid around double the original value for the assets, although this was clearly too much. At the same time, some enterprises were sold below their value and transactions were sometimes flawed. Examples here include Energy Brix, cited by Woodward as being sold at A$20mn below its reported value, the secret sale of the A$182mn SECV Herman Research Laboratories to a high-profile businessman, and the unusual and quiet sale of A.H.Plant, with government staff involved in both buying and selling! A further dubious deal was the A$30mn consultancy advice contract on electricity privatization awarded without competitive selection (Russell *et al.*, 2000). Though a stain on the overall divestiture programme, these transactions represented only a small fraction of the overall state sale proceeds.[18] In the main, Victoria's divestitures, and more generally Australia's divestitures, were remarkably clean. On the broader matter of net overall community welfare resulting from these divestitures, there has been only a limited number of academic evaluations undertaken to date. These have most often been critical. Walker and Walker (2000), for instance, compare share prices at the end of 1999 with share prices at sale and suggest that a wealth transfer from public to private hands to the tune of around A$48bn occurred through the 1990s. While overstating the case, they are nonetheless correct that the initial share flotation for Telstra involved a huge wealth transfer to the private sector. They are also right in reflecting the general public disquiet surrounding the gaps between the high-sounding political promises made and the more modest achievements in terms of improved services to citizens following divestitures.

Other elements of Australia's privatization programmes have seen limited analysis. For instance, the logic of the early Victorian TAB flotation has been questioned by Collyer *et al.* (2001). The stated objective of this flotation was financial – to save payments on the public debt. Collyer *et al.*, though, point to figures suggesting that, whilst interest repayments on public debt of around A$77mn per year were indeed avoided, the state was also to forgo dividends after the sale of some A$110mn per annum. In a similar vein, Quiggin (1999), a staunch privatization critic, estimates that, for the first Telstra sale tranche, interest savings compared to the value forgone by the public as a result of the sale resulted in a net loss of A$400mn for the year 1997/98.

Another case subject to detailed scrutiny has been the early sale of CSL. This was seen by asset management firms as 'the best of the (Australian) privatizations by a stretch' (reported in Hughes, 1998), whilst the controversial sale itself was subject to no fewer than five separate inquiries and critiques. The main economic critique concluded simply that the CSL sale had been 'a fiscal scandal', and raised some larger questions 'about public accountability and the extent to which the Commonwealth Public Service can be relied upon to protect the interests of the public'.[19] Ideological fervour, as observed in the UK, has evidently been present to a degree in Australian privatizations too.

Not all the evidence has been one way, however. Harris and Lye (2001:315), in an analysis of revenues from a sample of five federal and four state divestitures between 1989 and 1997, suggest that the extent of underpricing varied, but that it was 'much less than experienced in other countries including the UK' (ibid.:319). Their analysis points to both gains and losses to the public sector, but with 'some overall net loss'. This was not quantified. Likewise, Quiggin (1999) also reports that for a sample of five electricity sales and three airports, privatizations as a whole were fiscally neutral or modestly beneficial, under the assumption that the discount rate is around that prevailing in the private sector.

This sparse information suggests that, whilst divestiture transactions may have been a short-term boon for the stockmarket and for privatization advisors and consultants, the overall net social welfare benefits from Australia's privatization programme have probably been, at best, modest.

Conclusions

This chapter has presented privatization and regulation experiences from Australia. Australia has undergone a sea change from public to private ownership, having been one of the OECD's biggest privatizers throughout the 1990s. The bulk of these transactions were trade sales, although the few public flotations undertaken were large in terms of sale proceeds. It is concluded that, in the case of the Victorian electricity supply restructuring, privatization and regulation to date, reforms appear to have been both a political and an economic success, though benefits to electricity consumers appear modest. In the case of the initial part divestiture of Telstra, the government has successfully floated a minority stake in the company, with citizens subsequently seeing reduced prices and stronger competition. In other privatization cases, the results appear to have been more mixed.

Whilst it has certainly been possible to restructure completely the ownership and operation of an entire sector such as electricity, significant care has been needed to achieve consumer benefits through strong and independent regulatory frameworks. It can also be concluded, on the basis of the little available independent research to date, that the divestitures have been generally well implemented, resulting in reasonable value for money for taxpayers and modest public welfare gains in some cases. Overall, it is concluded that, although Australia's divestitures have not been perfect, the performance has probably been better than for many earlier privatizations around the globe.

Notes

1. Examples of sectors privatized after a full decade of profitability have included, for instance, electricity provision in Victoria and the national telecommunications sector (aside from 1987/88 when a major change to accounting policies occurred). Enterprises privatized after profitability have included the Commonwealth Bank (where a full decade of profitability occurred) and Qantas (which returned profits in the nine years prior to its sale).
2. Australia's incremental approach to embracing privatization policies was quite different to the New Zealand experience. Their awakening stemmed from far more pragmatic pressures. Between 1974 and 1984, the New Zealand net public debt increased from 5 per cent to 32 per cent of GDP, with a sliding credit rating and living standard in world terms. A snap election in mid-1984 resulted in the possibility of a change of government and a change in the currency exchange rate. This caused such a massive outflow of capital that the Reserve Bank of New Zealand devalued the NZ dollar by 20 per cent. With this widely regarded as a crisis of confidence, the New Zealand government set about a comprehensive and speedy three-phase reform programme of commercialization and corporatization, deregulation of the financial and administrative environments and privatization (Mascarenhas, 1991; DeVries *et al.*, 1998). The final privatization phase, between 1987 and 1990, under Labor, marked the end of this reformation, which was undertaken in a decade, in contrast to the Australian experience.
3. See Hughes (1998) for more details of this idea.
4. The spectacularly poor performance of both of these state banks followed a century and a half of successful management under state ownership. In both cases, the banks were put under the 'aggressive and entrepreneurial' leadership of former private sector executives, who took the banks out of their traditional role of 'the people's bank for home finance' into the realms of commercial lenders to entrepreneurs (Collyer *et al.*, 2001:42). These entrepreneurs included characters such as Christopher Skase, Alan Bond and Allan Hawkins – all of whom have since become globally renowned as failed or jailed tycoons (Sykes, 1996). Importantly, privatization in both cases provided ammunition for governments eager to frame these failures as 'public' disasters as well as a source of much needed revenues for state coffers now required to better manage resulting state debts. In the words of Collyer *et al.* (2001:37), these two cases 'had an enormous impact on how politicians, officials and the public came to think about public enterprise and privatisation over the next decade'.
5. This followed the recommendations of the Hilmer report (Hilmer *et al.*, 1993).
6. A recent clear example of the role of the ACCC has been the legal proceedings begun by the Commission against Qantas, alleging use of Qantas's market power against its smaller rival Virgin Blue on one particular travel route in Queensland (Macfarlane *et al.*, 2002).
7. In Victoria, the Kennett government adopted a compulsory competitive tendering policy for all local government services with a requirement that 50 per cent of turnover must be competitively tendered. The resulting upsurge in contracting arrangements reinvigorated the potential for private provision through contracts and was widely regarded as

further support for privatization in addition to enterprise sales initiatives. Under this policy, targets were set at 20 per cent, 30 per cent and 50 per cent of local government services to be subject to competitive tender by mid-1995, 1996 and 1997, respectively. Over one half of all Victorian local government operating expenditure is spent on services now provided by external contractors.

8. This particular action was widely viewed by commentators as being a politically motivated manoeuvre aimed at reducing the state auditor general's power. It was arguably one of the reasons for the defeat of the reformist Kennett government in 1999, and the subsequent adoption by the new Bracks government of a 'Charter for Good Governance'.

9. Ring-fencing (the separation of business functions for regulatory purposes), requires that there must be a clear accounting and that there is operational separation of distribution and retail functions within a distribution business for reporting to the Office of the Regulator General (Department of Treasury and Finance, 1997).

10. Walker (1998) points to the demise of two former high-profile political figures, John Hewson and John Kieren, and their respective technical expertise in economics and finance.

11. A parallel appears to exist here with the experience of both the UK and New Zealand. In the UK, the incumbent British Telecom could not agree the level of interconnect charges to its challenger Mercury, with the matter being resolved only through a subsequent court finding against BT. Likewise, in New Zealand, Telecom's challenger, Clear, was able to connect only after a protracted legal battle (Suckling, 1999).

12. One outcome of the Kennett regime was the construction of three new private prisons. In consequence, Victoria now has the highest proportion of privately housed prisoners in the world. One of these new private prisons was subsequently issued with three default notices and threatened with contract cancellation in 2000 following poor performance.

13. In a recent instance, Myer (2002) reports that electricity retailers requested power price rises of between 12.4 per cent and 20 per cent, but that prices were capped at between 2.5 per cent and 4.7 per cent following ORG analysis.

14. Average minutes 'off-supply' per customer varied between businesses by a factor of about six, with Citipower at around 41 and Powercor at 249 minutes off-supply per annum (ORG, 1999:21; 2001:2).

15. See Department of Treasury and Finance (1997).

16. See, for instance, Bailey (1999).

17. Stevens (1999) for instance reports price reductions of 43 per cent for long-distance calls, 68 per cent–80 per cent for international calls, and 20 per cent for local calls. More recently, the Productivity Commission (2002) reports that 'real household prices for a consumption basket of telecommunications services including rental, fixed line and mobile calls, fell by around 20 percent' over the past decade, with around one-half of this reduction since privatization.

18. Interestingly, despite the Kennett government's culture of obsessive secrecy and disdain for transparency and public accountability, divestitures were not accompanied by rampant corruption, as has sometimes been the accusation elsewhere in the world; see Ralston Saul (1997:12). In fact, the electricity asset sales were remarkably clean, judging by the absence of complaints, and the fact that a subsequent audit review of some 66 transactions listed only 0.89 per cent of the asset sales figure as being 'of concern' in terms of due process or value for money.

19. Amongst other issues, this study found that the Commonwealth had entered into a new 10-year contract to buy blood products for an annual fee twice as high as in previous years (Collyer *et al.*, 2001:116).

References

Bailey, K. (1999) 'Who Has Gained From Privatisation?', letter to the editor, *The Age*, 20 August.

Bartholomeusz, S. (2002) 'Energy Market Shake-Out Points to the Limitations of Privatisation', *The Age*, Business, 19 April, p. 3.

Collyer, F., J. McMaster and R. Wettenhall (2001) 'Public Enterprise Divestment: Australian Case Studies', Pacific Institute of Management and Development, The University of the South Pacific, Suva, Fiji Islands.

Crosweller, A. (2002) 'Premier Left to Hold Kennett's "Time Bombs"', *The Australian*, 4 January, p. 4.

Davidson, K. (2001) 'A Failed Experiment', *The Age*, 13 December, opinion page.

Department of Treasury and Finance (1997) 'Victoria's Electricity Supply Industry Toward 2000', report prepared by the Energy Projects Division , June, Melbourne (this report is also available on the worldwide web at *http://energy.dtf.vic.gov.au/*).

DeVries, K., C. O'Reilly and R. Scoular (1998) 'The New Zealand Privatisation Experience', internal report, Monash Mt Eliza School of Business and Government, Melbourne, November.

Harris, M. and J.N. Lye (2001) 'The Fiscal Consequences of Privatisation: Australian Evidence on Privatisation by Public Share Float', *International Review of Applied Economics*, 15(3), 305–21.

Henderson, I. (2002) 'Alston Targets Broadband Pricing', *The Australian*, IT section, 6 March.

Hilmer, F., M. Rayner and G. Taperell (1993) *National Competition Policy, Report to the Independent Committee of Inquiry into Competition Policy in Australia* (Hilmer Report), Canberra: AGPS.

Hodge, G.A. (2000) *Privatisation: An International Review of Performance*, Theoretical Lenses on Public Policy Series (ed. by Paul A. Sabatier), Boulder: Westview Press.

Hughes, O.E. (1998) *Public Management and Administration: An Introduction*, 2nd edn, London: Macmillan.

Industry Commission (1991) *Energy Generation and Distribution*, Report Number 11, Canberra: AGPS.

Macfarlane, D., S. Creedy and A. Fraser (2002) 'Fels Swoops at Qantas', *The Australian*, 8 May, p. 1.

Macmillan, G.G. (1998) 'Public Sector Finance, Topic 4: Accountability and Regulation of Public Finance', course notes developed for the International Centre for Management in Government, Monash Mt Eliza School of Business and Government, Melbourne.

Mahboobi, L. (2001) 'Recent Trends in Privatisation: 2000', *Financial Market Trends*, 79(2).

Mascarenhas, R.C. (1991) 'State-Owned Enterprises', in J. Boston, J. Martin, J. Pallot and P. Walsh (eds), *Reshaping the State: New Zealand's Bureaucratic Revolution*, Oxford: Oxford University Press.

McIntosh, K., J. Shauness and R. Wettenhall (1997) 'Contracting Out In Australia: An Indicative History', Centre for Research in Public Sector Management, University of Canberra.

Myer, R. (2002) 'Throwing the Switch', *The Age*, 7 January, p. 9.

OECD (1997) 'Application of Competition Policy to the Electricity Sector', OECD/GD(97)132, Paris (this document is also available on the worldwide web at *http://www.oecd.org*).

Office of the Regulator General (1999) 'Electricity Distribution Businesses, Comparative Performance Report for the Calendar Year 1998', ORG, Melbourne, August.

Office of the Regulator General (2001) 'Electricity Distribution Businesses, Comparative Performance Report for the Calendar Year 2000', ORG, Melbourne, August.

Porter, M. (2002) 'Privatisation Is (Still) Good For Us', *The Age*, 1 March, opinion page.

Productivity Commission (2002) 'Trends in Australian Infrastructure Prices 1990–91 to 2000–01', *Performance Monitoring*, AusInfo, Canberra, May.

Quiggin, J. (1999) 'The Future of Public Ownership in Australia: Privatisation or Renationalisation?', in Committee for Economic Development of Australia (ed.), *Privatisation: Efficiency or Fallacy?*, Melbourne.

Ralston Saul, J. (1997) *The Unconscious Civilisation*, Melbourne: Penguin Books Australia Ltd.

Reserve Bank of Australia (1997) 'Privatisation in Australia', *Reserve Bank of Australia Bulletin*, December, pp.1–8.

Roarty, M.(1998) 'Electricity Industry Restructuring: The State of Play', Parliamentary

Library of Australia, 25 May (this document is also available on the world wide web at *http://www.aph.gov.au/library/pubs*).

Romeril, B. (1997) 'Cut Off: The Losers in Utility Privatisation – A Study of Disconnections in the Victorian Electricity Industry', *Consumer Rights Journal*, 1(5), July–August,7–10.

Russell, E.W. (1990) 'Builders of Public Enterprise in Victoria', Address to the Royal Historical Society of Victoria, Melbourne, 23 October.

Russell, E.W., E. Waterman and N. Seddon (2000) *Audit Review of Government Contracts: Contracting, Privatisation, Probity and Disclosure in Victoria 1992–1999, An Independent Report to Government*, Volume 3, May, Melbourne: State Government of Victoria.

Stevens, N. (1999) 'Telecommunications Reform in Australia', presentation to the Telecommunications Reforms – Challenges and Opportunities Conference', 28 September, Jakarta.

Suckling, A. (1999) 'Regulating Vertically Integrated Incumbents', unpublished thesis for Master of Public Policy and Management, Centre for Management in Government, Monash Mt Eliza School of Business, Monash University, Melbourne.

Sykes, T. (1996) *The Bold Riders: Behind Australia's Corporate Collapses*, 2nd edn, Sydney: Allen and Unwin.

Usher, L. (1997) 'Ghost Towns Rise in the Wake of Privatisation', *Common Cause*, N.S.W., September.

Walker, B. and B.C. Walker (2000) *Privatisation: Sell Off or Sell Out? The Australian Experience*, Sydney: ABC Books.

Walker, D.J. (1998) 'Privatisation: Some Political Perspectives', presentation to Privatisation Workshop, Monash University, Caulfield, 2 August.

Wettenhall, R. (1965) 'Public Ownership in Australia', *Political Quarterly*, 36 (4), 426–40; also in R. Wettenhall (1987) *Public Enterprises and National Development: Selected Essays*, RAIPA (ACT Division) monograph.

Wettenhall, R. (1983) 'Privatisation: A Shifting Frontier Between Private and Public Sectors', *Current Affairs Bulletin*, 69(6), 114–22.

Woodward, D. (1999) 'Privatisation: A Policy or an Ideology?', in B. Costar and N. Economou (eds), *The Kennett Revolution: Victorian Politics in the 1990s*, Sydney: UNSW Press.

9 Postal privatization in the United States
Michael A. Crew and Paul R. Kleindorfer

Introduction

In this chapter we examine the role of privatization in postal services, with the main emphasis being on the role of privatization in the case of the United States postal service (USPS). The problem is not an easy one. USPS has an inefficient organizational and governance structure that precludes alignment of market and efficiency incentives with investments and operations. At the same time, USPS has a universal service obligation (USO), which is both a curse and a blessing, in that it is the source of large costs but also represents the basis for legitimating its letter monopoly and other privileges. Finally, in the face of both of these factors, USPS has additionally an institutional governance structure with respect to its primary input, labour, that effectively precludes an efficient response to changing market conditions, especially any such conditions requiring a smaller labour force.

Under the circumstances, it is exceedingly difficult to sort out what elements of USPS behaviour are absolutely essential for the viability of the USO and what elements are unnecessary infringements on the market in the form of anticompetitive behaviour. This is not a new problem in network industries. In the case of USPS it may be more severe because of the nature of the postal service, the nature of the USO and the politicization of decision making resulting from the public ownership in the USA and the oversight role exercised by the legislative and executive branches of government. Given these arguments, it might seem that privatization is the obvious solution and, only recently, Crew and Kleindorfer (2000) argued for it. However, a little over three years later, no progress has been made towards privatization and, at least in the short term, it appears less feasible. In some respects, however, the case is stronger. How can this be when other post offices (POs), notably those of the Netherlands and Germany, are partially privatized and most of the POs in advanced economies are becoming increasingly commercialized?

This chapter, in exploring the potential future privatization of the postal service, begins with a short discussion of privatization and some background on the nature of the postal service. The chapter then examines some of the approaches taken, including comparing the experience in the USA with that of other countries, especially the privatized postal services of Germany and the Netherlands. The discussion then turns to examine the option of privatization of USPS and, later, the way forward, particularly for USPS. The chapter ends with a brief summary and conclusion.

Background on the postal service and privatization

'*Privatisation* is not only an inelegant term; it is also lamentably imprecise . . . One major source of confusion is the difference between privatisation in the United States and the rest of the world' (Donahue, 1989). Privatization, at its most general, is the transfer of services that were formally under government control to private control. At one extreme it may involve the government selling its ownership rights in the form of an initial public offering (IPO) of stock to individual shareholders, notable examples being the sale by the United Kingdom of its telephone, electricity, gas and water utilities to individual shareholders. At the other extreme, privatization may not involve selling any assets and may mean as little as contracting out certain tasks that were previously performed within the public enterprise. A municipal water undertaking might contract out the management of its operation to a management company, which may itself be a subsidiary of a privately owned company. Many municipal services may be contracted out to franchisees. All these kinds of activities can be a privatization of varying degrees that falls short of government actually divesting its ownership so that the equity is privately held. Many privatization arrangements of this kind exist. A prison system might contract out the operation of one or more of its penitentiaries to a private company, or a private company might own and operate the prison properties itself, charging a fee per inmate to the government. We are not going to describe such arrangements in any detail as they have been extensively analysed elsewhere (for example, Shleifer, 1998). However, the lesson for the postal service is that privatization can take many forms and is not just confined to divesting the equity ownership to the private sector.

Privatization, in the sense of divestiture of the equity from public to private hands in the form of an IPO, has never been seriously considered by policy makers in the debate to reform the postal sector in the United States. However, USPS has privatized extensively, more than any other PO, individual pieces of the value chain through contracting to private companies and by encouraging entry of privately owned competitors into the upstream value chain. This includes not just barcoding and pre-sorting but also downstream access, namely, drop shipment to the delivery office. Reform of the postal sector was precipitated by crises in the late 1960s resulting in the Postal Reorganization Act of 1970, which provided the basis for the current organization of the US Postal Service and the Postal Rate Commission. Although the 1970 Act abolished the United State Post Office because of a crisis, which had been largely the result of mismanagement stemming from running it as a government department, it still retained public ownership in the form of a public enterprise, USPS. The new entity was intended to be more independent of political interference than the old USPO, with its own board of governors appointed by the President of the USA. However, it has proved impossible for USPS, organized as a public enterprise, to avoid operating in a political manner. It remains a public enterprise and, despite fairly widespread concerns about the state of USPS and many potential advantages in having a privatized postal service, it is unlikely that USPS will be privatized in the near future, at least in the sense of ending public ownership.

The arguments that private ownership is likely to be more efficient than public ownership are well known and so we will summarize them only briefly here with USPS in mind. Not all economic activities are more efficiently supplied by the private sector. For example, it is not clear that prisons, law enforcement, national defence and tax collection should be privatized in any significant manner. So we confine a discussion of the advantages, in principle, of privatization to the case where there are no strong reasons for public ownership and operation. Postal service clearly meets this test. There are no strong technological, strategic or economic reasons why the postal service should be publicly operated. Postal service is a network industry. Other network industries, for example, electricity, gas and telecommunications, are privately owned and operated.[1] Postal service is arguably relatively less important to the economy than any of the other network industries. It is an old industry with its origins before the industrial revolution. While it has changed dramatically in certain respects, it has not changed anywhere near as much as the rest of the communications sector, making it relatively less important than in its early days. It would be much more painful if the lights went out for half a day than if the postal service ceased for an extended period. There would be inconvenience if the mail did not get delivered, but the ready availability of (imperfect) substitutes would mean that severe disruption could be avoided. On the face of it, therefore, the postal service looks like an excellent candidate to reap the advantages of privatization.

In principle, residual claimants drive the benefits of privatization and the inefficiency (X-inefficiency) of public enterprise arises from the lack of residual claimants (see Chapters 2 and 3). Residual claimants readily exist in the case of private companies whose objective is profit. The stockholders are the recipients of the residual in this case, namely profits. Management, by means of appropriate executive compensation schemes, for example stock options, can be made to face incentives such that they share the stockholders' objective to maximize profits. The board of directors is intended to provide oversight of the management of the company and act as the fiduciaries of the stockholders.[2] The capital market also operates to provide further incentives to management to maximize profits. The market punishes poor management by driving down the price of the stock and by the threat of takeover. Competitive product markets further sharpen the incentives to operate efficiently. The objective of profits – the excess of total revenues over total costs – provides an incentive for cost economy and therefore X-efficiency.

By contrast, incentives in public enterprise are much softer, given the absence of effective residual claimants. The government's interest is entirely too diffuse. Moreover, with public enterprise, the discipline of the capital market is absent. On a priori grounds, the case that private ownership is likely to promote greater X-efficiency is very strong. The question is whether it is supported empirically. Donahue (1989: 76) cites a number of studies in the 1970s and 1980s that show no significant differences between private and public electric utilities. However, as Crew and Kleindorfer (1990) noted, there may be problems with the treatment of the cost of capital in these studies. Most of the public entities had tax advantages that lowered their cost of capital, thus diluting the credibility of arguments made that costs of public enterprises were lower. In addition, the period covered was when electric utilities were subject to cost of service regulation, also known as rate of return regulation (ROR). This type of 'cost-plus' regulation was likely to attenuate the incentives for efficiency and cost economy. Recently, regulation has moved very strongly towards incentive regulation (see Chapters 22 and 23), and it is not by accident that this trend has been tightly linked to privatization and the residual claimancy it embodies. For example, Littlechild's (1983) proposals for incentive regulation, specifically price-cap regulation, clearly presuppose residual claimants. Indeed, they were applied almost exclusively to privately owned companies, rather than public enterprises. Notably in the UK, price cap regulation (PCR) was the regulatory scheme adopted for the newly privatized enterprises, not only among network industries, viz. gas, electricity, telephone and water, but also for other industries such as Britain's major airports. Similarly, in the USA, price caps have been applied primarily to telecommunications companies. The fact that these companies are privately owned largely explains the potential of price caps in achieving more efficient operation than cost of service regulation. Under price caps, shareholders and top management, as residual claimants, have the opportunity to enjoy the extra profits that result from increasing the efficiency of operations.

Megginson and Netter's (2001) survey of the studies of recent instances of privatization provides a comprehensive study of whether private firms are likely to be more efficient than public enterprise. Their paper provides comparative longitudinal evidence from a number of sectors on performance before and after privatization. Moreover, incentive regulation, which specifically aims to encourage efficiency, was extensively employed for many of the companies during the period surveyed. Megginson and Netter conclude, 'Research now supports the proposition that privately owned firms are more efficient and more profitable than otherwise-comparable state-owned firms' (ibid.: 380).

Given the generally promising effects of privatization, it seems that privatization of USPS at a minimum has the potential to improve efficiency relative to the current situation. In view of the concern for the situation currently faced by USPS, the time would appear to be apposite to consider privatization as a possible reform strategy. To understand whether and how this might occur, however, we must first consider the central problems now confronting USPS and other POs worldwide. USPS and most postal services face three major problems which policy makers are aware of, and we now consider them.

First, the USO is generally, but by no means universally, recognized as a significant burden.[3] In addition, the postal service is not the only industry with a USO. It is a burden imposed by government on almost all other regulated network industries.[4] In the case of postal service it has two features, ubiquity and uniformity. Ubiquity means that it must collect and deliver everywhere in the country, to every address. Uniformity means uniformity of price irrespective of where the delivery or collection takes place. Letters (not parcels) are subject to the price uniformity requirement. All letters of the same weight carry the same postage. Similarly, service standards are subject to uniformity standard, in that they are managed within narrow limits. First class mail in the USA is delivered overnight within a defined area and otherwise within two or three days depending on distance and the outlying nature of the delivery point. The success in meeting the service standards is evaluated by an independent consulting company.

Second, X-inefficiency is a major problem for postal services, including USPS. Part of the inefficiency can traced to the absence of residual claimants as drivers of efficiency. Another source is the nature of postal service. It is extremely labour-intensive, with over 80 per cent of total costs being labour. It is at least strongly arguable that these problems may be relatively greater for USPS than for most other POs. Similarly, in the absence of privatization and residual claimants, there is little incentive on the part of postal management to address the issue of the current labour relations framework within which USPS operates. Unless there is a change in labour practices, the improvements in efficiency are likely to be small or non-existent. The current system involves binding arbitration. Thus approximately 80 per cent of the postal service's costs are effectively subject to the decision of an arbitrator. The arbitrator is not obliged to abide by considerations of USPS finances, and has little incentive to do so as USPS is a public enterprise that does not face the discipline of bankruptcy.

Third, postal service, especially the delivery of letters, is faring badly as a result of technological change in the economy that has improved the prospects of other sectors at its expense. Optical fibres and computers have had a dramatic impact on the economy. A new sector, the Internet, has grown from a tool used by scientists to a ubiquitous phenomenon. The marginal costs of employing the Internet, for example, are near zero, in contrast to the marginal cost of a traditional letter. The impact of the Internet is truly monumental and it will be a significant and continuing threat for the traditional postal service. In addition, while the Internet and associated developments in information technology have had a considerable impact on cost reduction, quality and new product offerings in other sectors, the same cannot be said for the postal sector. Notably, USPS has not benefited much on the production and marketing side from the information technology (IT) revolution and it has been hurt significantly on the demand side. By contrast, its major competitors, for example, United Parcel Service (UPS) and Federal Express (FEDEX), continue to benefit from improvements in IT and the Internet by introducing features that enable the shipper to arrange pick-ups, receive bills and track and trace their packages over the Internet. Unfortunately for USPS, the adverse effects on the demand side show no signs of abating and may even be growing in magnitude.

These three problems are considered central to most postal services worldwide. The first two have existed for many years. The third is more recent and its importance has only started to be understood in recent years. Indeed, it is still being addressed. We might have listed a fourth problem, namely the vulnerability of postal service to terrorist attack, as dramatically illustrated by the very recent episode of anthrax in the mail and the major disruption that this caused for the affected postal facilities and customers. As yet this has been a phenomenon confined to the USA and so we have not listed it as a general problem. In addition, since we are concerned with reform efforts generally, we will leave this problem until we discuss potential reforms for USPS. Reform efforts in the USA have attempted to address the three problems highlighted, as have the reform efforts of other countries. Countries have, in effect, addressed these problems in a variety of ways. In the next section we compare and contrast the approach taken by the USA to the privatization approach taken by the Netherlands and Germany.

Privatization and postal reform
The forces of technological change, increased competition and a changing approach to monopoly regulation mean that the time is ripe for serious reform of the postal sector. Privatization of USPS and other POs has the

potential to play a major role in transforming POs into successful, efficient and innovative postal networks. In the USA, while there has been a significant interest in reform, serious debate and a high degree of legislative activity, little has been achieved, in contrast to some of the changes in Europe.[5] The reforms in the Netherlands and Germany have been far-reaching and include privatization. This has not been the case in the USA. We will review the reforms in these three countries in turn.

Despite the reforms of 1970, operating USPS as a public enterprise remains a political matter that is in the hands of the government. It continues to be a public enterprise despite the many advantages of having a privatized postal service. For example, a private sector Postal Service would be subject to different competitive rules than a public enterprise and would have the potential of being more efficient than a public enterprise. In the USA, the proposed legislation, H.R. 22, was the most significant attempt at reform since 1970 and it failed ultimately, being abandoned in 2001. It had a number of innovative and significant proposals, the most important being a change in regulation from the current system, which is a form of cost of service regulation, to price cap regulation (PCR). PCR differs from traditional cost of service regulation in that it does not restrict the profit that the firm can make to the cost of service including an allowed rate of return on its capital. It sets the maximum price level[6] that the regulated firm may charge and then allows the firm to keep the profits that it makes. It also allows the firm to raise its prices over time by a specified amount, namely, the annual increase in the index less X, where X is a percentage deduction from the annual increase in the index. The setting of X involves some judgment on the part of the regulator and its level is closely related to the expected changes in efficiency of the company, as examined in detail in Crew and Kleindorfer (1996). Thus, by regulating the price level without direct regard for costs, PCR appeals to the firm's incentive to maximize profits and, in so doing, minimize costs and otherwise operate efficiently. The efficiency of PCR comes in the form of lower costs as a result of the operation of the profit motive. To be effective PCR requires the profit motive, which requires residual claimants if it is to operate. Absent residual claimants, PCR lacks the incentives for efficiency that support its implementation.

Residual claimants readily exist in the case of private companies whose objective is profit. The stockholders are the recipients of the residual, namely profits. Management, by means of appropriate executive compensation schemes, using stock options and performance-based bonus payments, can be made to face incentives such that they share the stockholders' objective to maximize profits. The capital market also operates to provide further incentives to management to maximize the value of the firm, notably through punishing poor management by driving down the price of the stock and by the threat of takeover.

With public enterprise there is effectively an absence of residual claimants, as the government's interest is entirely too diffuse, and the discipline of the capital market is absent. H.R. 22, in proposing PCR, failed to take into account the absence of residual claimants in the public sector. In addition, it completely ignored lessons learned elsewhere. It is no coincidence that incentive regulation, and specifically price cap regulation, has been applied almost exclusively to privately owned companies, rather than to public enterprises. The fact that these companies were privately owned largely explains the potential of price caps in achieving more efficient operation than cost of service regulation. Under price caps, shareholders and top management, as residual claimants, have the opportunity to enjoy the extra profits that result from increasing the efficiency of operations. However, if USPS were subject to price cap regulation with no change in ownership or residual claimants, there is absolutely no guarantee that efficiency would be improved, as there would otherwise be no, or at best weak, residual claimants to benefit from increased profits. Indeed, additional profits might arguably be counterproductive, in that they might send a signal to postal employees that the postal service could pay higher wages. Unlike a private company, the postal service, absent any other strong residual claimants,[7] would have little incentive to stand firm against wage demands, as management would have little to gain from doing so. In addition, a public enterprise is not subject to the pressure of competition in the same way that a private company is, in that it is insulated from bankruptcy. This insulation from the discipline of bankruptcy also means that a public enterprise, unless subjected to certain restriction, can undertake on favourable terms competitive ventures, which may include ill-conceived and risky ventures and have the potential for competing unfairly and inefficiently with privately owned companies.[8]

The importance of residual claimants has not been ignored completely in the postal sector. Short of privatization, the usual approach has been to promote strong management incentives for performance through executive profit targets as, for example, has been the case in Australia and New Zealand, where the post offices are still public enterprises. However, the government's powers to punish failure are weak compared to those of the market. The problem is that a public enterprise cannot go bankrupt and bankruptcy is an important stick in private enterprise that encourages management to be cost-conscious and avoid overly risky ventures. Without this stick, it is more difficult to design incentive contracts for top management because of the asymmetry implied by the carrot alone. This stands out in contrast to Germany and the Netherlands, where this problem should be absent and the incentives for efficiency should be stronger, as in both cases they are well advanced on their schedule for postal service privatization with a significant portion of the equity already privately owned. The implications for the US postal service are clear. Absent privatization or a schedule to privatize, the benefits to be expected from incentive regulation are likely to be reduced significantly.

Similarly, in the absence of privatization and residual claimants, there is little incentive on the part of management to address the issue of the current labour relations framework within which the US postal service operates. Unless there is a change in labour practices, the improvements in efficiency are likely to be small or non-existent. The current system involves binding arbitration.[9] With almost 80 per cent of the postal service's costs effectively subject to the decision of an arbitrator and with the arbitrator not obliged to abide by the price cap, this drastically reduces the likely efficiency gains from a price cap. The arbitrator may award wages significantly in excess of the rate of increase allowed by the price cap. If this happened, the postal service would have no alternative but to seek rate relief on the grounds of impending financial exigency! With this system of labour relations, which arises from the public enterprise status of the US postal service, there is little likelihood that the benefits of cost economy, promised by price caps, would be achieved in the postal service.

Although well intentioned, H.R. 22 was fatally flawed, as was argued in Crew and Kleindorfer (2000). This stands in contrast to the experience in Germany and the Netherlands. For at least a dozen years the Netherlands has been a force for change in the postal sector. The Netherlands and New Zealand were among the first of the POs to recognize the importance of becoming more commercialized, as examined by Toime (1991). The Netherlands embraced privatization, while New Zealand Post adopted a corporate structure that was wholly owned by the government. It continued to be innovative, but privatization is not expected to be part of its future. The Netherlands and Germany have been the only major POs to embrace privatization. We will therefore briefly review their experience and possible lessons learned.

The process that led to privatization of the Netherlands' PO traces its roots to 1989, when its structure was changed from a state enterprise to a private company whose stock was entirely owned by the government. Shortly after this, a close commercial relationship began to develop between the PO and TNT, an international express carrier with its origins in Australia. In 1994, the Dutch government sold 30 per cent of its shares in KPN, the combined postal and telecommunications operator, and in 1996 another 25 per cent, making it a minority stockholder. In 1996, KPN acquired TNT. In 1998, KPN divested its postal and telecommunications into two separate companies. Over the next two years or so it formed alliances with other POs, perhaps the most significant being the formation of a joint venture with the UK and Singapore POs to provide service in cross-border mail. In 2000, it acquired CTI LOGISTX. Its various businesses are grouped together in a holding company called TPG. Although it is a large company with around 130 000 employees and with revenues of almost €10 bn, it has not been the subject of major litigation. Its success has arisen from a solid base of mail upon which to build. Its USO is less onerous than most, the Netherlands being a small, densely populated country. In addition, it has traditionally received favourable treatment in its reserved area. The weight limit for mail reserved as a monopoly until recently was 500 grams, but is now 100 grams in line with the limit set for January 2003 for the entire European Union. While the Dutch may no longer be able to count on relaxed regulation, they are likely to remain the beneficiaries of a minimally burdensome USO.

A dozen years or so ago the Deutsche Bundespost was in poor shape. It was an extremely ungainly bureaucracy, whose position was made more difficult by the unification of East and West Germany. The East German PO was very overmanned and assimilating it into the new Germany looked like a very difficult task unless something drastic was done. The solution adopted by Germany was to hire a successful manager and businessman, Klaus Zumwinkel, to commercialize the operation. This culminated in the sale of around a third of the equity in 2000 and the transformation of the bureaucracy into a major multinational corporation.

The transformation of Deutsche Post World Net from a bureaucracy to a multinational corporation was a major one and was achieved in a number of ways. The internal organization was transformed by changing the compensation structure and importing managers from other industries, by modernization of the mail and parcels network within Germany, by developing new products, for example, hybrid mail and e-commerce, and by acquisition. Deutsche Post World Net has interests in not only the traditional mail and parcels businesses but also express mail, logistics, banking and more. With total revenue of €32.4 bn in 2000 and total employment in excess of 300 000, it is one of the world's largest corporations.

The path from bureaucracy to one of the world's largest companies began with major internal changes and encountered a number of hurdles on the way, some of which still remain. The company will face many more difficulties in the future as a result of its policy of aggressive growth and its size. It is and will continue to be a competitive threat not just to other POs including USPS but also to other major players in the delivery and logistics business. It has already been the subject of litigation from major companies, notably UPS. The principal cases before the European Commission involved alleged anticompetitive conduct, from cross subsidy and from improper state aid. The allegation was that it cross-subsidized competitive products, notably parcels, from its monopoly in letter mail. On 20 March 2001, a ruling of the Commission stated that cross-subsidy took place only prior to 1996 and no fine was imposed. However, a fine was imposed for the use of a loyalty rebate.

A case on state aid is pending. This case alleges that Deutsche Post improperly used state aid and the funding that it earned from its letter mail monopoly to acquire other companies. At first sight this seems to be the traditional red flag that is raised about public enterprise 'playing with the house's money' to the unfair advantage of private companies competing without the benefit of state aid. One argument would be that a public enterprise cannot go bankrupt and so if it is allowed to enter competitive businesses it has a huge advantage over private companies, who have to raise funds without government guarantee and who face the real threat of bankruptcy and takeover. However, this argument loses a considerable amount of its force in the situation where a government has made and announced an irrevocable decision to privatize, which the German government has done in the case of Deutsche Post. It even went as far, in 2001, as to change the German constitution to underline the credibility of its commitment to privatize. Without the change in the constitution, the sale of the equity would have been limited to 50 per cent. The amendment to the constitution makes it possible for the government to sell the entire equity. It is this credible commitment to privatization that weakens the force of the allegation of improper state aid. A commitment to privatize having been made, and a CEO having been charged with the task of bringing this about, the duty of the CEO becomes that of maximizing the value of the entity. One rather obvious implication of this duty to maximize value would be that the CEO should maximize the proceeds of the IPO and the subsequent tranches of equity to be sold.[10]

The state aid case and the cross-subsidy case have implications for the privatization of USPS. Currently, USPS is extremely restricted in its ability to enter other businesses and its rates are strictly scrutinized by interveners in cases before the Postal Rate Commission. If it were privatized, USPS would be at least twice the size of Deutsche Post and would almost certainly be subject to litigation on the grounds of improper state aid or using funds from its letter monopoly to enter competitive ventures. This would place the US government on the horns of a dilemma. Either it could keep USPS as a public enterprise, with perhaps some regulatory changes, or it could privatize it, but in such a restrictive manner that the value of the IPO would be severely affected. We now examine the privatization option for USPS.

The privatization option for USPS

We first examined the privatization option for USPS in Crew and Klein-dorfer (2000). We will start in this section by sketching this framework and then examine the feasibility of getting from here to there, to foreshadow our conclusion, 'You can't get there from here!'

In this section we will sketch a possible scenario for the future of a privatized postal service, the United States Postal Service, Inc. (USPSI).[11] We see USPSI as a continuing regulated monopoly, with details on proposed regulation below. However, we would propose reducing the monopoly from the current arrangement under which competitors cannot charge less than three dollars or twice the postage, whichever is greater, and we would confine the monopoly to a monopoly in local delivery.

We see our proposal as part of an evolving process. Entry has been taking place in postal services and fixed network industries over the last 10 years or so. Indeed, the US postal service faced entry into its business at an early stage in the form of worksharing, namely discounts for pre-sorting. Unlike privately owned companies, it did little to oppose market entry in this form. Similarly, its parcels business was devoured by UPS and FEDEX, who came to dominate the courier service. Now postal administrations in Europe and the USA are beginning to face more serious threats to their traditional and basic letters business. The issue of regulatory governance when entry is allowed is now becoming as important as it is in the other network industries.

Entry by competitors in network industries has not been complete, as some part of the value chain is a natural monopoly. Some parts of the industry can be successfully subjected to competition, but there is a residual monopoly, bottleneck or essential facility. As was argued in Crew and Kleindorfer (1998), making network industries more competitive may require the acceptance of some residual monopoly. We argued that, in these circumstances, the feasible approach was to recognize the inevitability of some regulation of the residual natural monopoly. The approach we proposed was to pare down the residual monopoly to the bone and regulate using a form of price cap or incentive regulation. This is the approach we would propose for the regulation of USPSI.

Currently, the postal monopoly or reserved area is usually defined in terms of either a monetary limit or a weight limit. Increasingly, in Europe the trend is to move to a limit based upon weight, which varies from country to country, subject to an upper limit of 500 grams required by the EU. Many countries are operating significantly below this level. In addition, USPS has a mailbox monopoly, which means that other carriers delivering items are not allowed to put them in the receptacle provided for the sole use of USPS.[12] We would propose a new approach to the regulation of USPSI. We would argue that many of the upstream services such as collection, transport and mail processing could be subjected to increased competition, with local delivery remaining as a regulated monopoly. The postal monopoly would be confined to the local delivery network only. Local delivery would be the core or residual monopoly. USPSI would take on the role of supplier of services wholesale and would not have any retail customers. Under our proposal, USPSI would provide only the local delivery networks and the sorting needed for local delivery.

Although we are not going into the details at this stage, we should emphasize that our proposal would not affect the rights of couriers and parcel operators to deliver as they do currently. They would be under no obligation to use USPSI's network for their existing services. USPSI would have a monopoly on local delivery of letter mail and small packets up to some weight limit. This weight limit would likely be less than the current limit.

The problem with this proposal, if this were the extent of it, is that it would potentially leave most residential postal customers high and dry for some services. Unlike the other network industries, it is unlikely that in postal service the competitive market has the potential to rebundle the services required for residential and other small customers to obtain fully integrated or end-to-end service. In the postal service there may be major problems of bundling together the various parts of the postal value chain needed to provide end-to-end single piece service for residential or other small customers. This is because a postage stamp is an extremely low value item leaving very little scope for competitors to bundle the services.[13] This is likely to be an even more important problem in rural areas, which receive service only because of cross subsidization from low-cost urban areas. These areas are highly vulnerable not only when it comes to delivery but also when it comes to collection. Similarly, very small residential customers, the Aunt Minnies, might be almost completely cut off from sending letters absent the 'lifeline' offered by POs. We are saying, in effect, that we cannot see much, if any, interest by new entrants in end-to-end single piece service for residential customers. However, because of potential scale economies arising from their collection networks, most postal administration could handle this kind of business and receive a contribution over variable costs. We would therefore argue that the postal monopoly or reserved area should consist of local delivery but that USPSI would also be required to provide single piece end-to-end service.

This requirement to provide end-to-end service does not result in an increase in postal monopoly power but, rather, forms a large part of USPSI's USO. While it would be obliged to offer single piece end-to-end service, there is nothing to stop consolidators from collecting mail from small customers into large batches of mail for presorting or barcoding. For large users this is done now. Some small customers might have this option if the market offered sufficient profit to make it attractive to entrepreneurs. Indeed, customers who would be the target for this option would likely be USPSI's profitable customers; that is, the potential for cream skimming would exist. However, the gains from competition here are likely to be greater than the losses from cream skimming. Given that the postal administration has a monopoly in local delivery, through which it would fund its USO, we are not concerned that such losses, if any, would affect the financial viability of the postal administration or threaten its ability to meet its USO. Another reason for taking this route is that funding the USO in the postal context through uniform pricing and the local delivery monopoly would likely be preferable to setting up a universal service fund, as is the case in telecommunications, as analysed in Crew and Kleindorfer (1998).

In common with most privatization proposals, we would envisage that USPSI would be subject to a form of PCR. Again without going into details, it is clear that the choices are between pure price cap regulation and hybrid price cap regulation.[14] Pure price cap regulation allows the regulated firm to keep any profits it earns within the price cap constraint. Hybrid price cap regulation allows the firm to retain only a percentage of the profits it makes above a certain return on its assets. Such hybrid forms of regulation provide considerable flexibility. Irrespective of the form of price cap regulation adopted, setting the starting point is a critical part of the process. The most likely approach is to have an initial rate case, which essentially takes a traditional cost of service approach based upon expected expenses and a rate of return on the invested capital or rate base.

The initial rate case is likely to be a highly contentious matter, in that USPSI would have every incentive to maximize the amount of expenses to be placed on the regulated sector. The aim would be to have a solid base of the reserved area on which to build, presumably with a view to pursuing a strategy similar to TPG, Deutsche Post and the massive Bell operating companies, all of whom were able to move into new businesses on the solid foundation of an underlying and relatively robust monopoly. In the case of USPSI, the current rate-making process is going to be stretched to the limit. Large numbers of interveners will oppose the expenses placed on the monopoly area. The potential for litigation will be huge, with protests of improper state aid and use of the monopoly along the lines faced by Deutsche Post, except that the protests will be much louder. It will be exceedingly difficult to reach agreement and to develop a funding package that will lead to a successful IPO. We will expand on this in the next section, but for the moment we will assume that the process is successful. With this heroic assumption, the rest of the process is relatively straightforward.

On the assumption that the initial rate case produced an allocation of expenses, it would be possible, on the basis of this allocation, to establish the initial prices that would then become subject to a price cap index. The individual products would have to be placed in 'baskets' for purposes of the price cap.[15] One approach would be to have two regulated baskets, for example, an 'access' basket and a 'single piece' basket. Each of these baskets would be subject to the price cap index. The index would be based on, say, the consumer price index (CPI) minus X. Setting the X factor would be quite important. It would have to recognize that, unlike telecommunications, technological change and demand growth are not rapid in posts. This would imply a low X factor. After a period of, say, five years, the price cap period, prices and the X factor would be reviewed, following standard practices in the implementation of price cap regulation (see Chapter 23).

While, in principle, it is possible to design a regulatory scheme for a privatized USPSI not dissimilar to those employed in other network industries and for privatized POs, as we just noted, there are non-trivial problems to be addressed. However, when the details of the situation currently faced by USPS are examined, the situation looks much more serious, as we now discuss.

The way forward for USPS

Currently, USPS faces some very serious problems. It faces major competition from the Internet. It faces severe financial problems and institutional constraints that prevent it from controlling its most important factor of production, labour. Recently, added to these problems has been the recognition that USPS is also very vulnerable to terrorist activity. Together these difficulties raise serious questions about how to bring about a successful privatization of USPS, which we now examine.

As the recent use of the mail to deploy anthrax has highlighted, mail service is extremely vulnerable to terrorism, especially bioterrorism. However, even before this, its vulnerability to terrorism has been apparent. For a number of years it has restricted items that can be placed in public mail boxes to those weighing less than one pound unless affixed with machine postage. This meant that individuals and small businesses had no choice but to mail items above one pound through a postal counter. While this is a small inconvenience, it makes the product less valuable. Postal service is anonymous and low priced. Both of these features mean that individual pieces receive minimal attention on the part of mailers and on the part of POs. Terrorism takes advantage of these features, raising postal costs and making the product less valuable. The losses imposed by terrorism are likely to make the operation of USPS much less attractive to the private sector. Investors may be unwilling to take the risk at prices that are feasible.

The financial problems facing USPS are particularly severe, as described by Robinson and Rawnsley (2002). The future looks even bleaker, as the situation has deteriorated rapidly since their study, due to both bioterrorism and a drop in postal volume. In addition, extra off-balance sheet liabilities have come to light and there is reason to believe that the liabilities actually stated on the balance sheet may be understated significantly. Off-balance sheet liabilities have recently received worldwide interest with the Enron bankruptcy and the web of off-balance sheet transactions that in the case of Enron served to hide billions of dollars of losses and liabilities. In the case of the USPS accounts, the problem is also a serious one. Robinson and Rawnsley note a liability of US$32.02 bn for deferred retirement costs out of total assets reported of US$59.09 bn. Included in the latter figure is the former figure, which appears on both sides of the balance sheet! Thus, by an accounting fiction, USPS is solvent! This accounting fiction is quite legal for regulated companies and is in accordance with generally accepted accounting principles (GAAP). The idea is that the regulated monopoly will provide for the funding of these liabilities as they occur in the future.[16] The ability of the letter monopoly to provide for this deferred liability is clearly called into question by the increased competition from the Internet and related forms of e-commerce.

Robinson and Rawnsley draw attention to off-balance sheet items that are of almost as serious a nature as the deferred pension obligations listed on the balance sheet. The most important of these off-balance sheet items is unfunded deferred retiree healthcare obligations. These are significant for USPS and for major US private sector companies. In the case of large private corporations, the treatment is the same as with USPS. For both they are treated as off-balance sheet items. Robinson and Rawnsley provide their estimate of the capitalized value of retiree healthcare liabilities of USPS at various discount rates, ranging from 5.5 per cent to 9 per cent. At the bottom end of this range the liability is around US$27 bn and at the upper end around US$47 bn. Given current interest rates, the 5.5 per cent discount rate may, if anything, be a little high. So, in some respects, US$47 bn might be considered a lower bound on liabilities.

These are serious financial problems that will be extremely difficult to overcome whether USPS continues as a public enterprise or is privatized. A decade ago the problems might have been manageable. USPS's unfunded liabilities would have been much less and the value of the monopoly would have been much more. If USPS had been subject to the kind of reform efforts undertaken in Germany at that time, the result might have been very different. Single piece postage rates, at least, would almost certainly have been higher and postal workers' wages might have been lower. Now privatization does not seem feasible without a major injection of funding from the US government, including a guarantee of the deferred retiree obligations accompanied by a large increase in rates. Such a package is likely to be opposed by strong forces.

The same pressure groups that prevented reform when the situation was more manageable still exist. Three major groups mean reform efforts are likely to flounder. Organized labour is concerned that a privatized USPS would pay lower wages and demand different work rules. Competitors are quite comfortable with a weak competitor like USPS, and they undoubtedly have an adverse effect through the current regulatory process on USPS's ability to price competitively. Under privatization and price caps they might face a competitor of the muscle of Deutsche Post and have to resort to more costly litigation in the courts as opposed to working through the regulatory process. The third group is mailers. Many businesses are built on the foundation of cheap but basic mail services provided by USPS. Opposition to major increases in rates is likely to be significant. All of these are powerful forces that will be overcome with great difficulty. It is not surprising, therefore, that reform efforts in the House of Representatives have not included privatization; however, they have included various forms of incentive regulation, though the residual claimant of a private firm would be absent.

Is there a scenario that might result in reform, a situation so severe that serious reform has to take place and might result in appropriate action being taken? This situation would need to be such that the pressure groups were overcome by a greater force. This is possible, but it has not yet happened. In the Spring of 2002, USPS is about to obtain a significant rate increase, though its revenues may not increase by the amounts that the forecasts predict. The seriousness of the situation may then be realized and real reform may take place. Possibly this should take the form of privatization. The benefits of this would be that the postal service would be less politicized and that labour relations would be changed significantly. A privatized postal service would, in such circumstances, be a much more powerful competitor. It would probably be a company similar to Deutsche Post with a range of operations not just confined to traditional mail. To satisfy its USO, it would presumably continue with some regulated monopoly protection. It would have powerful scale and scope economies and would be subject to complaints of unfair competition that do not exist under the present framework. It would, therefore, need to be subject to different competitive rules than a public enterprise and would have the potential of being more efficient than a public enterprise. But there are serious barriers to privatization, as we have noted.

Conclusions

Privatization in the postal arena could significantly improve static and dynamic efficiency relative to existing public enterprise. This is likely to be the case with USPS. However, the reform process is currently highly politicized in the USA, resulting in the inefficiencies examined here and elsewhere. Moreover, the highly politicized nature of USPS means that there are huge barriers in the way of any significant change. The USO, slow technological change, severe financial problems and the presence of powerful pressure groups, consisting of labour, competitors and mailers, make meaningful reform, including privatization, extremely difficult. A big bang may be needed. Deteriorating finances and technological change may be sufficient to precipitate such a crisis fairly soon. Alternatively, current reform efforts before Congress plus a continued willingness to provide government support, particularly in the area of underfunding deferred retiree obligations, may make it possible to paper over the cracks and delay the crisis for a considerable period. During this period USPS will shrink and privatization, if it ultimately arrives, will involve a much smaller company.

Notes

1. Water utilities in the USA are mostly publicly owned but there is a trend towards privately managed operations through contracts with privately owned utilities.
2. Unfortunately, not all boards perform their fiduciary function very effectively, as the Enron bankruptcy indicates.
3. Cohen *et al.* (2002) argue that the burden of the USO is heavier in some countries than in others. In particular, they argue that Italy is at the heavier end of the spectrum, while the USPS is at the lighter end.
4. In electric utilities it is known as the default service obligation (DSO).
5. For a recent survey and critique of reform efforts in the postal sector, see Campbell (2001).
6. This is normally based on a price index, for example, the Laspeyres index, which allows the firm to set its prices within the limits of the index.
7. It is difficult to argue in a credible manner that taxpayers are meaningful residual claimants.
8. Under private ownership these issues might be at least as serious. The revised H.R. 22 recognized some of these problems. However, the approach proposed in H.R. 22 may be exceedingly difficult to administer. It has a number of provisions requiring clear accounting separation of competitive and non-competitive products. Given the common resources used to provide many of the most obvious competitive products, attempts at accounting separation will undoubtedly lead to many complexities and additional regulations to sort out what resources are used for various products and what cost responsibilities are to be assigned to these products. The potential for strategic behaviour to discourage entry exists in public enterprise, as a recently documented example of cross-subsidies of competitive products by monopoly products in the case of the Federal Reserve Board illustrates (Cavalluzzo *et al.*, 1998). Thus we would not be sanguine about the ability of regulators to achieve either efficiency or clear separation in the provision of competitive and non-competitive products if the USPS continues as a public enterprise.
9. In addition, it is difficult to introduce practices that might reduce cost, for example, more part-time workers.
10. Interestingly, in defending the case this argument did not figure prominently. A major argument employed was that there was no improper state aid because of Deutsche Post's obligation to finance the USO.
11. We are confining our attention to regulation of USPSI and will not discuss major open

issues, such as finance and labour relations. See Froelke (2000) for some ideas on possible reform of postal labour relations as a prelude to 'privatization'.

12. Note that this is strictly a *mailbox* monopoly. It does not apply to residences with mail slots. Anyone is allowed to deliver if they can get their letter through the slot.

13. Compared to an electricity bill, a stamp is an extremely low value item. However, in the case of residential electricity customers, absent subsidies, getting companies in the USA interested in supplying such customers has proved difficult.

14. These terms are discussed in Crew and Kleindorfer (1996) and Kridel *et al.* (1996).

15. The index would apply to each basket separately. For example, if USPSI chose to raise the price of one basket by less than the allowed amount this would not be allowed as a credit to the other basket. One of the purposes of baskets is to restrict cross-subsidization of competitive products by monopoly products.

16. It is obviously a little more involved. The underlying principles are described in Robinson and Rawnsley (2002).

References

Campbell, J.I., Jr (2001) *The Rise of Global Delivery Services*, Washington, DC: JCampbell Press.

Cavalluzzo, K., C.D. Ittner and D. Larcker (1998) 'Competition, Efficiency and Cost Allocation in Government Agencies: Evidence on the Federal Reserve System', *Journal of Accounting Research*, 36(1), Spring, 1–32.

Cohen, R., C. Pace, M. Robinson, G. Scarfiglieri, R. Scocchera, V.V. Comandini, J. Waller and S. Xenakis (2002) 'A Comparison of the Burden of Universal Service in Italy and the United States', in M.A. Crew and P.R. Kleindorfer (eds), *Postal Delivery Services: Pricing, Productivity, Regulation and Strategy*, Boston, MA: Kluwer Academic Publishers.

Crew, M.A. and P.R. Kleindorfer (1990) *Private versus Public: Alternative Ownership Scenarios for Electric Utilities*, Santa Monica, CA: Reason Foundation.

Crew, M.A. and P.R. Kleindorfer (1996) 'Incentive Regulation in the United Kingdom and the United States: Some Lessons', *Journal of Regulatory Economics*, 9(3), 211–25.

Crew, M.A. and P.R. Kleindorfer (1998) 'Efficient Entry, Monopoly, and the Universal Service Obligation in Postal Service', *Journal of Regulatory Economics*, 14(2), 103–25.

Crew, M.A. and P.R. Kleindorfer (2000) 'Privatizing the U.S. Postal Service', in E.L. Hudgins (ed.), *Mail @ the Millennium: Will the Postal Service Go Private?*, Washington, DC: Cato Institute.

Donahue, J.D. (1989) *The Privatization Decision*, New York: Basic Books.

Froelke, R.D. (2000) 'Labour Market Outcomes of Postal Reorganization', in E.L. Hudgins (ed.), *Mail @ the Millennium: Will the Postal Service Go Private?*, Washington, DC: Cato Institute.

Kridel, D.J., D.E.M. Sappington and D.L. Weisman (1996) 'The Effects of Incentive Regulation in the Telecommunications Industry: A Survey', *Journal of Regulatory Economics*, 9(3), 269–306.

Littlechild, S.C. (1983) *Regulation of British Telecommunications Profitability*, London: Department of Trade and Industry.

Megginson, W.L. and J.M. Netter (2001) 'From State to Market: A Survey of Empirical Studies of Privatization', *Journal of Economic Literature*, 39(2), 321–89.

Robinson, A. and D. Rawnsley (2002) 'USPS Finances: Is there a financially viable future?', in M.A. Crew and P.R. Kleindorfer (eds), *Postal Delivery Services: Pricing, Productivity, Regulation and Strategy*, Boston, MA: Kluwer Academic Publishers.

Shleifer, A. (1998) 'State versus Private Ownership', *Journal of Economic Perspectives*, 12(4), 133–50.

Toime, E. (1991) 'Competitive Strategy for New Zealand Post', in M.A. Crew and P.R. Kleindorfer (eds), *Competition and Innovation in Postal Services*, Boston, MA: Kluwer Academic Publishers.

PART III

PRIVATIZATION IN DEVELOPING ECONOMIES

10 Assessing the impact of privatization in developing countries
Paul Cook and Colin Kirkpatrick

Introduction

Privatization has been a major element of the economic reform programmes pursued by developing countries during the past two decades.
Beginning in the late 1970s, the level of privatization transactions in developing countries has risen rapidly, and at the same time the range of developing countries and sectors involved in privatization has increased.
Between 1990 and 1999, total global privatization proceeds amounted to
$850 bn. Although developed countries accounted for the bulk of these pro-
ceeds, the share of developing countries is estimated to have been almost 30
per cent during this period (Mahboobi, 2000; Kikeri and Nellis, 2002).
Much of the privatization revenue has come from infrastructure privatization, mainly telecommunications and power, followed by the primary
sector, including petroleum, mining, agriculture and forestry. In regional
terms, Latin America accounts for the largest share of non-OECD privatizations, although Central and Eastern Europe and Central Asia sold the
largest number of enterprises. By comparison, privatization activity has
been modest in sub-Saharan Africa and the Middle East regions.

What has been the impact of privatization in developing countries? Have
the objectives which were set for privatization been met, and to what extent
has privatization contributed to the goal of achieving sustained economic
and social development in lower-income countries?

Impact assessment is a method of both ex ante appraisal and ex post evaluation, and is increasingly being used as a tool for evidence-based policy
analysis, in both developed and developing countries (Kirkpatrick, 2001;
Lee, 2002). In this chapter, impact assessment is deployed for purposes of
evaluation. Ex post impact assessment can be used to inform and refine future
policy formulation. It can also be used as a means of improving accountability processes, thereby contributing to broader goals of better governance.

The remaining sections of the chapter are as follows. The methodological issues of impact assessment as applied to privatization policy in developing countries are first examined. The following section surveys the
objectives of privatization and examines the arguments relating to ownership and performance. The next section considers the empirical evidence on

209

the impact of privatization in developing countries, relating the outcomes (impacts) to the objectives of privatization. The final section provides a summary and conclusions.

Assessing the impact of privatization

Assessment of the impact of privatization encounters a number of method-ological difficulties. The first relates to the choice of impact indicator. Ideally, performance should be assessed in terms of the objectives set for privatization. There may be multiple objectives, however, and the relative weight to be given to each objective may not be clear, or may shift over time. In some cases, the objective of privatization is broadly defined in terms of expanding the share of the private sector and encouraging market develop-ment. In other cases, the aim may be to improve macroeconomic per-formance, such as economic growth, fiscal balance or investment. More commonly, performance is assessed at the micro or enterprise level, in terms of economic efficiency and financial profitability. A further approach is to assess the outcome of privatization using a cost–benefit approach, where the social impact of privatization, particularly in terms of employment, is included in the evaluation.

The importance attached to these various objectives has varied between countries and over time. Privatization can contribute to one objective while at the same time making it more difficult to achieve another, presenting the policy maker with potential trade-offs. For example, the price that the private sector is willing to pay for the enterprise will depend on expected future profit performance, which in turn varies inversely with the level of competition in the market. In order to maximize the privatization sales revenue, the government may need to give the purchaser a guarantee of market protection, which is likely to mean a lower efficiency performance by the privatized enterprise. Also the impact which privatization has in terms of any particular objective will often depend upon broader macroec-onomic stability and market-strengthening measures, which increase private sector confidence in the government's commitment to the privatiza-tion programme. Where privatization is poorly planned and implemented, or where the sustainability of the reform programme is in doubt, the poten-tial gains from privatization will be compromised.

A second methodological challenge is the familiar one of establishing the counterfactual; that is, what would have happened in the absence of privatiza-tion? Two approaches have been widely used. The first is to compare perfor-mance of public and private enterprises in the same industry. The second is to study the performance of enterprises before and after privatization. Both approaches have their drawbacks and provide only an approximation to the ideal, but hypothetical, counterfactual position (Cook and Kirkpatrick, 1994).

Objectives of privatization

As noted already, policy makers have had a variety of objectives in mind for privatization. First, given the widespread evidence of the poor economic performance of state-owned enterprises, reflected in economic inefficiency, low productivity and lack of competitiveness, it was hoped that, by switching from public to private ownership, economic performance would improve. Second, many individual public enterprises, and the public enterprise sector as a whole, have operated at a financial loss, requiring various forms of subsidization, including direct transfers from central government. Privatization was seen, therefore, as a means of reducing the fiscal burden associated with loss-making public enterprises. Third, privatization was sometimes used as a means of raising revenue, which could be used to finance a fiscal deficit and relieve the government's liquidity constraint. Fourth, privatization has been adopted for broader macroeconomic reasons, for example, to increase the share of the private sector in the economy.

The theoretical argument for privatization rests on the hypothesis that, in a competitive market environment, enterprise performance will be superior under private ownership, as compared to public ownership; in other words, property rights are assumed to be the primary determinant of enterprise performance. But where there are significant market failures, such as market power or externalities, the public enterprise may produce socially efficient results which maximize social welfare, whereas the private manager will maximize private profits and welfare. This case for public ownership assumes, therefore, that bureaucrats and politicians will act in a way that maximizes social welfare. Public ownership has also been used to pursue other social objectives, beyond that of addressing market failures. These objectives have included reduced income inequality, increased employment, accelerated technology transfer and regional development.

The idea that public ownership is the solution to market failure has been challenged on several grounds. First, it is argued that government can deal with market failure by regulating private enterprises and/or contracting with a private firm to provide the social product. A similar argument can be made with respect to the non-market failure objectives, namely that there may be other more efficient ways of achieving social goals besides public ownership. Second, the merits of public ownership are further challenged by those who argue that bureaucrats and politicians do not seek to maximize social welfare but instead act to maximize their own utility. From this public choice perspective, politicians and enterprise managers use state-owned enterprises to benefit themselves, at the cost of inefficient enterprise performance. A closely related argument draws on principal–agent theory, maintaining that the owners (principals) of public enterprises have little incentive to monitor the managers (agents), with the result that the public enterprises have lower internal efficiency than private enterprises (also see especially Chapters 2 and 3 above).

For both private enterprises and state-owned enterprises, ownership is typically separated from control. Since managers' objectives are likely to differ from those of owners, a conflict arises between the two groups. Advocates of privatization argue that these problems are more acute, and thereby more costly, in public enterprises, where the threat of takeover or bankruptcy as a spur to managerial performance is absent.

The extent to which competition affects performance has important implications for the case of privatization. Competition is viewed as a key determinant of economic performance, improving allocative and productive efficiency. If market competition is the only determinant of performance, and affects all enterprises equally, then the focus for policy will be on increasing the level of competition in the market rather than changing the ownership of enterprises. In many developing countries, however, monopoly conditions are pervasive, and privatization is likely simply to replace a public monopoly with a private one. In the absence of market competition, regulation of the privatized monopoly will be needed if post-privatization economic (as distinct from financial) performance is to improve. However, if the previous arguments about the superiority of performance under private ownership are valid, the focus of policy should be on privatization *and* increasing market competition, though this is not a policy option in cases of 'natural monopoly', where attempts to introduce competition would lead to economic inefficiency.

To summarize, the argument for privatization is based on a number of related hypotheses: competition is not the sole determinant of enterprise performance; public ownership may not be the most efficient way of dealing with market failure or meeting social objectives; and because of public choice and principal–agent problems, public ownership is likely to produce an inferior performance compared to private ownership.

Empirical evidence on the impact of privatization in developing countries
Ownership and performance
Accepting that theory has failed to settle the debate over ownership and performance (Laffont and Tirole, 1993), a review of the evidence from empirical studies on the relative performance of public and private enterprises may help to remove the ambiguities of the theoretical literature. Empirical work has faced the standard methodological problem, however, of isolating the influence of ownership on performance from the impact of other determinants of performance. For this reason, the empirical evidence can also be challenged, and the debate on ownership and performance continues.

The most recent comprehensive review of the empirical work in this area is that undertaken by Shirley and Walsh (2001). They reviewed a total of 52 studies on private–public enterprise performance, spanning the period from 1971 to 1999, covering developing and developed countries and both similar private and public enterprises, and pre- and post-privatization enterprise performance, in a variety of competitive environments. Of the 52 studies, 32 (61 per cent) conclude that the performance of private and privatized firms is superior to that of public enterprises, while 15 studies find either that there is no significant relationship between ownership and performance, or that the relationship is ambiguous. Five studies conclude that publicly owned enterprises perform better than private enterprises. Similarly inconclusive results emerge from the 31 studies that compare private and public enterprises in the same industry. Here 18 studies conclude that private enterprises have better performance, while eight report mixed results and five find superior public sector performance.

Comparing performance in different market conditions, Shirley and Walsh identify 16 separate studies of public and private enterprise performance in competitive markets. In such markets, there are 11 cases which find superior private performance, and five which show no difference. The advantage of private ownership is less pronounced, however, in monopolistic markets, where six studies find private performance is superior, five find neutral results, and five find publicly owned enterprise performance to be superior.

The empirical evidence on ownership and performance does not resolve the theoretical ambiguities. The weight of evidence supports the view that private ownership will produce superior results in competitive markets, but is less conclusive about the effects of ownership in monopoly markets.

Macro-level impacts
Has privatization reduced the 'burden' of the public sector in developing countries? The evidence on the share of state enterprises in GDP shows no sign of a decline over the period 1978–91, when privatization was being widely adopted (World Bank, 1995). Public enterprises contributed about 11 per cent of GDP in developing countries throughout the period, with the highest share in sub-Saharan Africa (14 per cent), followed by 10 per cent in Latin America and 8 per cent in Asia. A similar pattern is observed for public enterprise employment, where the share in total employment remained unchanged at around 10 per cent. Regional variations are much greater for employment than for output, however, with the public enterprise sector in Africa accounting for perhaps 20 per cent of formal sector employment, compared to around 3 per cent in other developing country regions.

The case for privatization is based in part on the assumption that an 'overextended' public enterprise sector lowers economic growth. However, the empirical evidence fails to show a significant relationship between the size of the state sector and economic growth performance (Jalilian and Weiss, 1997). The literature on growth in developing countries suggests that a set of policy variables – particularly fiscal discipline, price and trade liberalization and privatization – are important in determining a country's growth performance, but, when taken individually, these variables have only a limited effect on growth (Aziz and Wescott, 1997).

Attempts to measure directly the relationship between privatization and economic growth in developing countries have been few, and have provided conflicting results. Studies by Plane (1997) and Barnett (2000) find a significant and positive relationship between privatization and economic growth. The study by Plane covered 35 developing countries over the period 1984–92. Using Probit and Tobit techniques, it was found that privatization positively contributed to GDP growth, and the effect on growth was more significant with respect to industry and infrastructure privatization. On average, privatization increased economic growth in 1984–8 and 1988–92 by 0.8 per cent and 1.5 per cent, respectively. The study by Barnett (2000) used 18 countries (including 12 developing countries) to examine the effect of privatization on real GDP growth. Again, privatization was positively correlated with economic growth, although it was indicated that the privatization variable was likely to capture the positive impact of a general regime change towards 'better' economic policies. Contrary results were obtained in a recent study by Cook and Uchida (2003). They used an extreme bounds analysis (EBA) to estimate the relationship between privatization and economic growth in 63 developing countries between 1988 and 1997. In this case there was a robust negative partial correlation between privatization and economic growth.

Clearly, the negative and positive findings between privatization and economic growth do not rule out the possibility that the wider economic and sociopolitical environment may have important effects on economic growth, and on the success of privatization. The Barnett (2000) study, using a limited number of countries, implies that the positive relationship between privatization and economic growth could be explained by privatization acting as a proxy for a range of structural measures signifying changes in the economic environment. In contrast, the study by Cook and Uchida (2003) attempted to control for the risk of the privatization variable reflecting other policy and structural reforms at the aggregate level.

The impact of privatization on growth is likely to be linked to a change in investment levels. Privatization has contributed to inflows of foreign investment to developing countries. Foreign direct investment and portfolio investment amounted to about 42 per cent of the total value of privatization transactions in developing countries over the period 1988–94, with Latin America receiving much of the inflow (Sader, 1994). Enterprise-level data on capital expenditure showed a significant increase (as a proportion of sales) in the majority of enterprises studied (Megginson *et al.*, 1994; Boubakri and Cosset, 1998). But privatization-related foreign capital inflows are a small proportion of total inflows, and foreign capital, in turn, accounts for less than 10 per cent of total investments in most developing countries.

The fiscal impact of privatization has been equally difficult to assess. While revenues from asset sales have been large, in many cases the net revenue gain has been significantly reduced by debt write-offs, costs of reconstruction, recapitalization and transaction costs. The contribution to the budget has also been found to be much less than sales proceeds, where privatization revenues are treated as extrabudgetary funds. The fiscal impact of privatization will depend on the amount, and the use made, of the proceeds and the subsequent changes in financial flows – taxes, transfers and dividends to and from the budget. A pioneering study in this area was that of Pinheiro and Schneider (1995), using the cases of Mexico, Argentina, Brazil and Chile. At the time, these countries accounted for nearly 60 per cent of total developing country privatization and, therefore, provided a representative picture. Using a comprehensive model that incorporated long-term time preferences and indirect effects of fiscal impact, the authors concluded that the objective of improving the fiscal balance through privatization was not achieved. The proceeds from privatization were too small and received too late to have a significant impact on the fiscal balance.

In contrast, using a sample of 18 developing and transitionary countries, Davis *et al.*, (2000) found that, on average, privatization proceeds transferred to the budget are saved, and used to substitute for other sources of domestic financing. The case studies also suggested that, over time, the fiscal situation tended to benefit from privatization. In particular, both the enterprise level and more aggregate data show positive impacts on revenue and a decline in transfers following periods of privatization; broader indicators of consolidated public enterprise accounts indicate a large decline in deficits (ibid.).

Micro-level performance
Micro-level evidence on the impact of privatization is derived mainly from enterprise data on performance 'before and after' privatization. Table 10.1 summarizes the results from a wide range of recent studies of enterprise level performance in developing countries. The evidence in the table supports the notion that, on average, privatization has led to an improvement in financial and economic performance. This holds for enterprises in both competitive industries and less competitive settings, although in the latter

case the evidence is less strong (Megginson and Netter, 1999). These findings are consistent with the 'survey of surveys' findings reported by Shirley and Walsh (2001) and discussed above.

Table 10.1   Summary of studies of firm-level impact of privatization in developing countries, 1980s to early 1990s.

	Mean before privatization	Mean after privatization	Share of firms with improved performance (%)
Profitability (net income/sales)	0.05	0.11	63
Efficiency (real sales per employee)	1.92	1.17	80
Output (real sales)	0.97	1.22	76
Leverage (total debt/total assets)	0.55	0.50	63
Dividends (cash dividends/sales)	0.03	0.05	76

Source: Davis et al. (2000, Table 8), based on Megginson *et al.* (1994); Boubakri and Cosset (1998); D'Souza and Megginson (1999); Megginson and Netter (1999).

The findings reported in Table 10.1, and in other similar studies, however, also suggest variation in *post*-privatization performance (see final column: 'share of firms with improved performance'). Megginson *et al.* (1994) found that the most significant improvements in performance occurred in those enterprises where there were major changes in management and enterprise governance structures.

Social impact of privatization
State-owned enterprises that are protected by soft budget constraints and non-competitive markets may be overstaffed and pay excessive wages and salaries, and part of the efficiency and financial gains from privatization, therefore, may result from a reduction in the workforce employed by the privatized enterprise. But these long-term economic benefits also represent short-term social costs as labour is retrenched. The impact of privatization on labour markets is therefore an important consideration in assessing the impact of privatization, particularly in the short and medium term. Privatization, particularly if accompanied by market deregulation, may result, however, in sufficient growth in demand and new businesses to offset the reduction in employment in the former state-owned enterprises. Some of the evidence at the aggregate and enterprise level suggests that privatization has not been associated with large-scale job losses. Davis *et al.* (2000) examine cross-country evidence for 18 countries and find that privatization has been associated with a reduction in both the contemporaneous and

lagged unemployment rate. Megginson *et al.* (1994) found that, for 61 enterprises in predominantly industrial countries, employment tended to increase after privatization. In a sample of developing countries, Boubakri and Cosset (1998) found a similar result, with about 60 per cent of the enterprises in their studies experiencing an increase in employment following privatization. White and Bhattia (1998), in their study of the impact of privatization in Africa, failed to find a correlation between privatization and job losses. They document instances when 'downsizing' resulted from the loss of subsidies and the application of hard budget constraints for public enterprises rather than privatization.

In contrast, Bhaskar and Khan (1995) analysed the impact of privatization on employment and output in the jute industry in Bangladesh. They found that privatization reduced employment, particularly among white collar employees, indicating that this category of employees was overexpanded when the jute mills were publicly owned. Using a database consisting of 218 privatized non-financial enterprises in Mexico between 1983 and 1991, La Porta and Lopez-de-Silanes (1999) found that productivity rose because employment had been halved. Khan (1999) also examined whether social welfare was affected by different types of ownership arrangements after privatization and found that employment was reduced after privatization, irrespective of the type of ownership. However, even if privatization does not have a major adverse impact on total employment over time, there will inevitably be short-term job losses and labour adjustment costs. This makes it important to consider the measures needed to mitigate the adverse social impact of privatization (Gupta *et al.*, 1999; Van der Hoeven and Sziraczki, 1997; Estache *et al.*, 2000).

Conclusions

This chapter has evaluated the impact of privatization in developing countries. The result has been to reveal a complex and sometimes contradictory picture, with major theoretical disagreements on the predicted outcomes and significant differences in the empirical evidence across sectors and countries, and over time. The experience with policy and performance has been diverse, making it difficult to identify common patterns of experience or to draw general lessons for policy.

What is apparent, however, is that improvements in public enterprise performance and in the contribution to economic development involve more than simply changing ownership from the public to the private sector. Privatization can be an effective instrument for bringing about significant economic and developmental gains, but, besides ownership, it involves a set of interlinking issues which include corporate governance, institutional capacity, market competition and political economy.

References

Aziz, J. and R. Wescott (1997) 'Policy Complementarities and the Washington Consensus', IMF Working Paper, 97/118, IMF, Washington, DC.

Barnett, S. (2000) 'Evidence on the Fiscal and Macroeconomic Impact of Privatisation', IMF Working Paper, July, IMF, Washington, DC.

Bhaskar, V. and M. Khan (1995) 'Privatisation and Employment: A Study of the Jute Industry in Bangladesh', *American Economic Review*, 85(1), 267–73.

Boubakri, N. and J.C. Cosset (1998) 'The Financial and Operating Performance of Newly Privatised Firms: Evidence from Developing Countries', *Journal of Finance*, 53(3), 1081–110.

Cook, P. and C. Kirkpatrick (1994) *A Report on the Experience with Privatisation and a Methodology for Assessing the Results*, Geneva: UNCTAD.

Cook, P. and Y. Uchida (2003) 'Privatisation and Economic Growth in Developing Countries', *Journal of Development Studies*, 39(6) (forthcoming).

Davis, J., R. Ossowski, T. Richardson and S. Barnett (2000) 'Fiscal and Macroeconomic Impact of Privatization', IMF Occasional Paper, no.194, IMF, Washington, DC.

D'Souza, J. and W.J. Megginson (1999) 'The Financial and Operating Performance of Privatised Firms during the 1990s', *Journal of Finance*, 54(4), 1397–438.

Estache, A., A. Gomez-Lobo and D. Leipziger (2000) 'Utility Privatisation and the Needs of the Poor in Latin America: Have we Learned Enough to Get It Right?', mimeo, World Bank, Washington, DC.

Gupta, S., C. Schiller and H. Ma (1999) 'Privatization, Social Impact and Social Safety Nets', IMF Working Paper, 99/68, IMF, Washington, DC.

Jalilian, H. and J. Weiss (1997) 'Bureaucrats, Business and Economic Growth', *Journal of International Development*, 9(6), 877–85.

Khan, S. (1999) 'Comparative Privatisation Experience: Employee and Private Ownership', in S.R. Khan (ed.), *Do World Bank and IMF Policies Work?*, Basingstoke: Macmillan.

Kikeri, S. and J. Nellis (2002) 'Privatisation in Competitive Sectors: Record to Date', World Bank Working Paper, no. 2860, World Bank, Washington, DC.

Kirkpatrick, C. (2001) 'Regulatory Impact Assessment in Developing Countries: Research Issues', Centre on Regulation and Competition Working Paper, no. 5, University of Manchester.

Laffont, J. and J. Tirole (1993) *A Theory of Incentives in Procurement and Regulation*, Cambridge, MA: MIT Press.

La Porta, R. and F. Lopez-de-Silanes (1999) 'The Benefits of Privatisation: Evidence for Mexico', *Quarterly Journal of Economics*, 114(4), 1193–242.

Lee, N. (2002) 'Developing and Applying Regulatory Impact Assessment Methodologies in Low and Middle Income Countries', mimeo, University of Manchester.

Mahboobi, L. (2000) 'Recent Privatization Trends', mimeo, OECD, Paris.

Megginson, W.L. and J.M. Netter (1999) 'From State to Market: A Survey of Empirical Studies in Privatization', draft paper prepared for joint references of SBF Bourse de Paris and the New York Stock Exchange, Paris.

Megginson, W.L. and J.M. Netter (2001) 'From State to Market: A Summary of Empirical Studies on Privatization', *Journal of Economic Literature*, 39(2), 321–89.

Megginson, W.L., Nash, R.C. and M. van Randenborgh (1994) 'Financial and Operating Performance of Newly Privatised Firms: An International Empirical Analysis', *Journal of Finance*, 49, (2), pp. 403–52.

Pinheiro, A. and B. Schneider (1995) 'Fiscal Impact of Privatisation in Latin America', *Journal of Development Studies*, 31(5), 751–85.

Plane, P. (1997) 'Privatisation and Economic Growth: An Empirical Investigation from a Sample of Developing Market Economies', *Applied Economics*, 29(2), 161–78.

Sader, F. (1994) 'Privatisation Techniques and Foreign Investment in Developing Countries, 1988–93', mimeo, World Bank, Washington, DC.

Shirley, M. and P. Walsh (2001) 'Public versus Private Ownership: The Current State of the Debate', mimeo, World Bank, Washington, DC.

Van der Hoeven, R. and G. Sziraczki (eds) (1997) *Employment and Privatisation*, Geneva: International Labour Office.

White, O. and A. Bhattia (1998) *Privatisation in Africa*, World Bank, Washington, DC.

World Bank (1995) *Bureaucrats in Business: The Economics and Politics of Government Ownership*, London and New York: Oxford University Press for the World Bank.

11 The privatization experience of Brazil
Werner Baer

Introduction

To understand the process and impact of Brazil's privatization in the 1990s, one must understand the reasons for the rapid growth of the state in the economy prior to that time. This chapter therefore begins with a brief review of the growth of state enterprises in Brazil, their contribution to the country's development, and the circumstances that ultimately resulted in state firms being considered as obstacles to growth, leading to the privatization programmes of the 1990s. This is followed by a description of the privatization process and its impact on efficiency and equity.

The growth of state enterprises in Brazil

State enterprises were present in Brazil in colonial times.[1] Their influence over the economy, however, was minor. This began to change considerably during the Great Depression of the 1930s. The institutional changes that led to a greater role of the state in the economy stemmed from the Brazilian government's desire to protect the economy from the full impact of the world depression and to support and speed up the process of import substitution industrialization (ISI). The latter became the major development strategy after the Second World War. When it became clear that neither the domestic private sector nor foreign groups had an interest in building an integrated steel mill, which was deemed necessary as a requirement for a vertically integrated industrialization process, Brazil's government became involved in that sector.[2]

State firms were started in the 1940s and 1950s with the intention of guaranteeing Brazilian control over the country's non-replaceable resources, such as oil and iron ore.[3] Over the three decades following the Second World War, the Brazilian government (both federal and local governments) founded and/or took over firms in the public utilities sector.[4] The motivation was the need for public utility services to expand along with the rapidly growing urban centres and industry, while private domestic and foreign firms were not interested in the modernization and expansion of these sectors, whose regulated tariffs resulted in low rates of return which discouraged further investments.

State involvement in the financial sector, which dated back to the late nineteenth century, grew rapidly during the ISI and post-ISI periods. The federal and state governments established commercial banks to provide credit to sectors such as agriculture or the regions which were neglected by private banks. As ISI proceeded in the post-Second World War period, there was an increasing necessity for long-term financing, while the country's capital market was still very weak. This led the government to create a development bank (BNDE),[5] which would make long-term loans and/or buy stocks in newly established or expanding industrial enterprises.

Various quantitative measures show the importance the Brazilian state had acquired in the economy by the 1970s and 1980s. In the early 1970s, almost 50 per cent of total gross investment was accounted for by government and state enterprises; this rose to 65 per cent by the early 1980s. In 1985, the federal and state commercial banks accounted for 40 per cent of bank deposits and 44 per cent of commercial loans of the 50 largest banks. In the same year the development bank (BNDES) and other government development banks (such as the development bank for Brazil's northeast) provided 70 per cent of all loans destined for investment purposes. In the same year, a survey of the 8094 largest incorporated firms revealed that state enterprises controlled 48 per cent of combined assets, 26.1 per cent of sales and 18.9 per cent of employment. Finally, in 1990, examining the 20 largest firms by sector, it was found that state enterprises had the following percentages of total sales (Baer, 2001:276–9): public utilities, 100 per cent; steel, 67 per cent; chemicals and petrochemicals, 67 per cent; mining, 60 per cent; transport services, 35 per cent; fertilizers, 26 per cent; transport equipment, 21 per cent.

For many decades, the large presence of the state in Brazil's economy was viewed as beneficial. It had a 'crowding in' effect, since it complemented the domestic private and foreign sectors by providing them with crucial inputs, often at low prices, and the private domestic sector was able to receive relatively cheap official financing. This benign perception of the state was acceptable in many quarters from the 1950s to the 1970s. For example, most of the loans from the World Bank and USAID to Brazil were made to state enterprises and development banks.

By the 1970s and 1980s, the state's presence in the economy had an increasingly negative impact on Brazil's economy. The decadence of state firms was due to a number of factors: having monopoly positions in many markets, state firms became inefficient and many abused their monopoly positions in dealing with their private sector clients; the government used state firms as instruments of macroeconomic policies (for example, forcing firms to charge low prices in order to fight inflation, or to obtain unnecessary foreign loans), causing large deficits in their operations and forcing the government to provide large subsidies; many state firms succumbed to political pressures to overemploy; and, as the state sector contributed towards increasing the government's budget deficit, it produced a 'crowding-out' phenomenon in relation to the private sector.

Privatization

Brazil's movement towards privatization began in the late 1970s, when a declining rate of growth resulted in increasing competition between public enterprises and the private sector for scarce capital resources – both domestic and foreign. As state enterprises were in the midst of large investment projects to which the government was giving full support, resources available for the private sector were in short supply. This ended the previous 'tripod harmony'[6] and led to a movement in favour of privatization.

The first attempt to control the expansion of Brazil's state-owned enterprises (SOEs) occurred in 1979 with the creation of the National Programme of Debureaucratization and the Special Secretariat for the Control of State Enterprises (SEST) (Castelar Pinheiro and de Oliveira Filho, 1992:337). These early programmes did not have much of an impact on the privatization process, however. The government used SEST to get greater centralized control over the SOEs. In fact, this institution made it easier for the government to use SOEs as instruments of macroeconomic policies.

In the first half of the 1980s, some effort was made to privatize the SOEs. The Special Commission for Destatization, which was established in 1981, identified 140 privatizable SOEs and recommended the selling of 50 in the immediate future. Of these, 20 were sold in the years 1981–4, bringing in total proceeds of US$190mn (ibid.:338–9). Many of these represented a 'reprivatization' process, as most of the firms concerned had fallen into the hands of the government development bank (BNDES) when they were on the verge of bankruptcy. The BNDES then reorganized these firms with a view to selling them back to the private sector. Most of the firms were small or medium-sized. At the time, the large SOEs were not thought to be privatizable.

There were various reasons for the lack of a forceful privatization programme in the 1980s. First, there was no political commitment, as the government in the early 1980s was more interested in controlling the expansion of the state than in changing its role. Second, as the first half of the decade was a period of deep economic recession, it would have been impossible to find buyers unless the SOEs were sold at politically unacceptable discounted prices. Third, the sale of SOEs was restricted to Brazilian firms. Fourth, to be effective, a large-scale privatization process would have made it necessary to institute a liberalization of government controls (especially price controls), which at the time was not acceptable to the government (ibid.: 338).

In the second half of the 1980s, the government paid lip service to privatization, but did not push for a massive programme. This might have been politically motivated. President Sarney's administration, which was the first civilian government in 21 years, was very sensitive to pressure groups. The latter included employees of SOEs, earning salaries that were substantially higher than market averages; private firms that sold goods to SOEs at great profit; firms that received goods and services from SOEs at subsidized prices; and politicians who made use of SOEs for their own purposes.

In the period 1985–9, 18 SOEs were privatized, bringing in government receipts of US$533 mn. Most were relatively small firms that been revitalized by the BNDES.

Privatization during the Collor and Itamar Franco administrations, 1990–93

The privatization programme of the Collor administration, which was introduced on 14 April 1990, proved to be of a much larger dimension than previous programmes. Not only was the government planning to privatize large SOEs, but the privatization process was viewed as being an integral part of a programme that was meant to modernize the Brazilian economy through a general market liberalization process.[7]

Most sales occurred at public auctions and 'currencies' acceptable from a buyer could be the old and new Brazilian currencies, various types of government debt certificates, foreign debt papers and foreign currencies. Foreign participation in SOEs to be privatized was limited to 40 per cent of voting capital and unlimited for non-voting capital and the maximum discount for debt conversion was set at 25 per cent. Other restrictions included a rule that foreign capital had to remain in Brazil for 12 years and that the sale of stocks acquired could only occur after two years. By 1992, some of these restrictions were modified: the 40 per cent maximum voting capital could be changed after auctions on a case-by-case basis; the requirement of sale of stocks and remittance of profits only after two years was eliminated; and the requirement that capital must stay in the country for 12 years was reduced to six years. The average time for privatizing an SOE took about nine months.

By mid-1993, 20 companies had been privatized and 21 others were on the privatization list. Most SOEs on that list were in the petrochemical, steel and fertilizer sectors; also under consideration at the time were the railroad system, the state aircraft manufacturer (EMBRAER) and a computer firm.

With the change of government in September 1992, due to the impeachment of President Collor, the new president (Itamar Franco) was at first reluctant to continue the privatization programme. However, after a three-month halt, the new administration decided to continue the process. The law that created the National Privatization Programme (PND) was changed to allow for unlimited participation by foreigners, and by the end of the Itamar

Franco presidency, at the end of 1994, more SOEs had been privatized than under the previous administration. Most manufacturing SOEs were privatized in the 1991–4 period.

Under President Fernanco Henrique Cardoso's administration, which began in 1995, the speed of privatization picked up further and included such sectors as mining and public utilities. In the last half of the 1990s, privatization was also extended to include firms which were owned by individual states and municipalities. Institutional changes were made in January 1995, when the National Privatization Committee was replaced by the National Privatization Council, which increased central control over the privatization process. While the PND was preserved, changes were made in the legal and institutional framework. In February 1995, the Concessions Law (Law 8987) was enacted, and constitutional amendments were approved later on in the year. The Concessions Law (regulated by Article 175 of the constitution) introduced changes in the rules applying to concessions in the public utilities sector.[8] Constitutional amendments discontinued public monopolies in telecommunications and gas distributed by pipeline; they also abolished the distinction between Brazilian companies owned by domestic and foreign capital. These changes paved the way for the privatization process in the mining and power generation sectors.

Privatization at the state and municipal levels was important because of its fiscal impact. Non-federal public companies were responsible for most of the SOE deficit. In 1994–8, while federal SOEs had a surplus amounting to 0.4 per cent of GDP, state and municipal SOEs had a deficit of 0.7 per cent of GDP. Thus privatization was important in the process of debt restructuring.[9] The privatization of roads and telecommunications was carried out by ministries that were directly concerned with those sectors rather than going through the PND.

The privatization of LIGHT, the electric utility that services Rio de Janeiro, in 1996, represented an important breakthrough in the sale of a large public utility. This was followed, in 1997, by the privatization of Vale do Rio Doce, which was the largest Brazilian exporter (of iron ore). As this was considered at the time to be the most efficient SOE, there was considerable opposition to its sale and the government had to win 217 lawsuits before the sale could be finalized. In the second half of the 1990s, the government increasingly required that most of the means of payment for privatizing firms were to be in the form of cash. According to Castelar Pinheiro and Giambiagi (2000: 19), 'As Brazil remained in the non-investment category internationally and the risk of large devaluation of the *real* loomed on the horizon, borrowing in foreign markets could only provide a partial solution. Therefore, the government stepped in, financing borrowers directly by the sale in installments or through the BNDES.'

It is also noteworthy that a new approach was taken to the privatization of roads, bridges, sanitation and railways. These were sectors with substantial amounts of externalities and lower profitability. In these cases an increasing emphasis in the auctions was placed on commitments to make substantial new investments in these sectors.

With the broadening of privatization into the public utilities sector, the value of the sales increased, to such an extent that they became crucial to the government's macroeconomic policies and, in particular, defending the currency under the *Real Plan*, especially given the impact of the Asian and Russian crises of the late 1990s. Thus 'privatization would give the country an edge over other countries that had been or might become prey to speculative attack. In this respect, privatization was seen as a kind of 'safety net' or "bridge to stability", affording the country some leeway for resolving its two main disequilibria, the current account and fiscal deficits' (ibid.).

Privatization results, 1991–2001

In the period 1991–2001, 121 SOEs (both federal and state-level firms) were sold, amounting to US$103bn (of this sum, US$84.9bn amounted to cash receipts and US$18.1bn represented debts that were transferred to the private sector).[10] It is noteworthy that, while privatization was restricted to manufacturing firms, revenues were relatively small, averaging US$2.7bn a year in 1991–5. Beginning in 1996, with the extension of privatization to public utilities and the participation of states, revenues surged. In 1997 alone, proceeds were greater than in the previous six years. Up to 2000, the domestic private sector dominated the privatization process, acquiring about 61.2 per cent of the shares auctioned. The share accounted for by foreign investors, however, increased considerably in the second half of the 1990s. In 1998, foreign investors were responsible for 59 per cent of total proceeds. On an overall basis, foreign participation rose from less than 1 per cent in 1994 to 43.8 per cent in 2001.

In sum, by the beginning of the twenty-first century, privatization had extended to all of the sectors of the economy in which the state had previously been active. The largest sector for privatization was the telecommunications industry, most of which was auctioned in July 1998. Table 11.1 shows the breakdown of Brazilian privatizations at the federal level in the period 1990–2000, by sector.[11] It may be noted that the telecommunication proceeds accounted for more than half of the federal revenues, or over a third of all privatization receipts. State government privatizations, which became significant during the Cardoso government, were dominated by sales of state-owned electric power companies, which accounted for over two-thirds of the value of state-level privatizations.

The relatively small amount of revenues received from privatization of the railroads and other transport infrastructure (included in 'Others' in Table 11.1) reflects the fact that in this case the Government's priority was not to maximize revenues from sales but rather to increase capacity in the sector. The decline in public spending in this sector in the preceding decade, and the continuing inability of the government to finance necessary investments, made privatization the only alternative.

Table 11.1   Brazil: total privatizations by sector, 1990–2000

Sector*	Number of companies	Revenue received (US$mn)	Revenue (per cent of total)
Steel	8	5562	8.0
Petrochemicals	27	2698	3.9
Railroads	7	1698	2.5
Mining	2	3305	4.8
Telecommunications	24	26644	38.6
Electric Power	3	3907	5.7
Others	18	1471	2.1
Sales of minority positions	—	1040	1.5
Total privatizations Federal government	89	46325	67.1
State government	28	22736	32.9
Total	117	69061	100.0

Notes: Data through to January 2000.
* A sectoral breakdown was not available for state privatizations. However, the author's estimate is that, between 1996 and 2001, 40 state enterprises were privatized, of which seven were state banks, while the rest were public utility enterprises in electricity and gas distribution, sanitation enterprises and the Rio de Janeiro Metro.

Source: BNDES, *www.bndes.gov.br/pndnew*.

The wealth effects of privatization
In the analysis of economic distribution issues, it is useful to distinguish between policy effects on wealth (stocks) and on income (flows). Although often closely related, these effects may sometimes diverge significantly.[12] In the context of privatization, wealth effects are alterations in the ownership of the country's economic assets. This is a once-and-for-all change, occurring at the time of privatization. Income distribution effects, however, are the continuing consequences of privatization on the real earnings and income of various groups in society, among them the new owners, workers and consumers of the products of the privatized firms. In this section, the

wealth distribution effects of privatization are considered. Income distribution effects are addressed in the following section.

The distribution of corporate wealth in Brazil has been divided traditionally into the *tripé* (tripod) of state-owned, private domestic and foreign enterprises (Baer, 2001: 279–82; Evans, 1979). Well before the major privatizations of the 1990s, many sectors of Brazilian industry were dominated by a small number of either private domestic firms or foreign firms. This was the case, for example, in the motor industry, where the top four firms accounted for 94 per cent of net receipts of that sector in 1998. In the same year the top seven firms in the cement industry accounted for 60 per cent of net receipts. In heavy construction, motors and components, electric appliances and steel, the top eight (four, four, and seven) firms accounted for 67 per cent (64 per cent, 75 per cent and 82 per cent) of net receipts in their respective industries.[13]

The privatization programme of the 1990s was largely driven by the government's need to maximize its revenues from the sale of state-owned enterprises by selling to the highest bidders. It is not surprising, therefore, that most of these bidders were either foreign enterprises or the largest domestic private firms. This suggests that the Brazilian privatization process, of selling to the highest bidder to relieve the fiscal stress on the public sector, may have had either a negligible or even negative impact upon the distribution of wealth in Brazil. Had the privatization policy attempted to divide the value of the formerly state-owned firms among Brazilian citizens or taxpayers, it is possible that the effects of privatization on the distribution of wealth might have been more positive. Even though some provision was made for workers and their pensions to share in the privatization process, this share was relatively modest. In December 1997, only 7.5 per cent of the shares of the privatized firms were held by employees and their pension funds (De Mello Jr., 2000: 85).

This trend in wealth distribution may have been reinforced, moreover, by the parallel trend in major mergers and acquisitions throughout the 1990s. These rose from 58 in 1992 to 212 in 1995 and to 351 in 1998 (Siffert Filho and Souza e Silva, 1999: 383). Some of these mergers were motivated, in part, by the need for private domestic firms to form strategic alliances large enough to make successful bids for enterprises that were being privatized. An example was the association among the Grupo Votorantim, Brazil's major cement producer, the large construction firm, Camargo Correia, and Brazil's largest private domestic bank, Bradesco, to participate in the privatizations in the energy sector (ibid.: 385).

Some insight into the possible effects of privatization on the distribution of corporate holdings and organization during the 1990s is provided by Table 11.2, which shows changes in the ownership of Brazil's hundred largest non-financial firms between 1990 and 1998. It classifies private domestic Brazilian firms into three sub-categories, corresponding to the degree of concentration of ownership. It should be noted that even the 'lower concentration' firms shown in the table include many which would not be considered 'widely held' in the North American sense. Even though no one individual or family had more than 20 per cent of the voting shares of the firms in this sub-category, a small number of owners could easily dominate the firm.

Table 11.2   Brazil: ownership distribution of 100 largest firms, 1990–98

	1990		1998	
	Number of firms	Share of total revenues %	Number of firms	Share of total revenues %
Private, lower ownership concentration*	1	1	4	3
Private, medium ownership concentration*	5	4	23	19
Private, high ownership concentration*	27	23	26	17
Public	38	44	12	21
Foreign	27	26	34	40
Cooperatives	2	2	1	0
Total	100	100	100	100

Note: * Lower ownership – no controlling owner; medium ownership – minority ownership that dominates the firm; high ownership – majority owners that dominate the firm.

Source: Siffert Filho and Souza e Silva (1999:402).

Several trends are evident in the data of Table 11.2. Privatization had little or no impact on either cooperatives or the least concentrated of Brazil's top hundred private firms, whose combined share of revenues (3 per cent of the total) remained unchanged. The major beneficiaries of the decline in the relative importance of the public enterprises over the 1990–98 period were both foreign owners and those domestic private Brazilian firms in which one individual or family owned at least 20 per cent of the voting shares (firms with medium ownership concentration).[14]

Some specific cases illustrate well the dominance of large domestic firms and foreign buyers in the privatization process. In the case of the steel firms COSINOR and Piratini, 99.8 and 89.8 per cent of the shares, respectively, were acquired by the private Gerdau steel group.[15] In the sale of the larger Companhia Siderúrgica de Tubarão steel company, 45.4 per cent of the shares were acquired by the private financial groups of Bozano Simonsen and Unibanco. In other sectors, such as telecommunications, alliances between private Brazilian groups (Construtura Andrade Gutierrez, Bradesco, Globopar, Banco Opportunity) and foreign purchasers (Telecom de Portugal, Banco Bilbao Vizcaya, Stet International, Iberdrola) were important (ibid.: 392). In the electric power sector, Brazilian firms allied themselves with foreign enterprises from the USA, Chile, France, Spain and Portugal (Leal Ferreira, 2000: 154).

The income distribution effects of privatization
Whatever the initial motivations for the establishment of Brazil's network of state enterprises, by the 1960s they had become a significant source of employment in terms both of numbers employed and of salaries. The social and political pressures generated by rapid labour force growth and a high level of rural migration to Brazil's cities contributed to the willingness of successive governments to absorb labour in the public sector in excess of real needs. The gradual recognition of significant overstaffing in many of the state enterprises was in fact one of the motivations for the establishment of the Special Secretariat for the Control of State Enterprises (SEST) in 1979.

Privatization reversed this trend in public sector employment. In a number of cases, even before firms selected for privatization were put on the auction block, they were 'fattened up' to make them more attractive to potential buyers by eliminating excess employment. In the Federal Railroad System (RFFSA), about half of the 40000-strong labour force was made redundant even before actual privatization. And, once in charge, private operators of the railroads further reduced the labour force to about 11500 employees, while actually increasing the level of services. In the major public ports, the number of workers employed was reduced from 26400 in 1995 to about 5000 in 1997, with further reductions projected to bring the labour force down to 2500 workers (de Castro, 1999: 111). A substantial reduction in the workforce also took place in the steel sector after privatization. The number of employees in the Companhia Siderúrgica Nacional fell from 24463 in 1989 to 9829 in 1998; in Cosipa from 14445 to 6983; and in Usiminas from 14600 to 8338.[16]

Foguel *et al.* (2000) show, using data from the 1995 PNAD, that, even when age, education, years on the job and other factors are taken into consideration, public sector wages in Brazil exceed those for similar employees in the private sector. The wage gap is particularly high for federal employees. The authors' findings suggest that the privatization programmes of the

1990s, especially those involving federal public enterprises, may have produced declines in the incomes of employees.

Analysis of the income distribution effects of the reduction in employment that resulted from privatization is complex, however, even if the economic efficiency arguments for eliminating overstaffing are straightforward. Had the income gains resulting from greater economic efficiency been distributed to Brazil's poorest, then privatization would have made an unambiguously positive contribution to equity as well as to efficiency. But there is little or no credible evidence that the efficiency gains were in fact distributed in this manner. What scant evidence does exist, notably the substantial increase in the profits of the recently privatized firms, suggests that much of the income gain from increased efficiency was captured by the new owners. Thus in both 1997 and 1998 the magazine *Exame* listed four privatized firms among the 20 top profit-making firms of the country (Vale do Rio Doce, Usiminas, CSN and Light). A decade earlier some of these firms, especially CSN and Vale do Rio Doce, had been on the list of the biggest loss-making firms. A significant share of these profits, moreover, accrued to foreign purchasers of the privatized firms. Some of the sharp increase in remittances of profits and dividends in Brazil's balance of payments, which rose from US$1.6 bn in 1990 to $2.5 bn in 1994, and to $7.2 bn in 1998, may reflect the profits realized by foreign firms that participated in the privatization process.

The other major link between privatization and income distribution runs through the regulatory system and its resulting impact on prices. As noted above, a large part of the privatization process centred on public utilities, notably telecommunications, electric power generation, highways, railroads and ports. An essential element in the privatization process was the restructuring of the regulatory system so as to attract private operators who would adequately maintain and expand services.

This raises the classic question in public utility regulation: what tariff rates can generate adequate funds for maintenance and expansion and provide an attractive enough return for private investors while not excessively burdening consumers? The government had used many state-owned public utilities in Brazil, at least from the 1960s, as weapons in the fight against inflation. This was done through the regulation of their prices, which were forced to lag substantially behind the increase in the general price level, with consequent reductions in plant maintenance and new investment. By the mid-1980s, the fall in public investment had resulted in serious deficiencies in the capital stock of a number of public utilities, including railroads, ports and electric power generation.[17]

Privatization forced a drastic revision of public utility rates. In telecommunications, for example, tariffs were raised dramatically in 1995, well before the actual auctioning of the Telebrás system. Residential subscriptions were raised by a factor of five, with the cost of local calls rising by 80 per cent. The maintenance of these rates facilitated the privatization of the system in July 1998 (Novaes, 1999:111).

A similar catch-up pattern may be observed in the electric power sector, in which rates had lagged behind overall inflation until 1993. In the following years, with successive privatizations of the power companies, electricity tariffs rose considerably faster than most other prices. The *Estado de São Paulo* reported, for example, that the price index used to adjust electricity prices increased twice as fast in 1999 as did the index used for wage adjustment.[18]

The evidence available to date suggests that the regulatory climate in Brazil moved substantially in favour of the new private owners of the public utilities. From an income distribution point of view, these regulatory changes shifted income to the new private concession holders from a much larger group of consumers. In the city of Rio de Janeiro, for example, while the Consumer Price Index rose by 189.7 per cent between August 1994 and February 2000, the price index for public services rose by 264.7 per cent (Conjuntura Econômica, January 2000).

One of the most frequently mentioned arguments for privatization is that private firms are better positioned to make gains in efficiency than is the public sector. In principle, in a competitive market system such efficiency gains should result in a fall in the relative price of the outputs of those sectors in which these gains are greatest. It appears indisputable that the productivity gains in some of Brazil's public service sectors were in fact well above average productivity gains for the economy as a whole. Labour productivity for Brazil increased at an annual rate of 3.9 per cent between 1994 and 1997, while labour productivity in public utilities increased at annual rate of 16.3 per cent over the same period (IBGE, *Anuário Estatistico do Brasil 1998*, Table 7.61).

When we compare the evident fall in costs implied by the increase in labour productivity in many of the newly privatized public utilities with their success in raising relative output prices, it is apparent that the Brazilian regulatory process heavily favoured producers and not consumers. The case of electricity is illustrative in this respect. The first concession contract, that of ESCELSA (the power generation and distribution company in the state of Espírito Santo), did not make clear the parameters to be used in readjusting tariffs and made no mention of the distribution of the gains from productivity improvements. These uncertainties were reduced in subsequent concessions, but almost entirely in favour of the concessionaires. In the case of Rio's LIGHT and later electricity privatizations, the gains from productivity were explicitly allowed to be retained by the concessionaire for a period of eight years before any renegotiation of the concession. Tariff adjustments, on the other hand, were allowed annually and were linked to the increase in the general price level (Leal Ferreira, 2000: 205–6).

One cannot ignore the potential political and social consequences of this recent pattern of development. A good example is provided by the 1999 confrontation between the operators of the highway concession and Brazil's truckers. The concession contracts had allowed operators to charge high tolls to finance maintenance and expansion. The truckers claimed that the tolls were excessive and that they threatened their livelihood. After a brief strike, in which the federal government even threatened possible military intervention, tolls were lowered substantially. This in turn led to court actions by the concession holders, who claimed contract violation. This example clearly shows the potentially divisive effects of a policy focus on efficiency, which implicitly assumes that income distribution effects can be ignored.

Conclusions

The growth of state involvement in Brazil's economy was an important aspect of the ISI process. For a long time, state enterprises and banks acted in a complementary fashion to the private domestic and foreign sectors. There came a time, however, when state enterprises entered a phase of decline as a result of their use as instruments of macroeconomic policy, an abuse of their monopoly positions and political interference in their management, which caused a fall in efficiency. The debt and fiscal crises of the 1980s contributed to the adoption of the privatization policies of the 1990s.

Privatization assisted Brazil's fiscal adjustment, substantially improved the efficiency of the sectors involved and resulted in an inflow of new capital. The downside of privatization, however, lies in the fact that it worsened a traditional problem of Brazil – inequality. Inequality in the distribution of income and wealth in Brazil has been discouragingly tenacious from colonial times to the present. The existing evidence suggests that the privatization programme of the 1990s, whose merits in terms of economic efficiency are undeniable, contributed little to change this pattern, and may even have worsened it.

As many economists have noted, the missing link between a more efficient economy and a more equitable distribution of income and wealth in Brazil during the twenty-first century may be found in human capital. As Brazil's economy follows the pattern of more advanced industrial economies, the employment needs of its agricultural and industrial sectors will continue to decline, while demand for skilled service jobs will rise. More equity will thus be attained by substantially increasing resources going to education and dramatically broadening the educational opportunities of the lower-income groups. In other words, the future distribution of income will be based increasingly on the distribution of human capital.

Notes

1. For greater detail, see Baer (2001:268–9).
2. Brazil's government founded a state steel firm (Companhia Siderúrgica Nacional) to do the job with technical help from the USA. In the 1950s, the state expanded its role in the steel sector by taking over locally started projects. This expansion would ultimately result in state enterprises being responsible for about 65 per cent of the country's steel output; see Baer (1969; 2001).
3. In the case of petroleum, Petrobras was given the monopoly over petroleum exploration. It became an industrial giant over the years, as it integrated forward, founding many subsidiaries in the petrochemical industry. The Companhia Vale do Rio Doce became the country's largest iron ore mining firm, also gradually diversifying into related fields such as cellulose and steel, and thus becoming a large state conglomerate.
4. State firms in railroads, telephone and electricity had already made their appearance much earlier, but a dramatic expansion, resulting in the almost total state takeover of these sectors, only occurred after the Second World War.
5. Banco Nacional de Desenvolvimento Econômico, which was established in 1953. It was later renamed Banco Nacional de Desenvolvimento Econômico e Social (BNDES).
6. The 'tripod harmony' was the mutually beneficial existence of the three ownership sectors – domestic private, multinational and state.
7. Law 8.031 established formal procedures for the privatization process. It created a Privatization Committee, consisting of five leading public officials and seven representatives from the private sector. The president of the BNDES was designated as head of the committee and the bank was to be the institution that would manage the privatization programme. The committee was to propose the names of state firms to be privatized and recommend the conditions of the sale. The law required consultants to be contracted through public tender; these would provide independent assessments of the value of the firm to be privatized. The committee would decide on the minimum price of the firm to be auctioned. See *Programa Nacional de Desestatização* (Rio de Janeiro: BNDES, May 1992).
8. It provided for penalties for delinquent concessionaires; created the possibility for large consumer groups to choose their suppliers (thus ending local monopolies); established that tariffs would be defined in the concession contract; stipulated that all concessions would be awarded for a fixed term and that renewal would be based on a new bidding process; prohibited public subsidies to concessionaires; and entitled consumers to participate in the supervision of the concession.
9. Castelar Pinheiro and Giambiagi state that the 'debt negotiation consisted of the transfer of state debts that pay market interest rates to the federal government, with future state revenues (over a 30-year period) as collateral. Since the real interest rate on the loan by the federal government to the states is 6 percent, and the market interest rate is greater, the arrangement involved some "federalization of state losses". In an attempt to minimize these losses and decrease the total deficit of the SOEs, the federal government required states entering into debt rescheduling agreements to settle 20 percent of the principal through the sale of assets. The requirement became a major inducement for the states to engage in their own privatization programs' (Castelar Pinheiro and Giambiagi, in Castelar Pinheiro and Fukasaku, 1999:18).
10. Of the US$103bn of privatization receipts, US$68.4bn represented federal firms which were privatized and US$34.6bn represented state firms.
11. In 2001, privatizations amounted to US$103bn, but a sectoral breakdown for that year was not available at the time of writing. Also, this sum includes both privatization receipts and transferred debts. Table 11.1 only gives the breakdown of receipts and not total transferred debts.
12. In theory, a complete set of perfectly functioning capital markets would permit all income flows to be translated into equivalent stocks of wealth. For all its theoretical appeal, such an assumption is totally at odds with the realities of an economy like Brazil's.
13. Calculated from data in *Gazeta Mercantil, Balanço Annual, 1999*.

234   *Privatization in developing economies*

14. One interesting example is provided by the privatization of the Companhia Siderúrgica Nacional (CSN) in 1993, in which the successful bid was put together by the medium-sized Grupo Vicunha, which had previously been active primarily in the textile sector. It forged an alliance with a number of domestic banks, pension funds and several foreign investors.
15. Biondi (1999: 42–7), provides an extensive list of the ownership structure of firms before and after privatization, based on BNDES data.
16. These numbers come from the magazine *Exame*, which has a yearly edition dedicated to 'Melhores e Maiores'.
17. See Coes (1995), Werneck (1987) or Baer and McDonald (1998) for a discussion of the decline in public enterprise investment.
18. *Estado de São Paulo*, 3 January 2000 (*www.estado.com*). This was due to the fact that the index used to adjust electricity prices was the General Price Index – Internal Supply (IGP–DI), which increased by 20 per cent in 1999. Wage adjustments were based on the Consumer Price Index (IPC), which in the same year increased by only 7 per cent.

References

Baer, W. (1969) *The Development of the Brazilian Steel Industry*, Nashville: Vanderbilt University Press.

Baer, W. (2001) *The Brazilian Economy: Growth and Development*, 4th edn, Westport, CT: Praeger.

Baer, W. and C. McDonald (1998) 'A Return to the Past? Privatization of Public Utilities: The Case of the Electric Power Sector', *The Quarterly Review of Economics and Finance*, Fall, 503–24.

Biondi, A. (1999) 'O Brasil Privatizado, São Paulo', *Fundação Perseu Abramo*.

BNDES (1992) *Programa Nacional de Desestatização*, Rio de Janeiro.

Castelar Pinheiro, A. and L. Chrysostomo de Oliveira Filho (1992) 'O Programa Brasileiro de Privatização: Notas e Conjecturas', *Perspectivas da Economia Brasileira*, IPEA, Brasília.

Castelar Pinheiro, A. and K. Fukasaku (eds) (1999) *Privatization in Brazil: The Case of Public Utilities*, Rio de Janeiro and Paris: Banco Nacional de Desenvolvimento Econômico e Social and OECD.

Castelar Pinheiro, A. and F. Giambiagi (2000) 'Os antecedentes macroeconomico e a estrutura institucional da privatizacao no Brasil', in *A privatizacao no Brasil: o caso dos servicos de utilidade publica*, Rio de Janeiro: BNDES.

Coes, D.V. (1995) *Macroeconomic Crises, Policies, and Growth in Brazil 1964–90*, Washington, DC: World Bank.

'Conjuntura Econômica' (2000) *Fundação Getúlio Vargas*, Rio de Janeiro, January.

De Castro, N. (1999) 'Privatization of the Transportation Sector in Brazil', in A. Castelar Pinheiro and K. Fukasaku (eds).

de Mello, Jr. and R. Luiz (2000) 'Privitização e Governanca Empresarial no Brasil', in *A privatização no Brasil: o caso des servicos de utilitade publica*. Rio de Janeiro: BNDES.

Evans, P. (1979) *Dependent Development: The Alliance of Multinational, State and Local Capital in Brazil*, Princeton: University Press.

Foguel, M.N., I. Gill, R. Mendonça and R. Paes de Barros (2000) 'The Public–Private Wage Gap in Brazil', Texto Para Discussão, No. 754, IPEA, Rio de Janeiro, August.

Leal Ferreira, C.K. (2000) 'Privatização do Setor Eletrico no Brasil', in *A privatização no Brasil: o caso dos servicos de utilidade publica*, Rio de Janeiro: BNDES.

Novaes, A. (1999) 'The Privatization of the Brazilian Telecommunications Sector', in A. Castelar Pinheiro and K. Fukasaku (eds).

Siffert Filho, N. and C. Souza e Silva (1999) 'As Grandes Empresas nos Anos 90: Respostas Estratégicas a um Cenário da Mudanças', in F. Giambiagi and M. Mesquita Moreira (eds), *A Economia Brasileira nos Anos 90*, Rio de Janeiro: Banco Nacional de Desenvolvimento Econômico e Social.

Werneck, R. (1987) *Empresas Estatais e a Política Macroeconômica*, Rio de Janeiro: Editora Campus.

12 Privatization in China
Joseph C.H. Chai

Introduction

Privatization has many different meanings. According to the count of Thiemeyer, there are at least 15 concepts of privatization in the literature (cited in Bös, 1991:2). Most studies of privatization have a narrow focus. First, they focus only on the outright sale of public assets to the exclusion of other forms of transfer, such as contracting out and leasing. Second, they focus only on public assets to the exclusion of collective properties. Third, they focus only on the non-agricultural sector. As a result, privatization in most of the literature simply means the sale of state-owned non-agricultural enterprises. Based on this concept of privatization, there is little doubt that privatization in China has made very little progress, as the core of Chinese state owned enterprises (SOEs), namely the large- and medium-sized industrial enterprises, which account for a significant proportion of national industrial output, assets and employment, have not been privatized. Yet, in spite of this lack of progress in privatisation, China has been able to outperform other transitional economies in most of the economic success indicators. Chinese GDP per capita not only did not suffer a dip but advanced at an annual average rate of 8 per cent between 1978 and 1995, which is one of the highest in the world according to the World Bank (1997). Chinese unemployment and inflation rates during the transition period were significantly higher than those during the pre-reform period. However, both were much lower than those experienced by the Central and Eastern European transition economies (Chai, 1997:195–6). In view of this, it has been suggested that the Chinese experience shows that privatization is not necessary for a successful transition from a centrally planned to a competitive market economy.

The purpose of this chapter is to take a closer look at the validity of this hypothesis. The chapter consists of three sections. The first examines the progress of privatization in China in its various economic sectors and focuses specifically on the nature of the Chinese style of privatization. The second assesses the economic impact. Finally, the lessons of the Chinese experience for other developing or transitional economies is considered.

The progress of privatization in China
The agricultural sector[1]
On the eve of Chinese economic reforms in 1978, most of the assets in the Chinese economy were either publicly or collectively owned. Since outright sale of these assets was considered ideologically and politically unacceptable, China had to adopt an alternative from of privatization in order to achieve its economic efficiency objective. This alternative way of privatizing was first introduced in the Chinese agricultural sector.

As shown in Table 12.1, in 1978, the collectives, known as the People's Communes, owned 93.5 per cent of the productive assets in China's agricultural sector, whereas the Chinese peasants owned only 6.5 per cent. Seven years later, the situation was completely reversed, with the Chinese peasants now owning more than 92 per cent of the assets in the agricultural sector. How was this swift privatization of Chinese agriculture achieved? It was achieved, not through the outright sale of collective farms to individual peasants, but rather through the introduction of the 'household responsibility system' (HRS). Under the HRS, the collectives and the present farmer entered into a contract, under which the collectively owned farmland was broken up and a fixed amount of it, together with the farm animals, implements and specified quotas and taxes, were assigned to the individual peasant households. The collective held out the promise that, once the specified quotas and taxes had been met, the household itself could retain any net output left over.

Table 12.1   Distribution of productive assets in the Chinese agricultural sector, 1978 and 1985 (in 100 million yuan)

Types of assets	1978			1985		
	Collective	Peasant	Total	Collective	Peasant	Total
Land	12 000	900.5[1]	12 900.5	0	20 000[3]	20 000
Fixed capital assets	1 615	negligible	1 615.0	1 146	1 554	2 700
Cash and reserves	56	69.4[2]	125.4	800	1 200	2 000
Others	329	0	329.9	0	0	0
Total	14 000	969.9	14 969.9	1 946	22 754	24 700
	(93.5)	(6.5)	(100)	(7.9)	(92.1)	(100)

Notes: Figures in parentheses are percentage distribution.
1. Private plots.
2. Includes cash of 32.09 yuan and 30 kilo grain per capita.
3. Under contract.

Source: Gaige Mianlin Zhidu Chuangxin (1988: 65–71).

The HRS was introduced in the Chinese countryside in the late 1970s in response to the worsening work incentives in the Chinese communes. Income distribution in the commune was formally work-based, using an elaborate system of work points. However, because of the difficulty of supervising agricultural work, the degree of work supervision in a commune was practically zero. As a result, each farmer received the same amount of work points for a given job, no matter how hard she or he worked; and income was distributed more or less in an egalitarian way. This poor work incentive system resulted in the undersupply of labour and work effort in the commune, and had a deleterious consequence for the Chinese agricultural sector and the standard of living. During the period 1957–77, Chinese agricultural growth stagnated and total factor productivity growth turned negative. Furthermore, the real average income of farmers declined during this period (Chai, 1997:3).

The HRS was chosen for two reasons. First, since the collectively owned land was not sold but contracted out to individual peasants, the reform was ideologically and politically acceptable. Second, the HRS was a more efficient incentive system than the former work point system. To begin with, all the transaction costs associated with work point measurement were eliminated. Furthermore, the household effort–reward function was made more direct and certain, as households were now allowed to retain the entire net income for themselves without having to share it with their co-farmers, after the fulfilment of all the obligatory deliveries to the state and collective as stipulated in the contract.

Though the HRS did not involve formal divestiture of collectively owned assets, it did lead to a de facto privatization of Chinese agriculture. Under the HRS. land and most of the fixed capital assets were transferred to individuals in one form and another. Large amounts of property, such as land, draft animals, agricultural machinery and implements, were transferred to the households through contracting out. Other properties were transferred through either sale or rent.

According to the government's policy guidelines, the mode of contracting out of land to the household was supposedly partly based on an egalitarian principle, that is according to the number of people in the household, and partly according to the number of labourers in the household. In practice, there was a tendency to divide the land on an egalitarian basis for two reasons. First, the attachment to land is deep-rooted in Chinese peasant culture. Most peasants equated the introduction of HRS to a second land reform. Hence individual peasants tended to press for an equal share of the land distributed. Second, and more importantly, the scarcity of land in China tended to make the assignment of land egalitarian. The proportion of land distributed on a per capita basis was mainly aimed at providing sufficient food grain production to satisfy the fixed grain ration for each person in the collective. Given the fixed grain ration per capita and the grain yield of land, the required proportion of land distributed on an egalitarian basis to satisfy the fixed grain rations for all households varied directly with the man–land ratio. Since the man–land ratio is known to be relatively high in Chinese agriculture, owing to the scarcity of land in relation to high population pressure, it can be deduced that most of the land must have been contracted out on a per capita basis.

The assignment of draft animals and agricultural machinery and farm tools to the households followed the assignment of the land. The method used is known as *zhejia daohu*, which worked in the following way: the total number of draft animals, D, was first assessed in terms of their market value, P_D, to arrive at the total value of the draft animals in the collective, $P_D D$. The latter was then divided by the total area of land, L_{Total}, to derive the average value of draft animals per unit of land assigned. The value of the draft animals to which each household was entitled, Q_D, then depended on the amount of land it had been assigned, L_D. Thus the following formula applies:

$$Q_D = (P_D D / L_{Total}) L_D.$$

Once the value of the draft animals to which each household was entitled had been determined, the household was usually given the option to receive its draft animals either in kind or in money. In the latter case, the household used the money to purchase draft animals from the market. Since most of the land was distributed on an egalitarian basis and the distribution of draft animals, agricultural machinery and farm tools was tied to that of land, it follows that a large proportion of collective properties were distributed mainly on an egalitarian basis.

Although most of the collective assets had been transferred to individual peasants, the collectives still maintained certain residual income, control and transfer rights over the properties transferred. Hence certain restrictions were placed on the holding and disposing of the properties transferred to a household. First, land was allowed to be held by the household for a specific period only. Initially, this was set at three to five years. Later on, this was extended to 15 years. Second, certain limits were placed on the use of land by the household. For instance, transferred land was to be used for cultivation only. Third, with respect to transferred draft animals, agricultural machinery and tools, the household had to maintain their book value if they were diminished by depreciation of other factors. Fourth, the household had to fulfil certain obligatory deliveries as stipulated in the contract. Finally, land assigned to the household was not allowed to be sold or rented. Later, to encourage a more rational distribution of farmlands, the subletting of land assigned to a farmer was allowed. However, since most of these restrictions were relaxed, watered down or not strictly enforced, most collective properties transferred to the household through contracting became in practice household private properties.

The non-agricultural sector[2]

On the eve of economic reform, the Chinese non-agricultural sector was dominated by SOEs (see Table 12.2), but, some 20 years later, the situation had changed. By 1998, the non-state enterprises (NSEs) had come to dominate the output and volume of transactions in the industrial, retail trade, transport and construction sectors. NSEs also dominated the service sector. Unlike the case of Central and Eastern European transitional economies, the privatization of the non-agricultural sector was achieved, not through the divestiture of the existing SOEs, but through the development of small and medium-sized NSEs. Chinese NSEs consist of both collective and private enterprises. The collective enterprises include both the urban and the rural collectives. The latter are also known as rural enterprises or the *township and village enterprises* (TVEs). Private enterprises consist of individually owned enterprises (IEs), privately owned enterprises (PEs) and

Table 12.2 Share of non-state enterprises in China's non-agricultural sector, 1980 and 1998 (%)

Sector	1980	1998
Industry (output)		
State	78.7	28.2
Non-state	21.3	71.8
Retail trade (volume)		
State	84.2	20.7
Non-state	15.8	79.3
Transport (volume)		
State	98.1[1]	NA
Non-state	1.9	NA
Construction (output)		
State	63.7[1]	33.3
Non-state	36.3	66.7

Notes:
1. 1975.
NA = not available.

Source: Ma (1982:68–9); *ZGTJNJ* (1999:421, 546, 457).

)

the foreign-funded enterprises (FEs). As discussed later, the distinction between the collective and private enterprises in the Chinese NSE sector is blurred. Chinese NSEs can be regarded as a collection of both genuine and quasi-private enterprises.

Table 12.3 gives an overview of the significance of the various types of NSEs in terms of employment. This table shows that NSEs accounted for 72.6 per cent of Chinese non-agricultural employment by 1998. It also reveals that, among the various NSEs, TVEs, PEs and IEs are the most important. These three types of NSEs were responsible for 62 per cent of China's total non-agricultural employment. The discussion below focuses on the factors that shaped the development of these three types of NSEs.

Table 12.3   Employment in China's non-agricultural enterprises, 1998

Sector	Employment (million)	Percentage share
A. State		
SOEs	90.6	27.4
B. Non-state	239.9	72.6
Urban collectives	19.6	5.9
TVEs	125.4	37.9
PEs	17.1	5.2
IEs	61.2	18.5
FEs	5.8	1.8
Other PEs[1]	10.8	3.3
Total	330.5	

Notes:
1. Includes shareholding units, jointly-owned units, limited liability corporations and limited shareholding corporations.
For information on PEs, IEs and FEs, see text.

Source: ZGTJNJ (1999: 136–7).

TVEs were created in the late 1950s as commune and brigade-run enterprises. These enterprises were one of the core elements of Mao's 'walking on two legs' policy, which envisioned the coexistence of labour-intensive, small-scale rural industrial enterprises beside the medium- and large-scale modern urban industrial enterprises. They were established at that time to mobilize surplus labour and other local resources in the countryside to achieve the goal of self-reliance and rural industrialization. With the collapse of the commune system in the early 1980s, they came under the administration of local government, namely the township and village governments. Hence they were renamed TVEs. Since 1984, the definition of

TVEs in Chinese literature and official statistics has broadened to encompass all enterprises established at or below the township level, regardless of their type of ownership. Hence the category includes collective and private enterprises.

Table 12.4   Development of TVEs, 1984–98

	Number (million)	Employment (million)	Output (billion yuan)
1984	6.1	52.1	169.8
1985	12.2	69.8	275.5
1986	15.2	79.4	358.3
1987	17.5	88.1	494.8
1988	18.9	95.5	701.8
1989	18.7	93.7	840.2
1990	19.5	92.6	958.1
1991	19.1	96.1	1 161.2
1992	20.8	105.8	1 769.6
1993	24.5	123.5	3 177.7
1994	24.9	120.1	4 537.9
1995	22.0	128.6	6 891.5
1996	23.4	135.1	7 790.3
1997	20.1	130.5	8 990.1
1998	20.0	125.4	NA

Note: NA = not available.

Source: *ZGTJNJ*, various issues.

As can be seen from Table 12.4, the development of TVEs since 1984 can be divided into four phases. TVEs experienced rapid growth during an initial spurt period in 1984–8, with the number of firms established tripling and their nominal output soaring by more than 300 per cent. There were two main factors behind this sudden spurt. The first factor was the de facto privatization of Chinese agriculture. As confirmed by various studies of the development of Chinese TVEs during this period (see, for example, Byrd and Lin, 1990; Zhang and Ming, 1999), the rapid growth of TVEs was a response to the supply and demand forces created by the success of rural reforms during this period. On the supply side, the success of the HRS increased agricultural productivity and released an enormous amount of surplus labour, which could not be accommodated in China's urban sector. This prompted the government to lift the restrictions on rural non-agricultural activities, and the surplus labour was absorbed in the rural sector by the development of rural NSEs. In addition, the success of the HRS in boosting rural incomes generated an enormous amount of savings, which provided a growing source of capital to finance rural industrial development. On the demand side, increased rural income as a result of the introduction of the HRS boosted the demand for consumer goods and housing construction, thereby increasing market outlets for the TVEs.

The second factor behind the rise of TVEs was fiscal decentralization (see, for example, Yusuf, 1994; Wong, 1992). China's fiscal structure at the time depended heavily on industry to generate fiscal revenues. The various fiscal reforms introduced after 1980 were aimed at fiscal decentralization and reassigned to local government virtually the entire surplus generated by local industry. Since local governments at the time were starved of revenue, they had an incentive vigorously to promote industrial development in an attempt to finance their growing expenditures.

During the period from 1989 to 1991, the development of TVEs entered a period of readjustment, with the number of TVEs declining in 1989 and experiencing very little growth thereafter. The tight monetary policy introduced by the government to control inflation in 1988–9 severely affected the supply of credit to TVEs. Furthermore, under the economic rectification programme of 1988–91, three million TVEs were closed down and the planned establishment of another 20000 was either abandoned or postponed (*ZGNYNJ*, 1990:43).

Rapid growth of TVEs resumed during the period 1992–4. Following the suppression of the democracy movement in Tiananmen Square, in 1989 local governments were extremely cautious about the development of NSEs as they were not sure about the central government's policy direction. Deng Xiaoping used his tour of the southern provinces in 1992 to reaffirm the Party's commitment to the establishment of a 'socialist market economy' and the promotion of the private sector. Thereafter, both the number and the output of TVEs rose rapidly.

After 1995, the development of TVEs in China entered a consolidation phase once again, with the number of establishments declining through closures and mergers (Lin and Yao, 2001:151). The main cause of this was the overexpansion of TVEs in the aftermath of Deng's 1992 tour.

As mentioned earlier, TVEs comprise both collective and private enterprises. Hence their property rights are ambiguous. This, coupled with the fact that TVEs, together with other NSEs, have been the major contributor to China's economic growth since 1985, has prompted a lot of theoretical speculation as to the causes of their success (see Weitzman and Xu, 1994; Li, 1994; Che and Qian, 1998). But, in fact, the distinction between TVEs and private enterprises is blurred and therefore ambiguous property rights are not such an important issue in practice. To begin with, many collective TVEs or township- and village-run enterprises are simply disguised private enterprises. They are set up as TVEs so as to avoid political persecution, a legacy of some continuing opposition to private ownership, and to gain access to preferred tax concessions accorded to collective enterprises. According to the survey of the State Industry and Commerce Administrative Bureau in 1995, about 21 per cent of collective enterprises were in fact, disguised private enterprises (Zhang and Ming, 1999:51). In another survey, cited by Han and Pannell (1999), the percentage of private enterprises disguised as collective enterprises is much higher, ranging from 20 to 50 per cent.

Also the private sector component of TVEs has been growing rapidly in recent years. As shown in Table 12.5, in terms of the number of establishments, most of the TVEs have been privately owned since 1984. In terms of output and employment, however, collective enterprises dominated in the earlier years. In contrast to SOEs, the collective TVEs are more efficient because they face a much harder budget constraint and their product market is less protected than that of SOEs (Jefferson and Rawski, 1994:56). But, compared with private enterprises, the property rights of collective TVEs are not well defined. They are owned by local government and enjoy less autonomy than private enterprises. A significant proportion of their after-tax profit is siphoned off for community expenditures or the development of other collective TVEs. Investment made by workers in TVEs cannot be inherited or returned as dividend to the workers. Finally, workers in collective TVEs are more protected than their counterparts in private TVEs. As a

Table 12.5   Percentage share of private TVEs in total TVEs in China, 1984–97

Year	Establishments	Employment	Gross output
1984	69.3	23.5	14.4
1985	84.5	38.0	24.7
1986	88.6	42.8	28.7
1987	91.0	46.4	32.1
1988	91.6	48.7	32.5
1989	91.8	49.6	33.6
1990	92.1	50.4	34.7
1991	92.4	50.4	33.6
1992	92.7	51.3	33.3
1993	93.1	53.3	35.7
1994	93.4	50.9	32.4
1995	92.7	52.9	35.9
1996	93.4	55.9	41.9
1997	93.6	59.2	51.2

Source: Lin and Yao (2001:161).

result, collective TVEs tend to be overstaffed and pay inflated wages. To counter this inefficiency problem, privatization has been launched in recent years. Thus, over the years, as shown in Table 12.5, the private ownership component of Chinese TVEs has soared. By 1997, they accounted for over half of the total output and employment.

Table 12.6   Development of IEs in China, 1981–97

Year	Number (10 000)	Employment (million)	Output (billion yuan)
1981	183	2.3	NA
1982	261	3.2	NA
1983	590	7.5	NA
1984	933	13.0	NA
1985	1 171	17.0	NA
1986	1 211	18.5	NA
1987	1 373	21.6	30.6
1988	1 453	23.1	51.6
1989	1 247	19.4	55.9
1990	1 328	20.9	64.2
1991	1 417	22.6	78.2
1992	1 534	24.7	92.6
1993	1 767	29.4	138.7
1994	2 187	37.8	163.8
1995	2 528	46.1	279.1
1996	2 704	50.2	353.9
1997	2 851	54.4	455.3

Note: NA = not available.

Source: Zhang and Ming (1999:93).

The average size of TVEs is relatively small compared to SOEs. In 1998, for example, an average TVE in the industrial sector employed only 11 workers, which was only 2.6 per cent of the level of employment in an average industrial SOE (*ZGTJNJ*, 1999:410–14). Nevertheless, the share of TVEs in total national industrial output rose from 9 per cent in 1978 to 58 per cent in 1997 (Lin and Yao, 2001:145).

An IE is officially defined as an individual proprietorship and a household firm employing not more than seven workers. The growth of IEs mirrors that of TVEs and can be divided into three phases. As shown in Table 12.6, during the first phase, 1981–8, the growth of IEs was rapid, with the number of establishments increasing by almost 700 per cent. During a readjustment in 1989–91, the number of IEs declined, reflecting the negative impact of the

Tiananmen Square incident. The growth of IEs received a heavy boost, however, after the southern tour of Deng Xiaoping in 1992.

Unlike TVEs, IEs are located in both rural and urban areas. In 1997, 64 per cent of IEs were found in cities and towns. In terms of sectors served, most IEs are concentrated in the service sector and in retail trade in particular. In 1997, for example, 84 per cent of IEs were engaged in the service sector, whereas only 12 per cent were found in the industrial sector (Zhang and Ming, 1999:94).

The growth of IEs in urban areas was initially triggered by the massive urban unemployment caused by the return of educated youth to the cities in the late 1970s. These young people were sent to the countryside during the Cultural Revolution (1966–76). In rural areas, the immediate stimulus to the development of IEs was the government's policy objective of soaking up the rural surplus labour generated by the increased labour productivity in agriculture after the de facto privatization of Chinese agriculture.

The growth of IEs in urban areas was later sustained by increased rural–urban migration. Prior to 1979, rural–urban migration was strictly controlled by the household registration scheme, under which farmers were not allowed to reside in cities or take up urban employment. Neither were they able to do so illegally, as they could not obtain foodstuffs in cities, which were strictly rationed on the basis of residential status. By the mid-1980s, however, with the introduction of a two-track price system (that is, official prices for planned outputs alongside market prices for surplus production), rural migrants in the cities were able to purchase food in the market. As a result, rural–urban migration soared. However, those who had moved to the cities were not acknowledged as urban residents by the urban authorities; indeed, they became known as the 'floating population'. This expanding floating population provided the major source of workers for the urban IEs.

According to Chinese official definitions, PEs are private firms with more than seven hired workers. PEs first appeared in China in 1980, and in 1984 official sanctions against them were lifted. But it was not until 1987 that they were formally recognized as a legitimate part of the Chinese economy, by the Thirteenth Party Congress. In the following year national laws and regulations for PEs were promulgated.

In spite of their formal recognition, the growth of PEs in the late 1980s was slow because of social prejudice against them and the numerous restrictions that they were still subject to. During the economic readjustment period of 1989–91, many PEs were forced to give up their businesses or disguised themselves as collective TVEs. After the southern tour of Deng Xiaoping in 1992, however, the growth of PEs experienced a sharp acceleration, fuelled by strong government support and the easing of

Table 12.7   Development of PEs in China, 1989–97

Year	Number (10 000)	Employment (million)	Output (billion yuan)
1989	9.1	1.6	9.7
1990	9.8	1.7	12.2
1991	10.8	1.8	14.7
1992	14.0	2.3	20.5
1993	23.8	3.7	42.2
1994	43.2	6.5	114.0
1995	65.5	9.6	229.5
1996	81.9	11.7	322.7
1997	96.1	13.5	392.3

Source: Zhang and Ming (1999:60).

restrictions on them. As can be seen from Table 12.7, between 1991 and 1997 the number of PEs jumped by almost 800 per cent.

Most PEs are registered as either sole proprietorships, partnerships or limited liability companies. Between 1990 and 1997, limited liability PEs as a share of total PEs increased from 4 per cent to 46 per cent (Zhang and Ming, 1999:48). Like IEs, most PEs are located in the urban areas. But unlike IEs, their industrial structure is much more balanced. In 1997, for example, 54 per cent of PEs were engaged in the service sector, whereas 45 per cent were in the industrial sector.

In 1999, the development of PEs received a further boost through a change to the Chinese constitution. In Article 11 of the constitution, the original clause, 'the private economy is a supplement to public ownership', was replaced by a new clause, 'the non-public sector, including individual and private business, is an important component of the socialist market economy'. In January 2000, the State Development Planning Commission declared that government would eliminate all restrictive and discriminatory regulations and practices against the PEs (Broadman, 2001:856). Of late, the government is even considering the admission of private entrepreneurs as members of the Chinese Communist Party.

The state sector
The main difference between the Chinese style of privatization and that of the Central and Eastern European countries has been the attitude to the state sector. Specifically, unlike its Central and Eastern European counterparts, the Chinese state sector remains basically unprivatized. Privatization in a narrow sense has been carried out in China's state sector since the 1980s, but this has involved only small SOEs, and in small- and medium-sized cities. By

the late 1990s, in some provinces almost 50 per cent of small SOEs had reportedly been privatized (Broadman, 2001:851). For the core of the Chinese state sector, however, namely the large- and medium-sized SOEs (LMSOEs), which still account for more than one-quarter of national output, two-thirds of the country's total industrial assets and more than half of urban employment, privatization in the narrow sense is still unheard of. However, it is not appropriate to conclude that there has been no privatization even in LMSOEs, for privatization in a broader sense or partial privatization has occurred in the core SOEs.

As in the agricultural sector, the problem facing the government is that the wholesale privatization of core SOEs is not ideologically and politically acceptable. Hence the government has had to search for an alternative incentive system to solve the agency problems in these enterprises. The alternative incentive system adopted has turned out to be very similar to that introduced in the agricultural sector. It is a kind of contracting out system known as the 'contract responsibility system' (CRS). A large variety of CRSs were practised in China during 1980 to 1994. In the early 1980s, a simple profit contract system was adopted. Under this system, the SOEs were contracted out to the enterprise management and the enterprise management undertook to pay the state a fixed sum, equivalent to the actual amount of profit delivered to the state in a base year. The state allowed the enterprises to retain all excess profits, which could be used to finance bonus payments and housing construction for the benefit of their employees (Chai, 1997:70–73).

After 1987, a management contract responsibility system (MCRS) was introduced. This system proved to be very popular and became the longest surviving incentive system in Chinese SOEs during the period from 1987 to 1994. Again, a large variety of MCRS were practised. The most popular form was the 'two-guarantee and one link-up' system (*lang bao yi gua*). Under this system, the enterprise management and the state entered into a contract, the duration of which averaged three to four years. During this period the enterprise management would guarantee the state the following: (a) the obligatory delivery of a certain amount of profits, (b) the completion of certain planned tasks of technical renovation of the enterprises, and (c) the link-up of the growth of the wage bill with that of enterprise efficiency indicators. The state held out the promise that the enterprise could retain any profits in excess of the obligatory delivery; the actual amount of profit delivered was set individually for each enterprise. The retained profit could be used to boost the collective consumption of the management staff and workers or could be used as either bonus payments or for reinvestment within the enterprises.

The two-guarantee and one link-up system was basically similar to the simple profit contract system. As in the latter, the enterprise was provided with strong incentives to maximize profits as they were allowed to retain all or most of the excess profit. However, as compared with the latter, they were subject to more constraints in order to avoid a conflict between the enterprise's objective of profit or production efficiency maximization and that of the state of welfare or allocative efficiency maximization. Thus, under the two-guarantee and one link-up system, an enterprise undertook not only to guarantee to deliver agreed profits but to achieve certain planned tasks, such as the technical renovation of the enterprises. In some cases other mandatory planned input and output indicators were included in the contract. Furthermore, an enterprise was supposed to limit the growth of its wage expenditures to that of its productivity, in order to prevent wage inflation.

In 1994, the MCRS was scrapped; in its place two new reform measures for China's SOEs were introduced. One was the restructuring of state ownership and the other the transformation of most LMSOEs into a 'modern enterprise system' through corporatization. Both measures amounted to a dilution of state ownership in China's state sector. Under the state ownership restructuring scheme, small loss-making SOEs could be declared bankrupt and low profit-making SOEs could be sold or leased, contracted out or merged with other enterprises. As for the LMSOEs, there would be a withdrawal of state ownership from competitive to strategic or natural monopoly industries. Since the competitive industrial sector accounted for 80 per cent of China's industrial output, the planned withdrawal of state ownership in this sector would substantially reduce the presence of state ownership in the industrial sector.

The scheme of transforming LMSOEs into a modern enterprise system was aimed at modernizing the corporate governance structure of the LMSOEs. To achieve this objective, LMSOEs would be incorporated as either limited liability companies or limited liability shareholding companies, in accordance with the company law adopted in 1994. According to this law, the main difference between these two types of companies lies in the following: first the size of equity capital (0.5 million v. 10 million yuan); secondly, the number of shareholders (2–49 v. 50 or above); and finally the liquidity of the shares. Only the shares of the latter can be traded on the stock exchange. The shares of both types of companies are classified into five categories: state-owned, institution-owned, individual-owned, collective-owned and foreign-owned. Only the last three categories of shares can be traded in the stock market (Lin and Zhu, 2001:310–11).

State ownership in the newly incorporated shareholding companies is no longer restricted to sole state ownership. It can be either sole, majority or a minority shareholding, depending on the significance and competitiveness of the industry (Chai and Docwra, 1997:170). Thus, for strategic industries, such as defence and rare material mining, sole state ownership is retained. For natural monopoly and basic industries, such as electricity, petroleum extracting and refinery, and certain high-tech industries as well as important service industries, majority state ownership is required. Finally, for competitive industries, only minority state ownership is necessary. Thus corporatization of the SOEs has the effect of diluting state ownership. This is confirmed by a recent study of the corporatization of 40 238 industrial SOEs based on a questionnaire survey of China's Statistical Bureau in 1998 (Lin and Zhu, 2001). This shows that, in most incorporated LMSOEs, the state retains majority ownership, but its ownership share has been reduced from 100 per cent to just above 50 per cent.

The state's shares in incorporated enterprises are, in principle, available for sale to both insiders (managers and ordinary employees) and outside investors. In practice, however, as a survey by China's Statistical Bureau showed, most of the non-state shares have been acquired by insiders (ibid.:325). In the newly incorporated shareholding companies where the state retains the controlling interest, the state exercises its ownership control through the following channels. For SOEs under central government control, the incorporated SOEs are administrated by the National Administrative Bureau of State-owned Property (NABSOP) and the State Asset Operating Companies (SAOCs) (see Figure 12.1). The NABSOP is responsible for general policy formulation with regard to the overall administration of the state ownership interest; SAOCs are responsible for the implementation of these policies through direct participation on the boards of directors of incorporated SOEs. For SOEs under local government control, there is an analogous two-tier control and management hierarchy: the municipal level state asset management bureau and the municipal level state asset operating companies.

An impact assessment
The results of Chinese-style privatization have been impressive. In terms of growth, as mentioned earlier, a World Bank study (1997) found that China's per capita income grew at an annual average rate of 8 per cent a year during 1978–95, based on Chinese official statistics. Chinese official data are known to have overstated the rate of China's economic growth during this period by about 1.2 per cent because of the GDP deflator used, which underestimated the actual rate of inflation in China. Hence the most plausible rate of economic growth in per capita terms during this period is between 6 and 7 per cent. Even if one adopts this lower estimate, however, China's growth performance is still very impressive. First, compared to the past, economic growth during this period has been 70 per cent faster than

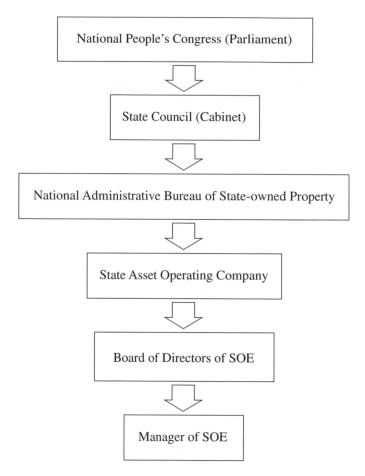

*Figure 12.1   Control of SOEs under China's modern enterprise system
reform*

that of the pre-privatization period, under Mao. Second, compared with
other countries during the same period, only South Korea and Taiwan have
been able to match China's economic growth. How was this high-speed
growth achieved? What has been the contribution of Chinese-style privatization?

China's rapid growth since the introduction of the first economic reforms
in the late 1970s can be divided into two phases (see Table 12.8). During the
first phase (1979–84), agriculture was undoubtedly a significant engine of
economic growth. It directly contributed almost one-third of aggregate
output growth. The main reason behind the rapid growth of agricultural

Table 12.8   Percentage contribution to GDP growth, by sectors in China

Sector	1979–84	1985–93	1994–98
Agriculture	32	12	9
Industry			
State enterprises	20	12	13
Non-state enterprises	14	46	44
Construction	5	6	6
Services	29	25	29

Source: 1979–93, Sachs and Woo (1997:74); 1994–98, own calculations based on data in *ZGTJNJ*, various issues.

output during this period was the de facto privatization of Chinese agriculture and the increase in state procurement prices for agricultural products. Lin (1992) provides an excellent decomposition of the sources of agricultural growth during this period. According to his estimates, almost half the agricultural output growth stemmed from the effective privatization of Chinese farmland through the introduction of the HRS. The HRS stimulated the growth of Chinese agriculture by enhancing both its allocative and productive or X-efficiency (Chai, 1997:26–7). X-efficiency rose under the HRS because, as mentioned earlier, the household effort–reward function was made more direct and certain because farmers were allowed to retain the entire net output for themselves without having to share it with their co-farmers. X-efficiency also rose because of the decentralization of income rights under the HRS. The assignment of income rights of collective assets to individual households made them responsible for the profits and losses and forced them to maximize the value of their assets. Allocative efficiency was also significantly enhanced under the HRS because farmers gained increased control rights over both the farmland and their labour and were able to deploy them according to the principle of comparative advantage. The increase in state procurement prices for agricultural products also contributed to Chinese agricultural growth. However, its contribution is limited, accounting for only about 16 per cent of agricultural growth during this period (Lin, 1992:47).

The close relation between the de facto privatization of Chinese agriculture and its rapid growth during 1978–85 is confirmed by the econometric studies of Jian *et al.* (1996) on China's regional growth. Using panel data from China's 28 provinces, they studied the factors which were responsible for the uneven economic growth of Chinese provinces during this period. The results of their studies, as shown in Table 12.9, reveal that provincial growth during the period was mainly driven by agricultural reform. The

Table 12.9   Regression results on determinants of China's provincial growth, 1978–85

Dependent variable: annual growth rate of per capita real GDP Sample size: 28 provinces	(1)	(2)	(3)	(4)
Log initial per capita real GDP	−0.023	−0.003	−0.006	0.002
	(−3.7888)	(−0.246)	(−0.507)	(−0.170)
Initial agricultural GDP share		0.116	0.110	0.107
		(1.931)	(1.818)	(1.745)
Coast (location)			0.008	−0.006
			(1.054)	(0.273)
Coast interacted with agricultural GDP share				0.047
				(0.697)
$\bar{R}^2$	0.271	0.394	0.397	0.384

Note: Figures in parentheses are *t*-values.

Source: Jian *et al.* (1996:35).

provinces with the higher share of agriculture in their GDP benefited disproportionately from the reform and, hence, were able to grow faster. Other factors that could have an impact on performance – initial per capita GDP and geographical (coast) location – were found to be non-significant.

The growth of Chinese agriculture levelled off after 1985, owing to a combination of factors (see Chai, 1991; Lin, 1992). First, the one-off effect of the de facto privatization of agriculture ended. Second, agricultural input and output prices started to rise under increased price liberalization. However, input prices increased much faster than output prices and, as a result, farmers found that farming activities became much less financially attractive than non-farm activities. Third, with the abolition of the system of compulsory state procurement of agricultural products, farmers no longer enjoyed the benefit of a price guarantee by the government and had to face increased price uncertainty. Finally, and not least, as Chinese agriculture approached its production frontier owing to the constraint of land shortage, the law of diminishing returns increasingly influenced output growth.

Thus, after 1985, Chinese economic growth was mainly driven by growth in the non-agricultural sector. Within the non-agricultural sector, as shown in Table 12.8, the NSEs were the biggest contributor to Chinese economic growth. They were responsible for approximately 45 per cent of GDP growth during this period. Another big contributor to growth was the service sector, which during these years accounted for about 27 per cent of GDP growth. Since the service sector was mainly dominated by NSEs, it can be inferred that, from 1985, NSEs in both the industrial and service sectors emerged as the biggest contributors to Chinese economic growth.

That the non-state sector has been the driving force behind China's rapid growth in recent years has been confirmed in a recent econometric study of China's regional growth by Stewart (2001). His study is similar to that of Jian *et al.* (1996). It focuses on the growth determinants of China's 28 provinces during the recent period, 1992–8. The results of his study show that, apart from the non-state sector variable and a western region dummy, all the other variables were not significant (Table 12.10). The coefficient of the non-state sector variable is strongly statistically significant and positive and suggests that an increase of 10 percentage points in the non-state sector's share in a province's total non-agricultural employment added more than one percentage point to that province's annual per capita GDP growth. The significance and negative value of the western dummy coefficient suggests that provinces located in western China were handicapped in exploiting non-state sector development because of their geographical isolation and comparative economic backwardness.

By contrast, in terms of their contribution to economic growth and efficiency, the limited or partial privatization of Chinese SOEs has not been very meaningful. However, neither has it been meaningless. Several studies (see Jefferson and Rawski, 1994; Groves *et al.*, 1994; Chai and Tisdell, 1999) confirm that the limited privatization of SOEs through the introduction of the CRS and MCRS achieved some success. According to these studies, SOEs gained increased autonomy in their input, output, finance and investment decisions. Their profit incentive was significantly enhanced as they were allowed to retain an increased proportion of their profits. Their behaviour increasingly resembled that of a private firm in a market economy and the increased autonomy and profit retention induced managers to strengthen workers' incentives. This, coupled with the increased competitive pressure from a growing non-state sector, resulted in increased productive efficiency. This is confirmed by several total factor productivity (TFP) growth estimates for Chinese SOEs. Laurenceson and Chai (2000), for example, found that, during the period 1980–96, TFP in Chinese industrial SOEs grew at an annual average rate of almost 2 per cent a year. In contrast, their TFP growth during the planning era under Mao was negative (World Bank, 1983).

In spite of the evidence of increased productive efficiency, there is little doubt that allocative efficiency in SOEs remains relatively low. Although the rate of growth of TFP in SOEs has been positive, it has amounted to only one-third to one-half of the corresponding rate achieved by the NSEs (Jefferson and Rawski, 1994: 56). Furthermore, the growth rate of TFP in Chinese SOEs has declined in recent years (Jefferson *et al.*, 2000). Meanwhile,

Table 12.10   Regression results on growth determinants of China's provinces, 1992–98

Dependent variable: average annual growth rate of real GDP per capita Sample size: 28 provinces	
Constant	0.0645
	(0.313)
Log initial real GDP per capita	−0.0031
	(−0.176)
Log rate of investment	0.0302
	(0.998)
Log $(n+g+d)$[1]	−0.0968
	(1.316)
Log post primary enrolment rate	0.0232
	(0.892)
Foreign direct investment	0.0121
	(1.029)
Size of non-state sector[2]	0.0012
	(3.863)
Fiscal balance[3]	−0.1649
	(−1.483)
Coastal dummy[4]	−0.0146
	(1.403)
Western dummy[5]	−0.0251
	(−2.429)
$\bar{R}^2$	0.665

Notes:
1. n is growth rate of labour; g exogenous technology growth and d the depreciation rate.
2. Share of the non-state enterprises in non-agricultural employment.
3. Provincial government fiscal deficits/surpluses.
4. Coastal province dummy.
5. Western province dummy.
Figures in parentheses are t-values.

Source: Stewart (2001:74).

the losses and debt of SOEs have continued to mount and the government has had to increase subsidies to bail them out. There is also strong evidence of a continued misallocation of investment, labour and other resources. For example, although the capital/output ratio of SOEs was twice that of NSEs, SOEs have received two-thirds of state industrial investment in recent years. Similarly, about 20 per cent of the workforce of the SOEs are regarded as redundant, yet these workers still continue to receive their pay. The result is that labour is employed in SOEs even when their wage is significantly higher than their marginal productivity. Also the 1995 national industrial census revealed that only 60 per cent of the factory capacity of the SOEs producing major consumer and industrial products was utilized (Broadman, 2001:856). Preliminary studies of recent attempts to modernize the corporate governance structure of Chinese SOEs through corporatization confirm that they have done very little to enhance the corporate governance standards in Chinese SOEs (see Chai and Docwra, 1997; Broadman, 2001). Worse still, they have led to the problem of 'insider control' of the firms, which has created new problems such as asset stripping, decapitalization, wage manipulation, privatization of assets and socialization of liabilities and corruption. In short, the partial privatization of SOEs has not been a viable substitute for wholesale privatization.

The biggest contribution of the limited privatization of the SOEs has been the maintenance of political, social and economic stability during the initial transition stage in China. The transition in the Central and Eastern European countries has been accompanied by increased economic instability, in the form of a large dip in output, employment and the standard of living and increased political and social unrest. In contrast, China has largely been able to avoid most of these short-run transition costs. As mentioned earlier, Chinese output not only did not suffer a dip but actually grew at an annual average of almost 8 per cent a year from the early 1980s. Similarly, China not only did not experience a dip in its standard of living but experienced a doubling of its living standards between 1978 and 1990 (Chai, 1991: 722–3). China's unemployment and inflation rates during the transition were significantly higher than those in the pre-reform period. However, both were much lower than those experienced by the Central and Eastern European transition economics (Chai, 1997, Tables 11.4 and 11.5). There has been increased political and social instability during the reform period in China, but compared with the Central and Eastern European countries China had been able to maintain a much more peaceful and stable political and social environment.

Why have China's short-run transition costs been much lower? One of the main reasons has undoubtedly been China's more gradual approach to privatization. To begin with, the delaying of the wholesale privatization of Chinese SOEs helped to maintain economic stability. The absence of wholesale privatization in the state sector meant that enterprise managers were spared supply-side shocks. Not only did their market remain sheltered from foreign competition but they continued to receive subsidies and soft bank loans from the state. Hence a large fall in output and employment was prevented. The delaying of the wholesale privatization of Chinese SOEs also helped to maintain political and social stability because the preservation of state ownership of LMSOEs softened the opposition of hardline communists to the economic reforms. Furthermore, it also quelled the opposition to reforms of those interest groups that benefit from SOE inefficiency in terms of either surplus workers, uneconomic prices or excessive factor payments. Finally, and not least, it also enabled the SOEs to continue to provide a social safety net for workers and thereby enhanced social stability. Unlike its western counterparts, the Chinese social welfare system is not state-based but enterprise-based. Each SOE operates like a small society providing a social safety net for its employees, which typically includes housing, education, medical care and retirement benefits. The conversion of an enterprise-based welfare system to a state-based one needs time because of the financial implications. Until a new state-based welfare system is in place, the scrapping of welfare benefits provided by enterprises under a wholesale privatization scheme would evoke widespread protests among workers, leading to dramatically increased social instability.

Lessons to be learned
What lessons can other developing and transitional economies learn from the Chinese privatization experience over the last two decades or so? The first important lesson is that privatization is absolutely necessary to achieve sustained intensive growth. Intensive growth is here defined as economic growth achieved through an increase of total factor productivity rather than through an increased use of inputs. As mentioned earlier, the lack of progress of wholesale privatization in China's state sector, coupled with the fact that China has been able to achieve a double-digit growth rate during some transition years, has led some analysts to conclude that privatization is not a necessary condition for a successful transition strategy.

The above review of Chinese privatization experience shows that this conclusion is untenable. It shows that China's rapid growth during the last two decades can be divided into two phases. During the first phase, 1979–84, rapid agricultural growth was a significant engine of high economic growth. The main driving force behind the rapid agricultural growth was the de facto privatization of China's collective agriculture through the introduction of the HRS, which increased total factor productivity in agriculture. Since 1985, agricultural growth has slowed down. The main source of growth during this second phase has been the growth of the non-agricultural sector, which in turn has been driven by the growth of China's non-state sector. This non-state sector consists of small and medium-sized enterprises under both collective and private ownership but with private ownership dominating. Thus, without the de facto privatization of the Chinese agricultural sector and then the rapid development of non-state enterprises in the non-agricultural sector, the high-speed growth of China during the last two decades would not have been possible.

The second most important lesson from the Chinese experience is that the build-up of a strong and vibrant private sector in an economy is achievable in many ways, ranging from the privatization of existing SOEs to the development of greenfield private enterprises. Similarly, the privatization of existing SOEs may also assume different forms, ranging from the narrow form of divestiture of existing SOEs to broader forms of privatization such as management contracts, contracting out and leasing. Policy makers in developing and transition economies need to be flexible and pragmatic in their choice of the specific forms of privatization and should choose those which are most suitable to their country's political, social and economic conditions.

With respect to the privatization of existing public enterprises, the Chinese experience is consistent with the experience of other developing countries. The narrow form of privatization, namely the divestiture of existing SOEs, was found to be of limited usefulness, except for small-scale SOEs. The most widely used form of privatization of existing SOEs has been the broader form of privatization, namely contracting out. As in other developing countries, the reasons for the limited usefulness of the narrow form of privatization are both practical and political (Cook and Kirkpatrick, 2000: xiv–xv). Specifically, the outright sale of existing public enterprises may be ideologically unacceptable to certain political interest groups and is likely to attract overt opposition. Furthermore, the outright sale of existing public enterprises invariably affects adversely the interest of powerful local groups, such as workers and managers of the enterprises, and thereby provokes opposition to privatization.

With regard to the development of a strong private sector, the Chinese experience is also consistent with the experiences of some Central and Eastern European countries. It shows that the rapid build-up of a strong private sector can be achieved through the development of small and medium-sized non-state enterprises instead of through privatization of existing SOEs. This greenfield approach has proved to be very popular in China because it has met with little opposition from local interest groups, namely workers and managers in the existing SOEs. Furthermore, the newly developed non-state sector has proved more efficient and productive than the partially privatized SOEs. Finally, the presence of the non-state sector has exerted strong competitive pressure on the SOEs, not only to improve efficiency but to change their objectives and behaviour in conformity with the rules of a competitive market economy.

The third important lesson from the Chinese experience is that some privatization in any form is better than none. As mentioned earlier, the broader form of privatization of China's existing SOEs had not been entirely meaningless. The practice of the contract responsibility system in

SOEs, coupled with the increased competitive pressures from a growing non-state sector, enabled the industrial SOEs to achieve an annual average rate of growth of total factor productivity of around 2 per cent. In contrast, the growth of TFP in the Chinese state industrial sector during the pre-reform period (1957–78) was consistently negative.

The fourth important lesson from the Chinese experience is that more privatization is better than less. The above review of the Chinese experience shows that Chinese SOEs, under both the partial and the broader form of privatization programme, have been able to raise efficiency and achieve productivity growth. Yet productivity growth in partially privatized industrial SOEs has reached only one third to one-half of that of the non-state industrial enterprises. Furthermore, there is evidence that the rate of growth of their TFP has been declining in recent years. Finally, preliminary studies show that the latest attempts by the government to enhance the corporate governance structure of the existing SOEs, through corporatization and restructuring, has met with little success. All this suggests that the partial privatization of existing SOEs is not a viable substitute for a wholesale privatization of the existing SOEs in the long run.

The fifth important lesson from China's privatization experience concerns the speed of privatization. The Chinese experience reveals that, though more privatization is preferable to less, the privatization should not be rushed through before the necessary conditions to ensure its successful implementation have been provided for. One of the important conditions is the establishment of a social safety net to protect the victims of full privatization. In the absence of this, as the Russian experience in particular shows, the laid-off workers of privatized SOEs inevitably experience increased poverty.

Another important condition is the establishment of a functioning capital market. In the absence of this, it is difficult to implement a full privatization programme. To begin with, the lack of a functioning capital market makes it difficult for the government to arrive at the real worth of the SOEs to be sold. Second, it also makes it difficult for the government to find sufficient domestic buyers. Theoretically, in the absence of domestic buyers, SOEs may be sold to foreigners, but this may not be ideologically and socially acceptable. Or they may be sold to insiders in the form of management–employee buy-outs, but this leads to the problems of insider control (see Chapter 17 and Havrylyshyn and McGettigan, 1999:8; Qian, 2001:313). These problems include the inequitable transfer of public assets to a handful of employees rather than the population at large; the diverting of resources from the firm for the benefit of employees, in forms such as asset stripping, excessive wage increases and insufficient investment; and privatization of assets and socialization of liabilities. Finally, mass privatization or equal-access voucher privatization may be an alternative method of divestiture in the absence of a functioning capital market. But this method of privatization, as the experience of Central and Eastern European countries shows, leads to a dispersed ownership structure, and this does little to improve corporate governance. Dispersed shareholders face collective action problems and lack the focus and power to achieve effective corporate management (see Chapter 16 and Havrylyshyn and McGettigan, 1999:9).

The performance of a modern private corporation depends not only on its effective internal governance and incentive systems, but also on its external incentive system and environment (see Chapter 2 and Vickers and Yarrow, 1989:44). Essential ingredients for an effective external incentive system and environment, which spur firms to achieve high economic efficiency, include, among other things, competitive product markets. Thus another important condition for a successful implementation of a full privatization programme is the establishment of a competitive market environment. This means the end of government support for privatized enterprises, the abolition of import protection, the conversion of a sellers' market into a buyers' market, and so on.

Privatized enterprises with market power need an effective regulatory framework since maximizing X-efficiency does not necessarily imply maximization of allocative efficiency (Bös, 1997:53–5). Hence yet another important condition for a successful implementation of a full privatization programme is the setting up of an effective legal and institutional framework and enforcement mechanism to regulate firms with market power (see Chapters 22 to 26). Finally, modern private corporations are required to increase efficiency because of the constant threat of takeover and bankruptcy. To make these threats credible, yet another necessary condition for a successful implementation of a full privatization programme is the establishment of a strong judicial system to enforce bankruptcy procedures and the development of a strong market for corporate control. The development of the latter is ultimately linked to the successful development of a functioning and competitive capital market.

Notes

1. This section draws heavily on Chai (1997: 15–20). The permission of Oxford University Press to make use of these materials in this volume is gratefully acknowledged.
2. This section draws heavily on Chai (1997: 169–70, 173, 176–8). The permission of Oxford University Press to make use of these materials in this volume is gratefully acknowledged.

References

Bös, D. (1991) *Privatisation: A Theoretical Treatment*, Oxford: Clarendon Press.
Bös, D. (1997) 'An Alternative to Privatisation: Coping with Managerial Slack in Public

Firms', in H. Giersch (ed.), *Privatisation at the End of the Century*, Berlin–Heidelberg: Springer Verlag.

Broadman, H.G. (2001) 'The Business(es) of the Chinese State', *World Economy*, 23(4), 849–75.

Byrd, W. and Q. Lin (1990) *China's Rural Industry: Structure, Development and Reform*, New York: Oxford University Press.

Chai, J.C.H. (1991) 'Agricultural Development in China', in E.K.Y. Chen and T. Maruya (eds), *A Decade of 'Open Door' Economic Development in China, 1979–1989*, Tokyo: Institute for Developing Economies.

Chai, J.C.H. (1997) *China: Transition to a Market Economy*, Oxford: Clarendon Press.

Chai, J.C.H. and G. Docwra (1997) 'Reform of Large and Medium State Industrial Enterprises: Corporatization and Restructure of State Ownership', in M. Brosseau, H.C. Kuan and Y.Y. Kueh (eds), *China Review 1997*, Hong Kong: The Chinese University Press.

Chai, J.C.H. and C. Tisdell (1999) 'Hardening the Budget Constraint to Control Inflation under the Two-Track System', in Y.Y. Kueh, J.C.H. Chai and Gang Fan (eds), *Industrial Reform and Macroeconomic Instability in China*, Oxford: Clarendon Press.

Che, J. and Y. Qian (1998) 'Insecure Property Rights and Government Ownership of the Firms', *Quarterly Journal of Economics*, 113(2), 467–96.

Cook, P. and C. Kirkpatrick (eds) (2000) *Privatization in Developing Countries*, Cheltenham, UK and Northampton, MA, US: Edward Elgar.

Gaige Mianlin Zhidu Chungxin (1988) *Economic Reform Facing Challenge of Institutional Innovation*, Shanghai: Joint Publishing Company.

Groves, T., Y. Hong, J. McMillan and B. Naughton (1994) 'Autonomy and Incentives in Chinese State Enterprises', *Quarterly Journal Of Economics*, 109(1), 183–209.

Han, S.S. and C.W. Clifton (1999) 'The Geography of Privatisation in China, 1978–1996', *Economic Geography*, 75(3), 272–96.

Havrylyshyn, O. and D. McGettigan (1999) *Privatisation in Transition Countries: Lessons of the First Decade*, Washington, DC: IMF.

Jefferson, G.H. and T.G. Rawski (1994) 'Enterprise Reform in Chinese Industry', *Journal of Economic Perspectives*, 8(2), 47–70.

Jefferson, G.H., T.G. Rawski, L. Wang and Y. Zhang (2000) 'Ownership, Productivity Change and Financial Performance in Chinese Industry', *Journal of Comparative Economics*, 28(4), 786–813.

Jian, T., J.D. Sachs, and A.M. Warner (1996) 'Trends in Regional Inequality in China', NBER Working Paper 5412, National Bureau of Economic Research, Cambridge, MA.

Laurenceson, J. and J.C.H. Chai (2000) 'The Economic Performance of Chinese State Owned Industrial Enterprises', *Journal of Contemporary China*, 9(23), 21–39.

Li, D. (1994) 'Ambiguous Property Rights in Transition Economies', *Journal of Comparative Economies*, 23(1), 1–19.

Lin, J.Y. (1992) 'Rural Reforms and Agricultural Growth in China', *American Economic Review*, 82(1), 34–51

Lin, J.Y. and Y. Yao (2001) 'Chinese Rural Industrialization in the Context of East Asian Miracle', in J.E. Stiglitz and S. Yusuf (eds), *Rethinking the East Asian Miracle*, Washington, DC: World Bank.

Lin, Y. and T. Zhu (2001) 'Ownership Restructuring in Chinese State Industry: An Analysis of Evidence on Initial Organisational change', *China Quarterly*, June, 305–67.

Ma, H. (1982) *Xiandai Zhongguo Jingji Shidan* (Contemporary Chinese Economy: A Compendium), Beijing: China's Social Science Publishing House.

Qian, Y. (2001) 'Government Control in Corporate Governance as a Transitional Institution: Lessons from China', in J. E. Stiglitz and S. Yusuf (eds), *Rethinking the East Asian Miracle*, Washington, DC: World Bank.

Sachs, J. and W.T. Woo (1997) 'Chinese Economic Growth: Explanations and Tasks Ahead', in Joint Economic Committee, US Congress (ed.), *China's Economic Future: Challenge to US Policy*, Amonk: M.E. Sharpe.

Stewart, B. (2001) 'Regional Development and Inter-provincial Income Inequality in China:

A Description and Analysis', unpublished economics honours thesis, School of Economics, The University of Queensland.

Vickers, J. and G. Yarrow (1989) *Privatisation: An Economic Analysis*, Cambridge, MA: MIT Press.

Weitzman, M. and C. Xu (1994) 'Chinese Township Village Enterprises as Vaguely Defined Cooperatives', *Journal of Comparative Economics*, 23(1), 121–45.

Wong, C.P.W. (1992) 'Fiscal Reform and Local Industrialization: the Problematic Sequencing of Reform in Post Mao China', *Modern China*, 18(2), 197–227.

World Bank (1983) *China: Socialist Economic Development*, vol. III, Washington, DC: World Bank.

World Bank (1997) *China 2020: Development Challenges in the New Century*, Washington, DC: World Bank.

Yusuf, S. (1994) 'China's Macroeconomic Management and Performance during Transition', *Journal of Economic Perspectives*, Spring, 71–92.

ZGNYNJ (*Zhongguo Nongye Nianjian*) (China's Agricultural Yearbook), various issues.

ZGTJNJ (*Zhongguo Tongji Nianjian*) (China's Statistical Yearbook), various issues.

Zhang, H. and L. Ming (1999) *Zhongguo Siying Qiye Fazhan Baogao 1978–1998* (China's Private Enterprise Development Report 1978–1998), Beijing: Social Science Literature Publishing House.

13 Privatization in Mexico and Chile: a critical perspective
Miguel D. Ramírez

Introduction[1]

The major countries of Latin America have been engaged for almost two decades in a process of radical market-oriented reform that has dramatically reduced state ownership and control of their domestic economies. Privatization of state-owned enterprises and the liberalization of trade and finance in countries such as Argentina, Brazil, Chile and Mexico have been carried out to such an extent that this has brought to an end the state-led development strategy known as import substitution industrialization (ISI). Deregulation of economic activity has also accompanied this process, as evidenced by the removal of what are deemed to be unnecessary controls and restrictions on the allocation of scarce resources in the product and factor markets of many countries of the region, notably Argentina, Chile and Mexico.

One of the major consequences of the privatization and liberalization movement, in recent years, has been the transfer of public sector firms to the domestic (and foreign) private sector in highly concentrated industries, such as airlines, banking, telecommunications, petroleum exploration and refining, where usually one or two firms dominate these markets. The inherent danger of doing this is that it may lead to a situation where private monopolies just replace public ones and where powerful foreign and domestic interests exert undue control (without public accountability) over key economic decisions in strategic sectors of the economy – a state of affairs that circumscribes the host government's room to manoeuvre and may compromise national sovereignty. Thus, unless an effective regulatory framework is in place to safeguard the public's interest against monopolistic abuses, the dominant firms in these markets may engage in both anti-competitive and anti-nationalist behaviour that could eliminate some or all of the purported benefits (including positive externalities such as loans and aid from international financial institutions, lower interest rates and so on) associated with privatization and liberalization.

This chapter will focus on certain key aspects of the privatization experience in Mexico and Chile and offer some suggestions for improving the legal–institutional framework within which these market-oriented reforms are undertaken. The layout of the chapter is as follows. First, it reviews some of the major theoretical premises upon which the logic of privatization stands. It then outlines a number of important regulatory issues and problems that arise when Latin American countries decide to privatize strategic public sector firms and/or natural monopolies. In the following two sections, it focuses on the regulatory, economic and social–political challenges and opportunities generated by the privatization of the banking and telecommunications industries in Mexico, and the privatization of telecommunications and energy in Chile. The conclusion summarizes the key findings, and proposes some corrective policy guidelines, designed to strengthen and improve the regulatory and legal environment in which market-oriented policies such as privatization are undertaken.

The rationale for privatization

It should be mentioned from the outset that the list of factors mentioned below is by no means meant to be exhaustive or conclusive; rather, it represents those conventional elements that most economists and political scientists believe to be of a decisive nature in the decision to privatize. Moreover, the relative importance of each of these factors varies from country to country, as well as over time, since each nation is faced with varying, and often unforeseen, internal and external circumstances, as the uneven process of privatization and economic deregulation unfolds. It should also be noted that, although this chapter tends to focus on the narrow definition of privatization, that is, the sale of state-owned enterprises to the private sector, it does not lose sight of the broader meaning of the term; that is, privatization refers to a social process which entails the progressive devolution of economic and financial activity to the private sector, including the deregulation of labour and financial markets, the liberalization of trade and the contracting out of quasi-public goods or services to private entities in accordance with government regulations and specifications. It is evident that all of these market-oriented reforms and policies are complementary in nature and are ultimately designed to reduce the direct and indirect role of the state in the economy and, in so doing, enable private agents to respond optimally to changing market opportunities and challenges.

From a strictly economic standpoint, then, the most important reason for privatizing economic activity (broadly defined) resides in the notion of a functionally neutral or minimalist state; that is, the public sector should confine its operations to those tasks which the private sector is unwilling and/or unable to undertake because of a lack of necessary capital, a dearth of technical/managerial expertise, sub-standard or non-existent economic infrastructure, unequal access to information about products and markets and, last but not least, the absence of an efficient legal–institutional framework for conducting business. There is a general presumption that the transfer of state-owned enterprises to the private sector takes place in a competitive environment that is devoid of major market failures. However, as shown in the case studies below, product market competition under optimal conditions exists rarely, if at all, in most Latin American countries, including Chile and Mexico. Undeterred, neoliberal enthusiasts contend that, even in those cases of private market failure, state intervention should be limited and confined to those operations where private sector participants cannot be found to assume the production, distribution and marketing of the goods and services in question. Any excessive prolongation and/or extension of government intervention into the 'rightful' domain of the market will invariably lead to public sector failure, which is, according to this view, always worse than market failure. Needless to say, this neoliberal agenda has gained a foothold in almost every country of Latin America over the past two decades, but its ferocity and hard-hitting edge, under military rule, was most visible in Chile, the country that experienced the greatest degree of polarization and working class struggle during the late 1960s and early 1970s. Mexico has also undertaken far-reaching market-oriented reforms that have effectively put an end to four decades of state-led industrialization, particularly during the administrations of Carlos Salinas de Gortari (1988–94) and Ernesto Ponce De Zedillo (1994–2000).

Closely related to the ideological explanation is the idea that economic efficiency can be improved if former state-owned enterprises are owned and managed by the private sector. Public firms, according to neoliberal advocates, are particularly susceptible to what, in the economics literature, is called the principal–agent problem. That is, the public firm, the agent in this case, is owned by 'society' at large (the principal), and is therefore potentially subject to a wide variety of politically and economically conflicting interests, particularly if the benefits and costs are distributed in a highly unequal manner across different social groups. In other words, when there is an uncoupling of beneficiaries and victims associated with the presence of state intervention in the form of tariffs, licensing agreements, price controls and the provision of public goods and services, economic groups that are directly affected have stronger economic incentives to capture the firm or agency and appropriate, through rent-seeking behaviour, the lion's share of the benefits (also see, in particular, Chapters 2 and 3 above). In sum, privatization enthusiasts contend that any attempt by the public sector to meet the varied and conflicting demands of its constituents would not only be politically costly and divisive, but economically inefficient as well.

However, these market advocates conveniently overlook the fact that the principal–agent problem is not exclusively confined to state-owned firms; it also arises when private sector firms are called upon to produce goods and provide services that display 'public good' characteristics, such as education, medical care, police protection, transport and communications, housing, banking services, mail service, refuse collection and national defence. Moreover, according to modern portfolio theory, private owners have an incentive to diversify their ownership of shares across several firms in different sectors in order to minimize risk. Larger firms will also tend to have a widely dispersed shareholding base, which means that any given shareholder will have neither the ability to exert influence on management nor sufficient incentive to monitor management's behaviour because of free-rider considerations. Although the threat of takeover and bankruptcy can prevent private managers from shirking their responsibilities or disregarding shareholder interests, the literature on the effectiveness of takeover threats on internal efficiency is far from settled and subject to considerable controversy.

The determining factor, insofar as allocative efficiency is concerned, seems to be the kind of market structure and regulatory framework within which the firm operates rather than ownership *per se*. As this chapter will show, the privatization movement in Chile and Mexico, in the absence of an effective regulatory framework, has led to an unwelcome situation where private monopolies just replace public ones.

The decision to privatize state-owned enterprises has also been rationalized along the lines that it helps send a 'credible' signal to the private sector that the government is serious about its commitment to market-based reforms. Formally, we have a situation that is characterized by asymmetric information because even though the government may be committed to market-based reforms, such as privatization and/or trade reform, it may be unable to communicate this effectively to the private sector. In this connection, Rodrik (1992:92) has shown in a formal model that the lack of credibility in market-based reforms, whether it be privatization and/or trade liberalization, can blunt incentives and 'interact with capital irreversibilities to produce a hefty tax on investment [and economic growth]'.

The credibility problem is even more pronounced if the government in question has initially lacked the ideological credentials of the Washington Consensus and/or if the country is emerging from a generalized economic crisis under International Monetary Fund (IMF) conditionality. To buttress their credentials, reform-minded governments of the region, including those in Chile and Mexico, have decided to go further than the recommendations of the conventional wisdom, by coupling their decision to privatize with a variety of economic and political incentives. For example, they have assumed the debt obligations of the public firm before sale as well as the direct costs associated with its sale, such as advertising and underwriting; they have often underpriced the shares of privatized assets and offered them to wealthy and influential economic groups; they have ensured a more flexible and deregulated labour market through the weakening and outright elimination of hard-won workers' rights; and they have concentrated on highly profitable, yet weakly regulated, priority sectors such as airlines, banking, telecommunications and energy.

The last, and perhaps most important, factor explaining the decision to sell state assets is that it generates an immediate financial transfer (the so-called *stock effect*) to the governments of the region even as it affects their future fiscal revenues (the *flow effect*). The trade-off, of course, will depend on whether the public firm is a perennial money loser or profitable enterprise, and whether the net revenues (if any) generated by the public firm before privatization are offset by the taxes paid by the privatized firm, assuming that the latter is profitable. More formally, the decision to privatize can be conceptualized by reference to the following expression:

$$W = (E + L + tV^*) - (T + V), \tag{13.1}$$

where W is the net gain to the state from privatizing the firm; E denotes the expected net value of externalities generated by the firm when it is privatized, including loans and aid from international agencies, the acquisition of new technology and managerial know-how and lower interest rates. The E variable may have a positive or negative sign. L refers to the lump-sum payment that the state expects to receive when privatizing the firm, while tV^* is the net present value of the future stream of profit taxes under private ownership, where t denotes the tax rate and V^* and V represent, respectively, the present value of the firm's future stream of net revenues under private and public ownership. Finally, T refers to the transaction costs associated with privatizing the SOE (for example, finding buyers, assessing the 'true value' of the firm's assets or 'sanitizing' the firm before sale by assuming its debt obligations: see Cantor, 1996).

Equation (13.1) above suggests that the state should choose to privatize the SOE if it anticipates high positive externalities, a high sales price, low transaction costs, a high revenue flow and a low present value (V) of the firm under state ownership. However, as indicated above, the lump-sum payment, L, received by the state may be offset by the long-term loss in government revenues if the tax rate is reduced significantly or eliminated. Moreover, the deficit-reducing effects of privatization may be offset completely if one includes the transaction costs, T, associated with 'sanitizing' the enterprises in order to render them more saleable to domestic and foreign buyers.

By and large, cash-strapped Latin American governments chose the privatization option because they were literally cut off from external private financial flows with the onset and aftermath of the 1980s debt crisis. Internal sources of funds were also unavailable to service their debt payments and bring down their ballooning public sector deficits because many of these countries were mired in economic crisis and, given their weak political and institutional setting, were incapable and/or unwilling to reform their structurally inefficient and highly regressive tax systems. Governments of the region were also constrained in using bond sales as a means of raising desperately needed revenues because, at the time, investors were fearful that these countries would default on their outstanding debt commitments, both internal and external.

Faced with no other politically and economically viable options, many governments of the region, including the Chilean and Mexican ones, proceeded to sell profitable public sector service firms under generous terms. This short-term strategy has proved to be an effective means to raise immediate revenues with which to service both internal and external debts, and thus reduce fiscal deficits, which often generate serious inflation and balance of payments problems. But, as indicated above, the short-term 'successes' of this strategy may come at the long-term price of a reduced flow of revenues in the future, a significant loss of employment opportunities, increases in poverty, the loss of economic autonomy and political sovereignty, and the further concentration of income and wealth in the hands of economically powerful and politically influential groups.

Problems and issues surrounding effective regulation
Several problems and issues surrounding effective regulation can be identified. First, the new regulatory systems that have arisen in Latin America to monitor the privatization of public firms are often plagued by administrative, financial and operational problems, and thus often find themselves in the difficult position of playing 'catch up' with the speed at which the privatization process is taking place. It should then come as no surprise that regulators often do not have access to timely and accurate information on consumer demand, the firm's costs and its degree of monopoly power, or the level of cost-reducing efforts undertaken by the newly privatized firm. Faced with asymmetric and undependable information, regulators are thus unclear as to what aspects of the firm's behavior should be regulated (for example, rate of return regulation versus price regulation: see Armstrong, 1994, and Chapters 22 and 23, below). Or, in the case of vertically integrated natural monopolists, regulators may be unable to regulate the firm's ability to manipulate costs via transfer pricing and thus move profits from regulated to unregulated activities.

Second, as indicated in the previous section, these administrative and operational problems are exacerbated by cash-strapped governments in the region, which view the privatization process more as a mechanism for converting future cash receipts into present cash sums to temporarily close destabilizing fiscal deficits and/or eliminate balance of payments problems, rather than in terms of efficiency considerations (Birch and Braga, 1993; Baer and Birch, 1992). Although some critics and legal scholars have attributed these problems to an inadequate system of property rights and contract law, they are more likely to be due to the fact that the newly created legal and administrative bodies are emerging with little or no track record, and with poor enforcement mechanisms, and are often underequipped and understaffed, with their personnel being poorly paid relative to the industry that is being regulated. Court cases thus take a long time to work their way through the legal system, supervision and monitoring costs are high, outcomes are often unpredictable, and regulators and judges may be susceptible to bribes and other forms of corrupt behaviour.

Third, government officials, faced with the operational inadequacies of the regulatory and legal systems in the region, are willing to substitute improved future technical efficiency of a newly privatized firm (assuming it is profitable) for potentially inferior allocative efficiency in the present; that is, the transfer of a poorly regulated public monopoly to the private sector involves a shift from marginal cost pricing to monopoly pricing that is often worse in terms of allocative efficiency and social welfare (Vickers and Yarrow, 1988). In effect, regulators are betting that the loss in allocative efficiency and social equity will be more than offset in the long run by the increased profitability and technological innovation expected from significant economies of scale, greater managerial incentives and shareholder monitoring (the principal–agent problem). Hence, for private firms to be superior in terms of economic and social welfare, the improvement in technical (internal) efficiency should be significantly higher than the loss in allocative efficiency (for a fuller discussion of this issue, see Chapter 4 above).

Finally, regulatory systems and antitrust laws have tended to emerge after, rather than before, the privatization of public firms in so-called 'strategic sectors' such as banking, mining, energy and public utilities. Under these circumstances it is not possible for regulators to establish a track record and rectify some of the worst administrative/operational problems and abuses that are likely to emerge: for example, underinvestment, technical inefficiency, restriction of output and entry, and unfair labour practices. That is, it is far more effective to prevent the emergence of monopolistic behaviour designed to create market power via mergers than it is to combat the anti-competitive practices of established monopolists, such as collusion and predatory pricing.

Privatization and regulatory reform in Mexico
The absence of appropriate antitrust laws and a strong independent regulatory agency with wide-ranging supervisory powers has led to suboptimal

outcomes in key sectors of the Mexican economy, particularly banking and finance. Financial liberalization and the deregulation of the financial sector during 1990–94, in the presence of little, if any, oversight over the country's financial intermediaries and their lending practices, has led to an unprecedented concentration of productive and financial resources in the hands of relatively few and powerful segments (*grupos*) of the private sector (including a growing foreign presence).[2]

The reprivatization of Mexico's 18 commercial banks is an excellent example of the distributional problems and economic pitfalls associated with a poorly designed and monitored programme. Although Mexican officials sought to distribute the country's financial power more equitably by prohibiting individual investors from owning more than 5 per cent of a privatized bank's shares, ex-bankers and new private financiers were able to create new financial controlling groups that circumvented the law and obtained up to 100 per cent of the shares of the newly privatized banks. For example, in a study of bank privatization, Mexican financial specialist Carlos Elizondo observes that only 44 economic *grupos* bid for the 18 nationalized banks, and the bulk of the savings of these privatized banks are now concentrated in a small number of individuals and firms. He reports that some of the same families that owned and controlled the banking system before the 1982 nationalization have returned, along with powerful industrialists and new private financiers. The latter are mainly owners of stock brokerage houses (*Casas de Bolsa*) who, according to Elizondo (1993), 'knew how to profit from the stock market much better than former bankers'.

In this connection, consider the case of Banamex, one of the three largest banks in Latin America and one of the oldest banks in Mexico, which at the time of its sale owned assets valued at more than US$15bn. Table 13.1 indicates that it was sold in 1991 for US$3.1bn to a *grupo* regional, which includes the country's largest brokerage house, Acciones Y Valores de Mexico. The group is headed by Alfredo Harp Helu (kidnapped in early 1994 and released later that same year), Roberto Hernandez Ramirez and Jose G. Aguilera Medrano. Hernandez Ramirez and Harp Helu are major partners in the Accival brokerage house, with controlling ownership of the company's equity capital of 39 and 36.23 per cent, respectively. The brokerage house is also a major stockholder in the telephone company Telmex (7 per cent) and – as a result of its merger with *grupo* Banacci – of the country's second largest bank, Bancomer (33.3 per cent). It should also be noted that Harp Helu is the former president of the stock exchange and a close friend of the (now disgraced) ex-president Carlos Salinas de Gortari (*Mexico Business Monthly*, 1991).

Bancomer, the country's second largest retail bank, was sold to individual

Table 13.1   Main privatizations in Mexico since 1991 (US$mn)

Year	Company	Sector	Equity share (%)	Amount	Purchaser
1991	Banca Cremi	Banking	66.7	241	Multivalores
1991	Banamex	Banking	70.7	3 131	Acciones y Valores
1991	Empresa Gamesa	Beverage	70.0	640	Pepsi Cola
1991	Bancomer	Banking	51.0	3 154	Valores Monterrey
1991	Telmex	Telecomms	20.7	5663	Grupo Carso, France Telecom, Southwestern Bell
1992	Multibanco Comermex	Banking	66.5	873	Augustin Legorreta Group
1992	Banco Internacional	Banking	72.0	480	Grupo Financiero Privado
1992	Banco del Atlantico	Banking	68.6	474	Grupo Bursatil Americano
1992	Banco Mex. Somex	Banking	81.6	605	Grupo Invermexico
1992	Banca Serfin	Banking	51.0	912	Grupo Financiero OBSA
1992	Banco Mercantil del Norte	Banking	66.0	573	Grupo Maseca
1993	Aseguradora Mexicana	Insurance	51.0	582	Grupo Mexival Banpais
1993	Channels 7 and 13	Television	100.0	645	Grupo Electra
1994	Telefonos de Mexico	Telecomms		530*	

Note: *Convertible offering.

Source: OECD (1995:81, Table 19).

investors (including Hernandez Ramirez and Harp Helu) led by Eugenio Garza Laguera, former owner of Banco Serfin and CEO of *grupo* Vamsa and Visa (see Table 13.1). Vamsa is a leading financial firm based in Monterrey, Mexico, with investments in securities, brokerage firms, leasing, factoring and warehousing. Its principal subsidiary, Seguros de Mexico, is Mexico's largest individual life insurer. *Grupo* Visa, on the other hand, is one of Mexico's oldest industrial concerns and an influential member of COPAR-MEX, a highly conservative and powerful business umbrella organization. It is the largest beverage concern in Mexico, with significant investments and market share in beer, soft drinks and mineral water. It is also actively involved in packaging, distribution and marketing.

Finally, Table 13.1 shows that even the relatively smaller banks have been sold to individuals and firms belonging to powerful financial and industrial *grupos*. For example, multiregional banks such as Banco del Atlantico (7th largest) and Banco Promex (12th largest) were sold to a group headed by Alonso de Garay Gutierres and Jorge Rohas Mota Velasco. The new owners are closely connected to *Grupo* Bursatil Americano, the country's second largest stock brokerage house. Banco del Atlantico is the largest multiregional bank, with assets of US$3.5 bn and a network of 204 branches spread over more than 26 of Mexico's 30 states. Finally, Banco Mercantil del Norte, the country's largest regional bank, was sold to a group of investors led by Roberto Gonzales, Juan Antonio Gonzales and Federico Graf. These investors are closely affiliated with *Grupo* Industrial Maseca, Mexico's largest tortilla flour producer.

The concentration of banking assets in a relatively small number of financial and industrial *grupos* with strategic economic and institutional associations has given rise to legitimate public concerns about the degree of competition present in the privatized banking system. One indication that the banking sector was expected to record persistent above-normal profits following privatization can be found in the price-to-book value paid for the banks by the new owners. According to Elizondo, 'The banks were bought at 14.07 times profit and 3.07 times book value. The same figures for banks bought in the US in the last five years have been on average 14 and 2.2 times' (Elizondo, 1993). A similar conclusion was reached by Gruben and McComb (1997: 23), who reported that between June 1991 and July 1992 – a period of only 14 months – all 18 government banks were sold, 'at the extraordinarily high average price-to-book value ratio of 3.49'. They went on to add that most of the buyers were large financial groups and broker-age houses who anticipated relatively little competition given that the three largest privatized banks alone, Banamex, Bancomer and Serfin, accounted for 60 per cent of all Mexican bank assets. Finally, McQuerry (1999) refers to anecdotal evidence which suggests that the new owners anticipated that their large investments costs would be easily defrayed in an environment of stifled competition.

Market power can also be measured by whether the industry exhibits sustained 'above-normal' profits. For example, the banks' profits, as measured by the real return on equity, rose from 18 per cent in 1992 to 23 per cent in 1993, and more than 26 per cent in 1994. Another measure of bank profitability reported by McQuerry (1999:25) is the return-on-average assets; it shows that, 'Whereas a solid return in the United States would be 1 percent, the average Mexican bank was attaining much more than this amount in 1993 [1.66 per cent]'. In a similar vein, Gruben and McComb (1997:23) observe that, when the last of the commercial banks was sold in 1992, 'the net return on assets for Mexican Banks was approximately 1.45 percent, versus 0.91 percent for U.S. banks'.

However, at the same time that the banks were registering record profits, they were also recording a dramatic deterioration in the quality of their loans. The ratio of past-due loans to total loans increased from 3.1 per cent in 1991 to 7.5 per cent in 1993, and then to over 8 per cent by the end of 1994 (see Table 13.2).[3] And although economic growth did slow from 3.6 per cent in 1991 to 0.3 per cent in 1993, it was gradual and it did pick up again in 1994 with an increase of 3 per cent. These figures suggest that, during the period in question, the newly privatized banks were engaged in heavy lending to the private sector in order to increase market share and, as a result, had overextended themselves. In fact, Gruben and McComb (1977:25) go as far as to argue that bank owners lent so much in the short run 'that they passed the point where marginal cost equalled marginal revenue, to a point where marginal cost exceeded marginal revenue'. Of course, they are quick to point out that the banks could not sustain this in the long run, but that, in the euphoria following the privatization of the banks, many inexperienced bank managers operating under weak accounting standards (to be discussed below) and bank supervision were expanding consumer credit on the basis of limited information and overly optimistic (herd-like) assessments of the future prospects for the Mexican economy.[4] Also, during a credit boom, borrowers can obtain funds from other creditors and use them as collateral to obtain additional funds from the banks for risky investments. In fact, the behaviour of Mexican bank managers is consistent with the hypothesis put forth by Hausmann and Gavin (1996:33) that, during a credit boom, 'good times are bad times for learning about the creditworthiness of borrowers' because 'even shaky enterprises will be liquid and appear solvent . . . and bank managers [particularly inexperienced ones] have a hard time determining which of their loans are going bad'.[5] And if this is the case for bank managers, it is even more so for the officials in charge of regulating the banking system, given that their knowledge set is a smaller subset of that available to bank managers!

One admittedly crude way of determining whether Mexican bankers were enmeshed in a credit boom is to focus on the performance of the banks' liquidity ratio, defined as the ratio of loans to deposits (see McQuerry, 1999). Table 13.2 shows that this ratio rose dramatically, from 110.3 per cent in 1993 to 130.1 per cent in 1995. In general, a lower ratio is preferable because the more deposits a bank has in relation to loans the more quickly it can convert them into cash to meet any unforeseen contingency, such as covering losses related to non-performing loans. The rapid increase in this ratio should have alerted government officials to the increasing fragility of the banking system, but it was only after the peso devaluation of 1994–5 and a severe economic contraction that it became apparent to government officials how undercapitalized (overleveraged) the banking system had become during the preceding credit boom.

Table 13.2   Performance indicators for the Mexican banking system (%)

	1993	1994	1995	1996	1997	1998
Past-due loans to total loans	7.50	8.4	12.1	12.0	11.6	11.8
Loans/deposits	110.3	116.5	130.1	119.1	101.7	103.1
Return on assets	1.66	0.49	0.31	−0.64	0.43	0.03

Source: McQuerry (1999); Bank of Mexico (1998).

In fact, one of the contributing problems to the rise in non-performing loans during the period in question stemmed from the inability of bank regulators to determine the quality of loans and the extent of self-lending within financial holding companies because Mexican accounting standards did not require consolidated reporting of banking assets and liabilities. To make matters worse, under the old accounting system Mexican banks severely underreported the percentage of past-due loans because, unlike the US system, Mexican banks only reported missed payments as past-due loans and not the outstanding balance on the loan to which interest could still accrue (see McQuerry, 1999:20). By the time the Mexican government proceeded to establish the Mexican National Banking and Securities Commission (CNBV), in May 1995, and adopt generally accepted accounting standards (GAAP), the damage to the banking sector was so severe that many banks were insolvent and the level of past-due loans had jumped to 12.1 per cent. Not surprisingly, bank profitability, as measured by return on assets, dropped sharply, from 0.49 percent in 1994 to −0.64 per cent in 1996 and, as Table 13.2 shows, had yet to recover to its pre-crisis level even as late as 1998.

Another, admittedly crude, indicator of enhanced competition and efficiency in the banking system is to determine whether the spread between lending and deposit rates has become progressively smaller. Contrary to expectations, Table 13.3 below shows that the spreads widened significantly immediately following the reprivatizations of the banks in 1992. For example, the table indicates that they rose from an already high 11.34 point margin in 1992 to 14.62 in 1993. It is also important to note that the rise in spreads occurred at the same time that the country's inflation rate fell significantly. Bankers were paying depositors considerably lower real interest rates in 1992–93 than in 1989–90 while, at the same time, they continued to charge borrowers high real interest rates. The high lending rates, in turn, contributed to the rapid rise in the percentage of non-performing loans reported above, particularly among small and medium-sized business firms and consumers, and ironically, made the banking system itself (with the exception of the three largest banks) susceptible to bankruptcy proceedings and government rescue packages, as evidenced by the near collapse of the banking system following the 1994–5 Mexican peso crisis (Peiro, 1996; Ramirez, 1995). A cautionary note is in order here. The rise in spreads reported above does not, in and of itself, constitute *prima facie* evidence that concentration has enhanced market power and economic inefficiency in the newly privatized banking system; other institutional and economic factors have to be incorporated into the analysis in order to determine whether the reprivatization process has undermined productive and allocative efficiency in the industry.

Table 13.3   Mexico: real interest rates and financial margins, 1987–96 (%)

Years	Deposit rates (CPP)	Average lending rates	Margins
1987	−14.61	−4.71	9.90
1988	−25.12	−14.18	10.94
1989	20.31	33.40	13.09
1990	8.54	19.08	10.64
1991	−0.22	11.58	11.80
1992	2.71	14.05	11.34
1993	6.18	20.80	14.62
1994	8.41	18.64	10.23
1995	−6.88	4.00	10.88
1996	0.33	6.31	5.98

Source: Bank of Mexico (1998); Calva (1995, Table 15, p. 92).

One of these factors has been the rapidly growing foreign banking presence in the market since the 1994–5 peso crisis. For example, the market share held by foreign banks was only 3 per cent in 1994, but rapidly increased in the following years, reaching a level of 22 per cent in 1999. It will be recalled that, when the North American Free Trade Area (NAFTA) was negotiated, the Mexican government anticipated that the foreign banks' market share would rise gradually to about 9 per cent in 1996 and to no more than 15 per cent by 1999.[6] The greater than expected foreign penetration was stimulated by the unprecedented financial difficulties of the smaller banks following the 1994 devaluation, many of which were caught in a tightening financial vice as a result of their rapidly deteriorating loan portfolio (in turn due to the country's economic depression and the imprudent lending practices of the banks) and the huge increase in their foreign currency debt, which stood at a staggering US$18 bn at the beginning of 1995.

Faced with the urgent need to raise capital for the troubled banks, the Mexican state actively promoted greater foreign participation in the purchase of the banks' equity shares. It introduced a new banking law in 1995 that permitted foreign banks to purchase a controlling interest in Mexican banks, without permission, provided that these banks' share of the total capital of the Mexican banking system is less than 6 per cent. However, with permission from the CNBV, foreign investors are allowed, in aggregate, to own up to 25 per cent of the total capital of the banking system, thus rendering null and void the old NAFTA rules, which set a limit of 9 per cent. In a further blow to nationalistic objectives, the Finance Ministry also allowed foreign banks to establish banks in the country that can, in turn, acquire between a 51 and a 100 per cent controlling interest in a Mexican bank.

The effects of these new banking laws and purchase limits has been to increase foreign ownership and control of the Mexican banking system. For example, in 1996, Banco Mexicano was taken over by Banco Santander of Spain, while, in June 1997, GE Capital Corporation took complete control of the equity of Banca Alianza. In 1998, Citibank went ahead with its takeover of Banca Confia, while Dresdner completed its acquisition of Bancrecer. Finally, JP Morgan and the Hong Kong Shangai Bank (HKSB) acquired close to 29 per cent of *Grupo* Financiero Serfin, S.A., owners of Banco Serfin which, as discussed below, had to be rescued by the Mexican government in mid-1999.

In addition to luring foreign investors to help shore up its ailing banking system, the government itself provided public funds to the system via *Procapte* (the Temporary Capitalization Programme). This rescue agency injected new capital into the distressed banks by allowing them to issue five-year convertible bonds that were then purchased by Fobaproa (the Bank

Fund for the Protection of Savings, to be discussed below). For example, Banco de Union, Banco Confia, Banca Cremi, Bancentro and Banpais, just to name of few of the smaller banks, have been provided with additional capital (as well as intervention in their administration) so that they can meet the internationally sanctioned capital-to-assets ratio of 8 per cent. Only the largest bank – Banamex – has managed to avoid serious financial difficulties (Fobaproa, however, did provide it with additional capital but without intervening in its day-to-day operations) and significant foreign ownership of their equity capital (*capital ordinario*). Mexico's second largest bank, Bancomer, on the other hand, recently announced that it intended to merge with Spain's second largest bank, banking giant Banco Bilbao Viscaya Argentaria, to create one of Latin America's largest financial entities. Even the third largest bank, Banco Serfin (owned by *grupo* Financiero Serfin) with a 13.4 per cent share of the market, was taken over by the Mexican government in July 1999 and is in the process of being recapitalized at taxpayer expense. It should be noted that this is not the first time that the government has stepped in to rescue the 'eagle' from falling (*grupo* Financiero's symbol is the 'eagle'). During the financial and economic crisis of 1995 it injected close to US$6.9bn in new .capital via Procapte and Fobaproa (*IL*, 1999b).

Basically, the Mexican state has de facto 'sanitized' these private financial enterprises and thus effectively subsidized their sale to powerful foreign and domestic interests. What makes the current wave of foreign takeovers and domestic mergers so worrisome, aside from their obvious impact on competition and national sovereignty, is the poor track record exhibited by the banking regulatory agencies during both the Salinas and the Zedillo *sexenios.* In their zeal to establish market-friendly (neoliberal) credentials, the banking regulators turned a blind eye to a number of excesses, ranging from allowing exorbitant spreads to permitting the second largest bank, Bancomer, to grant so many car loans that, when the crisis hit, its foreclosure rate on these loans meant that it became the de facto owner of the largest fleet of cars in Mexico (LAEB, 1995)! Perhaps most disturbingly, the 'blind eye' of banking regulators was not only confined to the banks' risky lending behaviour following privatization; it also failed to detect the extensive degree of criminal activity involved in the day-to-day operations of the privatized banks, particularly the smaller ones. The Mackey Report (1999) found extensive criminal activity in the operations of seven banks. For example, several bank managers knowingly accepted false information from debtors as well as illegally channelling funds to these debtors. In addition, documents relating to the operations of the banks were manipulated and falsified by bank managers with the full knowledge that, thereby, the financial health of the banks would be endangered. Finally, prominent members of Mexico's opposition parties, the PAN and the PRD, have charged Banco Union and its president, Carlos Cabal Peniche, with illegally financing the electoral campaigns of the assassinated presidential candidate, Luis Donaldo Colosio, his successor, President Ernesto Zedillo, and the governor of the state of Tabasco, Roberto Madrazo (see *IL*, 2000a, 2000b, 2000c). So far, criminal charges involving credit operations valued at US$638 mn have been brought against 40 bank managers, including prominent bankers such as Carlos Cabal Peniche, Jorge Lankenau and the notorious Angel Isidoro Rodriguez Saez (known as 'El Divino!' – see *IL*, 1999a – this shady character was extradited from Spain as he tried unsuccessfully to elude Spanish immigration authorities by jumping into the Mediterranean Sea from his yacht). It thus remains to be seen whether the regulatory mistakes, monopolistic abuses and criminal behaviour which have marred the Mexican banking system can be avoided in the near future. One can hardly blame a disinterested observer for being apprehensive about the eventual outcome.

The telecommunications sector
Telmex, Mexico's state-owned telecommunications firm, was sold in three major stages during the period 1990–4. In view of the fact that most members of the international business and financial community have viewed the sale of Telmex as a 'textbook' case of how state-owned companies in Latin America and elsewhere ought to be privatized, it is important to scrutinize the record carefully. The initial (December 1990) offering of 51 per cent of the company's equity (so-called 'AA' shares with full voting rights) was sold for US$1.757 bn to an international consortium led by *grupo* Carso, owned by Carlos Slim – the richest man in Mexico and Latin America with an estimated fortune of US$8 bn in 1999 and, at the time, a good friend of (and major political contributor to) the then president Carlos Salinas de Gortari. During the second stage, initiated in May 1991, the Mexican government sold 1.76 per cent of 'A' shares (with limited voting rights) to workers in exchange for concessions ranging from the elimination of numerous job classification categories to seniority clauses. Workers were also promised that no major lay-offs would take place following privatization and that the necessary reduction in the workforce would be achieved via limited relocation and normal attrition. By following this strategy, government officials clearly intended to avoid a major confrontation with the STRM, the Mexican Telephone union, perhaps learning a lesson from the rancorous labour–management relations associated with the privatization of Aeromexico and Mexicana airlines. It is also probable that Mexican officials anticipated efficiency gains in worker productivity given that the workers would now directly benefit from the company's

profitability. Finally, the state divested itself of all of its remaining interests in the company through international American Depository Receipt (ADR) stock offerings in the USA and global markets during the period 1992–4. It is estimated that these ADR offerings raised US$2.1 bn for the Mexican government. By and large, the proceeds from the sale of Telmex went into a contingency fund to pay off the Mexican government's internal and external liabilities.

Before its divestiture Telmex was the third largest company in Mexico and the second largest telephone company in Latin America. Telmex was also a highly profitable company because its monopolistic status enabled it to charge long-distance rates that were considerably higher than marginal cost and comparable international rates. In 1990, the state tried to correct the situation by lowering international long-distance rates, yet they remained considerably higher than their marginal cost. To make matters worse, not only were domestic long-distance rates increasing in real terms, but they were also increasing at a much faster rate than marginal costs. Obviously, the high rates on long-distance calls (used by wealthier Mexicans in urban areas) enabled the company to subsidize its local (and rural) markets by charging tariffs that were, in many instances, barely enough to cover their marginal cost.

Government officials justified the policy of cross-subsidization on the grounds that it offered greater telephone access to lower-income Mexicans in both rural and urban settings. The reality, however, was that the sacrifice in allocative efficiency was not offset by greater access to basic telephone services on the part of low- and middle-income Mexicans, or an improvement in services, such as reducing delays with telephone connections and repairs or, for that matter, a significant expansion in the telecommunications network (including satellite communication) of the country. In fact, before privatization, the rapid growth in Telmex's workforce was not accompanied by a greater increase in the number of new telephone lines. For example, the number of lines per employee was 96 in 1985, 89 in 1987 and 85 in 1988, before rising to 96 in 1989 – the year before privatization. Despite the increase in 1989, the number of new lines, particularly in the rural areas, did not keep pace with the growth of income in the economy. Moreover, the number of lines per 100 inhabitants was only 5.1 in 1989, below the number in countries such as Argentina (9.9), Costa Rica (9.0) and Uruguay (11.3), and far below that in the United States (with 60 lines per 100 inhabitants). Sanchez *et al.* (1993: 153) also report that 'there were [at least] 10,000 towns without a telephone service, about 60,000 of the country's public phones were out of order, and a large number of requests for repairs and new lines went unanswered'.

The aforementioned figures meant that massive investments of new capital were needed to improve and expand the company's telecommunications network in the near-to-medium term. For example, in 1989, it was estimated that, over the ensuing five years, Telmex would need an infusion of at least US$10 bn. The Salinas administration, however, contended that it was unable and/or unwilling to undertake the needed investment because it would divert needed resources away from high-priority social programmes, such as education, health and reducing poverty.

Notwithstanding the government's rhetoric, most of the income generated by the sale of Telmex went into a contingency fund to pay for the Mexican state's domestic debt rather than to increase directly 'social welfare'. Government officials claimed that paying off the internal debt (close to 11 per cent in real terms during 1990–91) produced substantial indirect benefits in the form of a reduction in domestic interest rates.[7] They also claimed that this more than offset the net fiscal loss resulting from the sale of the company: the Mexican government generated more than double what it had originally expected from the sale.[8] However, in the wake of the country's severe economic downturn and near financial collapse following the Mexican peso crisis of 1994–5, nominal interest rates soared to levels as high as 120 per cent with an inflation rate of 52 per cent, so any financial benefits that may have been generated by the sale of Telmex have long since evaporated.

The transfer of Telmex to the private sector was expected to improve the company's productivity as well as upgrade its woefully inadequate and substandard access to the network by consumers and other carriers, particularly in the long-distance market. Clearly, the Salinas administration did not help matters when it entered in 1990 into a concession agreement with the controlling private interests (*grupo* Carso) that gave them a monopoly over the provision of basic wire-line service for a period of seven years. Under the agreement, Telmex could continue its policy of 'rate averaging' (cross-subsidization), effectively preventing competitors from 'cream skimming' the long-distance market (where prices were considerably above short-run marginal cost), as well as forestalling their entry into the local telephone market, where rates were barely above short-run marginal costs (that is, excluding costs of capital and equipment). The industry 'regulator', the Secretaria de Communicaciones y Transportes (SCT), also instituted a system of ceiling prices designed both to protect the consumer and to keep the real level of prices (adjusted for inflation) charged for the various types of telephone service (long v. short-distance calls) constant during the seven-year period. The rationale behind the ceiling prices is that they would prevent Telmex from charging consumers a price higher than that which would prevail if the market were effectively contestable (competitive). SCT officials also hoped that this policy would minimize the distortions present when prices are set above marginal cost, and eventually move prices toward their 'optimal' (Ramsey) levels; that is, lower prices (still above marginal cost) would be set for services with a high price elasticity of demand (such as long-distance services) and higher prices for services with a low elasticity (such as local services). In reality, the pricing policy gave Telmex considerable latitude to set its own rate structure and, not surprisingly, the company continued its cross-subsidization policy. Nevertheless, the high inflation rates following the 1994–5 peso devaluation prevented the company from increasing its rates sufficiently (particularly in the local telephone market, where elasticity is low) to maintain constant prices in real terms.[9]

In exchange for this deterioration in allocative efficiency, the government demanded that the company 'move aggressively to modernize and extend the network' (for further details, see Pisciotta, 1997). Notwithstanding the rhetoric, it is not clear how this goal was to be achieved, given that there was no explicit legal framework in place regulating the pricing structure, the use and operation of radio frequencies, telecommunications networks, interconnection charges, resale and rules governing foreign investment in the country. The reason for this is that the Federal Telecom Law (FTL), which established such a legal framework, was not passed until 8 June 1995. To make matters worse, the regulatory agency in charge of promulgating and enforcing the rules of the game was created a year later by presidential decree. Until the creation of the Federal Telecommunications Commission (Cofetel), the Secretaria de Comunicaciones y Transportes (SCT) was 'in charge' of supervising the operations of Telmex. It is not apparent how the company was regulated because there was no comprehensive law governing key aspects of communications within the country at the time. One can only surmise that key decisions relating to classification of services, interconnection charges, resale, and licensing structure, as well as rules governing foreign investment in the telecommunications sector, were made on an ad hoc basis.

As things stand now, Cofetel, which sits wholly in the powerful executive branch of the Mexican government, must 'work closely' with SCT on competition policy and licensing procedures. In practice, this 'working relationship' has not turned out as expected because of the different agencies' overlapping jurisdictions and duplication of rules and regulations governing competitive operations and confusion about how concessions for phone services are to be awarded, and how interconnection is supposed to be negotiated between carriers. For example, the SCT has issued a different set of guidelines for the selection of long-distance carriers, accounting practices and interconnection charges than those of Cofetel. Not surprisingly, the lack of transparency and bureaucratic red tape present in the regulations governing the telecommunications market have led to disputes between carriers (for example, between cellular providers Iusacell – affiliated with Bell Atlantic – and Telcel, a subsidiary of Telmex, over the latter's cross-subsidization practices) that are currently being adjudicated in the Mexican courts instead of being resolved by the regulatory agencies.

Problems have also been encountered with the implementation of the FTL of 1995. It was supposed to encourage competition by allowing the entry of new private operators into the national telecommunications market in 1996, as well as permitting callers in Mexico to choose their own long-distance carrier by the beginning of 1997. Ostensibly, under the new law, Telmex would lose its local and long-distance monopoly, but in reality this has not taken place in the long-distance market because Telmex is still permitted to preclude the full participation of foreign companies in the resale of its capacity, in order to reach new (inter-state) locations within the country or the US market. This is a clear benefit to Telmex because the foreclosure of entry through pure resale limits the ability of Mexican consumers to choose between international carriers when placing calls to the USA (see *LAEB*, 1998). Mexican authorities, including the president of Cofetel, defend this practice by arguing that it will encourage new carriers to invest in the country's telecommunications infrastructure rather than use Telmex's existing capacity.[10] In fact, the SCT has persuaded foreign carriers interested in the long-distance market, such as AT&T, Alestra and Lusacell, to 'share' with Telmex the estimated costs (US$703mn) of improving the network over the next seven years. However, carriers such as Avantel, which competes with Telmex in the long-distance market and is owned by MCI and Banamex, has refused to sign up because in its estimation the proposal 'smacks of compulsion' (*LAEB*, 1998). Initially, Telmex also exercised considerable monopoly power over access to the public networks by charging very high interconnection tariffs to new long-distance firms for the use of its lines (US$0.057 per minute as late as August 1998). By comparison, India's interconnection charges during this period were $0.019 per minute, even though the volume of call traffic to Mexico is several times greater than to India (*LAEB*, 1998). In the local market, Telmex remains a de facto monopolist in most communities because foreign companies must use Telmex's bottleneck exchange facilities (local network) to deliver their services. Foreign carriers have complained to Cofetel that Telmex has set prices to use the 'local loop' that are higher than would prevail in a contestable market, thereby charging Telmex with abusing its dominant position in the market. In this connection, ECLAC (2000:130) reports that 'between 1997 and 1998, over a million phone lines were withdrawn because of the high prices charged by Telmex'. Telmex's dominant position is further strengthened by the fact that the cost to new firms of constructing their own local network is considerably higher than in the case of long-distance services.

In view of the above, it is obvious that the regulatory framework needs to be more transparent and efficient. It is not possible to achieve this when there are two regulatory bodies (housed in different branches of the Mexican government) issuing conflicting regulations on competition policy, interconnection charges, resale and licensing procedures. One should not be surprised, then, that many of the carriers bypass the regulatory agencies when disputes arise and, instead, go directly to the Mexican courts, where decisions can be held up for a number of years (as in the case of Iusacell's longstanding suit against Telcel – a subsidiary of Telmex – regarding the latter's rate averaging practices).

The Chilean experience with privatization

The privatization of public utilities in Chile took place between 1985 and 1990. The government sold 30 state-owned enterprises, in telecommunications, electricity generation and distribution, water and sanitation facilities, and the airline sector. Once the equity shares of these enterprises were publicly traded in the stock market, the Chilean state proceeded to employ a number of institutional and market procedures in their privatization. For example, in the case of *'capitalismo popular'*, which comprised between 5 and 10 per cent of the outstanding shares, workers were induced to buy underpriced shares by receiving an advance of up to 50 per cent of their severance payments. The state also guaranteed that, provided the workers held the shares until the age of retirement, they would receive a sale price which would not fall below the original purchase price, thus minimizing the risk of loss.[11] Through this privatization method, the number of direct shareholders in the privatized companies rose from around 26000 to over 200000 in 1989, with workers comprising about 15 per cent of the total.[12]

At this juncture it is important to observe that, from an economic standpoint, the total number of shares directly sold to workers was relatively small, yet from a political perspective it was highly successful because it gave workers a financial stake in the profitability of the firms that they own, thereby making it more difficult for future governments to reverse privatization.

Another method utilized by the Chilean government to privatize public sector firms during this phase was labelled *institutional capitalism*. Under this approach, stock of privatized firms were sold to institutional investors in general and to privately run pension funds (AFPs), in particular. This procedure also served to promote, indirectly, a wider share of ownership among the Chilean public via the investment of their pension funds. In order to minimize the risks to the newly created pension system, the Chilean government created a supervision of AFPs that set an ownership limit for each AFP. This stipulated that the shares of the privatized firms could not represent more than 5 per cent of the AFP's total investment portfolio. Chilean economist Patricio Meller (1993) observes that, in spite of 'these limitations and regulations, the AFP acquired (by 1990) around 25 percent of the shares of the privatized firms' (Meller, 1993; also see Hachette and Luders, 1993).

The Chilean government also invited foreign investors to acquire shares of the privatized firms via stock market and international open auctions. According to Meller (1993), when employing the former method, foreign bidders were not allowed to acquire a controlling interest in the privatized firms (no more than 10 per cent of the outstanding shares could be bought by a single buyer), while in the open auction method they could, as happened with the privatization of the large Chilean telephone company, CTC. Foreign investors were also encouraged to use external debt paper to acquire shares in the privatized firms. This process was heavily subsidized by the Chilean government because the debt paper, at the time, was trading in the secondary market at 30 to 40 per cent of its face value, yet it could be presented to the Chilean Central Bank and redeemed at par value in local currency. Moreover, the favourable exchange rate prevailing at the time and the underpricing of shares of the traditional SOEs enhanced the effective subsidy of this debt–equity swap programme. In total, between 1985 and 1991, the programme accounted for about 50 per cent of foreign investment in the shares of privatized enterprises and contributed significantly to reducing Chile's accumulated external debt (Hachette and Luders, 1993). Notwithstanding the relative success of the second phase of the second round of the Chilean privatization process, Meller cautions that 'the divestment of public firms has been so rapid that there has been no time to establish a regulatory framework within which the natural monopolies will operate' (Meller, 1993:107). This is clearly exemplified by the operational and regulatory problems associated with the privatization of the large Chilean telephone company, CTC.

The telecommunications and power sectors
The privatization of CTC began in December of 1987 and was completed in 1990 when Telefonica de España acquired a controlling interest in the company. Although from a broad economic standpoint the privatization of CTC has been a success, in terms of relatively higher rates of return in the post-privatization environment, an improvement in call completion rates and repair responses, and a decrease in the practice of subsidizing domestic rates through higher international rates, the lack of clearly defined rules regarding entry into the industry and what type of communications services it should specialize in has created confusion and diminished allocative efficiency. The problem arose when CTC, a natural monopoly controlling about 91 per cent of local phone services (as of 31 December 1997), decided to enter the lucrative international long-distance market by installing an optical fibre

network and its own long-distance satellite-based operations, CTC Mundo. This occurred even though Empresa Nacional de Telecommunicaciones (ENTEL) was originally established by the Chilean government to provide long-distance services for the country. ENTEL for its part challenged CTC's decision to enter this market because of the latter's dominant position, arising from the fact that all long-distance operators must get approval for new connections from the local phone company. ENTEL believed that this could lead CTC to discriminate in favour of its own affiliated long-distance operator (Bitran and Serra, 1994).

In October 1994, the Chilean Supreme Court ruled that CTC could compete in the long-distance market along with ENTEL and four other long-distance operators, Bellsouth, Chilesat, VTR and Lusatel. Initially, the liberalization of the long-distance telephone market (including domestic and international long distance) led to a dramatic fall in the rates for calls for example to the USA, Spain and Japan. In fact, at the height of the price wars in 1994, rates plunged by more than 80 per cent to as little as US$0.02 per minute for calls to the USA. By 1998, however, prices to the USA had risen and stabilized at a peak-hour rate of slightly more than US$1 per minute. Despite this increase in rates, they were relatively low by international standards, and the many discounts available to consumers enabled them, de facto, to secure even lower rates.[13]

The Supreme Court's decision, along with the multi-carrier system that allows consumers to select a carrier for each long-distance call, has also led to greater competition. Four more companies, CNT telefonica, Telefonica Manquehue, Transam and Carrier, have entered the long-distance market since 1994. The resulting 10 long-distance service providers are projected to invest heavily in Chile's long-distance business.

In the beginning, the benefits to the consumer from the price-cutting war came at a heavy cost in terms of the balance sheets and profit margins of the long-distance operators. For example, Table 13.4 shows that, during the first four months of 1995, the operators had jointly lost more than US$52mn, with 78 per cent of this accounted for by ENTEL, CTC and Bellsouth. In recent years, however, profit margins have recovered, as prices have risen, and stabilized for the larger carriers such as CTC Mundo and ENTEL, though they remain tight for the smaller companies.

The intense competition that followed the Supreme Court's ruling also led companies to cut labour costs drastically, seek additional capital from abroad and, not surprisingly, consider merging with their rivals to acquire market share. An estimated 1900 jobs were eliminated in 1995, of which 1100 were accounted for by ENTEL and CTC alone. In addition, VTR – a company belonging to Chile's Luksic group – took on a foreign partner, Southwestern Bell, in order to raise needed capital and offer a full range of activities such as cellular telephony and cable television. The fierce competition also led to mergers between rival firms and further concentration. For example, in 1995, CTC and VTR merged to form Startel, the only cellular company with a nationwide licence, in order to provide wireless phone services such as cellular, paging, mobile data transmission and radio trunking services. This strategic alliance between CTC and VTR enabled them to capture a 55 per cent market share of the cellular market from their nearest competitors, Bellsouth and ENTEL, with respectively, 33 and 12 per cent of the market. In December 1997, the 'strategic alliance' came to an end when CTC bought VTR's 45 per cent share in Startel for US$45mn, thus gaining total control of the company and further enhancing CTC's dominance of the long-distance market (Valenzuela, 1999).

Table 13.4   Performance of Chile's long-distance operators in early 1995

Company	Losses (US mn, 1995)	Share prices (% var.)	Job losses
ENTEL Chile	16.5	−42.4	500
CTC Mundo	12.5	−25.0	600
Bellsouth	12.1	—	—
TelexChile	7.2	−30.0	550
VTR	2.6	—	—
Lusatel	1.6	—	—
Total	52.5		

Note: — indicates that the data is not available.

Source: *Latin American Weekly Report*, 5 May 1995, WR-95–16.

In this connection, it is important to point out that, apart from its 43.6 per cent share in CTC, Spain's Telefonica also had a minority participation (20 per cent) in ENTEL. This led to a situation in which Chilean regulators, concerned about the likely exercise of monopoly power, ordered the foreign company to divest from either one of the companies (Birch and Braga, 1993). Telefonica initially appealed the decision to the Chilean Supreme Court, but in view of the court's decision in October 1994 it proceeded to divest itself of its shares in ENTEL. Again, this example serves to illustrate the fact that is it far more effective to prevent the emergence of anti-competitive practices aimed at creating market power than it is to combat through regulation the anti-competitive practices of established domestic and foreign monopolists.

Today, the Chilean long-distance market is characterized by a high degree of competition and lower rates for end-users, but these have come at the price of a higher degree of concentration by the three main carriers, ENTEL, CTC Mundo and Chilestat, whose market share was 90 per cent for domestic long distance and 73 per cent for international calls. Subtel (Subsecretaria de Telecommunicaciones), the country's regulatory and supervisory body for all telecommunications, must therefore maintain a watchful eye on future rates and services in order to preclude anti-competitive practices and the abuse of the considerable market power of the 'big three' (Valenzuela, 1999).

Another example of regulatory failure that could lead to monopolistic abuses has arisen in the Chilean electricity industry. It is now a well-established fact that competition can be introduced in the generating and distributive operations of the industry. Only the transmission network need be a natural monopoly. However, when Chile's ENDESA was privatized, regulators allowed the company to maintain its monopolistic position in activities where competition is not only viable but should be encouraged. For example, ENDESA provides 65 per cent of the power generation, owns the Central zone transmission grid, and its controlling company, ENERSIS, owns the largest distribution firm (CHILECTRA). Moreover, ENDESA owns most of the water rights for hydro-electric projects that will be developed over the next 20 years (Bitran and Serra, 1994). Finally, regulators have followed a pricing regulation scheme that sets rates based on the operating costs of a simulated efficient firm and ensures a real return of at least 10 per cent over the replacement value of assets. The replacement value of assets is obtained as a weighted average of estimates provided by both the firms in the industry and the regulatory agency. Not surprisingly, Bitran and Serra report that this has given private managers an incentive to alter the estimates of costs and replacement value of assets in their favour, resulting in large deviations from the estimates of the regulator, sometimes exceeding 50 per cent.

Obviously, the Chilean experience demonstrates that the present market structure and regulatory deficiencies have induced delays in investment patterns, diminished allocative efficiency, and created conflicts of interest, discriminatory behaviour and suboptimal patterns of development at the sectoral level.

Conclusions

The case studies reviewed in this chapter for Chile and Mexico are by no means meant to be exhaustive or entirely representative of what is occurring in the privatization and liberalization movement sweeping Latin America. However, they do point to actual and potential problems that have arisen when privatization and liberalization efforts have taken place without efficient and credible legal and regulatory frameworks in place. Far too often the privatization programmes in these countries have generated clear 'winners and losers', without the former, economic theory notwithstanding, having to compensate the latter. The streamlining of the Chilean and Mexican economies has yet to produce clear and sustained increases in economic efficiency and productivity, while it is apparent that privatization has come at the steep cost of increased economic concentration, anti-competitive practices, economic and financial instability, corruption and criminal behaviour. It is therefore not surprising that in many countries of the region, including Chile and Mexico, public opinion is opposed to the idea of more privatizations, particularly when overly generous terms are offered to domestic and foreign investors in a non-transparent and inefficient manner. The public rightly suspects that, when state firms in priority and strategic sectors, such as energy and telecommunications, are sold to powerful economic interests (*grupos*) with little, if any, public oversight and accountability, the outcome is likely to be one where collective interests are sacrificed in order to serve narrow individual aims. The government's loss of credibility with the public erodes the latter's support for further privatization.

Privatization by itself is not enough to improve industrial performance and distribute economic benefits to the consumer in the form of lower prices and better-quality products and services. Privatization also requires an effective regulatory system and enforceable antitrust laws to discipline firms *before* the privatization and deregulation of a given industry. At a minimum, it would be wise to avoid the simultaneous privatization of several public service sectors that have newly emerging regulatory systems and where administrative and operational flaws are likely to be discovered only after privatization. Otherwise, the result may be a situation like that which emerged in the Mexican telecommunications sector and the Chilean electricity industry, where, in the presence of inadequate regulatory supervision and the absence of adequate antitrust laws, the privatized firms were able to consolidate quickly and exercise considerable monopoly power. Another important pitfall that needs to be avoided by government regulators is the sale of public service firms with guaranteed, uncontested access to the market for several years before competition is introduced. The consumer was ill-served by the sale of Mexico's Telmex and Chile's ENDESA to the private sector with monopoly power *before* a legal/institutional framework was in place to regulate the operations.

Finally, both the Chilean and the Mexican privatization experiences suggest that the decision to give workers the option to participate in the purchase of the company's equity was a sound one, not only because it was crucial in securing labour's cooperation during the privatization process, but because it may contribute to improving the internal efficiency of the company by improving worker morale.

Notes

1. Sections of this chapter are based on my article, 'The Mexican Regulatory Experience in the Airline, Banking and Telecommunications Sectors', *The Quarterly Review of Economics And Finance*, 41 (2001), 657–81.
2. The OECD reports that the distribution of household income in Mexico during the 1989–92 period became more skewed. For example, the top quintile increased its share of household income from 53.5 per cent in 1989 to 54.2 per cent in 1992. At the same time, the remaining bottom deciles – with the exception of the third and fourth lowest (where their respective shares remained unchanged) – recorded a drop in their shares of household income. The OECD also finds that the Gini coefficient for Mexico rose from 0.46 in 1989 to 0.48 in 1992. For further details, see OECD (1995, Table 23). Undoubtedly, the rapid and unprecedented concentration of banking assets in relatively few industrial and financial *grupos* that accompanied the privatization of the Mexican banking system aggravated this unwelcome trend in income (and wealth) inequality in Mexican society.
3. For a radical perspective on the Mexican banking crisis, see Cypher (1996).
4. Gruben and McComb (1997) report that 'after the privatizations it was not unusual for those taking a lunchtime walk in nearby Alameda Park (in the downtown area) to be accosted by hawkers trying to enroll passers by for credit cards'.
5. See Mishkin (1999), who argues that the prevention of banking and financial instability in developing nations requires not only a strong regulatory and supervisory system 'to prevent excessive risk-taking on the part of financial institutions', but the use of selective capital control to avoid the 'vicious pendulum of capital inflows and lending booms' that are followed by massive capital outflows and the near collapse of the banking and financial system. In this connection, also see Ffrench-Davis and Agosin (1999) who make a compelling argument for the (temporary) use of non-interest-bearing reserve requirements to deter short-term capital flows and prevent, *inter alia*, excessive risk taking and exchange rate appreciation.
6. The growing participation of foreign capital is by no means confined to Mexico. The *Latin American Weekly Report* reports that between 1993 and 1995 the share of foreign capital in government revenues from privatizations in Latin America rose from 37.6 per cent (US\$4.1 bn) in 1993 to 61.8 per cent (\$2.7 bn) in 1996. For further details, see *LAWR* (1995, 1997, 1998a, 1998b, 1998c).
7. Data obtained from Sanchez *et al.* (1993).
8. The government hoped to collect around US\$2 bn, but by end of 1992 it had received over US\$4 bn from the sale of Telmex. See Sanchez *et al.* (1993).
9. For further details on Telmex's pricing policy, see Sanchez *et al.* (1993), and Alarcon (1998).
10. In fact, the Mexican government has not even established the basic guidelines governing the conditions under which a foreign operator may obtain a permit to utilize resale in order to reach additional locations; see Alarcon (1998).
11. For an informative assessment of Chile's privatization process between 1974 and 1990, see Luders (1991).
12. See Larroulet (1995). In this connection, Hachette and Luders (1993) estimate that, if share holdings through the private-non pension funds, AFPs, are taken into account, the number of shareholders rises to over three million.
13. See Grosse (2000) for an informative discussion of the challenges and opportunities facing privatized firms and government regulators in the Chilean telecommunications sector.

References

Alarcon, J.L. (1998) 'The Future of the Mexican Telecom Industry', a presentation by Javier Lozano Alarcon, President, Federal Telecommunications Commission (Cofetel), at the Economic Strategy Institute, Mexico City, 11 September.

Armstrong, M. (1994) *Regulatory Reform: Economic Analysis and the British Experience*, Cambridge, MA: MIT Press.

Baer, W. and M. Birch (1992) 'Privatization and the Changing Role of the State in Latin America', *Journal of International Law and Politics*, 25(1), 1–25.

Bank of Mexico (1998) *The Mexican Economy*, Mexico City: Bank of Mexico.

Birch, M. and C.A.P. Braga (1993) 'Regulation in Latin America: Prospects for the 1990s', *Quarterly Review of Economics and Finance*, 33 (Special Issue), 119–33.

Bitran, E. and P. Serra (1994) 'Regulatory Issues in the Privatization of Public Utilities: The Chilean Experience', *Quarterly Review of Economics and Finance*, 34 (Summer), 179–98.

Calva, J. (1995) 'El Nudo Macroeconomico de Mexico. La Pesada Herencia de Ernesto Zedillo', *Problemas del Desarrollo*, 26, Numero Especial (Enero-Marzo): 63–95.

Cantor, P. (1996) 'To Privatize or Not to Privatize', *Review of Radical Political Economics*, 28(1), 96–111.

Cypher, J.M. (1996) 'Mexico: Financial Fragility or Structural Crisis?', *Journal of Economic Issues*, 30(2), 96–111.

ECLAC (2000) *Foreign Investment in Latin America and Caribbean, 1999 Report*, Santiago, Chile: United Nations.

Elizondo, C. (1993) 'The Making of a New Alliance: The Privatization of the Banks in Mexico', *CIDE*, 5 (Documentos de Trabajo), 1–20.

Ffrench-Davis, R. and M. Agosin (1999) 'Capital Flows in Chile: From the Tequila to the Asian Crises', *Journal of International Development*, 11(4), 121–39.

Gavin, M. and R. Hausmann (1996) 'The Roots of Banking Crises: The Macroeconomic Context', in R. Hausmann and L. Rojas-Suarez (eds), *Banking Crises in Latin America*, Washington, DC: Inter-American Development Bank.

Grosse, R. (2000) 'Moving Beyond Privatization in Latin America: The Government/Business Relationship', *The North–South Agenda Papers*, 40, 1–16.

Gruben, W.C. and R. McComb (1997) 'Liberalization, Privatization, and Crash: Mexico's Banking System in the 1990s', *Economic Review*, First Quarter, Federal Reserve Bank of Dallas, 21–30.

Hachette, D. and R.J. Luders (1993) *Privatization in Chile: An Economic Appraisal*, San Francisco: ICS Press.

Informe Latinoamericano (IL) (1999a) 'Rescate de Bancos Descubre Fraudes', pp. 46–99.

Informe Latinoamericano (IL) (1999b) 'Labastida Emerge Con Amplia Ventaja', pp. 48–99.

Informe Latinoamericano (IL) (2000a) 'Fusion Apura Puesta a Punto', pp. 00–10.

Informe Latinoamericano (IL) (2000b) 'Alentara Fox a los Competidores de Telmex', pp. 00–27.

Informe Latinoamericano (IL) (2000c) 'Zedillo Abre Archivos del Banco Union', pp. 00–34.

Larroulet, C. (1995) 'The Impact of Privatization on Distributional Equity: The Chilean Case 1985–1989', in V.V. Ramanadham (ed.), *Privatization and Equity*, London: Routledge.

Latin American Economy and Business (LAEB) (1995) 'Which Mexican Banks are in Trouble?', LAEB-95-04 (April).

Latin American Economy and Business (LAEB) (1998) 'The Telecoms Deal in Mexico', LAEB-98-09 (September).

Latin American Regional Report – Mexico and NAFTA (RM) (1998) 'Fobaproa: Making Progress', RM-98-06 (9 June).

Latin American Weekly Report (LAWR) (1995) 'Chile's Long-Distance Operators', WR-95-16 (5 May).

Latin American Weekly Report (LAWR) (1997) 'FDI in the Region's Privatizations', WR-97-30 (29 July).

Latin American Weekly Report (LAWR) (1998a) 'Fobaproa Debt Plan Meets Opposition', WR-98-22 (2 June).

Latin American Weekly Report (LAWR) (1998b) 'The Telecom Deal in Mexico', September, p. 11.

Latin American Weekly Report (LAWR) (1998c) 'A Telmex Favour for the Competition', WR-98-34 (1 September).

Luders, R.J. (1991) 'Massive Divestiture and Privatization Lessons from Chile', *Contemporary Policy*, 9(4), 1–19.

Mackey, M.W. (1999) 'Report of Michael W. Mackey on the Comprehensive Evaluation of the Operations and Functions of the Fund for the Protection of Bank Savings FOBAPROA and Quality of Supervision of the FOBAPROA Programme 1995–1998', mimeo, submitted to the Congress of Mexico.

McQuerry, E. (1999) 'The Banking Sector in Mexico', *Economic Review*, Federal Reserve Bank of Atlanta, Third Quarter, 14–29.

Meller, P. (1993) 'A Review of the Chilean Privatization Experience', *The Quarterly Review of Economics and Finance*, 33 (Special Issue): 95–112.

Mexico Business Monthly (MBM) (1991) 'Banking and Finance', October, 6–7.

Mishkin, F.S. (1999) 'Global Financial Instability: Framework, Events, and Issues', *Journal of Economic Perspectives*, 13(4), 3–20.

OECD (1995) *OECD Economic Surveys: Mexico, 1995*, Paris: OECD Publications.

Peiro, I.R. (1996) 'A Cambios en la Actividad Empresarial del Estado Mexicano', in A. Giron and G. Roldan (eds), *Mexico: Pasado, Presente y Future*, Mexico City: Siglo XXI Editores.

Pisciotta, A.A. (1997) 'Telecommunications in Mexico: A Market in Transition', *CHH Mexico Law & Business Report*, 1(8), 1–6.

Ramirez, M.D. (1995) 'The Political Economy of Privatization in Mexico, 1983–92', *Organization*, 2(1), 87–116.

Rodrick, D. (1992) 'The Limits of Trade Policy Reform in Developing Countries', *Journal of Economic Perspectives*, 6, 1 (Winter): 87–105.

Sánchez, M., R. Corona, O. Ochoa, L.F. Herrera, A. Olvera and E. Sepúlveda (1993) 'The Privatization Process in Mexico: Five Case Studies', in M. Sánchez and R. Corona (eds), *Privatization in Latin America*, Washington, DC: Inter-American Development Bank/Johns Hopkins University Press.

Valenzuela, I.M. (1999) 'Chile: The Telecommunications Sector', *Industry Sector Analysis Series*, U.S. & Foreign Commercial Service and U.S. Department of State, Washington, DC.

Vickers, J. and G. Yarrow (1988) *Privatization: An Economic Analysis*, Cambridge, MA: MIT Press.

14 Privatization in South Africa
Erwin Schwella

Introduction

Privatization in South Africa is a hotly debated issue. In *The Shopsteward* of September 2000 (the official mouthpiece of the Congress of South African Trade Unions (COSATU)), the editor comments: 'COSATU rejects the argument put forward in the media and by Government ministers that they must be "realistic" and that "there is no alternative to a free market, neo-liberal capitalist solution, as advocated by the World Bank and the International Monetary Fund" (COSATU, 2000:2).

It should be noted that COSATU, a trade union federation, has been part of the tripartite government alliance in South Africa since 1994. The other two parties are the African National Congress (ANC) and the South African Communist Party (SACP). COSATU is therefore in the same government as the minister(s) to whom the editor refers in the above quotation.

In the quoted editorial, the editor is also highly critical of the Growth, Employment and Redistribution (GEAR) strategy of the government, to which it is partner, as this strategy 'has created neither growth, employment nor redistribution'. There should, according to the editorial, rather be a return to the only realistic alternative for workers, which is to put socialism back on the agenda with policies that put the interest of the workers and the poor first and not the interests of business and the rich. In South Africa, according to COSATU, this would mean going back to the Reconstruction and Development Programme (RDP) and implementing it vigorously to redress the inequalities and injustices from the apartheid years that still haunt the members of COSATU today. This is followed by a demand to the partners of COSATU in government – and more particularly to the ANC – that they should take the tripartite alliance seriously in these issues. The partner(s) must stop unilaterally imposing policies without even consulting the trade union wing, COSATU, of the alliance. All three partners should be brought into the structures of the policy-making process.

The South African Minister of Public Enterprises, Jeff Radebe, a member of the SACP, shows political sensitivity for the concerns of his government alliance partners when he carefully formulates his foreword to a policy document, 'An Accelerated Agenda towards the Restructuring of State-owned Enterprises', in August 2000 (page 1), by stating:

In summary, Government's policy with regard to State Owned Enterprises is more properly referred to as a restructuring programme, and not in the more simplistic terms of privatization. The programme was and remains designed around a multiple array of strategies, or mixes of options, that are designed to ensure the maximization of shareholder interests defined in economic, social and development terms. Thus restructuring refers to the matrix of options that include the redesign of business management principles [*sic!*] within enterprises, the attraction of strategic equity partnerships, the divestment of equity either in whole or in part where appropriate, and the employment of various immediate turnaround options.

The goal of this chapter is to focus upon and explore the fascinating context, challenges, policies and prospects in respect of privatization or, alternatively, the restructuring of the public sector economy in South Africa. To complement and support these goals in terms of focus, the following objectives will be pursued:

- a description and analysis of the context for privatization in South Africa with reference to the historical developments and the internationally and nationally relevant aspects of this context;
- a focus on the challenges faced in respect of privatization in South Africa, especially in respect of development, equity and service delivery, effectiveness and productivity issues and challenges;
- a discussion of the South African policy responses to the context and challenges in respect of privatization in South Africa, linked to the current state of implementation of these policies; and
- possible future scenarios in respect of privatization in South Africa.

In the following section the South African context of privatization receives attention.

Privatization in South Africa: the context
In this section different aspects of the context of privatization in South Africa will be focused upon. As a first step, a brief description of the history in respect of privatization in South Africa will be given. Thereafter, some reference will be made to the international as well as some relevant national aspects of the political, economic and social contexts of South African privatization.

Privatization in South Africa: a historical perspective
Privatization as a policy option came on the agenda under the previous South African regime. According to Fine (1997:5–9) privatization as a potential policy measure rose rapidly to prominence during the mid-1980s.

This prominence cannot only be explained by the upsurge of interest in such policies in a global context. South African policies in respect of privatization have to be seen against the background of the peculiar economic and social structures of apartheid, heavy state economic intervention, a peculiar industrial structure and a high level of concentration in the ownership of capital. The question of privatization in South Africa concerned to some extent, from its inception, how apartheid would survive, if at all.

This approach to the understanding of privatization in South Africa is also supported by Hentz (2000:1) where he states that the logic of privatization in South Africa can only be understood by juxtaposing the economic efficiency argument with the logic of political expediency. This need for juxtaposition holds true for both the apartheid and post-apartheid eras.

Brynard (1995:3–5) provides a brief summary of the privatization efforts and results in the era from the inception of these efforts until the first democratic elections in South Africa during May 1994. The intention to start the privatization process in South Africa was first announced by the former State President, P.W. Botha, on 5 February 1988. The first four public enterprises identified for privatization were the South African Iron and Steel Corporation (ISCOR), the Phosphate Development Corporation (FOSKOR), the South African Transport Services (later named Transnet), and the South African Post (SAPO) and Telecommunication (Telkom) Services.

Fine (1997:10) adds that in 1988 the state share in the oil from coal industry, SASOL, had already been sold and that the aluminium extraction company, ALUSAF, was also a candidate for privatization. He also points out that the then government stated very clearly that it would retain 51 per cent ownership of the privatized industries, indicating that revenue raising was the prime motive for the policy rather than releasing market forces. This is corroborated by Fine (ibid.), who quotes the minister of finances at that time, Barend du Plessis, who said that the emphasis should, amongst other things, be on the opportunity offered by privatization to release government funds that were locked up in the state owned enterprises (SOEs). Such released funds could then be used by government for alternative purposes.

From the above there are indications that in South Africa, at least initially, the primary reason for privatization as a policy option was a need for revenue on the part of the apartheid government. That government was feeling the pressures of international sanctions, decreased growth and increasing defence and security expenditure needed to sustain apartheid policies.

For a number of reasons these privatization plans of the National Party (NP) government delivered very little. Fine (ibid.: 12–14) refers to some of the reasons why only ISCOR really reached the state of privatization, where it was taken to the market via a public offering of shares:

- the state of the stock markets worldwide after the 1987 crash;
- the specific, even worse, state of the Johannesburg stock market at the time;
- the sheer volume of the transactions and the capital requirements to afford and purchase the stock in a depressed market;
- the international market climate in a period of boycotts and sanctions against South Africa severely limiting the potential for foreign investment;
- the possibility of labour action against the privatization option; and
- a realistic assessment under these circumstances of relatively small gains over large potential costs by the to-be-privatized industries.

All these factors probably made government and the industries hesitant to go ahead with the privatization process. This contributed to a stalling of the process except for the denationalization of ISCOR.

According to Fine (ibid.:14) the privatization programme failed to satisfy the goal of bolstering the ailing apartheid regime's short term finance needs. This was the status quo in respect of privatization at the time of the speech to Parliament made by President F.W. de Klerk, on 2 February 1990, when he announced the start of the democratization process in South Africa and the release from jail of Nelson Mandela. The period from 2 February 1990 up to the first democratic elections, held in May 1994, when the ANC in alliance with the SACP and COSATU gained a substantive majority in the Government of National Unity (GNU), was characterized by serious and difficult negotiations between all the role players. These negotiations also effectively put a halt to any continued efforts at privatization during this period.

After 1994, the ANC moved away from its previously held socialistic policies and adopted a more neoliberal economic programme. The first attempts at new economic and development policies delivered the Reconstruction and Development Programme, or the RDP.

The RDP Policy Framework 1994, *inter alia*, aimed at building the South African economy, departing from the view that the South African economy faced a deep-seated structural crisis which required fundamental reconstruction. This crisis developed because, for decades, forces within the White minority used their exclusive access to political and economic power to promote their own sectional interests at the expense of Black people. The South African Black people were systematically exploited and oppressed economically, resulting in the situation that South Africa, even in 2001, had one of the world's most unequal patterns of distribution of income and wealth. The economy is characterized by an excessive concentration of property in the hands of a tiny minority of the population. A contributory factor in this, according to the RDP Policy Framework 1994, was that:

> the apartheid state's economic agencies have been contradictory and secretive, and were subordinate to apartheid's logic and the siege-economy mentality. Parastatals such as the Industrial Development Corporation (IDC), Development Bank of Southern Africa (DBSA) and the Small Business Development Corporation (SBDC) could be immensely important in driving industrial, socioeconomic and infrastructural development. But in recent years, under the cloak of secrecy, the apartheid state privatized or commercialized many agencies in the public sector (such as Transnet, Eskom, Telkom, Iscor, Foskor, SAA, the SAPO and others). Often this policy, unilaterally imposed for ideological reasons, harmed basic services to the poor or reduced the ability of the state to mobilize resources for development. (Republic of South Africa, 1994)

To alleviate these problems, the RDP Policy Framework document provided the following institutional reform prescriptions:

1. The processes of commercialization and privatization of parastatals must be reviewed, to the extent that such processes may not be in the public interest. For this the elaboration of more appropriate business plans and the publication of these business plans for open debate will be required. The democratic government will reverse privatization programmes that are contrary to the public interest (paragraph 4.4.4.1).
2. To promote greater accountability in parastatals, lines of funding and reporting must be restructured to ensure that each parastatal is directly accountable to a particular ministry. This means that funding and reporting lines must be the same (paragraph 4.4.4.2).

The RDP Policy Framework 1994, paragraph 5.11, refers to what should happen in South Africa in respect of parastatals and state development institutions, but has no reference to their potential or real privatization. Rather, it states unequivocally that 'Parastatals, public corporations and advisory boards must be structured and run in a manner that reinforces and supports the RDP.' These recommended actions, which were probably not accepted by the inner circle of government, as well as the assessment of the state of privatization in South Africa at the time, should be seen as a significant indication of thinking at that time.

In contrast to the RDP, the Growth, Employment and Redistribution (GEAR) strategy document of June 1996 provides, *inter alia*, for 'Corporate governance and asset restructuring' and states:

> Within the context of government policy and in accordance with the procedures agreed in the National Framework Agreement with organized labour, the process of restructuring state assets is now proceeding. The nature of such

restructuring may involve the total sale of the asset, a partial sale to strategic equity partners or the sale of the asset with government retaining a strategic interest. Work is in progress to deal with the issues outstanding on the restructuring of the remaining state enterprises. (Paragraph 7.2 of the GEAR strategy, Republic of South Africa, 1996c)

From the above it is therefore clear that a major policy shift occurred from the time of the 1994 RDP and the time of GEAR, 1996. In the RDP very little, if any, space is created for privatization, while in GEAR the restructuring of state enterprises is definitely provided for, even to the extent that for any objective observer the results seem very close to privatization!

The National Framework Agreement (NFA) referred to in the GEAR strategy is significant here. This agreement was entered into as the National Framework Agreement (NFA) on the Restructuring of State Assets between the Government of National Unity (GNU), represented by the minister of public enterprises, and Labour, comprising COSATU, the Federation of South African Labour Unions (FEDSAL) and the National Council of Trade Unions (NACTU). This agreement was signed on 7 February 1996. The NFA established an agreed process between the parties in regard to the restructuring of state assets. The NFA states that the restructuring of state assets is part of the process of implementing the RDP. It is not, however, necessarily geared towards reducing state economic involvement in the country. The NFA states very clearly (Republic of South Africa, 1996b, para. 5.3) that restructuring should not occur at the expense of workers in state enterprises and should especially benefit the workers from previously disadvantaged communities (ibid., para. 5.5). The NFA then creates a set of structures and a process by which consultation has to take place between labour and the GNU in any envisaged process of restructuring.

Given the content and intention of the RDP and GEAR policies and the nature of the relevant positions of labour and government as well as the NFA – which preceded the GEAR strategy – government has proceeded with the restructuring endeavour since 1996. The results have not been spectacular.

The Economist of 9 November 1999 heads its article on South African privatization as 'The Painful Privatization of South Africa'. In this article there is reference to Minister Stella Sigcau who, according to *The Economist* (p. 49), presided over privatization in a regal but undynamic and uninspired way from 1994. She was replaced in 1999 by Minister Jeff Radebe – a member of the SACP – who is more effective and shows evidence of plans to jolt the privatization programme out of its coma.

The Economist reviews the state of privatization in South Africa at the time. Swissair bought 20 per cent of the South African Airways (SAA) in June 1999 as an equity partner; 30 per cent of Telkom, the state-owned telecommunications company, was divested during 1997, and the intention in

1999 was to sell off a further 10 per cent; intentions were also expressed to sell chunks of the forestry and arms SOEs during 1999 and to use the expertise of the British and New Zealand postal services to enhance efficiency in the South African Post Office.

These intentions were followed up in some aspects, but the main policy and implementation thrust culminated in the policy framework, National Framework Agreement (NFA) on the Restructuring of State Assets (1996b), which was launched at a presentation by Minister Radebe on 10 August 2000. This policy statement and its effects will be further discussed in the policy section of this chapter. For the present it suffices to note that the vision for restructuring is, according to Jeff Radebe, based on the RDP, GEAR and NFA as points of departure. Restructuring objectives for the transport, telecommunications, defence and other SOEs are covered in the policy document and will receive more detailed attention under the appropriate headings in this chapter.

It is useful to note here that the policy implementation – as can be expected – is not without its own challenges. The practical implementation of policies is influenced by international and national events. Internationally, the business climate subsequent to the World Trade Center attacks on 11 September 2001 will have a substantial influence on aspects of restructuring in respect of matters such as the attracting and retaining of international investors. It should be noted that the 20 per cent share in the SAA bought by Swissair will probably revert to the South African government subsequent to Swissair's financial crisis during 2001. Because of this crisis, Swissair defaulted on the agreement to pay for the shares, resulting in legal proceedings that will probably deliver the shares back to the original owners. Nationally, the ANC has recommitted itself to the tripartite alliance with the SACP and COSATU, after a series of anti privatization strikes by COSATU during August 2001.

After this introduction to the history of privatization in South Africa, it is now possible to give attention to the other contextual issues in respect of the international, political, economic and social context for privatization in South Africa.

Privatization in South Africa: the international context
Megginson and Netter (1998: 2–6) provide an overview of the most important international developments in respect of privatization. Germany, under Konrad Adenauer, led privatization when, during 1961, the German federal government sold off a majority stake in Volkswagen in a public share offering favouring small investors. In the UK, the Thatcher government drove privatization through a series of massive share issues during the 1980s and 1990s. The objectives for this privatization programme were to

raise revenue for the state, to promote economic efficiency, to reduce government interference in the economy, to promote wider share ownership, to create competition and to expose SOEs to market discipline (see Chapter 3). As the UK programme was perceived to be successful, it was also introduced in many other European countries. Notable examples are France, Germany and Italy (see Chapter 6).

In Asia, the patterns are not as neat as in Western Europe. Japan has sold relatively few SOEs, but those that were sold were enormous. The People's Republic of China is in the process of major economic reform and liberalization (Chapter 12), but has not, to date, done so by means of the outright privatization of SOEs. There is a pledge from the government to introduce such a programme, but owing to the social welfare responsibilities of Chinese SOEs, the implementation of these policy objectives may prove difficult. In India, there has also been a serious attempt at a major economic reform and a liberalization programme since 1991. The programme was adopted in response to perceived highly disappointing SOE performance, but privatization outright has so far not figured prominently on the reform agenda. Latin American countries have shown some enthusiasm for privatization with Chile, Mexico, Bolivia and Brazil taking diverse and substantive initiatives to privatize (Chapters 11 and 13). In Brazil, several very large SOEs have been sold in spite of fierce political opposition.

In sub-Saharan Africa, leaving South Africa out of the picture for the moment, there has been some privatization. The most likely situations in which it occurred were where countries had high budget deficits, high foreign debt and a high dependence on international agencies, such as the World Bank or IMF. For a fuller discussion, see Chapter 15.

The former Soviet-bloc countries of Central and Eastern Europe went through dramatic economic reforms, as their new governments attempted to create rapidly something resembling a market economy. The results of these privatization strategies are still being assessed and the evidence seems – at best – to be contradictory in respect of their success (Chapters 16–21). From the above, it is clear that privatization across the world was associated with strong pressures in the international context to follow suit from the perspective of the example set and through international trends, as well as because of the policies of international financial institutions. The phenomenon can even be described as a 'craze' for privatization. These trends in the international context are also mediated and transferred in South Africa through the relatively well-connected nature and sophistication of South African commercial institutions, such as banks and multinational corporations.

The international context in respect of privatization has, therefore, provided strong cues for the South African policies of restructuring. This point was recently confirmed by Minister Jeff Radebe, the South African

Minister of Public Enterprises. At a presentation he made in Pretoria on 10 August 2000, on a policy framework for an accelerated agenda towards the restructuring of state-owned enterprises, he first quoted extensively the former World Bank chief economist, Joseph Stiglitz. Stiglitz was quoted to emphasize that privatization is important and that institutional preconditions should be set up so that market incentives can operate effectively. According to the minister, the benefits of such a programme for South Africa are that, through the transfer of ownership of SOEs, fiscal impacts such as the lowering of the cost of state debt can be achieved. The increased fiscal resources that are made available can also be used for other social and economic programmes (Ministry of Public Enterprises, 2000:2).

From this international context we can move on to consider the most important elements of the national context, in respect of the potential impact of trends there that may influence the national policies and implementation of privatization in South Africa.

Privatization in South Africa: the national context
In the discussion of privatization from an historical perspective in South Africa, above, some of the issues emanating from the South African context with regard to privatization started to emerge. This South African context will now be briefly further focused upon. South Africa, even subsequent to democratization in 1994, is a country characterized by inequality, poverty, diversity and division. Politically, the country is now a well-established democracy, as set out in the Constitution of the Republic of South Africa, 1996 (Act 108) (Republic of South Africa, 1996a). The dynamics of the political situation are, however, still indicative of political division, often along continuing racial lines. Schwella (2001:371) refers to the oft-made comment that the 1994 general election results in South Africa represented an 'ethnic census', because analysis shows that Black people mostly voted for the ANC, who gained almost 63 per cent of the ballot, whereas White, Coloured and Asian voters voted for the National Party (NP), who took 20.4 per cent of the ballot. These trends were largely reconfirmed in the 1999 general election. The only major shift was that the ANC increased its percentage of the ballot to 66 per cent and the New National Party (NNP) lost support, mainly to the Democratic Party (DP), resulting in the DP gaining 9.5 per cent of the ballot and the NNP 6.9 per cent.

Although the above figures on the election results may actually indicate a rather unified, if not hegemonic, support for the ANC, three further factors need to be taken into account for current purposes. Firstly, the racial dividing lines which are apparent in these support bases are very prominent. Secondly, and as has already been indicated, the ANC is part of a tripartite alliance with the SACP and COSATU. This alliance has major differences about policy options and specifically about GEAR and the RDP and therefore about privatization. Thirdly, the political parties in South Africa hold markedly different ideological views. The ANC tends towards democratic centralism, the Democratic Alliance (DA) – which was formed after an alliance between the DP, the NNP and the very small Federal Alliance (FA) and which, in 2001, was in a process of turmoil – propagates a federalist and market orientation in its policies. Taken together, there are still major divisions in the South African polity along racial, ethnic and policy lines.

The economic context is also summarized in Schwella (ibid.:368–9). South Africa is a developing country with serious economic problems such as poverty, unemployment, inadequate economic growth, lack of investor confidence and an extremely unequal distribution of wealth. With regard to poverty (ibid.:6–39), the position in South Africa can be summarized as follows: approximately half of all South Africans live in poverty; and there is a distinct poverty bias towards rural Blacks, Africans, women and children.

Unemployment in South Africa has increased markedly since 1995. Unemployment rates increased by almost one million between 1997 and 1998 (Roux, 2000). The number in 1999, however, was unchanged compared to 1998, resulting in a marginal decline in the percentage unemployment rate. The 1999 rate was, nonetheless, at 23.3 per cent, substantially higher than the 1995 rate of 16 per cent. Unemployment trends in 1999, according to population and gender, reveal that the overall Black/African unemployment rate is 6.2 times higher than that for Whites; and there is a clear unemployment bias towards females.

The above trends are illustrated by the fact that during 1999 the highest unemployment rate was recorded for Black/African women at 35 per cent, in contrast to the lowest rate, which was for White males, at 4.4 per cent. It should also be noted that official unemployment rates are often disputed and said to be too low by credible non-government sources.

Economic growth in South Africa, subsequent to the 1994 democratic elections, has been disappointing. The government aimed at average growth rates of 6 per cent per annum. These growth rates were not met. The growth rate from 1995 to 2000 averaged a mere 1.8 per cent a year (*SA Reserve Bank Quarterly Bulletin*, March 2001:2). Wealth distribution in South Africa also remains highly skewed. The Gini coefficient for South Africa during 1995 was 0.59, indicating a very high degree of income distribution inequality. Further analysis of this figure indicates that in 1995 the poorest 20 per cent of households had 3 per cent of all household income at their disposal, while the richest 20 per cent had 65 per cent. Once again these figures coincide with the racial (White/Black) divide in the country. Indications are also that there are now increasing numbers of Blacks who are becoming higher earners, but that the percentage of extremely poor is not really decreasing.

The above facts indicate that serious economic issues face South African society and policy makers generally and in respect of privatization policies. This situation is also compounded by and has an impact upon the social context in South Africa, which shows the characteristics of a deeply divided society. These divisions were amplified and encouraged by apartheid policies, for ideological reasons. According to Schwella (2001:370–1) the Constitution of the Republic of South Africa, 1996, provides for 11 *official* languages, and a further analysis of the language situation reveals the following:

- no single language can claim majority status for the whole population;
- Zulu, Xhosa and Afrikaans are the three largest language groups in South Africa;
- the majority of South Africans do not speak English at all; and
- the clear preference of the present policy makers is for English and indications are that English will become the de facto official language of South Africa.

Over and above the language division, the diverse population is also divided along ethnic, religious and political lines. All in all, South Africa is a highly divided society with serious political and economic challenges.

The political, economic and social context of South Africa necessarily affects the government of South Africa and its policies, including policies in respect of privatization and restructuring. The divisions are also reflected in the very different and deeply held views on privatization of the various role players in South Africa. In summary, it can be stated that policy makers in South Africa are faced with challenging political, economic and social contexts, in which they have to deal with development and service delivery issues. The development issues demand a developmental capacity-building approach in South Africa. Primarily, the focus has to be on creating equity through policies enhancing Black empowerment, income redistribution, improved equity in service delivery in favour of previously disadvantaged groups, and poverty alleviation.

Simultaneously, government policies must also be aimed at improved service delivery by means of increased effectiveness, efficiency and productivity in service delivery. The imperatives with regard to equity enhancement and effectiveness and efficiency are, at least sometimes, in tension with each other. This is a fundamental policy and systems challenge for South African policy makers also with regard to privatization. In the next section,

South African policy responses to the context and challenges of privatization are discussed.

Privatization in South Africa: policies and implementation
From the above discussion it should be clear that privatization policies and their implementation are highly challenging and that the history of South Africa indicates a rather fragmented, haphazard and difficult approach to these matters. Subsequent to the appointment of Jeff Radebe as minister of public enterprises during 1999, he made serious attempts to advance policy changes involving restructuring in South Africa. After preliminary work had been done during 1999, the minister presented the South African government's policy framework for 'An Accelerated Agenda towards the Restructuing of State-owned Enterprises' (hereafter referred to as 'Policy Framework 2000') to the country on 10 August 2001. During the presentation of Policy Framework 2000 the minister elaborated on various aspects of restructuring.

Background
To enhance the policy capacity of the South African government in respect of restructuring, the previous Office for Public Enterprises was upgraded to a fully fledged government department in September 1999. The department and ministry engaged in a number of consultative processes during 1999 and 2000, leading to Policy Framework 2000. The aspects covered are vision, the economic and social effects of restructuring, promoting appropriate regulatory and competitive frameworks, promoting empowerment, improving corporate governance and ensuring improved ethics and probity, improving the restructuring process, restructuring the key enterprises of energy, transport, telecommunications and the defence-related industries, and other restructuring initiatives.

Vision
The vision has as its starting point in the RDP, some aspects of the GEAR strategy, and the NFA. SOEs in South Africa need to be restructured in such a way that the restructuring should maximize the contribution of state assets to development in a mixed economy that is responsive to market incentives. The restructuring needs to be aimed at the integration of public, private and social capital to ensure that the developmental objectives for South Africa are achieved.

The economic and social effects of restructuring
Restructuring at enterprise and sector levels must increase efficiency and effectiveness, and mobilize private sector capital. At the macroeconomic

level, the aim is to attract foreign direct investment and to assist in the development of an economic context that promotes competitiveness and growth. This must be done in the context of competitive markets, which has to be the most important policy component of the restructuring policy initiatives. It is accepted that the immediate impact of restructuring may result in some employment losses. To mitigate the negative social impacts, the Cabinet has approved a Social Plan Framework. The restructuring will also be managed in accordance with the NFA, which requires continuing consultation with organized labour and where the leadership of COSATU in particular will be consulted.

The key principles to be adhered to in respect of the vision of government for restructuring are as follows:

- the promotion of competition and competitive markets, to increase efficiency while transferring the efficiency gains to the population;
- where competition is not feasible, a regulatory framework to accompany the restructuring initiative;
- continued proper relationships according to the Policy Framework between government and the SOEs;
- utilization of different options for restructuring, from equity sales to employee participation and community partnerships, to ensure productivity, profitability, investment and innovation;
- optimal returns to be achieved from the proceeds of equity sales, dividends and/or tax returns;
- restructuring proposals to include social impact assessments and taking into consideration the legacy of apartheid, which disadvantaged the poor and marginalized parts of the country;
- transparency in the process.

Promoting appropriate regulatory and competitive frameworks
Restructuring policy in South Africa has competition as a key element and the government wants to ensure competition and an appropriate degree of regulation in respect of SOEs. Economic regulation is relevant where competition is lacking and cannot be guaranteed to provide optimal outcomes for consumers, the environment or related industries. Sectoral regulation must also satisfy the need that restructured SOEs function in the interest of the well-being of the public as consumers and indirect 'shareholders'. Where necessary, the Competition Commission of South Africa, as competition authority, should function in consultation with sectoral regulators to deal with competition issues, and the relevant jurisdictions of the Competition Commission and sectoral regulators are to be clarified.

Promoting empowerment

The policy of government on the restructuring of SOEs will entail new, creative and diverse strategies for genuine empowerment, in order more effectively to spread the benefits of restructuring. The National Empowerment Fund (NEF) Trust, which has to address the economic inequalities of the past, will be capitalized primarily through receiving shares from SOEs undergoing restructuring. Empowerment through the Trust will then take place by means of the following mechanisms:

- an investment trust, which will market investment units to historically disadvantaged individuals;
- a portfolio trust as a 'warehouse' of shares of SOEs, after which these shares can be sold to historically disadvantaged individuals; and
- an equity management fund, to provide venture capital for empowerment initiatives by historically disadvantaged groups.

Ownership and participation in the business of SOEs must be broadened to include the South Africans who were previously disadvantaged, through a range of equity schemes based on international best practice. A number of measures such as training, affirmative action, management development and the provision of entrepreneurial opportunities will also be incorporated into the strategy of empowerment. In similar ways, employees will also be given empowerment opportunities, including employee share ownership plans. Finally, community trusts, such as producer and consumer cooperatives, mutual companies and not-for-profit firms for the benefit of the disadvantaged, will also be established in the process of empowerment. In all of these processes the policy also has the clear objectives of improving corporate governance and ethics in SOE governance and advancing the restructuring process.

The restructuring of key enterprises

Policy Framework 2000 also sets out the policy intentions of government in respect of the restructuring of key enterprises. The Policy Framework states that the intention is to complete these restructuring processes by 2004 (page 6). For this reason it is complemented by a detailed set of business plans and initiatives for each entity to be restructured. These business plans, however, have not been made public. The Policy Framework then highlights the intentions of government in respect of certain major sectors (pages 6–8).

In respect of energy, the electricity utility Eskom will be incorporated as a limited liability company. By restructuring the transmission, distribution and generation activities of Eskom, each stage of production will be placed in separate entities. Competition will then be created in the generation industry. Initially, different generating companies will be formed to create internal competition. Subsequently, the private sector will be brought in to participate in generation and completely independent power producers will be encouraged. The separated transmission entity will probably remain in state ownership to provide equitable access to the power grid for all via a power pool. Distribution will be regionalized and decentralized in locally owned regional electricity distributors. A search is on currently for strategic equity partners for the different Eskom Enterprise business units.

With regard to transport, the restructuring of Transnet is impeded by huge pension fund debts inherited from the previous dispensation. This matter is to be addressed through legislation, guarantees and the selling of shares in companies such as M-Cell, a cellular phone company. The funds generated in this way will then be used to reduce Transnet's debt, after which more restructuring options will become available. Internal re-engineering and management and business improvements are necessary to ensure improved financial and other results. Spoornet – the railroads company – will be commercialized and a public offering and/or the involvement of a strategic equity partner will be considered. Portnet – the company managing South African ports – will be divisionalized into two business entities, the port authority and port operations. Port operations can then be privatized. New regulatory frameworks will also be devised for Transnet's and Portnet's activities. Initial public offerings are also being prepared for SAA and the airports company (ACSA). Petronet, the pipeline company transporting fuel, will be incorporated. Many of the other non-core businesses of Transnet are under investigation for restructuring and will probably be divested.

With regard to telecommunications, the main concern is with matters affecting the telephone company, Telkom. An initial public offering of Telkom shares is to be handled by an IPO office established in the Department of Public Enterprises. There are finalized plans to involve a second national telecommunications operator in the South African telecommunication market.

Turning to defence, the discussion of defence-related industry involves policies to incorporate the arms manufacturing company, Denel. There are processes to find and conclude deals with strategic equity partners for Denel Aerospace and Denel Ordnance. These equity partners will provide capital and access to technology and markets. Non-core business units in defence-related industry will be continuously disposed of.

Many other restructuring initiatives, but on a smaller scale, are under way in the forestry, mining and public resorts sectors.

Policy Framework 2000 is a comprehensive policy statement aimed at providing an effective and efficient process for the restructuring of SOEs in

South Africa. How successful the implementation of these policies will be, however, will depend on the way the contextual factors are incorporated into the process and the extent to which the important decision makers and stakeholders define and defend their interests. Historically, in South Africa many ambitious policy initiatives have run aground on the shores of these contextual realities, introduced into the process through the power plays between important stakeholders. The policy intentions are clear. But there are questions in respect of the expeditious implementation of the policy given the contextual, power and implementation capacity variables in South Africa.

The road ahead: possible future scenarios in respect of privatization in South Africa

In this section the discussion will be developed and systematized in an attempt to provide a speculative assessment of the possible road ahead in respect of privatization in South Africa.

When considering the context of privatization in South Africa, the national and international contextual factors, reviewed earlier, need to be considered. Internationally, globalization has led to the spread of privatization from the developed world since the second half of the twentieth century. For the developing world, these trends were mediated and sometimes amplified by means of (a) the policies of the World Bank and the International Monetary Fund; (b) the need of developing countries for international funding and direct foreign investment; and (c) policy and financing conditionalities based upon these factors.

Currently, there seems to be a re-evaluation of globalization and its effects, *inter alia*, as a result of the emerging anti-globalization lobby and serious disturbances at international economic meetings in Seattle, Prague and Genoa. Simultaneously, there also seems to be a case for reconsidering the near-panacea status conferred upon the economic strategy of privatization and more specifically the impact of its effects on developing economies.

The joint impact of these trends may lead to a situation where there is less pressure on developing countries, such as South Africa, to pursue privatization in the short and medium term. These trends are also reinforced by the state of world economic markets subsequent to the 11 September 2001 events in New York, as well as the general depreciation in technology stocks in the world's leading stock markets. These factors affect the international marketability of SOEs in the energy, transport, telecommunications and even defence technology sectors.

Some of these international trends are complemented by South African contextual trends. The growing international lobby against globalization and its alleged effects are vociferously introduced into the South African privatization debate by COSATU. They argue that the effects of privatization are detrimental to South African local interests and merely benefit the already (global) rich. According to COSATU, the results of South African policies and programmes are that the rich grow richer at the expense of the poor and that unemployment and poverty have increased. These trends will continue even further if privatization programmes are pursued. For these reasons, COSATU is putting serious pressure on their alliance partners in government to abandon the GEAR-oriented restructuring programmes in favour of larger state intervention and control, as foreseen by the RDP policy programme.

These differences between the government alliance partners have come very close to creating a final rift in the alliance. Government, in the form of the ANC and Cabinet, seem to have made some concessions towards COSATU to heal the conflict, but have subsequently then pursued the restructuring policy through the actions foreseen in Policy Framework 2000.

The national political contextual factors are also complemented by national economic issues, such as the crisis of the declining Rand, rising inflation and the collapse of the market for technology stocks. These can be linked to a lack of investor confidence in emerging markets, not least as a result of the political crisis in Zimbabwe and the January 2002 economic crisis in Argentina. These matters create serious difficulties for economic initiatives such as public offerings and the finding of credible international and/or local equity partners. Even in cases where international interests are already bound into transactions, such as the Swissair/SAA transaction, international partners can still default, as was the case in this transaction. These trends do not indicate rapid short- and medium-term successes in respect of privatization in South Africa, as underlined by the continual postponement of initiatives such as the public issue in respect of Telkom and the sell-off of stakes in other SOEs to equity partners.

Nationally, there is still pressure from the private sector for the continuation and even acceleration of the restructuring process. There are also some indications of political will in this regard, as evident in statements from President Mbeki and Minister Radebe. However, when addressing the potential rift with COSATU in the government alliance, the ANC tends to make either conciliatory or obfuscating comments to sooth COSATU sentiments. In this situation, there are at best indications of ambiguity and hesitancy on the part of the South African government in respect of privatization in South Africa.

A further factor in respect of the national situation is the need for sophisticated implementation institutions and competencies to implement privatization policies. There is capacity in the South African private financial, banking and legal sectors in this regard, and this capacity is well supported by international instructions. But, with respect to the public sector, these capacities are more limited. There have been improvements in the government's capacity after the establishment of the Department of Public Enterprises, but it is a questionable whether current capacity in this department is sufficient. If the policy institutions within government are not strong enough to sustain a privatization process, probabilities of successful policy implementation diminish. This is especially so in cases such as South Africa where there is substantial internal political opposition and resistance to restructuring programmes.

Conclusions

Privatization is deliberately referred to as 'restructuring' in South African government circles. This is significant as it indicates the extent to which the issues surrounding privatization in South Africa are complex and highly politicized. The current situation is also a reflection and continuation of the historical developments in respect of privatization in South Africa.

Historically, the apartheid government used the worldwide trends in respect of privatization as a justification for its attempts to privatize. It can be safely accepted that the previous National Party government needed the revenue from privatization in a last attempt to finance its policies. For these and many other reasons, the ANC opposed the privatization efforts, in conjunction with COSATU. After the coming to power of the ANC, COSATU and SACP alliance, the position changed. The ANC moved from the critical positions it held in the RDP towards a much more positive approach towards privatization foreshadowed in the GEAR policy, to a nuanced view expressed as official policy in Policy Framework 2000. In this shift, the ANC has been vigorously opposed by its alliance partner in government, COSATU.

Given a number of contextual and current realities in respect of the political, economic and social situation and trends in South Africa, progress with privatization will probably remain careful, slow and even haphazard. The policy intentions are clear, but the conditions and capacity for their implementation are problematic and highly contested by differing political and economic role players. Developments will retain a fascinating dynamics and warrant continued observation and analysis. This chapter presents an initial attempt to analyse this.

References

Brynard, P. (1995) 'Privatisation in South Africa', *Politeia*, 14(2) (Online journal), (*http://www.unisa.ac.za/dept/press/politeia/142/petrusw.html*).

COSATU (2000) 'Crush Poverty! Create Quality Jobs!', *The Shopsteward*, 9(3), 7 June, 1–3 (*http://www.cosatu.org.za/shop/shop0903/shop0903.htm*).

The Economist (1999) 'The Painful Privatisation of South Africa', 352(8136), 49.

Fine, B. (1997) 'Privatisation and the restructuring of state assets in South Africa: a strategic view', NIEP Occasional paper series, no. 7, National Institute for Economic Policy, Johannesburg (*http://www.niep.org.za/resart6.htm*).

Hentz, J.J. (2000) 'The two faces of privatisation: political and economic logics in transitional South Africa', *The Journal of Modern African Studies*, 38(2), 203–23 (*http://uk.cambridge.org/journals/moaj*).

Megginson, W.L. and J.M. Netter (1998) 'From State to Market: A Survey of Empirical Studies on Privatisation', New York Stock Exchange: Working Paper 98–05, 7 June (*http://www.nyse.com/about/NT00039702.html*).

Ministry of Public Enterprises (2000) 'An Accelerated Agenda Towards the Restructuring of State-owned Enterprises', Policy Framework, August, Department of Public Enterprises, 26 October (*http://www.dpe.gov.za/docs/policy/policyframework01.htm*).

Republic of South Africa (1994) 'The Reconstruction and Development Programme: A Policy Framework', Johannesburg (*http://www.polity.org.za/govdocs/rdp/rdpall.html*).

Republic of South Africa (1996a) 'Constitution of the Republic of South Africa Act 108 of 1996', Johannesburg (*http://www.polity.org.za/govdocs/constitution/saconst.html*).

Republic of South Africa (1996b) 'National Framework Agreement (NFA) on the Restructuring of State Assets', Government of National Unity. 15 June 2001 (*http://www.gov.za/reports/1996/nfa.htm*).

Republic of South Africa (1996c) 'Growth, Employment and Redistribution (GEAR) – A macroeconomic strategy', Johannesburg (*http://www.polity.org.za/govdocs/policy/growth.html*).

Roux, A. (ed.) (2000) *Business Futures*, Institute for Future Research, University of Stellenbosch.

Schwella, E. (2001) 'Public Sector Policy in the New South Africa – A Critical Review', *Public Performance Management Review*, 24(4), 367–88.

South African Reserve Bank (2001) 'Quarterly Economic Review', *Quarterly Bulletin*, 219, March (*http://www.resbank.co.za/Economics/qbulMar01/Pdf/qb.pdf*).

15 Privatization in sub-Saharan Africa
Paul Bennell

Introduction
Sub-Saharan Africa (SSA) is the least developed region in the world. Over 80 per cent of its 45 nations are classified as low-income developing countries with per capita incomes of less than US$400 per annum. Around two-thirds of the total population of 650 million in the region earn their livelihoods from smallholder agriculture.

For the large majority of SSA countries, economic growth and development has been poor since the 1970s. Post-independence, governments adopted statist development strategies and many nationalized the 'commanding heights' of their economies. A combination of serious economic mismanagement, poor governance with high levels of corruption and other rent-seeking activity, and limited economic diversification resulted in deep economic and increasingly political crises throughout the region.

Beginning in the early to mid-1980s, governments embarked on national economic reform programmes in order to rectify these policy shortcomings (Bennell, 1997). As elsewhere, privatization of both ownership and control of state-owned enterprises (SOEs) has become a central feature of these programmes. Privatization should be seen as part of a wider process of private sector development, which entails the nurturing of an indigenous capitalist class and attracting significant inflows of foreign direct investment. Reducing the fiscal burden of the public sector and improving economic efficiency are the other key related objectives.

The following discussion reviews the overall form of the privatization process in SSA from the mid-1980s to the late 1990s.[1] It then focuses on a number of key areas and issues, including the politics of privatization, foreign direct investment and promoting local ownership.

Overview
For expositional convenience, the overview of the privatization process in SSA will be divided into two time periods: 1980–95 and 1996–9.

The early phase: 1980–95
National privatization programmes (NPPs) were first introduced in the region during the late 1970s and a decade later well over half of all countries had some kind of NPP. Table 15.1 summarizes privatization

transactions in SSA during this period. Three groups of countries can be delineated:

- major privatizers (most notably, Benin, Guinea and Mali), where the majority of SOEs were divested;
- modest privatizers, where typically less than 10 per cent of the total value of public productive assets was divested (including Côte d'Ivoire, Nigeria and Ghana in West Africa and all countries in East Africa);
- minimal and non-privatizers, totalling some 25 countries.

Table 15.1 Privatizations and other SOE divestitures in SSA, 1985–95

	Divestitures		
Sub-region	Sales	Liquidations	Other
West Africa	363	127	125
East and Central Africa	252	91	29
Southern Africa	1372	231	225
Total	1987	449	379

Source: Bennell (1997).

During the 1980s, only a handful of governments were seriously committed to privatization. Although most programmes were instigated by the major international finance institutions (IFIs), the IMF and World Bank, the main preoccupation at this time was with macroeconomic reform. Performance targets for NPPs were rarely met. However, the pace of privatization began to pick up markedly from the early 1990s as a result of increased IFI pressure and greater commitment of governments to public sector reform. Three times as many SOEs were partially or completely sold during 1988–95 than in the preceding eight-year period.

The importance attached to privatization also depended to a considerable extent on the relative size of the public sector. In SOE-dominated economies, such as Ghana, Mozambique, Tanzania and Zambia, the role of privatization programmes in the overall process of economic restructuring was very much greater than in countries such as Botswana, Kenya, Mauritius and South Africa, where the private sector was much stronger.

In global terms, the privatization process in SSA was of marginal importance during this period. Between 1998 and 1995, total privatization transactions totalled US$2.73 bn, which was approximately 1 per cent of the value of all divestitures worldwide.

While the total number of SOEs decreased from 6100 in 1990 to 4100 in

1995, almost all of these divestitures were small and medium-sized enter-prises. Among those that were sold, the median value of a transaction was only US$370000. The five largest transactions accounted for 60 per cent of total proceeds. In value terms, three countries dominated the privatization process: Ghana, Nigeria and South Africa. Half of all transactions were in the manufacturing sector. Five industries – food processing, alcoholic bev-erages, textiles, cement and other non-metallic, and metal products – accounted for 60 per cent of total sale proceeds among privatized manu-facturing enterprises

A half of all transactions were private sales using open-tender proce-dures. Public flotations were rare and were confined to a handful of coun-tries that have well functioning stock markets (in particular, South Africa and Nigeria). Half of all receipts were in foreign exchange. Foreign capital tended to predominate in larger transactions (above US$1 mn) and in coun-tries which had weak indigenous business classes. Foreign involvement was highest in agriculture (69 per cent), mining (94 per cent), utilities (100 per cent), and hotels and tourism (68 per cent).

The mid-to-late 1990s
With the successful completion of the relatively easy first phase of the pri-vatization process in a reasonably large number of countries in SSA, the IFIs and other donor agencies increasingly focused their attention on the major public enterprises, which accounted for the bulk of public sector assets and employment and were the largest fiscal drain. These included post and telecommunications, airlines, ports, bus and truck companies, railways, water and electricity, and banks and other financial institutions. Unlike the case of the small to medium production enterprises, privatiza-tion of these SOEs was dependent on foreign companies taking the lead with sizeable commitments of new capital and foreign management and technology.

It was widely expected therefore that the scale and scope of NPPs would increase rapidly during the mid-1990s. Table 15.2 shows that the value of transactions did increase, from around US700mn in 1996 (less than US$200mn in 1995) to US$2.4bn in 1997. However, this was still much less than expected and the value of transactions then fell to US$1.3bn in 1998 and only US$556mn in 1999. There are a number of key reasons for the failure of the privatization programme to take off in these years, which will be considered below.

Privatization continued to be dominated by a relatively few large divesti-tures and was concentrated in a few countries (see Table 15.3). The proceeds from the 10 largest privatizations accounted for almost half of the total transactions. In value terms, a number of the largest privatizations were in

Table 15.2   Value of privatization transactions, by sub-region, in SSA, 1996–99 (US$ mn)

Sub-region	1996	1997	1998	1999	Total
West and Central Africa					
Bénin	0	0	0	0	0
Burkina Faso	0	0	0	1.1	1.1
Cameroon	41.1	0	72	0	113.1
Cap Verde	0	0	0	81.1	81.1
Côte d'Ivoire	111.4	254.6	80.1	21.6	467.7
Gabon	0	49			49
Ghana	185.7	67.6	20.7	39.5	313.5
Guinea	0	45	0	0	45
Mali	21.9	0	0	0	21.9
Mauritania	0	0	0	0	0
Nigeria	0	0	0	0	0
Senegal		191.4	150.3	69	410.7
Togo	10.6	0	0	NA	10.6
Regional sub-total	370.7	607.6	323.1	212.3	1 513.7
East Africa					
Eritrea	0	0	2	0	2
Ethiopia	0	0	172	50.4	222.4
Kenya	90.8	24.1	29.6	6.6	151.1
Madagascar	0	0	0	9	9
Rwanda	0	35	0	0	35
Tanzania	13.6	16.3	110.8	NA	140.7
Uganda	30.2	20	14.8	8.1	73.1
Regional sub-total	134.6	95.4	329.2	74.1	633.3
Southern Africa					
Angola	3.8	0	2.4	0	6.2
Lesotho	0	0	0	16.2	16.2
Malawi	8.9	0	10.7	5	24.6
Mozambique	37.8	21	28.6	NA	87.4
South Africa	122	1287	247	235	1891
Zambia	29.4	302	408.8	NA	740.2
Zimbabwe	0	109.8	0	20.5	130.3
Regional sub-total	201.9	1 719.8	697.5	276.7	2 895.9
Totals	707.2	2 422.8	1 320.2	556.5	5 006.7

Source: World Bank data base on privatization transactions.

Table 15.3   *Privatization transactions in SSA exceeding US$25mn,*
1990–99

Country	Enterprise	Sector	Value
Bénin	La Béninoise	Manufacturing	28.4
Cap Verde	Banco Commercial	Banking	33.2
Cap Verde	Electra	Power	47.9
Cameroon	Hevecam	Rubber	41.1
Cameroon	SOCAPALM	Agroindustry	50.0
Côte d'Ivoire	CIDT	Cotton/textiles	90.7
Côte d'Ivoire	Domaine Heviecole de l'Etat Bettie	Agriculture	45.5
Côte d'Ivoire	Blocs Palmier	Agriculture	66.6
Cote d'Ivoire	Société pour le Développement de Canne Sucres	Agriculture	41.2
Côte d'Ivoire	Palmindustrie	Agriculture	27.0
Côte d'Ivoire	CI-Télécom	Telecom	193.0
Ethiopia	Lega Dembi Gold Mine	Mining	172.0
Gabon	Société d'Energie et d'Eaux du Gabon	Power/water	NA
Ghana	Ashanti Goldfields	Mining	628.2
Ghana	Tomos Ghana	Services	30.2
Guinea	SOTELGUI	Telecom	45.0
Kenya	Kenya Airways	Airline	46.3
Kenya	Kenya Commercial Bank	Finance	29.4
Nigeria	NPCC oil field	Petroleum	500.0
Nigeria	Lagos Federal Palace	Hotel	72.4
Nigeria	Tourist Company of Nigeria	Tourism	49.8
Rwanda	King Gaisal Hospital	Medical	35.0
Senegal	SOCOCIM	Manufacturing	39.2
Senegal	SONATEL	Telecom	191.4
Senegal	SENELEC	Power	69.0
South Africa	SABC-commercial radio stations	Broadcasting	122.0
South Africa	Telkom	Telecom	1261.0
South Africa	Airports Company of South Africa	Transport	245.7
South Africa	South African Airways	Airline	235.0
Tanzania	Tanzania Cigarette Company	Manufacturing	55.0
Tanzania	Tanganyika Portland Cement	Manufacturing	48.0
Tanzania	Tanzania Breweries	Manufacturing	38.0
Uganda	Nile Hotel Complex	Hotels	26.9
Zambia	Zambia Sugar Company	Agroindustry	50.0
Zambia	Nkana and Nchanga copper mines	Mining	220.0
Zambia	Zambia Oxygen	Manufacturing	60.0
Zambia	Chambishi cobalt plant	Mining	50.0
Zambia	ZCCM-Baluba mine	Mining	70.0
Zambia	ZCCM-Luanshya copper and cobalt mines	Mining	245.0
Zimbabwe	Delta Corporation	Manufacturing	75.0
Zimbabwe	Commercial Bank of Zimbabwe	Finance	43.7
Zimbabwe	Cotton Company of Zimbabwe	Agroindustry	48.3

South Africa. Four other countries (Côte d'Ivoire, Ghana and Senegal in West Africa, and Zambia in Central Africa) accounted for another 20 per cent of privatization proceeds.

Despite the increased focus on the 'strategic' SOEs, only limited progress was made with privatization in these sectors. The main privatizations were as follows:

- agriculture: Côte d'Ivoire;
- airlines: Kenya, South Africa (sales), Zambia, Lesotho, Uganda (liquidations);
- finance: Cap Verde, Cameroon, Madagascar, Tanzania, Uganda, Zimbabwe;
- mining: Ethiopia, Zambia;
- power generation: Cap Verde, Gambia, Guinea, Senegal;
- telecommunications: Côte d'Ivoire, Gabon, Guinea, Lesotho, Senegal, South Africa;
- water: Côte d'Ivoire, Gabon, Gambia, Niger.

The devaluation of the African Financial Community (CFA) franc by 100 per cent in 1994 gave a major impetus to the privatization process in Francophone African countries. The overvalued CFA had been a serious deterrent to foreign investment for decades.

A major constraint in the privatization of the large SOEs has been the significant amount of preparatory work needed to make them saleable, including the establishment of robust regulatory frameworks for the natural monopolies. Sorting out the large debts of most SOEs has been time-consuming and costly. Interest by foreign companies has been weak in key sectors, including airlines and finance. The incentives to buy old state land-line telephone organizations have also been much reduced because most governments have awarded licences to private companies in the very high-growth mobile phone market. Government reluctance to dispense with asset-based valuations has also been a major issue in some countries.

The most far-reaching and successful NPPs were in Côte d'Ivoire, Mozambique and Zambia. The latter two countries are very heavily aid-dependent. In Mozambique, the privatization process was largely complete by 2000. SOEs accounted for 67 per cent of industrial output in 1990, but less than 20 per cent by the late 1990s. In Zambia, 254 out of a total of 280 SOEs were privatized, but major utilities still remained in public ownership. Privatization of the copper mines involved protracted negotiations with the eventual buyer, the Anglo-American Cooperation.

The economic and political environment

The overall economic and political climate for wide-ranging privatization programmes is the most fundamental constraint in most SSA countries. These remain fragile capitalist economies with limited entrepreneurial and management capacity in the key industrial and service sectors. During the last 25 years, inflows of foreign direct investment (FDI) have been very limited and have been concentrated in the three oil-producing countries (Angola, Gabon and Nigeria). There was widespread disinvestment in many countries, especially during the 1980s. Liberalization of foreign trade regimes has resulted in widespread deindustrialization, with the failure of both state and private enterprises to cope with import competition.

While the general political environment has become more conducive to comprehensive privatization, the actual saleability of SOEs has remained a key constraint in most SSA economies. The overall economic climate is of paramount importance and investors focus on the fundamentals of the overall economy as well as the particular sector they are interested in. For most countries and sectors, these fundamentals have not changed dramatically, as demonstrated by the fact that the annual economic growth rate averaged only 2.2 per cent per annum (in real terms) for the African continent as a whole during the 1990s.

Serious economic and political crises have undermined NPPs in a relatively large and growing number of countries in SSA. The most seriously affected countries are Angola, Burundi, Central African Republic, Congo (Brazzaville), Democratic Republic of Congo, Guinea-Bissau, Lesotho, Liberia, Rwanda, Sierra Leone, Somalia, Sudan, Togo and, more recently, Côte d'Ivoire, Eritrea, Ethiopia, Madagascar and Zimbabwe.

Economic and political conditions for privatization programmes are only conducive in a relatively small minority of SSA countries. Some of these, such as Botswana and Mauritius, have only relatively small numbers of SOEs. Nigeria and South Africa are the economic giants in the region. After a good start in the late 1980s, the privatization process in Nigeria completely stalled after 1994. Serious efforts to resume the NPP only began with the return of a democratically elected government in mid-1999.

Corruption and lack of transparency remain major concerns for prospective investors in many SSA countries.

The politics of privatization

As elsewhere, privatization is an intensely political process in SSA. However, during the 1990s, the political constraints in many SSA countries became less critical. Whereas most governments in the mid-to-late 1980s questioned whether they should privatize at all, the majority are now primarily concerned about the way NPPs can be designed and implemented most effectively. The fact remains, however, that privatization continues to be heavily externally driven in most countries. As the authors of a World Bank study themselves indicate, 'it is unlikely that there would have been much privatization without donors' (Bhatia and Campbell White, 1997).

The international finance institutions and donor agencies
Most countries in SSA are heavily aid-dependent. Consequently, economic policy is strongly influenced by the IMF and the World Bank. As noted earlier, since the mid-1990s, nearly all governments in SSA have come under increasing pressure from the IMF and World Bank to accelerate the privatization process. This has been driven by the recognition that the long-term success of the economic reform process is dependent on basic supply-side reforms, which entail the major restructuring of all the main economic sectors and the promotion of economic efficiency.

Enforcing donor conditionalities has proved to be highly problematic in most SSA countries. However, the ability of increasingly aid-dependent governments to resist and evade increasingly stringent conditionalities, which are directly linked to complete and rapid privatization, is now relatively limited.

Politicians and bureaucrats
During the initial phase of privatization up to the mid-1990s, the ideological commitment of African political elites to privatization in most SSA countries was weak. Many were openly hostile to privatization. A further political problem is that the costs of privatization are borne fairly immediately by relatively small but powerful groups, whereas the benefits for the population as a whole are only likely to become apparent in the longer term. Thus collective action is easier to organize against reform than for it. However, with accelerating economic and political reform, outright political resistance has largely died away. With the advent of multi-party democracy, many newly elected governments have distanced themselves from the statist policies of their predecessors. The continuing financial drain of supporting state enterprises has increased the resolve of governments to privatize them as quickly as possible.

It also the case, however, that greater democracy can slow down the privatization process. A notable example is in Uganda, where the Parliament suspended the privatization programme for nearly 18 months in 1998–9. This was due to serious concerns about inadequate legal and institutional arrangements, including ill-defined responsibilities and accountability, lack of transparency in a number of transactions, failure to collect payments from buyers, and the financial burden of retrenchment packages.

Furthermore, governments still shy away from the difficult economic and political issues which have to be addressed with respect to major privatizations. The higher the social cost, the greater the likelihood of delay. State holding corporations have also obstructed and delayed privatization programmes in a number of countries.

Producers and consumers
Democratization has also empowered sections of civil society to mount campaigns against high-profile privatizations. The general perception of the public in many countries is that the principal beneficiaries of privatization, are the rich and foreigners. During the early phase of privatization, opposition came mainly from workers in directly affected SOEs. However, privatization is increasingly being challenged by consumers as well as producers. This is particularly the case for basic services, which have a major impact on the well-being of the poor. The provision of these basic services is a key to the achievement of poverty reduction objectives, which have come to dominate the development agenda in SSA. Convincing the public that poverty reduction and privatization are mutually consistent has not been easy. For example, the privatization of the urban water supply in Ghana has been strongly opposed by powerful voices in civil society supported by international development non-governmental organizations based in the north. Privatization is also highly contested in South Africa. Given the legacy of the anti-apartheid struggle, trade unions and other, mainly urban-based, civil society organizations are particularly well organized and powerful.

Programme management
Many privatization programmes in SSA have been characterized by inadequate design and preparation. Privatization committees, commissions, units and other types of implementation agencies have invariably lacked sufficient legal authority and resources and have been hampered by excessive government interference. As a consequence, privatization transactions have been very protracted, with a high proportion of incomplete transactions and low transparency.

The World Bank has committed very substantial resources to support the implementation of NPPs and build national capacity. The majority of countries in SSA now have private sector support and privatization projects that are directly funded by the World Bank and other major donor agencies rely heavily on foreign technical assistance (in particular, the main international accountancy firms and management consultancies). The total cost of current World Bank projects in this area is in excess of one billion US dollars. The current privatization support project in Nigeria alone is US$114.3mn.

Foreign direct investment
Foreign companies and individuals have been involved in the large majority of privatizations in SSA. Although foreign investment policy regimes were liberalized in most countries, inflows of FDI continued to be concentrated in the three main oil-producing countries. The 1997–8 Asia crisis also had a significant impact, especially because of the sizeable involvement of investors from Malaysia in large privatizations in SSA.

The growing dominance of South African capital is also another noticeable feature of the NPPs in the region. This is particularly the case in the alcoholic beverages, mining, retail and fast food and hotel and tourism sectors in Eastern and Southern Africa.

Promoting local ownership
A key political objective has been to broaden the involvement of nationals in NPPs. However, given the limited development of capital markets, it has not been possible to rely on public flotations (IPOs) and mass voucher schemes to ensure the involvement of small investors. Privatization trust funds and management/employee buy-outs are also rare. Most reliance has been placed on deferred sales, but these have become controversial when purchasers have failed to meet payment dates, as has commonly happened in Ghana and Uganda.

Post-privatization performance
A key conclusion of a World Bank study is that, 'while a number of privatized businesses have failed, the overall impact of privatization at the enterprise level is encouraging with clear evidence of improving performance' (Bhatia and Campbell White, 1997). However, there is virtually no robust evidence on the post-privatization performance to substantiate assertions of this kind. None of the NPPs in SSA have adequate monitoring and evaluation systems.

Most information is therefore anecdotal and impressionistic. While there are some well-publicized success stories (such as Kenya Airways and Tanzania Breweries), virtually nothing is known about the number of privatized enterprises that have subsequently closed down. Certainly, however, larger enterprises have had much better access to capital, which was a critical constraint prior to privatization. Also wider fiscal and macroeconomic benefits will remain limited so long as the large corporations remain in the public sector.

Given the serious overstaffing that existed in most SOEs, it is not surprising that newly privatized enterprises have shed labour. For example, the workforce at Tanzania Breweries has been reduced from 4000 to 400 workers, but, with new investment, output has increased fourfold. With sales of assets and liquidations, employees have to be dismissed. In Zambia, formal sector employment fell by 61 000 between 1992 and 1995, although only 6000 of these job losses were directly attributable to privatization.

Future prospects

Since 2000, the pace of privatization has picked up markedly in a number of SSA countries, including Nigeria. While many of the basic economic and political constraints remain, most governments are genuinely committed to completing their privatization programmes as quickly as possible. Privatization conditionalities also feature prominently in Poverty Reduction Strategy Papers, which are now the focus of the IFIs and other donor agencies.

Five years ago, it was widely anticipated that major SOEs would be privatized by the end of the 1990s. For the reasons discussed earlier, this did not happen. However, it now seems likely that this will be achieved in most countries in SSA within the next five years.

Note

1.   Unfortunately, data for 2000 to 2002 are not yet available.

References

Bennell, P.S. (1997) 'Privatisation in Sub-Saharan Africa: Progress and Prospects during the 1990s', *World Development*, 25(11), 1785–803.
Bhatia, A. and O. Campbell White (1997) *Privatization in Africa*, Washington, DC: World Bank.

PART IV

PRIVATIZATION IN THE TRANSITION ECONOMIES OF CENTRAL AND EASTERN EUROPE

16 Privatization and corporate governance in transition economies: theory and concepts
Igor Filatotchev

Introduction

After many decades of centrally planned and state-controlled development, managers of industrial companies in the former command economies are now confronted by a growing pressure to restructure their organizations that affects, to different extents, all major sectors in the former command economies (Puffer, 1994). Although there may be different causes of this problem (the collapse of a highly integrated system of production and distribution, competition from imports, severe cuts in state subsidies and defence spending and so on), it produces a serious threat to an organization's viability when managers fail to diagnose successfully the causes of their firm's decline and respond with strategies appropriate for the demands of an evolving and changing environment (Peng and Heath, 1996).

Large-scale privatization was expected to enhance restructuring in failing SOEs through the elimination of the major constraints on managerial actions imposed by state ownership and central planning (Boycko *et al.*, 1995). Privatization has been an important tool of economic reform throughout former Communist Bloc countries, although particular privatization modes differed from country to country. For example, Hungary focused on sales of state assets to foreign owners, whereas the Czech and Slovak Republics employed equal-access voucher privatization (see Carlin and Aghion, 1996, for a summary of privatization programmes in Central and Eastern Europe). Russia used a combination of voucher insider privatization with auction sales of shares in former state-owned companies to outside individual and institutional investors (Blasi *et al.*, 1997). The form, but not the scale, of the Russian mass privatization model, involving the distribution of vouchers to citizens and eventual insider control, was imitated in Belarus and Ukraine (Filatotchev *et al.*, 2000). Despite the obvious differences in terms of coverage and timing, privatization in the three countries was essentially a 'give-away' process without any elements of genuine financial sacrifice.

As a result, privatization programmes in the former communist countries have created a diverse range of ownership structures and corporate governance mechanisms at company level, with Russia having the world's largest population of newly privatized companies. Bearing in mind these dramatic changes in the organizations' environments and ownership structures, one might expect that managers of the former state-owned enterprises, now liberated from the rigid control of the central planning bureaucracy, would engage in a substantial restructuring process aimed at the rapid adaptation of their businesses to the new economic conditions.

However, a growing number of studies, based on detailed surveys of enterprises and outside investors in the region, have indicated that the process of post-privatization restructuring of ownership is not speedy, nor is there strong evidence of the development of conventional systems of corporate governance (see, for example, Blasi *et al.*, 1997; Blasi and Shleifer, 1996; Earle and Estrin, 1996; Filatotchev *et al.*, 1996; Frydman *et al.*, 1996). What is less clear is the degree to which this reflects active collusion by insiders to retain control of firms in the course of privatization, even though insider control may make it very difficult to obtain the capital required for increasing productivity. Moreover, where outsiders were allowed to buy shares in would-be privatized state-owned firms, the rights of new minority shareholders were poorly protected. There is a growing concern among investors, analysts and policy makers about frequent cases of abuse of minority investors by controlling shareholders that might take the form of share dilution, pyramids of cross-shareholdings, related-party transactions and so on. Against this background, external investors have been cautious in providing finance, and the lack of sufficiently developed legal mechanisms that would protect the rights of minority shareholders and promote investment have hindered post-privatization enterprise restructuring.

This chapter explores the dynamic interrelationships between privatization, emergent corporate governance and performance in transition economies. In the following section, the main theoretical underpinnings of the privatization programmes of the reforming governments of Central and Eastern Europe (CEE) and the former Soviet Union (FSU) are outlined, and a summary of different privatization modes used in the privatization process is provided. The next section is focused on an analysis of the economic effects of 'insider privatization'. This is followed by a discussion related to the problems of ownership concentration and 'private benefits of control' that may be obtained by dominant owners at the expense of minority shareholders. Finally, the role of 'relationship investors', such as financial–industrial groups, investment funds and so on, that have emerged in the course of outsider privatization in a number of transition economies is discussed, followed by conclusions.

Privatization in transition economies

Derived from the principles of Marxism, previously, planned economies were characterized by the exclusivity of state-owned property, resulting in acute inefficiencies at the firm as well as the macro level (Kornai, 1992). A major objective of reforms in countries undergoing transition to a market economy is to increase the productive efficiency of former planned enterprises and to make their outputs competitive on world markets (Sachs and Warner, 1995). Privatization emerged as central to effecting such reform thanks to its sociopolitical importance and potential macroeconomic benefits. It was designed to enhance restructuring in failing state-owned companies through the elimination of the major constraints on managerial strategic actions imposed by state ownership and central planning, and to provide new incentives for managers to make important strategic decisions.

Typically, programmes have used a mixture of privatization methods, with the dominant approach varying between countries (Brada, 1996). In the former Soviet Union (FSU), countries have generally imitated Russia in the application of 'give-away' privatization to incumbent management and through vouchers distributed to adult citizens, which are then used to bid for shares in enterprises (Estrin and Wright, 1999).[1] In most cases, these privatizations were accomplished without any additional infusion of new capital. Direct sales to inside management and employees as 'privatization buy-outs' or to foreign investors as 'privatization divestments' have been a secondary method of transfer to the private sector. The results of the 'voucher privatization' in Russia are particularly impressive. By the end of June 1994, some 13 000 medium and large state-owned enterprises had been privatized, accounting for 76 per cent of total industrial employment (*Russian Economic Trends*, 1995:40). In most of the privatizations that occurred before July 1994, employees were able to acquire shares without significant borrowing through the use of vouchers, in what amounted to a 'give-away' scheme. Voucher privatization in Russia clearly gave much greater scope for insider control than, for example, the Czech privatization scheme, where 70 per cent of voucher points were allocated by individuals to investment funds (Takla, 1994). The workforce in Russian companies had a choice of three 'variants' when privatizing their company. These variants involved employees, managers and outsiders able to obtain varying total amounts of shares and at varying prices in terms of vouchers and cash (see, for example, Boycko *et al.*, 1995; Blasi *et al.*, 1997, for a detailed discussion of the Russian privatization programme). The popularity of variant 2, which gave the incumbents the possibility of obtaining 51 per cent or more of their firm's shares, was for the most part due to the fears of incumbents that external buyers could obtain a majority stake in their firm and thus exert pressure on managers to undertake unwelcome, job-threatening restructuring (see, for example, Earle and Estrin, 1996).

Among the FSU countries, only Estonia has pursued a policy primarily focused on direct sales and therefore one likely to encourage widespread outsider ownership. In the countries of Central Europe, direct sales or voucher privatizations, often in favour of outside owners, have predominated (EBRD, 1998). For example, in Hungary, the privatization process was coordinated by the State Property Agency (SPA) that was created in March 1990.[2] It was responsible for both management and supervision of the ownership transformation. The shares in state enterprises were transferred to the SPA, which was then entitled to exercise ownership rights and appoint a board of directors. The process implied initial ('pre-privatization') transformation of state enterprise into a corporate form, supervised by the SPA, and outright divestment or transfer of assets of the state-owned enterprise to a new joint stock company of equivalent value. At the first stage of the privatization programme that was launched in January 1990, 20 large and well performing companies were valued by international consultants and then offered for sale. However, this stage also demonstrated a difficulty of privatization via an open market flotation and certain limitations of widespread shareholder ownership. It turned the attention of the policy makers to the search for strategic investors. Direct state involvement remained a defining feature of the privatization programme and the majority of subsequent methods relied on sales for cash. Frydman *et al.*, (1993:178) document that Hungary had created a very liberal climate for foreign investors already, at the beginning of 1990s, by allowing repatriation of profits and 100 per cent foreign ownership.

A fundamental theory, underlying the discussion of privatization effects on restructuring in the economics of transition literature, is agency theory. This predicts that privatization will lead to greater efficiency by improving monitoring systems and providing managers with better incentives to perform (see Chapter 2 and Jensen and Meckling, 1976). Arguably, the principal benefit of large-scale privatization was the 'depoliticization' of economic life (Boycko *et al.*, 1995:7). Since in former command economies political interference in the economy was considered a fundamental source of inefficiency, the main objective of privatization was to sever the links between enterprise managers and politicians, including both the ministerial bureaucracy at the centre and local officials in the regions. Ultimately, ownership transfer from the state to new private owners would lead to the development of western systems of corporate governance that discipline incumbents either through the threat of takeover or through the 'voice'-based mechanisms of monitoring and control (Frydman *et al.*, 1993).

Studies on emerging economies have also uncovered important contextual factors that may contribute to agency-theoretic explanations of firm restructuring in a transitional context. These factors include the development of market institutions, (high) levels of government involvement, industry structures, ownership patterns and enforcement of business laws

(Khanna and Palepu, 2000; La Porta *et al.*, 1998; North, 1990). For instance, privatization of formerly state-owned enterprises often resulted in the emergence of different organizational forms, such as networks, 'recombinant properties', or heterarchies (Peng and Heath, 1996; Spicer *et al.*, 2000; Stark, 1996). These organizational forms represent the redefinition or recombination of previously state-owned organizational assets, blurring the boundary between public and private property in transition economies (Stark, 1996). An important reason for these restructuring outcomes might be the limited impact of new private owners on firm restructuring. The study by Filatotchev *et al.* (2000) indicates that managerial opportunism during 'downsizing' is not controlled effectively by the institutional owners of the firm. These suboptimal outcomes of firm restructuring are often explained by the fluid state of the institutional environment in transition economies (Newman, 2000; Whitley and Czaban, 1998). A study by La Porta and colleagues (1998) also substantiates the importance of contextual examination. These authors found that variations in ownership protection and enforcement of the laws in different countries may affect the potential impact of owners on firm strategy.

Although the adaptation of firms in CEE involves a complex set of agency problems, studies agree that the shift from state to private ownership is one of the most important contextual factors associated with firm restructuring in these countries. There is substantial evidence in earlier studies of the positive performance effects of privatization (see Chapter 2). These benefits might be due to the improved effectiveness of ownership control in privatized firms, as government bureaucrats had little interest and expertise to control managerial opportunism in the formerly state-owned firms (Kornai, 1992). In addition to much-needed capital, private owners may provide skills and effective control mechanisms for the management of firms. Indeed, privatized firms sold to foreign owners have been found to outperform state-owned firms (Frydman *et al.*, 1996). D'Souza and Megginson (1999) have also reported significant post-privatization performance improvements in the areas of profitability, sales, operating efficiency and dividend payments. Sachs *et al.* (2000) note that the benefits of privatization may be related to parallel institutional reforms, such as improved legal frameworks, better enforcement, hardened budget constraints and new industry entrants (also see Chapters 10, 24 and 25).

Despite the well-documented performance gains of privatizations in the region, little research has focused on the effectiveness of different privatization methods in a variety of environments. This extension is important, since CEE governments, that are expecting to gain macroeconomic benefits (for example, employment, enhanced local supply and trade balance) from improved firm performance, have experimented with a diverse set of privatization methods. Moreover, the outcome of restructuring is of interest to the new owners, concerned about designing proper control systems within newly privatized firms.

Insider privatization, managerial entrenchment and restructuring[3]
There has been considerable debate about the first stage of economic reforms in CEE and the FSU concerning the possible restructuring benefits from privatizing enterprises through transfers of ownership to incumbent managers and employees. Any market-based restructuring is taking place in a situation where, although management has significant stock holdings, the body of employees, including managers, holds the majority of the equity (see Blasi and Shleifer, 1996). This debate is rooted in the agency theory literature on the importance of managerial equity ownership for firm strategies. In particular, the extent of managerial equity ownership has been identified as a crucial aspect of managerial willingness and capacity to implement strategic change. The private nature of shareholdings provides manager-owners with the incentive to consider the consequences of their actions for the market value of their property rights and the proper motivation of managers through incentive alignment may prove a powerful mechanism to ensure that managers implement value-enhancing restructuring actions (Holderness and Sheehan, 1988; Jensen and Meckling, 1976).

The insider privatization model would seem to have benefits regarding the amount of conflict within firms over decision making, as the 'them-and-us' scenario which existed under central planning management structures would no longer be in place. But while decisions that are geared towards employees' interests may be more universally acceptable in an employee-owned firm, the question remains as to whether these decisions are optimal from the firm's value-maximizing point of view. Employees may avoid taking otherwise necessary painful restructuring decisions in order simply to protect their jobs and incomes in the short run (see Estrin, 1986; Earle and Estrin, 1996; Hansmann, 1996, for a general discussion of problems of employee ownership and control). Hansmann (1990) suggests that employee shareholders may prefer investment projects in which the upside gains accrue primarily to employee owners, while the downside risks are borne primarily by the providers of capital.

Many observers regarded insider privatization as a first step towards a better alignment of residual claims and control rights (Boycko *et al.*, 1995). Employee ownership is arguably a costly governance structure, bearing in mind the costs of the collective choice mechanism (see Hansmann, 1990, for a survey of worker ownership costs). If a decision by the majority of workers to acquire shares arose from pure asset motives, such as insiders' information about a firm's prospects, or the anticipation that a concentrated holding would prove to be more liquid (because of fixed transaction costs per employee, or because proximity to other shareholders would attract potential buyers who might otherwise be difficult to find), then employees would be content to sell shares to outside buyers once private information had been reflected in share valuations. The expectations of excess returns would then disappear and risk aversion would dictate portfolio diversification. Even if the primary motivation for acquiring shares was to secure insider control, the employee owners of a firm might still be tempted to transfer their ownership rights to outside 'core' investors, since dispersed internal ownership makes it difficult for them to exercise the control component of their property rights (Earle and Estrin, 1996).

The expectation that insiders' shareholdings would be fairly rapidly reduced, and that outside shareholders would come to dominate, was not unreasonable given the experience of employee management buy-outs (EMBOs) in market economies (Wright *et al.*, 1995; Pendleton *et al.*, 1998). Typically, employee shareholders in EMBOs gradually sell out. Unfortunately, this analogy overlooks one important difference between western EMBOs and privatization experiences in transition economies, which is that, in the west, insiders generally only have control of the firm if they also have the confidence of outside investors. In the west, employee share ownership of EMBOs is often rather unimportant, with employees rarely even having as much as 49 per cent of the voting equity. Even though the managers may be majority shareholders, EMBOs are usually supported by some combination of venture capital and bank debt, so outsiders have a very significant voice in decision making from the outset.

Alternatively, in the circumstances of transition economies, incumbents may have made a conscious decision to invest in insider control as an insurance against unemployment and loss of access to the social facilities provided by the company (Aghion and Blanchard, 1998; Blanchard and Aghion, 1996; Estrin, 1983). This entrenchment element would give the shares greater value to insiders than to outsiders, and so would imply retention of shares by insiders. The problem is amplified by the weak state of the external labour market and bond-posting by the firm's employees, in the form of reliance by employees on the ex-state firm not only for an income but also for housing, healthcare, recreation and so on (Richman, 1965). Combined with the underdeveloped nature of the Russian stock market, where share prices of even officially quoted companies rarely reflect the economic value of businesses, this may seriously slow down the post-privatization dynamics of insiders' shareholdings.

To illustrate these arguments, Filatotchev *et al.* (1999) consider a theoretical model of the insider-controlled firm under the explicit assumption that only if outsiders gain control will capital be provided to restructure the firm and raise efficiency. This model demonstrates the conditions under which insiders may choose to retain control, despite the capital gains on offer should they decide to sell out.

Suppose that, under insider control, the firm employs n workers and produces an output of x per employee. If the firm was controlled by outsiders, a new set of workers would be employed at the market wage of w, and the output would be y per employee, provided that the firm is restructured at (one-off) restructuring costs of e per employee. In that event, the former insiders would be unemployed for an uncertain length of time before obtaining work at the wage w, a state of affairs to which they attach the value R. Outsiders will only attach positive value to the firm if

$$y - e > w. \tag{16.1}$$

On the other hand, if

$$R < x, \tag{16.2}$$

insiders feel better off in the firm than in a state of unemployment. If shares are freely traded, outsiders will offer a sum of $(y - e - w)$ for each worker's shares. If, however,

$$y - e - w < x - R, \tag{16.3}$$

this bribe will not be sufficient to induce workers to give up control. The retention of insider control does, however, require collusion, since if each individual believes that she can sell her shares without insider control being lost, she will do so at any positive price even if (16.3) holds; that is, there is a free-rider problem.

We may now turn to the issue of why restructuring requires outsider control. Let us assume that, with the same injection of capital of ne, the managers can raise output from nx to ny, whether insiders or outsiders have control. This is profitable for insider-controlled firms provided that

$$y - e > x. \tag{16.4}$$

The problem facing potential lenders is that these are not the only circumstances in which an insider-controlled firm may choose to borrow. The insiders might effectively use the sum borrowed to supplement their own incomes, rather than to invest in new equipment, and then allow the firm to go into liquidation, leaving the bank or outside investor with a loss of ne. This will be profitable for insiders whenever

$$R + e > x. \tag{16.5}$$

If this condition holds, it will be a more profitable action than restructuring, provided that

$$y - R < 2e, \qquad (16.6)$$

in which case the provision of outside capital becomes a bribe to liquidate the firm rather than to restructure it. Since the value of R is private information to insiders, lenders cannot verify with certainty whether (16.6) holds, so that they will be unwilling to make loans. This moral hazard aspect of insider control is well known (Hansmann, 1990, 1996).

Even where equation (16.3) holds, so that insiders collude in order to keep control, there is an argument that sooner or later outsiders will gain control anyway. The argument is that, provided that $x < w$, insiders would be better off getting a private sector job elsewhere than staying in the firm. An insider who gets an outside job no longer has an incentive to hold on to her shares, but will sell them at any positive price. If the remaining insiders are liquidity-constrained and not in a position to buy these shares, eventually outsiders will gain control by buying them as they come on the market.

This is where the distinction between employees and managers may become important. One argument for a rapid transformation of insider-controlled firms into outsider-controlled ones is based on the assumption that managers are keen to rationalize the firm as rapidly as possible, and attract outside finance which can facilitate this restructuring. According to this view, managers' objectives are similar to those of outside investors and they consider employee ownership an obstacle to restructuring. Hence managers will be very tempted to form a coalition with potential core investors and they will welcome sales of shares by employees (Shleifer and Vishny, 1997; see also Barberis *et al.*, 1996, for a survey of changing managerial attitudes in Russian privatized retail trade units).

However, some researchers indicate that managerial shareholding may create a trade-off between managerial incentives and entrenchment (Morck *et al.*, 1988). More generally, the fact that manager-owners are reluctant to allow influence and involvement by outsiders is well-known (Ang, 1991). A major criticism which can be levelled at large-scale, rapid privatizations in transitional economies is that, while ownership changes, management largely does not (Brada, 1996). Managers may still be the same 'Red Directors' from the past, and their entrenched attitude to outsiders may be linked to the fact that most of them have been appointed before privatization, under the previous *nomenklatura* system (Linz, 1997). They may fear that, if outside investors gained control, the top management would be replaced and that their firm-specific investments, which have been built up over previous years, would be irretrievably lost. Consequently, the principal objective of managers in this case would be to retain insider control, and they would be happy to form a coalition with other employees to keep their support (Filatotchev *et al.*, 1999; 2000)

Let us assume that, if outsiders gain control, managers obtain a managerial position (either in this firm or another) with probability p, and with probability $1 - p$ they can only be employed in non-managerial work at a wage w. The value which managers attach to a managerial position is m. Assume further that initially employees, managers and outsiders all own some shares. Then managers will prefer insider control if

$$\lambda n(y - e - w) < (1 - p)(m - w), \qquad (16.7)$$

where λ is the proportion of shares which managers need to hold to ensure insider control (that is, 0.5 minus the employees' share). The left-hand side of (16.7) is the opportunity cost of this shareholding, whilst the right-hand side is the expected loss of employment income to managers if outsiders gained control. Two points stand out: one is that managers' perceptions of their own chances in the managerial labour market (p) are important; the other is that the larger the proportion of shares they need to own to secure insider control (λ), the more likely they are to sell out to outsiders.

The argument just given assumes a perfect market in shares so that employees can sell directly to outsiders. There is considerable evidence of imperfections in the market for shares in privatized firms across the CEE and FSU. There is mounting anecdotal evidence that restrictions on share transfers are prevalent and take many different forms, ranging from a free transfer of companies' shares to management-controlled, closed mutual trusts, to a formal requirement that employees can only offer their shares to other managers and employees. It seems likely that in practice these imperfections make it easier for managers than other parties to trade shares. If managers can prevent direct trades between other parties, then it is likely that, if they prefer outsider control, they can make excess profits by purchasing shares from employees wishing to sell and subsequently resell to outsiders. This is because employees may be liquidity-constrained and prepared to sell at below market price rather than wait for the market imperfections to disappear. The possibility of purchasing shares more cheaply does not, however, alter the preferences of managers as expressed in equation (16.7), since this depends only on the price at which the shares can be resold to outsiders.

To summarize, 'give-away' privatizations, where insiders become majority shareholders, are unlikely to create efficient governance systems because they tend to promote managerial entrenchment and opportunism. A survey from Russia indicates that managers use their equity as a deterrent against outside investors who may threaten them with dismissal (Filatotchev *et al.*, 1999). Diffused share ownership among individual, inexperienced shareholders is unlikely to provide an effective constraint on self-serving behaviour by former 'Red Directors'. Moreover, the give-away nature of the distribution of equity means that insiders have insufficient investment to motivate them to protect their firm, thus further encouraging shirking (Filatotchev *et al.*, 1996). Privatization buy-outs that involve insiders purchasing the firm's assets and thus taking on a commitment to reimburse outside funding may introduce a stronger pressure to restructure. However, these pressures may be weakened where budget constraints remain relatively soft.

Ownership concentration and 'private benefits of control'[4]
When entrenched former 'Red Directors' are unable to introduce the very often painful restructuring measures, 'externally imposed change may be the only way to bring the organization back into fit with its environment' (Dunphy and Stace, 1988:320). For example, outside shareholders may be powerful enough to engage in screening and managerial selection mechanisms, when inefficient managers are identified and replaced by more able and better trained corporate entrepreneurs (Holderness and Sheehan, 1988).

There is a growing body of research in the economics and management literature that links the pattern and amount of stock ownership with managerial behaviour and, eventually, corporate performance (see Jensen and Warner, 1988; Short, 1994, for a comprehensive survey). Within this research, the vast majority of studies have been focused on ownership concentration effects in large, publicly traded firms. These studies suggest that large-block outside ownership may be an effective counter-balance to managerial opportunism. Companies may have large, undiversified shareholders that play a critical leadership and monitoring role. They have both the incentives and the means to restrain the self-serving behaviour of managers (Maug, 1998; Zeckhauser and Pound, 1990). For example, using structural equation modelling, Hoskisson *et al.* (1994) showed that block shareholders may not allow a poor strategy such as diversification to evolve into poor performance, therefore decreasing the magnitude of restructuring. Wruck (1989) provides empirical evidence that suggests that, when managers have an opportunity to conduct a self-serving deal that damages shareholders, the decision to sell a block of securities to non-management investors increases shareholder wealth. Finally, the study by McConnell and Servaes (1990) suggests a positive relationship between institutional share ownership and Tobin's Q.

Therefore privatization divestments through sales of large blocks of shares in the former state-owned firms to dominant ('strategic') investors may be a viable alternative to insider privatizations from the enterprise efficiency point of view. However, previous research has recognized several possible governance roles for large-block shareholders, some of which are likely to be value-enhancing while others are likely to have negative effects (see Hansmann, 1996; Shleifer and Vishny, 1997, for an extensive discussion).

A fast-growing literature on the optimal ownership structures of firms, depending on the levels of 'private benefits of control' (for example, Grossman and Hart, 1988; Harris and Raviv, 1988), has extended research beyond the conventional US/UK environment and has recently become a focal point of theoretical and policy debates. This research is particularly important for countries with a relatively low protection of minority investors and where expropriation of minority shareholders by the controlling shareholders is extensive. This expropriation may take various forms, such as related-party transactions, use of transfer pricing, asset stripping and other forms of 'tunnelling' of revenue and assets from firms (see Morck *et al.*, 1998; La Porta *et al.*, 2000b, for an extensive discussion). As a result, the primary agency problem in this environment is not the failure of professional managers to satisfy the objectives of diffused shareholders, but rather the expropriation of minority shareholders by the controlling shareholders (La Porta *et al.*, 2000a; Shleifer and Vishny, 1997).

However, the willingness of controlling shareholders to expropriate minority investors is constrained by their financial incentives. Following the agency framework developed by Jensen and Meckling (1976), a number of authors link these incentives to equity ownership by controlling shareholders that enhances their interest in a non-distortionary distribution of dividends. Other things equal, ownership concentration should lead to lower expropriation and, as a result, countries with poor investor protection would typically exhibit more concentrated control of firms than countries which have good investor protection (La Porta *et al.*, 2000b). In addition, Bebchuck (1994; 1999) develops a rent-protection theory of corporate ownership structure, suggesting that, when private benefits of control are large in countries with weak legal protection, concentrated ownership is the only viable arrangement. In his model, controlling shareholders will tend to maintain control because surrendering it would attract attempts to assemble a controlling stake by rivals seeking to capture these private benefits. Dyck (2000) extends this analysis by suggesting that ownership concentration is not only more stable, it may even be less costly, since it prevents quick and destructive equity dilution in the situation where dispersed shareholders are uncertain about future control. He provides evidence that countries that had dispersed ownership at the time of privatization, such as the Czech Republic, report steady increases in concentration over time. This evidence is consistent with the view that in established publicly traded firms ownership concentration is a substitute for legal protection in providing the functions of corporate governance (La Porta *et al.*, 1998).

Some researchers have indicated, however, that concentrated shareholding may create a trade-off between incentives and entrenchment (La Porta *et al.*, 2000a; Short, 1994). In particular, a lack of diversification and limited liquidity mean that large shareholders are affected adversely by the company's idiosyncratic risk (Maug, 1998). To compensate for this risk, they may use an opportunity to collude with managers or shift wealth from minority shareholders to themselves. For example, Pound (1988) argues that large institutional investors and unaffiliated blockholders are likely to side with management ('the strategic-alignment' hypothesis) or they can be influenced by existing business relationships with management ('the conflict-of-interest' hypothesis).

Building on this research, some authors point out that ownership concentration *per se* may negatively affect the value of the firm when majority shareholders have a possibility to abuse their position of dominant control at the expense of minority shareholders (Bebchuk, 1994; Stiglitz, 1985). As a result, at some level of ownership concentration the distinction between insiders and outsiders becomes blurred and blockholders, no matter what their identity is, may have strong incentives to divert resources in ways that make them better off at the expense of other shareholders (Wruck, 1989). La Porta *et al.* (1998) suggest that, in this environment, firms with concentrated owners would face difficulty raising equity finance because minority investors fear expropriation by managers and concentrated owners. Modigliani and Perotti (1997) also suggest that poor protection of minority shareholder rights and the ability of controlling shareholders to extract a 'control premium' in excess of their legal residual claims reduce the ability of the firm to raise equity capital and, as a result, profitable new ventures will be forsaken.

To summarize, there may be a trade-off between incentives and rent-seeking effects associated with concentrated shareholding. On the one hand, the entrenchment perspective suggests that large-block shareholders may abuse their power and try to extract a control premium at the expense of other shareholders, and this opportunistic behaviour would deter outside investment and negatively affect the firm's value. On the other hand, the greater the concentration of cash flow rights in the hands of large-block shareholders, the greater are their incentives to distribute dividends in a non-distortionary way (La Porta *et al.*, 2000a). A balance between these two types of behaviour depends not only on the firm's idiosyncratic characteristics (the level of diversity, control systems, and so on) but on the firm's environmental factors, such as the prevailing legal and regulatory frameworks.

To illustrate these arguments, Filatotchev *et al.* (2001) suggest a simple theoretical model that illustrates ex ante effects of concentrated ownership on outside investment decisions and the firm's value. In this model, the firm can pursue value-enhancing investment projects under the explicit assumption that its current internal investment resources are limited, and only outside investors can provide capital to restructure the firm and raise efficiency. Since enterprise restructuring and modernization in transition countries may be associated with potentially high moral hazard costs of debt finance, it is assumed that all investment projects will be financed by equity.

Suppose that an investment project would create the output Y, provided that the firm is restructured at restructuring costs of I. The firm's output is related to investment through a simple production function:

$$Y = \alpha \, I^{\beta}, \tag{16.8}$$

where $0 < \beta < 1$ because of the diminishing returns on investment. In a single-period model, and under the assumption that investors are risk-neutral, an investment project is efficient if:

$$I \leq Y. \tag{16.9}$$

Assume that a controlling shareholder ('the entrepreneur') has a majority of voting rights associated with cash flow or equity ownership λ in the firm, $0 < \lambda < 1$. In the environment of low protection of minority shareholders' rights, the controlling shareholder is able to extract the control premium s, and we define s as the share of corporate income that can be appropriated to the controlling shareholder before pro rata distribution ($0 < s < 1$). Following Modigliani and Perotti (1997), Bebchuk (1999) and La Porta *et al.* (2000a), let us also assume that the controlling shareholder will sell equity only up to the point where s/he retains a majority of voting rights because s/he values the ability to extract the control premium. Outside investors will only attach positive value to the firm if:

$$I \leq Y(1 - \lambda)(1 - s). \tag{16.10}$$

And, using (16.8) we obtain an equilibrium condition:

$$I = [\alpha(1 - \lambda)(1 - s)]^{1/1 - \beta}. \tag{16.11}$$

It is clear that investment is a decreasing function of s:

$$dI/ds = -\alpha[(1-\lambda)/(1-\beta)][\alpha(1-\lambda)(1-s)]^{\beta/1-\beta} < 0.$$

In other words, the greater is the control premium, the less will be the volume of externally funded investment.

Filatotchev *et al.* (2001) develop this framework further by suggesting that the expropriation of minority shareholders may have costs implications, since the controlling shareholder has to engage in legal but costly manoeuvring to divert profits, such as setting up intermediary companies, facing legal challenges, taking risks of being fined and soon. If $C(s,\lambda)$ is the share of the profits that the controlling shareholder wastes when s is diverted, $C_s > 0$, $C_{ss} > 0$, then s/he only receives

$$U = sY + \lambda(1-s)Y - C(s,\lambda)Y.$$

The controlling shareholder maximizes U with respect to s, and an optimal value of s^* which must satisfy the following equation:

$$C_s(s^*,\lambda) = 1 - \lambda. \tag{16.12}$$

If we differentiate the first order condition (16.5) with respect to λ we obtain:

$$ds^*/d\lambda = -(1 + C_{s\lambda}(s^*,\lambda))/C_{ss}(s^*,\lambda). \tag{16.13}$$

This gives us important comparative static information. Following La Porta *et al.* (2000a) let us assume that $C_s(s^*,\lambda) = C_s(s^*) = constant$ for all λ. Then

$$ds^*/d\lambda = -1/C_{ss}(s^*,\lambda) < 0.$$

In other words, if the marginal costs of expropriation are independent of λ, then the higher is the cash flow ownership by the controlling shareholder, the lower are the incentives to expropriate. This is a counterpart to the Jensen and Meckling (1976) analysis of the incentive effect of concentrated entrepreneurial ownership on the consumption of perquisites (see Shleifer and Wolfenzon, 2000, for a detailed discussion).

However, the effect of ownership concentration on the size of the control premium is more ambiguous when the marginal costs of expropriation are falling with an increase in λ; that is, $C_{s\lambda}(s^*,\lambda) < 0$. For example, concentration of cash flow rights may be accompanied by a more than proportional increase in voting rights (Claessens *et al.*, 1999; Bebchuk, 1999; Bebchuk *et al.*, 1999), and this concentration of voting control may make expropriation less costly because it reduces the probability of minority shareholders effectively colluding against the controlling shareholder. In addition, the separation between cash flow and control rights also reduces the extent of the incentive effect of concentrated ownership (Bebchuk *et al.*, 1999; La Porta *et al.*, 1998). In a particular case when $1 + C_{s\lambda}(s^*,\lambda) < 0$, that is, the marginal costs of expropriation are falling relatively faster compared to an increase in the cash flow rights, we have a situation where $ds^*/d\lambda > 0$. In other words, an increase in the cash flow ownership will lead to an increase in expropriation. By differentiating (16.11) with respect to λ and using (16.13) it is easy to show in this particular case that $dI/d\lambda < 0$; that is, investment diminishes with an increase in ownership concentration. Since the firm's performance is directly related to outside investment, it follows that an increase in λ will also reduce the value of the firm Y, and this illustrates the entrenchment effect of concentrated ownership discussed by Morck *et al.* (1988; 1998), Wruck (1989) and others.

This simple model illustrates that privatization's impact on the firm's investment and performance depends on the interaction between the entrenchment and incentive effects of concentrated ownership. The balance between these two opposite effects is determined by expropriation costs and these costs largely depend on how far country-specific circumstances, such as the legal protection of minority shareholders and reputational considerations, limit the opportunism of controlling shareholders (Claessens *et al.*, 1999; Dyck, 2000). In addition, constraints on the tradeability of shares may also change the balance between the incentive and entrenchment roles of concentrated ownership: the private benefits of control may be more valuable for an entrenched controlling shareholder when s/he is wholly insulated from any takeover threat (Bebchuk *et al.*, 1999).

Privatization and governance roles of 'relationship investors'
In the case of the weak legal and regulatory framework and the large relative weight of intermediated credit to direct equity financing in many countries around the world, the relationship governance of either the Japanese or the German model may substitute for open capital markets of the US/UK type. A number of authors raise the issue of the governance role of debt and debtholders (Hart, 1995; Jensen, 1986). Debt can provide a hard efficiency incentive mechanism for management, in the sense of the need to meet interest payments and the bankruptcy procedures which can be invoked when there is a failure to meet such payments. It can also be associated with the provision of active monitoring through bank–corporate relationships, involving regular information provision, face-to-face management meetings, flexible interpretation of covenant breaches and so on (Booth and Deli, 1999; Myers and Majluf, 1984). More generally, Dewatripont and Tirole

(1994) show that there is a complementarity between debt and equity in terms of corporate governance functions.

Aspects of an integrated system of monitoring of management by banks in the west may be more important in enforcing performance than a simple reliance on default. Banks and other relationship shareholders are generally found to develop intimate and well-informed relationships with company executives, which facilitates provision of funds for company expansion (Franks and Mayer, 1997). This process is particularly suited to the contingency where the firm's activities are opaque to outsiders, either because of high technical complexity (such as is evidenced by high levels of R&D expenditure – see Zeckhauser and Pound, 1990; Roe, 1990) or when the firm is crucially dependent upon idiosyncratic personal relationships with clients or suppliers, thus hampering active monitoring by outside investors.

Another stream of research highlights the relevance of large diversified corporate groups in less developed economies. These groups may serve the function of creating a private capital market, where smaller firms have access to finance inside the group. Modigliani and Perotti (1997) suggest that the ability of a holding company or an 'in-house' bank to capture the benefits from control ensures a steady supply of financing. These groups may also develop long-term relations with lenders to attenuate the risk of moral hazard. Empirical evidence indicates that Japanese firms associated with financial *keiretsu* are not as credit-constrained in their investment choices as independent firms (Berglöf and Perotti, 1994). Khanna and Palepu's (2000) 'institutional voids' theory suggests that the development of diversified groups in emerging markets may be a response to market and legal imperfections that increase the transaction costs of external funding.

Building on this research, some authors suggest that 'relationship investors', such as customers, suppliers of inputs and finance, and so on, should be a target group of investors in the process of the privatization of state-owned enterprises in transition economies (Frydman *et al.*, 1993). In particular, bank ownership and control of industrial firms may offer significant economies of scope that may be crucial to particular stages of privatization development. In privatization buy-outs in Hungary, banks providing finance have the power to obtain information and control rights in the company as a condition of extending the loan (Karsai and Wright, 1994). Further evidence from Hungary indicates that venture capital firms play an important role in financing privatization buy-outs and attach great importance to board membership and their role in helping to form and manage the board, monitoring financial performance and managing crises and problems (Karsai *et al.*, 1997). However, banks may be more likely to monitor investments through receipt of regular reports than through active board involvement (Karsai and Wright, 1994), so that board composition may still be weak. Similarly, the expertise of venture capital firms may be immature in Hungary compared to developed markets and contextual factors may mean that their board role may be significantly reduced if they do not have majority ownership (Karsai *et al.*, 1997). In their analysis of the privatization of Russian shops, Barberis *et al.* (1996) found that those shops which were sold to outsiders were significantly more likely to lay off managers. Although the authors concede that their findings may not be directly applicable to industrial firms, this evidence suggests that privatization divestments to financial institutions and foreign strategic investors, in contrast to privatization to insiders, could be followed by the development of more effective systems of corporate governance and control that identify and remove underperforming managers.

Although they provide firms with ready access to funds for expansion, relationship investors have been criticized for personal involvement with executives in failing companies, where 'rescue packages' are the norm (Macey and Miller, 1997). In particular, Harris and Raviv (1990) provide evidence that German banks are reluctant to discipline managers in client companies, especially when they are linked to these companies through a system of cross-shareholding. Banks with board seats and/or shares in a firm have been seen to protect their investments by advocating massive internal cash transfers within German firms into hidden reserves, that can be used to smooth declining firm income in a crisis. This amounts to banks forming a coalition with managers to keep down dividends payable to outside shareholders (Baums, 1993). In addition, there is some evidence that bank holdings distort investment decisions: Thomas and Waring (1999) report that investment decisions in large, bank-controlled firms in Japan and Germany are influenced more by liquidity considerations than by expected investment returns, as is the case in the USA.

Therefore there is an ambiguity concerning the corporate governance effects of relationship investors with dual (or multiple) roles within the firm. There may be either positive spillover effects or efficiency loss as shareholders perform other roles simultaneously (for example, banks as shareholders, suppliers of credit and financial advisers), enjoying information advantages as 'insiders' (Myers and Majluf, 1984). As a result, sophisticated financial institutions and legal provisions are needed to discourage the abuse of multiple roles. In terms of access to outside financing, banks and other fixed-claim holders with existing roles in the company must also be trusted (Barney and Hansen, 1994) as shareholders not to indulge in short-term opportunism and/or collude with dominant shareholders, thus raising their own economic rents in relation to their fixed-payment services, at the expense of the residual incomes of minority shareholders. For example, Frydman and colleagues (1996) show that, although voucher investment funds in Russia have board representation in at least some of the enterprises in their portfolio, they are either passive investors in insider-dominated enterprises or attempt to find some way of working with management in order to have some limited influence.

These arguments also help us to reassess the consequences of the most recent trends in the transition economies associated with the rapid development of holding companies. A particularly characteristic example of this trend is found in the oil and gas industries in Russia, which are dominated by holding companies such as Gazprom, Sibneft, Tyumen Oil Company (TNK) and YUKOS. Most of these conglomerates have been created at the second stage of the Russian privatization programme, when the State Property Committee used a 'loan-for-shares' scheme as a privatization method. These companies are fixing the boundaries of their empires through intra-holding consolidations, mergers and single-share swaps. They are also characterized by concentrated ownership. Moreover, outside shareholders in each of them have suffered a dilution of their holdings, at different stages and to various degrees. In addition, many industries in Russia have also experienced a rapid development of financial–industrial groups (FIGs) that represent large diversified holding companies owned by banks, trading companies and so on. Very often FIGs and other holding companies are actively trying to fend off pressure for their members to restructure, and sometimes become simply a vehicle for creating pyramidal ownership structures. La Porta *et al.* (1999) suggest that these structures can be used by controlling shareholders to make existing shareholders pay the costs but not share all of the benefits of new ventures. Therefore, instead of being the 'flagships' of the fledging Russian private economy, these holding companies and FIGs may turn into examples of poor corporate governance and inefficiency.

A possible collusion between the dominant owners and providers of debt (or a passive acceptance by debt-holders of the fact that the dominant owner is abusing its power at the expense of minority shareholders) not only produces a negative impact on the firm's value, but can also create serious resource constraints for the development of entrepreneurial firms. This is so, in particular, in emerging market economies without developed equity markets and large numbers of investors willing to fund initial public offerings.

Conclusions

Firms in transition economies have been privatized to generate various macroeconomic benefits, such as employment, competitiveness and an inflow of direct foreign investment. In addition to the macroeconomic benefits, privatization (using financial markets and infusion of new capital) has been linked directly to improvements in firm performance. Recent studies on CEE, however, have found that firm performance may depend on additional factors (Filatotchev *et al.*, 2000; Sachs *et al.*, 2000), underlining the importance of continued contextual examinations of privatization (Cuervo and Villalonga, 2000).

This chapter outlines the theory and policy debates concerning the corporate governance implications of various ownership patterns. It provides further support for the case of strong regulatory and capital market institutions and effective enforcement of 'good corporate governance' rules, especially concerning the protection of minority shareholders (OECD, 1999). So far, most studies of corporate governance problems have focused on issues related to the consequences of opportunistic behaviour of insiders and their opposition to outside control. This chapter shows that the protection of minority shareholders from the blockholders' opportunism is as important for enterprise restructuring and development of an efficient system of corporate governance as protection against entrenched management. In addition, this conclusion is extended to an environment where debt finance is predominant and equity finance plays a minor role. In such an environment, the collusion between dominant owners and financial institutions may lead to further efficiency distortions. Further research on the post-privatization evolution of ownership and control may help understanding of the complex and dynamic relationships between ownership patterns and economic performance in transition economies.

Notes

1. In this chapter, restitution, another specific form of privatization in CEE, is not discussed. Despite its political importance, returning state assets to their original owners has been difficult in CEE owing to either inadequate or conflicting ownership records (Brada, 1996; Megginson and Netter, 2001).
2. Later becoming the Hungarian Privatization and State Holding Company, APVRt.
3. This section is based on I. Filatotchev, M. Wright and M. Bleaney (1999) 'Privatization, insider control and managerial entrenchment in Russia', *Economics of Transition*, 7, 481–504; reproduced with permission of Blackwell Publishers.
4. This section is based on I. Filatotchev, R. Kepelyushnikov, N. Dyomina and S. Aukusionek (2001) 'The effects of ownership concentration on investment and performance in privatised firms in Russia', *Managerial and Decision Economics*, 22, 299–313; reproduced with permission of John Wiley & Sons Limited.

References

Aghion, P. and O. Blanchard (1998) 'On privatisation methods in Eastern Europe and their implications', *Economics of Transition*, 6(1), 87–99.

Ang, J. (1991) 'Small business uniqueness and the theory of financial management', *Journal of Small Business Finance*, 1(1), 1–13.

Barberis, N., M. Boyko, A. Shleifer and N. Tsukanova (1996) 'How does privatisation work? Evidence from Russian shops,' *Journal of Political Economy*, 104(4), 764–90.

Barney, J. and M. Hansen (1994) 'Trustworthiness as a source of competitive advantage', *Strategic Management Journal*, 15 (Special Issue), 175–90.

Baums, T. (1993) 'Takeovers versus institutions in corporate governance in Germany', in D.D. Prentice and P.R.J. Holland (eds), *Contemporary Issues in Corporate Governance*, Oxford: Clarendon Press.

Bebchuk, L. (1994) 'Efficient and inefficient sales of corporate control', *Quarterly Journal of Economics*, 109(4), 957–94.

Bebchuk, L. (1999) 'A rent-protection theory of corporate ownership and control', National Bureau of Economic Research Working Paper 7203, Cambridge, MA.

Bebchuk, L., R. Kraakman and G. Triantis (1999) 'Stock pyramids, cross-ownership, and dual class equity: The creation and agency costs of separating control from cash flow rights', National Bureau of Economic Research Working Paper 6951, Cambridge, MA.

Berglöf, E. and E. Perotti (1994) 'The governance structure of Japanese keiretsu', *Journal of Financial Economics*, 35, 45–57.

Blanchard, O. and P. Aghion (1996) 'On insider privatisation', *European Economic Review*, 40, 759–66.

Blasi, J. and A. Shleifer (1996) 'Corporate governance in Russia: an initial look', in R. Frydman, C.W. Gray and A. Rapaczynski (eds), *Corporate governance in Central Europe and Russia*, Vol. 2, Budapest: Central European University Press.

Blasi, J., M. Kroumova and D. Kruse (1997) *Kremlin Capitalism. Privatizing the Russian Economy*, Ithaca and London: Cornell University Press.

Booth, J. and D. Deli (1999) 'On executives of financial institutions as outside directors', *Journal of Corporate Finance*, 5, 227–50.

Boycko, M., A. Shleifer and R. Vishny (1995) *Privatising Russia*, Cambridge, MA: MIT Press.

Brada, J. (1996) 'Privatization is transition: Or is it?', *Journal of Economic Perspectives*, 10, 67–86.

Carlin, W. and P. Aghion (1996) 'Restructuring outcomes and the evolution of ownership patterns in Central and Eastern Europe', *Economics of Transition*, 4, 371–88.

Claessens, S., S. Djankov, J. Fan and L. Lang (1999) 'Expropriation of minority shareholders: Evidence from East Asia', World Bank Policy Research Working Paper 2088, World Bank, Washington, DC.

Cuervo, A. and B. Villalong (2000) 'Explaining the variance in the performance effects of privatization', *Academy of Management Review*, 25, 581–90.

Dewatripont, M. and J. Tirole (1994) 'A theory of debt and equity. Diversity of securities and management–shareholders congruence', *Quarterly Journal of Economics*, 109(4), 1027–54.

D'Souza, J.D. and W.L. Megginson (1999) 'The financial and operating performance of privatized firms during the 1990s', *Journal of Finance*, 54, 1397–438.

Dunphy, D.C. and D.A. Stace (1988) 'Transformational and coercive strategies for planned organizational change: beyond the OD model', *Organization Studies*, 9, 317–34.

Dyck, I. (2000) 'Ownership structure, legal protection and corporate governance', mimeo, Harvard Business School, Boston, MA.

Earle, J. and S. Estrin (1996) 'Employee ownership in transition', in R. Frydman, C.W. Gray and A. Rapaczynski (eds), *Corporate governance in Central Europe and Russia*, Vol. 2, Budapest: Central European University Press.

EBRD (European Bank for Reconstruction & Development) (1998) *Transition Report, 1998: Enterprise performance and growth*, London: EBRD.

Estrin, S. (1983) *Self-management: economic theory and Yugoslav practice*, Cambridge: Cambridge University Press.

Estrin, S. (1986) 'Long-run supply responses under self-management: Reply', *Journal of Comparative Economics*, 10(3), 342–5.

Estrin, S. and M. Wright (1999) 'Corporate governance in the former Soviet Union: An overview', *Journal of Comparative Economics*, 27(3), 398–421.

Filatotchev, I., T. Buck and V. Zhukov (2000) 'Downsizing in privatized firms in Russia, Ukraine and Belarus', *Academy of Management Journal*, 43, 286–304.

Filatotchev, I., M. Wright and M. Bleaney (1999) 'Privatization, insider control and managerial entrenchment in Russia', *Economics of Transition*, 7, 481–504.

Filatotchev, I., R. Hoskisson, T. Buck and M. Wright (1996) 'Corporate restructuring in Russian privatizations: Implications for US investors', *California Management Review*, 38, 87–105.

Filatotchev, I., R. Kepelyushnikov, N. Dyomina and S. Aukusionek (2001) 'The effects of ownership concentration on investment and performance in privatised firms in Russia', *Managerial and Decision Economics*, 22, 299–313.

Franks, J. and C. Mayer (1997) 'Corporate ownership and control in the UK, Germany and France', *Journal of Applied Corporate Finance*, 9(4), 30–45.

Frydman, R., K. Pistor and A. Rapaczynsky (1996) 'Exit and voice after mass privatisation: the case of Russia', *European Economic Review*, 40(3–5), 581–8.

Frydman, R., E. Phelps, A. Rapaczynski and A. Shleifer (1993) 'Needed mechanisms of corporate governance and finance in Eastern Europe', *Economics of Transition*, 1(1), 171–207.

Grossman, S.J. and O.D. Hart (1988) 'One share–one vote and the market for corporate control' *Journal of Financial Economics*, 20, 175–202.

Hansmann, H. (1990) 'The viability of worker ownership: an economic perspective on the political structure of the firm', in M. Aoki, B. Gustafsson and O. Williamson (eds), *The firm as a nexus of treaties*, London: Sage.

Hansmann, H. (1996) *The Ownership of Enterprise*, Cambridge, MA: Harvard University Press, pp. xi, 372.

Harris, M. and A. Raviv (1988) 'Corporate governance. Voting rights and majority rules', *Journal of Financial Economics*, 20, 203–35.

Harris, M. and A. Raviv (1990) 'Capital structure and the information role of debt', *Journal of Finance*, 45, 321–50.

Hart, O. (1995) *Firms, Contracts and Financial Structure*, Oxford: Oxford University Press.

Holderness, C.G. and D.P. Sheehan (1988) 'The role of majority shareholders in publicly held corporations', *Journal of Financial Economics*, 20, 317–46.

Hoskisson, R.E., R.A. Johnson and D.D. Moesel (1994) 'Corporate divestiture intensity in restructuring firms: Effects of governance, strategy and performance' *Academy of Management Journal*, 37, 1207–51.

Jensen, M. (1986) 'Agency costs of free cash flow, corporate finance, and takeovers', *American Economic Review*, 76, 323–9.

Jensen, M.C. and W. Meckling (1976) 'Theory of the firm: Managerial behavior, agency costs, and ownership structure', *Journal of Financial Economics*, 3, 305–60.

Jensen, M.C. and J.B. Warner (1988) 'The distribution of power among corporate managers, shareholders and directors', *Journal of Financial Economics*, 20, 3–24.

Karsai, J. and M. Wright (1994) 'Accountability, Governance and Finance in Hungarian Buyouts', *Europe–Asia Studies*, 46, 997–1016.

Karsai, J., M. Wright and I. Filatotchev (1997) 'Venture capital in transition economies: The case of Hungary', *Entrepreneurship Theory & Practice*, 21, 93–110.

Khanna, T. and K. Palepu (2000) 'The future of business groups in emerging markets: Long-run evidence from Chile', *Academy of Management Journal*, 43, 268–85.

Kornai, J. (1992) *The Socialist System*, Princeton, NJ: Princeton University Press.

La Porta, R., F. Lopez-de-Silanes and A. Shleifer (1999) 'Corporate ownership around the world', *Journal of Finance*, 54, 471–517.

La Porta, R., F. Lopez-de-Silanes, A. Shleifer and R. Vishny (1998) 'Law and finance', *Journal of Political Economy*, 106, 1113–55.

La Porta, R., F. Lopez-de-Silanes, A. Shleifer and R. Vishny (2000a) 'Investor protection and corporate valuation', mimeo, Harvard University, Boston, MA.

La Porta, R., F. Lopez-de-Silanes, A. Shleifer and R. Vishny (2000b) 'Investor protection and corporate governance', *Journal of Financial Economics*, 58, 3–27.

Linz, S. (1997) 'Russian firms in transition: Champions, challengers and chaff', *Comparative Economic Studies*, 39(2), 1–36.

Macey, J. and G. Miller (1997) 'Universal banks are not the answer to America's corporate governance "problem": A look at Germany, Japan and the US', *Journal of Applied Corporate Finance*, 9(4), 57–73.

Maug, E. (1998) 'Large shareholders as monitors: Is there a trade-off between liquidity and control?', *Journal of Finance*, 53, 65–92.

McConnell, J.J. and H. Servaes (1990) 'Additional evidence on equity ownership and corporate value', *Journal of Financial Economics*, 27, 595–612.

Megginson, W. and J. Netter (2001) 'From State to Market: A Survey of Empirical Studies on Privatization', *Journal of Economic Literature*, 39, 321–89.

Modigliani, F. and E. Perotti (1997) 'Protection of minority interest and the development of security markets', *Managerial and Decision Economics*, 18, 519–28.

Morck, R., A. Shleifer and R. Vishny (1988) 'Management ownership and market valuation: An empirical analysis', *Journal of Financial Economics*, 20, 293–316.

Morck, R., D. Strangeland and B. Yeung (1998) 'Inherited wealth, corporate control and economic growth: The Canadian disease?', National Bureau of Economic Research Working Paper 6814, Cambridge, MA.

Myers, S.C. and N.S. Majluf (1984) 'Corporate financing and investment decisions when firms have information that investors do not have', *Journal of Financial Economics*, 20, 187–221.

Newman, K. (2000) 'Organizational transformation during institutional upheaval', *Academy of Management Review*, 25, 602–19.

North, D.C. (1990) *Institutions, institutional change and economic performance*, Cambridge: Cambridge University Press.

OECD (1999) *Principles of Corporate Governance*, Paris: OECD Publications.

Pendleton, A., N. Wilson and M. Wright (1998) 'The perception and effects of share ownership: Empirical evidence from employee buy-outs', *British Journal of Industrial Relations*, 36(1), 99–124.

Peng, M.W. and P.S. Heath (1996) 'The growth of the firm in planned economies in transition: institutions, organizations and strategic choice', *Academy of Management Review*, 21, 492–528.

Pound, J. (1988) 'Proxy contests and the efficiency of shareholder oversight', *Journal of Financial Economics*, 20, 237–65.

Puffer, S. (1994) 'Understanding the bear: a portrait of Russian business leaders', *Academy of Management Executives*, 8, 41–54.

Richman, B. (1965) *Soviet Management*, Englewood Cliffs, NJ: Prentice-Hall.

Roe, M.J. (1990) 'Political and legal restraints on ownership and control of public companies', *Journal of Financial Economics*, 27, 7–42.

Russian Economic Trends (1995) Volume 4, Number 1. London: Whurr Publishers.

Sachs, J. and A. Warner (1995) 'Economic reform and the process of global integration', *Brookings Papers on Economic Activity*, 2, 1–118.

Sachs, J., C. Zinnes and Y. Eilat (2000) 'The gains from privatization in transition economies: Is change of ownership enough?', CAER II Discussion Paper 62, Harvard Institute for International Development, Cambridge, MA.

Shleifer, A. and R. Vishny (1997) 'A survey of corporate governance', *Journal of Finance*, 52, 737–83.

Shleifer, A. and D. Wolfenzon (2000) 'Investor protection and equity markets', mimeo, Harvard University.

Short, H. (1994) 'Ownership, control, financial structure and the performance of firms', *Journal of Economic Surveys*, 8, 203–49.

Spicer, A., G.A. McDermott and B. Kogut (2000) 'Entrepreneurship and privatization in Central Europe: The tenuous balance between construction and creation', *Academy of Management Review*, 25, 630–49.

Stark, D. (1996) 'Recombinant property in East European capitalism', *American Journal of Sociology*, 101, 993–1027.

Stiglitz, J.E. (1985) 'Credit markets and the control of capital', *Journal of Money, Credit and Banking*, 17, 133–52.

Takla, L. (1994) 'The relationship between privatization and reform of the banking sector: the case of the Czech Republic and Slovakia', in S. Estrin (ed.), *Privatisation in Central and Eastern Europe*, London: Longman.

Thomas, L.G. and G. Waring (1999) 'Competing capitalisms: Capital investments in American, German and Japanese Firms', *Strategic Management Journal*, 20(3), 729–48.

Whitley, R. and L. Czaban (1998) 'Institutional transformation and enterprise change in an emergent capitalist economy: The case of Hungary', *Organization Studies*, 19, 259–80.

Wright, M., S. Thompson, K. Robbie and P. Wong (1995) 'Management buy-outs in the short and the long term', *Journal of Business and Finance Accounting*, 22(4), 461–82.

Wruck, K.H. (1989) 'Equity ownership concentration and firm value. Evidence from private equity financing', *Journal of Financial Economics*, 23, 3–28.

Zeckhauser, R.J. and J. Pound (1990) 'Are large shareholders effective monitors? An investigation of share ownership and corporate performance', in R.G. Rubbard (ed.), *Asymmetric Information, Corporate Finance and Investment*, Chicago and London: University of Chicago Press.

17 Privatization in Russia

Paul Hare and Alexander Muravyev

Introduction[1]

In all countries privatization programmes are pursued to fulfil a range of state and/or social objectives. The methods adopted are commonly influenced by the priority ranking of these objectives, and this can change over time for either political or economic reasons. In any case, the outcome of a privatization programme is a set of privatized firms whose subsequent economic behaviour and performance will depend not only upon their new private sector status, but upon many other features of the economic environment that have little or nothing to do with privatization *per se*. This, of course, is why privatization in the transition economies, where much of the institutional environment for a market-type economy is still under construction (see Hare, 2001), sometimes turns out to be disappointing in its impact on the economy, as compared to privatization in a long-established market-type economy such as the UK. Russia is a case in point.

Overall economic performance, even in an economy like Russia's that was predominantly state-owned for decades under the communist system, depends both on the way the former state-owned firms function post-privatization and on the activities of wholly new firms. At the start of transition, the importance of the latter factor was seriously underestimated, with the result that external advice as well as official policies paid rather more attention to organizing privatization and implementing it speedily than now appears justified. Later, attention shifted to new firm formation and the policies and institutions needed to support that aspect of building a private sector. Growth in the economy is then generated as a result of a dynamic process that includes the following elements: (a) entry of new firms (one hopes of relatively high productivity); (b) growth, restructuring and transformation of existing businesses (both state-owned enterprises (SOEs), former SOEs, and new entrants); and (c) the orderly closure of failing businesses (and one hopes that these are overwhelmingly low productivity businesses).

The balance between these elements can vary a good deal between countries and over time. For instance, if too many firms close at a time when few new ones are being established, the result will be rapidly rising unemployment rates and withdrawals from the labour market, with costly implications for public expenditure. There could also be political unrest if such change was perceived to be too rapid. On the other hand, if there is little new entry and there are few closures, the economy is not likely to be growing very successfully. This is closer to the Russian pattern over the 1990s, at least up to the end of the decade.

In what follows, we proceed as follows. First, we set out the basic facts about Russian privatization since 1991. Then we consider some of the barriers to change in Russia, focusing on the banks, financial markets more generally, and the labour market. Further barriers associated with the maintenance of traditional networks, the use of barter and similar payment mechanisms, and the linkages between enterprises and the state are examined later. This discussion helps to explain why restructuring has been relatively slow in Russia thus far. Changing tack a little, the chapter then addresses the particular issue of the public utilities in Russia and how they are being or are likely to be privatized. Finally, the chapter concludes by outlining some practical policy proposals through which Russia could yet develop a thriving private sector.

The process of privatization in Russia

'Voucher privatization . . . was a large-scale programme largely of a socio-political rather than an economic character. It was a fundamental means to create the socio-political preconditions for solving economic problems' (Anatoly Chubais, Head of the State Committee for the Management of State Property, 1994).

According to the conventional wisdom of transition economics, it was necessary first to achieve macroeconomic stabilization, then (or in parallel) to liberalize domestic prices and foreign trade, moving on finally to privatization and enterprise restructuring (for example, see Portes, 1991; for a more critical view of early transition mistakes, see Portes, 1994). Throughout the whole process, a great deal of institutional change would also be going on to enable the emerging market economy to function well (see Hare, 2001). In practice, many countries, including Russia, liberalized first and then found that the ensuing burst of inflation, together with losses of tax revenue, required even more stringent stabilization efforts than initially anticipated. Thus the Gaidar reforms initiated in January 1992 substantially – though far from completely – liberalized prices and trade, and the ensuing burst of inflation was not quickly brought under control (see OECD, 1995; 2000; EBRD, various years). Hence, when Russia embarked upon its programme of mass privatization, in the period 1992–4, it did so in an economy that was still experiencing high inflation and substantial government deficits, and in which financial discipline at the enterprise level was practically non-existent (see Leijonhufvud and Craver, 2001).

The task of privatizing the Russian economy was of an enormous scale.

As described in Blasi *et al.* (1997), the Russian economy in the late 1980s was dominated by large and medium-sized industrial enterprises that had more than 200 employees. These firms employed about 95 per cent of the industrial workforce and produced 95 per cent of production. Large firms with more than 1000 employees accounted for 75 per cent of employment and production. At the beginning of 1991, the Russian Federation had approximately 24000 medium-sized and large industrial enterprises and about 170000 smaller ones – astonishingly few businesses for such a large and diverse economy. Moreover, virtually all these businesses were in the state's hands.

As OECD (1995) explains, measures taken towards the end of the communist period in Russia had allowed a variety of cooperatives and leasehold enterprises to be established, often using the assets and labour force of existing SOEs to set up these new, quasi-private businesses. These measures gave rise to a wave of *spontaneous* or *nomenklatura* privatization. This spontaneous privatization took a variety of forms: from nomenklatura–bureaucratic privatization to managerial privatization and employee lease buy-outs (see Radygin, 1995 for an account of spontaneous privatization). The last scheme was especially widespread – the USSR law on leasing enacted in 1989 provided employees (worker collectives) with the opportunity to lease state enterprises with the right of buy-out; the enterprises were then re-established as 100 per cent insider-owned closed corporations. Formally, the lease buy-out privatization was stopped in mid-1991, when the law on privatization was passed; however, it de facto continued through 1991 and even 1992. The incidence of the lease buy-out scheme was particularly large in the retail trade and consumer services sectors, in light industry and some others. By February 1992, 9451 state enterprises accounting for 8 per cent of total employment were leased by their workers and managers (Blasi *et al.*, 1997).

Partly in order to regain control over this process, the Russian government launched its main privatization programme in mid-1992 (see Sutela, 1998). The programme classified enterprises into three categories: (a) small enterprises, to be sold by competitive bidding or lease buy-out; (b) large enterprises, to be converted to joint stock companies first (corporatization), then privatized through the mass privatization programme; and (c) medium enterprises, which could use either method. Some enterprises, such as most public utilities and firms in the defence sector, were exempted from this round of privatization. However, firms in retailing and consumer services, which had already been transferred to municipal ownership in 1991, were required to take part in the small privatization (that is, category (a), above), and mass privatization was required for about 5000 large enterprises and over 15000 medium-sized ones. In what follows, we mostly deal with the privatization, restructuring and performance of medium-sized and large firms.

Mass privatization

The process referred to as mass privatization in Russia implied, de facto, a combination of two main techniques: management–employee buy-outs and the mass privatization itself. Surprisingly, the main role in the process turned out to involve the former rather than the latter technique. Besides, some elements of the competitive sale of enterprise shares for cash – through cash auctions and investment tenders – were also incorporated in this stage of privatization.

Associated with the mass privatization, the Russian government distributed to the population, for a nominal fee of 25 roubles per voucher, around 150 million vouchers, each with a face value of 10 000 roubles. Since vouchers were freely circulating securities, people could use them as a means of payment when purchasing shares of enterprises at voucher auctions, or could sell them or invest them in specially created voucher investment funds. The management–employee buy-out component stemmed from the substantial privileges given by the state to managers and employees of the enterprises offered for privatization. The programme granted these groups the opportunity to receive a significant fraction of shares either for nothing or with substantial discounts.

Privatization of each enterprise started with a development of a privatization plan, which determined the procedures for the sale of shares as well as the proportions offered to various groups of potential investors, most importantly, employees and managers within the limits allowed in the privatization regulations. The plan was to be approved by the State Committee for the Management of State Property (GKI), the main Russian privatization agency, or its regional offices. The next step involved corporatization, which transformed state enterprises into open joint-stock companies wholly owned by the state. At this stage the charter capital of each firm was calculated as the book value of its assets other than land (and net of any outstanding debt), and the board of directors was appointed comprising the general manager with two votes, a representative of rank-and-file employees, and one representative each of the federal and local governments. Shares of newly created companies were transferred to the Federal Property Fund (FPF) and its regional branches, which acted as the sellers of enterprises.

Given the generous entitlements offered to managers and employees in the Russian privatization, these insiders were able to choose from among three options, or privatization methods, at a general meeting of their enterprise.

Option 1   Workers and managers were to receive 25 per cent of equity in the form of preference (non-voting) shares for nothing, plus the right to purchase a further 10 per cent of ordinary (voting) shares using cash or vouchers (at 30 per cent discount on the January 1992 book value). Senior managers of enterprises could purchase an additional 5 per cent of the stock in the form of ordinary shares.

Option 2   Workers and managers could buy – for cash or vouchers – 51 per cent of voting shares at 1.7 times the book value of the enterprise on January1992.

Option 3   A managing group (that could include existing management and workers, or any other physical or legal person) that took responsibility for the execution of the privatization plan and the prevention of enterprise bankruptcy could buy 30 per cent of the voting shares; a further 20 per cent could be purchased by management and workers (regardless of whether they were part of the managing group) at a 30 per cent discount.

In addition, employee shareholdings could be increased through so-called Employee Privatization Funds (*Fond Aktsionirovaniya Rabotnikov Predpriyatiya* – FARP). Ordinary shares amounting to 10 per cent of a firm's charter capital (if an enterprise followed the second option of privatization, the limit was 5 per cent) could be assigned to these funds for subsequent sale to employees on preferential terms. These funds could be created only if the application for privatization was submitted before 1 February 1994.

Option 1 was first proposed as the main approach, but it met with strong resistance from managers who, through regional leaders and through their representatives in the parliament,[2] were able to put sufficient pressure on the government to have Option 2 included in the programme (Åslund, 1995). Option 3 was also included as a result of pressure from the managerial lobby, but in practice the government banned its use at large enterprises and by imposing a 'no bankruptcy' condition finally made it rather unattractive for the managers. In all three options, given the rapid inflation in Russia during the relevant period, the prices that insiders were asked to pay for enterprise shares were scarcely more than nominal. In this sense, the mass privatization really was a give-away operation.

As for the mass privatization component, the programme envisaged that not less than 29 per cent of shares of each firm would be sold at a voucher auction, though in reality the figure was closer to 20 per cent. How people disposed of their vouchers was interesting: about half were invested by employees (and, as a rule, their relatives) in their own enterprises, either through closed subscription or through voucher auctions. A quarter of the vouchers were sold, and the remaining quarter was invested in voucher investment funds. These were closed-end funds that issued their own shares in exchange for vouchers invested by people; they were not obliged to repurchase the issued shares. The number of voucher funds peaked in 1994, amounting to 662. About 25 million people – over 16 per cent of citizens – became shareholders in these funds, which acquired over 10 per cent of the assets of the firms offered for privatization.

The last component of privatization, the competitive sale of shares at investment tenders or cash auctions, typically involved 10 to 20 per cent of the shares of enterprises. In an investment tender, which was a competition between investors to buy a block of shares, bidders had to agree to provide the company with additional assistance in the form of capital investments or technology. Similarly, cash auctions also produced capital for enterprises.

What were the results of this privatization programme? Quantitatively, they were extremely impressive. Firstly, within two years the programme transferred the majority of state-owned firms to private ownership, representing an unprecedented privatization effort in the world. As a result, by September 1994 there were already 100 000 privatized firms in Russia (outside agriculture), accounting for over 80 per cent of the industrial workforce (OECD, 1995). Most small enterprises had been privatized, and of the 24 000 or so medium and large enterprises, most had been corporatized and over 15 000 privatized by the end of 1994. Privatization then lost momentum to some extent, and continued at a much slower rate in subsequent years. Nevertheless, the main goal of separating the business sector from the state to limit the scope for state interference in enterprise activity was formally achieved.

Secondly, the privatization programme resulted in substantial ownership by managers and employees. Over 70 per cent of the firms offered for privatization chose Option 2, just over 21 per cent chose Option 1 for their privatization, giving insiders – managers and workers taken together – an overwhelming degree of control at most enterprises (see also Earle and Estrin, 2001). It is worth noting, however, that the incidence of employee ownership was much smaller in large enterprises, which represented the jewels of the economy. While, for example, 61 per cent of all enterprises that were privatized through corporatization in 1994 chose Option 2, their share in the total charter capital of all privatized firms was only 19 per cent (IET, 2001). In other words, in large, capital-intensive enterprises, insiders were unable to accumulate enough funds to buy 51 per cent of shares under Option 2; as a result, these firms mostly followed Option 1 privatization.

Thirdly, outsider control over firms was rare immediately after privatization. Outside ownership was typically spread among numerous investors, so that none had enough votes to influence corporate decision-making processes significantly. In particular, the role of voucher investment funds, which were originally considered as a potentially important locus of outsider control and a vehicle of restructuring, was limited. The most visible manifestation of this was the sharp reduction in the number of funds, so by mid-1997, only 350 funds remained out of the 662 existing in 1994. More importantly, the funds only played a minor role in the governance of privatized firms, mostly because their shareholdings in individual companies were limited by privatization regulations. Even when they had enough shares, they often lacked the necessary expertise in managing industrial enterprises. Finally, the funds could not provide enterprises with financial resources as they often held relatively illiquid shares in poorly performing privatized firms which did not pay dividends. The Russian experience simply confirms many of the concerns regarding the role of voucher investment funds in privatization expressed in Ellerman (1998).

Foreign involvement in this stage of Russia's privatization was virtually negligible, and most of the FDI entering Russia, whether for wholly new undertakings, or related to privatization and restructuring, was heavily concentrated in just four areas: Moscow City, Moscow oblast', St Petersburg and Leningrad oblast' (Broadman and Recanatini, 2001a). More recently, it is clear that FDI inflows remain highly differentiated by region, being concentrated in those areas already relatively developed and in receipt of most western technical assistance (Bradshaw, 2002).

Other steps towards a private sector economy
During the same period, 1992–4, several million apartments in Russian cities were privatized – usually to their existing tenants – either free or at highly subsidized prices. However, as Starodubrovskaya (2001) points out, the opportunity was not taken to make the new owners responsible for the maintenance of common areas and external structures of apartment blocks, nor were the prices paid by residents for their public utility services (water, electricity, heating, gas) raised to anywhere near their costs of supply. After a number of adjustments, the current position is that these prices are set to cover costs by 2008.

Little progress was achieved in the early 1990s in privatizing land. The right to hold land as private property first appeared in the RSFSR (Russian Soviet Federative Socialist Republic) Law on Property adopted in 1990. In 1993, private property in land appeared in the new constitution that was approved through a referendum. However, the detailed regulation of land sales and purchases and, more importantly, the mechanisms for registering and protecting individual property rights in land, have not been in place for almost a decade since then. The result has been a very modest turnover of land. Moreover, the fact that property rights in land were so poorly defined has meant that most transactions took the form of leasing.

One of the consequences of the deficient regulation in this area was that privatization of state enterprises was not accompanied by the privatization of the land on which the enterprises were located (the land was not counted as one of the enterprise's assets). Hence, even now, most privatized firms in Russia do not own the land which they use, this being leased from municipalities or oblast' authorities (OECD, 1995:69). Though the privatization of these lots was permitted by a Presidential Decree as early as 1992, the process was rather slow. During 1995–9, only 327 transactions were registered. As for the amount of land purchased, during the period 1994–9 (the official statistics are only available from 1994–5) this only amounted to 366 square km (with 296.3 square km of this in 1995 alone) (see IET, 2001).

In agriculture, progress was limited by opposition from associations of *kolkhoz* and *sovkhoz* managers, as well as by the parliament's reluctance to pass a comprehensive land law legalizing the private ownership of land and establishing a functioning market (Åslund, 1995; see also Leonard and Serova, 2001). With the reorganization of collective farms (*kolkhozy*) into joint-stock companies at the beginning of the 1990s, most residents of the rural areas (primarily collective farmers or *kolkhozniki*) gained the right to a share in the arable land of their farms. The outcome of the process was that about 12 million people became owners of land. However, no mechanism for identifying and separating off the land belonging to particular individuals was created, so in effect they merely owned abstract shares of fields and these could not be bought and sold. Moreover, various laws contained contradictory provisions concerning the use of agricultural land. For example, the law on mortgage directly banned the use of this land as collateral, while the law on agricultural cooperation allowed such transactions.

It was only in the year 2000 that land reform really started to be discussed seriously. Then, in 2001, the parliament adopted a Land Code regulating the market for non-agricultural land (in industrial areas, cities and settlements, accounting for about 2 per cent of the land resources of the country). A principal condition of the new law was that the land on which immovable property is located is now automatically treated as part of the asset concerned. Hence such property can no longer be privatized without privatizing the associated land, unless some special restriction is imposed. With respect to agricultural land, the breakthrough occurred in 2002 with the adoption of a new law that envisaged clear procedures for separating off the plots of agricultural land already privatized to rural residents, as well as clear rules for buying and selling land.

Aside from creating a private economy through its privatization policies, Russia also experienced a considerable upsurge in new business formation.

By late 1993, Goskomstat statistics showed that Russia had over 700 000 new private businesses (accounting for over 11 per cent of total employment). By 1999, however, there was only about one business entity per 55 people in Russia, scarcely one-fifth of what one would expect from the corresponding statistics for Central and Eastern European economies, or for typical, developed market economies. In Russia's case, entry of new businesses was almost certainly discouraged by bureaucratic obstacles and various forms of corruption and criminal behaviour, together with the factors discussed in the next two sections. Åslund (2001) suggests that mafia-type activities have been more predictable, and hence less damaging to new business formation, than the arbitrary interference of government agencies, which is an interesting observation. Further, the lack of adequate bankruptcy laws, and a great deal of official protection for firms deemed 'too big to fail' ensured that the turnover in the enterprise sector remained low: there were too few 'exits', and there was too little 'entry'. The result was continuing soft budget constraints, even for privatized firms (Kornai, 2001).

Loans-for-shares
1995 was a turning point in the Russian privatization programme. With the accomplishment of the mass privatization programme, the government announced a shift of priorities. The emphasis was placed on maximizing privatization revenues. The first manifestation of this change of direction was the loans-for-shares privatization, which was at best controversial, if not actually rigged. An excellent account of the loans-for-shares scheme is provided in Lieberman and Veimetra (1996), and a brief description follows below.

The idea of the scheme was advanced by a consortium of the largest Russian banks in March 1995. The scheme envisaged that the banks would lend funds to the government, taking blocks of shares in large and strategic enterprises as collateral. Blocks of shares would be auctioned separately to the banks, and the bank that offered the largest loan would be the winner. It was required to hold the shares until 1 September 1996 and within two years after that date could sell the shares and take one-third of the capital gains. While holding the shares, the banks had the right to vote at shareholder meetings, except over certain issues such as reorganization, liquidation and the issue of new equity.

Two reasons are typically put forward to explain the use of the loans-for-shares scheme. On the one hand, the Russian government was desperate in 1995 to increase its revenues from privatization, but it was facing severe difficulties in achieving its budget targets for privatization revenues, given the increasing uncertainty due to approaching parliamentary elections, as well as a direct ban on privatizing enterprises in the oil industry, which had been imposed by the parliament. On the other hand, the banks wanted to gain control over some of the largest Russian companies as cheaply as possible.

The implementation of the loans-for-shares privatization was questionable, to say the least. The auctions were administered by the banks, which could also participate in them as both bidders and depositors for bids. The participation of foreigners was restricted and competing bids were often disqualified on technical grounds. For example, Oneximbank administered the auction for Norilsk Nickel and won it for US$170.1mn, only US$0.1mn above the starting price, by disqualifying a bid for US$350mn on a technicality. The transactions frequently represented either buy-outs of enterprises by their own managers supported by banks or – in most cases – direct, non-competitive sales of blocks of shares to the interested banks or financial–industrial groups (FIGs) (see IET, 1997).

The initial plan was to apply the loans-for-shares scheme to 29 enterprises, but only 12 enterprises finally took part, of which half belonged to the oil sector. All the transactions were implemented within a two-month period, from 3 November to 28 December 1995. All but two blocks were sold by the banks in 1996–8, mostly to the banks' affiliates.[3] The government raised over a billion US dollars, but the non-transparency of the auctions immediately caused a public uproar over privatization. In subsequent years, there were a number of attempts to revise the results of the loans-for-shares privatization, mostly on the part of the communist-influenced parliament. This contributed to the insecurity of property rights and delayed the restructuring of some of the companies concerned.

Case-by-case privatization: 1996–2001
Since 1996, the policy of privatizing firms to maximize state revenues was continued, but privatization was increasingly implemented on a case-by-case basis. Typically, most revenues came from one or two major transactions in a given year, but their size varied dramatically from one year to the next. Most privatization transactions were prepared with a known buyer in mind, typically insiders, since the presence of controlling shareholders in Russian companies reduced the interest of potential external buyers in purchasing minority ownership stakes.

The echoes of the scandalous loans-for-shares scheme, presidential elections in 1996, and President Yeltsin's heart troubles resulted in no major transactions in 1996. Revenues from privatization were less than US$300mn, which is the lowest figure for the entire period 1995–2001. In terms of privatization revenues, 1997 was the most successful year so far. The revenues exceeded US$3bn, of which US$1.875bn came from the sale of a 25 per cent plus one share stake in Svyazinvest, the national telecommunications holding company. Little progress was achieved in 1998, except for the sale of

2.5 per cent of Gazprom shares to Ruhrgas for US$660mn. Revenues from privatization did not exceed US$1 bn. The financial crisis resulted in the suspension of privatization tenders after 17 August. In 1999, the federal government conducted two major privatization transactions, the sale of 10 per cent of the shares in Lukoil and 49.806 per cent of the shares in the Tyumen Oil Company (TNK). Total revenues from privatization were less than US$400mn. In 2000, the list of potential privatizations included 242 companies belonging to 24 sectors, as well as shares in about 1500 recently corporatized enterprises. However, most revenues again came from two transactions: the sale of 85 per cent of the shares in the ONAKO oil company for US$1.08bn, and the sale of 0.5 per cent of Lukoil shares for about US$50mn. Overall, privatization activity in 2000 yielded revenues of somewhat more than US$1.1 bn.

According to BOFIT (2002), Russian privatization in 2001 involved divesting stakes in 125 enterprises, mostly sold at auction. Most stakes were less than 25 per cent of the companies involved, but the sales contributed about US$350mn to the federal budget in 2001. The largest deal was the sale of almost 80 per cent of the coal company, Kuzbassugol, through two auctions, and the sale of the state insurance company, Rosgosstrakh. These two transactions accounted for revenues of over US$200mn. For 2002, the privatization of shares in 426 corporations and about 150 unincorporated entities is expected to yield over US$1 bn, with two large transactions – a 20 per cent stake in the oil and gas producer, Slavneft, and a 6 per cent stake in LUkoil – accounting for over 85 per cent of the expected revenues.

Performance of the privatized economy
There are two levels at which to think of Russia's economic performance, the macroeconomic and the microeconomic. The former (the *macroeconomy*) concerns overall activity levels, as reflected in aggregate growth trends, employment and unemployment levels, and similar indicators. Looking at such measures of performance, it is clear that, until the past three years or so, Russia's economy has done very badly. This is not the place to go into detailed explanations for the economy's aggregate behaviour, but the general trends and some related analysis can be followed in EBRD (various years), and OECD (1995, 2002). Here it is enough simply to note that, whatever beneficial effects privatization might have had in Russia, they are not yet particularly evident in the aggregate data. The situation is summed up in Table 17.1 below.

At the *microeconomic level*, what we are interested in is evidence of beneficial restructuring. Has privatization stimulated firms to undertake restructuring, or have privatized firms somehow managed to survive without much restructuring? Have persistently loss-making firms been compelled by market pressures to retire capacity, and in extreme cases even to close? The evidence is rather mixed, but on balance quite negative. Numerous enterprise surveys, some of which are referred to in the next two sections, show that many firms have not experienced much pressure. They have survived despite being unprofitable and are most probably non-viable in the longer term. Interestingly, whether firms are still state-owned or already privatized seems to make rather little difference to the extent and nature of the restructuring undertaken.

Various studies report that the post-privatization ownership structure with its dominant role for insiders, primarily employees, seriously inhibited restructuring efforts. It is no exaggeration to say that the Russian experience with employee ownership confirms many of the concerns expressed in the theoretical literature. Firstly, regarding such an important dimension as employment restructuring, employee-owned firms proved to be more inclined towards labour hoarding than outsider-owned firms. Secondly, employee-owned firms had much more limited opportunities to raise external funds. The core problem here is the risk facing potential investors that their funds would be used to sustain existing levels of labour inputs rather than to undertake modernizing investment. No less important is the fact that employee ownership often results in little or no control over the managers, who may therefore pursue their own personal objectives, including personal enrichment (Frydman and Rapaczynski, 1994). Evidence for such adverse consequences of employee ownership in Russia can be found in Blasi (1996) and Earle (1998).

Ownership by the second group of insiders, namely managers, in the transition economy of Russia has typically been considered beneficial in terms of its likely impact on enterprise performance and restructuring (Earle, 1998; Klepach *et al.*, 1997). However, a serious caveat associated with managerial ownership in Russia is the possibility of entrenchment of old managers who are simply unable to run firms in a market economy.

Using a sample of firms from Sverdlovsk oblast', Perevalov *et al.* (2000) concluded that privatization 'on average' produced decent improvements in operating profit margins and, to a lesser extent, in labour productivity. At the same time they found that corporatization was no worse than privatization *per se* because the performance of companies wholly owned by the state scarcely differed from that of privatized firms with little or no residual state ownership. Thus, according to Perevalov *et al.* (ibid.), the transfer of ownership from the state to private owners is of secondary importance as compared to the initial step of separating enterprises from the state through corporatization, since this already starts to harden the budget constraints facing firms.

To extend the argument, imperfections in the internal mechanisms of

Table 17.1   Indicators of Russia's macroeconomic performance, 1991–2001

	1991	1992	1993	1994	1995	1996	1997	1998	1999	2000	2001
GDP growth (% p.a.)	-5.0	-14.5	-8.7	-12.7	-4.1	-3.5	0.9	-4.9	5.4	9.0	5.0
Inflation (%, Dec. to Dec.)	160.4	2 509	839.9	215.1	131.3	21.8	11.0	84.4	36.5	20.2	18.6
Government balance (consolidated budget, % of GDP)	NA	NA	-4.7	-9.4	-5.7	-8.9	-8.8	-4.5	-1.0	2.8	2.9
Unemployment (% of labour force)	NA	5.2	5.9	8.1	9.5	10.4	11.8	13.2	12.6	9.8	8.9

Note: NA = not available
Sources: Goskomstat.

359

governance emphasize the important role that must be played by external mechanisms, primarily bankruptcies and closures of badly performing enterprises and an active takeover market. The evidence on the role of these mechanisms, however, is rather mixed and often negative.

Barriers to change 1: banks, financial markets and the labour market
From the previous section it is evident both that Russia privatized a large part of its economy at an astonishing, indeed unprecedented, speed, and that the outcome of the process has been disappointing, characterized by weak and often poorly directed restructuring efforts, and the survival of many enterprises that should have disappeared long ago. In this and the next section, we sketch some of the factors that help to explain such lack-lustre performance.

Banks and financial markets
In a normally functioning market economy, the banks – and the financial sector more generally – provide resources for enterprise sector investment and, through the resulting financial discipline, contribute to the imposition of hard budget constraints on all business entities. In Russia, this type of mechanism worked very badly during the 1990s, for several reasons. First, before August 1998, the banks themselves could make more money from lending to the government or through their foreign transactions than from lending to business. Second, the demand for bank credit for investment remained low, with most firms either not investing at all or relying on their own resources such as retained profits, reserves and so on. This was primarily due to the high interest rates that resulted from the state's aggressive borrowing. (In passing, however, it is worth remarking that the lack of business sector borrowing is a reason why Russia's business sector was not greatly affected by the 1998 financial crisis.) Third, even when banks did lend, they were inclined to lend to traditional customers and were sometimes amenable to government 'requests' to go on lending to firms that were technically insolvent. Fourth, quite aside from government pressure, the banks' own incentives often encouraged them to hide bad debts by continuing to lend more to ailing enterprises, in the expectation that sooner or later they might well be bailed out by the government.

Since the 1998 financial crisis, the banking sector remains underdeveloped and consists of over 1000 banks, most of which are small and undercapitalized. Moreover, the crisis resulted in a loss of confidence in the banking sector on the part of depositors and the creation of a virtual monopoly for the state-controlled Sberbank or Savings bank, which now has 72 per cent of the retail market (RET, 2002). Overall, therefore, the Russian banking sector functioned extremely poorly for much of the past decade, and contributed to the endemic 'soft budget constraint' culture (see, however, OECD, 2000, which suggests that budget constraints are slowly getting harder).

Similarly to the banking sector, the Russian stock market has never played an important role in providing enterprises with financial resources. The number of listed equities is about 200, of which only a few dozen are regularly traded. Most equities are illiquid. For example, while the market capitalization of several individual companies amounts to billions of dollars, the average daily turnover in the Russian Trading System (RTS) – the largest over-the-counter market in Russia – has not exceeded US$100mn.

As Kogut and Spicer (2002) have emphasized, the Russian style of privatization that gave rise to substantial insider control and extremely dispersed share ownership outside the firm, with weak legal and institutional protection for minority shareholders, has itself seriously discouraged financial market development in Russia. Effective corporate governance of enterprises requires concentrated ownership of shares. Although some concentration has occurred since the privatization 'rush' of 1992–4, insiders have often managed to inhibit such processes. 'In the absence of institutional mechanisms of state regulation and trust,' even those financial markets that came into existence in Russia often became 'arenas for political contests and economic manipulation' (ibid.: 1).

The labour market
The behaviour of the Russian labour market during the 1990s has been one of the big surprises of the country's transition. First, the general decline in output in virtually all sectors from the start of the 1990s, and continuing through the mid-1990s, was not accompanied by a parallel decline in employment, with the result that labour productivity declined sharply in much of the economy. The unemployment rate rose slowly during the 1990s and only reached the levels of 10–15 per cent of the labour force by 1997, in contrast to Central Europe, where such levels came about far more rapidly.

Second, the Russian labour market was characterized by a high turnover of labour – higher than in other post-socialist countries – but at the same time surprisingly low rates of job destruction. In other words, even in firms whose demand had collapsed severely, workers who left of their own accord were frequently replaced, and few workers were made compulsorily redundant.

Third, specific adaptation techniques were developed by Russian firms. For instance, instead of cutting employment, most Russian enterprises cut wages (in practice, by allowing money wages to rise more slowly than the general price level), delayed the payment of wages, or placed workers on various forms of leave, often unpaid or on reduced pay. The latter arrangements were not equivalent to dismissal, since the workers concerned remained on the enterprise payroll and they and their families retained their entitlement to whatever social benefits were supplied through the firm. In many cases, these benefits were substantial (on the start of this process, see Commander *et al.*, 1995).

Fourth, the interregional mobility of labour remains low as a result of administrative barriers, the lack of reliable information about employment opportunities in other regions, the underdevelopment of the housing market, the low density of the transport network and the high costs of moving to other regions (Kapelyushnikov, 2001).

More recently, some of these trends have been investigated in detail in Broadman and Recanatini (2001b). By using data from around 70 enterprise case studies in eight Russian regions, and Goskomstat data on over 125000 firms for the period 1996–9, the authors found that, on average, firms had only 'downsized' their employment by about 12 per cent by 1999. Since 1998, there has been some job creation in sectors benefiting from stronger export incentives, or sectors more able to compete with imports (import substitution). However, downsizing and other aspects of restructuring are still often constrained by the restrictive Labour Code,[4] by local political pressures and by poor incentives. Indeed, rates of job destruction have actually declined markedly in the last few years, suggesting that labour market barriers to restructuring are not diminishing.

Barriers to change 2: networks, non-monetary transactions and the role of the state

Continuing the analysis of the previous section, we next turn to outline those factors that can be regarded as hold-overs from the socialist system, or revivals of socialist era practices, and also touch on the role of the state in hindering or promoting enterprise restructuring.

Networks and non-monetary transactions

How do firms survive in circumstances where demand collapses, and when what had been a rather stable economic environment suddenly becomes exceptionally turbulent? Several strategies can be envisaged, depending on many features of the economic landscape. Under *competitive conditions* with very hard budget constraints, firms would essentially have to 'sink or swim'. Many would certainly fail, but a surprising number of Russian firms would probably have discovered that they could adapt to the new conditions, and some would even be prospering already.

A less risky approach would be to rely on the *business networks* established under socialism, both horizontally (across an industrial branch) and vertically (up and down the supply chain). Exploiting these networks, and sometimes building new ones, firms in trouble can then assist each other by agreeing to trade with each other, by accepting products in lieu of monetary payments, by granting each other credits, and so on. This process was facilitated in Russia by the willingness of the state to accept tax payments in the form of commodities, and by the toleration by the major public utilities either of non-payment or of payment in kind. These interrelated transactions were mutually reinforcing, and have contributed to the survival through the 1990s of many Russian enterprises. By the mid-to-late 1990s, the share of inter-enterprise transactions in Russia that involved non-monetary payment rose to somewhat over two-thirds, though since the 1998 economic crisis, and with the tougher approach to economic policy adopted by President Putin, the phenomenon has been steadily declining since then.

This is just as well, because in our view the combination of networks and non-monetary payment seriously restricted, and still does restrict, the development of competition in the economy. One aspect of this, even more damaging from the standpoint of longer-term performance, is that new entry is strongly deterred, since many potential entrants will rapidly discover that there are no customers for their output, these being already committed to the existing trading and production networks.

The role of the state
How has the new Russian state operated during the 1990s, and how have its actions hindered or supported enterprise restructuring, both pre- and post-privatization? Right from the start of transition it was acknowledged that the state's all-pervasive role in the economy was a key factor explaining widespread inefficiency, slow responses to market pressures, lagging innovation and the like. While privatization, as described above, was a major part of the response, this was commonly preceded by corporatization, the conversion of SOEs into joint-stock companies, still with 100 per cent state ownership but with management/enterprise boards somewhat distanced from day-to-day political concerns. But separating the *economy* from the *state* in this way often did not turn out to produce much real change in business behaviour, for two reasons: (a) in Russia, as elsewhere, it was quickly discovered that business behaviour depends not only on formal ownership and management structures, but also on other aspects of the business environment, notably those to do with *competition*; and (b) it turned out that there remained in place many other *channels of influence* over enterprise behaviour through which government – at all levels – could operate, and these frequently served to undermine the initially stated goals of corporatization and privatization.

As regards *competition*, various laws and decrees governing competition policy in Russia were passed during the 1990s, but their effectiveness was weakened by their poor and inconsistent administration, the discretion remaining with government bodies (such as ministers) to determine whether a particular situation would be governed by the general policy or allowed to stand as an 'exception', and the practice of forming networks noted above. Under pressure from sector lobbies, or from regional elites nervous of the political repercussions of high unemployment in their areas, government frequently allowed such exceptions. Further, local governments were also not slow to restrict trade in diverse ways in order to protect 'their' enterprises. Such interventions seriously inhibited competition, enabling far too many existing SOEs (even after their privatization) to survive, even while failing to undertake substantial restructuring. The counterpart to this is that new entry was also discouraged, a factor that tended to reinforce officials' desire to protect existing businesses.

While these remarks refer largely to Russia's domestic markets, and the problems facing new Russian entrants, much the same points also apply to many of the foreign companies seeking to enter the Russian market. Despite nominally low tariffs in most sectors, companies have faced a diverse plethora of non-tariff barriers that have served to protect many Russian firms, even poorly performing ones. Much of this informal/implicit protection will need to be removed as Russia completes its negotiations to join the World Trade Organization (WTO) (see Hare, 2002) and this might finally improve the all-important competitive environment in Russia.

The other channels of influence through which firms' behaviour could be affected were more indirect and selective. They included the following:

- toleration by the government of *non-payment of taxes* and/or social security contributions;
- toleration by government of *non-payment of other obligations*, principally utility bills;
- selective provision of *subsidies* either directly via the state budget or indirectly via directed bank credits (or even more indirectly via toleration of the delayed servicing or non-servicing of outstanding credits). Such subsidies could be paid directly to specific enterprises, or could take the form of import duties to protect domestic producers (these act as a subsidy by allowing the domestic prices to be higher than they otherwise would be);
- the complex and fluid relationships between the federal government and the 89 federal 'subjects' providing opportunities for intervention in the affairs of many enterprises not only from the centre, but, often more importantly, through regional/oblast' authorities. The latter often introduced local trade restrictions to 'protect' their enterprises, or offered tax reliefs or other favours, sometimes contrary to the rules

already in place at federal level. Since Putin became president, these inconsistencies between federal and regional/local policies are slowly being brought under more rational control.

The public utilities: steps towards privatization and issues of regulation
'We work in the situation of strong monopolies and a weak state' (Andrey Sharonov, Deputy Minister for Economic Development, explaining the threat that the monopolies will block the reform, 2001).

Public utilities reform started in 1992, but is still far from complete. Different degrees of progress can be observed in different sectors. First, many of the natural monopolies have undergone corporatization and partial privatization (for example, power utilities sector, telecommunications – fixed networks). Others still exist in the form of governmental agencies or state enterprises (for example, railway transport is undertaken by the Ministry of Railway Transport, water supply is provided by local state-owned enterprises). It is important to note that the existing organizational forms were mostly created in the first half of the 1990s, and that since then the government has not taken major steps to corporatize or privatize public utilities.

Regardless of the organizational form and ownership, to date the government has failed to establish a sound system of monopoly regulation. For many sectors, the main problem is that the existing public utilities operate in both potentially competitive and monopolistic sub-sectors, like UES, the national electricity holding company, which owns both the grid (monopolistic) sub-sector and power-generating stations (potentially competitive). Thus monopolistic businesses are not yet separated from the potentially competitive ones. As a result, it is difficult to estimate the costs of production of public utilities and to regulate their tariffs. It is also impossible to create competition in the potentially competitive sectors, as independent producers have no guaranteed access to the grid in the case of power utilities or to the pipelines in the case of the gas industry. This issue of the appropriate mode of restructuring public utility industries, and the extent of vertical integration that should be retained in post-privatization industry structures, is examined in Pittman (2001). In general, the best outcome depends on three factors: (a) capabilities of regulatory bodies; (b) effectiveness of the judicial system in enforcing regulatory orders; and (c) effectiveness of the country's information systems (which in turn depends on telecommunications and IT systems). For Russia, one would have to rate all three of these dimensions rather poorly, and the design of public utility structures should take this fully into account.

Besides such regulatory problems, the government often forces public utilities to take into account its social objectives, which are often unjustifiable from an economic viewpoint and can even be damaging in terms of their impact on the utilities themselves and the economy as a whole. For example, the government establishes and maintains low prices of electricity for households. The resulting losses are then expected to be covered through higher tariffs for industrial consumers, giving rise to a price structure for electricity exactly the opposite of what is normally found in developed market economies (where prices paid by households are generally far higher than those paid by industrial and commercial customers). The same sort of cross-subsidization still exists in other sectors.

Other restrictions on public utilities include the requirement to continue supplying several categories of consumers even if they do not pay for the services. This restriction applies primarily to sectors regarded as strategic, such as national defence. Obviously, however, these sectors should be financed by the state in such a way that they are able to cover all their costs, including those associated with the consumption of public utility services. In practice, this has not always been the case in Russia (for an example of this in the higher education sector, see Hare and Lugachev, 1999). It is evident that tariff regulation is meaningless if some consumers are, in effect, permitted not to pay, since these entities will be able to treat the service in question as if it were a free good. In economic terms, this is an extremely inefficient practice.

After assuming power in 2000, the Putin government declared that public utility reform would be one of its priorities. But, given the enormous difficulty of the task, few major practical steps have been taken so far. Limited progress has been achieved in the field of tariff regulation. Thus, in 2000, the government established a special body to regulate tariffs in railway transport, and quite recently a unified tariff body was created. But the major issue of how to separate potentially competitive sub-sectors from monopolistic ones remains unresolved. Without this separation, the costs of production can hardly be controlled.

In some sectors, progress is more tangible. In particular, the government announced a number of measures to reform the power utilities and railway transport sectors. On the other hand, there is much less clarity concerning other sectors, including the gas industry. The rest of this section therefore focuses on the major utilities that remain in federal state ownership, namely UES, the Ministry of Railway Transport and Svyazinvest, representing the power utilities, the railways and the telecommunications sector, respectively. We also refer briefly to the gas industry, specifically the company Gazprom, although the state no longer holds a majority stake in it.

Price regulation: 1992–2001
With price liberalization in 1992, the government determined the list of goods and services whose prices would continue to be regulated by the state and

introduced maximum limits for their permissible price increases. However, several services, such as telephone network services for business entities, which were provided by natural monopolies, and which were not considered as socially important, were omitted from the list. Aside from introducing in 1992–3 a variety of price ceilings and maximum limits for price increases, the government also established maximum profitability levels in some cases.

At that time most sectors were still regulated by the relevant sector ministries and regional authorities. Outside the ministries there existed only one system of regulatory bodies, namely the Federal Commission and Regional Commissions for Energy, which were created in 1992 to regulate prices in the electric power and heat-and-power sectors. However, even in this sector the legal basis for such regulation was not formally established until 1995.

Price regulation underwent substantial change in 1995. Firstly, natural monopolies were distinguished as special sectors which, owing to their economic nature, required special regulation. Three governmental agencies were created to deal with price regulation in the energy sector, in transport and in telecommunications. In 1998, the responsibility for regulating the latter two sectors was transferred to the Ministry for Antimonopoly Policy.

Secondly, a division of authority and responsibilities was introduced between the federal centre and the regions on price regulation issues. The list of goods and services whose prices were to be regulated by regional authorities was announced. It included electricity and heating, natural gas for residential use, and charges for mail and telephone communications at the regional level. This created the conditions for tariffs to differ between regions. At the same time, the reform weakened the coordinating role of the centre and this resulted in substantial tariff differences for the same services in neighbouring regions. The level of tariffs in a particular region depended on the ability of regional monopolies to justify their cost levels and the required rate of return to their local government. The lack of any agreed methodology to assess the validity of costs, and the substantial uncertainty regarding external factors affecting costs (such as unpredictable inflation), ensured that an objective revision of the tariffs was virtually impossible.

The next major step in developing methods of price regulation was the 1997 government decision to reform monopolistic industries. The government had several objectives in mind: to separate off potentially competitive activities; to introduce common, non-discriminatory rules for using network infrastructure (electricity grid, pipelines and so on); and to reduce the extent of inefficient cross-subsidization. However, the reform largely failed owing to resistance from the sectoral lobbies, as well as the impact of the 1998 economic crisis.

The most recent attempt to reform the system of price regulation commenced in 2000, with the adoption of an ambitious governmental programme of reforms, known as 'Gref's programme' (Gref being the leading economic minister). According to this programme, establishing a system of price regulation should take place in parallel with reforming the monopolies. The latter, however, causes disputes both between the government and the monopolies and within the government itself. To date, almost the only visible outcome of the new programme is the establishment of a unified body for tariff regulation, with responsibility for regulating tariffs in sectors such as oil, gas, energy and transport.[5]

Power utilities

The sector was corporatized and partially privatized under a special scheme set up in accordance with a Presidential Decree issued in 1992. Under the scheme, the government distributed the grid and all non-nuclear electricity-generating stations among the 72 regional companies and Unified Energy System (UES), the national holding company operating in the sector. Typically, all enterprises operating in a particular region were included in large regional companies. The number of regional companies is, however, fewer than the number of subjects of the federation (89). This is due to the fact that some regional companies operate across several regions; for example, Lenenergo supplies electricity to both the city of St Petersburg and the Leningrad region, and these are two independent subjects of the federation. The scheme also envisaged that controlling blocks of the regional companies would be held by UES. As a consequence, each regional company became a monopoly in a particular region in regard to distribution and inherited most electricity-generating assets (except for nuclear stations, which remained state-owned).

According to the recently announced governmental programme, reform in the sector will include the separation of electricity generation from electricity transmission and measures to induce competition among independent producers. Rather than keeping majority ownership in the UES, the state will only control the company established to own the main power lines (that is, the grid). Generating capacity, as well as the local distribution networks, will be transferred to private ownership. As with other monopolistic sectors, the reform will also deal with the price imbalances referred to above, by removing cross-subsidization and ensuring that the general level of electricity prices is economic.

Gazprom

Gazprom is a single company which controls the major share of Russia's gas reserves; it operates both in gas extraction and in transport, owning all the major pipelines. The main problems currently facing the gas industry are similar to those in other monopolistic sectors, namely the interweaving of competitive and monopolistic sub-sectors and extensive cross-subsidization (the domestic price for gas being several times lower than its export price). Hence the proposed reform package is similar to those in other industries, involving non-discriminatory access by independent producers to the pipelines and greater competition among producers. But the case of Gazprom is different from other utility industries in one key respect: the state does not have a majority ownership stake, controlling less than 40 per cent of the voting shares in the company. Therefore reforming the gas industry is likely to be a difficult process because any major reorganization of the company will require the consent of minority shareholders.

Railway transport

Currently the Ministry of Railway Transport performs two functions: it is the governmental body with responsibility for determining state policy in the rail sector, and it is the business entity that actually operates the railway system in Russia. The conflict of interests is apparent. Therefore the government plan for restructuring of the industry envisages several steps. The first step entails establishing a 100 per cent state-owned joint-stock company to operate the railway transport business. At this stage it is planned to transfer all the assets to the new joint-stock company. Second, it is planned to separate different types of business activity within the company; thus passenger transport would be distinguished from freight transport. One benefit of this is that it would become possible – perhaps for the first time – to calculate their respective costs in a way that would facilitate major improvements in the tariff structure. The next stage envisages a sub-division of the company, with different businesses being transferred to a number of separate subsidiaries. The company would thus be transformed into a state holding company, which would own the entire railway infrastructure (track, signals, stations and the like) together with shares in the various subsidiary companies. The latter might then be privatized, partially or fully.

The government also plans to abolish gradually the practice of cross-subsidizing passenger transport through higher tariffs on freight transport. It is planned that, by 2005, the budget will contain a separate item to compensate fully for passenger transport losses. Such subsidies are not feasible now, as the real losses from passenger transport are unknown because of the lack of transparency in the ministry's operations and accounts.

Telecommunications

Reform in the sector started with the establishment of 88 regional operators and the national operator, Rostelecom (which covers long-distance and international backbone traffic). In 1995, controlling blocks of shares in regional operators were transferred to a specially established holding company, Sviazinvest, which became responsible for channelling investments into the sector. In 1997, as noted above, a 25 per cent plus one share stake in Sviazinvest was sold to private investors. Repeated efforts by the government to sell a second 25 per cent minus two shares stake met with apathy from potential investors and were finally abandoned. The 1998 economic crisis severely hit the sector as many operators held hard currency loans for their equipment purchases while collecting all of their revenues in roubles.

The effective tariffs, which were among the lowest in the world in dollar terms even before the crisis, were substantially reduced by devaluation of the rouble. The tariffs charged to residential users for local calls have remained artificially low for political reasons. After the crisis, average local monthly fees, which represent the major source of operators' revenues (there is no per minute charge on local calls), were about two US dollars and tariff increases were postponed in view of the forthcoming elections. As in most sectors subject to anti-monopoly regulation, the telecommunications sector has been characterized by extensive cross-subsidization. Losses from the low tariffs on local calls continue to be offset by revenues from international and long-distance calls as well as from higher tariffs for business entities, which account for most revenues in the sector. This sharply contrasts with the situation in more developed markets where local calls are the major source of revenues in the sector.

Reform in the telecommunications sector appeared on the policy agenda in 2000, based on the idea of increasing growth through attracting more investments. The reform envisages mergers among the existing regional operators to form seven larger companies, with the main aim of raising their market capitalization and liquidity to increase their ability to attract additional funding for new investment (from both domestic and foreign sources, through the issuance of American Depository Receipts). A further important component of the reform will be the introduction of per minute tariffs on local calls all over the country and the gradual abolition of cross-subsidization.

Conclusions

Competition is something that economists like and firms generally detest. In elementary accounts of the economists' conception of competition – for instance in the models of perfect competition or the Chamberlinian model of imperfect competition – competition is there in the background, forcing firms to organize their production in a way that keeps costs at a minimum, and giving rise to an efficient, static market equilibrium. More sophisticated accounts regard competition more as a process, giving rise to the entry, exit and incumbent restructuring referred to in the introduction to this chapter. In principle, the process should result in an evolving population of firms producing a changing mix of products with growing productivity. But as we saw above, especially when looking at the barriers to change, there are many reasons why such a benign[6] process might not function properly in a country such as Russia. Entry of new firms has been very sluggish compared to the more dynamic transition economies of Central Europe, and this in turn has made it easier for existing enterprises to apply political pressure to secure their protection through the various mechanisms noted above.

Related to this, some very interesting points are made in the survey paper by Megginson and Netter (2001). These authors find that privatization is usually beneficial, and that it is often associated with general improvements in governance at all levels in a society; but they do note that the position in the transition economies is extremely mixed at present, and suggest some areas for further research.

First, can reforms other than privatization serve as a precursor or substitute for privatization? Their discussion suggests that responsible governments will not wish to push forward a risky and difficult policy such as privatization without being sure that other supporting policies are in place. Concerning the Russian case, this raises questions about the possible need to have achieved stabilization, and to have implemented important legal and institutional reforms, prior to privatization. It also raises the question whether extensive pre-privatization restructuring should have taken place. In our view, Russian privatization was pursued in excessive haste, with poor results in terms of the subsequent enterprise behaviour and performance. However, the situation can be 'rescued' to a large extent as the government implements and enforces measures to deal with the problems highlighted above.

As regards pre-privatization restructuring, this is a hotly debated issue in the privatization literature, but for Russia we seriously doubt the merits of such a policy. Why should we have expected the state, which created Russia's medium and large enterprises under conditions of central planning, suddenly to develop a capability to restructure these entities into units that would be viable and competitive in the market? Instead, we prefer to see the emergence of conditions in which many enterprises will undertake post-privatization restructuring under new management, or at least in a new market environment.

The second research area concerns the labour economics of privatization: does privatization lead to big lay-offs; can the social costs of restructuring be handled through retraining, relocation or support for new businesses, and so on? In Russia, wages have fallen sharply and enforced lay-offs have been surprisingly few. The social and political costs of restructuring have been perceived as unacceptably high in many instances, with the result that we noted above, namely slow and limited restructuring so far. However, these costs might have been perceived as far lower had positive policies to encourage and support new business been pursued earlier and more vigorously.

The last area is more forward-looking, to do with the role that privatization can play in preparing an economy to meet new challenges, such as globalization, the increasing role of information-based industries, IT and the like. It cannot be claimed that much of Russia's privatization during the 1990s was motivated by such concerns, but perhaps the subsequent – and long delayed – restructuring of the economy will be.

In the light of these observations, we offer a few conclusions concerning the Russian privatization process. First, the institutions and procedures to manage Russia's privatization process were established quite early in the Russian transition. While they have evolved over time, and gradually eliminated or reduced the incidence of various abuses, the basic structures have achieved a virtually unprecedented volume of privatization transactions within an exceptionally short period. Much of the Russian economy is now privatized, across virtually all sectors.

Second, the principal exceptions are defence industry enterprises and much of the public utilities, involving firms mostly exempted from the first privatization 'rush' of the mid-1990s. However, even here there have been some significant moves towards privatization, and substantial efforts to strengthen economic regulation to constrain the abuse of monopoly power.

Third, nevertheless, the huge volume of privatization activity in Russia has not yet been accompanied either by sufficient restructuring of production or by dramatically improved economic performance as measured by a whole range of microeconomic indicators: profitability, productivity, export performance and the like.

Fourth, the rush to implement mass privatization (which was motivated by political considerations) resulted in the emergence of firms substantially owned by their employees and managers, an ownership structure that has proved to be inefficient from the viewpoint of enterprise restructuring and performance. Though the incidence of employee ownership decreased in the years following the mass privatization, it still remains a significant obstacle to the revitalization of Russian firms.

Finally, we find that this weak performance is not only due to deficiencies within the privatization process *per se* (such as the resulting preponderance of insider/employee ownership), but also relates to a combination of institutional, political and economic policy shortcomings. These have to do with the political inability to tolerate high rates of unemployment, even temporarily, in many areas, the accompanying soft budget constraints that remained pervasive, and the very slow evolution of the necessary legal and regulatory institutional structure to support a well functioning market-type economy. Thus the poor outcomes are also due to the lack of competition throughout the Russian economy.

Notes

1. The authors are grateful to Saul Estrin and the editors of this volume for helpful comments and suggestions on earlier drafts. Remaining errors are our own.
2. We use the term 'parliament' here and later to avoid possible confusion. The institution has had different names at different times, such as Supreme Soviet under the communist system, Duma or State Duma more recently.
3. Two remaining shareholdings are 26.7 per cent of voting shares in Novorossiysk Sea Shipping Company and 25.5 per cent in North-Western River Shipping Company with loans of US$22.5mn and US$6.05mn, respectively. In 2001, the government decided to repay the loans in order to regain these shareholdings. The loans are to be repaid from federal budget revenues in 2002.
4. The old Labour Code was replaced in 2002. The new Code appears to be less restrictive for employers; for example, it envisages a broader range of reasons for dismissals and restricts the power of trade unions.
5. Note, however, that the issue of Russia's domestic energy pricing is likely to be critical for WTO entry, see Hare (2002).
6. It is benign, of course, only for those firms that prosper. For those that fail, it can be quite brutal. However, from a social point of view even failure is not so bad, since people and assets can be, and usually are, redeployed into other, more productive activities.

References

Åslund, A. (1995) *How Russia Became a Market Economy*, Washington, DC: The Brookings Institution.

Åslund, A. (2001) 'The Development of Small Enterprises', in B. Granville and P. Oppenheimer (eds), *Russia's Post-Communist Economy*, Oxford and New York: Oxford University Press. Ch. 12.

Blasi, J. (1996) *Corporate Ownership and Corporate Governance in the Russian Federation*, Moscow: The Federal Commission for the Securities Market.

Blasi, J., M. Kroumova and D. Kruse (1997) *Kremlin Capitalism: The Privatization of the Russian Economy*, Ithaca, NY and London: Cornell University Press.

BOFIT (2002) 'Russian and Baltic Economies – The Week in Review', issue 7, Bank of Finland, Helsinki.

Bradshaw, M.J. (2002) 'The Changing Geography of Foreign Investment in the Russian Federation', *Russian Economic Trends*, 11(1), 33–41.

Broadman, H.G. and F. Recanatini (2001a) 'Where has all the Foreign Investment Gone in Russia?', World Bank Working Paper, World Bank, Washington, DC.

Broadman, H G. and F. Recanatini (2001b) 'Is Russia Restructuring? New Evidence on Job Creation and Destruction', World Bank Working Paper, World Bank, Washington, DC.

Commander, S., J. McHale and R. Yemtsov (1995) 'Russia', in Simon Commander and Fabrizio Coricelli (eds), *Unemployment, Restructuring and the Labor Market in Eastern Europe and Russia*, EDI Development Series, Washington, DC: World Bank.

Earle, J.S. (1998) 'Post-Privatization Ownership Structure and Productivity in Russian Industrial Enterprises', paper presented at the ACES-ASSA meeting, Chicago, January.

Earle, J.S. and S. Estrin (2001) 'Privatization and the Structure of Enterprise Ownership', in B. Granville and P. Oppenheimer (eds), *Russia's Post-Communist Economy*, Oxford and New York: Oxford University Press. Ch. 6.

EBRD (various) *Transition Report*, London: EBRD.

Ellerman, D. (1998) *Voucher Privatization with Investment Funds: An Institutional Analysis*, Washington, DC: World Bank.

Frydman R. and A. Rapaczynski (1994) *Privatization in Eastern Europe: Is the state withering away?*, Budapest: Central European University Press (in cooperation with Oxford University Press).

Hare, P.G. (2001) 'Institutional Change and Economic Performance in the Transition Economies', *Economic Survey of Europe in 2001*, issue 2, Geneva: UN Economic Commission for Europe.

Hare, P.G. (2002) 'Russia and the WTO', draft paper for the Centre for European Reform, London, and RECEP, Moscow, mimeo, May.

Hare, P.G. and M. Lugachev (1999) 'Higher Education in Transition to a Market Economy: Two Case Studies', *Europe–Asia Studies*, 51(1), 101–22.

IET (1997) *Russian Economy in 1996: Tendencies and Perspectives*, Moscow: Institute for the Economy in Transition.

IET (2001) *Ownership Transformation and Comparative Analysis of the Russian Regions*, Moscow: Institute for the Economy in Transition.

Kapelyushnikov, R. (2001) *The Russian Labour Market: Adaptation without Restructuring*, Moscow: State University – Higher School of Economics Press.

Klepach, A., P. Kutnezsov and P. Kryuchkova (1996) 'Corporate Governance in Russia in 1995–1996 (from the Soviet-type Enterprise to the Manager-controlled Firm)', *Voprosy Ekonomiki*, No. 12, pp. 73–87.

Kogut, B. and A. Spicer (2002) 'Capital Market Development and Mass Privatization are Logical Contradictions: Lessons from Russia and the Czech Republic', *Industrial and Corporate Change*, 11(1), 1–37.

Kornai, J. (2001) 'Hardening the Budget Constraint: The Experience of the Post-Socialist Countries', *European Economic Review*, 45(9), 1573–99.

Leijonhufvud, A. and E. Craver (2001) 'Reform and the Fate of Russia', *OFCE Working Paper*, 2001/3, May, Observatoire Français des Conjonctures Economiques, Paris.

Leonard, C.S. and E. Serova (2001) 'The Reform of Agriculture', in B. Granville and P. Oppenheimer (eds), *Russia's Post-Communist Economy*, Oxford and New York: Oxford University Press. Ch. 13.

Lieberman, I. and R. Veimetra (1996) 'The Rush for State Shares in the "Klondyke" of Wild East Capitalism: Loans-For-Shares Transactions in Russia', *George Washington Journal of International Law and Economics*, 29(3).

Megginson, W.L. and J.M. Netter (2001) 'From State to Market: A Survey of Empirical Studies on Privatization', *Journal of Economic Literature*, 39(2), 321–89.

OECD (1995) *The Russian Federation 1995*, OECD Economic Surveys, Paris: OECD (October).

OECD (2000) *Russian Federation*, OECD Economic Surveys, Paris: OECD (March).

OECD (2002) *Russian Federation*, OECD Economic Surveys, Paris: OECD (February).

Perevalov, Y., I. Gimadi and V. Dobrodey (2000) 'The Impact of Privatisation on the Performance of Medium and Large Industrial Enterprises', EERC working paper 2K/01E.

Pittman, R. (2001) 'Vertical Restructuring in the Infrastructure Sectors of Transition Economies', *World Development Report 2002 – background paper*, World Bank, Washington, DC.

Portes, R. (1991) 'The Path of Reform in Central and Eastern Europe: an introduction', CEPR Discussion Paper No. 559, London: Centre for Economic Policy Research.

Portes, R. (1994) 'Transformation Traps', *Economic Journal*, 104(426), 1178–89.

Radygin, A. (1995) *Privatisation in Russia: Hard Choice, First Results, New Targets*, London: CRCE – The Jarvis Print Group.

RET (2002) *Russian Economic Trends*, vol. 10, no. 1, Moscow: RECEP.

Starodubrovskaya, I. (2001) 'Housing and Utility Services', in B. Granville and P. Oppenheimer (eds), *Russia's Post-Communist Economy*, Oxford and New York: Oxford University Press. Ch. 14.

Sutela, P. (1998) *The Road to the Russian Market Economy: Selected Essays, 1993–1998*, Helsinki: Kikimora Publications.

18 Privatization and corporate governance in the Czech Republic
Michal Mejstrík

Introduction[1]

A characteristic feature of quickly transforming post-communist econo-mies is the imbalance of their economic development arising from a stage of economic and social restructuring that can be described as a process of 'creative destruction' (if we are to paraphrase the concept introduced by Joseph Schumpeter in 1942). The imbalances are, on the one hand, caused by the conscious economic policy diagnosis of various participants in the political process; on the other hand, they themselves lead to the unfolding of unexpected new imbalances, the solution of which requires major new economic policy responses (see Mejstrík, 1997).

The transition to a market economy inevitably has to include several aspects such as macroeconomic stabilization and trade and price liberaliza-tion. Privatization and the rapid formation of a private sector were added to this list by economic reformers as the only way to avoid the 'reform pitfall'. The problems of this policy were most significantly demonstrated in the key aspect of changes of ownership relations in strategic businesses. A privatization process which would gain and maintain the popular support of a substantial group of voters, and which at the same time would affect the critical core of companies to a sufficient depth, was unable to be achieved in many transforming economies for an extensive period of time (for example, in Ukraine, but also in the Czech Republic, and to a lesser extent in Hungary: see Chapters 20 and 21).

Except for demonopolization of their administratively formed monop-oly conglomerates, Czech political representatives in the first half of the 1990s prevented a government restructuring of state-owned enterprises before privatization as a matter of principle. This was because rapid and wide privatization was expected to cut the 'umbilical cord' of central pater-nalism and former personal and political alliances, born in the hierarchies of a communist economy. The direction of restructuring thereafter was intended to be left to the will of owners, following their private interests.

However, a different approach had been accepted for the telecommuni-cation, energy, mining and bank sectors prior to their privatization – mostly in the form of organizational and financial restructuring and the creation of a regulatory framework for natural monopolies. Finding the political will and consensus for the development of this regulatory framework for natural monopolies proved to be very difficult, slow and costly, and blocked the privatization and actual restructuring of companies until the second half of the 1990s.

The privatization programme

The types of ownership transformation in the Czech Republic are summarized in Table 18.1. The Czech programme was both a top-down and a bottom up approach and originally developed as the Czechoslovak (or CSFR's) privatization programme, which was later divided into separate programmes for the Czech and Slovak Republics (Czechoslovakia split voluntarily into the Czech and Slovak Republics in January 1993). The process was initiated by acceptance of a programme of small and large restitutions (100 000 restitution claims were settled and the return of property to the original owners or their heirs was an important if not a controversial part of all large privatization projects) as well as small privatizations (over 30 000 small units, such as shops, were auctioned in the small privatization programme). These developments are described in detail in Mejstrík (1997). The momentum of the Czech process was maintained by the massive privatization of over 6000 large companies and the rapid development of a small and medium-sized enterprise (SME) sector (see McDermott and Mejstrík, 1993; Benacek, 2001). In the privatization process foreign participation was encouraged, in the second half of the 1990s, through improved institutions and the government's FDI incentive programme. As a result, a huge amount of FDI flowed into the country.

The original top-down and bottom-up organization of the Czech privatization process can be illustrated through the fact that, with some strategic exceptions, between 1991 and 1993 managers of state-owned enterprises (SOEs) or bidders for them were supposed to prepare their own privatization plan, which was then reviewed by the Founder Ministry (i.e. relevant branch Ministry controlling the state enterprise subject to the foreseen privatization) and by the Ministries of Privatization in both the Czech and Slovak Republics. An excessive number of competing proposals were presented (on average three competing projects were submitted for each scheme in the first privatization wave) and this resulted in a great variety of privatization methods. Moreover, the volume of the work, involving evaluation and approval, transferred a great degree of authority to the relevant ministries. These, however, mostly selected projects submitted by the managers.

After announcing that its mission in transition had almost been completed, the existence of the Czech Ministry of Privatization and Property Administration ended in June 1996. It reportedly evaluated over 24 000 of

Table 18.1 Types of ownership transformation in the Czech Republic

Type	Method	1991–4	1995–6	1997–2002
Top-down ownership transformation	property restitution	intensive	limited	unfinished
	small privatizations	completed	—	—
	property sales of different forms	intensive	intensive	completed
	shareholding sales	limited	mostly domestic, FDI in telecom	intensive for banks, utilities mostly through FDI
	coupon privatization	completed	—	—
	land ownership transformation	partial	partial	partial
	municipalization	intensive including stakes in utilities	limited	limited
Bottom-up enterprise development	domestic start-ups	very intensive	moderate	moderate
	greenfield foreign direct investments	very limited	limited	very intensive
Consolidation of ownership	mergers and acquisitions	mostly domestic leveraged buy-outs	intensive domestic leveraged buy-outs	intensive domestic and FDI
Bankruptcies	amended bankruptcy law implementation	limited	limited	intensive after banks enforced loan repayments

nearly 28000 submitted projects, covering over 6000 companies. Each company project contained a decision on privatization in respect of individual privatization units, and their various divisions, which often independently used various alternative transformation methods; of these, over one-third had been approved. Remaining privatization projects were to be reviewed later by a smaller privatization department included in the Ministry of Finance.

Completion of the privatization programme
As of 31 May 2002, out of a total of 6623 privatization projects approved by the relevant governmental bodies and submitted to the Czech Fund of National Property (later 'the Fund' or FNP) and containing 16407 economic units with a total book value of over €32 bn, 98 per cent had already been at least partially privatized. This amounted to 6468 privatization projects containing 16172 units; see Table 18.2. The transformation of the ownership of property in section A of the table, as well as restitutions and small privatizations, had almost been completed, mostly in the 1990s; the

Table 18.2   Implementation of privatization projects by 31 May 2002

A. Sale and restitution of property in the Czech Republic

Approved method of transformation	Number of units by 31.5.2002		Total value of property in CZK mn by 31.5.2002	
	submitted	completed	submitted	completed
Public auction	1210	1200	8.5	8.5
Public tender	1380	1334	33.9	33.0
Direct sale	6680	6550	68.6	67.0
Gratuitous property transfer or restitution, restitution with additional purchase	5264	5216	71.9	71.6
A. Total	14534	14300	182.8	180.0

B. Foundation of joint-stock companies or takeover of ownership interests

B. Total	1873	1872	798.2	798.2
A+B. Total	16407	16172	981.0	978.2

Note: Book value data are based on the accounting data included in privatization projects (in contrast to Table 18.3).

Sources: The Fund of National Property of the Czech Republic, web page *www.fnm.cz.*

implementation of privatization projects in part B, especially for shareholdings, by the implementation body FNP was in principle completed by coupon privatization between 1992 and 1994. However, the final privatization of core shareholdings in most of the strategic companies was only completed in 1997–2002 (see Table 18.3).

The majority of large corporations transformed into joint-stock companies represented only 11 per cent of business units, but as they were mostly large companies, they accounted for over 82 per cent of the total book value of privatized property. This has kept the share of property value approved for coupon privatization close to 43 per cent of the total book value of privatized shares of joint-stock companies and around 35 per cent of the total approved volume. Table 18.3 provides further details on the different methods used to transfer shares.

The most notable development is found in the book value of 'shares intended for sale', which more than doubled between December 1996 and May 2002, as a result of the sale of banks and utilities (most notably the gas sector) to foreign parties. This is described more fully below.

Mass privatization
For medium and large state-owned enterprises (SOEs) the initial emphasis was on partial privatization through a coupon scheme, although other methods of sale emerged through competing or combined privatization plans, including directly negotiated sales, public auctions and tenders and transfers to municipalities. In reality the coupon method left the core of strategic companies intact and its implementation resulted in a number of serious problems.

Details on the coupon privatization are provided in Table 18.4. Each adult citizen was eligible to purchase a book of coupons both in the first and second large privatization waves – 1000 points of investment 'money' with limited maturity – for a registration fee of CZK1000. This fee, amounting at the time to around US$34 or 25 per cent of the average monthly wage, enabled self-financing of the scheme; net revenues of the FNP in 1995 included over US$110mn that originated mainly in registration fees. For the first wave of large privatizations, some 8.56 million Czech and Slovak citizens purchased coupons out of 10.5 million eligible citizens. This massive scale of participation, involving nearly three-quarters of all eligible citizens, was quite unexpected and somewhat rare in Central and Eastern Europe. These coupons entitled every citizen to bid, through a somewhat complex central auction process, for shares in a SOE of their own choosing in either round of sales, or to allocate their investment points to a financial intermediary, notably the investment privatization funds (IPFs), which emerged independently. These intermediaries, in turn, bid for

Table 18.3   Transformation of shares of joint-stock companies in the Czech Republic

Structure of assets and stages of the transformation, in total nominal value	From commencement of privatization, CZK bn (nominal book value)	
	31 December 1996	31 May 2002
1. Shares submitted to FNP	713.7	758.1
as part of privatization projects	696.1	
the FNP's contribution to companies (subscriptions)	13.2	
otherwise obtained shares (capitalization of claims)	4.4	
2. Implementation of share privatization:	500.3	616.3
shares intended for sale	68.6	173.5
public offer	12.6	27.7
direct sale to Czech parties	22.2	both to foreign and Czech
direct sale to foreign parties	13.7	117.1
employee shares	2.2	2.2
public tenders	17.8	26.5
shares intended for gratuitous transfer	431.8	442.8
coupon privatization	341.4	341.9
gratuitous share transfer to municipalities	52.3	55.7
shares for Restitution Investment Fund (RIF)	19.7	19.8
shares for restitution cases	1.8	1.8
Foundation fund (NIF)	0.5	1.9
Agricultural and forestry fund, and others	16.1	21.7
out of which reduction of registered capital	−3.6	−8.0
RIF shares	6.1	9.6
3. Shareholdings held by FNP	208.9	142.5
strategic holdings FNP	170.1	127.5
other holdings FNP	35.4	15.0
RIF	3.4	0

Note: Book value data are based on regularly updated accounting data.

Source: *Annual Report of the Fund of National Property of the Czech Republic 1996*, web page www.fnm.cz for 2002.

blocks of shares in the SOEs through the same auction process. Some 429 coupon investment funds were legally registered in the two republics, attracting 72 per cent of all coupons placed. However, 55 per cent of coupons placed with the IPFs went to just 14 investment fund groups, mainly subsidiaries or affiliates of the large commercial banks, savings banks and insurance companies. The incentives and governance structures of the IPFs, and in particular their financial relationship with banks, greatly influenced the restructuring outcome in the privatized sector (see EBRD, 1995). The accelerated creation of a capital market for over 2000 publicly tradeable shares held by more than 6 million small investors resulted in significant transaction costs, in particular the temporary expansion of numerous servicing personnel, such as 520 securities dealers, hundreds of investment funds and 153 investment management companies.

Table 18.4   Coupon privatization

	First wave	Second wave
Supply		
Number of shares	973	867
Book value of shares (CZK bn)	200	155
Eligible citizens over 18 (mn)	7.62	7.62
Demand		
Total coupon holders (mn)	5.95	6.17
Coupons invested through firms (mn)	4.33	3.92
Number of funds	264	353
Average book value per coupon holder (CZK)	33 600	25 700

Note: Some shareholdings that remained unsold in the first wave of privatization were sold in the second wave.

Source: Own calculations (Mejstrík, 1997).

The majority of shares in Czech companies (842 out of 973) offered for sale in the first wave were accounted for by coupon purchases. Coupon shares therefore became the most important block of shares in these companies, followed by non-coupon investors such as direct investors. The expected share ownership dispersion did not characterize the initial ownership pattern of companies, however. Instead, key companies were dominated by several institutional owners or funds that represented the interests of the investment company owners. Under the Czech Commercial Code and the characteristics of corporate governance given the institutional framework described below, the views of the investment funds prevailed at shareholders' general meetings over the remaining, unorganized (and usually absent) dispersed shareholders. Table 18.5 provides an analysis of the effective voting strength of different investors at selected general meetings. The table is based on a study of 919 Czech firms privatized in the first coupon privatization wave (the votes of very small shareholders who had usually not taken part in voting were omitted). The results show, for example, that coalitions of one to four investment funds could have achieved a majority of the votes at general meetings in 727 joint stock companies. Hence, as a result of coupon privatization, a substantial portion of the Czech and Slovak economies was effectively controlled by a relatively small number of privatization funds. Moreover, in spite of a diversification rule, which required a 20 per cent ceiling on any single IPF's ownership of the total nominal value of securities issued by the same issuer, the promoters of funds found ways to obtain control over companies by placing the ownership of additional share parcels in other entities that they established.

Table 18.5   Relative power of investors in Czech companies after the first coupon privatization wave

Investors' voting strength	50%	40%	30%	20%	10%
Foreign investors	33	40	45	45	51
Domestic direct investors	24	30	40	47	58
Temporary holdings of FNP	56	88	135	173	293
Permanent holdings of FNP	3	7	11	11	21
Shares to be sold by banks	12	17	30	47	61
Additional restitutions	4	6	7	11	52
Single largest fund	146	231	442	737	895
Two largest funds – cumulative	473	644	782	974	916
Three largest funds – cumulative	669	760	847	892	918
Four largest funds – cumulative	727	790	860	897	918
Five largest funds – cumulative	754	809	867	900	918
Six largest funds – cumulative	761	817	869	902	918
Ten largest funds – cumulative	768	821	872	903	919

Source: Laštovicka *et al.* (1995).

Mass privatization usually includes the distribution of shares in SOEs to the public, either free or for a minimal charge, generally through a coupon allocation scheme. The coupon model holds out the promise of both rapid privatization and widespread involvement of the population and, to some extent, an equitable initial distribution of former state-owned wealth. In the case of the Czech Republic, on one hand, the high number of new investors created new constituencies in favour of a market economy and the ruling political representation. On the other hand, the coupon schemes proved to be complex, held many pitfalls, and paradoxically, during and after their implementation phase, resulted in an undermining of public support for privatization, restructuring and their political sponsors. The first very problematic matter was a lack of relevant legislation that would develop a standard financial market framework. As a result, the official transfer of shares into private hands was not conducive to effective corporate governance. The wide dispersion of ownership led to a lack of effective corporate governance at a time when strong shareholder control was necessary to discipline firms' management. An inadequate protection of ownership rights and a weak institutional structure led to a corporate governance style under which companies could continue to behave in inefficient ways. These developments are described more comprehensively below.

A second issue was that coupon privatization provided neither the enterprises nor the state treasury with needed finances. This was not as urgent a problem in the Czech Republic as in some other countries at the time, because of the state's budgetary surpluses; however, little of the required capital for industrial restructuring was raised through registration fees for coupon sales. At the same time, coupon distribution did not add to the financial burden typically caused by privatization through leveraged buy-outs.

The third issue is that the capital market generated overnight through the coupon scheme was thin and heavily artificial. The mass initial public offering (IPO), overlooking the role of fresh cash, led to a terribly undercapitalized market that was bound gradually to die unless it could create a more normal environment and attract new external and financially strong investors. Finally, other shortcomings of the voucher privatization system can be suggested, such as complexity and exposure of inexperienced citizens to undue risks. The lesson from the Czech example is that countries beginning their privatization programmes should examine the various options open to them, taking full advantage of the experience to date.[2]

Czech case-by-case privatizations
Of the various available privatization methods, public auctions gained the highest possible financial returns to the government and guaranteed fairness and transparency in determining the eventual owner. Nonetheless, this method was hampered by the fact that typically there was not a sufficient amount of money among the population to allow for successful auctions. Additional finance, widely provided by banks, often resulted in the granting of risky credits (see Mejstrík, 1997: ch. 6). In the beginning, often the contracts signed with buyers were incomplete and this meant that some privatization proceeds were not collectable. Also, an exclusive focus on the money a potential buyer was willing to pay meant that other factors were neglected.

Smaller blocks of shares in the hands of the FNP were regularly sold on the capital market through public offerings. Looking at Table 18.3 above, the remaining 'other' minority holdings of the FNP, valued at CZK 15 bn (in 55 companies) in May 2002, might be subject to privatization as soon as the market allows by a variety of techniques. However, in the recent past another 60 companies have gone bankrupt or have been liquidated.

A public auction or tender in which other criteria than money are used (such as a willingness to develop the industry with committed investment, maintain levels of employment, protect the environment, reinvest future profits and so on) resolves some of these problems and is more sensitive to the character of the privatized property. But it is more vulnerable to subjective decision making, favouritism and perhaps even corruption. It has also created the grounds for incomplete contracts, leading to a limited chance of the government getting paid in full.

Direct sales, on the other hand, involve no organized competition among buyers. Rather, a sale is made to a predetermined buyer. The Czech Republic requires the specific approval of its government for direct sales to be made. Nonetheless, in cases where many different projects were submitted, which all proposed direct sale within similar rules, the FNP took the decision and thus projects proposing direct sale were encouraged.

Privatizations of strategic companies: the last, but moving, target
In May 2002 the Fund received €4.1 bn for the majority government gas sector stake, a sum equivalent to triple the book value at the enterprise and representing an unprecedented single privatization revenue. However, the remaining strategic holdings of the Czech FNP (CZK 127 bn) include majority stakes in 21 strategic, mostly partially privatized, companies, seen so far as natural monopolies or 'family silver' (for example, utilities such as telecommunications, energy generation, oil and energy transmission and wholesale distribution, airports and post). While privatization of telecommunications companies is being completed, the government is about to propose sales of certain parts of the remaining strategic shares, but only after implementation of a regulatory and privatization framework for these natural monopolies.

In the traditional strategic but dying sectors, such as metallurgy or machinery, which rely heavily on government interventions, problems continue. In general, across the whole of Central Europe political factors have for a long time blocked the preparation of an adequate regulatory regime for natural monopolies in the power and gas sector, as well as privatization of the banking and industrial core through sale to strategic investors. Political pressures and lobbying, frequently revived by the appearance of incomplete contracts, has usually limited offers of businesses to be sold to strategic investors in terms of number and quality. Governments, being under public pressure, have gradually limited themselves to sale of peripheral businesses, while the key businesses and their core have remained protected by the 'umbilical cord' of state paternalism with soft budget constraints. All over the world state ownership brings a significant side-effect consisting in easier and cheaper access to credit resources, as credits to companies co-owned by the state are *ceteris paribus* considered to be lower risk even by private banks. There is always the opportunity of a state guarantee, bridging subsidies, tax and customs advantages, and favourably set state-regulated prices that crowd out investment in private companies. This type of 'state insurance' is especially visible in the traditional, over-manned and inefficient Czech metallurgy sector. It encourages the continuation of non-efficient behaviour on the part of companies co-owned by the state, as well as irresponsible entry into high-risk activities due to 'moral hazard'. The banks are not saved from moral hazard either.

Another consequence or concomitant of state paternalism, which has occurred in the Czech Republic from the beginning of 1995, is a significant slow-down in the process of the removal of non-viable, especially 'strategic' or 'too big to fail' companies through bankruptcies; restructuring that might have indirectly resulted in increased productivity and competitiveness for domestic manufacturers. For example, out of 8700 bankruptcy petitions filed in the Czech Republic, only 1900 bankruptcies were declared, often after several years' delay. As a result, soft budget constraints for hugely inefficient companies are retained and a chain deterioration of payment discipline occurs across the economy. However, the exceptional bankruptcy and reprivatization of the traditional machinery producer CKD Transport Systems, in 2001, may mark a turning point and open a new era.

In conclusion, the Czech Republic has adopted a system which allows for a variety of privatization techniques, not simply the coupon model as quoted by many analysts. This system has provided flexibility, but at the same time it has concentrated much decision-making power in the hands of the government's project evaluators. In order to cover the gradually emerging transformation costs, the importance of the privatization proceeds for governments has increased, which in turn has increased the importance of case-by-case sale methods (see below).

Privatization and corporate governance in the Czech Republic

The emergence of tradeable shares and the opening of the capital market created certain prerequisites for establishing efficient corporate governance. Major corporate governance issues have been raised, however, by the Czech process of transition to a market economy. Most authors share the view that the pure act of transferring ownership of assets from the state to the private sector does not of itself establish the conditions for enhanced corporate governance, which would in turn generate greater enterprise efficiency. Problems arise for a number of reasons.

- Privatization is a one-off process and has conflicting economic, financial and political objectives reflecting particular interest groups (for example, foreign v. domestic buyers, insiders or outsiders).
- In coupon privatization, the government administratively enforced the initial public offering of nearly 2000 share issues and their public tradeability. Among most of the participants this created an expectation of the overnight emergence of a liquid and functioning capital market with shares for all investors, no matter how small. Naturally, those expectations could hardly be met at once. The government, however, had not supplemented administrative rules applied in a centralized, 'laboratory phase' of share distribution, with the implementation of an institutional market framework that would generate involvement of at least the best corporates in public share trading and a willingness of investors to invest in the companies. The government has withdrawn for quite a long time from its role in cultivation of the institutional and legal framework for capital markets and the creation of relevant expectations within the investing public and enterprise management.
- The assumptions of well-functioning markets, particularly the markets for capital, management labour and corporate control, have not been met.
- Banking institutions effective in either the Anglo-Saxon or the German sense have been absent.
- Underdeveloped institutional and legal frameworks have meant that the important necessary conditions for effective corporate governance have been absent. For example:
  — most contracts have an incomplete character and it is difficult to enforce them;
  — non-banking financial institutions have been left without proper regulation and supervision. These include the collective investment vehicles (mutual or investment funds, pension funds, insurance companies) that resulted from coupon privatization. Moreover, there has been no political will to enforce the existing laws;
  — monitoring and accountability procedures have been weakly performed, both inside companies and outside;
  — superficial auditing rules (for example absence of any explanatory notes to the accounts) have led to poor and misleading audits even for the most important corporations;

— rating quotations by recognized rating agencies have been unavailable and external investors have had to invest under conditions of significant uncertainty. It is not surprising, therefore, that portfolio investors, both domestic and from abroad, have lost their appetite for Czech shares. The field has thus been left open to insider investors and insider trading. This development has been neither effectively monitored nor sanctioned.

— business courts were flooded by minor cases that should have been dealt with in a different manner. Cumbersome rules of procedure and evidence meant that cases took too long to resolve, while the backlog of leases kept increasing and eventually exceeded several years. A first-come-first-served system has meant that major cases have been dealt with only after long delays unless intensive lobbying was applied. Judges, apprehensive about making a decision, have further delayed cases by abusing the procedural rules. Judicial independence and irremovability has, in practice, often meant that even the blatant misbehaviour of judges has been punished only rarely. Czech judges are not bound by decisions reached in similar cases by their colleagues and there is little attempt to judge the cases in light of the intention of the legislation. The employment of a formalistic approach by the judges has meant that collusion or intention to defraud has been virtually impossible to establish, except where the accused confessed – a rare outcome;

— business courts have registered changes in statutory bodies only with long delays and this has increased the lack of transparency. Challenges to registering changes in the registered share capital have also been dealt with slowly. This has hampered both financial restructuring and the initial public offering of equity;

— the bankruptcy code has been incomplete and was not fully enforced until 1999;

— payments of unpaid promissory notes or bills of exchange have been hard to enforce when institutions, such as an executor, were missing.

Within such a difficult institutional framework, western corporate governance models need to be assessed in a different light.

The Anglo-Saxon principal–agent approach
This approach to corporate governance has met insurmountable challenges in the Czech Republic, owing to the absence of its preconditions. There has been no access to liquid stock markets that would give the shareholder unrestricted, low cost exit opportunities. In particular, the liquidity of

trading for small fragments of shareholdings has been negligible. There has been no takeover barrier to management discretion and enormous acquisition premia. Only in 1996 was a mandatory bid in the case of a takeover by a majority 50 per cent shareholder introduced. Buy-out prices, based on the easily manipulable public market price, have been low. In most cases, however, distribution of shareholding into the hands of two or three legal entities was sufficient to preclude any buy-out at all.

Minority investors have not been protected. They have been unable to rely either on sufficient information or on profit sharing, to which they were entitled. The extremely limited role for shareholder voice in this model, through the right to vote at company general meetings, has been further limited because at general meetings no proxy voting has been allowed. Decisions, such as on takeovers – an issue of such importance that most authors agree that shareholders should always have a right to decide – have been decided at remote locations with limited and very costly access for small shareholders. Class actions have not been allowed, which has further increased the transaction costs for dissenting shareholders. While some attempts had been made to create associations of small shareholders (for example, OSMA – Ochranné Sdružení Malých Akcionáru), in practice the only action a small shareholder can take is to exit with a loss.

There has been a general tendency to leave public markets and go private not only for small to medium-sized companies but for many large corporations, either to escape the restrictions on their activities which a share listing entails or, in the case of companies taken over by foreign capital, in adherence to the parent company's policy. Of the originally 'publicly tradeable' companies in the Czech Republic, 90 per cent have been delisted. At the same time, the limited number of IPOs taking place so far has involved cases of income transfers from controlled companies rather than a genuine share subscription from new investors. In the case of genuine IPOs, the par (minimum issue) value of almost all listed Czech companies would have to be lowered to obtain P/E (price/earnings) ratios acceptable to new investors. However, the existing rules for changing the issued share capital are very cumbersome when it comes to lowering the par value. In any case, companies are not interested in behaving in a way which would give them a chance to obtain capital on the share market because they anticipate that no one would risk their money in a joint stock company over which they do not have control. This, in turn, has served to further confirm the suspicions of outside investors about investing in privatized corporations, thus setting up a vicious circle.

Companies have not accommodated small shareholders since the gains from so doing were lower than the costs. The unethical behaviour of companies has made the cost of financial intermediation through the stock market prohibitive.

The stakeholder model
In the Czech Republic, it has been explicitly intended that this model should be applied in a limited number of cases, such as in the partial privatization of large and small corporates with a regional monopoly (such as the local distribution companies of energy, gas and water). Their important clients – municipalities – were allocated registered (non-tradeable) shares according to the number of inhabitants. These shares were intended to represent a blocking minority vote, according to Czech law, of 34 per cent, in order to increase their 'voice' in company management. However, limited minority shareholder protection and a weak voice in practice, plus the expected low dividends and the temptation to sell out to international investors, led most municipalities to sell their shares. They sold options to their registered and barely transferable shareholdings through entering into very complex option, future or loan contracts. Cash-hungry municipalities disregarded the stakeholder model, providing evidence of mistrust and lack of interest in the administratively enforced stakeholder model of corporate governance.

If we take the stakeholder model in its more general meaning, that is companies behaving in a way which does not maximize only the direct interest of its shareholders, it must be said that little official encouragement has been given to the notion of 'good corporate citizenship'. This is propagated in countries such as Germany or Japan, which actively advocate the social contract model of public life. Nevertheless, companies did on many occasions go beyond their legal duties in curbing environmental emissions and in supporting sporting and other welfare activities in their communities.

The single owner model
The single owner–manager approach is typical for closely-held or privately-held companies and its adoption has become widespread. It is often considered as the most straightforward way to govern an enterprise that does not have access to public financial markets, with the added benefit of a reduction in the firm's direct information costs. The limited reporting by the firm, however, makes it less transparent to its business partners, while (non)compliance and low information disclosure requirements can lead to further difficulties. The decisive role in external financing is taken by bilateral loans provided by banks, which are the only monitoring institutions. Worldwide, this model has been used by SMEs or strategic investors, while until recently in the German or Japanese environment such a model reflected the governance of many large corporates.

Large shareholders behaving as a single owner
The markets for capital and corporate control transform themselves into a bivalent form when only '0' or '1' are the values for corporate control. As

there was no market for 'smooth' quantities of shareholdings, only a market for majorities or control in the Czech corporate world, gaining a voting majority gave the majority shareholder the ability to dispose of the entire profit, not just its share of it. This was possible because the controlled company could be forced to enter into disadvantagous contracts with trading vehicles set up by the dominant shareholder. Profits, and not infrequently assets, were stripped away from the company. In the opinion of commercial lawyers, police prosecutors and judges, there was no viable way in which this practice could be deemed illegal. Managers of many investment management companies were able to replace passive investors' behaviour and enjoy all the advantages of controlling industrial holdings without the consent of the mass of their minority shareholders, and often to the detriment of their interests. Quite a number of investment companies conducted themselves in a manner that would elsewhere be deemed unethical, to say the least. Nevertheless, they escaped any adverse repercussions.

News that a controlling portion of a company's shareholding was held by one shareholder was almost invariably followed by a rapid decline in that company's share price. In effect, the costs of takeovers in the Czech Republic were reduced by half because the acquisition of 50 per cent (sometimes less) of the issued shares allowed the dominant shareholder to appropriate all of the potential profit. Although legislation was eventually implemented requiring a shareholder to make an offer to purchase the shares of the other shareholders after passing the 50 per cent threshold, it was easily circumvented by acting through more than one corporate entity. As a result, the dominant shareholder came to possess all the advantages of a single owner on the backs of those remaining shareholders who had been unwilling or unable to sell while the dominant shareholding was built up. Moreover, since the acquisition was typically financed by bank loans, there was no downside risk if the company subsequently failed through bad management or asset stripping. The loans would remain unpaid and the banks ended up owning worthless shares that had been pledged as the security for the loan.

Many dominant shareholders went a stage further and used their voting power to cancel the public tradeability of the shares, a practice only possible before legislation was passed mandating an offer to purchase the shares of the other shareholders at net equity value. This spared the dominant shareholders the cost and nuisance of having to comply with the informational requirements imposed on publicly traded companies, though these were negligible in comparison with the requirements prevailing in Anglo-American capital markets.

Given the unrepeatable character of privatization and the incompleteness of most contracts and of the institutional framework itself, many actors in the corporate sector, and not just the managers but also investment funds and asset management companies, played a one-shot game at the expense of the managed companies and their minority shareholders. The dominant strategy was 'cheating': that is, exploiting any contractual incompleteness in a largely unregulated environment to one's own advantage. Such a model also describes the wider Central and Eastern European environment in the recent past.

Leveraged Buy-outs (LBOs), the failure of state-owned commercial banks and the behavioural formulae of owners
The large state-owned financial institutions that gave birth to the biggest groups of managed funds and their investment companies were not completely privatized until the end of the 1990s. These, as well as the companies which they controlled, effectively remained in state ownership. The portfolio companies that they directly and indirectly controlled were influenced by the state-owned banks' policies and by management appointed by the state, both of which were heavily guided by a desire to accommodate what the management perceived to be the wishes of governmental agencies. The banks' ownership of these companies had a long-term impact on their asset quality owing to the violation of the principles of prudential banking and the efficient allocation of savings. This resulted in the granting of bad loans 'secured' by collateral agreements based on large amounts of production assets, which were often obsolete and hence with a potential market value much lower than the loan.

Between 1994 and 1996, large banks provided credits enabling ownership transfers between domestic investors and the consolidation of shareholdings in enterprises formerly privatized by coupons. This was a serious failure of the banks, with the rare exception of Czeskoslovenska obchodni banka (CSOB) observable mostly at the banks 'controlled' by the state. Instead of enforcing discipline amongst the largest debtors (for example, enterprises Chemapol, CKD Holding Praha and SKODA Plzn, controlled by Czech 'would-be' capitalists) and pushing them towards enterprise restructuring, banks granted debtors further loans. These included loans for leveraged acquisitions of coupon privatized companies and even of foreign companies. Such subversion of hard budget constraints, something to which the government as the main shareholder of those banks had publicly committed itself, arguably imposed greater subsequent costs on the state budget, and on the minority shareholders of the banks, than if these enterprises had gone through a bankruptcy process earlier. The larger the relevant enterprises were, the more political and economic power they represented and this slowed down the use of bankruptcy legislation because of the misuse of the argument 'too big to fail'.

The enterprises inevitably faced a poor future, and usually crashed at the first recession.

The atmosphere of tempting acquisition opportunities undoubtedly contributed to the above mentioned 'bivalent form' of Czech corporate governance focused on majority control. The prisoner's dilemma can explain relevant behaviour of a number of indebted Czech corporate owners and creditors. It also strengthened the conflict of interests between corporate owners' and creditors' roles within all financial groups. Under an imperfect governance structure, the ownership alliances of banks have not supported, either domestically or abroad, any IPOs of indirectly owned corporates that injected into them the external equity which was needed for restructuring. Banks have been afraid of the dilution of their shareholdings, which might eventually lead to a loss of corporate control.

Disregarding a handful of cases of share capital increases, all of which retained the existing ownership structure because shareholders exercised their right to subscribe, Czech companies have had to rely on their internal financial sources and other credit lines. This has worsened their corporate capital structure and interest rate sensitivity and in turn slowed down innovation and increased the firms' cost of capital. This development might have been avoided in view of the experience of countries exposed to similar corporate governance problems.

Privatization of key bank shareholdings
After lengthy political discussions and delays, the privatization of bank shareholdings began in response to the banks' management failure. Bank privatization finally helped to break the vicious circle described earlier. The first direct privatization deal involved financial institutions (excluding Investicni a postouni banka (IPB)) and the most successful one was CSOB. Its shareholders sold their shares to a Belgian bank (KBC) for €1.2bn in June 1999. IPB was affected later by an enforced privatization to Nomura. The sale appears to have been unsuccessful and the company was quickly reprivatized in 2000 to CSOB, controlled by KBC, after being placed in receivership in July 2000, and with a resulting negative effect on the state budget (the estimated costs were over €3bn). Privatization of Ceska sporitelna to Erste Bank Sparkassen for over €600mn in 2000 and Komercni banka to Société Générale in 2001 were affected by large cleaning-up operations of their non-performing loans before their privatization. In general, for all of the banks privatized their net balance was negative, as demonstrated in Table 18.6, which emphasizes the cost of the pre-sale balance sheet clean-up. The revenues from and costs of Czech bank privatizations in the second half of the 1990s are summarized in Table 18.6. However, both the pre-sale clean-up and an attractive Czech depositary and corpo-

Table 18.6   The cost of and revenues from Czech bank privatizations in the second half of the 1990s

	Revenues (CZK bn)	Estimated cost (CZK bn)
Komercni banka	42.8	51.4
CSOB	1	43.2
Ceska sporitelna	20	23.4
IPB	3	
Total	106.8	217

Note:
* Current estimate of costs for workout of IPB bad loans guaranteed by the Czech state.

Source: Estimate, *www.cnb.cz*, CERGE-EI (2001: 87) and Ceska sporitelna.

Table 18.7   Comparison of privatizations of banks in Central and Eastern Europe

Privatized bank	From	Shares for sale (%)	Buyer	Price/ book value	Date of transaction
CSOB	Czech R.	65.69	KBC Bank	2.2	June 1999
Pekao	Poland	52.10	UCI/Allianz	2.2	August 1999
Bank Handlowy	Poland	56.00	Citibank	1.8	January 2000
Ceska sporitelna	Czech R.	52.07	Erste Bank	1.6	March 2000
Bulbank	Bulgaria	98.00	UCI/Allianz	1.5	October 2000
Slovenska sporitelna	Slovakia	87.20	Erste Bank	1.8	January 2001
Zagrebacka Bank	Croatia	55.00	UCI/Allianz	1.5	May 2001
Komercni banka	Czech R.	60.00	Société Générale	3.0	June 2001

Source: National Property Fund of the Czech Republic, mimeo.

rate market generated sufficient interest in the privatization tender auctions, and this led to fairly high price-to-book value ratios in the case of CSOB and Komercni banka, especially in comparison with other bank privatizations in Central and Eastern Europe (see Table 18.7).

Foreign direct versus portfolio investment
One of the developments reflecting the 'Czech structure' of privatization and corporate governance has been a rapid but fluctuating inflow of foreign direct investment (FDI), into both privatized companies and greenfield projects. These are reflected in the country's balance of payments account

(Table 18.8). This has contrasted with the limited and fluctuating amount of foreign portfolio investments into the non-transparent environment of the Czech capital market. Foreign investors have adjusted their behaviour to the Czech institutional framework. Strategic owners have been able to control their companies much more directly through FDI, leading to a much smaller agency problem.

FDI volume and fluctuations are due to three sources: privatization sales (95 per cent in 1995, but 60 per cent in 2000), reinvestments and greenfield investments, all of which are influenced both by government policies, such as the tax level and FDI incentive policy, and by other factors, such as country creditworthiness or territorial differentiation targets of investors. While the largest individual foreign direct investments usually resulted from a limited number of case-by-case privatizations, the coupon privatization inspired large numbers of medium-sized investments by strategic investors, who gradually took over many companies privatized through the coupon and temporarily controlled by investment funds. Since 1997, there has also been a growing number of greenfield foreign investments attracted by government FDI incentives. At the end of 2001, the Czech stock of FDI in the form of equity capital totalled US$23.6 bn. The overall FDI volume including reinvested earnings and credit relations with foreign investors stood at US$26.7 bn. The Czech Republic achieved the highest figure per capita for FDI within Central and Eastern Europe in the 1990s, as evidenced by the figures in Table 18.9. The FDI inflow for 2002 will be fostered by several large acquisitions, especially by the €4.1 bn privatization proceeds for the gas sector. Foreign investors have derived confidence from the political stability of the country, its almost completed privatization programme and an improved legal environment gradually incorporating elements of the EU's *acquis communautaire*.

Over the period 1990–2000, FDI has been highly diversified by sectors with a focus on the service and production sectors (60 per cent and 38 per cent, respectively, of total FDI until 2000) and to a lesser extent on the trade and repairs sector (15 per cent) financial intermediation and insurance (15 per cent), transport and telecommunications (11 per cent) and real estate (9 per cent), which has generated a certain mix of positive and negative structural and trade impacts. As a result, today around 3400 enterprises are either owned or co-owned from abroad, with 64 per cent of these companies having 100 per cent foreign ownership, another 25 per cent having more than 50 per cent foreign ownership and 11 per cent having a 10–50 per cent foreign stake. It is particularly significant that over 94 per cent of banking sector assets are now foreign-controlled. The major investors in the Czech Republic have come from the Netherlands, Germany, Austria and the USA, which respectively have accounted for 30 per cent, 26 per cent, 11 per cent and 7 per cent

Table 18.8 Balance of payments of the Czech republic

US$bn	1992	1993	1994	1995	1996	1997	1998	1999	2000	2001
1. Current account	−0.3	−0.5	−0.8	−1.4	−4.1	−3.6	−1.2	−1.5	−2.7	−3.3
2. Financial and capital account	0.0	3.0	3.4	8.2	4.3	1.1	2.9	3.1	3.8	4.5
Direct investments	1.0	0.6	0.7	2.5	1.4	1.3	3.6	6.2	4.9	4.8
Portfolio investments	−0.03	1.6	0.9	1.4	0.7	1.1	1.1	−1.4	−1.8	5.4
Long-term capital	0.3	0.8	1.1	3.4	3.1	0.9	−2.0	−0.7	−0.1	0
Short-term capital	−1.3	0.06	0.7	1.0	−0.9	−2.2	0.2	−1.0	0.8	−1.7
3. Errors, exchange rate differences	0.2	−0.1	−0.3	0.6	−0.8	0.3	0.3	0	−0.3	0.4
4. Decline in foreign exchange reserves	0.08	−3.0	−2.4	−7.5	0.8	1.8	−1.9	−1.7	−0.8	−1.8

Source: Czech National Bank.

Table 18.9   FDI inflow into the Czech Republic

			FDI into Central and Eastern European countries per capita (US$)			
Year	FDI into Czech Republic (US$mn)	% of GDP	Czech Republic	Hungary	Poland	Slovenia
1997	1 275	2.4	126	214	127	189
1998	3 590	6.0	361	202	165	125
1999	6 234	11.6	615	196	188	91
2000	4 934	9.3	447	170	233	91
2001	4 820	8.6	—	—	—	—
1990–2000 cumulated FDI per capita			2 082	1 782	1 018	803

Source: Czech National Bank (2002), quoting WIIW Vienna for per capita comparative data.

of FDI. Thus the Czech Republic now has deeply integrated private owner-ship rights within European and worldwide ownership networks.

Privatization and enterprise restructuring
An additional financial debt burden had accumulated as a result of the cost of privatization and subsequent leveraged acquisitions, accelerated espe-cially by the chain acquisitions of a number of firms by the largest domes-tically controlled companies in 1995–6. This has worsened the capital structure of many Czech firms and increased their cost of capital. In this environment, sectors and branches of the economy have been restructured to very different degrees; in particular, a neglect of restructuring is widely recognized in the railways and some other non-privatized industries. Lobbying by trade unions and other vested interest groups in the unrestruc-tured sectors has prevented change and kept, for example, wage growth par-allel with the inflation rate, in spite of a sharp decline in labour and capital productivity. The experience of the Czech Republic, along with that of Poland and Hungary (see Chapters 19 and 20), suggests that this situation in the unrestructured industries permanently threatens negotiations about rational wage increases in other industries. Very limited restructuring has also taken place within large heavily indebted domestic conglomerates (for example, Chemapol Group, Skoda Plzn, CKD Holding Praha), which accumulated debt due to chain acquisitions financed by credits. These firms have become financially distressed and have responded to the reduction of their cash flow by letting their arrears grow. Their stretched budgets have been heavily hit by recession, such as the slowing down of government pro-

jects in 1997–8. Trying to avoid bankruptcy, these conglomerates have taken advantage of the incomplete legal framework within this 'one-shot game', relied upon their size to exercise political influence, diversified their risk through the formation of subsidiaries, and adopted creative accounting to hide their troubles. No management energy has been left to focus on the development of key competencies and rationalization through the sale of unmanageable subsidiaries. Given their financial weakness, most of the restructuring projects that occurred were badly managed and the confidence of customers became seriously eroded. By 1999, most of these companies had finally gone bankrupt.

Some industrial companies, mostly foreign-controlled, have responded to demand and market signals properly with deeper restructuring, with cost adjustments (including a temporary cut in real wages, succeeded by quick wage growth after rapid productivity growth was achieved), by introducing new products and technologies and by more active marketing – all within the framework of a new 'contract architecture'. They have significantly increased their non-price competitiveness (for example, Škoda cars owned by Volkswagen) and have become the engine of an outward-looking, export-led growth stimulated by foreign demand. Sectors with competitive market segments and higher value-added products have been able to sell in the highly competitive OECD markets. These companies have also had a lower cost of capital because they have been able to borrow in international markets via their parent companies. As illustrated in Mejstrík and Zemplinerová (1998) and a CNB report of 2002 and other recent research reports, a significant amount of enterprise restructuring (both reactive and proactive) has already been achieved, both within sectors of the Czech economy and within some firms.

Results of research surveys have confirmed the positive impact of foreign-owned companies on restructuring, but also some problems. Czech analysts sometimes talk of a two-speed economy, where the more rapidly growing segment is represented by the more effectively governed, more deeply restructured, foreign-controlled companies. In 2001, profitability, measured by average return on equity (ROE) in (non-financial) foreign-controlled corporates, reached over 9.9 per cent, while the ROE was only 4.3 per cent for domestically controlled, large private non-financial companies. The same sort of gap was reported in the previous period, 1997–2000, and for the indicator return on assets (ROA) (see Table 18.10). Foreign-controlled companies also performed better in terms of capital productivity and foreign trade, both importing and exporting a larger share of production. While they contributed 42 per cent of 2001 total industrial value added, employing 32 per cent of labour and 34 per cent of assets, they generated 51 per cent of total net profit and 50 per cent of corporate taxes.

The most important point to stress here is that, over time, these corporates have applied much more demanding external 'contract architecture' in relationships with their suppliers and customers than other Czech companies. Customers have had to pay their liabilities on time and suppliers have had to deliver their products at audited quality and 'just in time'. This has required innovations in processes and capital expenditures. If these conditions were not met, they were excluded from suppliers' lists, which meant their departure from the few 'islands of stability' within the wilderness of the Czech enterprise sector. Yet even these few 'islands' have eroded. Since 1997, the Czech Statistical Office has published data suggesting that the payment discipline of large foreign-controlled firms has seriously deteriorated; their payables overdue have doubled. In this respect they have got closer to Czech company 'standards', under which companies unfairly gain competitive advantage and lower their cost of capital at the expense of their suppliers.

Table 18.10   Performance of foreign-controlled and domestically-controlled enterprises in 2001

	Domestic economic controlled (%)	Foreign controlled (%)
ROA	5.1	8.7
ROE	4.3	9.9
Value added/assets	21.5	29.3
Equity/assets	50.9	43.6
Imports/cost of sales	19.0	54.0
Exports/sales	22.4	57.0

Source: Neumaier (2002).

Conclusions

The key task to transform state-owned enterprises (SOEs) into value-maximizing concerns in the Czech Republic was first addressed in terms of a change of ownership, through both enterprise sales and coupon privatization. The coupon privatization was a form of artificial primary issue or IPO as a means of transforming ownership interests from the state to private hands. Transfer of stock into the hands of coupon shareholders (natural persons or legal entities) did not mean, however, finding definite owners and did not necessarily increase corporate capital.

Until 1997, the government rigidly relied upon the laboratory environment of the first privatization stage, where an imperfect legal framework was totally inadequate for the efficient functioning of a market economy. Supported by the strong voice of a number of Czech would-be capitalists, later often bankrupted owing to excessive debts and neglect of restructuring, the government accepted the prevalence of 'incomplete contracts'. Incomplete contracts led to a general unenforceability of assumed contractual obligations, and an unassailable position of debtors vis-à-vis creditors and of majority shareholders vis-à-vis minority shareholders. This trend was reinforced by the destructive effects of poorly and slowly functioning courts.

Even after some of the inadequacies in capital market regulation were removed, starting in 1994–5, the government did not manifest a political will to supervise compliance with the regulatory rules covering the behaviour of the most important institutional owners, mainly the investment funds and investment management companies. Those in control of funds and investment management companies were allowed to abuse the existing contractual incompletenesses to their individual benefit. Collective investment vehicles were transformed to the advantage of the investment management companies without the consent of the mass of their minority shareholders and to the detriment of minority interests. Many of the investment management company executives pursued short-term profit rather than the long-term interests of their investors. A variant was enterprise ownership by alliances of funds sponsored by the large state-controlled banks. They usually supported at least a reactive restructuring and viable enterprise development. A deeper restructuring was, however, impeded by the banks' conflict of interest as owners and creditors and they had no interest in external injections of additional equity capital.

Economically, this contributed to a seriously biased corporate governance regime in the Czech Republic, the departure of many portfolio investors, and the poor performance of the Czech capital market. In turn, this further limited the possibility of restructuring the SOEs privatized by coupon. Consolidation of shareholdings in a non-transparent environment attracted leveraged takeovers by financially weak but well-connected players, who counted on making short-term speculative gains by reselling their shares. The more stable ownership structures were dominated by foreign, strategic shareholders.

Typically, economic relationships have either a cooperative game or a prisoner's dilemma characteristic: full cooperation maximizes the participants' joint pay-off in the long-term 'repeated game', but 'cheating' – that is, exploiting any contractual incompleteness to one's own advantage – remains the dominant strategy in a one-shot game. With the example of foreign-controlled companies in the Czech Republic, the hypothesis that firms which build a reputation for ethical collaboration, are able over a long period to substitute cooperative outcomes for unsatisfactory cheating ones, is illustrated. These relationships of the firm – the internal and external 'contract architecture' – are undoubtedly the source of considerable competitive advantage. Furthermore, firms which have fostered such a reputation have established themselves as islands of microeconomic institutional stability. They have enjoyed an advantage in attracting new trading partners (as customers, suppliers or employees) precisely because the latter know that the former can be expected to maintain their reputation. Nevertheless, the one-shot advantages based on legal imperfections (such as capital market legislation relating to mandatory bids) can hardly be ignored by rational foreign investors in spite of their long-term orientation. Ethical temptations are always present in situations characterized by unrepeatable opportunities for individual gain, such as a privatization process based on incomplete contracts within an imperfect institutional framework.

The Czech example shows that a cheating strategy based on contract incompleteness leads to the outflow of needed capital from companies, undermines their restructuring and deepens their indebtedness. Economic recession then arises, followed by the collapse of holding company structures, with serious economic losses. As we have already mentioned, in historical situations of this type there is an acute need for government activity to speed up institutional changes that clarify rules and prevent unacceptable behaviour on the part of managers and owners. Von Mises saw the basic institutional characteristic of a market economy as the owner himself being liable, as it is he who absorbs the damage caused by mismanagement of the enterprise. This characteristic of a market economy should be taken into account both in the long-run policies (amended bankruptcy law) and in the short-run policies (revitalization programmes) of Central and Eastern Europe. The Czech experience also suggests that the government should enter into well-defined privatization contracts, preferably with serious foreign investors whose influence leads to a more widespread adoption of responsible corporate governance and corporate behaviour in the economy.

Bank privatization finally helped to break the vicious circle described earlier. Many hidden and unsolved problems had, however, accumulated in the meantime. The existing approach to pension funding was left intact and restructuring steps, such as early retirements, helped contribute to its gradual collapse. Restructuring problems to tackle a sizeable bad debt problem (25 per cent of GDP) as well as environmental guarantees issued by the FNP during the privatization process (over €4.5 bn) have had secondary effects. They require urgent treatment in the next five years.

A number of institutional changes have lately been discussed and adopted by the Czech parliament. A new, less imperfect, capital market regulation has been foremost among them. Since April 1998, the capital market supervision by the Ministry of Finance has been replaced by an independent regulatory Securities Exchange Commission. That Commission might be complemented step-by-step by self-regulated organizations of market players based on a binding code of conduct. An amended business code and Security Act adopted by Parliament in September 2000 have reshaped the institutional environment further. A 'legislative storm', demonstrated by over 800 new or amended acts passed by the parliament between 1999 and 2002, has introduced a number of reforms on the road to implementing and perfecting new laws along the line of the EU's *acquis communautaire*. However, the road ahead is still a long one.

Notes

1. This chapter is based on the results of an EU-ACE Research Project P96–6171–R, 'Corporate Governance, Privatization and Industrial Policy' and grant GAČR No. 402/99/06066. I would like to thank Vladimir Halama of EEIP and the editors for their work on the English version of this paper and for a number of invaluable suggestions made. The remaining errors and omissions naturally remain my responsibility.
2. A critical, more detailed technical analysis of the Czech coupon model briefly presented above can be found in Mejstřík *et al.* (1997) and especially in Mejstřík (1997).

References

'Annual Report of the Fund of National Property of the Czech Republic 1996–2001', Prague (*www.fnm.cz*).

Benacek, V. (2001) 'The Generic Private Sector in an Economy of Transition: Developments and Impacts on the Czech Economy', research Report IR 01–046, IIASA, Laxenburg.

CERGE-EI (2001) *Czech Republic 2001: Mixed Blessings*, Prague: CERGE EI.

Czech National Bank (2002), 'Balance of Payments Report', Prague (*www.cnb.cz*).

EBRD, *Transition Report 1995, Investment and Enterprise Development (Economic Transition in Eastern Europe and the former Soviet Union)*, London: EBRD.

Laštovicka, R., A. Marcincin and M. Mejstřík (1995) 'Corporate Governance and Share prices in Voucher Privatizatized Companies', in J. Švejnar (ed.), *The Czech Republic and Economic Transition in Eastern Europe*, New York: Academic Press.

McDermott, G. and M. Mejstřík (1993) 'Czechoslovak competitiveness and the role of small firms', in D. Audretsch and Z. Acz (eds), *Small Firms and Enterpreneurship*, Cambridge: Cambridge University Press.

Mejstřík, M. (1997) 'Privatization in the Czech Republic and Russia: The Voucher Model', in H. Giersch (ed.), *Privatization at the End of the Century*, Berlin: Springer-Verlag.

Mejstřík, M. and A. Zemplinerová (1998) Final report of EU-ACE Research Project P96–6171–R, 'Corporate Governance, Privatization and Industrial Policy', mimeo, Prague.

Mejstřík, M., A. Zemplinerová and A. Dervis (eds.) (1997) *The Privatization Process in East–Central Europe: The Evolutionary Process of Czech Privatization*, Dordrecht/Boston/London: Kluwer Academic Publishers.

Neumaier, I. (2002) 'Are we going to be just an Assembly Line?', *Ekonom Weekly*, 25, Prague.

19 All roads lead to outside ownership: Polish piecemeal privatization

Tomasz Mickiewicz and Maciej Baltowski

Introduction

The purpose of this chapter is to provide an economic discussion of privatization, privatization policy choices and actual results in Poland. First, it explains why the privatization of state enterprises was implemented with delay, as compared with other elements of the economic transformation programme introduced at the beginning of 1990. Next, it examines the choice of privatization methods, the political economy of privatization and the three major policy issues: namely, the pace of privatization, sequence of privatization and the authority to initiate and carry out privatization. Initially, employee buy-outs (EBOs) played a significant role in privatization programmes, yet, in the later stage, outsider privatization gained more significance. In addition, post-privatization ownership transfers resulted in a convergence of ownership structures towards those controlled by outside institutional investors. The appendix presents a detailed technical guide on privatization methods in Poland and a basic set of figures illustrating the outcome.

Privatization in the political context of a reform programme

Even before the first post-communist ('Solidarity') government was formed, the round table talks between Solidarity and the communist government, in Spring 1989, revealed the polarization between 'liberal' views (a relatively new trend) and 'socialist self-governing' views on privatization. The latter was a well established tradition within the Solidarity union. It originated in the earlier programme of limited reforms (1980–1). Apparently, the economic section of the round table talks was dominated by the adherents of employee self-government, whose aim was more to remedy the failings of the socialist system and to improve management of the state property than to carry out radical ownership transformation. Instead of privatization, they talked about the socialization of the public sector and about ownership pluralism. The only concession made to the potential privatization programme adherents was the adoption of the uniform 'state property fund', a notion which was to encompass a departure from the existing form of state enterprises supervised by their founding bodies. The implicit rationale

402

behind this arrangement was not only to create an entirely new model of ownership supervision, but to ensure a basis for ownership transformations and for efficient use of the assets at the disposal of the existing state enterprises. The agreed programme of reforms stipulated the liquidation of the structure of state enterprise 'founding bodies' by the end of 1990.

The first post-communist government, headed by Tadeusz Mazowiecki, commenced its mission in the summer of 1989. At that time the attention of the political and economic elite was not concentrated on privatization; the focus was on stabilization, internal liberalization and external liberalization. Regarding macroeconomic policy issues, choices were more obvious and there was at least general agreement on the direction of policy. Ownership transformation, however, was a subject characterized by a lack of consensus and this resulted in a delay in political decisions. Hence privatization of state enterprises was not considered a priority in drafting the guidelines for Poland's economic reform. The Balcerowicz plan, submitted to the *Sejm* in October 1989 and adopted at the end of the year in the form of a package of statutory legislation, assumed that 'it is essential to solve such macroeconomic problems as the budget deficit, inflation, foreign exchange reserves and foreign debt before taking necessary measures to combat economic inefficiency which was identified as a crucial, though difficult and time consuming problem' (Lukawer 1994:739–40; see also Balcerowicz, 1995). It was also decided that the problem of macroeconomic stability and liberalization should be solved by means of a 'shock therapy', while privatization and institutional changes should be carried out gradually. Moreover, the Balcerowicz Plan assumed that the 'hard' financing of enterprises and the development of market competition would ultimately foster higher productivity in state enterprises and enforce a mode of functioning similar to that of private entities. The realization of these goals would precede a slower privatization process.

While the theoretical elaboration for this strategy was provided three years later by Balcerowicz (1995), in the autumn of 1989 the practical rationale for adopting such a sequence of measures was simple. Macroeconomic stabilization policies, as well as introducing a greater degree of economic freedom, have always been included in a standard set of activities undertaken by governments of countries that take advantage of financial support provided by the World Bank and the International Monetary Fund. Those practically tested instruments of economic policy were applied in Poland with a relative degree of success. Yet, with respect to radical institutional changes, and to a large-scale privatization scheme for state enterprises in particular, a recourse to existing western practices was impossible since there was no previous experience of this scale of ownership change. At the same time, the existing proposals by foreign advisors[2] (for which no political consensus existed yet) were more directional in nature than operational, and as a rule could not be immediately submitted to the *Sejm* for legislative consideration. Marek Dąbrowski is right to say that, with the disappearance of the political barriers that blocked privatization for years, 'new obstacles of a conceptual and organisational nature appeared' (Dąbrowski, 1991:406). Indeed, among the top economic tiers of the government, and more specifically between Mazowiecki and Balcerowicz and their foreign and domestic advisors, there was no consensus concerning the direction of the privatization process, let alone about the details of a comprehensive programme of reform.

Privatization options

In addition to various ideas for improving the existing state enterprises, there were three main categories of privatization blueprint in Poland. They were two concepts of non-equivalent privatization – the so-called 'public' (mass, voucher) privatization and employee privatization – both consisting of free or partially free disposal of property, and a concept of equivalent privatization, that is, making state property available to private owners through the sale of firms or assets, preceded by an evaluation process.

Mass (public, voucher) privatization

The concept of public privatization, was formulated at the end of the 1980s in Gdańsk-based liberal circles. In the autumn of 1988, Janusz Lewandowski and Jan Szomburg presented a coherent blueprint of mass privatization based on privatization vouchers, summarized as a 'genuine and radical transfer of ownership rights to the public at large' (Lewandowski and Szomburg, 1989:72). These authors proposed a uniform distribution of shares of privatized state enterprises to the Polish adult population totalling 28 mn.[3] Their original project contains many features that were later adopted in the limited version of a mass privatization programme (see appendix). The authors proposed that inscribed and non-tradeable privatization vouchers would be issued. The mass privatization programme was to be carried out by *Towarzystwa Wspólnego Inwestowania* (Joint Investment Societies) that would function as mutual funds. This idea of voucher privatization was, one way or another, later executed in most countries of the former communist block (Hungary being a notable exception; see Chapter 20).[4]

Employee buy-outs

The concept of employee buy-outs was promoted in Poland by Rafał Krawczyk as early as in 1986.[5] He argued that priority should be given to enterprise employees, who would receive 51–60 per cent of shares, which for the period of three to five years would generate no income. Public sector employees would participate in the privatization of state banks. The justification provided by Krawczyk was that this was the only feasible privatization path. Any other option would be strongly resisted by the employees and, in effect, the whole process of privatization would come to a standstill (according to the provisions of the Act on State Enterprises of 1981, employees were granted significant control rights). Thus Krawczyk's argument provides the same intuition as that later formalized by Blanchard and Aghion (1996).[6]

At the turn of the 1980s, a large and influential group of economists, politicians and employee self-government activists perceived employee ownership plans in privatization as the essence of a structural and ownership transformation of the Polish economy. The group included representatives of the political opposition (such as Ryszard Bugaj, Marek Dąbrowski, Władysław Frasyniuk, Jerzy Osiatyński and Szymon Jakubowicz) and members of the ruling elite (Marcin Święcicki and Leszek Gilejko). They demanded preferential terms for the employees of state enterprises in the process of ownership transformations. It was argued that those demands were justified historically, because of the contribution of the 'Solidarity' trade union to the abolition of the communist system, and also it was believed that preferential terms granted to the workforce would ensure vital social support for privatization as well as other structural reforms.

In the summer of 1989, the parallel American idea of ESOPs (*Employee Share Ownership Plans*) appeared in Poland and won immediate approval amongst Solidarity union activists, though more among the lower tiers of union members than in the National Commission. The concept of ESOP and other employee ownership schemes[7] was widely promoted, particularly among union and self-government activists in major industrial sites (Ludwiniak, 1989; Kurowski, 1989). ESOP advocates held that the ideas of universal employee stock ownership perfectly matched both the existing expectations and specific characteristics of the Polish economy. These ideas were perceived as a remedy for social problems resulting from the structural transformation that was under way. Thus, in a sense, employee ownership was perceived as an implicit guarantee that the manufacturing sector retained responsibility for welfare functions, as under communism.[8] With the benefit of hindsight, we may say that this view was rather naïve and neglected the fact that the role of employee ownership is rather marginal in highly developed OECD economies, where the share of such firms does not exceed a mere 1 per cent of ownership. The proponents of the idea of employee self-government cited a variety of arguments, including economic theory, statements supporting the positive implications of employee ownership,[9] such as '*Laborem exercens*' (the Pope's encyclical in which John Paul II advocated the supremacy of labour over capital), and practical experience of the German socially oriented market economy with its '*Mitbestimmung*' – employee participation in management.

Equivalent privatization

The idea of 'equivalent privatization' was announced officially in the so-called 'Beksiak Group Programme' prepared by Professor Janusz Beksiak, in association with a group of economists affiliated to the Catholic University of Lublin. The scheme was devised at the request of the presidium of the Citizens' Parliamentary Club ('Solidarity') in August–September 1989, and it was promptly submitted to the government headed by Tadeusz Mazowiecki for consideration. Privatization constituted a relatively substantial part of the scheme (Beksiak *et al.*, 1989: 29). According to the scheme, all enterprises over 250 employees were to be transformed into joint stock companies as of 1 January 1990. Of the shares, 20 per cent were to be allocated free to the employees, whereas the remaining 80 per cent were to be taken by the State Treasury and subsequently made available to private investors (on either a mass or limited scale of sale depending on the type and financial standing of a given enterprise). The scheme allowed for the exclusion of some major national corporations (such as the Polish State Rail and Polish Mail) as well as the military sector. With respect to smaller state enterprises, that employed under 250 persons, the scheme proposed the establishment of the National Property Fund (in other words, a state enterprise 'liquidation commission') with area offices. The aim of the Fund was to take over supervision from the 'founding bodies' of these enterprises with a view to prompt sale thereof. This procedure was referred to as 'direct privatization' (see appendix).

Thus the Programme assumed a free-of-charge transfer of 20 per cent of company shares to the employees. This figure became an immutable canon of ownership transformation in Poland (see appendix). These share transfers could be primarily considered as a form of employee compensation for their initial control rights in state enterprises, guaranteed in previously existing employee self-government legislation.[10]

Equivalent versus non-equivalent privatization

The political decision to opt for the procedure of non-equivalent privatization of state enterprises (that is, mass privatization or employee privatization) was perceived as highly probable in the autumn of 1989, given the fact that the consensus at the 'round table' talks was not pro-capitalist in character. In addition to that, there were social expectations concerning the participation of employees and all citizens in the privatization of the national property. Surprisingly, these two concepts met with a barrage of criticism from Krzysztof Lis, who, in October 1989, became Government Plenipotentiary for Ownership Transformations. The group headed by Lis claimed that such solutions could seriously hinder the development of a market economy and consolidate the inefficient mode of firms' operations, based on 40 years of 'real socialism' and eight years of employee self-government structures. The idea of a 'trust', that is, collective ownership of shares (an important element of the ESOP system), seemed particularly dangerous, since lack of share transferability could block the development of both the capital market (including the stock exchange) and financial mechanisms of investment allocation. Accordingly, contrary to the predominant public mood, the final decision of Mazowiecki's government was to opt for the equivalent privatization model with some concessions for employees. This mode of thinking was reflected in the State Enterprises Privatization Act adopted by the *Sejm* on 13 July 1990. Yet, while equivalent privatization was adopted in principle, in practice this was not quite the case.

Most importantly, given the conditions of the Polish economy during the first two years of market reforms, it was difficult to distinguish between equivalent and non-equivalent privatization. It turned out that the supply of national property offered for sale exceeded the market demand. The latter was largely limited, owing to some restrictions imposed on foreign capital and to lack of interest from both foreign and domestic investors, resulting from economic instability. Thus the equilibrium sale price was low. This led to a situation where the owners of any financial resources benefited tremendously, since within the framework of formally 'equivalent' privatization they could transform their resources into 'non-equivalently' large parts of the national property, thanks to its low market price.[11] Thus equivalent privatization was in reality non-equivalent, with preference given to existing owners of financial resources. The problem is that those who benefited were either (1) former *nomenclatura* members, (2) participants in the so-called 'shadow' (that is, illegal) economy, and/or (3) representatives of the old, licensed private sector, many of them directly linked to the former communist power structures. As in the other transition countries, 'this reallocation of property rights is regarded as unjust by broad segments of the population, because the acquisition of competence, information and assets by former members of nomenclature is not perceived as legitimate' (Brucker, 1997: 103).

Thus the choice between equivalent and non-equivalent privatization was, in political terms, the choice between different social groups that would obtain economic gains. In the case of non-equivalent privatization, the group of beneficiaries would include either all adult citizens of Poland, enterprise employees or former property owners and their heirs. Experience of other transition countries demonstrates that all these groups were politically acceptable, yet in Poland the third group was practically excluded from the privatization process owing to lack of sufficient political support. More generally, the impossibility of 'equivalent privatization' in the early phase of the process implied strong preference for politically acceptable beneficiaries of the process (that is, employees and the general public). Only at a later stage did stronger interest from foreign owners and the emergence of domestic institutional investors shift the balance towards equivalent privatization, as the prices became more acceptable.[12]

Dilemmas concerning privatization procedures

Even when the basic pattern of ownership transformation had been decided, there remained three dilemmas of an apparently more technical nature, yet their settlement was vitally important to the final picture of the privatization path. The issues to determine, were (a) the pace of privatization, (b) the sequence of privatization, and (c) the authority to initiate and carry out privatization processes.

The pace of privatization

The pace of privatization is linked to the mode of privatization. Practically speaking, only mass, non-equivalent privatization can guarantee rapid and radical changes in the formal ownership structure of the economy. On the other hand, however, this model of privatization carries the risk of weak corporate governance and does not result in access to new finance (see Chapter 16). Therefore its effects on restructuring are usually rather insignificant. In contrast, a slower pace of privatization may result in implementation of more efficient corporate control structures, immediately after ownership change. Thus slower formal privatization may, in fact, result in faster convergence towards efficient post-privatization control structures with well-defined (outside) owners, capable of introducing effective restructuring programmes.

At the same time, however, slower privatization may be arrested by political decisions before its completion. This results from the fact that the state sector may regain its position as a strong pressure group affecting government administration. Delay to privatization may result in consolidation of the industrial lobbying after the initial period of 'extraordinary politics'[13] and government financial support for unrestructured industries.

Following the opinion of the Minister of Privatization in 1992, Gruszecki (1995:81), one can safely add that one more cause of the slow pace of the privatization process in Poland lay not so much in the lack of adequate structural solutions and shortages of capital resources, but in the lack of 'entrepreneurs', that is, people who knew how to lead and manage enterprises. Given the pattern of privatization adopted, there was almost no one to sell the national property to: there were not enough potential managers because the old post-socialist traditional 'private sector', represented by craftsmen, sole traders and farmers, was completely unprepared to take over the state enterprises.

The sequence of privatization

The next issue relates to the sequence in which privatization projects were to be implemented. In theory, given the limited processing capacities of privatization agencies, the focus of early privatizations should be on branches with high relative gains in terms of efficiency: the effect of the form of ownership on profitability depends on the type of industry in which enterprises are operating.[14] In the case of emerging industries, where innovation is rapid or where competition for products is high (or may be introduced fast, as in trade and services), privatization leads to faster and much better results. Competition potential is high in the consumer goods sector of industry. On the other hand, potential efficiency gain related to privatization is relatively smaller in some well-established sectors and industries where monopolistic practices are relatively difficult to remove. It follows that the transformation should commence in those branches of the economy that guaranteed the best results. This was the case in Poland. Again, typically, these were also branches with a lower value of assets per employee, which strengthered the initial tendency towards employee buyouts. Outside manufacturing, the privatization of the banking sector was initiated early and carried out in a steady and careful way. While the privatization process was slow, it was still faster than in most other transition countries and that had obvious implications for the efficiency of financial flows, including investment.

More difficult privatizations were saved 'for later'. Yet, as a result, the traditional manufacturing industries as well as the sectors responsible for the economic infrastructure, characterized by a strong position and high lobbying potential, became ardent defenders of state ownership, making privatization a long and complicated process. The subsequent cost of restructuring programmes and the impact of continuous poor fiscal discipline in some of the largest state enterprises (rail, coal mining, metallurgy) were important factors resulting in the fiscal crisis of late 2001. In the late 1990s, over ZL4bn were spent on the mining sector restructuring programme, with generous financial allowances for voluntary redundancies. Yet, after significant downsizing, by late 2001 the sector still paid only 86 per cent of due VAT and 65 per cent of local taxes. Another major problem area related to state rail (ZL3bn in overdue obligations), metallurgy (ZL1.2bn in overdue payments in taxes) and the sugar industry (the debts of just one sugar refinery regional cartel – Silesian – amount to ZL450mn) (Mickiewicz, 2001).

Thus, given piecemeal privatization methods and the limited technical capacity of privatization agencies, the strategic choice implied a trade-off between a focus on sectors where the potential immediate gain in efficiency from privatization was highest and sectors where early privatization could

prevent entrenchment and eliminate the subsequent impact of poor financial discipline.

Authority to initiate and carry out privatizations
The last issue which required settlement concerned the choice of bodies
authorized to initiate and carry out privatization. After long discussion, the
Sejm finally rejected plans for stringent parliamentary control of the privatization process, a measure that would have a detrimental and delaying
effect on the efficiency of privatization in general. It was decided that
because the state was the owner of national property, the government
administration would be responsible for ownership transformation, with
provisions requiring the self-government body of state enterprise to give its
consent to an initiation of the relevant procedures (see appendix). The
management of state enterprises that faced privatization had the power to
influence the path of proposed privatization, and they exercised this right
in a variety of ways. There were also examples of companies that did not
meet the objective criteria for a given privatization path, yet, despite the
initial negative opinion of their 'founding body', exerted considerable pressure and successfully executed privatization procedures. There are also
examples of successful actions to stop privatization of economically sound
state enterprises that generated interest among serious investors, yet where,
owing to strong resistance from trade unions and/or the workers' council,
privatization processes were not initiated, even when additional concessions were subsequently offered.

The selection and the course of privatization could be hampered by the
presence of not two, but three or even four parties involved. These comprised the founding body representing the interests of the State Treasury,
the workers' council representing the vital interests of employees, and the
outside buyer who could submit bids and trigger privatization. There was
also the management of the enterprise, who might support the interests of
any of these three parties, though, in practice, managers were likely to take
the point of view either of the prospective owner or of the employees, but
hardly ever that of the State Treasury. The following patterns could therefore be distinguished during the privatization procedure:

1. the buyer siding with the founding body against the employees – a sit-
    uation found frequently during direct privatization with the participa-
    tion of outside capital;
2. employees and managers against the founding body – occurring most
    frequently when an employee lease was under negotiations;
3. employees and the founding body against the buyer and the manage-
    ment team – usually occurring during the 'quick transaction' procedure.

Thus a privatization procedure led to the dispersion of competence and responsibility. It caused tensions, mutual suspicions, accusations and more generally increased transaction costs and delayed the process. Yet the procedure also had advantages, which are typically overlooked by outside observers. It made it difficult for the parties to engage in secret agreements and thus substantially reduced the risk of corruption. The distribution of privatization competence between the four parties discussed above internalized the interests of all those involved and constrained the potential for political influence. At the same time, it introduced mutual control. This control was exercised by the interested parties who jointly had a complementary, full picture of a given privatization process and all its intricacies, which could be hidden from any external audit. It is also worth stressing that the existence of strong independent trade unions was advantageous from this point of view. While in some cases trade unionists colluded with management, in many others they created strong checks on illegal/semi-legal asset stripping by managers.

The influence of the three non-governmental parties in privatization procedures could counter-balance the impact of state supervision over these processes, which is, given the inadequate standards of public administration in Poland, most tainted by short-term politics. Indirect privatization (through corporatization, see appendix) was and still is a more vulnerable method of privatization in this respect, and this threat looms over mass privatization programmes, such as those already administered by the National Investment Funds. Wieslaw Kaczmarek (1997), Minister for Ownership Transformations in the years 1993–6, did not hide his disenchantment when he wrote upon leaving office: 'Politics remains the chief enemy of privatization. It happened many times that economic considerations in favour of privatization gave way to the realisation of political aspirations or goals. . . . Parliamentary debates, questions and interventions of MPs and senators or some articles in the press revealed all too clearly that the criticism of privatization was actually but a "cover" for various private interests.'[15]

Transfer from insiders to outsiders and the residual state property
The results of existing research show the positive impact of privatization on performance. Studies have confirmed that privatized enterprises invest more, create a long-term development strategy, introduce state-of-the-art production methods and launch new products. They also improve and enhance their management systems, pay attention to human resource management and recruit adequate personnel (Megginson and Netter, 2001). Yet these positive effects of privatization on enterprise restructuring clearly depend on the specific ownership structure resulting from such transformations. In particular, companies that do not have a strategic investor operate

differently from strong companies with a private outside investor. The results in the latter group are better, as they are in the companies where the institutional owner is its principal shareholder, usually a leading domestic or international corporation (Havrylyshyn and McGettigan, 1999; Djankov and Murrell, 2000).

The results confirm that preference for outside investors was reasonable from the economic point of view, but proved to be difficult to implement. The stronger than expected role of EBOs resulted (a) from pressure coming from industry insiders; but even more importantly, from (b) the identity of potential outside owners, which was difficult to accept from the political point of view, (c) insufficient demand from outsiders, especially in the first years of transition, and (d) the complexity of flotation/evaluation procedures. Wherever attractive outside investors were present, it was possible to compensate the employees for their loss of control rights via a free allocation of minority shares, wage increases at the time of privatization and employment guarantees.

Secondary transfers of ownership, post-privatization convergence
The empirical studies seem to point out that secondary ownership transfers are under way in Polish privatized enterprises (Kozarzewski and Woodward, 2001; Kozarzewski, 2002). This process consists of another significant wave of ownership transformation that is sweeping through already privatized enterprises and leading to a convergence of various ownership structures created as a result of the different paths of privatization. This phenomenon largely pertains to employee-owned enterprises, which make up approximately 60 per cent of all privatized enterprises in the country (yet far less in terms of the value of assets – see appendix). After two to three years of operations, the ownership structure in the privatized companies is undergoing noticeable changes that seem to follow two directions: the emergence of a dominant group of shareholders from inside the companies, usually made up of persons linked to top management; and the taking over of control of enterprises by a major entity from outside that incorporates these enterprises into its holding company (or capital group).

This second process, the takeover of ownership control of privatized companies by a major external entity, usually follows a certain course, as follows:

1. An employee-owned company, which is heavily burdened with lease-related obligations experiences a shortage of financial resources; in particular its development needs are not satisfied.
2. The management of the company begins to seek strategic outside investors ready to put up considerable capital. This search, carried out

primarily within the same industry and alongside existing cooperation links, usually leads to companies that used to be members of former industrial conglomerates or foreign trade corporations, which have developed and maintained a strong presence in international markets.

3. Such potential investors are themselves successful companies, often listed on the stock exchange, and which wish to extend their activities throughout Poland by capitalizing on their former connections.

4. Facing the pressing need to increase the company's capital, the owners (or principal shareholders) of leasing companies are willing to accept equity participation by a strong partner who has already been in the market for several years. Thus the initial owners frequently abandon their principal ownership rights in return for a more secure future in a stronger organization.

Survey results reported by Kozarzewski and Woodward (2001) compare the ownership structure of employee-leased companies immediately after privatization with the most recent evidence available (1999). The most interesting changes relate to the following:

- a rapid decrease in the share of equity held by non-managerial employees, from 58.7 per cent to 31.5 per cent;
- an initial increase of the share held by executive board members, from 8.7 per cent to 15.1 per cent in 1998 – yet the share seemed to decrease or at least stabilize in the following year (14.2 per cent in 1999);
- a rapid increase of the share of ownership held by strategic outside investors (both foreign and domestic), from 1.4 per cent to 17.1 per cent; this is the most significant category of outside owners;
- increase in the share of all other outside investors, except 'corporatized firms'.[16]

The political character of residual state property

As the state sector shrinks, the pace of privatization slows down because the fewer state enterprises are left to be privatized, the more difficult it is to privatize them (a corollary: the fewer the enterprises owned by the state, the stronger their political character becomes).

The completion of each privatization process reduces the domain of the state, which in fact is the domain of the bureaucracy. It is also a fact that the number of state officials who deal with ownership transformation processes, and who supervise state enterprises on behalf of the state, is not reduced in proportion to the spread of privatized enterprises. At the same time, in Poland the political involvement of high-ranking officers in the ministry or regional authority levels is on the rise, as recent years seem to demonstrate. In fact, experience shows that various new forms of *nomenclatura* have developed covering medium- or low-ranking managerial posts in the bodies of economic supervision, whereas at the beginning of the 1990s only top managerial positions were counted in that number. It follows that the growing 'concern' for political influence in the economy must concentrate on the ever decreasing number of enterprises – hence the political intensification. This view is confirmed by the fact that, during the past few years, practically every single decision concerning the selection of members of supervisory boards in joint stock companies (under State Treasury control) required political approval, whereas at the beginning of the structural transformation specialists with no affiliations to political parties were selected (that is, so-called 'computer-aided' selection was applied).

Conclusions
The privatization of state enterprises in Poland, which began 10 years ago, is coming to an end. Private ownership in the economy, measured by its contribution to the GNP, is now approaching 75 per cent – a level comparable to that of the West European countries.

The privatization process in Poland has encompassed a diversity of methods and the adoption of the principle of a case-by-case privatization. Yet the share of employee buy-outs in privatization was significant. It resulted not necessarily from the strong position of insiders (as they could be compensated during any outsider privatization) but from lack of interested outside investors, particularly in the early phase of the privatization process. Fast insider privatization has one important advantage as compared with the continuation of state-owned enterprise: even if there is no initial improvement in efficiency, the privatization triggers secondary ownership transfers. Here the Polish experience confirms theoretical intuitions in this respect developed by Blanchard and Aghion (1996), Aghion and Blanchard (1998) and Filatotchev *et al.* (1999).

The variety of the privatization procedures adopted and their pace distinguish Polish privatization from the privatization processes in other countries of the former communist bloc, where the pace of formal privatization was faster (especially voucher privatization, as in Russia and the Czech Republic – see Chapters 17 and 18) and more uniform in nature.[17] It seems, however, that irrespective of the adopted patterns of privatization and the manner of the departure from the legacy of socialism in the economy, the economic systems of the majority of Central and Eastern European countries are becoming very much alike. In particular, control in the privatized sector is shifting towards institutional investors, both foreign and domestic companies. This trend is strengthered in Poland by the increased role of outsider privatizations in the later stages of the privatization process. At the same time, it is not the privatization outcomes, but the problem of entrenched sectoral interests in the residual state property which is developing into a serious economic problem. Continued financial support for the residual state sector, mainly in the form of tax arrears, is one of the factors negatively affecting Poland's fiscal balance (Mickiewicz, 2001).

While the privatization-related legislation proved highly efficient, the two weak points of the entire privatization venture in Poland relate to (a) organizational shortcomings (no independent privatization agency, a failure to find a viable solution to the problem of unwanted property, insufficient personnel and resources involved in carrying out the privatization processes), and (b) a deficient information policy: little effort was made to inform public opinion and win support for privatization to ensure a satisfactory atmosphere for the realization of ownership transformation.

Appendix: privatization methods in Poland

Two clusters of privatization methods are applied in Poland: indirect privatizations through corporatization, and direct privatization paths via liquidation. They will be discussed in turn.[18]

Indirect privatization (through corporatization)

As a first step of the privatization process, state-owned enterprises (SOE) are converted into a standard joint stock company, governed by the rules of the Commercial Code rather than the old Law on State Enterprises. In this new company, 100 per cent of shares is initially owned by the State Treasury. This transformation is called 'commercialization' or 'corporatization'.

At the same time, the firm is transferred from the register of the parent government agency ('the founding body', either regional authorities – *wojewoda* – or branch ministries) to the jurisdiction of the Ministry of Privatization. According to 1990 legislation, the Minister of Privatization was obliged to make the shares publicly available to buyers within two years from the date of the corporatization. This was not respected in practice and the condition was removed in 1996.

There are two paths leading to corporatisation. The Minister of Privatization transforms the enterprise either upon the joint request of its managing director and workers' council, following consultation with the general assembly of all employees and the parent government agency ('founding body'), or upon the request of the parent government agency ('founding body') with the consent of the director and the workers' council, again following consultation with the general assembly of the employees. There is also an exceptional path, where the Prime Minister, upon the request of the Minister of Privatization, transforms a state enterprise without the consent of insiders, although their opinion must be solicited by the minister.

Corporatization leads to the diminution of workers' control over the enterprise, as the workers' council ceases to exist. It is replaced by the standard supervisory board, where only one-third of members is elected by the employees and two-thirds are appointed by the Ministry of Privatization (and employees lose their right to elect one-third of the members after privatization, that is, when over 50 per cent of the shares is transferred to private hands). Some incentives were created to gain insiders' support:

- 15 per cent of shares were reserved for employees, who are authorized to buy them on preferential terms (before 1996: 20 per cent);
- there was a 20 per cent reduction in the restrictive excess wage tax (*popiwek*) levied on wage increases above allowable limits in state enterprises (the tax has now been completely abolished);

- corporatized enterprises may be exempted from an asset tax ('dividend') levied on a portion of the book value of the capital of state enterprises.

There are some additional rules under the mass privatization scheme.

After corporatization, three alternative methods of privatization were applied, namely: the capital method, mass privatization and bank-led restructuring.

The capital method is always preceded by an individual assessment for each privatized company. It can be implemented using three different methods: (a) initial public offerings (IPOs) via the stock exchange, (b) public offerings outside the stock exchange (for smaller companies, where either individual offers from investors are collected and compared or an auction is organized), and (c) open invitation to negotiations (typically, for the largest and most strategic companies in good financial condition).

In the case of negotiations, the resulting privatization contract includes three other dimensions, in addition to price. All were important criteria for the choice of strategic investors:

- an investment programme, with priority for export-enhancing restructuring;
- 'social' programme, which relates to employment guarantees, typically for a period of 24–36 months (yet sometimes longer – in some cases even up to seven years) and any other social benefits for employees;
- environmental programme, with commitments related to natural environment protection and regeneration; this is particularly important in view of more stringent EU regulations being imposed on countries such as Poland that are candidates for EU membership.

In practice, the three methods of capital privatization might be used simultaneously.

Amongst 225 companies that were recently quoted on the Warsaw Stock Exchange, 70 per cent were privatized companies and 30 per cent new private companies. The first group includes 50 companies[19] for which initial public offering was a method of entry to the stock exchange and 90 companies that were floated on the stock exchange by the new owner after privatization. However, even for the latter group, at the time of flotation the Treasury would typically sell the residual shares. Thus the privatization process was critical for the emergence of the Warsaw Stock Exchange.

Warsaw's stock exchange has performed relatively well, compared with other countries. In 2000, liquidity was relatively high, as measured by the ratio of market turnover to market capitalization (132 per cent), which was the second highest after Hungary (204 per cent). In addition, the Warsaw Stock Exchange has a good record of being used for new equity issues (Pajuste, 2001).

Mass privatization programme[20]
Participation in the programme had to be accepted by insiders. After the initial selection by government, an open invitation was sent to enter the programme and either the enterprise director or workers' council could raise objections within 45 days. In July 1995 and December 1995 (in two waves), the shares of 512 participating companies (equivalent to 10 per cent of the production potential of all the initial state sector) were distributed among 15 national investment funds (NIFs), the Treasury and employees, for each company: 33 per cent of shares went to one leading NIF, 27 per cent to the remaining 14 NIFs, 25 per cent were retained by the Treasury, and 15 per cent was transferred free of charge to employees. (In certain cases, a further 15 per cent went to entitled individuals, such as farmers and fishermen, who had contractual relations with the company concerned, and the percentages above were adjusted.)

National Investment Funds (NIFs)   NIFs were established as joint stock companies, and thus as closed-end investment funds. Initially, 100 per cent of their shares was owned by the Treasury, then 85 per cent of their share capital was transferred to certificate holders (see below) between mid-1997 and the end of 1998. The remaining 15 per cent of equity was retained by the state to be used for compensating the fund management. During this transitory phase, all dividends were allocated to a fiscal account for the benefit of certificate holders, who were entitled to receive them after the final transfer of ownership.

The NIF organs consist of a supervisory board, a management board and the general assembly of shareholders. However, the actual management of the assets can be delegated to 'management firms'. Self-managed funds were strongly discouraged. In particular, funds managing their assets without the help of a management firm are not eligible for a performance fee, unlike those that are externally managed.

NIFs could conclude management contracts exclusively with management companies included on the list selected through competitive tender by the Selection Commission, according to publicly announced selection criteria. Yet there was little competition after the list of management companies was compiled, as the number of companies included was only marginally higher than the number of funds.

Of the 15 NIFs, 14 had an initial contract with a management company.

Later, there were disputes in three cases between management companies and the funds; two ended with the cancellation of the management contract. In the third case, the Ministry of Privatization dismissed most members of the supervisory board (management contracts are concluded for a period of 10 years but can be terminated at 180 days' notice) (Uvalic *et al.*, 1998).

In most cases, management companies were sponsored by a consortium of domestic and international banks and consulting companies, foreign managers and consultants (the role of foreign financial institutions was thus much greater than in the Czech case). Also there is no cross-ownership as Polish banks, which were co-sponsors of management companies, were either already privatized or too big to be an object of significant investment by NIFs (and it is not feasible as there are limits on NIFs' borrowing).

Privatization certificates   All adult citizens of Poland with permanent residence in the country were entitled to buy the privatization certificates, between November 1995 and November 1996. The certificates could be obtained for a token price of ZL20 (approximately £5). Of the people who were qualified, 96 per cent (25.9 mn people) bought the certificates. From the onset, certificates were freely tradeable and foreign exchange offices specializing in trading them. From July 1996, the certificates were also listed on the Warsaw Stock Exchange.

The certificate bought for £5 had an initial street price of around £20 and could be sold on the spot. It was estimated that around a half of participants sold their certificates immediately. The stock exchange price increased to £30 by the end of 1996, but later decreased to below £20. Ultimately, around 90 per cent of certificates were placed on the stock exchange. This was a necessary condition for their exchange for a package consisting of one share from each of the NIFs. Shares of NIFs were introduced on the stock exchange parallel to certificates in June 1997; that is, one year after the certificates. Conversion of certificates for shares was left to owners' discretion, but the deadline for this operation was the end of 1998.

Bank-led restructuring
This programme was designed to tackle the problem of bad debts. The corresponding law was introduced three years after the start of the privatization process (that is, in 1993), as the existing bankruptcy/liquidation procedures were not effective in enforcing efficient restructuring (see Baer and Gray, 1996). The programme was also intended as groundwork for the privatization of seven major banks out of nine that were created from the monobank system in 1989.

The programme required the banks to establish internal specialized work-out units and based on their assessment to take subsequent action by

March 1994 to recover loans classified as doubtful or bad at the end of 1991. A course of action had to be chosen from several options (if the debtor had started to service the debt over at least the previous three months, no further action was required):

- a court or bank conciliation agreement (see below);
- the debtor was declared bankrupt;
- liquidation was initiated under the privatization law or under the law on SOEs, where the enterprise is shut down and assets are directly sold (see the section below on direct privatization);
- the debt was sold on the emerging debt market; that is, the bank sold its claims against enterprises by public auction or in negotiations undertaken on the basis of a public invitation (however, in practice, selling of debt was hardly used).

The most interesting and popular method is the conciliation agreement. It allows banks to institute special accelerated conciliation agreement procedures in relation to indebted enterprises, in order to reduce their indebtedness or spread it out over time on more favourable terms. Banks are empowered to negotiate a restructuring agreement on behalf of all creditors, and the state Treasury loses its superiority; only the national and secured creditors retain priority. In addition, it is possible to convert the claims into shares (Baer and Grey, 1996).

Creditors who hold at least 30 per cent of the total claims against a company or state enterprise have the right to use this 'debt for equity swap' procedure. Alternatively, the law allows banks to use it. Conciliation agreements were signed for 122 companies up to the end of 1998,[21] yet, in 26 per cent of companies, the state share of equity remained above 50 per cent; therefore it is arguable whether those cases can be described as genuine privatizations.[22]

Since 1997, an additional route for debt–equity swaps has been introduced on the basis of section IV of the new privatization law of August 1996. However, the impact of this new route has been negligible. Up to the end of 2000, related debt–equity conversions had been introduced in only 16 companies, of which nine were transformed from majority to minority government shares. In addition, all of those companies were small and medium-sized enterprises and of marginal significance for the economy.

Direct privatization methods
Here the SOE is directly liquidated and ceases to exist as a legal entity; that is, there is no intermediate phase of corporatization. It is the major method used to privatize small- and medium-sized companies in Poland and may

be carried out through alternative legal procedures. First, a company's assets (or organized parts of its assets) may be leased to a new company set up by its employees: the enterprise is let out for use against lease payments and the property is transferred after full repayment. This liquidation procedure has been by far the most popular privatization method since the privatization process began. However, it applies to enterprises whose financial situation is relatively good and which are able to meet the charges related to the buy-out.

Second, a company's assets may be sold to a domestic or foreign investor, following the formal announcement of bankruptcy. In a so-called 'express sale', which can be used in the case of enterprises that employ up to 300 people, enterprises can be privatized with the use of a simplified procedure by tender or as a result of negotiation. This offer was addressed to the Polish private sector, but it met with only moderate interest. Finally, a company's assets may be used as a contribution in kind to the initial capital of a joint venture company set up by the Treasury and a private investor.

It is also possible to privatize a firm using a procedure that is a combination of these three methods.

Genuine liquidations A separate privatization path is reserved for companies which go into genuine (that is, not only legal/formal) liquidation as a result of poor financial and economic performance. Poor financial condition is defined by law as a situation where either (a) the after-tax profits are not sufficient to cover the obligatory 'dividend' to the state budget or (b) in the case of a firm which is exempted from paying the 'dividend', the firm operates at a loss that formally triggers the liquidation. In relation to such enterprises the government may undertake 'reform' procedures by appointing a 'curative commission' (two representatives chosen by the workers' council, two from the Ministry of Finance, one from the bank creditors and two from a parent government agency ('the founding organ'). The commission replaces the previous management of the enterprise and is in charge of implementing the programme of restructuring. If the enterprise still remains unable to pay all past and current dividends to the government, the Ministry of Finance is required to liquidate the enterprise. Alternatively, the government may immediately institute liquidation procedures. A liquidator is appointed who replaces the previous management. The assets of these enterprises are sold by the liquidator to third parties in a public auction and the proceeds go to pay off the creditors (in practice, the assets are typically sold to enterprise insiders; usually, however, there are lay-offs, so the employees suffer real costs of financial distress).

State enterprises with insufficient assets to pay off all debts may also be declared bankrupt. The assets belonging to these companies are sold.[23]

Other privatization methods
It is often overlooked that a significant number of companies were privatized by methods different from those included in the privatization law described above. The most typical privatization processes included:

- *Individual Treasury decisions on state assets to form new companies, typically joint venture firms with foreign partners.* This relates to several major privatizations in manufacturing with a strategic foreign investor. Most significant examples include the takeover of the manufacturing plant in Bielsko-Biala by Fiat, Daewoo's investment in a track factory in Lublin and ABB's investment in ZAMECH-Elblag.
- *Takeover of companies with an initial majority Treasury share, on the basis of commercial law and without invoking privatization procedures.* This relates primarily to the former foreign trade organizations, which were corporatized already in 1990 and in the presence of minority institutional investors. In those enterprises state shares were either sold to existing minority shareholders or the private majority stakes were acquired by issuing new equity, with new capital provided either by existing or new institutional investors.
- *Privatization of dependent companies after privatization of mother companies.* In some cases, state companies held 100 per cent shares in other companies. Yet the privatization process of the latter could be entirely different from the former.
- *Separation and independent privatization of parts of the state companies.* Examples include Stalprodukt SA (in Bochnia), a large publicly quoted company that until 1992 was part of the Cracow Steelworks and was subsequently separated and privatized. Similarly, at the time of the Bielsko-Biala plant takeover by Fiat, some elements of the state company were privatized separately.

None of these four privatization paths is included in the official privatization statistics, which relate only to privatizations that follow standard methods envisaged in the privatization law.

This richness of privatization methods makes Poland different from all other post-communist countries except Hungary. However, it may be noticed that, since 1997, the privatization process has became more standardized, for at least three reasons: (a) the process of privatizations via bank conciliation agreement was practically completed, (b) the mass privatization (NIF) programme was completed, and (c) the new privatization law narrowed down applications for miscellanous direct privatization methods.

Since then, capital privatizations and public offerings in particular have dominated in the privatization of large enterprises. Direct privatization methods have been applied only in the case of small companies; their number may still be large, but their aggregate share of manufacturing output is small.

Some basic figures on Poland's privatization programme[24]

At the beginning of privatization, in mid-1990, there were over 8500 state enterprises in Poland. By mid-2001, the number of state enterprises had decreased to 1268 functioning firms, including 402 corporatized state firms; that is, only 15 per cent of the initial number of companies still operate as state-owned. In addition, 608 state firms were undergoing bankruptcy procedures.

The privatization process included:

- 1500 companies, which were corporatized to form 1446 new entities. This included 289 capital privatizations (in this, 101, or 35 per cent, involved a share of foreign capital) and 512 firms were in the mass privatization (NIF) programme.
- 1813 companies included in the direct privatization programme. In this, 1195 (66 per cent) of privatizations were completed by employee leasing, 391 (22 per cent) were privatized by direct sale, 172 (9.5 per cent) by the contribution of assets to a new company with outside investors, and 55 (3 per cent) by a mixed form of privatization.
- 804 companies were liquidated.
- 1437 employee-owned companies were formed as a result of both leasing and direct liquidation procedures.
- All 1662 state farms were liquidated by 1995; property and land were sold or leased.

The share of the private sector in gross value added was 70 per cent by 1999 and its share of employment was even higher: 73 per cent by 2000. However, the share of the private sector in the value of capital was smaller, at only 47 per cent in 1999. This resulted from the fact that the privatization of the most capital-intensive branches of industry had been slow. On the other hand, the private sector's share of investment was 62 per cent by 1999. This meant that capital has been accumulating faster in the private sector.

Notes

1. The authors are grateful to Taylor and Francis Ltd for granting permission to use some sections from Bałtowski and Mickiewicz (2000). More details on the latter text may be found at *http://www.tandf.co.uk* (*Post-Communist Economies*).
2. These proposals largely came from foreign advisors such as R. Frydman, A. Rapaczyński and J. Sachs, as well as W. Amiel.
3. See also Lewandowski and Szomburg (1990a; 1990b).
4. For a concise summary of mass-privatization programmes, see Estrin and Stone (1996). For an assessment of the results, see Megginson and Netter (2001).

5. The main tenets of his ideas had been presented in several seminars, public lectures and articles (esp. Krawczyk, 1988) and in Krawczyk (1990). See also Jasiński (1994:143–4).
6. See also Aghion and Blanchard (1998); Filatotchev *et al.* (1999).
7. For example, ESOT – Employee Stock Ownership Trust; mutual funds and so on. For more details of such schemes, see Błaszczyk (1997).
8. On the social functions of enterprises under communism and the subsequent separation of the economic and welfare systems, see Rein *et al.* (1997).
9. For an overview of the theoretical discussion of employee ownership in the context of post-communist transition, see Earle and Estrin (1996).
10. Again, that corresponds to the simple theoretical model presented in Blanchard and Aghion (1996); Aghion and Blanchard (1998). However, compensation could also include explicit employment clauses provided in privatization contracts (see appendix) and implicit wage compensation.
11. M. Guzek estimated that the value of supply amounted to approximately US$100bn, balanced against the demand valued at US$10bn (Guzek, 1995:156).
12. On the other hand, a large inflow of FDI in the late 1990s led to new political tensions.
13. For the concept of 'extraordinary politics', see Balcerowicz (1995: ch. 9).
14. This view can be traced back to the classic paper by Alchian and Demsetz (1972).
15. Yet there is some irony in the fact that, when Kaczmarek had returned to office in late 2001, his first decisions resulted in the replacement of whole supervisory boards of the largest companies under Treasury control, and replacement by political affiliates as new members. All this just copied the practice of his predecessors, regardless of political affiliation.
16. For similar results from a different survey, see Kozarzewski (2002). Also Błaszczyk *et al.* (2001) discuss parallel developments in the portfolio companies of the National Investment Funds.
17. Hungary is similar to Poland in this respect. However, the main difference between the two economies is that the share of FDI in Hungarian privatization was higher and inflows of foreign capital played a significant role much earlier in Hungary. On the post-privatization evolution of ownership structures in Hungary, see Bishop *et al.* (2002) and Chapter 20 below.
18. We do not discuss here small privatization, that is, privatization of small economic units in trade and other services; see Frydman *et al.* (1993).
19. In fact, there were 52 initial public offerings, but two companies were withdrawn from the stock exchange subsequently.
20. This section draws on Bałtowski (1998), Gesell (1998), Hashi (1999), Ławniczak (1997), Uvalic *et al.* (1998).
21. Seven more were signed by the end of 2000.
22. On the early assessment of the performance results of the bank-led restructuring programme, see Chudzik (1998), Gray and Holle (1998).
23. Baer and Gray (1996) discuss the advantages and disadvantages of this procedure.
24. All data are from the Central Statistical Office of Poland and relate to 30 June 2001, unless stated otherwise.

References

Aghion, P. and O. Blanchard (1998) 'On Privatisation Methods in Eastern Europe and Their Implications', *Economics of Transition*, 6(1), 87–99.

Alchian, A. and H. Demsetz (1972) 'Production, Information Costs, and Economic Organization', *American Economic Review*, 62(5), 777–95.

Baer, H.L. and C.W. Gray (1996) 'Debt as a Control Device in Transitional Economy', in R. Frydman, C.W. Gray and A. Rapaczyński (eds), *Corporate Governance in Central Europe and Russia*, Budapest: Central European University Press.

Balcerowicz, L. (1995) *Socialism, Capitalism, Transformation*, Budapest: Central European University Press.

Bałtowski, M. (1998) *Prywatyzacja przedsiębiorstw państwowych. Przebieg i ocena*, Warsaw: Wydawnictwo Naukowe PWN.

Bałtowski, M. and T. Mickiewicz (2000) 'Privatisation in Poland: Ten Years After', *Post-Communist Economies*, 12(4), 425–43.
Beksiak, J., T. Gruszecki, A. Jędraszczyk and J. Winiecki (1989) 'Zarys programu stabilizacyjnego i zmian systemowych', mimeo, Warsaw.
Bishop, K., I. Filatotchev and T. Mickiewicz (2002) 'Endogeneus Equity: Determinants of Ownership Structure in Largest Hungarian Firms', *Working Paper in Business and Economics*, no. 6, Centre for the Study of Social and Economic Change in Europe, SSEES, University College London (forthcoming in *Acta Oeconomica*).
Blanchard, O. and P. Aghion (1996) 'On insider privatisation', *European Economic Review*, 40(3–5), 759–66.
Błaszczyk, B. (1997) 'Perspektywy i zadania prywatyzacji w Polsce na najblizsze piec lat', in H. Boahniarz and S. Krajewski (eds), *Sektorowe programy restrukturyzacji i prywatyzacja majatku panstwowego*, Warszawa:
Błaszczyk, B., M. Górzyński, T. Kamiński and B. Paczoski (2001) 'Secondary Privatization in Poland (Part II): Evolution of Ownership Structure and Performance in National Investment Funds and their Portfolio Companies', *CASE Report No. 47*, Center for Social and Economic Research (CASE), Warsaw.
Brucker, H. (1997) *Privatisation in East Germany. A Neo-Institutional Analysis*, London: Frank Cass.
Chudzik, R. (1998) 'Banks as "Agents of Change" – the Experiences with Restructuring of Bad Debts in Poland', mimeo, Frankfurt Institute for Transformation Studies, European University Viadrina.
Dąbrowski, M. (1991) 'Od gospodarki planowej do rynkowej: tempo i etapy transformacji systemowej', *Ekonomista*, 4–6.
Djankov, S. and P. Murrell (2000) 'The Determinants of Enterprise Restructuring in Transition: An Assessment of the Evidence', Working Paper, University of Maryland.
Earle, J. and S. Estrin (1996) 'Employee Ownership in Transition', in R. Frydman, C. Gray and A. Rapaczyński (eds), *Corporate Governance in Central Europe and Russia*, vol. 2, Budapest: CEU Press, pp. 1–61.
Estrin, S. and R. Stone (1996) 'A Taxonomy of Mass Privatisation', *Transition*, 7(11–12), 8–9.
Filatotchev, I., M. Wright and M. Bleaney (1999) 'Privatisation, insider control and managerial entrenchment in Russia', *Economics of Transition*, 7(2), 481–504.
Frydman, R., A. Rapaczyński and J.S. Earle (1993) *The Privatisation Process in Central Europe*, Budapest: Central European University Press.
Gesell, R. (1998) 'Polish Mass Privatisation – Success or Failure', paper presented at the Workshop on Privatisation, Corporate Governance and the Emergence of Markets, Frankfurt Institute for Transformation Studies, Frankfurt/Oder.
Gray, C.W. and A. Holle (1998) 'Classical Exit Processes in Poland: Court Conciliation, Bankruptcy, and State Enterprise Liquidation', in L. Balcerowicz, C.W. Gray and I. Hoshi (eds.), *Enterprise Exit Processes in Transition Economies*, Budapest: Central European University Press.
Gruszecki, T. (1995) 'Prywatyzacja – dokonania i perspektywy', in R. Kostro and M. Matraszek (eds), *Program dla Prezydenta*, Warsaw: Grupa Windsor.
Guzek, M. (1995), 'Privatization in Poland', *Bedingungen Ökonomischer Entwicklung*, Marburg: Marburg Universität.
Hashi, I. (1999) 'The Polish National Investment Fund Programme: Mass Privatization with a Difference?', paper presented at the CEPR/ESRC Workshop on Transition Economies at EBRD, London.
Havrylyshyn, O. and D. McGettigan (1999) 'Privatization in Transition Countries: A Sampling of the Literature', IMF Working Paper, WP/99/6.
Jasiński, P. (1994) *Z powrotem do kapitalizmu. Problemy przekształceń systemowych i własnościowych*, Warsaw: CASE and PWN.
Kaczmarek, W. (1997) 'Inne spojrzenie na prywatyzację', *Rzeczpospolita*, 27 January.
Kozarzewski, P. (2002) 'Changes in Corporate Governance Structures in Polish Privatised Companies', Working Paper in Business and Economics, no. 8, Centre for the Study of Social and Economic Change in Europe, SSEES, University College, London.

Kozarzewski, P. and R. Woodward (2001) 'Secondary Privatisation in Poland (Part I): Evolution of Ownership Structure and Company Performance in Firms Privatized by Employee Buyouts', CASE Report no. 47, Center for Social and Economic Research (CASE), Warsaw.

Krawczyk, R. (1988) 'Uwłaszczyć', *Przegląd Tygodniowy*, 35.

Krawczyk, R. (1990) *Wielka przemiana*, Warsaw: Oficyna Wydawnicza.

Kurowski, S. (1989) 'Idea wlasnosci pracowniczej', *Tygodnik Solidarnosc*, 20.

Ławniczak, R. (1997) 'A Polish Experiment in Corporate Governance – the National Investment Funds (NIFs)', *Corporate Governance*, 5(2), 67–76.

Lewandowski, J. and J. Szomburg (1989) 'Uwłaszczenie jako fundament reformy społeczno-gospodarczej Zarys programu', *Propozycje przekształceń gospodarki polskiej*, Warsaw: PTE.

Lewandowski, J. and J. Szomburg (1990a) 'Model transformacji gospodarki polskiej', IBnGR, *Transformacja Gospodarki*, 1.

Lewandowski, J. and J. Szomburg (1990b) 'Strategia prywatyzacji', IBnGR, *Transformacja Gospodarki*, 7.

Ludwiniak, K. (ed.) (1989) *Pracownik właścicielem*, Lublin: Catholic University of Lublin.

Łukawer, E. (1994) 'Poglądy polskich ekonomistów na ogólne założenia transformacji systemowej', *Ekonomista*, 6, 739–40.

Megginson, L. and J. Netter (2001) 'From State to Market: A Survey of Empirical Studies on Privatisation', *Journal of Economic Literature*, 39, 321–89.

Mickiewicz, T. (2001) 'The Polish Economy: Budget Crisis and Beyond', *The Stockholm Report on Transition*, 11(4), SITE, Stockholm School of Economics.

Pajuste, A. (2001) 'Corporate Governance and Stock Market Performance in Central and Eastern Europe: A Study of Nine Countries, 1994–2001', in K. Liuhto (ed.), *Ten Years of Economic Transformation. Volume II – Markets, Companies and Foreign Business in Transition*, Lappenranta University of Technology, pp. 193–224.

Rein, M., B. Friedman and A. Worgotter (eds) (1997) *Enterprise and Social Benefits after Communism*, Cambridge: Cambridge University Press.

Uvalic, M., D.M. Nuti and S. Estrin (1998) 'The Impact of Investment Funds on Corporate Governance in Mass Privatisation Schemes: Czech Republic, Poland and Slovenia', mimeo, London Business School.

20 Privatization in Hungary and its aftermath
Iván Major

Introduction: analytical framework[1]

After 13 years of political and economic transformation in Central and Eastern Europe (CEE) the time has come to assess the main results and possible shortcomings of the changes. This chapter sums up the history of Hungarian privatization at the company level and the ensuing restructuring of the Hungarian economy at the macroeconomic level. The political aspects of the transformation are deliberately avoided, in spite of their potential importance. The focus is on the issue of whether Hungarian privatization – its scope, speed and actual methods – resulted in efficient companies and in a healthy economy. These aims were set out at the beginning of the transition. There have been numerous other goals of the privatization policy than those mentioned, but the analysis will be kept within this narrower framework, for even these issues are more complex than what could be exhaustively addressed in a brief study.

The structure of the chapter is as follows: initially, a brief overview of the history of Hungarian privatization is provided, followed by a discussion of its initial conditions, targets and methods. The main results of the privatization policy are then considered. The main findings of the core analysis of this study are provided, along with a follow-up analysis of the economic performance of the Hungarian companies with different ownership structures to that in Major (1999).

A brief history of privatization in Hungary
How it all began

Hungary arrived at its political and economic transformation in 1989 with a series of partial changes in market institutions and in ownership structure already behind it. The legal institutions had been in place even before the more recent changes: the law on foreign investments of 1988 provided full guarantees to international investors on their investments and profit repatriation. The law on commercial banking of 1987 created the basic framework for flexible financial operations for private businesses. The law on 'company transformation' and 'corporatization' defined all the legal forms of business ventures – joint stock, limited liability, individual, partnership, state-owned and municipal company – that are common in advanced market economies. Moreover, the managers of state-owned Hungarian enterprises had already had some autonomy in their decision making for two decades. The companies also had long-term technical and commercial ties to firms in advanced market economies. Thus Hungarian managers and workers had been more or less ready for private enterprise long before the political transition.

There was, however, no 'blueprint' readily available for the new democratic forces describing how to replace the collapsing economic system with a viable and efficient one within a tolerable period of time. It seemed clear what kind of an economy the Hungarians wanted, but nobody really knew how to get there. After a short period of entertaining the idea of an 'ownership reform' that would have left the state-owned property with the workers' collectives, with municipal governments and with state-owned holdings, the main political parties agreed to launch a comprehensive programme of genuine privatization. The State Privatization Agency (SPA) was established and it was subordinated to the Hungarian parliament before the first democratic elections in January 1990. It initiated two large sales transactions, one of them, the largest Hungarian travel agency IBUSZ, through the Budapest and Vienna stock exchanges.

The new democratically elected government put the SPA beyond parliamentary control and under its own supervision and the government declared its commitment to selling state-owned property rather than freely distributing it among the people. The government's decision was partly necessitated by the fact that Hungary was heavily indebted to western and Asian – mainly Japanese – banks, by an amount of US$21.2 bn gross and US$19.8 bn net in 1990. The foreign debt of the country peaked at US$31.7 bn gross and US$19.7 bn net in 1995. Hungary's GDP amounted to US$34.6 bn in 1990 and it was US$41.7 bn in 1995. Thus the ratio of net indebtedness to the advanced market economies had been 58 per cent in 1990 and was 48 per cent in 1995.[2] And there was no relief in sight. Hungary's traditional markets – the Soviet and other CMEA economies – had collapsed. In addition, the high level of uncertainty within the Hungarian economy and the lack of free resources within the firms, prevented the Hungarian companies making a swift restructuring of their products, technology and marketing activities. The only restructuring that took place was a massive decline in employment. Consequently, the inflow of government revenue from the companies dramatically declined, while government spending on unemployment benefits rapidly increased, creating huge imbalances in the state budget.

Beside the objective constraints on a free distribution of assets, the government also accepted the views of those economists who strongly argued that the sale of the state-owned property to private owners should be viewed, not just as a source of government revenue, but also as a method to strengthen the commitment of new owners to a responsible and efficient use of their newly acquired assets.[3]

In addition to the urgent need to accumulate government revenue, the governing parties pursued other goals when they started the privatization programme. They had three main targets to achieve: to create a new middle class that would act as a solid basis for political democracy; to do justice to those whose properties had been confiscated by the communist regime; and to use privatization as a lever to enhance economic efficiency at the macro-economic level as well as at the company level. The accomplishment of these often contradictory goals resulted in a peculiar blend of privatization strategies. The government decided to sell the large state-owned companies to foreign investors. To avoid a massive reprivatization, it distributed 'compensation coupons' to the former private owners of agricultural land, real estates and smaller industrial assets. In addition, it used cheap loan facilities to support Hungarian private entrepreneurs who wished to buy state-owned assets. Both compensation and the support of the Hungarian entrepreneurs were aimed at 'buying' loyal clients to the right-wing government. But the government also wanted to retain a large part of the state-owned property – especially public utilities and the 'flagships' of Hungarian industry – to cement the economic basis of its political power.

There is no need for a lengthy discussion of the Hungarian privatization process, for it has been documented extensively by Hungarian and foreign authors.[4] In particular, the State Privatization and Asset Management Holding Ltd (SPAM) organization supported the publication of a series of books, written by Hungarian authors, that give a fairly comprehensive account of the privatization process. Hence only a brief overview of the main areas of Hungarian privatization is provided here.

Privatizing industry: the players and the rules of the game
The total asset value of large and medium-sized state-owned industrial companies amounted to HUF2600bn in 1990. The number of companies for privatization was 1857.[5] Initially, the first government of the transition tried to sell a 'package' of about two dozen companies, but the interest in the package was very weak. A few months later, a second package of construction companies was offered for sale by the SPA, but this resulted in even less interest than the first attempt. Then the SPA turned its privatization programme into a case-by-case sale. Although much more slowly than had been envisaged, the SPA was able to sell the largest industrial companies (mostly to multinationals) by 1994.[6] The main reason for this slowness was the bureaucratic character of the bargaining process. The SPA had to get consent from other government agencies – the members of the government, the Ministry of Finance, the National Bank – to every single transaction. It

was also fiercely attacked by influential populist groups for selling the 'family silver' too cheaply to foreigners. Moreover, the staff of the SPA was not well trained to sell companies on a large scale. Also the framework and the rules for the transactions were unclear.[7] A special kind of cycle could be observed in Hungarian privatization. When the government found the process – and the inflow of revenue – too slow, it instructed the SPA to decentralize the transactions. Managers of the companies to be privatized were given extensive rights to look for potential buyers and to discuss the details of the sale, but as soon as strong political pressure groups objected loudly and attacked the 'red barons' (the company managers) for stealing state-owned property, a recentralization campaign began.[8]

There was interest from foreign investors in acquiring Hungarian state-owned companies, but those investors usually wanted to buy only the best Hungarian companies, which had large domestic markets and markets in the former CMEA countries. Investors were rarely interested in the machinery or plant of the other Hungarian companies. They frequently praised the Hungarian workers and managers for their skills, but they were not ready to save jobs in abundance. In addition, they required tax privileges and infrastructure facilities – for instance, new roads and rail tracks to the gates of the plant – from the state agencies.

Large state-owned companies were sold to foreign investors in manufacturing: for example, Tungsram to GE, Lehel (white products) to Electrolux and Telephone Works and Ganz Turbines to Siemens.[9] The price that was paid by the buyers averaged around the book value of the companies, but the guarantees, for instance for the necessary environmental investments, and the tax privileges from the Hungarian state often exceeded the sale price of the company. The longer-term impact of foreign acquisitions is considered later in the chapter.

An important lesson of Hungarian privatization was that 'greenfield investment' by foreign investors played a role at least as important as genuine privatization itself. The whole Hungarian car industry, a large part of manufacturing, the bulk of the computer industry and information technology, the core of wholesale and retail trading, a considerable share of the food industry, commercial and investment banks and other financial services were created anew by foreign investors. While the whole privatization process generated an inflow of revenues of US$7.8bn, the total amount invested in Hungary by foreign investors added up to US$23bn between 1990 and 2000.[10]

Privatizing agriculture: the compensation coupons
Hungarian agriculture was hit by the collapse of the CMEA (Council for Mutual Economic Assistance) market. The formerly state-owned agricul-

tural cooperatives produced mostly wheat and meat for the Soviet market. Agricultural products were regarded as 'hard goods' in Hungary, for the country could buy Soviet oil and other raw materials in exchange for agricultural products. The right-wing Hungarian governments of 1990–94 and 1998–2002 had an ideological zeal to weaken and ultimately demolish the agricultural cooperatives and to support family farms. Although cooperatives were fully transferred to the ownership of their own members, the conservative parties still considered them nests of old socialism. The history of agricultural transformation is a sad saga of creating confusion and uncertainty among agricultural producers and their business partners.[11]

Those who or whose antecedents had had agricultural property before communism could receive compensation coupons for their lost property.[12] They could participate in open auctions for land with these coupons, but compensation coupons were traded under the counter too. Finally, many bidders who had lost any kind of contact with agricultural production several decades earlier, or who never had any affection for agriculture, acquired agricultural land. These people lived in industrial towns and worked in a factory and now became 'farmers', in a fortnight! There was no efficient market for land, therefore they could not and they would not sell their property. Foreigners could not legally buy agricultural land in Hungary and successive governments resisted creating an open market for real estate. Foreign investors could only acquire land via so-called 'pocket contracts', that is, by using Hungarian 'buyers' as mediators, and they faced fierce opposition from the government.

Compensation coupons were not only used for acquiring land but were introduced into the Budapest stock exchange as 'toy money' too. The price of these coupons never reached their face value and frequently declined to 30–35 per cent of it. The depressed and declining price of the coupon made it less and less attractive to those who held it. Most of these, especially the elderly, decided to get rid of their newly acquired 'wealth' quickly. Consequently, those people who received the coupons as a compensation for their earlier suffering lost out. Brokerage agencies specialized in buying the compensation coupons in large quantities, and then used the coupons to acquire the shares of companies who were traded on the stock exchange. In addition, the government had to spend billions of Hungarian forints to sterilize the compensation coupons that could not be used for such acquisition.

The largest state farms are still in the hands of the state privatization agency and the economic basis for agricultural cooperatives has been undermined. The family farms are too small to be able to produce efficiently, most of the families that cultivate the land are too poor to invest in productive machinery, and potential foreign buyers are scared away from buying into farming. In its accession negotiations with the European

Union (EU), Hungary has asked for a seven-year derogation from opening up its market for agricultural land to foreign buyers. But until Hungary can join the EU there is little hope that Hungarian agriculture will recover.

Privatizing small businesses and retail trading

At the dawn of the transition it seemed an easy task to turn the state-owned retail stores, small service units and state-owned apartments over to private hands. But it took about four years for the privatization of small businesses and real estate to be actually concluded.[13] The slowness of the process can be explained partly by the large number of business units that had to be sold. About 14000 shops and commercial facilities were put up for sale, many of them belonging to a chain of stores. Also, until 1993, every single small privatization transaction was administered and concluded by the SPA and the state agency lacked the bureaucratic and business capacity to evaluate the assets individually. In addition, small privatization was very much the focus of political attention. The government intended to channel small business facilities to its supporters. This also added to the cumbersome nature of the transactions. Another reason why small privatization was slow was the role municipal government played in the transactions. Local government owned a part of the businesses or they were the owners of the real estate where the companies were located. Consequently, in most cases the SPA and the potential buyer had to agree with the local government the details of the transaction.

There was no substantial revenue for the state budget generated from small business privatization. Moreover, it did not take long for the privatized retail shops to lose their market share and they were then usually taken over by newcomer large chain stores. Several multinational companies, such as Tesco from Great Britain, Auchan from France, Metro and Cora from Germany, Ikea from Sweden, Kaiser and Julius Meinl from Austria, have built huge shopping malls in the capital and in other large cities of Hungary. They have swallowed up the business of the smaller shops. A similar development has occurred with petrol stations and with warehouses and high-tech services.

In conclusion, small business privatization took a lot of effort from government agencies and from potential private buyers. It contributed to the birth of a lively market in businesses and services, but its economic impact was much smaller than the influence of the greenfield investment of a few multinational companies.

The privatization of public utilities

When economic transformation started in 1990, only a few Hungarian economists believed that the public utilities would have an important role in privatization. The most liberal-minded were not against turning over the public utilities to private hands, but they assumed that there would be no interest in those assets and markets. What actually occurred in the privatization of the telecommunications system, electricity and gas generation and distribution, the transport sector and municipal services between 1993 and 1998 was a complete surprise. The largest companies in these industries competed for the ownership title 'Hungarian public companies'.[14] Privatization of public utilities generated more than 50 per cent of government revenue from privatization between 1990 and 1998. Moreover, the privatization of public services and companies put Hungary well ahead of most member countries of the EU in terms of the opening up and liberalizing of public utility markets.

The sale of 30 per cent of Malév's (the Hungarian airline's) shares to Alitalia started the series of transactions in large public companies in 1993. It was then followed by an auction for the concession rights to provide mobile and fixed network telecommunications services. US and North-European companies acquired shares in the mobile telecommunications market. A third service provider, Airtouch-Vodafone, with the Hungarian Post Office and the Hungarian Broadcasting Company, obtained a concession to start mobile telecom services in GSM-900 and in DSC-1800 technology in 1999.

British Telecom, Cable and Wireless, France Telecom, the Italian Stet (now Telecom Italia), Telefónica from Spain and Deutsche Telekom with its US partner, Ameritech International Ltd, submitted bids for the market of the Hungarian Telecommunications Company (HTC) in early 1993. Ultimately, Deutsche Telekom and Ameritech received an exclusive concession and a 30.2 per cent share of HTC for US$875 mn. In addition, US and French companies acquired exclusive concessions for public switched telecom services in another 19 local telecom regions. A further 35 per cent of HTC's shares was bought by the German–American consortium for US$850 mn in 1996. The shares of the company were introduced onto the New York and Budapest stock exchanges in 1997. The only company among the Hungarian telecom firms whose privatization has failed so far was the Hungarian Broadcasting Company (Antenna Hungaria).

The energy sector, which had the largest share of fixed assets and in employment among public utilities, also participated in large-scale privatization. A nationwide holding company (MVM) – a company managing the nationwide electricity network (OVIRT), 10 power-generating plants, six regional distribution companies and four back-up service units – had operated in the electricity industry in Hungary before the transition. After privatization, 46 to 49 per cent of the shares of each distribution company, 38 to 81 per cent of the shares of six power generating companies and 90 per cent of the network planning company were sold to German, French, British and Italian power-generating and distribution investors in 1995.[15]

Similarly to the electricity industry, up to a 50 per cent share of six natural gas distribution companies was sold to large US, German, Austrian and Italian core investors in the same year.[16] Finally, a 55.5 per cent stake in the Hungarian Oil and Gas Works (Mol Rt.) was privatized to a dispersed group of financial and institutional investors between 1995 and 1997.

The partial privatization of public utilities resulted in a large inflow of government revenue and powerful multinational core investors entered the Hungarian energy market. Since public utilities usually show economies of scale (that is, they have increasing returns to scale) and there exist entry barriers to potential newcomers in these sectors, the markets for public services need economic regulation. The institutions for a comprehensive and advanced market regulation did not exist in Hungary before the transformation. Also the successive governments after the changes did not fully comprehend the importance of introducing efficient regulation. Consequently, privatization of the telecommunications market, the energy market and the banking sector occurred within a fragmentary and contradictory framework of regulatory regimes. The backwardness of regulation resulted in perpetual conflicts between foreign investors and the government and among the companies themselves.[17]

Privatizing the banking sector
Since Hungarians lacked the financial means that would have been necessary to acquire substantial shares in large banks and other financial institutions, the only potential buyers of the banks and insurance companies came from abroad.[18] However, the two Hungarian governments immediately before and after the transition were against the privatization of commercial banks to foreign owners. Their main argument was that the commercial banks had lent huge loans for investment in the state-owned enterprises (SOEs) under socialism, and the SOEs would never be able to repay those loans. Consequently, the banks would exercise a decisive influence upon the companies and would become de facto owners of, the SOEs even before privatization. In addition, foreign banks along with foreign investors who intended to acquire the shares of the SOEs could create an all-encompassing net of cross ownership of Hungarian companies that would give them full control of the Hungarian economy. A 'hidden privatization'[19] of the largest insurance company (Állami Biztosító, or National Insurance Company) to the German insurance company Allianz was concluded by the last socialist government before the democratic elections, but no other privatization took place in the banking sector until 1994. As a consequence, foreign-owned 'greenfield' banks were established by German, French, US and British banks between 1990 and 1994.

The state-owned commercial banks accumulated huge debts because of poor business operation and because of the growing indebtedness and collapse of their client companies. Thus a very expensive clean-up of the banks and the indebted companies had to precede any attempt to privatize the banks. The costs of the so-called 'bank and loan consolidation programme' of the Hungarian government amounted to HUF350bn (about US$3.5bn) until 1993. When the government decided to privatize the banks in 1993–5, it had to put additional financial resources into the banks to make them look lucrative for foreign investors. Ultimately, US, Dutch, German, Irish and Belgian core investors acquired majority shares in four out of the six largest Hungarian commercial banks. Foreign investors followed the German–Japanese rather then the Anglo-Saxon model of banking. They created general banks rather than specialized financial institutions – such as investment banks, venture capital banks and retail banks – from their newly acquired assets. All banks provide a wide range of services to companies and the population. The majority share of financial services for the population, however, remains in the hands of the two large commercial banks, OTP (National Savings Bank) and Postabank (Postal Bank). While OTP has been fairly successful, Postabank has needed successive infusions of government money to cover its losses.

The 'big six' international auditing and consulting agencies also established offices in Hungary. In addition, the largest law firms of the USA and Western Europe, specializing in business law and in the creation of legal institutions for the market, set up offices too. The market for financial services has become the most vibrant and the most lucrative segment of the service sector in Hungary.

The main results of privatization
Privatization was concluded in Hungary by the end of 2000. A few companies, such as Hungarian Airlines, Antenna Hungaria (the broadcasting monopoly) and the large agricultural farms still await acceptable buyers, but the bulk of state-owned property has been transferred to private hands. Some 75 to 80 per cent of the country's fixed assets are now owned by, and two-thirds of employees work in, private sector companies. Balance sheet data for the year 2000 show that 59 per cent of company equity has been acquired by foreign investors.

Government revenues from privatization have turned out to be much smaller than what had been expected at the start of the privatization process, however. Consequently, privatization has not contributed significantly to the reduction of Hungary's tremendous debt. The only exception was in 1997, when the government sold shares in large public utilities and US$1.5bn, about half of the obtained revenues, was used to reduce government debt.[20]

The most important result of privatization has been a massive restructuring of the companies and an ensuing increase in the companies' productive and 'X efficiency'.[21] While Hungary avoided a 'shock therapy'-type financial stabilization programme at the beginning of its transition, the way it privatized the state-owned property and its very strict bankruptcy law of 1992, along with an austerity programme, the so-called 'Bokros package' in 1995,[22] not only restored the financial discipline of the companies, but set the basis for a sustainable growth path for the country, as presented in Table 20.1.

Hungarian privatization put the emphasis on creating the basic institutions of a market economy rather than swiftly changing the ownership title of the SOEs. The direct sale of assets along with a dominant role for foreign investors in the acquisitions forced the organic development of all the necessary economic and legal institutions.[23] Foreign ownership had a crucial impact on the Hungarian economy. More than 60 per cent of total exports and GDP has come from foreign-owned companies since 1996. The presence of foreign companies in investment and in employment has been more moderate, however, showing that foreign investors still regard the Hungarian economy as a risky place for long-term investment. Nevertheless, Hungary is meeting or will soon meet all of the criteria of the Maastricht and Copenhagen treaties to qualify for EU accession.

Time and again, respected analysts have tried to prove that Hungarian privatization did not result in the emergence of genuine private ownership, but ended up with a strange network of cross-ownership among state-owned banks and companies – the so-called 'recombinant ownership' structure (Stark, 1996) or 'managerial capitalism' (Szelényi, 1995). Stark's and

Table 20.1   *Main economic indicators for Hungary, 1990–2000*

Year	1990–95 annual average	1996	1997	1998	1999	2000
GDP, annual growth (%)	−1.6	1.3	4.6	4.9	4.2	5.2
Unemployment rate (%, annual average)	9.2	9.9	8.6	7.9	6.0	6.4
Rate of CPI inflation (%)	25.3	23.6	18.3	14.3	10.0	9.8
Exports, annual growth (%)	0.2	4.6	29.9	22.1	15.9	21.7
Net foreign debt relative to GDP (%)	41.0	32.6	26.4	26.4	25.0	24.7
Investment, annual growth (%)	−3.2	5.2	8.5	12.7	5.3	6.5

Source: The National Bank of Hungary, *Annual Report 1999*, 61; *Annual Report 2000*, 176, 178, 183–6, 188, 192, 196–7, 251, 254.

Szelényi's hypothesis is that the Hungarian managers of the formerly state-owned companies and banks used their privileged position to grab controlling roles in the companies after privatization. Szelényi even argues that management rather than ownership matters in controlling a company. He goes further, saying that Hungarian managers did not want to become the owners of their companies, but they very much wanted to remain on the 'captain's deck'. But a series of empirical research has shown that neither the recombinant property nor the managerial capitalism model is dominant in the Hungarian economy.[24] Their underlying assumption is unfounded because of the dominant role of foreign ownership in the Hungarian company sector.

To suggest, however, that Hungarian privatization has been a fairy tale, a Hollywood success story without any repercussions, would be far from the truth. The discussion in the following sections of the chapter shows that privatization and company restructuring were much slower, and their costs were much higher, than had been expected at the start of the transition. In addition, turning the state-owned property into private hands – especially into foreign private hands – created a negative reception and a strengthening xenophobia among the Hungarian people. While most Hungarians were aware of the fact that state ownership had been the strongest pillar of the communist political regime, they responded to the actual demolition of state ownership with growing resistance. An economic explanation for this phenomenon is provided below.

Post-privatization company restructuring and its results
Most SOEs of the former socialist Hungarian economy had been loss makers because of the low level of allocative and productive efficiency, encouraged by poor financial discipline in the companies and in the public administration. Losses were ultimately financed by the population, who paid the price in terms of limited consumption, poor services and perpetual shortages, and by foreign lenders, whose loans were used to finance Hungary's debt. It has been a widely shared expectation among members of the economics profession that privatization, foreign ownership and an extensive company restructuring would considerably improve companies' economic performance and their financial discipline. But there is no consensus among the analysts as to what should be meant by 'company restructuring' and how to measure and assess company performance.

Many outstanding analysts of the transforming economies use company restructuring in a narrow sense. These authors focus on changing the company's employment structure and they measure the success or failure of restructuring by the speed and extent of the employee lay-offs.[25] Major and colleagues applied the term 'restructuring' in a much wider sense

(Major, 1999), meaning the change of the company's corporate governance structure, its production and marketing activity, its investment activity and its financial policy.

The other issue that has received a lot of attention lately is how to measure company performance. Initially, most authors who wrote about the accomplishments of the CEE companies used *profitability* as a leading indicator of economic performance.[26] Another line of research emphasized *production, factor productivity* and the companies' *market shares*. According to the latter approach, productive efficiency rather than profitability properly reflects the companies' economic performance.[27] Major (1999) emphasized the different role of both approaches and applied a complex analysis to assess company performance.

The efficiency approach is based on Nickell (1996:725), whose main argument in favour of efficiency is simple, but seemingly convincing: 'The question I am directly concerned with here is the impact of competition on the efficiency and productivity growth rates of companies. This a question that is very rarely pursued, much greater attention having been paid to profitability, which competition probably reduces, rather than to efficiency and productivity growth, which, it is hypothesized, competition increases. Since it is productivity growth that is the cause of the "wealth of nations", this emphasis on profitability is rather curious.'[28]

Is there really a conflict between the 'profitability approach' and the 'efficiency approach'? Are competition or market conditions in general more directly related to the companies' efficiency than to companies' profitability? By 'market conditions' is meant more than just the degree of competition. Also included is the notion of the level of integration of an industry's market in the international economy, the regional features of the market, the presence or absence of market regulation and the level of concentration of the companies' assets – besides their sales – which operate in a certain industry. To formulate this in economists' jargon: is the (frontier) production function a more appropriate model for a company's efficiency analysis than a profit function?

It is a textbook truism that competition reduces or eliminates monopoly rent, while the lack or feebleness of competition makes room for economic profits. Consequently, company profits will decrease rather than increase with efficiency improvements. Competition fosters economic efficiency, while efficiency gains result in growing market shares of the more efficient companies; but growing market shares mean larger market concentration, that is less competition, and less competition reduces efficiency. We are therefore potentially in a vicious circle. Moreover, the production function reflects a company's *technical* efficiency – especially the level of its capacity utilization and the composition of its production inputs – while it disregards other aspects of *economic* efficiency, that is, the relation of revenues to *economic* costs. If companies behave in a rational profit-maximizing manner, they *always* minimize costs; that is, conditional factor demand is always efficient at any production level. However, if companies maximize profits at given factor prices, they must select that production level which is not only efficient but also is the profit maximizing output. Thus the change of CEE companies' profitability is originally a relevant indicator of their performance alongside the indicator of technical efficiency.

In addition to the very complex relationship between the efficiency and profitability of a company, the assessment of the CEE companies' performance is made even more complicated by companies undergoing a radical change of their ownership structure. Hence we must address the issue of how important a role ownership plays in the economic performance of companies. Several studies of CEE economies show that market conditions rather than ownership affect economic performance. At the same time, numerous authors have tried to show that private companies (and especially foreign-owned companies in the CEE countries) are significantly more profitable and efficient than SOEs.[29] A new test of this issue is provided below.

Productive efficiency and profitability in privatized and state-owned companies

The same company balance sheet data base for the Hungarian corporate sector as described in Major (1999), but extended with balance sheet data for 1999 and 2000, is used for the test. Balance sheet data of all Hungarian enterprises with double entry book-keeping (CDEs) for the years from 1988 until 2000 are therefore used, except for those companies whose fixed assets, total revenues from sales or number of employees were negative or zero, whose data were omitted. First, the data were recalculated from nominal to real values, applying the relevant price indices. The consumer price index (CPI), the producer price index (PPI) of the industries, the price index of investment goods and the GDP deflator were adopted to make company-level data comparable with 1988 as the base year. It is a matter of judgment how far one goes in aggregating or disaggregating the industry structure of an economy. Here 78 industries were grouped into seven large sectors:

- agriculture and food industry;
- heavy industry (including mining, metallurgy, construction materials industry);
- human services (including financial services, real estate, personal services, repair, education, health and cultural services);
- light industry (including textile, dressing, paper industry and printing);

- manufacturing (including pharmaceuticals, engineering, vehicles industry and computer industry);
- production services industry (including energy generation and distribution, transport, telecommunications and postal services); and
- trade (including wholesale and retail trading).

Four groups of the CDEs were formed according to their ownership structure:

- *foreign private company*: where the majority of the assets are in private hands and the share of the foreign owner(s) is larger than the share of the domestic owner(s);
- *domestic private company*: where the majority of the assets are in private hands and the share of the domestic owner(s) is larger than the share of the foreign owner(s);
- *SOE with minority foreign ownership*: where the share of the state in the assets is larger than 50 per cent, but the company has a minority foreign co-owner with no less than 10 per cent of the shares;
- *SOE*: the state owns more than 50 per cent of the assets and the share of foreign ownership is less than 10 per cent.

The companies' profitability was measured using return on assets (ROA), which is the ratio of the companies' gross profits to their fixed assets. Efficiency was measured as the ratio of the companies' value added to their total costs. The indicators of profitability for the four ownership groups are presented in Table 20.2.

The message from the profitability indicators seems straightforward: after the turbulent era of mass privatization and the financial stabilization of the Hungarian economy, which lasted until 1995–6, foreign companies achieved higher profitability than SOEs though not domestic private firms. As Halpern and Körösi (1998) showed, the export performance of companies had a significant impact on their profitability level. Since foreign companies had stronger positions on the international markets, this was reflected in their economic performance.

Domestic private companies had fluctuating profitability. The ups and downs can be explained by these companies' unstable markets and financial positions. By contrast, SOEs struggled for survival and the trend of their profitability declined. But the picture is not entirely clear. Foreign companies performed better than the SOEs between 1995 and 1998, and in 2000, but they did not do so between 1990 and 1992 or in 1999. A usual argument to explain the setbacks of foreign companies is that these companies started huge investments in order to restructure the acquired and collapsing firms

Table 20.2 Profitability indicators of the CDEs, by ownership group, 1988–2000

Ownership groups	1988		1990		1991		1992		1993		1994	
	Number of CDEs	ROA (%)	Number of CDEs	ROA (%)	Number of CDEs	ROA (%)	Number of CDEs	ROA (%)	Number of CDEs	ROA (%)	Number of CDEs	ROA (%)
Foreign private	—	—	4715	3.9	7713	0.0	11911	−0.5	15948	0.0	17420	0.5
Domestic private	—	—	16626	3.8	28374	0.0	40504	−0.9	50528	−0.5	59037	0.0
SOE with minority foreign ownership	—	—	17	7.9	3	−0.1	311	0.2	169	0.4	90	0.2
SOE	7185	0.1	1770	4.8	1720	0.0	3898	−0.5	2951	−0.7	2199	0.1
Total	7185	0.1	23128	4.4	37810	0.0	56624	−0.6	69596	−0.5	78746	0.2

Ownership groups	1995		1996		1997		1998		1999		2000	
	Number of CDEs	ROA (%)	Number of CDEs	ROA (%)	Number of CDEs	ROA (%)	Number of CDEs	ROA (%)	Number of CDEs	ROA (%)	Number of CDEs	ROA (%)
Foreign private	18879	0.5	19764	0.5	20201	1.4	21104	0.4	20926	2.8	37040	3.8
Domestic private	68443	−0.1	81421	0.5	94508	1.4	107107	0.6	114134	4.9	99101	3.8
SOE with minority foreign ownership	68	0.0	46	0.3	40	0.1	31	0.0	28	4.7	119	4.9
SOE	1761	0.2	1627	−0.2	1552	−0.6	1582	0.2	1597	5.7	823	0.1
Total	89151	0.2	102858	0.4	116301	1.0	129824	0.2	136685	3.9	137083	3.8

Note: CDEs = enterprises with double entry book-keeping; ROA = return on assets.

and this explains their low profit levels. But the periods of the setbacks do not match the periods of large increases in their investments.

One could argue that Hungary has been on a sustainable path of economic growth since 1997, as indicated earlier in Table 20.1, and the locomotive of economic growth has been the foreign-owned sector within the Hungarian economy. The share of foreign companies in total exports in GDP and in investments increased during the 1990s. Hence this confirms the better performance of the foreign companies. But even in the year 2000, when the number of foreign-owned firms was above 37000, while the number of the SOEs had radically declined, from 7185 in 1988 to 823, the number of foreign-owned companies whose profitability surpassed 10 per cent was only 4175, while 9745 foreign-owned companies operated with below-average but non-negative profitability, and 7985 foreign companies had negative profitability indicators. We may conclude from these data that it was not the foreign-owned sector as a whole that fuelled Hungarian economic growth, but a minority core of foreign-owned companies, mostly the multinationals.

The possible reasons for the private companies' mixed performance have been discussed in earlier studies (Major, 1999). The issue is referred to briefly in the next section, but first the efficiency of companies under different ownership structures is discussed. The efficiency indicators for the four ownership groups are shown in Table 20.3.

The efficiency indicators for each ownership group, measured as value added relative to total costs, show the opposite trend to that shown by the profitability data. Domestic and foreign private companies generally performed better than the SOEs until 1994, but they usually tended to achieve lower economic efficiency than state-owned firms between 1995 and 2000. Domestic and foreign private firms also changed rankings: domestic private companies showed better results than foreign firms between 1990 and 1994, but their position deteriorated thereafter. What can explain these results? One explanation is provided in Major (1999), where it was shown that the fall of GDP in Hungary between 1990 and 1995 was due to a cost explosion as the contraction of production reinforced the impact of increasing costs on company revenues and profits. Hungarian companies with different ownership structures reveal decisive differences in their cost structures. Foreign companies have spent relatively more on overheads, they have paid higher wages and the share of 'purchased products to be sold' has been much larger in their costs than is the case for the other ownership groups. This last cost item especially is interesting, for this is a way in which a company can reallocate its profits via 'transfer pricing'. Wages and depreciation have been a relatively smaller part of the costs of SOEs, while financial and banking costs have had a larger share. The high share

Table 20.3 Efficiency indicators for the CDEs, by ownership group, 1988–2000

Ownership groups	1988		1990		1991		1992		1993		1994	
	Number of CDEs	Factor efficiency (%)	Number of CDEs	Factor efficiency (%)	Number of CDEs	Factor efficiency (%)	Number of CDEs	Factor efficiency (%)	Number of CDEs	Factor efficiency (%)	Number of CDEs	Factor efficiency (%)
Foreign private	—	—	4715	22.5	7713	23.7	11911	19.2	15948	9.5	17420	12.8
Domestic private	—	—	16626	36.0	28374	38.6	40504	17.1	50528	29.4	59037	18.3
SOE with minority foreign	—	—	17	35.2	3	5.3	311	27.5	169	10.1	90	3.4
SOE	7185	21.2	1770	11.9	1720	13.3	3898	19.0	2951	10.4	2199	10.1
Total	7185	21.2	23128	20.2	37810	20.9	56624	18.5	69596	19.4	78746	14.2

Ownership groups	1995		1996		1997		1998		1999		2000	
	Number of CDEs	Factor efficiency (%)	Number of CDEs	Factor efficiency (%)	Number of CDEs	Factor efficiency (%)	Number of CDEs	Factor efficiency (%)	Number of CDEs	Factor efficiency (%)	Number of CDEs	Factor efficiency (%)
Foreign private	18879	21.8	19764	22.9	20201	26.1	21104	20.1	20926	18.6	37040	13.9
Domestic private	68443	18.4	81421	18.0	94508	21.0	107107	15.4	114134	16.9	99101	12.1
SOE with minority foreign	68	26.7	46	25.4	40	24.1	31	20.7	28	25.5	119	7.9
SOE	1761	31.0	1627	31.8	1552	25.7	1582	26.4	1597	16.7	823	33.5
Total	89151	21.8	102858	21.6	116301	24.0	129824	18.4	136685	17.5	137083	13.3

of financial and banking costs reflects the fact that SOEs converted their fixed assets into more liquid and – until recently – more lucrative financial investments. While the investment climate was poor and new investments in production too risky to start, investing in government bonds and other securities seemed safe. Domestic private companies have had the least stable cost structure, with sometimes very high then low shares of purchased products to be sold, a fluctuating share of wage costs and an oscillating share of financial costs.

There is a positive aspect to the foreign companies' higher costs relative to their value added. It reflects the fact that foreign companies have spent the most on restructuring as regards the reorganization of labour, redeployment of activities, the upgrading of production technology and marketing, and the reorganization of company management. And as we learn from the experience of all the CEE countries, these are the types of restructuring that are very expensive and take a fairly long time. We may conclude that foreign companies as a group did not perform very well as regards their economic efficiency, but the cost explosion can be explained by the huge expenses of restructuring. On the other hand, the economic efficiency of the SOEs seems higher than for the other ownership groups, which may be interpreted as a sign of retreat rather than as a signal of their long-term dynamic development.

Profit functions of Hungarian companies

We have seen in the tables above that ownership has not been an unquestionable and positive factor in company profitability and efficiency.[30] But which are the factors, then, that influence the companies' profitability and economic efficiency the most? We used log-linear extended profit functions to trace the significant factors in companies' profitability. The idea behind this model was as follows: if the companies' production function is of a Cobb–Douglas type (CD function), then – applying Hotelling's lemma[31] – the profit-maximizing output levels can be expressed as a CD function, too. Then profits will depend on output prices and on the companies' returns to scale.[32] Our model was as follows:

$$\log Gpr = \log Phys + \log Mon + \log Mat + \log GRW + exsh + privsh + forsh + \varepsilon,$$

where log is the natural logarithm, Gpr = gross profit; $Phys$ = physical assets; Mon = financial assets; Mat = material costs; GRW = gross wage costs, including social security; $exsh$ = the company's export to sales ratio; $privsh$ = the ratio of private shares in stockholders' equity; $forsh$ = the ratio of foreign-owned shares in stockholders' equity, and ε is the disturbance term. There is one problem with loglinear CD-type profit functions: a firm can have negative profits. Hence we separated the companies with negative gross profits from those that achieved positive profits and estimated the parameters of the following function:

$$-\log(-GPr) = \log Phys + \log Mon + \log Mat + \log GRW + exsh + privsh + forsh + \varepsilon.$$

Since $-\log(-GPr) = \log(1/-Gpr)$, estimated parameters with negative signs indicate that the larger the value of the independent variable, the smaller the amount of negative profits will be.

Ordinary least squares (OLS) regression was used to estimate the parameters for the year 1988, then for the period between 1990 and 2000. Estimated parameters and statistics are summarized in Tables 20.4 and 20.5. As can be seen from Table 20.4, there is a fairly good fit between our model and the companies' data, with modest variances in the disturbance term; R^2 values indicate a reasonable model selection. As regards the estimated parameters, we expected significant and positive values for the companies' physical and financial assets ($\log Phys$ and $\log Mon$), and the results fulfilled our expectation. It is important to note that financial assets have had a larger impact on gross profits than the companies' tangible, physical assets. It was a surprising result for us that the companies' export shares did not have a significant impact on profitability in most years, and the sign of the parameter is not stable. It was also unexpected that wage costs are not significant and the variable had positive parameters in most years.

As regards the companies' ownership structure, the results can be taken as expected, but at the same time they are surprising. Private ownership had a significant impact on the companies' profitability after 1994, but this impact was negative. A more detailed analysis would probably show that the large number of domestic private companies and their very modest economic performance are the decisive factors behind this fact. Foreign ownership has had a more limited impact on profitability – this variable was significant only in a few years – but in most years when foreign ownership was a significant factor it had a positive impact on profitability.

Data on companies with negative profits in Table 20.5 show that physical assets and financial assets had a significant but inverse impact on profits. That is, a company with larger fixed assets was less likely to become bankrupt. The companies' ownership structure, especially foreign ownership, was also statistically significant in relation to profits. But in this case the larger the share of foreign ownership, the more probable it was that the company would incur losses.

Table 20.4 *Gross profit functions (firms with positive profits), 1988–2000*

Dependent variable: lngpr	1988	1990	1991	1992	1993	1994	1995	1996	1997	1998	1999	2000
(Constant)	−4.540**	2.188**	−3.784**	1.096*	−0.023	−0.740	−0.681	−0.964*	−2.982*	−2.140**	−0.223	−1.126**
LNPHYS	0.064**	0.118**	0.052	0.230**	0.281**	0.287**	0.111	0.166**	0.180	0.210**	0.268**	0.149**
LNMON	−0.158**	0.553**	0.285**	0.343**	0.365**	0.115	0.442**	0.335**	0.226	0.398**	0.303**	0.352**
LNMAT	0.041*	−0.059	0.120	−0.029	0.097	0.015	−0.067	−0.025	0.364	−0.047	0.153**	0.283**
LNGRW	1.006**	0.122	0.337**	0.208*	0.040	0.064	0.029	0.097	0.214	0.045	0.212**	0.158**
EXSH	0.469**	0.109	−0.624	−0.244	−0.617*	0.076	0.350	−0.022	1.111	−0.053	0.122	0.362*
PRIVSH	–	0.191	−0.297	0.041	0.020	−0.158**	−0.180**	−0.175**	−0.024	−0.205**	−0.052*	−0.095**
FORSH	–	0.127	−0.008	0.436**	0.135	−0.143**	−0.088	−0.053	−0.032	−0.015	0.085*	0.062**
Number of companies	7185	19181	23911	30572	35967	49468	58352	84750	96465	99600	99422	113557
R^2	0.935	0.552	0.604	0.530	0.544	0.592	0.659	0.634	0.747	0.740	0.791	0.819
SEE	0.505	1.462	1.388	1.471	1.611	1.496	1.443	1.544	1.368	1.331	1.214	0.890

Note: * significant at 0.05 level; ** significant at 0.01 level; SEE = standard error of the estimation.

446

Table 20.5 *Gross profit functions (firms with negative profits), 1988–2000*

Dependent variable: −ln(−gpr)	1988	1990	1991	1992	1993	1994	1995	1996	1997	1998	1999	2000
(Constant)	—	−2.669**	3.166**	−0.745	−0.691	0.835*	0.131	1.618**	−0.450	1.513**	−0.262	0.531
LNPHYS	—	−0.185**	−0.079	−0.239**	−0.337**	−0.072	−0.174**	0.011	−0.169	0.035	−0.219**	−0.278*
LNMON	—	0.134	−0.008	−0.235**	−0.403**	−0.110	−0.226**	−0.307**	−0.456	−0.355**	−0.004	−0.265*
LNMAT	—	−0.390*	−0.349**	−0.066	0.045	−0.016	0.007	−0.071	−0.459*	0.034	−0.063	−0.129
LNGRW	—	−0.140	−0.288*	−0.196	−0.047	−0.100	−0.025	−0.036	−0.449	−0.141	−0.135	−0.140
EXSH	—	−0.769	−0.587	−0.229	0.634	−0.012	1.200**	0.279	−2.302	0.754	−0.190	−0.303
PRIVSH	—	−0.153	0.083	0.072	0.128*	0.054	0.130**	0.180**	−0.260	0.107**	0.094*	0.121
FORSH	—	0.171	0.282*	0.082	0.001	0.452**	0.202**	0.250**	0.283	0.207**	0.202**	0.003
Number of companies	—	3947	13899	26052	33629	29278	30799	18108	19836	30224	37263	23526
R²	—	0.515	0.635	0.521	0.569	0.671	0.647	0.691	0.691	0.619	0.735	0.681
SEE	—	1.513	1.443	1.592	1.657	1.388	1.443	1.484	1.657	1.538	1.273	1.374

Note: * significant at 0.05 level; ** significant at 0.01 level; SEE = standard error of the estimation.

447

Indicators of the companies' market share, market concentration indices (Herfindahl–Hirschman index, HHI) by industries and asset concentration in the industries were experimented with as explanatory variables, but none of these variables seemed relevant to profitability. The only variable that had some impact in certain years was asset concentration (defined by the HHI index for asset concentration).

We may conclude that the companies' profit function can be reasonably described by a CD-type extended function, which indicates that the companies' profitability and their efficiency are closely related. The results obtained are not completely unexpected, but they are somewhat surprising. First, profits are influenced by the same factors as output levels, although the weights of these factors are different in the production functions and in the profit functions. Second, the companies' endowment in terms of production factors has a smaller impact on profitability than financial assets. This finding is compatible with our earlier study (Major, 1999), but it shows that the traditional production function approach may need some revision. A really surprising result is the ambiguous role of the companies' export activity in profitability. This phenomenon needs further research. Finally, we need to know more about the impact of ownership on the companies' efficiency and profitability. Our findings do not match the widespread assertion that private companies, especially foreign companies as a whole, considerably improved their performance during the economic transition.

Conclusions
Hungarian privatization has been successfully concluded, in the sense that more than 80 per cent of the state-owned property has been transferred to private hands in a more or less organized manner. The way Hungary privatized its state-owned property largely contributed to the emergence of the fundamental institutions of a market economy. Private property rights now have firm roots in the Hungarian economy. Corporate governance structures in Hungarian companies usually match the most advanced techniques of ownership control and management.

Foreign investors – among them multinationals, medium-sized companies and small ventures – contributed to the success of the Hungarian privatization. Foreign-owned companies have been the driving force in Hungary's economic growth since 1996. Foreign owners and managers have introduced a variety of new business cultures and they took the lead in restructuring the acquired SOEs.

Company restructuring started with reorganization; that is, a reduction and redeployment of labour, a crucial task after decades of 'hidden unemployment' and ensuing managerial and employee 'slack' in the former socialist Hungarian economy. But the restructuring of the Hungarian companies turned out to be a more complex task than just laying off abundant labour. The whole governance and management structure of the companies had to be changed. Huge investments were needed to upgrade both obsolete technology and products. Also, after the collapse of the former socialist common market (CMEA), new market strategies had to be implemented and new markets had to be found for Hungary's production. This process took much longer than was expected at the beginning of the transition.

The decisive role of foreign companies in the Hungarian economy increased both the scope and the speed of Hungary's opening up and integration into the international economic community. But inside Hungary, foreign companies have rarely been integrated into domestic production and R&D networks. In fact, R&D departments of Hungarian companies were closed, with a few exceptions, and know-how in Hungarian firms is now supplied by foreign-based companies.

Although foreign investors were active in Hungarian privatization, large foreign companies fostered greenfield investments when creating their production base in Hungary. A large number of new companies were established in the vehicle industry, in the new technology industries, in the food industry, in engineering, in financial services and in other manufacturing. Some multinationals have built their companies on the basis of existing organizations in the public utilities sector. The privatization of public utilities was a real surprise to most analysts. Only a few of them believed that Hungarian public utilities – telecommunications, the transport sector, electricity and gas distribution – would attract considerable attention. In fact, the sale of shares in these companies reaped the highest revenues for the government, and the privatization of public utilities had a decisive impact on the whole restructuring process.

Privatization and company restructuring considerably improved the companies' productive efficiency and profitability, but the improvement was not without setbacks, and the benefits of restructuring only slowly penetrated the wider Hungarian economy. A core group of foreign companies produced most of the improvement, while a large number of domestic and foreign private companies still struggle for survival. As the analysis shows, profitability and economic efficiency of enterprises did not always improve with the expansion of private ownership.

Finally, since mass privatization started about 13 years ago, Hungary has gone a long way towards joining the West European economic community. The accession process to the EU has meant innumerable tasks to accomplish, but the efforts would have been wasted had Hungary not been ready to dismantle its old state-owned economy and create a healthy market economy on the basis of private property rights. It would not be correct to say that the Hungarian economy today has no efficiency gaps and that

Hungarian companies are competitive in every area of the international economy. But tens of thousands of domestic and foreign private companies have created an economy that is ready and mature enough to join the EU. We can rightfully expect from accession that competition and market pressure on Hungarian companies will increase, which will further facilitate company restructuring and efficiency improvement. Should accession be delayed, it would weaken the competitive pressure on the Hungarian economy and give disturbing signals to companies and to the country as a whole.

Notes

1. I should like to thank Ákos Róna-Tas, Mihály Laki and Kálmán Kőhegyi for their valuable ideas that helped formulate my hypotheses and research methods. I am also grateful to Helga Fenyvesi, a student of mine at the University of Veszprém, for her research assistance. The responsibility for all the remaining errors and vagueness is mine.
2. *Annual Report of the National Bank of Hungary (NBH), 1997*, p. 265.
3. The most prominent and influential among them was János Kornai, who published his 'manifesto' in Hungarian in 1989 (Kornai, 1990).
4. See, for instance, Frydman *et al.* (1993), Frydman and Rapaczyński (1994), Major (1993; 1999), Mihályi (1998a), van Brabant (1992) and Voszka (1997).
5. Mihályi (1998a:405).
6. Privatization of the industrial companies was extensively discussed by Diczházi (1999), Eszes (1998), Szalavetz (1998), Szanyi (1999) and Voszka (1997, 1998).
7. I discussed the non-conventional features of the market for state-owned assets in Major (1999:43–58). Laki (1993) described Hungarian privatization as an 'end-of-season sale'.
8. 'Wild privatization', 'nomenklatura privatization' and 'spontaneous privatization' were the most frequently used terms to describe or, rather, stigmatize the transactions that had been concluded by company managers. The attacks on these privatization transactions were strongest in Poland, but they were present in Hungary too (Voszka, 1998).
9. An extensive account of the role of FDI in Hungarian privatization was given by Hunya (1996) and it was also discussed by Diczházi (1999).
10. Calculated from Mihályi (1998a: 409) and the *Annual Report of the National Bank of Hungary*, 1997.
11. The change of ownership titles in Hungarian agriculture was described by Lovászy (1999).
12. An in-depth discussion of the compensation schemes can be found in Mihályi (1998b).
13. On the details of the long and controversial process, see, for instance, Earle *et al.* (1994: 99–174). Important contributions to the analysis of small privatization on a theoretical and an empirical level are Róna-Tas (1997) and Laki (1998).
14. On the privatization of the telecommunications industry, see Major (1998). On the privatization of the energy industry, see Mihályi (1998a).
15. See Mihályi (1998a:286, 298).
16. Ibid.: 303–5.
17. Kiss *et al.* (2000) discussed the shortcomings of market regulation in the Hungarian telecommunications industry. Newberry (1997) outlined the weaknesses of market regulation in the Hungarian energy sector. Várhegyi (1998) and Ábel and Bonin (1994) pointed to the premature state of banking regulation.
18. A detailed account of the privatization of the financial sector is given in Várhegyi (1998).
19. 'Hidden privatization' means that the government concluded the transaction with the Allianz Company in secret.
20. A meticulous calculation of the change in asset values and government revenue from privatization was conducted by Mihályi (1998a).

21. The notion of 'X efficiency' is attributable to Leibenstein (1962).
22. The austerity programme was named after its elaborator, Finance Minister Lajos Bokros.
23. Hungary can be regarded as an excellent example of the role of institutions in economic development in terms of North's theory of institutions (North, 1991).
24. See, for instance, Tóth (1999) and Mihályi (1998a).
25. See, for instance, Aghion, Blanchard and Carlin (1994), Aghion, Blanchard and Burgess (1994), Borish *et al.* (1995), Carlin and Aghion (1996).
26. For Hungary, see, for instance, Halpern and Kőrösi (1998) and Major (1999).
27. Brada *et al.* (1997) discuss enterprise efficiency in Czechoslovakia and in Hungary and Halpern and Kőrösi (2001a) conduct an efficiency study of Hungarian companies based on frontier production functions.
28. Another important article on the subject is Nickell *et al.* (1997).
29. See, for instance, Pohl *et al.* (1997) and, for Hungary, Halpern and Kőrösi (1998).
30. Major (1999) and Vezzoni (1999) have come to a similar conclusion.
31. See, for example, Varian (1992: 43). When profits are at maximum, input levels are set so that they minimize costs. Consequently, with given output prices,
$$\pi(y(\mathbf{x})) = p \cdot y(x) - \mathbf{w} \cdot \mathbf{x}.$$

    But $\mathbf{w}_i = \dfrac{\partial y(\mathbf{x})}{\mathbf{x}_i}$. Thus $\pi^*(y^*) = \left(p - \sum_{i=1}^{n} a_i\right) \cdot y^*$,

    where π is profits, p is the output price, y^* is the profit-maximizing output, $\mathbf{x}$ is the input vector and $\mathbf{w}$ is the vector of input prices. The profit function is more complicated if companies are not obliged to be price takers. Then market demand – especially its elasticity – also has an impact on profits.
32. See, for instance, Carlton and Perloff (2000: 236–59). Halpern and Kőrösi (2001b) analysed the relationship between market power and mark-up pricing in the Hungarian corporate sector, that is, how far away the companies' output prices are from their marginal cost. Working with 'Solow residuals' and the Lerner index they showed that foreign-owned companies, as dominant players in most markets, can and do apply monopolistic pricing practices much more frequently than firms with domestic owners.

References

Ábel, I. and J.P. Bonin (1994) 'Financial Sector Reform in the Economies in Transition: On the Way to Privatizing Commercial Banks', in J.P. Bonin and I. Székely (eds), *The Development and Reform of Financial Systems in Central and Eastern Europe*, Aldershot, UK and Brookfield, US: Edward Elgar.

Aghion, P., O. Blanchard and R. Burgess (1994) 'The behavior of state firms in eastern Europe, pre-privatisation', *European Economic Review*, 38(6), 1327–49.

Aghion, P., O. Blanchard and W. Carlin (1994) 'The Economics of Enterprise Restructuring in Central and Eastern Europe', CEPR Discussion Paper, no. 1058, November.

Annual Report of the National Bank of Hungary, 1996 (1997) Budapest: National Bank of Hungary, pp. 216, 248.

Annual Report of the National Bank of Hungary, 1997 (1998) Budapest: National Bank of Hungary.

Annual Report of the National Bank of Hungary, 2000 (2001) Budapest: National Bank of Hungary.

Borish, M.S., F.M. Long and M. Noel (1995) 'Restructuring Banks and Enterprises: Recent Lessons from Transition Countries', World Bank Discussion Papers, no. 279, Washington, DC.

Brada, J., A. King and C. Ma (1997) 'Industrial Economics of the Transition: Determinants of Enterprise Efficiency in Czechoslovakia and Hungary', *Oxford Economic Papers*, 49, 104–27.

Carlin, W. and P. Aghion (1996) 'Restructuring Outcomes and the Evolution of Ownership Patterns in Central and Eastern Europe', *Economics of Transition*, 4(2), 371–88.

Carlton, D.W. and J.M. Perloff (2000) *Modern Industrial Organization*, 3rd edn, Reading, MA: Addison-Wesley.

Diczházi, B. (1999) *A külföldi tőke szerepe a privatizációban* (The role of foreign direct investment in privatization), Budapest: ÁPV Rt. and GJW Consultatio Ltd.

Earle, J.S., R. Frydman, A. Rapaczynski and J. Turkewitz (1994) *Small Privatization – The Transformation of Retail Trade and Consumer Services in the Czech Republic, Hungary and Poland*, Budapest, London and New York: Central European University Press.

Eszes, I. (1998) *A Hungalu privatizációja* (The Privatization of Hungarian Aluminum Works), Budapest: ÁPV Rt. and Kultúrtrade Ltd.

Frydman, R. and A. Rapaczyński (1994) *Privatization in Eastern Europe: Is the State Withering Away?*, London and Budapest: Central European University Press.

Frydman, R., A. Rapaczyński and J. Earle (1993) *The Privatization Process in Central Europe*, London and Budapest: Central European University Press.

Halpern, L. and G. Kőrösi (1998) 'Corporate Performance in Transition: Econometric Analysis of Hungarian Exporting Firms, 1985–1994', in L. Halpern and C. Wyplosz (eds), *Hungary: Towards a Market Economy*, Cambridge: Cambridge University Press.

Halpern, L. and G. Kőrösi (2001a) 'Efficiency and market share in the Hungarian corporate sector', *Economics of Transition*, 9(3), 559–92.

Halpern, L. and G. Kőrösi (2001b) 'Mark-ups in the Hungarian Corporate Sector', William Davidson Working Papers no. 411, William Davidson Institute, University of Michigan, Ann Arbor.

Hunya, G. (1996) 'Foreign Direct Investment in Hungary', Working Paper: Forschungsberichte, no. 226, Vienna: Wiener Institut für Internationale Wirtschaftsvergleiche.

Kiss, F., I. Major and P. Valentiny (2000) *Információgazdaság és piacszabályozás* (Information economy and market regulation), Budapest: Akadémiai Kiadó.

Kornai, J. (1990) *The Road to a Free Economy*, New York: Norton.

Laki, M. (1993) 'The Chances for the Acceleration of Transition: the Case of Hungarian Privatization', *East European Politics and Societies*, 7(3), 440–51.

Laki, M. (1998) *Kisvállalkozás a szocializmus után* (Small ventures after socialism), Budapest: Közgazdasági Szemle Alapítvány.

Leibenstein, H. (1962) 'Allocative Efficiency vs. X-Efficiency', *American Economic Review*, 56, 392–415.

Lovászy, Cs. (1999) *Termőföld tulajdonosváltás Magyarországon* (Ownership change of the agricultural land in Hungary between 1988 and 1998), Budapest: ÁPV Rt. and GJW Consultatio Ltd.

Major, I. (1993) *Privatization in Eastern Europe: A Critical Approach*, Aldershot, UK and Brookfield, US: Edward Elgar.

Major, I. (ed.) (1999) *Privatization and Economic Performance in Central and Eastern Europe: Lessons to Be Learnt from Western Europe*, Cheltenham, UK and Northampton, MA, USA: Edward Elgar.

Major, Iván (1998) *A távközlés privatizációja* (Privatizing Hungarian Telecommunications), Budapest: ÁPV Rt. and Kultúrtrade Ltd.

Mihályi, P. (1998a) *A magyar privatizáció krónikája* (The chronicle of Hungarian privatization 1989–1997), Budapest: Közgazdasági és Jogi Könyvkiadó.

Mihályi, Péter (1998b) *Kárpótlás* (Compensation), Budapest: ÁPV Rt. and Kultúrtrade Ltd.

Newberry, D. (1997) 'Privatisation and liberalisation of utilities', *European Economic Review*, 41(3–5), 357–83.

Nickell, S. (1996) 'Competition and Corporate Performance', *Journal of Political Economy*, 104(4), 724–46.

Nickell, S., D. Nicolitsas and N. Dryden (1997) 'What makes firms perform well?', *European Economic Review*, 41(3–5), 783–96.

North, D.C. (1991) *Institutions, Institutional Change and Economic Performance*, Cambridge: Cambridge University Press.

Pohl, G., R.E. Anderson, S. Claessens and S. Djankov (1997) 'Privatization and Restructuring in Central and Eastern Europe. Evidence and Policy Options', World Bank Technical Paper, no. 368, Washington, DC.

Róna-Tas, Á. (1997) *The Great Surprise of the Small Transformation: The Demise of Communism and the Rise of the Private Sector in Hungary*, University of Michigan Press, Ann Arbor.

Stark, D. (1996) 'Recombinant Property in East European Capitalism', *American Journal of Sociology*, 101(4), 993–1027.

Szalavetz, A. (1998) *Az energetikai gépgyártás privatizációja* (The privatization of the energetic machinery industry), Budapest: ÁPV Rt. and Kultúrtrade Ltd.

Szanyi, M. (1999) *Csöd, felszámolás, végelszámolás, mint a privatizáció módja* (Bankruptcy, liquidation and final closure as privatization techniques), Budapest: ÁPV Rt. and GJW Consultatio Ltd.

Szelényi, I. (1995) *The rise of managerialism: The 'new class' after the fall of communism*, Budapest: Collegium Budapest.

Tóth, I.J. (1999) 'Ownership Structure, Business Links and Performance of Firms in a Transforming Economy: The Case of Hungary', Discussion Paper, no. 3/1999, Institute of Economics, the Hungarian Academy of Sciences, Budapest.

van Brabant, J. (1992) *Privatizing Eastern Europe: The role of markets and ownership in the transition*, Dordrecht: Kluwer.

Várhegyi, É. (1998) *Bankprivatizáció* (The privatization of the banking sector), Budapest: ÁPV Rt. and Kultúrtrade Ltd.

Varian, H. (1992) *Microeconomic Analysis*, 3rd edn, New York: Norton.

Vezzoni, C. (1999) 'Factors of the Companies' Profitability and Efficiency: the Result of a Multi-regression Analysis', in I. Major (ed.), *Privatization and Economic Performance in Central and Eastern Europe: Lessons to be Learnt from Western Europe*, Cheltenham, UK and Northampton, MA, USA: Edward Edgar, pp. 225–64.

Voszka, É. (1997) *A dinoszauruszok esélyei* (The Chances of Dynosauruses), Budapest: Pénzügykutató Rt. and Perfekt Publishers.

Voszka, É. (1998) *Spontán privatizáció* (Spontaneous privatization), Budapest: ÁPV Rt. and Kultúrtrade Ltd.

21 Privatization in Ukraine
Saul Estrin and Adam Rosevear

Introduction

This chapter discusses the process of privatization in Ukraine.[1] Ukraine left
the former Soviet Union to become an independent country in 1991, with
a seemingly valuable structure of economic and agricultural assets owned
by the state (see Hare *et al.*, 1999). In addition, Ukraine was able to call
upon financial and technical assistance from the international community,
thanks to its advantageous geopolitical position between Russia and
Europe. The new democratic government under President Kravchuk had a
popular mandate to chart the future course of Ukraine, following the 90
per cent vote for independence from Russia. The government could have
followed the example of transition already established in neighbouring
Poland or Hungary by institutionalizing the necessary reforms to commence the transformation of Ukraine into an economically successful and
pluralistic society. However, this apparently good starting position was
wasted. Ukraine has instead suffered a large fall in national output, near
hyperinflation and a series of political corruption scandals.

In this chapter, we will examine in detail the progress in one crucial aspect
of the transition process: privatization (see Blanchard *et al.*, 1991; Estrin,
1994; Nellis, 2000; Djankov and Murrell, 2002). We will chart the complex
and tortuous process whereby privatization was accomplished in Ukraine,
as well as employ new evidence from a recent enterprise-level survey to
establish empirically the consequences of the ownership change. There was
significant achievement in terms of the growth of the private sector:
according to the EBRD, the private sector share of GDP increased from 10
per cent in 1991 to 60 per cent in 2000 (see EBRD, 2000; 2001). However,
privatization faced significant political and social opposition, which meant
that the process was very lengthy and did not lead ownership to be transferred to the private sector in forms likely to enhance company productivity. Moreover, the political immaturity of the new Ukranian state (see Hare
et al., 1999) and the resulting problems of corruption and state 'capture' by
powerful industrial interests (see Johnson *et al.*, 1999; Aslund, 1999) meant
that privatization was not accompanied by the emergence of necessary supporting institutions, such as a sound independent banking sector, effective
anti-monopoly legislation (see EBRD, 2001) or the required legislative
framework to support free market exchange (see Estrin and Wright, 1999).

The chapter is organized as follows. We first set the context for studying privatization in Ukraine by exploring its importance in the transition process, and its particular relevance in the Ukrainian environment. We then go on to outline the convoluted Ukrainian privatization process, to illustrate the practical problems of building a market economy in a situation where the state is relatively weak and the relevant stakeholders – managers, workers and politicians – are at the very least wary of the process and, at the worst, bitterly opposed. This led to privatization being undertaken in such a way that the state was frequently replaced as owner by managers and workers, almost certainly because the authorities needed to give significant or even majority ownership stakes to insiders, in order to induce them to accept the concept of privatization at all (see Boycko *et al.*, 1995). Later, we use a large new enterprise level survey of Ukrainian firms to illustrate the pattern of primarily insider ownership which emerged, and to explain the problems that insider ownership can cause for enterprise restructuring and performance. We also illustrate the implications of the weak Ukrainian institutional environment by establishing that the ownership pattern which emerged immediately post-privatization has persisted to the current day. It was hoped that the ownership structure would adjust through capital market pressures to a more conventional outsider-dominated pattern. The consequences of this poor ownership structure and the unsatisfactory institutional environment for enterprise performance and productivity in the 1990s are also presented. There seems little doubt that the failure of the enterprise sector to restructure is at the heart of the poor Ukrainian economic performance during the 1990s.

Transition and privatization
While privatization everywhere raises particular problems and dilemmas, it is important to note that it represents merely one element, though an important one, in the broader process of transition from a socialist to a capitalist economy. The other major components of a successful reform programme, like that in Poland, are macroeconomic stabilization following price liberalization; opening the economy to foreign trade and competition; developing effective and liquid capital markets and institutional reform, including the legal system and the functioning of the state (see EBRD, 2001, for an evaluation of progress in these areas). Though privatization cannot be considered in isolation, private ownership of firms is usually argued to be pivotal to the success of market reforms (see Nellis, 2000).

The primary argument in favour of privatization concerns incentives (see Chapters 2, 3 and 4); in transition, it is also the potential dissonance between the task of restructuring state-owned firms and the motivation of management. In all firms where owners do not directly control decision making themselves, mechanisms of governance are required to ensure that hired managers maximize profits. In the west, these issues are usually addressed through the disciplines of the capital market. The share price, which itself reflects a market-based evaluation of the future profitability of the firm, is publicly available information upon which to evaluate the performance of one management team against another. Share prices can also form the basis for takeovers, where alternative management teams replace poorly performing ones, or provide the basis for high-powered incentive schemes for managers. Other 'solutions' for managerial deficiencies include bankruptcy or associated financial restructuring. Perhaps most importantly, people monitoring the companies' performances are motivated to get it right by the prospect of their own financial gain if they can guess better than the market a firm's future prospects; the incentives are decentralized but powerful.

In contrast, state firms have no market-based evaluation of their performance. Managers in state-owned firms are aware that governments may not be particularly interested in profits, but have in mind a variety of objectives, many political and social. They can exploit this lack of focused purpose to their own advantage, for example enjoying an 'easy life' or failing to keep a tight grip on costs, especially labour costs. Also state firms do not face the threat of takeover or bankruptcy. Hence the literature has concluded that company performance can be sharply improved by privatizing state-owned firms. The empirical evidence certainly appears to support this view for most countries, including most emerging markets (see Megginson and Netter, 2001). There is also quite strong evidence that privatization has improved company performance in Central Europe (for example, Frydman *et al.*, 1999). However, as we will show below, the results are much less clear-cut for the former Soviet Union, including Ukraine (also see Estrin and Wright, 1999; Djankov and Murrell, 2002).

The state as owner usually has neither the interest nor the power to impose a profit orientation on managers. This problem has particular force in the formerly socialist economies of Central and Eastern Europe because the state owned such a large proportion of GDP. This meant that countervailing forces, such as domestic and import competition, which keep the problem in check in capitalist economies, are largely absent. The state owned virtually all firms in the former Soviet Union as recently as 1991 (EBRD, 1994) and this set the context for privatization in Ukraine. Effective change has probably been hindered because the former socialist managers are often still in place in many enterprises, and their most likely interest in the face of all the changes is to attempt to preserve the status quo, especially with respect to employment and the local community. Even if they had the appropriate skills and experience, such managers would probably not have the incentives to restructure their organizations to face competition on world markets. They might instead work in the interest of major stakeholders – the labour force as a whole; the local community to which the firm may be a major supplier of public goods, services and housing as well as jobs; and perhaps even to networks of suppliers of intermediate inputs (Earle and Estrin, 1996). There is no one in this list concerned to defend the return to capital, which can be assumed to take a relatively low priority.

Alternatively, such managers could choose to exploit the weak monitoring and absence of effective governance to appropriate corporate assets for themselves (see Boyko *et al.*, 1995). For instance, consider the situation in an enterprise that the reform process has left clearly non-viable, for example a supplier of defence components whose market has disappeared. Managers and workers in such companies could realize that, once capital market forces are operating effectively, the company will be closed. In the interregnum, they have incentives to decapitalize the company and to use its (possibly not insignificant) credit lines in order to absorb assets from more productive uses. It may be noted that negative net worth will be no constraint provided the firm has positive gross assets. More generally, in situations where corporate governance is weak, managers have incentives to steal company assets through legal, semi-legal and criminal activities. This has been a persistent problem in the former Soviet Union (see Johnson *et al.*, 1999; Aslund, 1999).

Privatization is important for the practicalities of restructuring state-owned firms and enhancing productivity and performance. Restructuring involves investment and, in all the transition countries, the government has had few resources to make available to the enterprise sector. Privatization, at least in principle, holds out the promise of access to relatively cheap new funds from the new owners through the issuance of shares. If associated with the development of a private banking sector, debt financing might also become available. Perhaps even more enticing is the hope that the new owners will be foreign firms, in part or in full, bringing simultaneously capital and access to western design, technology, markets and managerial expertise. Foreign direct investment has been an important element in privatization in the leading transition economies such as Hungary and Poland (see, for example, Meyer, 1998). However, external owners will not invest funds if there is a risk that their funds will be wasted, expropriated by insiders or stolen. For privatization to work in the context where significant investments are required, there must be adequate legal and institutional safeguards for external investors in firms, through a corporate legal code that is effectively enforced, an operating and liquid capital market and proper rules for corporate governance, including rules ensuring the rights of minority shareholders and debt holders. Many countries of the former

Soviet Union, including Ukraine, have been very slow in introducing such rules (Estrin, 2002).

Privatization in Ukraine
The economic performance of Ukraine since independence has been poor. Real GDP fell 60.7 per cent between 1989 and 1999, worse than the CIS (Commonwealth of Independent States) average of a 44.5 per cent fall in GDP from 1989 to 1999 (UN, 2000). In addition, Ukraine was the only transition country that experienced a fall in GDP in every single year from 1989 to 1999, before GDP finally began to grow again in 2000, when a rate of 6 per cent was achieved. The extent of GDP decline is probably exaggerated, however, owing to two factors: firstly, the growth of the informal economy, which is estimated to account for around 50 per cent of GDP (Kaufmann, 1996); secondly, the move from overreporting to meet and exceed plan targets in the Soviet system, to underreporting under the current system in order to minimize tax payments. Over this same period, Ukraine experienced the fourth highest annual average inflation rate in any one year after wartorn Yugoslavia, Bosnia Herzegovina and Armenia (UN, 2000), with hyperinflation for several months in 1993. The inflation performance has improved since 1997, however. Even so, on most measures, Ukraine remains a reform laggard (EBRD, 1999) and has only achieved limited success in transforming its institutional environment. Respect for the law is low, corruption is rife, bankruptcy is rarely enforced and the majority of firms use complex barter arrangements in lieu of cash (Aslund, 1999). Problems of weak governance by the state, as owner, also apply in an extreme form in Ukraine.

Privatization in Ukraine took place in these inauspicious economic conditions. The political environment was hostile, with a majority of parliamentarians being opposed, to a greater or lesser extent, to the concept of privatization of large enterprises or the privatization of land. One can obtain an insight into the political process by considering in detail the chronology of the various privatization programmes. Ownership change began in Ukraine during the last three years of the Soviet period. The laws 'on individual working activity', 'on cooperation' and 'on enterprise', passed in 1988–1991, all increased the independence of economic agents and reduced the role of the state (Leshchenko and Revenko, 1999). Following the declaration of independence in 1991, the Ukrainian Supreme Soviet adopted the 'Concept on Destatization'. The first programme of privatization quickly followed and was adopted by the Supreme Soviet on 7 July 1992. The stated presidential target was to privatize 40 per cent of state property. In September 1993, the programme was altered and this goal was increased to 70 per cent. However, privatization actually remained slow for the remainder of the Kravchuk presidency (1991–4) because of political opposition. 'Mass privatization'[2] – the distribution of shares at a zero or nominal price, which elsewhere was being introduced at this time to speed up the privatization process (for example, in the Czech republic: see Estrin, 1994, and Chapter 18; or in Russia: see Boycko *et al.*, 1995, and Chapter 17) – was not attempted in Ukraine in this period.

The election of President Kuchma in mid-1994 marked a political turning point in the privatization process. Privatization moved up the political agenda. Kuchma appointed a new chairman of the State Property Fund (SPF), which had the responsibility for state-owned firms, and passed over to him control of the privatization process (Drum, 1996). The privatization process was streamlined and, with the removal of many bureaucratic obstacles, the mechanics of a mass privatization programme were put in place: automatic valuation procedures, creation of bid collection sites nationwide for use in the privatization auctions, a public information/advertising campaign and the issue of privatization certificates (PCs). In this Ukrainian version of mass privatization, designed to create the liquidity to 'sell' state-owned firms to private owners quickly, each citizen was entitled to one certificate valued at Krb 30000 (equivalent to less than one US dollar during 1994). This could be used to bid for shares in the privatization auctions/sales. The privatization programme began in November 1994 for large enterprises and in December of the same year for small enterprises.

In 1991, it is estimated that Ukraine contained 18000 state-owned large and medium-sized enterprises and 45000 state-owned small enterprises (Drum, 1996). The figures for the evolution of the private sector are provided by the SPF; only 30 firms were privatized in 1992, and 3555 in 1993, and these were mostly small firms. SPF figures state that the total number of privatized enterprises had risen to 11552 in December 1994, 28272 in December 1995, 48225 in December 1996 and 57009 in December 1997. The number of privatized enterprises had increased to 73349 by December 2000. These figures include the splitting up of pre-existing large state enterprises into several smaller privately owned firms.

Figure 21.1 indicates that the pace of private sector development has been decelerating over time. This has particularly affected large and middle-sized firms. The reasons for this can be traced to the conditions of privatization. Following the hyperinflation of 1993, the value of the vouchers and Privatization Deposit Accounts was increased by 3500 per cent to Krb 1050000. The valuation of enterprises, which was based on 1991 book value, was also uprated to take account of inflation. This led to many enterprises being overvalued (Hare *et al.*, 1996). Ukrainian privatizations were not such 'good value' as in Russia. This is one of the major reasons why the privatization process in Ukraine has been slower than in its neighbour (see Estrin and Wright, 1999).

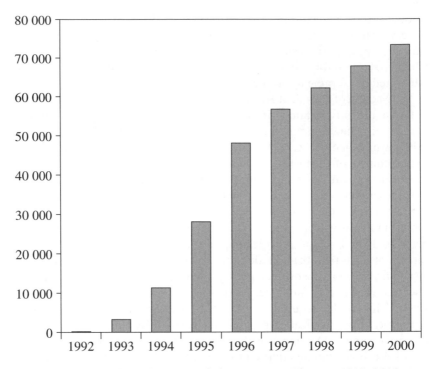

Figure 21.1   Number of privatized enterprises in Ukraine, 1992–2000

A solution to the problem of overvaluation was the creation of compensation certificates (CCs) in 1996.[3] CCs supplemented PCs and could be used to bid for up to 30 per cent of a company in the privatization auctions. Unlike the practice of the PC auctions, CCs could be used to bid for shares below the 'floor price'. Also in contrast to the PC, the CC was a 'bearer' certificate and could be sold for cash, arguably making it a money alternative. While this posed a danger of inflation because of the implicit rise in the money supply, it allowed investors to accumulate CCs and thereby facilitated privatization.

Privatization slowed down further, however, during 1997 and 1998, partly owing to unrealistic pricing of enterprises sold for cash, but also as a result of increased political obstruction from parliament. The uncertainty generated by the economic crisis following the Russian default in August 1998 also reduced the appetite of investors for Ukrainian assets. However, an interesting new feature of the 1998 privatization programme was that the branch ministries were required to justify any continued state shareholdings in individual enterprises. This was based on the assumption that full privatization would yield a higher benefit than a partial one, as it would reduce interference from the state. The cost of government intervention in a private firm is more difficult for politicians to hide than it is in a state-owned company. Although this policy seemed sensible, it had limited effect in the immediate aftermath of the Russian default in summer 1998.

From 1998, it became imperative for the government to find new sources of revenue. Up to then, the Ukrainian government had relied on foreign financing to meet its budget deficit. Following the rescheduling and partial agreed cancellation of its sovereign loans in 1998, this option was no longer available. These difficulties were exacerbated by a shrinking tax base. This meant that revenue-raising targets began to play an increasing role in the conduct of privatization. The use of privatization receipts to reduce the budget deficit had only begun in 1993; before then this was forbidden. The share of privatization proceeds allocated to the budget rose steadily, from 50 per cent in 1993 to 90 per cent in 1999. After 1998, the focus of privatization increasingly turned to cash sales. However, companies continued to be over-priced, which contributed to the continued slowdown in the pace of privat-ization. There were two main planks to the 1999 programme. The first was the divestiture of the remaining minority state stakes in enterprises. The other was the sale of significant state share holdings in large strategic enterprises. These sales were conducted through a 'mass cash auction' programme.

The prime minister and the cabinet of ministers instructed the SPF to maximize revenues by offering as many shares as possible for cash. Accordingly, during 1998, the SPF reallocated some share package offerings from certificate auctions to cash auctions. However, as this was accompa-nied by a reluctance to offer shares below nominal prices, it actually led to a decline in the number of medium and large enterprises being privatized.

Thus, perversely, the shift towards cash privatization was partly respon-sible for the deceleration of the pace of privatization in 1998. As the SPF was reluctant to proceed with the sale of the most attractive (and poten-tially most lucrative) enterprises, the purpose of raising more revenue was defeated. Some less attractive enterprises were being offered, while a number of potentially high revenue-yielding enterprises were put on a list of companies that must remain state-owned. Privatization, therefore, failed to generate the expected revenues. Privatization has also been slow because companies have been overvalued. However, lowering the asking prices would have also caused difficulties, as this would have risked even stronger opposition to the sales in parliament.

The slow pace of privatization gave increased bargaining power to enter-prise insiders. The lack of progress led to the establishment of strong *de facto* control by the employees and managers over enterprises. This was due to the vacuum of authority and monitoring left by the reduction in the power of the planners in the sectoral ministries. This de facto control of managers and workers was transformed by the privatization process into *de jure* control, as insiders took majority ownership in many enterprises in the subsequent three years.

The impact of privatization, ownership structures and enterprise performance

Insiders versus outsiders

In theory, the impact of voucher privatization on company performance depends on who are the beneficiaries of the mass privatization. There are two categories of people to whom the authorities could sell, or freely distribute, shares. The first are 'insiders' to the firm: managers, workers or both. The second are members of the general population, either as a whole or those specifically discomfited by the previous nationalization and who seek redress from the new regime. In Ukraine, there have been serious attempts to ensure significant outsider stakes. This was in contrast to Russia, where the voucher privatization favoured insiders from the start (Earle and Estrin, 1997). However, even in Ukraine, insider privatization has predominated in practice.

One needs to consider who would in principle make better owners of firms, outside capital holders exercising their influence through the stock exchange and financial institutions along Anglo-Saxon lines, or the existing stakeholders in the firm – managers and workers (also see Chapter 16 for a further discussion of insider and outsider ownership in transition economies). The arguments in favour of allocating dominant or majority shareholdings to insiders in the Ukrainian environment are very clear. Such an approach is very fast and easy to administer, since the target group of buyers is already identified. It could even raise some revenue because managers and workers may be willing to make some contribution towards the value of the assets that they are receiving. The insider approach also ensures that the existing scarce managerial experience, and this is a severe constraint in Ukraine, continues to be exploited.

There are a number of major problems with insider privatization, all of which have important implications in Ukraine (see Earle and Estrin, 1996). In the first place, insider ownership raises numerous questions about enterprise motivation and performance, especially if there are significant employee shareholdings. Many regard employee ownership as inextricably linked to the consumption of assets by workers in the form of higher wages. In Ukraine, worker ownership is usually taken to imply managerial control and the dangers from managerial ownership and control are considered less dramatic (see Boycko *et al.*, 1995). However, in the absence of a capital market allowing managers to withdraw their equity, the motivational impact on company performance is not as positive as one might hope.

Management may be forced to consume capital at the end of their life cycle in order to recoup previous investments. There is also the danger, if the government does press to sell off all its assets immediately, that the fledgling private firms will carry excessive debt. Perhaps most seriously, diffused ownership among workers combined with managerial control gives incentives and opportunity for managers to expropriate assets. The same problems can arise if outsider ownership is highly diffused so that no single shareholder or group of shareholders has an incentive to monitor management effectively.

Moreover, managerial or employee-managerial ownership is not the most suitable ownership form for enterprises about to embark on the major restructuring that is needed in Ukraine. Decision-making authority is given to groups who might be removed, or at least find their position fundamentally altered, by more dispassionate analysts of enterprise needs. Thus workers in overmanned plants will be loath to vote themselves out of a job, while former socialist managers, now owners of the firm, will be unlikely to countenance choices that increase the importance of colleagues in the hitherto insignificant finance, accounting and marketing divisions, let alone choices leading to financial reliance on local banks or suppliers.

Privatization to insiders also fails to bring new funds to the company, at a time when additional resources are the crucial ingredients for deep or 'strategic' restructuring (see Roland, 2000, on forms of restructuring). This contrasts with the situation if the new owners are external to the firm, when they may have both the instruments and the control to bring in the additional funds they consider to be required. Insider ownership thus brings little additional funding from the new owners and creates such serious agency problems that the management may be unable to raise external financing.

The key problem with all types of mass privatization is, thus, that they fail to create effective forms of corporate governance. The difficulty is that any attempt to distribute shares widely to the general public, either workers or shareholders, must imply that ownership rights will become widely diffused among the population as a whole. But highly diffused ownership rights, and the absence of any dominant block of shares, means that control over managers will necessarily be weak. The objective of voucher privatization – to spread the new ownership rights as widely as possible among the new population – therefore conflicts with the aim of bringing effective external capital market pressures to bear on managerial decision making. When ownership rights are widely diffused, so that managers do not need to fear the dissatisfaction of a controlling block of shares acting in unanimity to remove them from their jobs or to enforce, for example, more radical restructuring policies, they may feel empowered to resist threatening changes, including the prevention of outsiders from building dominant stakes.

In practice, the 'working collective' of each enterprise – the workers and the managers – received priority rights and privileges in acquiring shares in Ukraine through the early lease buy-out privatization method (see below). However, these were taken away in an effort to reduce insider influence, with priority rights being reallocated to employees as individuals, in several ways. Firstly, there was a mechanism for the free transfer of social assets of the firm: recreation centres, cafeterias, holiday homes and day care centres. Secondly, workers could use their privatization certificates and then a further 50 per cent in cash to purchase shares in the enterprise. Any remaining shares were offered for competitive sale. If the workers formed a buyer's association with a minimum of 50 per cent of the workforce, they could become the preferred buyer. Payment by instalments over three years was allowed, with an initial payment of 30 per cent. Managers were able to buy a further 5 per cent of the enterprise share capital for a low price (Drum, 1996).

The Act of Leasing of State Enterprises of April 1992 gave employees the right to lease their enterprise with an option to buy at a later date, and 3500 enterprises were leased to workers and managers with a buy-out provision free or at a low price (Drum, 1996). This early period thus saw the privatization of enterprises predominately to managers and workers. In theory, the post-1994 programme should have resulted in the sale of enterprises to 'outsiders', such as citizens, investment funds, other enterprises and foreigners. In practice many enterprises continued to be sold to managers and workers.

The privatization process also aimed to encourage the existence of investment funds to offset the outsider dispersion problem (see Coffee, 1996, for a critique of the use of investment funds in the Czech case). These organizations collected vouchers from the population in order to buy blocks of shares. It was hoped that, as concentrated 'blockholders' of shares, these investment funds would be able to monitor management strategy and behaviour. However, the funds have allegedly concentrated on trying to make profits from share trading and have rarely tried to monitor or influence managerial objectives or actions.[4] By 1997, there were over 350 investment funds, though 80 per cent of vouchers collected were controlled by under 40 funds (Drum, 1996). Despite this concentration of control in the hands of a few investment funds, they need to own larger blocks of shares in total if they are to provide a counterweight to the 'insider dominance' of many share registers, as we will see below.

As the state still retains a significant stake in many enterprises, the question of how these shares are managed, and what impact they have on emerging corporate governance arrangements, is important. Management of state shares is carried out by the relevant branch ministry or, after the company has been slated for privatization, by the SPF. The cabinet of ministers can decide to transfer the right to manage state shares to other entities. This can be a government body, a private individual chosen through a tender process or the winner of a bid for a package of shares to whom the option of managing the state stake is given. However, in the past the SPF has not actively managed the continuing state shareholdings. It has often given its proxy votes to the management. The 1999/2000 privatization programme aimed to change that by requiring the SPF actively to monitor management and exercise the voting power of the shares during company Annual General Meetings (AGMs).[5]

Ownership structures in Ukraine, post-privatization
We have outlined the different privatization programmes in Ukraine. We have shown that enterprise insiders were given massive advantages before 1995 that lessened but did not disappear afterwards. We have also seen how the state has since tried to increase the revenue raised from privatization and attempted belatedly to manage the remaining state share stakes by monitoring management and using its vote in AGMs to change company strategy.

To explore questions of enterprise ownership and performance further, we undertook an enterprise-level survey of Ukrainian firms in 1999. We visited 230 enterprises in all regions of Ukraine. Each interview took an average of four hours to complete. We made the appointments with a senior manager (often the general director), who would usually assign an employee, often an accountant, to help us collect the quantitative data. The manager answered the qualitative questions him or herself. The quantitative data were taken from the financial reports that the enterprises send to the government each year.

The sample of firms was drawn from the population of firms listed at the local SPF offices. These lists included firms of all ownership types, and were the most complete lists of firms available in Ukraine. However, they have two drawbacks. Firstly, some 'sensitive' companies from the military–industrial complex are not listed. This omission removes some of the firms which are reputedly worst performing because they have lost the majority of the military market of the FSU. This provided a 'positive' bias to the survey. Secondly, a large proportion of firms in Ukraine operate in the informal economy. By definition, these firms would not appear on any official lists. This is likely to bias the survey in the other direction. The most dynamic firms in neighbouring Poland have been small *de novo* firms. In Ukraine, stifling bureaucracy and endemic bribe seeking have forced many of the *de novo* firms into the informal sector (Kaufmann, 1996). Even if we could locate them, it is unlikely that these firms would give answers on ownership, restructuring and performance to an interviewer. This is because they are subject to legal censure and also extortion by organized crime. As a result of this omission, there are likely to be some more dynamic, forward-looking firms in Ukraine which were not covered by the sample. Thus the survey excluded some of the best and some of the worst performing firms in Ukraine. Despite this, the SPF lists remain the most complete ones available.

The industrial fabric differs between the regions of the Ukraine. Although heavy industrial firms are located all over the country, they are more concentrated in the east. Similarly, there are more agribusinesses, including food processing, in the south and west. We visited firms in all regions with a small bias towards the Central and Eastern regions, which have a higher share of industrial production in Ukraine.

Turning to ownership structures, the sample was constructed to ensure that enterprises where the state has a majority share holding are relatively few, as can be seen in Table 21.1. Retained majority state ownership is rather higher than implied by this sample; according to EBRD (2001) only some 55 per cent of Ukrainian GDP was produced by private firms in 1999. However the survey was aimed at privatized enterprises. When we consider sectoral variation, in Table 21.2, we find that state-dominated enterprises account for a significant part of metallurgical enterprises (around 14 per cent of the total). Textile and food processing are the only other branches where majority state-owned companies have a noticeable presence, and collectives are also quite important in these sectors.

Table 21.1   Ukraine: enterprises, by ownership (%)

Joint-stock company (mainly privately owned)	85.6
Cooperative	0.4
Joint-stock company with majority state ownership	6.1
Leasehold	0.4
Other	7.4
Total	100

Table 21.3 gives a breakdown of ownership structure of the sample as a whole and also by insider and outsider dominated companies. We consider a particular group to be the dominant owner when more than 50 per cent of shares are owned by that group. Thus a firm is 'insider-owned' when at least half the shares are in the hands of managers, workers and former workers and also where these groups hold more than 40 per cent of the shares and the next largest shareholder holds less than 40 per cent. Outsider-owned companies are defined in the same way (outsiders own

Table 21.2   Ukraine: ownership, by industrial branch (%)

	Metallurgy & engines	Chemical & pharmaceu- ticals	Construction materials, wood processing	Food processing	Textiles
Joint-stock company	84.6	95.2	81.8	89.2	82.9
Cooperative	—	—	—	1.4	—
Joint-stock Company with majority state ownership	13.9	—	—	4.1	5.7
Leasehold	—	—	3.0	—	—
Other	1.5	4.8	15.2	5.4	11.4

more than 50 per cent of shares in total) with the qualifying groups of shareholders being Ukrainian banks, Ukrainian firms, Ukrainian investment funds, Ukrainian citizens, foreign individuals, foreign companies and agricultural producers. Table 21.3 reports the ownership structure now and at the time of the first shareholders' meeting. It allows us to ask whether ownership patterns, and more importantly changes in ownership patterns since the time of the first shareholder meeting, immediately after privatization, are affected by the nature of majority ownership.

Just after privatization, when firms held their first shareholder meetings, ownership was concentrated in the 'Workers' Collective'. Some 56 per cent of shares were in the hands of managers and workers, in the proportions 10 per cent to 90 per cent (and some 90 per cent of shares held by insiders were held by current workers and around 10 per cent by former workers). This tremendous concentration of shareholding in the hands of insiders is consistent with the findings from a previous enterprise survey conducted by the authors in 1997 (see Estrin and Rosevear, 1999a; Estrin and Wright, 1999). Of the remaining 44 per cent of shares not in insider hands, on average, around a quarter were retained by the state and a further quarter were in the hands of citizens. Only around 9 per cent of other shares were in the hands of investment funds and a further 8 per cent owned by other Ukrainian firms, potentially fairly concentrated external owners. Foreign ownership of companies was very low, amounting to 2 per cent of the total holding.

When we disaggregate by category of shareholdings at the time of the first shareholders' meeting into insider-dominated and outsider-dominated firms, some interesting patterns emerge. Firstly, the predominant shareholders in outsider-owned firms are Ukraine citizens (18.8 per cent), firms

Table 21.3 Ukraine: shareholding, by ownership (%)

Shareholder type	Now			First shareholder meeting		
	All firms (%)	Insider owned firms (%)	Outsider owned firms (%)	All firms (%)	Insider- owned firms (%)	Outsider- owned firms (%)
State	7.6	2.7	7.1	10.1	5.3	11.7
Workers' collective	55.1	82.2	22.6	55.8	78.9	27.2
Of which:						
managers	7.5	10.3	3.8	5.8	7.5	3.6
workers	34.1	50.4	13.9	44.0	61.8	21.5
former workers	13.2	19.7	4.8	6.8	8.7	4.4
Ukrainian firms	10.8	2.3	23.4	8.0	2.2	16.9
Ukrainian banks	0.8	0.4	1.7	0.5	0.0	1.1
Ukrainian investment funds	7.3	1.7	15.5	8.8	3.0	15.9
Ukrainian citizens	12.7	7.2	21.6	10.8	5.8	18.8
Foreign individuals	0.2	0.7	0.4	0.2	0.0	0.4
Foreign companies	3.2	1.9	4.7	2.0	1.5	2.6
Agricultural producers	2.1	1.6	3.1	2.7	2.3	3.5

(16.9 per cent) and investment funds (15.9 per cent). Thus external ownership, even when it occurred, was rather widely dispersed. Foreign firms held
at best a modest stake, even in outsider-dominated firms – less than 3 per
cent. Interestingly, the state retained on average a higher stake in outsider-
than in insider-owned firms (11.7 per cent as against 5.3 per cent, on
average). It would also appear that potential strategic owners were aware of
the dangers of excessive insider ownership in Ukraine, even at the time of
the first shareholder meeting. Thus we find the non-state outsiders' stake to
be only on average 14.8 per cent in insider dominated firms, with more than
one third of these shares owned by citizens, and 20 per cent or less by either
investment funds, Ukrainian firms or agricultural producers. Very few
shares were held by foreign firms in insider-dominated firms. Once again,
this strongly suggests that, from the outset, outside owners, including
foreigners, were well aware of the dangers and corporate governance problems of investing in insider-dominated firms. The predominance of insider
ownership may, therefore, explain the unwillingness of strategic investors,
domestic or foreign, to invest in Ukrainian firms.

The survey allows us to explain how the ownership structure has
changed from the time of the first shareholders' meeting until the spring
of 1999, a period which includes the Russian crisis of August 1998. If the
legal and institutional infrastructures were in place and capital markets
were functioning, we would expect movement in the ownership structure
post-privatization, with workers selling to outsiders and managers, insiders selling to outsiders, the state reducing its share by selling to outsiders,
and finally some clear emergence of concentrated majority outsider ownership as strategic blocks of shares changed hands. It can be seen that there
is little evidence of this in Ukraine. Insider ownership remained, on
average, virtually constant at 55 per cent, though there is some evidence
that workers are either selling their shares to managers or keeping their
shares as they change job (hence becoming 'former workers'). However,
there was no overall shift from insider to outsider ownership, or from
workers to outsiders, and only a very small shift from the state to outsiders. The evolution in ownership structure that privatized Ukrainian firms
probably require to enable restructuring had not yet emerged by 1999,
according to our survey.

Moreover, there is little evidence of increasing concentration of ownership
among outside owners. In fact, on average, investment funds had proportion-
ately fewer shares than at the time of the first shareholder meeting, though
other firms and citizens had increased their share. There was, however, some
increase in the average shareholding of foreign firms, which is an encouraging sign, though only from 2 per cent to 3.2 per cent on average. The very
limited role played by Ukrainian banks in enterprise corporate governance

is also highlighted in Table 21.3; their share increased slightly but remains on average below 1 per cent.

Table 21.3 also suggests that the evolution of ownership structure may have been different in insider- and outsider-owned firms. This could be a crucial indicator of the likely future path of ownership. In insider-owned firms, which of course represent a majority of all firms in our sample, the Workers' Collective has actually been increasing its shareholdings since the first shareholders' meeting; the insider stake has increased from around 79 per cent to 82 per cent on average, primarily because of an increase in the shareholding of managers. Managers' shareholdings increased, by 30 per cent of their original holding, as they bought shares from workers, and probably from investment funds and agricultural producers. Thus, far from gradually evolving towards the traditional structure of an outsider-owned firm, our survey provides evidence that Ukrainian firms were instead retrenching into managerial ownership and control, at least in the majority of cases where insiders already had a dominant stake.

In outsider-owned firms, however, the picture is different. Here insiders were selling their shares, notably workers who reduced their stake, on average, by 7.6 percentage points. The shares were not bought by managers or held by former workers, as we have seen occurred in insider-owned firms. Rather, they were sold to outsiders, notably other Ukrainian firms and foreign companies (who had almost doubled their share in outsider owned Ukrainian firms since the first shareholder meeting). Thus, in outsider-owned firms, we do find evidence of reduced insider stakes, increasing ownership concentration and rising (though modest) foreign investment. This is an encouraging sign for the Ukrainian economy, suggesting that market forces in ownership stakes will assert themselves if the initial ownership structures are conducive.

The survey also provides additional evidence on corporate governance and strategic ownership. We find that, in the average firm, the number of managers holding shares is around 15, while the number of workers is 599 and of former workers 302. Holdings by Ukrainian citizens and firms are also highly dispersed, at 1065 and 616 shareholders on average, respectively. However, the typical number of shareholders who are banks, foreign individuals and foreign companies is one, and of investment funds is two. Thus outsider holdings, though on average modest, are quite highly concentrated.

Given the poor structure of ownership and the weak institutional environment, it is perhaps unsurprising that there is little evidence that privatization has improved enterprise performance in Ukraine (see Estrin and Wright, 1999, for a survey). For example, Estrin and Rosevear (1999a) report the results from a survey of 150 firms undertaken in 1997. Their survey instrument contained 27 questions about enterprise and restructuring activities, from adjusting quality of product or product mix to asset disposals or financial restructuring. The observed level of restructuring in Ukraine was extremely low. On a scale of one (no restructuring) to five (very active in restructuring) the average score was less than 2.0 in 12 areas of restructuring and less than 3.0 (moderate change) in 23 out of 27 areas. The highest average score was only 3.8 (for changes in investment policy) and the lowest a mere 1.2 (effectively no change at all) for policy on loans.

The 27 questions were asked for a second time in our 1999 Ukrainian survey, discussed above. Once again, Ukrainian firms admitted to having undertaken little or no restructuring in most of the areas under discussion. On this occasion, a score of less than two (minimal change) on a scale of one to five was recorded for 11 out of the 27 activities, including reducing wage arrears, rescheduling loans or disposing of social assets. However, a further 13 categories scored between two and three (moderate change), a slight shift upwards since 1997. These restructuring activities included new investment, changing technology, increasing export efforts and reducing material inputs. Moreover, three activities scored more than three, including changing suppliers and distribution network. The latter yielded on average the highest score, at a level of 3.4. However, although there was slightly more restructuring indicated in the 1999 than in the 1997 survey, the pace remained very slow.

Estrin and Rosevear (1999b) seek to relate improved enterprise performance to ownership structure in Ukraine. They estimate a series of performance equations, using sales, profits and employment as indicators of company success. The explanatory variables used include factor inputs (labour, capital and capital quality), barter, export ratios and a detailed specification of ownership structure. Their equations indicate that there is no relationship between ownership and performance. To be precise, in their 1997 sample they find that privatized firms were not significantly more profitable or productive than state-owned ones, and that there was no significant difference in the performance of insider- and outsider-owned private enterprises in Ukraine.

The evidence is, therefore, that privatization is not yet affecting enterprise performance in Ukraine. As noted by Djankov and Murrell (2000) this may be because privatization was undertaken in such a way that appropriate private ownership firms did not emerge. It may also be that, for privatization to be effective, we require appropriate private market institutions and a competitive capital market, which are still developing in Ukraine. It may even be that improved economic performance actually comes primarily via *de novo* entry of private firms, more than the privatization of the large former state-owned industrial sector. *De novo* entry has been comparatively rare in Ukraine, at least in comparison with more advanced transition economies such as Poland (see Johnson and Loveman, 1995; Estrin, 2002; and Chapter 19).

Finally, if we regard changing senior management as an indicator of effective corporate governance, Table 21.4 provides important evidence that things may finally be beginning to improve. Using our 1999 sample, the table reveals considerable turnover in senior management. As we might have expected, outsider ownership yields more effective governance than insider ownership, with a considerably higher proportion of firms having changed their general managers since 1994. The state also appears to impose effective control over the firms it continues to own, with the vast majority of general managers having been changed since 1994. This is one of the few pieces of evidence that harder budget constraints and privatization are finally beginning to have an effect in Ukraine, although the management changes appear not to have filtered through to performance.

Table 21.4   Change of general manager, by ownership, since 1994 (%)

State owner-dominated	83.33
Private owner-dominated	45.83
Insider owner-dominated	39.20
Outsider owner-dominated	57.95

Conclusions

Privatization in Ukraine has been a slow, convoluted and politicized process. To have privatized 70 000 firms in eight years is an achievement. However, the performance of privatized enterprises has been disappointing. This poor performance may be linked to the fact that enterprise insiders own too much of Ukrainian industry. At the onset of the transition, many economists expected insiders to sell their stake to outsiders with the financial and managerial means to restructure and improve performance. Our survey shows that insiders are continuing to consolidate their hold over that majority of companies where they already have a dominant stake.

Ukrainian economic performance has not yet benefited substantially from privatization. Empirical evidence from the rest of the world shows that outside ownership usually results in improved performance. Therefore policy makers should encourage an evolution of the ownership structure towards outside ownership. To this end, the government should promote a deepening and widening of the stock market and of legislation to protect minority shareholders. The government should also consider adjustments to the tax system that would encourage share sales by insiders.

A key element in the economic growth of neighbouring Poland has been the development of *de novo* firms. Ukraine needs to encourage the development of new, small private enterprises. It could do this by reducing the number of bureaucratic signatures required before starting a business. It should then reduce opportunities for corrupt bureaucrats to extort monies from entrepreneurs by reducing regulation whenever possible.

Notes

1. The authors would like to thank Maria Bytchkova for research assistance, though any errors or omissions remain the responsibility of the authors.
2. See Estrin (1994) on mass privatization in Central and Eastern Europe, and the special issue of the *Journal of Comparative Economics*, Vol. 27, no. 3, 1999, for a discussion of mass privatization in the FSU (former Soviet Union). See also Roland (2000) for an overview.
3. During 1996, an additional form of privatization certificate, called a compensation certificate, was issued. It was given as compensation to savers who had lost the value of their money held in the State Savings Bank during the hyperinflation of 1992–4.
4. Information given during an interview between one of the authors and the deputy director of the SPF.
5. The problem of retained state share ownership in transition economies is analysed in Bennett *et al.* (2001).

References

Aslund, A. (1999) 'Russia's Collapse', *Foreign Affairs*, 78(5), 64–77.

Bennett, J., S. Estrin and J. Maw (2001) 'Mass Privatisation and Partial State Ownership of Firms in Transition Economics', CEPR Discussion Paper, no. 2895.

Blanchard, O., R. Dornbusch, P. Krugman and L. Summers (1991) *Reform in Eastern Europe*, Cambridge, MA: MIT Press.

Boycko, M., A. Shleifer and R. Vishny (1995) *Privatizing Russia*, Cambridge, MA: MIT Press.

Coffee, J.C. (1996) 'Institutional Investors in Transition Economies: Lessons from the Czech Experience', in R. Frydman, C. Gray and A. Rapaczyński (eds), *Corporate Governance in Central Europe and Russia*, vol. 1, Budapest: Central European University Press.

Djankov, S. and P. Murrell (2002) 'Enterprise Restructuring in Transition: A Quantitative Survey', *Journal of Economic Literature*, 40(3), 739–92.

Drum, B. (1996) 'Privatization, Enterprise Restructuring, and Capital Market Reform', in P. Cornelus and P. Lenian (eds), *Ukraine: Accelerating the Transition to the Market*, Washington, DC: IMF.

Earle, J. and S. Estrin (1996) 'Employee Ownership in Transition Economies', in R. Frydman, C. Gray and A. Rapaczyński (eds), *Corporate Governance in Transition*, vol 2, Budapest: Central European University Press.

Earle, J. and S. Estrin (1997) 'After Voucher Privatization: The Structure of Corporate Ownership in Russian Manufacturing Industry', CEPR Discussion Paper, no. 1736.

EBRD (1994) *Transition Report 1994*, London: EBRD.

EBRD (1999) *Transition Report 1999: Ten Years of Transition*, London: EBRD.

EBRD (2000) *Transition Report 2000: Employment, Skills and Transition*, London: EBRD.

EBRD (2001) *Transition Report 2001: Energy in Transition*, London: EBRD.

Estrin, S. (1994) *Privatisation in Central and Eastern Europe*, New York: Longman.

Estrin, S. (2002) 'Competition and Corporate Governance in Transition', *Journal of Economic Perspectives*, 16 (Winter)(1), 101–129.

Estrin, S. and A. Rosevear (1999a) 'Enterprise Performance and Corporate Governance in Ukraine', *Journal of Comparative Economics*, 27(3), 442–58.

Estrin, S. and A. Rosevear (1999b) 'Enterprise Performance and Ownership: The Case of Ukraine', *European Economic Review*, 43(4–6), 1125–36.

Estrin, S. and M. Wright (1999) 'Corporate Governance in the Former Soviet Union: An Overview', *Journal of Comparative Economics*, 27(3), 398–421.

Frydman, R., C. Gray, M. Hessel and A. Rapaczyński (1999) 'When Does Privatization Work? The Impact of Private Ownership on Corporate Performance in the Transition Economies', *Quarterly Journal of Economics*, 114(4), 1153–91.

Hare, P., J. Batt and S. Estrin (eds) (1999), *Reconstituting the Market: The Political Economy of Microeconomic Transformation*, Chur, Switzerland: Harwood Academic Publishers.

Hare, P., M. Ishaq and S. Estrin (1996) 'The Legacies of Central Planning and the Transition to a Market Economy: Ukrainian Contradictions', CERT Discussion Paper, no. 96/18.

Johnson, S. and G. Loveman (1995) *Starting Over in Eastern Europe*, Boston: Harvard Business School Press.

Johnson, S., D. Kaufmann, J. McMillan and C. Woodruff (1999) 'Why Do Firms Hide? Bribes and Unofficial Activity after Communism', SITE Working Paper no. 150.

Kaufmann, D. (1996) 'The Missing Pillar of a Growth Strategy for Ukraine: Reforms for Private Sector Development', in P. Cornelus and P. Lenian (eds), *Ukraine: Accelerating the Transition to the Market*, Washington, DC: IMF.

Leshchenko, L. and V. Revenko (1999) 'Privatization and Restructuring in Ukraine', in P. Hare, J. Batt, M. Cave and S. Estrin (eds), *Reconstituting the Market: The Political Economy of Microeconomic Transformation*, London: Harwood Academic Press.

Megginson, W. and J. Netter (2001) 'From State to Market: A Survey of Empirical Studies on Privatization', *Journal of Economic Literature*, 39(2), 321–89.

Meyer, K. (1998), *Direct Investment in Economies in Transition*, Cheltenham, UK and Lyme, US: Edward Elgar.

Nellis, J. (2000) 'Privatization in Transition Economies: What Happened? What's Next?', mimeo, World Bank, Washington, DC.

Roland, G. (2000) *Transition and Economics: Politics, Markets and Firms*, London: MIT Press.

UN (2000) *Economic Survey of Europe 2000 No. 1*, Geneva: United Nations Economic Commission for Europe.

PART V

REGULATING
PRIVATIZED INDUSTRIES

22 Regulation: theory and concepts
Dieter Bös

Introduction

Public utilities are enterprises which supply essential goods or services, where 'essential' means that they cannot be cut off without danger of total or partial collapse of an economy. From an allocative point of view these enterprises contribute to the infrastructure of the economy, while from a distributional point of view they contribute to providing consumers with necessities of life. The most important public utilities can be found in the areas of electricity, gas, water, telecommunication, postal services, radio, TV, airlines, railroads and urban public transport. It is not the ownership but the lack of competition which justifies regulation of the activities of public utilities. Accordingly, privatization does not necessarily imply the end of government regulation. If it is impossible to expose a public utility to competition, then price and quality regulation typically are regarded as inevitable, in spite of the government's interest in withdrawing from intervention in the particular field as signalled by the very act of privatization.

This raises the question of how far competition can be introduced in the supplies of telecommunication, rail and the like. For a long time this question was not asked, because all public utilities were thought to be 'natural monopolies', characterized by a subadditive cost function[1] and by sustainability:[2] it is cheaper to produce goods by a monopoly than by many firms, and potential market entrants can be held off without predatory measures. In such cases unregulated private enterprises would exploit the market. Therefore regulation is necessary. Contestability of monopolies is particularly relevant in the case of multi-product enterprises where market entry may refer to only one product or a subgroup of products of the public utility. Obviously, only rarely does the whole public utility exhibit the properties of a natural monopoly. In many cases only a network is a natural monopoly and competition is possible with respect to the other parts of production or distribution of services. Various companies which administer rolling stock could use the same railroad infrastructure. Various telecommunication companies can use the same network. Typically, however, a relatively long time is needed to establish competition in these fields successfully. The British market for telecommunications was characterized for a long time by British Telecom as the market leader and Mercury as the follower. Note that telecommunications is a good example of an erosion of natural monopoly positions: in practice the invention of the mobile phone implies that for particular services no fixed-line network is needed. This change in the technology, accordingly, leads to fierce competition in this field. A failure story, on the other hand, is the privatization of British Rail. Here, the railroad network was considered a natural monopoly that had to be regulated, but was not regulated carefully enough and quality deteriorated quickly. The train-operating companies responsible for providing passenger services have route monopolies under franchises.

Whenever there is no competition, or the competition is not strong enough to prevent a public utility from exploiting its customers, government regulation of public utilities remains on the agenda of economic policy and, therefore, remains an important subject of economic theory.

A very general framework for a theory of regulation of a public utility is as follows. The theory considers a two-person game between a regulator and a manager who represents the public utility. The objectives of the two players may vary. The regulator may alternatively be considered as a welfare maximizer, as a politician who wants to maximize votes or as a bureaucrat who wants to maximize his power and, therefore, is interested in a high budget of the utility or in a high output. The manager may be modelled as a profit maximizer or as an agent who is interested in his personal income and in the disutility of his effort. In this two-person relationship the players have to consider various constraints. First, the utility is typically obliged to meet all demand at the regulated prices.[3] Second, in many cases the public utility is explicitly restricted in its ability to maximize profits. Alternative regulatory models deal with direct profit constraints (profit must be smaller than some exogenously given threshold) or with indirect profit constraints, imposing 'caps' on prices or an upper boundary on the rate of return on investment. Third, the regulation must not eliminate the public utility. Regulation has failed if the regulator drives the utility into bankruptcy or, in an alternative formulation, induces the manager to leave his job (violation of the manager's participation constraint). Finally, whenever the regulator is not fully informed, he must induce the manager to operate in line with the regulator's intentions (incentive compatibility).

Any regulatory activity should be evaluated by comparison with a benchmark model. A fully informed welfare-maximizing regulator may be taken as the basis of such a benchmark. Which prices would he impose on the public utility? Let me present two very simple rules; many more refined rules can be found in Bös (1994). Consider first the simple maximization of the sum of consumer and producer surplus,[4] without any profit constraint. In this case the regulator will choose prices which are equal to the respective marginal costs. If the public utility operates under increasing returns to scale, these marginal-cost prices will lead to a deficit of the firm. If this deficit is considered too high, the regulator may choose prices which maximize the sum of consumer and producer surplus under a revenue–cost constraint.[5] In this case, Ramsey prices will be chosen.[6] Consider a two-product utility,[7] selling quantities x_1 and x_2 at prices p_1 and p_2. Denote marginal costs by C_i, $i = 1,2$. Ramsey pricing is characterized by the following marginal conditions:

$$\frac{p_1 - C_1}{p_1} = -\lambda\frac{\varepsilon_{22} - \varepsilon_{12}}{\varepsilon_{11}\varepsilon_{22} - \varepsilon_{12}\varepsilon_{21}}; \quad \frac{p_2 - C_2}{p_2} = -\lambda\frac{\varepsilon_{11} - \varepsilon_{21}}{\varepsilon_{11}\varepsilon_{22} - \varepsilon_{12}\varepsilon_{21}}, \quad (R)$$

where ε_{ij} $i,j = 1,2$ are price elasticities of demand[8] and $\lambda \in [0, 1]$ is a scale parameter which depends on the profit threshold. If $\lambda = 0$, we have marginal cost prices, if $\lambda = 1$, we have monopoly prices. Now consider the right-hand side of the first of the above equations:

$$-\lambda\frac{\varepsilon_{22} - \varepsilon_{12}}{\varepsilon_{11}\varepsilon_{22} - \varepsilon_{12}\varepsilon_{21}} = -\frac{\varepsilon_{22}/\lambda - \varepsilon_{12}/\lambda}{\varepsilon_{11}/\lambda \cdot \varepsilon_{22}/\lambda - \varepsilon_{12}/\lambda \cdot \varepsilon_{21}/\lambda} = -\frac{\eta_{22} - \eta_{12}}{\eta_{11}\eta_{22} - \eta_{12}\eta_{21}},$$

with $\eta_{ij} = \varepsilon_{ij}/\lambda > \varepsilon_{ij}$. A similar transformation holds for the second equation. Accordingly, the Ramsey utility behaves like a profit-maximizing monopolist who overestimates all price elasticities of demand by the same factor $1/\lambda > 1$.

Overestimation of elasticities implies that the utility will be more cautious than the profit-maximizing monopolist when it comes to raising prices above marginal costs: the prices are set more cautiously, the more easily demand is lost in the case of a price increase (and this is just the same problem a pure monopoly faces, hence the possibility to characterize Ramsey prices by a comparison with monopoly prices). In contrast to monopoly prices, however, the cautious behaviour of the Ramsey firm implies a lower price level than for a profit-maximizing monopolist, resulting from the fact that the profit constraint is lower than the monopoly profit (and higher than the deficit at marginal-cost prices). The most popular special case of Ramsey pricing is the so-called 'inverse-elasticity rule': if all cross-price elasticities are ignored, the relative deviation of any price from the marginal costs is lower, the higher the direct price elasticity of demand.

In contrast to the benchmark models, regulators are in practice never fully informed. There is, first, the moral hazard problem, which arises if the regulator and the manager of the public utility are equally badly informed when the decision on regulation is made. In this case both allocative and productive efficiency can be achieved by 'selling the store to the agent' and stipulating a Loeb-Magat (1979) mechanism: the regulator gives the consumer surplus to the manager in exchange for a lump sum compensation. The manager is allowed to retain the profit. Therefore, he will maximize the sum of consumer and producer surplus and attain the first best. In practice, this mechanism is not applied, because it shifts all of the risk to the manager and away from the regulator, and because it is too expensive in the case of asymmetric information, which is more plausible than symmetric information: it is highly likely that the manager of the public utility is better informed than the regulator. Therefore, most of the modern theory of regulation concentrates on the adverse selection problem, where the information is asymmetrically distributed when the decision on regulation is made. It has been shown that there is a special class of contracts between the regulator and the public utility whose result is always at least as good for the regulator as any other contract he could conceive. In this contract the manager is asked to announce the actual value of his private information and gets a specially designed incentive income which induces truthful revelation ('revelation principle'). The incentive income implies that the manager of the public utility gets an information rent for revealing his private knowledge. Seminal work on price regulation under asymmetric information is due to Baron and Myerson (1982) and Laffont and Tirole (1993).

The remainder of the chapter is organized as follows: we begin with the treatment of price regulation by simple regulatory rules. These rules require a minimum of information on the side of the regulator. In particular, he need not know the functional shapes of demand and cost functions or the probability distribution of some unobservable variable. Unfortunately, the simple regulatory rules typically raise negative incentive effects on the part of the regulated utility and, therefore, they are only rarely applied in economic practice. We shall discuss the iterative mechanisms of Vogelsang and Finsinger and yardstick regulation. Then we turn to informationally demanding price regulation, which avoids the negative incentive effects, but requires much more information on the part of the regulator and, therefore, is more of a fascinating theoretical exercise than an actually applied instrument of economic policy. Therefore, we devote another section to price cap regulation, which *is* practically applied, obviously because it implies a satisfactory compromise between information requirements for the regulator and negative incentive effects for the public utility. Finally, we turn to some problems of quality regulation. A brief conclusion follows.

Simple regulatory rules
Regulation by an iterative process
Consider the following regulatory adjustment process which leads to Ramsey prices.[9] Players of the game are a profit-maximizing public utility under increasing returns to scale, and a welfare-maximizing regulator who has only minimal information about the activities of the utility. At the

beginning of a period the regulator stipulates a set of prices which are at most cost-covering if applied to the quantities sold in the period before. Within this set the utility chooses those prices which maximize its profit; this profit may well be positive. The profit-maximizing prices and quantities of the present period serve as the basis for the regulatory set of prices of the next period, where the utility once again chooses profit-maximizing prices that belong to the regulatory set. This iterative process continues until break-even Ramsey prices are achieved.

Why can such an iterative process lead to optimal prices? Recall the Ramsey benchmark model. The optimal prices resulted from a maximization of the sum of consumer and producer surplus for a given profit constraint. By duality, the same prices result if the profit is maximized under the constraint that consumer surplus plus producer surplus should not fall below an adequately chosen threshold. Now consider the Vogelsang–Finsinger model. The utility maximizes profit. This maximization is constrained by a regulatory set of prices which are at most cost-covering if applied to the sales of the previous period. It is obvious that this regulation protects the consumers against exploitation from the profit-maximizing utility. Therefore, it has the same function as the minimum threshold on consumer plus producer surplus.[10]

The main advantage of this regulatory adjustment process is the minimal information requirement for the regulator. In order to stipulate the regulatory set of prices, he only has to know the prices, the quantities and the total costs of the past period. In particular, he does not need any information about the total shape of demand and cost functions, and he does not need any information about the distribution of particular non-observable variables. On the other hand, there are various disadvantages of the regulatory adjustment process. The utility may have an incentive to increase costs in the long run because waste today leads to a higher price level tomorrow and increases the long-run profits.[11] Moreover, the demand and cost functions must remain unchanged until the Ramsey optimum is achieved and this can only hold if the revision of the regulatory set of prices is made fairly frequently. Even annual revisions may be too infrequent.

Yardstick regulation
Yardstick regulation can be applied by a regulator who faces various similar utilities and, therefore, can use the information about one utility to regulate the others. The regulator asks one utility for the actual value of some variable which is private knowledge of this utility. However, he commits himself to use this piece of information only for the regulation of all the other utilities, not for the regulation of the particular utility itself. This utility, in turn, is regulated on the basis of the information acquired

from all the other utilities. Since the utility knows that telling the truth will not influence its own regulation, it has no incentive to give false information. Hence, it will tell the truth. Yardstick regulation applies a basic idea which has been used often in mechanism design literature, in particular in the mechanisms for the revelation of preferences for public goods.

A more detailed analysis of the yardstick mechanism is as follows.[12] Assume that there are *n* identical regional monopolies. The demand function is the same in every single region. The firms operate under constant production costs. However, these production costs can be reduced by R&D investments. A welfare-maximizing regulator sets the prices and a subsidy which is paid to each utility. If the regulator were fully informed, he would choose marginal-cost prices and equate the subsidy to the costs of the R&D investments. However, the regulator does not know the R&D technology. Therefore, he applies the following mechanism:

- At date 1 he announces the regulatory rules: for any single utility he will set prices that are equal to the mean of all other utilities' announcements of production costs. Every utility will receive a subsidy which is equal to the mean of all other utilities' announcements of the R&D investment costs. He also commits himself not to bail out any utility in the case of bankruptcy.
- At date 2 each firm invests in R&D and the regulator comes to know their investment costs and the associated production costs. This is made possible because under the announced regulation no firm has an incentive to hide information on R&D or production costs.
- Given his information on investment and production costs, at date 3 the regulator actually fixes the price and the subsidy for any single firm according to the regulatory rules announced at date 1.
- Finally, at date 4, the utilities produce, sell their products at the regulated prices and encash the subsidies.

This mechanism implements the first best, that is, marginal-cost prices and subsidies which cover the costs of the R&D investments.

The main advantage of this mechanism is its low information requirement for the regulator. He does not need any information about cost and demand functions. He just applies the insight that no firm is interested in cheating unless this improves the profit. Since the firm's own announcement has no influence on the profit, no firm will cheat and the regulator gets all the information he needs for a first best regulation. Moreover, the achievement of the first best is driven by the firms' profit-maximizing behavior and, therefore, there are no adverse incentive effects which might stop the firms from choosing their strategies which lead to the first best.

Unfortunately, however, yardstick regulation also has quite a few disadvantages. First, it is vulnerable to collusion, because collusion makes profits dependent on a firm's own announcements. This makes yardstick regulation questionable in all those cases where various privatized utilities have been created by splitting up the former monolithic publicly owned utility.[13] Similarly, for effective yardstick competition, there must be a number of firms in the industry with similar demand and cost conditions. This is why the UK regulators have opposed some proposed mergers in the electricity and water sectors. Second, it is difficult to understand how a regulator of a privatized utility can commit himself not to bail out a utility which he has driven into bankruptcy by his regulatory policy. (Regulators often have a legal requirement to ensure that the regulated firm can earn sufficient revenues to carry out its proper functions.) Third, the whole merits of using this form of regulation are called into question at the practical level if cost and demand functions are different.[14] This has drawn UK regulators into heated arguments with companies about the value of comparative competition.

Informationally demanding regulatory rules
The principal–agent model
The regulator as principal of the game is not able to produce the firm's outputs, so he needs the manager of the public utility as his agent. There is asymmetric information. Only the manager knows the actual realization of a one-dimensional characteristic θ which influences the costs or the demand.[15] We normalize θ by defining $\theta \in [\underline{\theta}, \bar{\theta}]$, where $\underline{\theta}$ is the worst case. Asymmetric information also prevails with respect to the manager's effort: it cannot be observed by the regulator. However, the above assumptions do not imply that the regulator is ignorant of the utility's special features. Far from it! He is assumed to be very well informed. This is the serious weakness of the informationally demanding regulatory rules compared with the simple rules of the preceding section. The regulator has to know the functional shapes of the public utility's cost and demand functions and of the manager's utility function. Moreover, he has to know the distribution function of the unobserved characteristic that influences costs or demand. Finally, it is assumed that the regulator, ex post, observes total costs[16] or at least the produced quantities.[17] The regulator's lack of information, therefore, refers only to the actual realizations of the managerial effort and the cost or demand characteristic. However, this very lack of information prevents the regulator from calculating how much total costs or total sales result from the agent's effort or from the actual realization of a cost or demand characteristic. Therefore, the agent can cheat. The agent's utility is $U(t, e)$, where t is the managerial income and e is the managerial effort, $U_1 > 0$, $U_2 < 0$: the agent feels better if he gets a higher income and if he

expends less effort. Therefore, the manager has an incentive to pretend that
there have been adverse cost or demand shocks and, thus, effort had to be
very high so that the manager should be compensated by a much higher
income. What should the regulator do in such a situation? The principal–agent theory proposes the following sequence of strategic moves.

- Stage 1: The manager is better informed. Only he knows the cost or
  demand characteristic. The regulator only knows the distribution
  function of this characteristic.
- Stage 2: The regulator offers a contract which implements a direct
  mechanism: the manager will have to announce the actual realization
  of the unobservable characteristic. For every possible announcement $\hat{\theta}$
  the contract stipulates an incentive income $t(\hat{\theta})$ which is defined so as
  to fulfil two requirements. First, the contract is *incentive-compatible*,
  that is, the manager achieves highest personal utility if he truthfully
  informs the regulator, $\hat{\theta} = \theta$. The incentive compatibility condition
  requires that the managerial utility be strictly increasing in the characteristic θ; that is, $U_{\theta} > 0$: when the manager is asked for the correct value
  of θ, he must not have an incentive to cheat by announcing a lower θ
  than is actually realized. Second, the contract takes care of the
  manager's *participation constraint;* managerial income and effort are
  traded off in such a way that it is attractive for the manager to stay at
  his job and not to leave to take up an outside position. The managerial
  utility $U(t,e)$ has to exceed the reservation utility $\bar{U}$ which is the highest
  utility level the manager could earn in an alternative job. In a full information benchmark the participation constraint is always binding:

$$\bar{U} = U(t^*(\theta), e^*(\theta)) \qquad \forall \theta \in [\underline{\theta}, \bar{\theta}],$$

where $e(\theta)$ means that the regulator correctly anticipates how the
manager will adjust his effort to the actual realization of θ ($\theta = \hat{\theta}$) In
the case of asymmetric information, however, the participation con-
straint binds only in the worst situation:

$$\bar{U} = U(t^*(\underline{\theta}), e^*(\underline{\theta})) < U(t(\theta), e(\theta)), \qquad \forall \theta > \underline{\theta}.$$

This result is rooted in the incentive compatibility constraint, which
requires utility to increase in θ. Hence, the participation constraint
can only bind at the lowest realization of θ.

It is a further part of the contract that the income will be paid at the end
of the game, but only if the produced outputs are exactly equal to those

quantities which the regulator has calculated on the basis of the truthful information from the manager.[18] This calculation also allows the regulator to announce the prices at which the outputs are to be sold.

- Stage 3: The manager informs the regulator about the actual realization of the cost or demand characteristic.
- Stage 4: The manager chooses his effort depending on the actual value of the characteristic, $e(\theta)$.
- Stage 5: The manager produces and sells the products at the regulated prices. He encashes his income.

Asymmetric information on costs[19]
Assume the following cost function:

$$C = C(x_1,...,x_n,e,\theta); \qquad C_i := \partial C/\partial x_i > 0, \partial C/\partial e < 0, \partial C/\partial \theta < 0.$$

Total costs depend on the vector of produced quantities $x_1,...,x_n$ the managerial effort e and an exogenous cost characteristic θ. This characteristic refers to the type of utility, from high-cost firms to low-cost firms: a particular set of output quantities requires high costs if θ is low, but low costs if θ is high. Now consider a regulator who maximizes welfare and takes account of market-clearing conditions and of a profit constraint. Furthermore, he writes a contract with the manager which is incentive-compatible and fulfils the manager's participation constraint. It can be shown that in this case the regulator chooses a special type of Ramsey prices. As in the full information benchmark model, he operates like a profit-maximizing monopolist who overestimates all price elasticities by the same factor. In the special 'inverse elasticity' case, as in the benchmark, the relative deviation of any price from the marginal costs is lower, the higher the direct price elasticity of demand. However, the marginal costs in the asymmetric information Ramsey formula comprise both the marginal production costs and an incentive correction term which copes with the manager's incentive compatibility problem.

The asymmetric information Ramsey formula differs from the benchmark formula *(R)* by the inclusion of incentive correction terms I_i, $i = 1,2$. It runs as follows:[20]

$$\frac{p_1 - C_1 - I_1}{p_1} = -\lambda \frac{\varepsilon_{22} - \varepsilon_{12}}{\varepsilon_{11}\varepsilon_{22} - \varepsilon_{12}\varepsilon_{21}}; \qquad \frac{p_2 - C_2 - I_2}{p_2} = -\lambda \frac{\varepsilon_{11} - \varepsilon_{21}}{\varepsilon_{11}\varepsilon_{22} - \varepsilon_{12}\varepsilon_{21}}.$$

The incentive correction terms I_i result from the differentiation of the manager's incentive compatibility constraint with respect to the ith quantity. Therefore, instead of considering the marginal production costs C_i, in the asymmetric information setting the regulator considers modified marginal costs $C_i^M = C_i + I_r$

How should one interpret the regulator's pricing decision? Will asymmetric information Ramsey prices be higher or lower than Ramsey prices in a full information benchmark (assuming identical profit constraints)? A first guess would hint at higher prices, because the badly informed regulator has to pay for the production costs plus the information rent of the manager. The fully informed regulator does not pay such a rent. It would be plausible to assume that in the case of asymmetric information the manager always gets a higher income, which would enforce higher prices. Typically, however, this simple plausibility is incorrect.[21] Since the incentive compatibility condition requires $U_\theta > 0$, the managerial income at some level θ^0 influences all incomes at higher levels of θ. This external effect is present for all realizations of θ except the best one, $\bar{\theta}$. Hence, at this point the income is chosen by the regulator so as to attain full efficiency and, therefore, the effort level is

$$e(\bar{\theta}) = e^*.$$

Recall that the manager's participation constraint is not binding at $\bar{\theta}$ (in contrast to the full information benchmark),

$$U(t(\bar{\theta}), e^*(\bar{\theta})) > U(t^*(\bar{\theta}), e^*(\bar{\theta})) = \bar{U},$$

where in the first term we have substituted $e = e^*$. However, this implies

$$t(\bar{\theta}) > t^*(\bar{\theta}).$$

In a low-cost firm the managerial income will be higher than the benchmark income.

Consider next the worst possible case, $\underline{\theta}$. Here it would be too costly for the regulator to enforce efficient effort (because of the external effect on all other incomes). Therefore, he settles for an effort lower than efficient,

$$e(\underline{\theta}) < e^*.$$

The participation constraint is binding,

$$U(t(\underline{\theta}), e(\underline{\theta})) = U(t^*(\underline{\theta}), e^*(\underline{\theta})) = \bar{U}$$

and, therefore, we have

$$t(\underline{\theta}) < t^*(\underline{\theta}).$$

In a high-cost firm the managerial income will be lower than the benchmark income. Therefore, the managerial income can be lower or higher than the benchmark income. Consequently, asymmetric information can imply a lower or a higher average of prices, depending on whether we have a low-cost or a high-cost firm.

However, a lower average of prices does not necessarily imply that all prices must be lower than their benchmark equivalents. A particular price will be higher than its benchmark equivalent if the marginal rate of transformation between the managerial effort and the cost characteristic responds positively to an increase in the supply of the respective good.[22] An increase in output in this case makes it easier for the manager to transform exogenous costs shocks into rents.

The incentive correction term which is part of the marginal costs in the modified Ramsey rule may vanish in particular cases. First, consider the manager's trade-off between effort and the cost characteristic. This trade-off indicates how far the manager can reduce his effort if the cost characteristic is improved. The incentive correction term vanishes if this trade-off does not depend on the supplied quantities.[23] In this case prices determine quantities, but not the relationship between effort and the cost characteristic. Therefore, there is no incentive correction term in the Ramsey formulas. Second, consider the best realization of the cost characteristic. Here, the regulator can choose the efficient solution since there is no external effect on larger values of θ. Therefore, in the case of $\bar{\theta}$, there is no incentive correction term in the Ramsey formula. Note that identical Ramsey formulas for regulatory prices typically will not imply identical prices in the benchmark and in the asymmetric information case. The cost characteristic will continue to influence the managerial effort and income, and the managerial income enters the profit constraint that determines the revenue that must be raised at the regulated prices. Hence, the absolute values of the prices will be influenced by the cost characteristic even though the Ramsey structure of prices is the same in the benchmark case and in the case of asymmetric information.

Asymmetric information on demand[24]

Assume the following compensated demand functions:

$$x_i^h = x_i^h(p, u^h, e_i, \theta), \qquad \partial x_i^h / \partial e_i > 0, \qquad \partial x_i^h / \partial \theta > 0.$$

The quantity of good i which individual h buys depends on the vector of consumer prices p, on his utility u^h, on a demand characteristic θ and on the marketing efforts which the manager of the public utility devotes to good i, that is, e_i. The derivatives with respect to prices and utility are assumed to follow the usual microeconomic convention.

Once again, the welfare-maximizing regulator will choose a modified Ramsey rule. However, the most plausible modification does not hold. Since the manager gets an information rent, one would have assumed that, once again, the regulator considers modified costs consisting of production costs plus costs of 'buying' the information on the demand characteristic. This is not the case, however. The modification occurs on the demand side: the factor by which the elasticities are overestimated in the Ramsey formula is changed by incentive correction terms. For the two-good case the modified Ramsey formula is as follows:[25]

$$\frac{p_1 - C_1}{p_1} = -\frac{(\lambda - I_1)\varepsilon_{22} - (\lambda - I_2)\varepsilon_{12}}{\varepsilon_{11}\varepsilon_{22} - \varepsilon_{12}\varepsilon_{21}}; \quad \frac{p_2 - C_2}{p_2} = -\frac{(\lambda - I_2)\varepsilon_{11} - (\lambda - I_1)\varepsilon_{21}}{\varepsilon_{11}\varepsilon_{22} - \varepsilon_{12}\varepsilon_{21}}.$$

There are different incentive correction terms for the different goods, so the extent of overestimation differs, depending on how price changes influence the manager's marginal disutility of effort and his trade-off between effort and the demand characteristic (how far he can reduce his effort if the demand characteristic improves).

In contrast to the case of asymmetric information on costs, decreasing marginal costs may require a totally different regulatory policy than that described in the preceding paragraph. In a simplified example,[26] the incentive compatibility of the regulatory scheme requires prices which are increasing in demand. On the other hand, first best marginal-cost prices would have to be decreasing in demand because of the decreasing marginal costs. Accordingly, from the welfare point of view, incentive-compatible price regulation becomes too costly. It can be shown that in this case it is optimal for the regulator to implement the same price for all realizations of the demand characteristic ('bunching'). It is too costly to elicit the true information from the manager of the firm and the price regulation is only based on the regulator's imperfect information.

Price cap regulation

The most widely used form of price cap regulation is the $RPI - X$ formula: a price index of the monopolistically supplied goods of a public utility must not increase by more than the retail price index minus a constant X, which has been set by the regulator.[27] The constant X was conceptualized as a factor that reflects productivity increases of the public utility. These increases should be passed on to the consumers. The productivity increases may refer to an outward-shifting production frontier that is due to technical progress. Accordingly, telecommunications should have a high X, gas should have a low X. Productivity increases may also reflect the fact that the firm has reduced slack in its production, producing nearer to the frontier than before (approaching productive efficiency).[28] This argument was often put forward when price caps were introduced in the course of privatization. The constant X should also take account of demand increases that allow price reductions in the case of increasing returns to scale.[29] In the regulatory practice, however, several other criteria have influenced the choice of X:[30]

1. Regulators often choose X so as to determine the profits of the public utility: X is increased if the profits have been high. If in such a case the regulator sets X so as to allow a fair rate of return to the firm, the $RPI - X$ regulation comes close to rate-of-return regulation.

2. If $RPI - X$ is introduced on the occasion of privatization of a public utility, the government will have an incentive to choose a low X because this increases the profits of the utility and, therefore, the revenue that the government gets from the sale of the shares of the firm.

3. How X is set depends decisively on the informational status of the regulator. The worse he is informed about costs or demand, the lower the X he must choose. Otherwise, the regulator could drive the firm into bankruptcy. At high levels of uncertainty, cost-plus regulation may be preferable to price cap regulation, since in such a case price cap regulation implies the concession of higher prices than cost-plus regulation.[31]

The constant X will be reviewed at regular intervals to cope with changes in the profitability of the public utility ('regulatory lag'). This lag implies a tension between achieving (and maintaining) allocative efficiency and the attainment of productive efficiency. Lags in adjusting price caps give the profit-maximizing public utility incentives to improve productive efficiency, but at the cost of allocative efficiency. Consider a regulator who has chosen a particular value of X and a regulated utility which reduces its costs to increase the profit. The firm may retain this higher profit. However, at the next revision of X, the prices are set so as to shift the gains from the efficiency increases from the producer to consumers. The firm's incentives depend on the length of the regulatory lag. If the interval between two revisions is too short, there will not be many incentives for innovative activities by the utility. If the interval is too long, too much profit goes to the firm and the consumers are exploited (also see Chapter 23).

If the regulator is imperfectly informed about the costs, the firm will make strategic use of the regulatory lag. Let us assume that the manager of the firm knows that the regulator will choose X so as to siphon off the utility's profits. Insofar as cost-reducing innovations are reversible, the firm has an incentive to be a high-cost firm at the moment of the regulatory reviews, but a low-cost firm in between. A sawtooth profile of the firm's cost-reducing innovations will result.[32] The issue of the timing of productive efficiency gains and price cap reviews can be overcome (to a degree) by the use of a 'glidepath' and similarly lagged adjustments of the cap rather than loading all of the adjustment into current price.

On the side of the firm, there may be imperfect information about the date of the next price revision. If the manager of the utility knows some exogenous probability of the regulatory revision, he will act too cautiously in his innovative policy. A better result is achieved if the probability of revision is endogenized. This is the case if the manager knows that a revision becomes highly likely if the profit exceeds a particular level that is considered fair by the regulator. The regulation converges to prices where there is no excess of current over fair profit. Moreover, cost minimization is achievable.[33]

Quality regulation
There have been many complaints about quality deterioration due to privatization and insufficient quality regulation. The UK rail privatization provides the most recent example. Quality regulation is more complicated than price regulation, because quality typically is multidimensional in nature. By way of example, the quality of local transport services should be measured by reference to the percentage of cancelled trains, waiting time (frequency of services), travelling time, comfort of rolling stock and cleanliness of the stations. The multidimensionality makes it impossible to find simple regulatory rules for quality regulation (like $RPI - X$ for price regulation). Simple rules can only be found if one-dimensional quality indicators are considered, for instance the reliability of supply measured in percentage of cancelled trains, or in percentage of breakdowns of electricity supply. Multidimensionality, however, implies weighting of various quality indicators, which in practice is a complicated cost–benefit analytical task.

From the theoretical point of view, the conventional neoclassical models could well be augmented in order to deal with both price and multidimensional quality regulation. However, to simplify the treatment, in this chapter we only consider one-dimensional quality indicators q_i which enter in the cost function C, the compensated demand functions x_i^h, and the consumers' expenditure functions r^h.[34] For a two-good firm we have the following specifications:[35]

$$C = C(x_1, x_2, q_1, q_2); \qquad C_i := \partial C/\partial x_i; \ C_{qi} := \partial C/\partial q_i, \qquad i = 1,2,$$
$$x_i^h = x_i^h(p_1, p_2, q_1, q_2, u^h); \qquad \phi_{ij} := \partial x_i/\partial q_j; \ x_i := \Sigma_h x_i^h, \qquad i = 1,2,$$
$$r^h = r^h(p_1, p_2, q_1, q_2, u^h); \qquad Q_i := (1 - \lambda)\Sigma_h \partial r^h/\partial q_i < 0, \qquad i = 1,2.$$

Let us begin with two full information benchmark models where quality regulation adjusts to marginal-cost pricing and to Ramsey pricing. In the first case, every single quality has to be expanded until the marginal quality costs equal the sum of marginal utility gains as measured by changes of the individual expenditure functions,

$$C_{qi} = -\Sigma_h \partial r^h/\partial q_i, \qquad i = 1,2.$$

Accordingly, the individual marginal utility gain can be interpreted as a marginal rate of substitution between quality and the individual income, where the income is measured by the expenditure function. The first best qualities, therefore, require the equality of a marginal rate of transformation (marginal quality costs) and the sum of individual marginal rates of substitution. This condition resembles the Samuelson condition on public goods. In the second case the qualities are adjusted to Ramsey prices. The best interpretation of the optimal qualities can once again be given by a comparison with a monopolist who chooses prices and qualities so as to maximize his profits. The respective first-order condition on quality of good 1 is as follows:

$$p_1 - C_1 = \frac{(C_{q1} + Q_1)\phi_{22} - (C_{q2} + Q_2)\phi_{21}}{\phi_{11}\phi_{22} - \phi_{12}\phi_{21}}.$$

An analogous condition holds for the second good. The first-order conditions are characterized by the consideration of the quality-correction terms $Q_i := (1 - \lambda)\Sigma_h \partial r^h/\partial q_i$. Once again, λ is a scaling parameter which is zero for marginal-cost prices and unity if we have an unconstrained monopoly. Therefore, the quality-correction terms Q_i vanish for the perfect monopolist: the profit maximizer neglects consumer welfare gains, the welfare maximizer takes them into account. As these gains are measured by the negative values of Q_i, we may conclude that the welfare-maximizing regulator behaves like a monopolist who underestimates the marginal quality costs by the sum of the individual rates of substitution between quality and income. This implies a tendency towards higher qualities.

Finally, let us briefly sketch the changes in the optimal qualities if an informationally demanding regulatory process is applied. The cost function will now depend on the quantities produced, on the quality indicators, on the effort variable and on the cost characteristic. An analogous extension holds for the demand functions. Differentiating the managerial incentive compatibility constraint with respect to the quality indicators gives *quality-induced incentive correction terms* (and there are still the usual quantity-induced incentive correction terms, which we have treated in the section on informationally demanding regulatory rules). The rules on price regulation remain unchanged, although the absolute levels of prices will, of course, change. However, we get new rules on quality regulation. Both in the case of asymmetric information on costs and in the case of asymmetric information on demand, a quality-induced incentive correction term is added to the marginal quality costs: the regulator considers the sum of the quality costs and the costs that are induced by the information rent of the manager. This holds for both cases of asymmetric information treated in this chapter – on costs and on demand.

Conclusions

The most important contribution of the new theories of price regulation has been the accentuation of the information and incentive structures. Imperfectly informed regulators may set wrong incentives for the managers of the regulated public utilities. The new theories of regulation show how to achieve the best possible results if the regulator lacks information.

This chapter has first presented various simple regulatory mechanisms. Vogelsang and Finsinger's iterative mechanism excels by its minimal information requirements: the regulator only needs information on past quantities, past prices and past realizations of total costs. Shleifer's yardstick regulation links the regulatory rules for some firm to performance indicators of other firms in a similar position: since truth telling does not influence a firm's own regulation, it will not cheat, and the regulator gets all the information. Unfortunately, however, in practical applications of these simple mechanisms, the regulated utility will be able to dodge the regulator's intentions by using strategic behavior. This has led us to a treatment of informationally demanding regulatory mechanisms that are incentive-compatible and, therefore, strategy-proof. Unfortunately, however, the regulator must be extremely well-informed to apply this sort of regulation: except for the actual realizations of a cost or demand characteristic and the effort of the manager, he must be perfectly informed about the situation of the regulated public utility. This must be the main reason why, in practice, the simple $RPI - X$ regulation prevails. Obviously, it represents an acceptable compromise between not too high information problems and not too high incentives for managerial strategic behavior. Finally, in this chapter we have emphasized the importance of quality regulation, which is a rather neglected field in regulation theory and also very often in the practice of regulation.

Notes

1. Good overviews of the precise meaning of subadditive cost functions can be found in Panzar (1989: 23–33) or Sharkey (1982: 54–83).
2. See, in particular, Baumol *et al.* (1982). A very clear treatment of the problem of the contestability of monopolies can be found in Sharkey (1982: ch. 5).
3. In the peak-load pricing literature it has been shown that under particular assumptions

rationing of the demand may be welfare-optimal. See Bös (1994: ch. 15).
4. The terms 'producer surplus' and 'profit' are used synonymously in this chapter.
5. This constraint requires either that the deficit should not be too high, or that the firm's revenue should at least cover the production costs, or that a minimum profit should be attained.
6. Ramsey (1927) considered the problem where a given tax revenue should be raised by indirect taxation at minimal welfare loss. However, for given producer prices indirect taxation means a choice of consumer prices and, accordingly, his theory can be directly transferred to the case of regulation of the prices of public utilities. It was Boiteux (1956, 1971) who first presented a general equilibrium model on public sector pricing with a given profit constraint.
7. The extension to the n-good case is straightforward; see Bös (1994: ch. 8).
8. We deal with compensated price elasticities, that is, the elasticities are defined along Hicksian demand functions $x_i^h = x_i^h(p_1,...,p_n,u^h)$ where u^h is the utility of the hth consumer, $h=1,...$ H.
9. See Vogelsang and Finsinger (1979).
10. It can be shown that the regulatory set of prices is tangent to the indifference surface of the welfare function. The convexity of welfare allows substitution of this tangent hyperplane for the actual welfare function in the various steps of the iterative process.
11. See Sappington (1980).
12. The standard paper on this mechanism is Shleifer (1985).
13. A good example is the British regional electricity companies.
14. For this case Shleifer (1985: 324–5) suggests a reduced-form regulation which uses predicted costs on the basis of a regression analysis linking marginal costs and exogenous characteristics of all utilities. However, the first best will then only be achieved if the regression explains 100 per cent of the variance of costs, which typically will not be the case.
15. Of course such a characteristic could also refer to other functions which are relevant for the utility. By way of an example, in Bös (1994: ch. 31), a model is presented where such a characteristic refers to a budget-appropriation function.
16. This assumption is typical of the Laffont–Tirole (1993) approach.
17. Baron and Myerson (1982) wrote about regulation with unknown costs. However, they assume that the quantities are ex post observable. For a nice presentation of the Baron-Myerson model, see Laffont and Tirole (1993: 155–8).
18. This assumes a modelling where ex post the regulator observes produced quantities. If he/she ex post observes the realized costs, but not the individual quantities produced, a similar story can be told.
19. This subsection presents only a very rough sketch of the relevant problems; for details, see Bös (1994: chs. 28 and 29).
20. Once again, the extension to the n-good case is straightforward; see Bös (1994: 316–20).
21. For the following treatment of managerial incomes, see Bös and Peters (1991: 39–41).
22. For constant total costs and constant quantities we consider the total differential of the cost function $C(x_1,...,x_n,e,\theta)$. We obtain $\partial e/\partial \theta = -C_\theta/C_e = -MRT(e,\theta)$ and, therefore, $MRT > 0$. If $\partial MRT/\partial x_i$ is positive, then the incentive correction term I_i is positive, which implies a tendency towards a higher price of good i.
23. This is the case if the cost function is $C(x_1,...,x_n,f(e,\theta))$.
24. Once again this subsection presents only a very rough sketch of the relevant problems; for details, see Bös (1994: chs. 28 and 30).
25. The extension to the n-good case is straightforward; see Bös (1994: 336–9).
26. See Lewis and Sappington (1988); for a particularly simple presentation of the problem, see Bös (1994: 303–4). Formally, consider the second-order condition of the managerial revelation problem. The managerial utility U depends, *inter alia*, on the announced value of the demand characteristic, called $\hat{\theta}$. To make truthful revelation a managerial utility maximum, we must have $U_{\hat{\theta}} = 0$ at $\hat{\theta} = 0$, where θ is the actual value of the demand characteristic. Furthermore, we must have $U_{\hat{\theta}\hat{\theta}} < 0$. It is comparatively simple to find plausible assumptions for this second-order condition to hold in the case of asymmetric

information on costs. However, this is not the case if there is asymmetric information on demand. Compare Bös (1994: 311 (cost side) and 331–2 (demand side)).

27. This form of regulation has been proposed by Littlechild (1983).
28. Leibenstein (1966) coined the term X-*inefficiency* for production below the frontier. Note that the X in X-inefficiency has nothing to do whatsoever with the X in the $RPI - X$ formula. To avoid misunderstanding, as a synonym for X-efficiency we will use the term *productive efficiency* in the text.
29. See Vickers and Yarrow (1988: 214–16).
30. Many further problems in the practical application of the $RPI - X$ formula are treated in Bös (1991: 67–8).
31. See Schmalensee (1989).
32. See Armstrong *et al.* (1991).
33. This has been proved for rate-of-return regulation by Bawa and Sibley (1980).
34. This presentation follows Bös (1994: ch. 16). For an explicit treatment of quality regulation, see also Laffont and Tirole (1993: ch. 4).
35. To simplify further the formal analysis, we suppress the dependence of x_i^h and r^h on the prices and qualities of goods other than the two goods produced by the public utility in question.

References

Armstrong, M., R. Rees and J. Vickers (1991) 'Optimal Regulatory Lag under Price Cap Regulation', mimeo, Nuffield College, Oxford.

Baron, D.P. and R.B. Myerson (1982) 'Regulating a Monopolist with Unknown Costs', *Econometrica*, 50(4), 911–30.

Baumol, W.J., J.C. Panzar, and R.D. Willig (1982) *Contestable Markets and the Theory of Industry Structure*, rev. edn. 1988, New York: Harcourt Brace Jovanovich.

Bawa, V.S. and D.S. Sibley (1980) 'Dynamic Behavior of a Firm Subject to Stochastic Regulatory Review', *International Economic Review*, 21(3), 627–42.

Boiteux, M. (1956, 1971) 'Sur la gestion des monopoles publics astreints à 'l'équilibre budgétaire', *Econometrica*, 24(1), 22–40. (English edition: 'On the Management of Public Monopolies Subject to Budgetary Constraints', *Journal of Economic Theory*, 3(3), 219–40.)

Bös, D. (1991) *Privatization: A Theoretical Treatment*, Oxford: Oxford University Press.

Bös, D. (1994) *Pricing and Price Regulation / An Economic Theory for Public Enterprises and Public Utilities*, Advanced Textbooks in Economics, vol. 34, Amsterdam: Elsevier, North-Holland.

Bös, D. and W. Peters (1991) 'A Principal–Agent Approach on Manager Effort and Control in Privatized and Public Firms', in Attiat Ott and Keith Hartley (eds), *Privatization and Economic Efficiency*, Aldershot, UK and Brookfield, US: Edward Elgar.

Laffont, J.J. and J. Tirole (1993) *A Theory of Incentives in Procurement and Regulation*, Cambridge, MA: MIT Press.

Leibenstein, H. (1966) 'Allocative Efficiency vs. "X-Efficiency"', *American Economic Review*, 56(3), 392–415.

Lewis, T.R. and D.E.M. Sappington (1988) 'Regulating a Monopolist with Unknown Demand', *American Economic Review*, 78(5), 986–98.

Littlechild, S.C. (1983) *Regulation of British Telecommunications' Profitability*, London: HMSO.

Loeb, M. and W.A. Magat (1979) 'A Decentralized Method for Utility Regulation', *Journal of Law and Economics*, 22(2), 399–404.

Panzar, J.C. (1989) 'Technological Determinants of Firm and Industry Structure', in Richard Schmalensee and Robert D. Willig (eds), *Handbook of Industrial Organization*, vol. 1, Amsterdam: Elsevier, North Holland.

Ramsey, F. (1927) 'A Contribution to the Theory of Taxation', *Economic Journal*, 37(1), 47–61.

Sappington, D.E.M. (1980) 'Strategic Firm Behavior under a Dynamic Regulatory Adjustment Process', *Bell Journal of Economics*, 11(1), 360–72.

Schmalensee, R. (1989) 'Good Regulatory Regimes', *Rand Journal of Economics*, 20(3), 417–36.

Sharkey, W.W. (1982) *The Theory of Natural Monopoly*, Cambridge: Cambridge University Press.

Shleifer, A. (1985) 'A Theory of Yardstick Competition', *Rand Journal of Economics*, 16(3), 319–27.

Vickers, J. and G. Yarrow (1988) *Privatization: An Economic Analysis*, Cambridge, MA: MIT Press.

Vogelsang, I. and J. Finsinger (1979) 'A Regulatory Adjustment Process for Optimal Pricing by Multiproduct Monopoly Firms', *Bell Journal of Economics*, 10(1), 157–71.

23 Regulating prices and profits
Thomas Weyman-Jones

Introduction

Regulatory theory concerns the behaviour of the profit-maximizing firm engaged in a game with a regulator who is often not well informed about the firm's costs. Regulatory practice is concerned with companies owned by investors and operating in specific markets under regulated accounting procedures. Dieter Bös (Chapter 22) has admirably surveyed the theory of regulation and this chapter complements that chapter by addressing the issues of regulatory practice in setting prices and their relationship with the company's profits. The context is largely that of price cap regulation, which is becoming widely adopted throughout Europe, Australia, New Zealand and parts of the USA, and in many other developing and transition economies, especially where international bodies such as the World Bank have a role in infrastructure financing.

Price cap regulation sets the maximum average revenue that a company is allowed to charge for its outputs for a specific price control period. This usually takes the form of $RPI - X$ price capping in which the initial price is allowed to escalate at an annual percentage rate equal to $RPI - X$, where RPI is the annual growth rate in the consumer price index and X is a productivity growth rate. Numerous major issues must be determined: the weights used to calculate the company's average revenue; the initial price or average revenue for the next period, P_0; the productivity growth X factor; the benchmark levels of operating expenditure, capital expenditure and depreciation allowed to the company; the weighted average cost of capital; the value of the regulatory asset base; and the target speed of adjustment to the benchmarks. Finally, regulation may be applied to the way the company charges other suppliers for access to its connected customers when a physical delivery network is provided, although this topic is not discussed in detail here. All of these issues must be evaluated within a corporate financial framework which is recognized by capital markets and related to the accounting information which is available for comparable unregulated companies. The classic paper by Beesley and Littlechild (1989) recognized these issues at an early stage, issues that continue to require large amounts of regulatory resources as regulation of privatized companies has evolved. This chapter begins with a short summary of the $RPI - X$ regulation model and highlights a range of issues that arise in its practical application. These issues are considered in turn, allowing us to arrive at a more detailed overview of the problems of price cap regulation.

RPI − X regulation: basic ideas

Privatization may represent the first opportunity for the company to respond to market-based incentives. However, this assumes too readily that the interests of managers and shareholders are perfectly aligned. Thus a lenient price cap may simply be taken by managers as a binding constraint rather than as a pure incentive. In fact, little attention has been given to whether the incentives in $RPI − X$ regulation are as attractive to managers as they are to the owners of the companies concerned. In fact, the traditions of public service associated with a state-owned monopoly may be hard to dispose of in the initial stages of privatization.

$RPI − X$ regulation is designed to combat the moral hazard which may cause management failure to exert cost cutting efforts. Since shareholders are the residual claimants to all efficiency savings, and efficiency savings are the way of generating additional rewards under $RPI − X$ regulation, the $RPI − X$ system has the potential to be a very effective form of incentive regulation. In practice, however, the application of the price cap idea has raised issues of both analysis and measurement. The underlying principles are set out here and these are based on the method of benchmark regulation used by UK, Australian and Netherlands regulators (OFGEM, 1999; National Audit Office, 2002; IPART, 1999; EC, 2002; DTE, 2000). The critical issues are:

- What is the nature of the price which is capped?
- What is the basic model for choosing X?
- What is the form of the control that results?

The model targets an average revenue figure for each year of the control period: $P_t = P_o(1 + RPI − X)^t$. The average revenue is usually either derived from a tariff basket index of the regulated company's individual prices or as a weighted average of the revenues from different activities. The average revenue is evaluated on the basis of a benchmarking exercise applied to operating expenditures, OPEX, and capital expenditures, CAPEX. The overall purpose is to calibrate the following discounted present value (PV) equation:

$$PV(revenues) \equiv PV(PQ) = PV(\text{costs}).$$

However, the regulator has to fit these calculated benchmarks into a financial model that recognizes the informational needs of shareholders and the wider capital market. The cash flow costs incurred by the company are:

$$PV(costs) = PV(OPEX + CAPEX + Interest\ and\ Dividend\ Payments).$$

Combined with the present value of revenues, this yields a financial model which maximizes the present value of the company's cash flows subject to meeting the price cap, the demand forecasts, and capacity and quality of supply constraints. Such a model has a long history in regulated industries (see Littlechild, 1970; Turvey, 1971) and it is relatively common in corporate finance theory to approximate the behaviour of present value cash flow maximization by a model of economic value added. This approximation is useful in the case of setting the financial model of a price control. The procedure can be set out as follows.

First, the companies being regulated are requested to report their operating costs at the beginning of the control period ($t = 1$) together with their capital expenditure projections up to the end of the control period ($t = T$). Different scenarios can be used relating to existing quality of supply standards and enhanced quality of supply. For example, in network energy companies, quality of supply may be measured in terms of *security*, which is measured as the number of interruptions of supply per customer, and *availability*, which is measured as the duration of interruption of supply per customer.

The regulator, together with appointed consultants, scrutinizes the operating costs and the capital expenditure projections, and may carry out a comparative efficiency analysis of the former, while drawing up its own capital projections based on agreed forecasts about demand growth. The outcome is a set of operating and capital expenditure projections and depreciation of the network (OPEX, CAPEX and D) which the regulator believes reflects the efficient frontier amongst the companies. A final ingredient in this financial model is the return on capital. The regulator calculates the companies' weighted average cost of capital (wacc) and determines an estimate of the company's regulatory asset base (RAB). The return on capital allowed in the cost projection is ($wacc \times RAB$). The weighted average cost of capital is also used as the discount rate in all of the present value calculations. A rolling series of opening regulatory asset values (RAB_{t-1}) and closing values (RAB_t) is determined by adding the capital expenditure flow and subtracting depreciation flow during the period to adjust the starting stock value:

$$RAB_t = RAB_{t-1} + CAPEX_t - D_t.$$

Consequently, in this financial model of regulatory economic value added, the company's costs are treated as falling into three categories: operating expenditures, depreciation and the return on capital: $OPEX + D + (wacc) RAB$.

The (key) ingredients in the financial model have become the P_0 settlement: this is the initial price which is to form the basis for the future revenue flows of the company from the start of the new control period, and the X factor implied in the projection of costs. Usually X is fixed to achieve cost savings over the control period that reflect the shift in the frontier efficiency of the companies, plus an element of 'catch up' for those firms in the industry not yet deemed to be at the efficiency frontier. The only undetermined number is the initial price correction, and this can be solved as P_0 in equation (23.1):

$$P_0 = \frac{PV[OPEX + D + (wacc)RAB]}{PV[(1 + RPI - X)Q]}. \tag{23.1}$$

Consequently, in this widely adopted regulatory financial model, the regulated price per unit of output may be considered as the sum of the following:

- the allowed forecast operating costs per unit of output adjusted for total factor productivity gains;
- an allowance for depreciation of the regulatory asset base per unit of output adjusted for total factor productivity gains;
- a return on the appropriate regulatory asset base per unit of output adjusted for total factor productivity gains.

The incentives explicit in the model can be illustrated for a hypothetical company as detailed in Figure 23.1, where two price control reviews are shown for 1995 and 2000, together with a pre-control initial price. The industry has been privatized since 1990, and initially price was allowed to rise. At the beginning of the first control period in 1995, the initial price is moved down by ΔP_0 to take account of the projected benchmarked cost efficiency savings and return on capital over the succeeding period. The price control for the period 1995–2000 is set as:

$$P^* = OPEX^* + D^* + (wacc^*)(RAB^*),$$

with the asterisks indicating that each element in the price cap has been benchmarked or otherwise determined by the regulator as a proportion of the productivity adjusted output forecasts.

The shaded area shows the operating and capacity cost savings above and beyond perspective savings actually made by the company during the control period 1995–2000. The company retains these benefits for share-

£/kWh

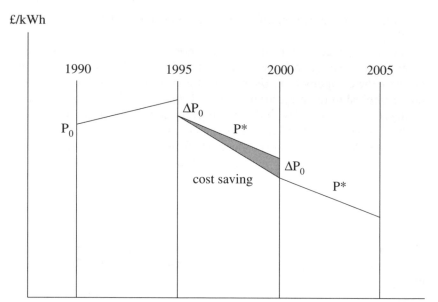

$$P^* = OPEX^* + D^* + (wacc^*) (RAB^*)$$
model of *RPI–X* review of price controls

Figure 23.1   Price adjustments under a price cap regime

holders during the period of the regulatory control. However, at the beginning of the second control period, in 2000, new forecasts and a new initial price are set, with the one-off price reduction ΔP_0 delivering to consumers the excess cost savings already achieved by the company, assuming no other changes have arisen in the company's circumstances that could endanger its financial viability at the new benchmarks set by the regulator. These one-off price reductions at the commencement of each new control period are referred to as the P_0 adjustments. In Figure 23.1 the focus is on a single company and all of the excess cost savings realized in a given period are passed to consumers in the P_0 adjustment for the next period, so that the company starts again with a price control that reflects a forecast return on the regulatory asset base equal to the weighted average cost of capital.

Two major issues of principle and one of practice arise in this price cap framework. The first issue concerns the difficulty of achieving an incentive-compatible and individually rational set of cost benchmarks and demand forecasts. These are essential to encourage participation in the regulatory process and to produce information revelation. The second issue is whether the explicit financial model which is used, and which is based approximately on standard corporate finance calculations of economic value added, adequately represents the decision making behaviour of a firm maximizing the present value of future cash flows and operating through agency relationships with the firm's managers.

The practical issue concerns the timing of the cost savings which a regulated company makes. The later in the control period these savings are achieved, the shorter is the time that the company can retain them. Suppose for convenience that consumers use the same discount rate (r) as the regulator's cost of capital ($r = wacc$). Assume that a price control period lasts for T years. Any cost saving ΔC achieved at the beginning of the control period and which will last forever has a present value of $\Delta C/r$. Its present value to the firm is $(\Delta C/r)(1 - (1 + r)^{-T})$ since the firm only receives it for T periods at most, and it has a present value to consumers of $(\Delta C/r)(1 + r)^{-T}$. The National Audit Office (2002) refers to the relative size of these two terms as the incentive power of the regulatory contract (see Bös, Chapter 22, for other interpretations of this term). However, n years into the control period the firm's present value of cost savings is reduced to $(\Delta C/r)(1 - (1 + r)^{-(T - n)})$. In practice, therefore, with regulatory reviews every T years, the incentive power of $RPI - X$ falls rapidly the later any cost savings can be achieved. Just prior to a price review, $RPI - X$ becomes a cost-plus or profit confiscation mechanism. Similarly, as the length of the control period, T, declines, the incentive power of $RPI - X$ regulation also declines because of the resulting reduction in the net present value of any cost reduction.

This description of a model of price controls in regulation reveals substantive issues of potential dispute between the regulator and the companies. These issues are the focus of the rest of the chapter and they concern the following:

- the choice of X factor and the extent of *frontier shift*;
- the allowed operating cost, OPEX, and *catch-up* to the frontier;
- the projected capital expenditure and related quality of supply targets, CAPEX;
- the allowed depreciation profile, D;
- the resulting regulatory asset base, RAB;
- the weighted average cost of capital, wacc;
- the P_0 or *glidepath* adjustment for individual companies, and the period for which cost savings can be retained.

Choice of X factor and frontier shift

In order to determine P_0, equation (23.1), the X factor was taken as fixed in advance by the regulator. However, the X factor is only one of the indicators of productivity and efficiency gains that have an impact on the companies being regulated because there are OPEX and CAPEX benchmarks in the model as well. A convenient way of regarding all of these benchmarks is to separate the potential productivity gains into efficiency change and technical change components. Moreover, this reflects common practice in efficiency and productivity analysis. Efficiency change reflects the way in which individual regulated companies may catch up with the industry frontier. Technical change reflects the shift over time of that frontier.

Bernstein and Sappington (1999) have tackled this issue of frontier shift in their survey of the ways of determining the X factor, and a simplified form of their argument can be presented using a format suggested by Knox Lovell (2002). The Bernstein–Sappington framework assumes that there is no technical inefficiency. In this case we can write the rate of profit in a competitive economy in terms of a ratio of revenues to costs:

$$\pi = \frac{p'y}{w'x}$$

and expressed as price and volume indices:

$$\pi = \frac{P(\circ)\,Y(\circ)}{W(\circ)X(\circ)} = \frac{P(\circ)}{W(\circ)} \times \frac{Y(\circ)}{X(\circ)};$$

that is, rate of profit = [price recovery] × [productivity]. However, in a fully competitive economy with every firm on its production frontier, the rate of profit growth (and indeed the level of economic profit) is zero:

$$\pi = \dot{P} - \dot{W} + \dot{TFP} = 0.$$

We use a dot over a variable to denote its rate of growth, and in this expression $\dot{TFP}$ is the economy-wide rate of total factor productivity growth. Rearranging, we have the result that the rate of change of output prices is given by the rate of change of input prices minus the rate of total factor productivity growth (Bernstein and Sappington, 1999, eqn 2.6, p. 9):

$$\dot{P} = \dot{W} - \dot{TFP}.$$

We now disaggregate this result over two sectors consisting of the small regulated industry sector (R) and the much larger remainder of the competitive economy (C):

$$\dot{P}_R = [\dot{W}_R - \dot{TFP}_R].$$
$$\dot{P}_C = [\dot{W}_C - \dot{TFP}_C].$$

Now we simply note that $\dot{P}_R = RPI - X$ and $\dot{P}_C = RPI$. Consequently, we have the Bernstein–Sappington result:

$$X = RPI - \dot{P}_R = T\dot{F}P_R - T\dot{F}P_C + \dot{W}_C - \dot{W}_R \qquad (23.2)$$

This tells us that, in a general equilibrium with every firm on its production frontier, the X factor is given by the difference between the total factor productivity growth potential in the regulated sector and that in the remainder of the competitive economy, plus the difference in the rate of growth of input prices in the two sectors. This is Bernstein and Sappington's (1999) equation (2.12), page 11. A prior stage is to set economic profit in the regulated sector to zero, which is precisely what equation (23.1) sets out to do. Then equation (23.2) determines X in terms of expected input price growth and potential total factor productivity growth.

There are, nonetheless, a number of assumptions underlying this result which may not apply, as discussed by Beinstein and Sappington (1999). We assumed that all of the regulated industry's prices are capped, but there may be a more limited span of control. We assumed no major structural changes in the two sectors, which may not be true. We assumed a small regulated sector and a large competitive sector, but RPI may itself be driven by the regulated industry's prices, with this qualification most likely to apply in transition and developing economies. Finally, we assumed that the rest of the economy was competitive, but in practice we may need to allow for second-best compensating distortions. Nevertheless, despite these qualifications, there is in general a clear framework for setting X. Thus X reflects the extent to which the regulated sector can achieve productivity growth in excess of the rest of the competitive economy when input prices are common to both. Since we assumed that the firms in question were all on their respective industry production frontier this means that the X factor reflects technical change or frontier shift. In practice, X reflects the total factor productivity growth of the most efficient firm in the regulated industry.

Benchmarking OPEX and frontier catch-up

The result in equation (23.2) for setting X ignores the possibility that regulated firms may not lie on the industry production frontier. The practice of making efficiency and productivity comparisons amongst public utilities has been strongly developed in the last few years, and most regulatory offices have provision for benchmarking or applying yardstick competition to the utilities under their remit. There are two areas of interest: comparing the efficiency of production amongst utilities at a specific point in time (efficiency analysis) and measuring the productivity growth of utilities over time (productivity analysis). Norway has been trying out data envelopment analysis (DEA)-based yardstick mechanisms for some time, and a similar mechanism to the OFGEM model can be seen in the work of the Netherlands regulator (DTE, 2000). In this case total costs were bench-marked using a DEA model with constant returns to scale. The value of the companies' assets (regulatory asset base) and the weighted average cost of capital were derived from financial models reflecting the circumstances of the deregulated companies and the derived P_0 and X factors. Since the P_0 figures were heavily constrained by the legislative form of the deregulation, more weight was given to the X factors. These were capped at 8 per cent, but differed significantly amongst companies in part because of their distance from the constant returns to scale DEA efficient frontier. This control is due to last until 2003, when it may be replaced by an explicit yardstick mechanism which bases X on national total factor productivity growth.

In fact, throughout Europe, there is growing interest in this form of price control for distribution networks. An informal group of European regulators has discussed the possibility of constructing internationally comparable databases for yardstick regulation using the model described here. There are arguments for and against the use of yardstick competition in benchmarking OPEX and CAPEX figures. Bogetoft (1997) shows that, generally, an optimal (individually rational and incentive-compatible) revenue cap contract which will minimize the amount of informational rent to be paid to the firms decouples the firm's revenue or price cap from its own costs and uses instead a figure which is a 'best practice cost norm' or 'minimal extrapolation cost standard', set to act as a benchmark for the firm in question. In Bogetoft's optimal incentive contract, the regulated firm is paid its observed input cost plus a proportion of the difference (positive or negative) between a benchmark of the cost of meeting the firm's observed output level and its observed input cost. This benchmark is 'the maximal cost of producing the firm's outputs that is consistent with the a priori assumptions about possible cost structures and the realised production plans [costs and outputs] of the other firms' (ibid.: 285). The role of the benchmark is to provide an upper bound on the costs of the firm, making it essential that it at least exceeds the minimal technological cost of production.

Bös (1991, 2002) is, however, critical of yardstick competition. He argues that 'the fascinating clarity and straightforwardness of yardstick regulation is flawed if the actual application is considered' (Bös, 1991:82). He offers four principal objections. First, the model assumes that the firms have the same characteristics. Although a regression-based approach to correcting for heterogeneity amongst the comparators is possible, this solution may be very imperfect if the regression has low explanatory power. DEA approaches do, however, allow for differences in the exogenous operating characteristics of different firms through the use of non-discretionary inputs and outputs. The effect is to add constraints to the problem so that, if a particular firm is penalized by its operating characteristics compared with the rest of the industry, it obtains a closer envelopment (higher efficiency score) than in the absence of the constraints. Bös's second argument notes that the model excludes information asymmetry relating to demand but this, too, is an area where the regulator may be poorly informed. The third argument points out that the solution assumes that the regulator is able to commit himself or herself not to support the firm if it is threatened with bankruptcy. However, the ability to commit oneself in this way is often ruled out in the legislation setting up regulatory offices, and the commitment is difficult to sustain with any credibility. The assumption of a credible commitment possibility is also a major criticism of such agency models, as voiced by Crew and Kleindorfer (2002). Finally, the model assumes no collusion amongst the firms, but this may be very unrealistic when we are dealing with a group of newly privatized utilities used to working together prior to privatization.

Nevertheless, the benchmarking approach is favoured by regulators because it is an attempt to overcome the problem of asymmetry of information and the lack of incentive mechanisms in purely prescriptive procedures such as cost of service or rate of return regulation. The majority of applications of benchmarking for efficiency have been applied to operating expenditure (OPEX), and this is true for all of the UK price-capped utilities where national or international comparators are available (National Audit Office, 2002).

Figure 23.2 illustrates efficiency benchmarking at a basic level. It shows the average firm at A with output and operating cost: (y_m, c_m), the point through which a fitted cost regression must pass. The lowest cost observation is at B and the regression line shifted down to pass through B is the cost frontier. Over time, the frontier can be expected to shift with technical change and this is what the X measures. The deviation of the average firm from the frontier is given by the residual e. Although the frontier is represented here by an ordinary least squares (OLS) regression line, it could just as easily have been constructed by data envelopment analysis – in which case it need not be described only by the two parameters (intercept and slope) assumed to underlie the whole sample.

A major issue in efficiency benchmarking is whether the residual representing the distance of the average firm from the frontier is a measure of only underperformance or inefficiency. Many regulators assume that this is the case. All deterministic DEA-based studies make this assumption, as do all comparisons which use corrected ordinary least squares (COLS). These certainly account for the majority of OPEX benchmarking exercises. A well-known example is the OFGEM (1999) study of UK electricity distribution,

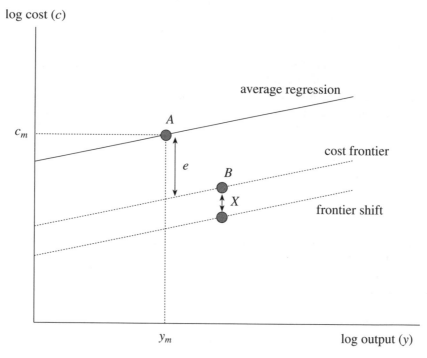

Figure 23.2   Efficiency benchmarking

while UK water regulation has made the most explicit use of this sort of regression-based model (National Audit Office, 2002).

Nonetheless, there is a strong possibility that the residual includes measurement and sampling error and an accumulation of other random influences, which cast doubt on the extent of measured inefficiency. There are methods for overcoming such a problem involving both stochastic DEA and regression-based stochastic frontier analysis (SFA) techniques (Lovell, 1993). Regulators have been unwilling or unable to make great use of these methods, probably because they have demanding data requirements. In fact the greater the variation in sampled cost, the more likely it is that stochastic methods will fail to reject the null hypothesis that there is no inefficiency in the sample at all, and consequently the investigator has to conclude that all variation is due to random error. In its 1999 review work, the UK water regulator did at least recognize the existence of the problem by requiring that 'inefficient' companies need only to catch up 60 per cent of the distance to the frontier in certain categories of OPEX. However, the 60 per cent figure seems to have been an arbitrary choice. In addition, a regulator may not require that all catch-up take place immediately, but instead may phase it to occur along a glidepath. Supposing that the length of time between regulatory reviews is T years, the firm may be given n years to achieve catch up. The benchmarking procedure for OPEX may therefore take the form:

reduce OPEX by a factor: $\dfrac{T-n}{T}\,(\gamma e) + X$, where the parameters are:

$$\frac{T-n}{T} = \text{glidepath},$$

$\gamma = $ percentage catch-up of distance e to frontier,

$X = $ frontier shift.

Benchmarking CAPEX

Benchmarking of CAPEX is still a difficult procedure and OFGEM (1999) indicated that it used relatively crude measures to distinguish amongst the UK utilities' provision. These measures simply compared each company with the industry average over time. Regulatory debate is extensive on the issue of whether OPEX and CAPEX should be benchmarked separately or together. Underlying the issue are two different models of the firm's cost structure. A *cash flow* model of total costs includes OPEX, CAPEX, dividends (V), and interest payments (I) to holders of the firm's equity and debt. Expressed in the same form as equation (23.2) it is:

$$P_0 = \frac{PV[OPEX + CAPEX + (V+I)]}{PV[(1 + RPI - X)Q]}. \tag{23.3}$$

Contrast the direct role of CAPEX on the regulated price in this cash flow model (23.3) with its role in the *financial* model underlying equation (23.1). In equation (23.1) capital expenditure projections minus the depreciation projections are added to the previous period's closing value of the regulatory asset base to produce the new regulatory asset base, which in turn produces the allowed return when multiplied by the weighted average cost of capital:

$$P_0 = \frac{PV[OPEX + (1 - wacc)D + (wacc)(CAPEX + RAB_{t-1})]}{PV[(1 + RPI - X)Q]}. \tag{23.4}$$

In the financial version the immediate effect of CAPEX changes is relatively small, but the size of the regulatory asset base is critical to the price control. The use of the financial model rather than the cash flow model focuses regulatory attention on the end of period asset base and in practice this has had the effect of encouraging regulators to take different views about the benchmarking of CAPEX from those applied to OPEX. There is a tension between the application of these two models, however. The regulated firms may be able to substitute OPEX for CAPEX, and vice versa, since the CAPEX–OPEX split is influenced by accounting conventions, with the result that some OPEX data refer to costs arising from the operating expenditures associated with asset construction in progress, and some OPEX data may be capitalized. In practice, regulators find it difficult to determine external benchmarks for CAPEX and may end up offering weaker incentives in CAPEX management. If there is a tight regulatory squeeze on OPEX but not CAPEX, there is an unintended incentive to substitute CAPEX for OPEX by biases in projecting future demand on the pipes and wires network and in the accounting treatment. However, regulators often worry about the opposite effect: bias against CAPEX in $RPI - X$. This may arise if there are strong incentives for OPEX reduction through benchmarking but weak rewards to CAPEX to reinforce and maintain the networks.

The National Audit Office (2002) reported that both regulators and companies in the UK context felt that in practice $RPI - X$ had a bias against CAPEX – a form of reverse Averch–Johnson effect. This arose from weak rewards for CAPEX and a failure to recognize some CAPEX, particularly that related to information technology, as contributing to the regulatory asset base. To avoid this problem, the regulator has to focus attention very closely on the quality of supply to customers. One important development in the UK context has been carried out by the electricity regulator (OFGEM, 2000; 2001). This applies incentives to the companies by making a percentage of the allowed revenue dependent on the company's performance on three measures of quality of supply: availability of load (duration of lost load), security of load (number of interruptions) and speed of response to complaints. To allow effective comparisons between companies, the regulator adjusts the measured performance for inherited capacity problems from before privatization and inherent capacity problems associated with geography and customer density. Other UK regulators have approached the issue differently. The water regulator carries out very detailed asset management monitoring of the network in a 'hands on' manner, and the transmission services in electricity are rewarded by a sliding scale mechanism. Other regulators, for example, in the Netherlands, have preferred to benchmark the total expenditures of the regulated companies, and regulatory debate on total cost benchmarking continues. It makes sense from the point of view of not introducing differential incentives, but runs into the problem that OPEX benchmarking is much simpler to model and execute than CAPEX benchmarking.

Depreciation allowances

Although depreciation does not enter a cash flow model of the value of a company, it has a role to play in the financial model of price cap regulation because it represents a cost associated with using the capital assets of the company to produce output. The role of the depreciation charge needs to be seen in terms of what is called *articulation* (Whittington, 1998). This requires that, in a consistent financial model, the treatment of depreciation in the regulated company's income flow is the same as its treatment in the calculation of the regulatory asset base. Depreciation is the return *of* the capital to the owners of the company. It also has an impact on the return *on* capital to the investors of the company through its effect on the current regulatory asset base. In practice, a major issue for regulators has been that the typical network industry has a spectrum of assets with very different asset lives, so that accounting details can have an important effect on the regulated price formula. More generally, the problems of calculating and benchmarking the appropriate depreciation allowance are related to the calculation of the regulatory asset base.

Valuation of the regulatory asset base (RAB)

At privatization a value has to be established for the regulated company. This value will play a critical role in the financial model on which future price regulation is based, and it is called the regulatory asset base or RAB. For many privatized utilities the equity market value of the companies' shares differs significantly from the replacement cost of the companies' assets. This arises partly from faulty investment decisions under state ownership, but also simply because the RAB is a forward-looking measure. In the case of the Netherlands privatization of electricity, for example, it was decided by the regulator that setting the RAB equal to the replacement cost of the distribution assets would lead to an increase in the overall price level, contrary to the requirement that initial prices in 2000 were to equal the 1996 level in real terms.

The debate on the RAB is concerned with the following issues. We begin the post privatization or regulated period with a set of productive assets previously owned by taxpayers and now owned by shareholders. The book value of these assets at current replacement cost is A. At the same time the shares have a market value M set by the stock market and which varies from day to day: $M = mA$ where m is the market to asset ratio, and usually $0 < m \leq 1$. For example, in the UK gas privatization, at flotation $m = 0.4$. It will be the case that $M = mA$ reflects the future profit stream anticipated by the stock market from the use of these assets in the context of the regulatory regime for determining revenues. The problem is to set a value for RAB. Should it reflect the usually higher figure for the replacement cost of the assets, A, or the usually lower figure for market value, $M = mA$? There is a direct effect on regulated prices because the lower is the value of RAB, the lower is the regulated price in equation (23.1) and the lower is the share of that price received by the regulated company as its return on capital.

The Netherlands regulator, DTE, arrived at a value for the initial RAB by assuming that in 2000 the rate of return, r_0, on invested capital, projected at that time from existing revenues and OPEX, was equal to the weighted average cost of capital, *wacc.* UK regulators have all taken as the initial value for RAB the market value of the shares averaged over a period following the privatization. Since many of these shares were deliberately priced low to attract small-scale buyers, with restrictions on large scale purchases, the immediate price was a poor basis for RAB. Different UK regulators took the market value averaged over a period of between eight months and five years to establish RAB for their first regulatory reviews. This initial calculation, once completed, cannot be repeated, otherwise, as Whittington (1998) argues, it becomes a circular exercise. Whittington emphasizes that the UK regulators have consistently seen the RAB as measuring the value of investors' funds and not the valuation of specific assets inherited from the state-owned industry. He also identifies three other critical problems with the RAB, related to the expression used earlier in the chapter:

$$RAB_t = RAB_{t-1} + CAPEX_t - D_t. \qquad (23.5)$$

The first problem is the annual adjustment to RAB for overall price changes. Maintaining the argument that RAB measures the value of investors' funds at opportunity cost, UK regulators use the RPI (retail price index) to revalue the RAB. They reject the use of a replacement cost of capital index for the same reason that they reject an asset measure of RAB. The second issue is the treatment of depreciation to maintain articulation, as described in the previous section. Whether depreciation is seen as a return of capital invested or a charge for replacing assets consumed, it is essential to maintain a consistent usage in both equations (23.1) and (23.5), otherwise price controls are distorted. The third issue is the measure of CAPEX. To maintain consistency this is regarded as investment *in* the firm rather than investment *by* the firm. As such, it is rolled forward at the same price index as RAB. However, the emphasis on the market value of CAPEX rather than its asset value at replacement cost is another reflection of the worry that $RPI - X$ may have a bias against upgrading the quality of the asset base, unless such quality-related investment is specifically rewarded by benchmarking CAPEX separately rather than as a part of total cost. Again the issue of whether price control has a bias against investment arises.

The cost of capital
The real pre-tax weighted average cost of capital for UK regulation has been calculated on a conventional basis for a number of years and incorporates risk-adjusted equity and debt rates. It has varied between 6 per cent and 7.5 per cent in the different controls applied to the energy utilities and was set at 6.5 per cent for the 1999 UK electricity distribution review (OFGEM,1999:43). In summary it is

$$wacc = \delta \ [real \ risk \ free \ cost \ of \ debt + drp] + \\ \varepsilon \ [real \ risk\text{-}free \ cost \ of \ equity + erp] \ \beta$$

where drp = debt risk premium; erp = equity risk premium, δ and ε are the ratios of debt and equity in financing the company and β is the equity beta on the distribution companies. The equity beta stems from the use of the capital asset pricing model to determine the cost of equity funds. It reflects the extent to which the company's share price varies with the overall value of the stock market, and the higher the beta value the more a company's share price will rise or fall when the market rises or falls. The National Audit Office (2002) has summarized the parameters used in different UK utility regulations between 1999 and 2001, and these are shown in Table 23.1.

β is set at 1.0 in UK electricity distribution to reflect 'the low risk nature of the distribution business which has the characteristics of a natural monopoly' (OFGEM, 1999:41).

Table 23.1   Real pre-tax weighted average cost of capital parameters used by UK regulators, 1999–2001

Parameter	Telecoms	Electricity transmission	Electricity distribution	Water
Risk-free rate (%)	3.0	2.5–2.75	2.5	2.5–3.0
Debt/(Debt + equity) ratio	0.3	0.6–0.7	0.5	0.5
Equity beta	1.29	1	1	0.7–0.8

Source: National Audit Office (2002).

Periodic P_0 adjustments, glidepaths and rolling mechanisms
We have already reflected on the problem of catch-up with the cost frontier, which is used in some but not all benchmarking exercises to reflect uncertainty and random error. We also noted that the incentive power of $RPI - X$ diminishes as the time approaches for the next regulatory review. These issues spill over into the nature of the P_0 price adjustment at review. Regulators have differed in the way in which cost savings have been passed

back to consumers, the two approaches being known as 'the helicopter' and 'the glidepath' (National Audit Office, 2002). The helicopter approach immediately delivers all of the cost savings achieved previously to consumers, with a single price adjustment at the start of the next regulatory period. It means that the actual rate of return on capital of the company is immediately adjusted to the weighted average cost of capital. This can severely reduce the incentive power of $RPI - X$, as discussed earlier, and an alternative is to stage the price control so that the actual rate of return is adjusted to the cost of capital over a period known as the glidepath. This may not always find favour with consumers, of course. Another way of looking at this incentive issue is to allow the company to retain cost savings for the whole length of a regulatory period with a rolling OPEX or CAPEX mechanism. In this way OPEX savings made in the last year of a regulatory review period would be retained for five years, say, into the next period. For CAPEX some form of regulatory 'logging' of actual investments in quality of the network can be used, which will be allowed to play a role in allocating rewards in the next regulatory review period. All of these devices are ways of mitigating the more crude aspects of price capping by $RPI - X$.

Conclusions

This chapter has discussed the principles of price cap regulation and issues arising, and has pointed to a number of possible problems. Price cap regulation has been challenged by other models of regulating prices and profits. These models often offer alternative forms of incentive regulation with different degrees of power. Crew and Kleindorfer (2002) offer one set of views, particularly about models based on agency theory such as price capping. They identify the problem of the assumption of regulatory commitment not to subsequently reset the price control, which has been accepted as a major difficulty of this approach. They argue that the perceived incentive power is greatly reduced when allowance is made for regulators retrospectively clawing back gains they had previously committed themselves to permitting. Cost of service or rate of return regulation does not rely so heavily on this assumption of regulatory commitment, but has far fewer claims for incentive power. Sliding scale mechanisms (for example, Burns *et al.*, 1998) offer intermediate incentive power regulation. They operate by offering the company a choice of regulatory contracts: choosing a high-powered mechanism will allow the company to retain a higher share of its economic profits, choosing a more lenient mechanism could result in profit confiscation. Such mechanisms usually return a share of the regulatory benefits to consumers on an annual basis. They offer a halfway house between cost of service and price capping for privatized utilities, avoiding some, but not all, of the measurement and benchmarking issues in price capping discussed in this chapter.

References

Beesley, M. and S. Littlechild (1989) 'The Regulation of Privatized Monopolies in the United Kingdom', *RAND Journal of Economics*, 20,(3), 454–72.

Bernstein, J. and D. Sappington (1999) 'Setting the X factor in price cap regulation plans', *Journal of Regulatory Economics*, 16, 5–25.

Bogetoft, P. (1997) 'DEA based yardstick competition: the optimality of best practice regulation', *Annals of Operations Research*, 73, 277–98.

Bös, D. (1991) *Privatization: a theoretical treatment*, Oxford: Clarendon Press.

Burns, P., R. Turvey and T.G. Weyman-Jones (1998) 'The Behaviour of the Firm under Alternative Regulatory Constraints', *Scottish Journal of Political Economy*, 45(2), 133–57.

Crew, M. and P. Kleindorfer (2002) 'Regulatory economics: twenty years of progress?', *Journal of Regulatory Economics*, 21(1), 5–22.

DTE (2000) 'Guidelines for price cap regulation of the Dutch Electricity Sector in the period from 2000 to 2003, February 2000', Netherlands Electricity Regulatory Service, The Hague: Dienst uitvoering en toezicht Elektriciteitset (DtE), (*http://www.dte.nl*).

European Commission (2002) *Implementing the Internal Energy Market: first benchmarking report*, Luxembourg: Office for Official Publications of the European Communities

IPART (1999) 'Regulation of Electricity Network Service Providers: incentives and principles for regulation', Discussion Paper DP-32, Independent Pricing and Regulatory Tribunal of New South Wales, Sydney (*http://www.ipart.nsw.gov.au*).

Littlechild, S. (1970) 'Marginal Cost Pricing with Joint Costs', *Economic Journal*, 80(3183), 323–35.

Lovell, C.A.K. (1993) 'Production Frontiers and Productive Efficiency', in H.O. Fried, C.A.K. Lovell and S.S. Schmidt (eds), *The Measurement of Productive Efficiency*, New York: Oxford University Press.

Lovell, C.A.K. (2002) 'Imperfect Optimisation', *Easter 2002 Workshop on efficiency and productivity analysis*, University of Leicester Management Centre (*http://www.le.ac.uk/ulmc/epu*).

National Audit Office (2002) *Pipes and Wires*, London: Stationery Office.

OFGEM (1999) *Distribution Price Control Review Final Proposals*, December, London: Office of Gas and Electricity Markets (*http://www.open.gov.uk/offer*).

OFGEM (2000) *Information and Incentives Project: output measures and monitoring delivery between reviews, final proposal*, September, London: Office of Gas and Electricity Markets (*http://www.ofgem.gov.uk*).

OFGEM (2001) *Information and Incentives Project: incentive schemes*, January, London: Office of Gas and Electricity Markets (*http://www.ofgem.gov.uk*).

Turvey, R. (1971) *Economic Analysis and Public Enterprise*, London: Allen & Unwin.

Whittington, G. (1998) 'Regulatory asset value and the cost of capital', in M.E. Beesley (ed.), *Regulating Utilities: understanding the issues*, IEA Readings 49, London: Institute of Economic Affairs.

24 Comparing regulatory systems
Anthony Ogus

Introduction

This chapter explores the institutional frameworks and legal forms which are used in different jurisdictions to implement the collective goals explicit or implicit in government regulation.[1] Its content is relevant to an analysis of the regulation of privatized utilities, though it goes beyond this. It will focus in particular on what has been generally called 'economic regulation', the regulation of prices and quality of services supplied in a market characterized by natural monopoly conditions. However, at points it will refer to 'social regulation', or those areas of state intervention generally justified by reference to externalities and information asymmetries (Ogus, 1994:4–5).

We will consider the characteristics of regulatory systems under two main headings:

- *institutional*, for example whether the regulator is a branch of government or an agency, to a greater or lesser extent independent of government, and the principles of accountability; and
- *procedural and managerial*, for example any requirements of transparency of decision making and internal systems of considering costs and benefits.

However, as soon as we leap into comparisons between national systems, we realize that there is a risk of oversimplification if little account is taken of the cultural and constitutional context in which the regime is to be found (Daintith, 1988). By way of illustration, take the case of licensing (say) taxis. We may find a strong resemblance between the regimes in two different jurisdictions: similar conditions may be stipulated for the grant of a licence, and similar processes may be laid down. But the *functioning* of the regulatory system may be strikingly different if, for example, state A has a panoply of process values incorporated into its general administrative law and enforced by an independent judiciary, whereas in state B the matter is simply one of bureaucratic *diktat*. So also the concrete decisions made may depend not only on the merits of applicants and the use of highly detailed legislative or administrative criteria, but also on the constitutional basis of the system (also see Chapter 25). State A may enshrine a general principle of freedom of economic activity, in relation to which the requirement for licensing constitutes a necessarily limited exception; state B may, in contrast, regard the system as simply an instrument facilitating government control of the economy.

Indeed, above and beyond substantive constitutional norms may be other significant aspects to be considered under what may be loosely called 'cultural' variables. Historically, different bureaucratic and regulatory traditions have emerged in different countries relating to the style of rule making and enforcement. Such traditions may stem from the cultures associated with different legal systems (for example, common law, civil law, Scandinavian, Latin American) or operate quite independently of the latter.

This chapter begins, therefore, with an attempt to identify how regulation fits into the constitutional and cultural environment.

The constitutional framework

Regulation, in our conception, involves individuals and firms being induced to outcomes which, in the absence of the instrument, they would not have attained. It therefore necessarily involves the exercise of power by the state or an agency of the state. Constitutions control power and allocate it between different organs of the state (Sajó, 1999), more specifically between legislature, executive and judiciary. Under most modern western constitutions, the power to regulate is acquired, if only implicitly, by the legislature.

If our interpretation of regulation as imposing collectivist goals is accepted, conferring sovereign power on the legislature to regulate might seem, in the light of democratic principles, to be obvious. However, democratic ideals must, to some extent, cede before other values and, in consequence, constitutional arrangements governing regulation are more complex (Daintith, 1997: 77–81).

First, and most obviously, in practice much regulatory power is delegated by legislatures to the executive; while primary legislation may lay down objectives and general principles, subordinate legislation or other administrative instruments provide the detailed rules. The costs of legislators being sufficiently informed to make good decisions and of the necessarily frequent technical amendments make this inevitable.

Secondly, in some countries, notably France (Bell, 1992), the power of the executive to regulate at least in some sectors is derived directly from the constitution. This may reflect a political or ideological choice in favour of limiting democratic influences on decisions in such areas, a tradition persisting from monarchist concepts of the state (Piettre, 1947).

A third exception, sometimes overlooked by political scientists and economists, is the residual power of the judiciary to regulate. In many jurisdictions, the courts refuse to enforce contractual obligations which are contrary to the *ordre public*, a concept sufficiently broad to encompass a large number of social and economic values (Lloyd, 1953). In the common law world, judges have developed principles not only to constrain monopolistic behaviour (Trebilcock, 1986) but also, under the doctrine of 'common callings' (Taggart, 1995:216–27), where such conditions are justified or inevitable – as in natural monopolies – to guarantee services and to regulate prices. In New Zealand, attempts have been made to apply the principles to post-privatization utility arrangements (Taggart, 1995). In the absence of a regulatory administrative authority, the approach may be justified, but it is problematic insofar as it requires a legal claim for it to be activated and (in modern times) makes great demands on the technical expertise of judges.

A fourth qualification arises from the possibility of an allocation of legislative competence between national and provincial legislatures under a federal system of government (Prince, 1999). Inspired by notions of political decentralization, these constitutional arrangements raise difficult questions, whether they inhibit trade across the federation and/or encourage 'regulatory competition' between regions, with beneficial or adverse economic consequences (Inman and Rubinfeld, 2000). The same issues arise in a transnational context, such as the European Union (Esty and Geradin, 2001).

Note too that in some countries the constitution itself may exert constraints on the power of the legislature to regulate; and this in turn will depend on the set of politicoeconomic values to which that document gives expression (Ogus, 1990). Thus we may have, as in the United States, a constitution which is interpreted as being based on a premise of freedom of economic activity. Then regulation has to find its constitutional legitimacy in the (admittedly broad) range of 'police powers' (for example, protection of the health, safety and welfare of the community), the exercise of which can interfere with that freedom. This approach may be contrasted with another tradition that defines the role of the state as in some way directed towards social welfare ends, which may diverge from unregulated market outcomes. Thus the German Basic Law of 1949 has, at its base, the concept of *soziale Marktwirtschaft* (social market economy) impliedly legitimizing more active regulatory interventions (Reich, 1977:82–6). But the language used to define such powers tends to be very vague, making constitutional challenges easy to resist. For example, Article 41 of the Italian Constitution provides that 'the law will set up appropriate schemes and controls in order that public and private economic activities may be directed and coordinated for the benefit of society'. This in turn should be distinguished from a third type of constitutional framework, which assumes a planned economy and gives the legislature or government all the powers necessary to control it (see, for example, Laptev, 1978)

Administrative law

Administrative law deals with the decisions and activities of public institutions and, in particular, specifies the means of challenging their validity and providing remedies for grievances. It plays a number of vital roles in relation to regulatory systems, ensuring that regulatory institutions use proper procedures and act not only within their legislative mandate, but also fairly and reasonably within the light of those objectives (Baldwin and McCrudden, 1987: ch. 3).

There are major differences between countries regarding the character and effectiveness of administrative law and an obvious variable is the strength and independence of the judiciary, who are primarily responsible for making and enforcing decisions against public institutions. In this connection, it would be wrong to assume that the power of judges to control administrative activity is a reflection of the state of the jurisdiction's economic development and therefore to be found predominantly in western industrialized countries. It has been persuasively argued that the world's most active judiciary, in this sense, is to be found in India (Baar, 1992).

In any event, there are important differences between administrative law systems in countries which show equal respect for the separation of powers and ensure the independence of judges (Tate and Vallinder, 1995). There are, on the one hand, the continental European, civil law jurisdictions, which have a system of public law tribunals, separate from the main judicial system; and, on the other, the common law jurisdictions, where administrative action is largely controlled by the ordinary courts, the state being regarded as simply *primus inter pares*.

Even within these two systems there are important variations. So, for example, the question whether a court has the power to annul legislation on the ground that it is inconsistent with the constitution is not one which receives the same answer within each tradition (McWhinney, 1986). The German *Verfassungsgericht* has the power, but that of the French *Conseil Constitutionnel*, which in any event is not a court, is more limited. The United States Supreme Court has the power, the British House of Lords has not.

Other differences may be questions of emphasis and therefore more difficult to categorize. German administrative law centres on the notion of the *Rechtsstaat*, the main principle being that all instances of public administrative activity must be legitimized by formal legal norms (Faber, 1992: 28–30). While this idea would not be treated as wholly alien to the French *droit administratif*, the latter takes as its focal point the 'public interest'. This not only enables constitutional texts to be interpreted in such a way as to justify appropriate administrative action; it also protects private citizens, in the sense of requiring public authorities imposing losses on individuals in the furtherance of the public interest to provide compensation (Brown and Bell, 1998: 175–6).

Then, as between two of the leading common law jurisdictions, the USA and the UK, administrative law has clearly diverged (Schwartz and Wade, 1972). American judges take a harder look at the reasonableness of administrative actions (so-called 'substantive judicial review'), whereas their English counterparts have rather concentrated on whether appropriate procedures have been observed. American administrative law has also gone further in terms of process values, requiring a greater degree of transparency of decision making and encouraging participation by interested third parties.[2]

Regulatory traditions and styles
Characterizing and placing what we have come to call 'regulation' within legal systems are highly problematic tasks, as an impressionistic comparison of the way law librarians classify books bearing that title would at once reveal. The question is not unconnected with the politicoeconomic basis of the law. Thus we find that civil law systems, which have rationalized the concept of the state and particularly its role in the economy, have developed formal legal categories for this purpose: for example, the French *droit public économique* (Delvolvé, 1998) and the German *Wirtschaftsverwaltungsrecht* (Jarass, 1984). These terms have been used to bring under a single umbrella the law relating to public enterprise, public finance, state controls of private enterprise and competition law – and therefore without difficulty have incorporated the regulation of privatized entities. In contrast, in Anglophone jurisdictions with their common law emphasis on the control of government power, equivalent classifications do not exist. Of course, the same areas of law can be identified, but there has been nothing in legal doctrine to link them. Rather, they have been seen as disparate aspects of administrative law, the main concern of which was to control executive discretion, rather than facilitate outcomes considered as economically desirable (see, for example, Allen, 1927). Interesting, but not entirely successful, attempts were made by German emigrants to impose continental patterns on the American (Freund, 1931; 1932) and British (Goldschmidt, 1937) systems.

Paradoxically, the concepts of 'regulation' and 'regulatory law' which became so dominant in the 1980s and afterwards were predominantly Anglo-American in origin. They had, as their base, the economic notion of public law responses to instances of market failure and, as such, were rationalized by legal scholars from a law-and-economics background (Breyer, 1982; Ogus, 1994). Undoubtedly, this literature had an impact on administrative lawyers, who began to forsake their traditional preoccupation with discretion and judicial review to join 'the economists' pilgrimage to the new Jerusalem, which beckons with responsive regulation, regulatory negotiation and regulation by performance outcome and through economic incentives' (Aronson, 1997). While public lawyers from the common law world were thus acquiring a vision which was closer to that of continental exponents of 'economic law', the latter were adjusting to the somewhat narrower notion of 'regulation', which became in French *réglementation* (Lévêque, 1998) and in German *Regulierung* (Reich, 1984).

Notwithstanding this convergence of the conception and rationalization of regulation between the two principal legal cultures, the practical application retained important differences. Most of these will emerge later in the chapter, but already here we can mention some examples which result from the historical traditions.

- The focus on the 'state' and the greater degree of state intervention in the continental tradition led to a culture of 'public interest' regulation which is somewhat broader than the Anglo-Saxon emphasis on 'market failure' regulation (Dyson, 1992b).
- The style of the legislation used for regulatory purposes in common law systems tends to aim at a high level of precision, thus generating lengthy and very complex provisions; the continental approach adopts more general and abstract language, leaving more room for discretionary interpretation (Dale, 1988). Historically, this can be explained as a consequence of the ideology that regulation was an incursion on the general principles of the common law and, thus, to be protected against judicial conservatism, required to be formulated in very specific terms (Ogus, 1980).
- Given their long tradition of state intervention and centralized bureaucracy, continental European systems have been less comfortable than common law jurisdictions with regulatory agencies which are, at least to some degree, independent of government (Majone, 1996: 10–12).
- While continental regulatory authorities are given powers themselves to impose sanctions for non-compliance, the British regulatory systems predominantly use the criminal justice process to enforce regulation (European Commission, 1994). The latter tendency appears to be a consequence of the fact that, before modern bureaucracies, regulation was enforced by justices of the peace, the local arm of the criminal law (Ogus, 1992).
- In common law systems, again because historically intervention was regarded as exceptional rather than routine, regulatory techniques and principles have tended to emerge piecemeal, with little attempt at coherence across different sectors. In some European continental jurisdictions, particularly Germany, attempts have been made to develop general principles of regulatory administrative justice (Boujong, 2000).

Institutional structure
In this section we consider a number of issues concerning the institutional structure of regulatory regimes. In relation to each, we shall examine current arrangements in the light of theoretical arguments.

Regulatory agencies and government
Regulatory systems must, of course, be enforced and therefore require some agency for this purpose. More than this, as we have seen, legislatures invariably delegate the task of detailed rule making and this is often undertaken by the institutions responsible for enforcement. The first important issue which has to be addressed is the extent to which such institutions should be independent of government. There is here a spectrum of alternative arrangements, ranging from complete government control to self-regulation. Although there are many possible variations, we can identify four main types.

1. An agency which is part of (central or local) government. External expert opinion may be consulted but the rules and decisions are made within the permanent bureaucracy, in relation to which a politician (the relevant minister) takes ultimate responsibility.
2. An agency which is semi-autonomous, in the sense that, while it is independent of, and not accountable to, government, the latter exerts some residual control through one or more of the following:
    — appointment of members,
    — some government representation,
    — an expectation, or requirement, that rules and decisions will be made in accordance with government policy or guidelines,
    — some form of ratification of decisions by ministers.
3. An agency which is independent of government, in the sense that few, if any, of the above controls exist. It is a public institution, acting under powers conferred, and in accordance with principles enacted by the legislature. Its members are experts drawn from non-government sources and without political affiliations.
4. An agency which is predominantly self-regulatory as well as independent of government, in the sense that a significant proportion of the members are drawn from and directly represent the regulated sector. Some degree of public control may nevertheless be exercised through one or more of the following:
    — some members represent the public interest,
    — the principles and/or procedures to be followed are determined by the legislature,
    — rules and decisions can be challenged by reference to the courts or some superior public agency.

At the risk of oversimplification, a survey of practice, both historical and interjurisdictional, can lead us to some interesting generalizations. In the first place, in the last three decades or so there has been a global tendency to shift along the spectrum away from central government control: this has been a main feature of what has been called the 'deregulation' movement (Ogus, 2000). Nevertheless, secondly, the extent to which that phenomenon has occurred has varied between different countries and in accordance with different regulatory cultures. Agency of type 3 above is the classic form of American regulatory commission, developed at the end of the nineteenth century to govern utilities. Public ownership had been expressly rejected as a mode of governance and so the notion of a body of independent experts was wholly consistent (Landis, 1938). In contrast, Japan (Vogel, 1996) and the European nations had typically adopted public ownership in this area, and when utilities were privatized new forms of regulatory agency emerged (see, for example, Demargny, 1996) but (except in Germany which had been influenced by the American model in its post Second World War reconstruction: Woolcock, 1996: 308) it was harder to sever the ties with governmental authority (Majone, 1996: 14–15).[3]

So, for example, in Spain the central government exercises direct control over the electricity industry and its prices. In Germany, the federal government establishes the general structure of tariffs for electricity, while the Länder governments control prices to consumers.[4] In France, such decisions are proposed by the Regulatory Commission, but taken by the Minister.[5] In Ireland, the minister can give directions to the Commission for Electricity Regulation for the performance of its functions.[6] In the UK, the minister has residual powers to revise any modifications by the Office of Gas and Electricity Markets of any conditions in a supplier's licence.[7]

A third generalization, and this applies to the USA as well as to Europe, is that agencies dealing with powers of social regulation, for example consumer protection and environmental protection, have more government involvement than those governing economic regulation, and indeed in many countries remain, as type 1 above. Nevertheless, this should not be taken as necessarily implying exclusively centralist decision making. In the important area of employment, and particularly health and safety at work, a tradition has long been established of a tripartite (state, employer representatives and employee representatives) governance structure (Baldwin and Daintith, 1992). In other areas, there is an increasing tendency for the details of regulatory policy to be worked out with the regulated industries on a consensual basis (Ogus, 2000). This last arrangement clearly involves some degree of self-regulation, which, in any event, can assume a large variety of forms (Page, 1986: 144–8). However, in its most blatant form (type 4 above), self-regulation is used in most jurisdictions mainly in the area of professional regulation (Faure *et al.*, 1993).

What then are the theoretical arguments regarding these issues? They mainly relate to the costs of the information necessary for good decision making and the ability to ensure that the agency's performance is consistent with the regulatory public interest goals; in other words, the principal–agent problem (Macey, 1992). We can begin by recognizing the advantages of delegating regulatory rule making and enforcement to an agency which is largely independent of government (Mashaw, 1985). Expertise can be concentrated in ways not always possible within a permanent bureaucracy and distance from government can reduce the degree of political interference – the history of public ownership has revealed too often that politicians are tempted to aim at short-term benefits, leading to, among other problems, uncertainty and instability (Zeckhauser and Horn, 1989). Nevertheless, a role for government may be justified if aspects of regulation require essentially political judgments. This helps to explain the preference for type 1 in relation to social regulation and for type 2 as regards utilities regulation: while the primary questions of efficient price tariffs are for the independent agency, any social dimension, for example subsidization and distributional preferences for certain customers, may more appropriately be determined by governments which are democratically accountable (Baldwin and Cave, 1999:289–91). Some residual government control or influence can also be justified on the basis that policy can thereby be coordinated with other relevant agencies and sectors.

One reason for the observed worldwide trend towards consensual, decentralized regulatory rule making is the growing recognition that governments cannot always be relied on to possess or properly to process the information necessary to meet the regulatory goals at low cost (Gunningham *et.al.*, 1998:44). We can clearly see the advantage, for example, of large firms formulating their own rule-book, which is then submitted to the regulatory agency to ensure compatibility with those goals (Ayres and Braithwaite, 1992). By themselves, however, these arguments do not justify adoption of the complete self-regulation model, type 4, because here unconstrained agencies can exploit their regulatory power to advance private, rather than public, interests, in particular by creating barriers to entry (Faure *et al.*, 1993). Such tendencies may nevertheless be checked if the self-regulatory agencies do not have monopoly regulatory power but rather have to compete with other self-regulatory agencies (Ogus, 1995).

Scope and super agencies
As one might expect, practice varies regarding the categorization of regulatory agencies and the scope of their remit.

So, for example, in the USA, the state of Wisconsin has a Public Services Commission responsible for telecommunications as well as electricity, gas and water. The Scandinavian countries have a single agency which deals with all aspects of energy, including the regulation of prices where monopolies persist. Italy and the UK (since 2000) have a combined regulator of electricity and gas (but not water). France, Germany, the Netherlands and Portugal have separate authorities for electricity, gas and water.

There are clear advantages in the broader remit if that leads to greater consistency in policy making, particularly where, as with gas and electricity, there is interaction between the two markets, and to a uniform approach to such technical matters as the method of estimating capital investment costs for the purposes of price controls (Baldwin and Cave, 1999: 296–8). But it may be the case that some form of competition between regulatory agencies serves to sharpen their responses and thus enhances accountability (Macey, 1992: 104–7).[8]

Liberalization of markets traditionally associated with natural monopolies has also given rise to another dilemma of institutional policy. In some areas, notably telecommunications but also the supply of gas and electricity, regulation in the form of price controls has been regarded as a temporary phenomenon pending the arrival of sufficient competition. Legislation then typically requires of regulatory agencies both to promote competition and, if the market is insufficiently competitive, to control prices. The dilemma arises because typically, within the jurisdiction, there are other regulatory institutions formulating and enforcing competition law generally. Two linked questions arise: should the competition aspects of utility regulation be integrated into the broader powers and responsibilities of the competition authority and removed from the sectoral utility regulator? And, when competition is deemed to be sufficient to remove the price controls, should that regulator be disbanded?

Across the jurisdictions we can observe a variety of responses to these questions. To some extent these may depend on the extent to which competition without price regulation has been, or is likely to be, achieved. So, for example, there is greater deference to the role of the competition authorities in the telecommunications sector where competition is more advanced; in the European context, the EU Commission's Directorate-General for Competition plays a most significant role (Coates, 1999). But even here there is tension created by concurrent and overlapping powers of national regulatory authorities and national competition authorities (Larouche, 2000). An even greater diversity exists in the energy sector. At one end of the spectrum is New Zealand, where no sectoral regulatory institutions have been retained and there are no explicit legislative powers to control prices (Taggart, 1995). Then there is Denmark, where such powers do exist but they are exercised by the Competition Authority, which has established price committees for this purpose.[9] But most jurisdictions seem to favour a dualist model in which there is a sectoral regulator applying competition law, but in the expectation that this will be informed by, or at least consistent with, the principles emanating from the competition authorities (Grenfell, 1999). Perhaps the most interesting example of such a model is to be found in Canada where the law provides devices for enhancing the relationship between competition and sector regulators (Doern, 1998b:268–72; Janisch, 1999).

> Notably: (1) the empowering of the competition regulator to appear before sectoral regulators to advocate or raise concerns about competition;[10] (2) the availability of a 'regulated conduct' defence to a firm facing allegations of uncompetitive practices by the competition regulator;[11] (3) the doctrine of 'regulatory forbearance' entitling a sectoral regulator not to regulate where effective competition exists.[12]

The arguments for and against merger of the sector regulator and the competition authorities seem to be well balanced (Prosser, 1997:272–7). On the one hand, there is a clear advantage in having a single agency deal with competition issues in whatever context they may arise and tensions can obviously arise if the sector regulator postulates principles and policy which are not consistent with those being applied more generally. On the other hand, a more general agency may have insufficient experience of, and be insufficiently sensitive to, the specific features of the utility industries, for example their social or service obligations, particularly where the balance between regulation and competition has not yet tipped decisively in the direction of the latter. It may also be that a sector regulator can more effectively fulfil the role of *promoting* competition, a function which is very different from that of *policing* competition, typically undertaken by competition authorities.

Another institutional question much mooted in recent years is whether there should exist some 'super' authority which takes some residual responsibility for a variety of regulatory regimes (Baldwin and Cave, 1999:296–8). Understandably, such institutions may exist in federal jurisdictions, where the sector regulators operate at a provincial or regional level and questions arise as to inter-state provision (see, for example, the Australian Independent Competition and Regulatory Commission and the Canadian National Energy Board); but as such they do not normally play an overseeing role and hence the sector regulators are in no way accountable to them. Another model is provided by the Administrative Conference of the United States which, from 1968 to 1995, monitored regulatory agency procedures and rule-making practice, and issued recommendation for improvements.[13] Building on this, one might envisage a two-tiered structure in which a general, overseeing body of experts reviews the powers and procedures of sector regulators and assists in resolving disputes between them and the regulated industries.

Discretion and accountability

We turn next to the power conferred on regulatory agencies, the nature of the discretion involved and the methods used to render them accountable. In theoretical terms, we are back with the principal–agent problem (cf. above, p. 522). To enable the agent, here the regulator, to apply the expertise which he or she is assumed to possess, a broad discretion must usually be conferred. So, for example, the British Gas and Electricity Markets Authority's principal objective is:

'to protect the interests of consumers in relation to electricity conveyed by distribution systems, wherever appropriate by promoting effective competition between persons engaged in, or in commercial activities connected with, the generation, transmission, distribution or supply of electricity'

and it should carry out its functions:

'in the manner which . . . it consider is best calculated
(a) to promote efficiency and economy . . .
(b) to protect the public from dangers . . .
(c) to secure a diverse and viable long-term energy supply'.[14]

However, the extent to which legislation further directs, by specific rules or guidelines, how the discretion is to be exercised varies significantly between jurisdictions. To illustrate this, we can examine the provisions governing the control of electricity prices. Now we know that, to achieve efficient pricing in monopoly conditions, regulators have tended to adopt either the long-standing American method of cost recovery based on a 'fair rate of return' or a price-capping technique, tied to inflation but incorporating productivity expectations, such as that devised by the Thatcher government for the privatized utilities in the 1980s (Ogus, 1994:305–13; also see especially Chapter 23). But there is considerable diversity as to whether the legislation prescribes an appropriate method and, if so, with what degree of detail.

One finds that common law jurisdictions tend to use general language and thereby confer a very broad discretion on regulatory agencies.

Typical state legislation in the USA simply requires that the regulator should ensure that the rates charged 'shall not exceed the actual cost of such . . . services including a fair rate of return'.[15] The UK regulators have mainly used variants of the famous $RPI - X$ price-capping formula (Rees and Vickers, 1995). However the formula is contained in no legislative instrument but only in the licences granted to individual suppliers, the terms of which may be amended by the regulator in accordance with the general principles governing the 'efficiency' of supply and quoted above (Grenfell, 1999:224). A similar approach is taken in Ireland.

The legislation of some continental European jurisdictions has been more specific.

> Thus in France, which broadly speaking adopts the US method, the permissible tariff of electricity prices is explicitly related to the recovery of costs in relation to which research and development costs are treated as particularly important.[16] Even more striking is the Italian law no. 481 of 14 November 1995, which specifically incorporates a price-cap formula almost identical to that used, but not legislatively prescribed, in the UK: the annual tariff growth is not to exceed the difference between the target inflation rate and the increased productivity attainable by the supplier (Avanzini, 2000:353).

The contrast may seem to be paradoxical in the light of what was said earlier about legislative styles, but it rather reflects differences of approach within administrative law, which themselves can be explained by reference to principal–agent theory. We may readily assume that everywhere the 'principal' is intended to be the public interest, justifying and therefore also constraining the regulatory system, but the extent to which the legislator is viewed as representing that interest is another matter.

The continental European tradition has always been to emphasize the link between legislatures and the public interest; particularizing administrative functions within a strong, prescriptive statutory framework is, therefore, unsurprising. The American approach is somewhat sceptical of this link, recognizing the key role that pressure groups and private interests play in the legislative process. Greater reliance is placed on ex post methods of constraint through the general principles of administrative law. The expectation is that those enabled, by such principles, to participate in regulatory procedures or to challenge regulatory decision making in the courts will be more representative of the 'public interest' than the politicians (and bureaucrats) responsible for the legislation (Breyer and Stewart, 1985:26–32). For a period of over a hundred years, clarification of the way regulators should control utility prices consistent with the notion of a 'fair rate of return' emerged not from a legislative or executive source but rather from judges and the huge case law which emerged from judicial review of regulatory decision making (Breyer, 1982, ch. 2).

> The British systems since the 1980s seem to be somewhat unhappily stranded between the European continental and the American traditions, having neither the prescriptive statutory framework of the former, nor the strong administrative law environment of the latter (Graham, 1998:351).

The above discussion leads us into a more general consideration of accountability, which can, of course, take a variety of forms, political and legal (Baldwin and Cave, 1999: ch. 21; Prince, 1999). Inevitably, in jurisdictions where governments retain a major degree of control, independent agencies, if they exist, are accountable to the executive.

> In South Africa, for example, the National Electricity regulator must 'furnish the Minister with such information and particulars as he or she may from time to time require'; and submit an annual report, containing *inter alia* information 'regarding the envisaged strategies of the regulator'.[17]

More typically, political accountability takes the form of submitting reports to the legislature, which may have a special committee to scrutinize and debate its contents. In this connection, one may note that the British practice, not much imitated in other countries, to designate the regulator as a single person, rather than a committee or a commission, may strengthen political accountability, as the individual concerned has in consequence a much higher profile (Doern, 1998d: 40–41).[18]

Legal accountability enables those aggrieved by a decision or an exercise of rule making to issue a formal complaint or appeal. Where an agency's powers include that of issuing licences or conditions for individual firms, it may well have its own appeals panel for such purposes.[19] Of greater significance is the right to bring claims to another institution. Here one observes a divergence between countries which establish specialist commissions or tribunals, such as the British Competition Commission,[20] having powers to determine disputes within the sector, or a related sector, and those which rely exclusively on institutions having competence over general administrative matters. Examples of the latter include not only the system of administrative tribunals in civil law jurisdictions, but also the ordinary courts in common law jurisdictions, with their powers of judicial review. The main advantage of a specialist institution is that it can bring expertise to bear on the relevant regulatory issues, particularly where, as in the cited example, it includes economists as well as lawyers and administrators. But, as we have already seen, the general jurisdiction of the American courts has not prevented them from developing a sophisticated approach to regulatory concerns (Foster, 1992: 187–97); and in the civil law systems the high standing and profile of institutions such as the French *Conseil d'Etat* and the German *Bundesverwaltungsgericht* ensure effectiveness as well as legitimacy (Dyson, 1992a: 12–13).

Procedures and management
The background: the legal character of regulatory systems
The choice of appropriate procedures and management systems is much dependent on the style and culture of regulatory systems and so, to explain their incidence, we must return to some of the fundamental aspects discussed earlier in this chapter. One is the distinction between social and economic regulation (above, p. 514), the importance of which tends to be underestimated by economists and political scientists. Social regulation, such as that governing health and safety and environmental pollution, has a long history, dating back to mediaeval times (Ogus, 1992) and is derived from the police powers of the state (Freund, 1932). As such, in its developed forms, it assumed the character of 'command and control', the machinery of government coercing desired behaviour from its citizens. Most of the procedures were therefore designed to ensure that the regulators did not exceed their legislative mandate, that the rules were reasonably required to meet the regulatory objectives, and that the enforcement processes complied with the demands of natural justice and did not discriminate unfairly against firms or individuals: the 'bread and butter' of traditional administrative law (Baldwin and McCrudden, 1987:ch. 3).

The origins of economic regulation are quite different. Although some form of inherent legal restraint on monopolies has existed in most jurisdictions, the control of prices and quality in natural monopolies has been a relatively recent phenomenon, simply because the most important instances of the latter have been associated with technological developments occurring after the industrial revolution. The strategies of governments in dealing with the problem were, at the outset, and at least in institutional terms, uncertain and incoherent (Arthurs, 1985). So, in the nineteenth century, exploitative behaviour by private monopolists might be combated by ad hoc inquiries and adverse publicity, rather than by any systematic application of legal norms (Foster, 1992:227–35), while the ever-expanding public ownership of natural monopolies became subject mainly to internal procedural directives, which did not always facilitate accountability to outsiders (Lapsley and Kirkpatrick, 1997:ch. 3).

The American distaste for public ownership led to the retention of private utilities but with regulatory commissions controlling prices. These institutions acquired two related characteristics (MacAvoy, 1979: ch. 2). Firstly, their principal function being to review price levels and structures proposed by the suppliers, they acted as adjudicators as much as rule makers. Secondly, the fact that typically they were dealing with monopolists, with therefore a 'one to one' relationship, some degree of cooperation from the regulated firms was necessary if they were to acquire the necessary information for good decision making, and that some interchange of personnel was not unknown, all led to a concept of 'negotiated regulation', very different from that normally associated with command-and-control (cf. Peacock, 1984). Not surprisingly, there were allegations and evidence of 'regulatory capture' (Bernstein, 1955), and efforts were made to contain the phenomenon by (as we shall see) stringent procedural requirements.

The wave of privatization in countries in the 1980s and 1990s and the need to create regulatory agencies raised the question of the extent to which the American model would be followed. Alternative strategies were to harness the new agencies to existing traditions of administrative proceduralism and management, and to imitate the institutions already existing for social regulation. However, the same period also witnessed major changes to the latter, there being a significant move away from command-and-control towards systems involving economic incentives and more freedom for firms in meeting regulatory objectives (Ogus, 2000).

Procedures
We may focus on three main categories of procedural rules designed to encourage transparency and third-party involvement in regulatory decision making (OECD, 1994:ch. 3): *notification*, the one-way communication between the regulator and the public; *consultation*, the collecting of information relevant to the decision; and *participation*, the use of public hearings to allow oral representations and discussion. As indicated above, American administrative law has taken a lead on all three aspects (Breyer and Stewart, 1985).

The obligation to notify the public of proposed regulatory policies and rules is routinely applied in all jurisdictions. A requirement to publish reasons for decisions or rules is less commonly encountered.

> The failure of the UK legislation to impose such a duty on utility regulators has been much criticized (Baldwin and Cave, 1999:315–16). In the USA, the threat of judicial review is sufficient to secure the practice.[21] In France, there is an obligation on the *Commission de régulation de l'électricité* to give reasons for its recommendations regarding prices, but not on the government which makes the decision consequent on the recommendation.[22] The Italian regulator publishes its decisions in a fully reasoned form.[23]

Publishing reasons obviously encourages good decision making and, as a measure to combat discrimination in favour of domestic firms, European law imposes such an obligation on member states in relation to the award of authorizations for the construction of electricity generators.[24] Nevertheless, if regulators will, in practice, give reasons for their decisions, it may be counter-productive to make this the subject of formal requirements since it may render the process unduly legalistic, causing additional costs and delay, and 'such procedures always work to the advantage of the regulated; they provide another route to regulatory capture' (Foster, 1992:274).

This need to achieve the right balance between overlegalism and informality applies also to the other procedural issues. In the case of utility regulation, formal provision is typically made for consultation with a body representing consumers (Locke, 1998) and reports from Japan and Portugal suggest that in those countries specialist advisory groups representing other constituencies play a key role in policy formulation (OECD, 1994:28). But it is not clear that the lines of communication thus made necessarily open prove to be more effective than consultation which operates in a more ad hoc manner and which appears to take place in most jurisdictions: 'consultation which focuses on only selected and well-organized interests may produce biased information which can skew regulatory decision-making' (ibid.). Of course, there is little that can be done to control the weight which regulators attribute to various third-party communications, but procedural devices can at least be introduced to restrain attempts to influence decision making by 'back-door lobbying': in the USA, this is done by requiring that all communications between third parties and regulators concerning proposals are placed on the official record (Breyer and Stewart, 1985:663–71).

Unsurprisingly, given its adversarial culture, American administrative law has gone furthest towards a model of regulatory process involving public hearings (ibid.: 561–9). Italy seems to be moving in the same direction.[25] But such an approach would seem to be less appropriate in systems in which governments play a role in decision making. Also it is arguable that oral debate can detrimentally oversimplify the complexities of some regulatory issues, including the determination of utility prices (Baldwin and Cave, 1999:318–19).

Managerial systems

'Regulatory management' is a relative newcomer to the language of regulatory theory and policy. It has had its greatest impact in relation to social regulation as a reaction to the widespread perception in the 1970s and 1980s that many systems had to a greater or lesser extent failed to meet their targets (Sunstein, 1990:ch. 3). This was a consequence of the fact that rules had become too numerous and too complex, that they imposed unnecessary burdens, especially administrative burdens, on firms and that they were too inflexible relative to changing technological and economic conditions (OECD, 1994:17). The impact on regulatory policy has been significant (OECD, 1992). As we have already seen (above p. 521), there has been the deregulation movement involving more flexible regulatory instruments and a degree of self-regulation, but equally important has been the introduction of practices and procedures aimed at the better management of regulatory systems (Hill, 1999).

Among these reforms, we should highlight measures designed to coax bureaucracies towards better regulation. In a number of jurisdictions, so-called 'regulatory checklists' have been introduced, requiring officials involved in regulatory policy and the drafting of regulatory rules to reveal their awareness of characteristics which are considered desirable (OECD, 1993). Thus in Norway the checklist includes questions such as the following:

> Is government action necessary?
> If so, is it preferable at national or regional level?
> Have different regulatory techniques been considered to determine which is the most appropriate?
> Are the regulations drafted in language and style which can be readily under-stood?
> Can they be effectively enforced? (Norway, 1994)

More ambitiously, in some countries, notably the USA, regulators must engage in some form of cost–benefit analysis of regulatory proposals, often known as *regulatory impact analysis* (Froud *et al.*, 1998). This is somewhat controversial if it effectively requires officials to demonstrate that a measure is justified in cost–benefit terms, because the benefits of regulatory intervention are more difficult to quantify than the costs (McGarity, 1991). But, typically, the instrument is used more as an information device, enabling policy makers to have a better understanding of the probable consequences of particular instruments.

In relation to areas such as environmental pollution and industrial health and safety, management systems of this kind have, it is claimed (for example, Gunningham *et al.*, 1998), promoted a better informed and a more sophisticated choice between regulatory instruments, and between regulatory and non-regulatory instruments. To what extent they have had an impact on economic regulation is somewhat less clear. Of course, the latter embraces the quality as the well as the price of monopolistic services and good management systems can assist in the devising of effective controls, such as performance indicators (Ogus, 1994:286–7). But, arguably, good management systems can also contribute meaningfully to what we have seen to be the crucial policy issue: the tension between price controls and competition policy, and, if price controls, the choice of an appropriate method for determining efficient prices.

Conclusions

This chapter has provided, not an evaluative study of regulatory systems, but rather a mapping exercise, attempting to characterize the institutional structure of economic regulatory systems in different jurisdictions and explaining the characteristics within historical and legal traditions.

What we have seen is that ideas about regulation have been evolving across jurisdictional boundaries. To some extent this may have been the consequence of the interaction between national regulatory regimes occurring within increasingly globalized markets (Braithwaite and Drahos, 2000) – a dimension which has not been explored in this chapter. But while there may be some convergence of regulatory objectives and substantive principles, the character of national regulatory institutions is still best to be understood within each jurisdiction's culture. In the words of Sir Christopher Foster, 'while the underlying economic principles and therefore the regulatory offences should be relevant in all economies, how the offences should be expressed, monitored and controlled can only be decided in the context of the constitution, laws and political habits of the individual country' (Foster, 1992:417).

Notes

1. For different modes of mapping regulatory systems, see Doern (1998b) and Doern *et al.* (1999).
2. It is nevertheless considered that within the last two decades British judges have become much more active in relation to judicial review (Richardson and Sunkin, 1996).
3. Government control can, of course, also be exercised by retaining shares in a privatized company. For general discussion of the various methods, see Chapter 2, and Graham and Prosser (1991:ch. 5).
4. Energiewirtschaftsgesetz 1998, §11.
5. Loi n°5. 2000–108 du 10.02.00, Art.4, al.I. For general observations on the relationship between government and regulator, see Lévêque (1998:75–6).
6. Electricity Regulation Act 1999, s.10.
7. Electricity Act 1989, s.11A, inserted by Utilities Act 2000, s.35.
8. Though Macey also recognizes that competition may induce the agencies to identify more with the industries they regulate.
9. See *www.ks.dk/eng/regnskab/1999/report.html.*
10. Competition Act 1986, ss.125–6.
11. *Attorney General of Canada* v. *Law Society of British Columbia* [1982] 2 Supreme Court Reports 455.
12. *Alberta Government Telephones* v. *Canada* (1984) 15 D.L.R. (4th) 515.
13. For a list, see *http://www.law.fsu.edu/library/admin/acus/acustoc.html.*
14. Electricity Act 1989, s.3A (1) and (5), inserted by Utilities Act 2000, s.13.
15. Iowa ST s.476 1C.
16. Loi 2000–108 of 10 February 2000, art.4(II).
17. Electricity Act 41 of 1987, s.5D, inserted by Electricity Amendment Act 60 of 1995.
18. See also on this aspect of regulatory systems, Wilks (1998:139–40).
19. For example, the Irish Electricity Regulation Act 1999, ss.29–30.
20. Competition Act 1998, ss.45–9.
21. See, for example, *Complex Consol. Edison Co. of New York* v. *F.E.R.C.* 165 F 3d 992 (1999).
22. Loi of 2000, above n.5, art.4(III).
23. For examples, see *www.autorita.energia.it/docs.*
24. Directive 96/92/EC, art 5.
25. An inference drawn from the practices described in *www.autorita.energia.it.*

References

Allen, C. (1927) *Law in the Making*, Oxford: Clarendon Press.

Aronson, M. (1997) 'A Public Lawyer's Responses to Privatisation and Outsourcing', in M. Taggart (ed.), *The Province of Administrative Law*, Oxford: Hart Publishing.

Arthurs, H.W. (1985) *Without the Law: Administrative Justice and Legal Pluralism in Nineteenth-Century England*, Toronto: University of Toronto Press.

Avanzini, G. (2000) 'Il sisteme elettrico in Italia', in E. Ferrari (ed.), *I Servizi a Rete in Europa: Concorrenza tra gli ioperatori e garanzia dei cittadini*, Milan: Raffaello Cortina.

Ayres, I. and J. Braithwaite (1992) *Responsive Regulation: Transcending the Deregulation Debate*, New York: Oxford University Press.

Baar, C. (1992) 'Social Action Litigation in India: The Operation and Limits of the World's Most Active Judiciary', in D.W. Jackson and C.N. Tate (eds.), *Comparative Judicial Review of Public Policy*, Westport: Greenwood Press.

Baldwin, R. and M. Cave (1999) *Understanding Regulation: Theory, Strategy and Practice*, Oxford: Oxford University Press.

Baldwin, R. and T. Daintith (eds) (1992) *Harmonization and Hazard: The Regulation of Workplace Safety in the European Community*, London: Graham and Trotman.

Baldwin, R. and C. McCrudden (eds) (1987) *Regulation and Public Law*, London: Weidenfeld & Nicolson.

Bell, J. (1992) *French Constitutional Law*, Oxford: Clarendon Press.

Bernstein, M. (1955) *Regulating Business by Independent Commissions*, Princeton: Princeton University Press.

Boujong, K. (ed.) (2000) *Karlsruher Kommentar zum Gesetz über Ordnungswidrigkeiten*, 2nd edn, Munich: Beck Verlag.

Braithwaite, J. and P. Drahos (2000) *Global Business Regulation*, Cambridge: Cambridge University Press.

Breyer, S. (1982) *Regulation and its Reform*, Cambridge, MA: Harvard University Press.

Breyer S. and R. Stewart (1985) *Administrative Law and Regulatory Policy*, 2nd edn, Boston: Little, Brown.

Brown, L.N. and J.S. Bell (1998) *French Administrative Law*, 5th edn, Oxford: Clarendon Press.

Coates, K. (1999) 'Regulating the Telecommunications Sector: Substituting Practical Co-operation for the Risks of Competition', in C. McCrudden (ed), *Regulation and Deregulation: Policy and Practice in the Utilities and Financial Services Industries*, Oxford: Clarendon Press.

Daintith T. (ed.) (1988) *Law as an Instrument of Economic Policy: Comparative and Critical Approaches*, Berlin and New York: De Gruyter.

Daintith, T. (1997) 'Regulation', *International Encyclopedia of Comparative Law*, Vol. XVII, State and Economy, Tübingen: Mohr Siebeck.

Dale, W. (1988) *British and French Statutory Drafting*, London: Institute of Advanced Legal Studies.

Delvolvé, P. (1998) *Droit Public de l'Économie*, Paris: Dalloz.

Demarigny, F. (1996) 'Independent administrative authorities in France and the case of the French Council for Competition', in G. Majone (ed), *Regulating Europe*, London: Routledge.

Doern, G.B. (1998a) 'The Interplay among Regulators: Mapping Regulatory Institutions in the United Kingdom, the United States and Canada', in G.B. Doern and S. Wilks (eds), *Changing Regulatory Institutions in Britain and North America*, Toronto: University of Toronto Press.

Doern, G.B. (1998b) 'Approaches to Managing Interdependence among Regulatory Regimes in Canada, the United Kingdom, and the United States', in G.B. Doern and S. Wilks (eds), *Changing Regulatory Institutions in Britain and North America*, Toronto: University of Toronto Press.

Doern, G.B., M.M. Hill, M.J. Prince and R.J. Schultz (1999) 'Canadian Regulatory Institutions: Converging and Colliding Regimes', in G.B. Doern, M.M. Hill, M.J. Prince and R.J. Schultz (eds), *Changing the Rules: Canadian Regulatory Regimes and Institutions*, Toronto: University of Toronto Press.

Dyson, K. (1992a) 'Theories of Regulation and the Case of Germany: A Model of Regulatory Change', in K. Dyson (ed.), *The Politics of German Regulation*, Aldershot: Dartmouth.

Dyson, K. (1992b) 'Regulatory Culture and Regulatory Change: Some Conclusions', in K. Dyson (ed.), *The Politics of German Regulation*, Aldershot: Dartmouth.

Esty, D.C. and D. Geradin (eds) (2001) *Regulatory Competition and Economic Integration: Comparative Perspectives*, Oxford: Oxford University Press.

European Commission (1994) *The system of administrative and penal sanctions in the Member States of the European Communities*, Brussels: Office for Official Publications of the European Communities.

Faber, H. (1992) *Verwaltungsrecht*, 3rd edn, Tübingen: Mohr.

Faure, M., J. Finsinger, J. Siegers and R. Van den Bergh (eds) (1993) *Regulation of the Professions: A Law and Economics Approach to the Regulation of Attorneys and Physicians in the US, Belgium, the Netherlands, Germany and the UK*, Antwerp: Maklu.

Foster, C.D. (1992) *Privatization, Public Ownership and the Regulation of Natural Monopoly*, Oxford: Blackwell.

Freund, E. (1931) *Standards of American Legislation*, Chicago: University of Chicago Press.

Freund, E. (1932) *Legislative Regulation*, New York: Commonwealth Fund.

Froud, J., R. Boden, A. Ogus and P. Stubbs (1998) *Controlling the Regulators*, Basingstoke: Macmillan.

Goldschmidt, H.W. (1937) *English Law from the Foreign Standpoint*, London: Pitman.

Graham, C. (1998) 'The Office of Telecommunications: A New Competition Authority', in G.B. Doern and S. Wilks (eds), *Changing Regulatory Institutions in Britain and North America*, Toronto: University of Toronto Press.

Graham, C. and T. Prosser (1991) *Privatizing Public Enterprise: Constitutions, the State, and Regulation in Comparative Perspective*, Oxford: Oxford University Press.

Grenfell, M. (1999) 'Can Competition Law Supplant Utilities Regulation?', in C. McCrudden (ed.), *Regulation and Deregulation: Policy and Practice in the Utilities and Financial Services Industries*, Oxford: Clarendon Press.

Gunningham, N. and P. Grabosky, with D. Sinclair (1998) *Smart Regulation: Designing Environmental Policy*, Oxford: Clarendon Press.

Hill, M.M. (1999) 'Managing the Regulatory State: From "Up", to "In and Down", to "Out and Across"', in G.B. Doern, M.M. Hill, M.J. Prince and R.J. Schultz (eds), *Changing the Rules: Canadian Regulatory Regimes and Institutions*, Toronto: University of Toronto Press.

Inman, R.P. and D.L. Rubinfeld (2000) 'Federalism', in B. Bouckaert and G. De Geest (eds), *Encyclopedia of Law and Economics*, Vol. V, The Regulation of Contracts, Cheltenham, UK and Northampton, MA, USA: Edward Elgar, pp. 661–91.

Janisch, H. (1999) 'Competition Policy Institutions: What Role in the Face of Continued Sectoral Regulation?', in G.B. Doern, M.M. Hill, M.J. Prince and R.J. Schultz (eds), *Changing the Rules: Canadian Regulatory Regimes and Institutions*, Toronto: University of Toronto Press.

Jarass, H.D. (1984) *Wirtschaftsverwaltungsrecht und Wirtschaftsverfassungsrecht*, 2nd edn, Frankfurt a.M.: Alfred Metzner Verlag

Landis, J.M. (1938) *The Administrative Process*, New Haven: Yale University Press.

Lapsley, I. and K. Kilpatrick (1997) *A Question of Trust: Regulators and the Regulatory Regime for Privatised Utilities*, Edinburgh: Institute of Chartered Accountants of Scotland.

Laptev, V.V. (1978) 'Socialist Enterprises', *International Encyclopedia of Comparative Law*, Vol. XVII, State and Economy, Tübingen: Mohr Siebeck.

Larouche, P. (2000) *Competition Law and Regulation in European Telecommunications*, Oxford: Hart Publishing.

Lévêque, F. (1998) *Economie de la réglementation*, Paris: La Découverte.

Lloyd, D. (1953) *Public Policy*, London: University of London Press.

Locke, S. (1998) 'Modelling the Consumer Interest', in G.B. Doern and S. Wilks (eds), *Changing Regulatory Institutions in Britain and North America*, Toronto: University of Toronto Press.

MacAvoy, P.W. (1979) *The Regulated Industries and the Economy*, New York: W.W.Norton.

Macey, J.R. (1992) 'Organisational Design and Political Control of Administrative Agencies', *Journal of Law, Economics and Organization*, 8, 93–110.

McGarity, T. (1991) *Reinventing Rationality: The Role of Regulatory Analysis in the Federal Bureaucracy*, Cambridge: Cambridge University Press

Majone, G. (1996) 'Regulation and its modes', in G. Majone (ed.), *Regulating Europe*, London: Routledge.

Mashaw, J. (1985) 'Prodelegation: Why Administrators Should Make Political Decisions', *Journal of Law, Economics and Organization*, 1, 81–100.

McWhinney, E. (1986) *Supreme Courts and Judicial Law-Making: Constitutional Tribunals and Constitutional Review*, Dordrecht: Nijhoff.

Norway (1994) *To Regulate – Or Not: Checklist for use when deciding on instruments and new regulation*, Oslo: Royal Ministry of Government Administration

OECD (1992) *Regulatory Reform, Privatisation and Competition Policy*, Paris: OECD.

OECD (1993) *The Design and Use of Regulatory Checklists in OECD Countries*, Paris: OECD.

OECD (1994), *Improving The Quality of Law and Regulations: Economic, Legal and Managerial Techniques*, Paris: OECD.

Ogus, A. (1980), 'Economics, Liberty and the Common Law', *Journal of the Society of Public Teachers of Law*, 15, 42–57.

Ogus, A. (1990), 'Property Rights and Freedom of Economic Activity', in L. Henkin and A.J. Rosenthal (eds), *Constitutionalism and Rights: The Influence of the United States Constitution Abroad*, New York: Columbia University Press, pp. 125–50.

Ogus, A. (1992) 'Regulatory Law: Some Lessons from the Past', *Legal Studies*, 12, 1–19.

Ogus, A. (1994) *Regulation: Legal Form and Economic Theory*, Oxford: Clarendon Press.

Ogus, A. (1995) 'Rethinking Self-Regulation', *Oxford Journal of Legal Studies*, 15, 97–108.

Ogus, A. (2000) 'New Techniques for Social Regulation: Decentralisation and Diversity', in H. Collins, P. Davies and R. Rideout (eds), *Legal Regulation of the Employment Relation*, Dordrecht: Kluwer, pp. 83–98.

Page, A.C. (1986) 'Self-Regulation: The Constitutional Dimension', *Modern Law Review*, 49, 141–67.

Peacock, A. (ed.) (1984) *The Regulation Game: How British and West German Companies Bargain with Government*, Oxford: Blackwell.

Piettre, A. (1947) *Economie Dirigée d'Hier et d'Aujourd'hui: du colbertisme à notre temps*, Paris: Médicis.

Prince, M.J. (1999) 'Aristotle's Benchmarks: Institutions and Accountabilities of the Canadian Regulatory State', in G.B. Doern, M.M. Hill, M.J. Prince and R.J. Schultz (eds), *Changing the Rules: Canadian Regulatory Regimes and Institutions*, Toronto: University of Toronto Press.

Prosser, T. (1997) *Law and the Regulators*, Oxford: Oxford University Press.

Rees, R. and J. Vickers (1995) 'RPI – X Price Cap Regulation', in M. Bishop, J. Kay and C. Mayer (eds), *The Regulatory Challenge*, Oxford: Oxford University Press, pp. 358–85.

Reich, N. (1977) *Markt und Recht: Theorie und Praxis der Wirtschaftsrechts in der Bundesrepublik Deutschland*, Neuwied: Luchterhand.

Reich, N. (1984) *Staatliche Regulierung zwischen Marktversagen und Politikversagen*, Heidelberg: Mueller Juristischer Verlag.

Richardson, G. and M. Sunkin (1996) 'Judicial Review: Questions of Impact', *Public Law*, 79–103.

Sajó, A. (1999) *Limiting Government: An Introduction to Constitutionalism*, Budapest and New York: Central European Press.

Schwartz, B. and H.W.R. Wade (1972) *Legal Control of Government: Administrative Law in Britain and the United States*, Oxford: Clarendon Press.

Sunstein, C.R. (1990) *After the Rights Revolution: Reconceiving the Regulatory State*, Cambridge, MA: Harvard University Press.

Taggart, M. (1995) 'Public Utilities and Public Law', in P.A. Joseph (ed.), *Essays on the Constitution*, Wellington: Brooker's, pp. 214–64.

Tate, C.N. and T. Vallinder (eds) (1995) *The Global Expansion of Judicial Power*, New York: New York University Press.

Trebilcock, M.J. (1986) *The Common Law of Restraint of Trade: A Legal and Economic Analysis*, Toronto: Carswell.

Vogel, S.K. (1996) *Freer Markets, More Rules: Regulatory Reform in Advanced Industrialised Countries*, Ithaca and London: Cornell University Press.

Wilks, S. (1998) 'Utility Regulation, Corporate Governance, and the Amoral Corporation', in G.B. Doern and S. Wilks (eds), *Changing Regulatory Institutions in Britain and North America*, Toronto: University of Toronto Press.

Woodcock, S. (1996) 'Competition Among Rules in the Single European Market', in W. Bratton, J. McCahery, S. Picciotto and C. Scott (eds), *International Regulatory Competition and Coordination: Perspectives on Economic Regulation in Europe and the United States*, Oxford: Clarendon Press, ch. 10.

Zeckhauser, R. and M. Horn (1989) 'The Control and Performance of State-Owned Enterprises', in P.W. MacAvoy, W.T. Stanbury, G. Yarrow and R. Zeckhauser (eds), *Privatization and State-Owned Enterprises: Lessons from the United States, Great Britain and Canada*, Boston: Kluwer.

25 Privatization and regulation of public utilities: problems and challenges for developing economies
David Parker

Introduction

In recent years market liberalization and privatization have been championed as a means of spreading the benefits of globalization worldwide (Ramanadham, 1993). Policies favouring market liberalization and privatization have been advanced by economists (for example, Aharoni, 1986; Hanke, 1987; Cook and Kirkpatrick, 1988; Vickers and Yarrow, 1988; Shapiro and Willig, 1990; Boycko *et al.*, 1996) and the main international aid and trade bodies, particularly the World Bank, IMF, OECD, Asian Development Bank and latterly the World Trade Organisation (WTO) (Ikenberry, 1990: 100; Ramamurti, 1992; World Bank, 1995). In 2000 global privatization receipts rose to a record US$200bn (*Privatization International*, January 2001).

Nevertheless, in spite of, and sometimes because of, privatization, state regulation of the economy continues to grow. State regulation exists because private markets can 'fail'. Market failure is likely where (a) markets are dominated by monopolies because of economies of scale or scope in production technology; (b) there are significant external costs and benefits, so that not all gains and costs are captured by the direct participants in the economic exchange; (c) markets are incomplete, so that price signals do not produce a socially optimal allocation of resources; for instance, where markets are 'missing' or underdeveloped; (d) there are information deficiencies in markets, so that markets do not allocate resources efficiently; (e) society may decide that free market outcomes are undesirable because of the resulting distribution of income and wealth; and (f) goods are 'public goods', that is, non-rival and non-excludable in consumption, so that the economic (opportunity) costs of extending supply to additional consumers is zero or negligible.

State regulation takes various forms reflecting the type of market failure that is being addressed. The primary focus of this chapter is economic regulation designed to overcome market failure resulting from monopoly or near monopoly provision. Economic regulation is particularly appropriate where firms have a natural monopoly. Natural monopolies exist where there are economies of scale or scope in production so that competition

537

raises supply costs. This is most likely where there are important fixed costs in the form of networks, pipelines and similarly high-cost infrastructure, as in the case of the public utilities. For a long time, natural monopoly has been a rationale for state ownership, but more recently it has been interpreted as an argument for state regulation of privately owned public utilities (Vickers and Yarrow, 1988). Examples of industries where competition is restricted by the technology and economics of the industry include electricity and gas transmission and distribution, rail infrastructure, fixed line telecommunications and water and sewerage services. Elsewhere, economic regulation is concerned with policing outputs and prices where competition is underdeveloped or under attack (Littlechild, 1983). Other forms of state regulation, such as environmental, health and safety, planning, employment and consumer protection regulation, are more usually associated with the existence of externalities, incomplete markets, information problems and socially unacceptable outcomes from market transacting.

This chapter considers the problems faced when public utilities are privatized in developing countries and there is continued state regulation of the industries. The study is based on a review of the literature and on experience of working as a consultant on privatization and regulation in a number of developing and transition economies.[1] The aim is to improve understanding of the current regulatory environment in developing countries and the methods by which this regulatory environment can be improved. Although the chapter is concerned with the regulation of privatized public utilities, a number of the issues are applicable to the other forms of state regulation. Around one-third of all privatizations in developing countries since 1988 have involved the public utilities (Cook and Uchida, 2001:2). A number of the issues explored may also be of particular relevance to the transition economies.

Regulation and competition

From the 1950s to the 1970s, state economic planning and nationalization were considered to be beneficial for economic development in developing countries. During the 1980s, attention switched to the encouragement of private enterprise as the key to sustainable economic growth. State industries are now seen as the cause of, rather than the cure for, economic stagnation. Opening up economies to private capital, including foreign investment, is considered to be good for economic growth because it improves both technology and management (*Financial Times*, 11 April 2001:15). Also a competitive private sector is considered to be more economically efficient than state enterprise (Megginson and Netter, 2001). Market liberalization and the resulting economic growth is seen as essential if the UN's commitment to have the number of people living on the equivalent of one dollar a day in developing countries is to be met by 2015.

The World Bank's Private Participation in Infrastructure Project Data Base shows that between 1990 and 1999 the private sector undertook more than 1900 projects in developing economies, involving a total investment of US$560 bn. It also shows that 80 per cent of low-income countries have had some form of private participation in at least one infrastructure sector (Izaguirre and Rao, 2000). The scale of private participation in low-income economies continues, however, to lag behind that in rich and middle-income countries. Fostering private enterprise requires a favourable environment for entrepreneurship and investment, whether in large, small or micro businesses. This in turn requires reducing impediments to investment including government laws and regulations that inhibit legitimate private enterprise. Many developing countries suffer from a legacy of heavy state intervention, leading to distorted markets and resource misallocation. Privatization in developing countries cannot, therefore, be usefully separated from the need to improve the regulatory and competitive environments for enterprise and investment. Regulation policy involves ex ante control over market transactions through formal and informal rules of conduct or behaviour. Formal regulations include laws, contracts and written codes of conduct that government can and does authorize. Informal regulations involve largely uncodified practices, norms of behaviour, self-regulation and the like, which are not necessarily directly under the control of the state or susceptible to short-term state influence.

Competition policy is a matter for government directly and is concerned with ex post regulation of the outcomes of private markets or with protecting consumers and improving economic efficiency by policing market behaviour. Whereas some countries, such as New Zealand and Australia, have emphasized competition policy at the federal level in order to control behaviour in privatized public utilities, most countries have recognized that competition law on its own may be inadequate to protect consumers from monopoly abuse. In consequence, formal regulatory systems have been created, including the establishment of either industry-level or multi-utility regulatory offices. Dedicated regulatory offices have been set up in Europe, the transition economies, Latin America, the Caribbean, parts of South and East Asia and in Africa, especially for the telecommunications and electricity sectors. The degree of 'independence' of these regulators from day-to-day political interference varies, however, and, even where there is intended to be a large degree of independence, this may be compromised at times of economic difficulty or political upheaval. For example, in Hungary electricity prices agreed with the regulator, the Energy Office, were later reduced by the government. It is important to appreciate, therefore, that regulation policy is nested within a framework of wider state actions, which are themselves nested within formal and informal rules of conduct and behaviour relating to enterprise and investment in the economy.

Where competition is restricted, costs may be inflated and, to maximize profits, prices will exceed marginal costs. It is therefore in the interest of economic welfare for the state to intervene to regulate prices and outputs in the market and to regulate the market to introduce and maintain competition. In public utilities, especially in the early years after the privatization of a dominant state-owned supplier, all of the problems associated with monopoly abuse may exist, notably lax cost control, poor attention to consumer wants and inflated prices. Also, even though over time competition may develop in some activities, conditions of 'natural monopoly' will continue to prevail where the costs of installing competitive networks (for example, electricity lines, gas pipelines or railway infrastructure) make competition uneconomic (Klein, 1998) or where the market is insufficiently large to sustain a number of competing operators operating on an efficient scale. In such cases a public policy response is required when firms are privatized: possible solutions involve the application of competition law to prevent anti-competitive behaviour (such as predatory pricing or other market 'entry barriers' used by the dominant firm) and the removal of trade controls through market liberalization measures. Another response is either to reconfigure existing regulatory institutions or to introduce new ones to promote economic efficiency. Sometimes all of these responses will be necessary if private markets are to develop successfully.

When competition exists, resource allocation through unimpeded markets will usually produce higher economic welfare than resource allocation through state planning. State ownership in developing countries has been associated with waste and, more specifically, the inefficient employment of labour and the squandering of capital. Prices and outputs are commonly politically rather than economically determined, resulting in lower social welfare (see Chapters 2 and 3). Recognition that competition can bring welfare gains, even in markets where production was thought to be a natural monopoly, has been a significant driver of privatization and market liberalization in the public utilities. At the same time, however, it should not be forgotten that, where the state or a state regulator artificially stimulates market entry, leading to production on a suboptimal scale, economic welfare will also be reduced.

Table 25.1 provides a general schema for assessing the regulation of public utilities. The general argument is that state ownership is associated with monopoly markets and 'low-powered' incentives to be efficient. The state is likely to be a more lenient supplier of capital for investment than private shareholders, who require a reasonable expectation of a sound

Table 25.1   A schema for assessing the regulation of public utilities

	State-owned & regulated	Privatized & 'independently' regulated	Private & non-regulated
Market	Suitable where natural monopoly	Suitable where natural monopoly	Market should be competitive
Efficiency incentives	Low-powered (non-profit)	Varies depending on private property rights the efficiency and effectiveness of the regulation	High powered (profits)
Potential for regulatory and political capture	High	Moderate	Low
Regulatory transaction costs	High	Varies depending on the efficiency and effectiveness of the regulation	Low
Regulatory risk (risk to taxpayers or investors)	High	Varies depending on the nature of the regulation	Low

return on their investments. In a competitive product market it is to be expected that inefficient suppliers will fail to attract customers and therefore will not survive. It is the case, however, that in developing countries both product and capital markets are generally underdeveloped and far from complete. Some firms may have large market shares and market entry may be difficult or impossible because of market dominance and state controls. Therefore the extent to which efficiency incentives improve under privatization will be heavily influenced by the type of competitive and regulatory environment that is put in place. In particular, inconsistent and opaque regulation is likely to frighten-off investors and stymie the development of both product and capital markets.

As Table 25.1 also indicates, whereas state ownership is associated with high regulatory risk arising from direct management of industry, privatization with 'independence' in regulation is intended to lower regulatory risk. Management then runs the enterprises within the regulatory constraints laid down. The more these constraints are set out clearly in statute or other official documentation, the more transparent the regulation becomes for both managers and investors. A written set of rules, especially when protected by statute, is generally less easy for politicians either to change or to ignore than an unwritten understanding. Some regulatory discretion will remain, however, because not all future events and contingencies can be foreseen and specified in advance and hence the 'regulatory contract' inevitably remains incomplete. The regulatory contract is the written and more often unwritten 'rules' of the regulatory game established when the regulatory system was set up. There will be scope for the regulator to use judgment and there should be some scope for learning and adaptation, as both regulator and regulated become more familiar with the nature of the regulatory environment and appropriate regulatory responses (Parker, 1999a). But a properly functioning regulatory system will avoid the high levels of regulatory risk that arise where there is inconsistent and therefore unpredictable political intervention in industries, as often has been the case under state ownership. Also an effective regulator is one that is not 'captured' by any particular interest group within or outside the ruling political party.

As a consequence, compared with direct state ownership and control, the transaction costs of regulating monopolies are theoretically reduced. The transaction costs of regulation are the costs of directly administering the regulations plus the compliance costs for industry, including distortions to investment and employment policies. The complexity and changing nature of priorities within government tend to push up transaction costs under state ownership. Under private ownership with regulation, the intention is that the transaction costs be reduced, although they will still exist; their degree will depend upon the efficiency of the competitive and regulatory systems in terms of minimizing administrative and compliance costs, while also remaining effective in promoting social welfare or the public interest. Regulatory offices should aim to operate efficiently, at low cost, and effectively in terms of achieving public interest objectives.

Regulation is a proxy for competition following privatization, attempting to achieve allocative and productive efficiency and therefore a Pareto optimal solution. However, in practice, 'perfect' regulation no more exists than 'perfect' markets. In practice, economic regulation involves a complex balancing act between promoting the interests of consumers (lower production costs and prices and good quality of service) and the interests of taxpayers (minimal tax-financed subsidies), ensuring adequate returns to investors so that the proper investment needs of the industry are met (shareholders should earn at least a normal return on capital invested) and encouraging the development of competition (competitors will be attracted to markets where super-normal profits are earned). Also the regulator has to identify those parts of the business where competition can thrive and has to take into consideration social and environmental issues (for example, when removing cross-subsidization of services). Achieving an acceptable balance between these regulatory objectives is never likely to be easy – for example, especially controversial is establishing the level of 'normal' profit – and for this reason regulators may have to expect criticism from both producers and consumers (Souter, 1994).

Given the various goals that regulators must balance, in general, although competition cannot be considered 'first best' if natural monopoly exists, regulation will be 'second best' to competition no matter what precise form it takes. For example, a perfectly implemented price cap form of regulation may overcome some of the economic costs of rate of return or cost of service regulation, used extensively in the USA and elsewhere – notably cost padding and overinvestment (Averch and Johnson, 1962; Kahn, 1995:47–112). A price cap provides what are recognized economic advantages in terms of providing incentives for management to pursue productive efficiency, but it still has important drawbacks. In particular, it has not proved, as intended (Littlechild, 1983), much less complex to administer than rate of return regulation (Foster, 1992; Vass, 1999). Price cap regulation requires information on, for example, the relationship between production costs and volumes produced, the scope for productivity improvements, future input price changes (such as wages), the state of the current asset stock and the optimal depreciation allowance, the correct method for allocating joint and common costs to the regulated activities, and the appropriate cost of capital (Armstrong *et al.*, 1994; Alexander and Irwin, 1996; Vass, 1999). These are much the same information needs as enter into the setting of profits under rate-based regulation and the same regulatory errors of judgment can arise (see also

Chapters 22 and 23). The result is likely to be disagreements over regulatory decisions and the means by which the decisions have been reached, sometimes spilling over into the political arena. In the UK, the price cap has been associated with an adverse public reaction to some of the profits the regulated companies have made: under the price cap, it is prices, not profits, that are directly regulated (Parker, 1997; Saal and Parker, 2001).

In general, the following are areas for potential conflict between regulator and regulated, irrespective of the precise form the regulation takes:

1. the rights of regulators to obtain information, which they consider they need to regulate effectively; this reflects the inherent information asymmetry in regulated markets, as discussed further below;
2. the proper valuation of the capital stock, asset values and the cost of capital when setting regulatory rates of return;
3. the extent to which the regulator should be allowed to alter 'the rules of the game', for instance over what is the level of depreciation charge that should be permitted to enter into a company's cost structure when setting prices;
4. the extent to which the regulator should favour new operators over the incumbent firm so as to promote competition where possible. The regulator may need to tilt 'the playing field' to encourage new entrants in the face of market dominance by the incumbent operator by providing especially favourable conditions for market entry, including obstructing a competitive response by the incumbent. The regulator will need to intervene to ensure that new entrants can access the incumbent's network at a reasonable charge by regulating network access and interconnection charges (Armstrong *et al.*, 1996).

An attempt may be made to measure the expected net welfare effects of privatization with regulation of public utilities using some kind of 'regulatory impact assessment' (Lee, 2002). But, while the intended benefits of a proposed regulation are usually well articulated, the costs may be much more opaque and speculative. The major costs are usually as follows:

●   *Reduced efficiency incentives.* Regulation produces distortion to prices and outputs. Prices are unlikely to be those that would have arisen in a competitive environment because the regulator lacks the information needed to set such prices and regulators can easily slip into being regulators 'of competition' rather than regulators 'for competition' (Burton, 1997).
●   *Costs of administration and compliance.* When assessing the economic impact of regulation two sets of costs need to be included: (a)

the compliance costs falling on the private sector, and (b) labour and capital costs borne by the regulatory agencies (these are passed on to the private sector in the form of taxation or levies). The costs to government of running regulatory offices will usually be accounted for in public spending, but often the larger economic costs involve the impact of regulation in terms of resulting economic distortions and the costs imposed on the private sector by having to comply with the regulations. These costs are often invisible or concealed and do not enter into national accounting statistics directly (Stein *et al.*, 1995; Hopkins, 1995). Where regulation compliance costs have been estimated, as in the USA, they are said to total around $700 bn (for a slightly lower estimate of $660 bn, see Leach, 2000: 78). This contrasts with a figure for direct regulatory costs borne by federal agencies of some $25 bn (Hopkins, 1996, cited in Blundell and Robinson, 2000), though to this needs to be added the costs of the large regulatory machine at the state level in the USA. However, any dampening effects of regulation on entrepreneurship, innovation and technological change are difficult to quantify.

- *Information asymmetries.* Information asymmetries lead to information rents or profits that reflect one party's information advantage over another (an example of what Williamson (1985) calls 'opportunistic behaviour'). The regulator and the regulated companies have different levels of information and the companies can be expected to exploit their advantage when negotiating prices, profits and outputs. The companies will have superior information about their costs of production, future investment plans and price elasticities, while the function of the regulators is to encourage and cajole companies to supply this information so that appropriate regulatory decisions can be made. For example, only when the regulatory office has a good idea about the price elasticities of the companies' outputs and their cost functions can it set prices to achieve a normal profit. This leads to increasingly detailed information requirements from firms in terms of annual returns, regulatory accounts and so on. The regulator may use comparative efficiency or 'yardstick competition' techniques to improve information, such as comparing performance across various domestic producers or domestic with international producers, and may undertake parametric and non-parametric estimations of production costs. In the UK, regulators have used all of these methods,[2] but the results are controversial and, for useful comparative analysis to be undertaken, there needs to be a number of firms operating under the same or at least similar cost and demand conditions.

- *Regulatory risk.* Regulatory risk is associated with the information asymmetries inherent in regulation. Regulatory risk arises from the nature of the regulatory rules (the degree of inherent risk implied by the form of regulation adopted) and uncertainty about the interpretation the regulator may place on the rules. The regulated companies must enter into investment programmes often involving appreciable sunk costs. Once having invested, the regulated companies can suffer from the 'hold up' problem (Hart and Moore, 1988). The regulator can drive down prices towards the short-run marginal (or avoidable) costs of production, leading to financial loss to investors. In other words, wherever there are sunk costs, as inevitably there are in public utilities which have large, dedicated investments in pipes, transmission lines, water treatment plants and so on, the regulated companies are at risk. This regulatory risk arises from uncertainty about the future actions of the regulator at the time of the investment decision. Management will need to take a view on the likely evolution of the regulatory environment over the life of a capital investment, which is a particularly hazardous piece of speculation when regulators and governments can and do change. In consequence, to compensate for the inevitable regulatory risk at the time of an investment, investors are likely to demand sovereign guarantees, thus transferring risk to the government, or require a 'risk premium' on their investments, leading to a higher cost of capital and therefore lower investment.
- *Regulatory capture.* Regulatory capture including political capture is a form of rent-seeking behaviour. Regulation may be captured by the interests of the regulated and therefore cease to work in favour of the general public interest (Stigler, 1971; 1988; Posner, 1974; Peltzman, 1976; High, 1991) or it may be manipulated by politicians to meet political goals or to pay off political supporters. In more extreme cases, regulation may be championed by special interests and designed to maximize their economic rents from the outset (Stigler, 1988). On cost–benefit grounds, individual taxpayers may feel that it is not worthwhile actively challenging the introduction of new regulations, whereas those likely to gain most from the new regulations (a much smaller number, perhaps a very small minority) will have every incentive on cost–benefit grounds to lobby hard for regulatory changes in their favour. Moreover, once the regulatory system is introduced, the regulators may themselves become active rent seekers, opposing any steps to reduce their power and perks: 'The self-interest of regulators will, in general, make them tend to exaggerate benefits, under-estimate costs and over-estimate the demand for action on their part' (Blundell and Robinson, 2000:11). Such

arguments lead to the conclusion that regulation will be expanded beyond the economically efficient level: 'there is a remorseless tendency for government regulation to be pushed to levels at which marginal social benefits are well below marginal social costs' (Ricketts, 2000: ix). These arguments suggest that state regulation will tend to be oversupplied. An oversupply of regulation is further encouraged by a lack of adequate national accounting for regulatory costs. If the bulk of regulatory costs are external, in the sense that they fall on other parties than government in the form of compliance costs, it is to be expected that regulation will be expanded by government beyond its economically efficient level. The expectation is that government will expand regulation to the level where the marginal benefit to government is equal to the marginal cost to government, which will be a level at which the marginal social cost of the regulation exceeds the marginal social benefit. This is likely to be particularly so where governments are not dependent on the ballot box for re-election. The ballot box acts as an indicator, albeit a crude one, of public opposition to regulatory costs.

The objective of regulation should be to protect the consumer; while providing an environment where the industry can invest with a high degree of confidence that profits legitimately made are not eroded by vexatious regulation. This is difficult to achieve for the reasons set out above. Also regulation influences the nature of the markets that evolve. Instead of resources being attracted to areas of greatest consumer demand, with potentially the highest welfare gains, they are attracted to areas where market access is permitted or encouraged by the regulator or short-term profits are highest given the regulatory constraints. In consequence, state regulation has the potential to distort economic activity severely. It also has the potential to crowd out market solutions to social and economic problems. For example, in the absence of state regulations, voluntary industry standards, market quality marques and private insurance might evolve to provide a superior (lower social cost, higher social benefit) solution to potential externalities and information problems (for examples, albeit from developed countries and mainly the USA, see Blundell and Robinson, 2000: 18–29; Yilmaz, 2000: 90–91). It is also suggested that, where the market introduces self-regulation or other forms of substitutes for state regulation, the result is much lower regulatory costs because of the resulting competition amongst suppliers of these alternative solutions. Moreover, such market alternatives may also be more flexible than state regulation, in the sense of more quickly evolving as the economic conditions change.

This line of argument suggests that the removal of state regulation could produce considerable economic gain (Winston, 1993; Molitor, 1996), but this is true only if efficient market solutions exist and this is not obvious in the case of privatized public utilities which retain considerable market power. Indeed, there will always be some natural monopoly, such as in distribution and transmission systems for power and pipelines for water and gas. In such cases attention needs to be paid to developing an efficient and effective state regulatory system to avoid monopoly abuse. Also, if the regulator is to be successful in promoting competition over time in areas of the public utilities' activities that are not naturally monop- olistic, such as electricity generation, attention needs to be applied to developing and policing network access rules and interconnection charges for those parts which are, such as access for generators to electricity trans- mission and distribution systems (Armstrong *et al.*, 1996). In general there tend to be three broad phases to the evolution of public utility reg- ulation after privatization, as illustrated in Figure 25.1. The first phase of privatization is associated with regulating the incumbent monopoly; a second stage involves policing the developing competition and establish- ing and monitoring infrastructure access rules to ensure that the domi-

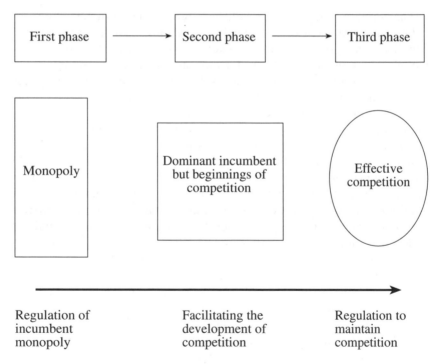

Figure 25.1   Privatization of public utilities: the three phases

nant firm does not crush new entrants to the industry; and a third stage is concerned with maintaining the effective competition that eventually develops. The latter stage is probably best served through the use of national competition laws rather than dedicated regulatory offices. In other words, the three phases are associated with a movement from ex ante to ex post regulation of markets. It is also important to appreciate that few developing countries appear to have progressed much beyond the first stage for any of their network industries. It may also be the case that, given the characteristics of developing country markets, especially their size, competition may be difficult to develop, although one possible way forward is concession agreements, franchising and so on to operate the monopoly for a given period. In this case, while there is no competition *in* the market, there is periodic competition *for* the market, though allocating contracts can quickly fall victim to regulatory capture and even outright corruption.

Institutions and institutional reform
The UK Department for International Development's Enterprise Development Strategy document (DFID, 2000) refers to the need for 'reasonable regulation' (para.3.2.1) and 'competent legal and regulatory institutions' (para.3.6.2) in developing countries. But to achieve this end requires a sensitive appreciation of institutional structures. There is a need to understand the meaning of 'reasonable regulation' and what are 'competent legal and regulatory institutions' within the specific context of each economy. Peter Evans warns that 'exogenous inspirations . . . build on indigenous institutional foundations' (Evans, 1995:243) and the institutional context is increasingly recognized by economists as being critical to any explanation of long-term economic performance.

One of the leading advocates of 'institutionalism', the Nobel prize-winning economist Douglass North (North, 1990, 1991), defines the term 'institution' widely to include any constraint that individuals devise to shape human interaction (North, 1990:4). Therefore institutions include formal constraints, notably laws, constitutions and rules, as well as informal constraints, such as norms of behaviour, customs, conventions and 'culture', including tradition and trust relationships (on the role of trust in economies, see Fukuyama, 1995; De Laat, 1997; on the related importance of 'reputation' in economic transacting, see Klein, 1997). What is common to all institutions is that they are a product both of history or cumulative social learning and of current conditions and they determine the context within which privatization and state regulation are embedded. For example, trust lies at the core of effective regulation. As Lapsley and Kilpatrick (1997:4) comment:

At the heart of the effective regulation of utilities sits the question of trust: the extent to which consumers, employees and the government can trust the individuals selected to act as regulators. In particular, the extent to which they can be trusted to discharge their discretionary powers effectively and the extent to which the regulator can trust the regulatee to act in a manner which may not exploit any advantage, e.g. informational, actual or perceived, which it has over the regulator.

Privatization and regulation policies can be distorted creating considerable economic damage, as discussed above, and the degree of such failure is governed by the institutional context (see also Chapter 24). Privatization and regulation in a country with poorly developed governmental institutions, including weak democratic and legal foundations, cronyism and outright corruption, are most likely to be associated with high economic net costs. Countries with weak governments and judiciaries and with histories that do not promote trust relationships are likely to produce high regulatory risk. In these countries decisions made behind closed doors and in response to minority political influences create an environment that is not conducive to private investment and enterprise. Regulatory and political capture, if not already endemic, will be a constant threat.

Trust is linked to regulatory risk and to wider issues relating to the context within which privatization and regulation are introduced and developed. The institutional context drives how and why privatization and regulation evolve, the forms they take and do not take, and their results. Private property rights may be ill-defined and ill-protected; for example, contracts may be difficult to negotiate and may be subject to repudiation with no or limited legal redress. In general, there may be a lack of respect for 'the rule of law'.

State regulation can both damage and benefit economic growth, depending upon its form and the manner in which it is implemented (Guasch and Hahn, 1999). Experience suggests that, to minimize regulatory risk and maximize regulatory effectiveness following privatization:

- the rules of the regulation game need to be set down clearly for regulators and investors, preferably by statute;
- to protect their 'independence' from special interests, regulators should not be open to summary dismissal;
- appointments to regulatory bodies should be on the basis of ability and not be the result of political patronage;
- regulatory offices should be adequately staffed in terms of required skills (economic, financial, engineering and administrative expertise) and should have adequate budgets to pay competitive wage rates to attract and retain skilled staff and to finance their proper functions.

Where regulators' budgets and the levels of pay of regulatory staff are subject to political whim, capture by politicians is more easily achieved; indeed, it may be inevitable.

The legitimacy of a regulatory system depends upon public confidence and is associated with proper *accountability, transparency, proportionality, targeting* and *consistency*: see Figure 25.2. Accountability means that regulators, while having a large degree of day-to-day operational independence, work within clearly agreed rules and are democratically accountable for their actions. Transparency requires that all relevant parties be involved in the process by which regulatory decisions are reached and that the way regulatory decisions are made be open and explained. Proportionality means that the regulation should be proportional to the market failure to be tackled – the regulations should not be excessive in relation to the problem. Targeting refers to ensuring that regulation is properly aimed at the problem and does not spill over into unintended areas. Consistency requires a high level of uniformity and continuity in regulation so as to avoid unpleasant surprises for investors, reduce regulatory risk and develop trust between the regulator and the regulated (Haskins, 2000:60)

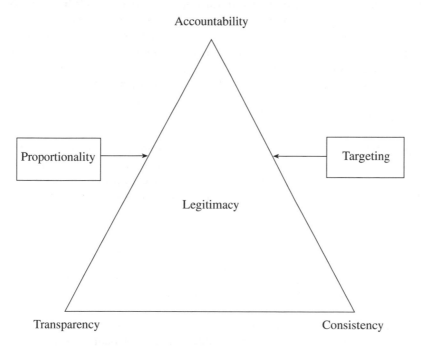

Figure 25.2   Regulatory legitimacy

Deciding on the most appropriate institutional structure for efficient and effective regulation in a particular country requires addressing the political and economic environment in which the regulation is to be established (Lapsley and Kilpatrick, 1997; Parker, 1999a; 1999b; 1999c). In some countries separation of regulation from day-to-day politics may be problematic, especially where prominent politicians and government supporters are appointed to positions of regulator. Eggertsson (1997:8) comments: 'In a society that lacks trust and commercial morality, where the rule of law does not constrain actors, where political checks and balances are weak, and where the enforcement of third party exchange is unreliable, control structures that are optimal for a ruling coalition may bring poor global economic results.' In general, regulation is most soundly based in countries where there is a tradition of professional public administration, low corruption and cronyism, and where a political decision to allow some degree of regulatory independence carries credibility. In many parts of the world, such conditions do not exist: a strong administrative tradition, continuity in democratic politics and an impartial administration and judiciary are absent (Levy and Spiller, 1996). In these countries, any attempt to introduce effective regulatory policies may at best be partial in its benefits and transitory in nature. For example, in Central and Eastern Europe, the institutional framework for an efficient market economy – from well-defined and protected property rights to business ethics conducive to mutually beneficial market transacting – did not exist in 1989, and in some of the countries they are still largely absent. The underlying political and economic uncertainty and the untested nature of these new 'democracies' has created a context in which regulatory legitimacy cannot be taken for granted. Equally, the recent economic crisis in East Asia has reintroduced political involvement in prices and investments in a number of countries. In Asia, Latin America and Africa, both traditions of political intervention in the economy and bouts of political and economic instability often undermine any likelihood of long-term regulatory consistency. Relevant in this context is a recent comment on the 1997 East Asian financial crisis in a publication from the World Bank:

> The East Asian financial crisis has shown how systemic failure of corporate governance can exacerbate macroeconomic difficulties. Above all, the crisis highlights the dangers of poor financial disclosure, inconsistent accounting standards, perfunctory board oversight, excessive corporate leverage, bad banking practices, thin and unregulated capital markets, and lack of expeditious bankruptcy and takeover laws. (Smith, 1999:1)

Regulation and poverty reduction
In developing countries, poverty reduction is a critical objective, with poverty defined in terms both of material deprivation and of a lack of

opportunity for individuals to contribute fully to their community. Competition and regulation policies can promote poverty reduction as well as detract from existing poverty alleviation policies. The result will depend upon the form the policies take and the existence of the necessary supporting economic and social institutions. This conclusion is consistent with the thrust of the reports of donor agencies such as the World Bank (1995) and the Asian Development Bank (*Financial Times*, 5 January 2001:11). In addition, although it is common to focus on regulation and large firms, for example the regulation of large telecommunications businesses, in the context of developing countries it is particularly important to consider how regulation affects small enterprises.

Competition and regulation policies can be beneficial for poverty reduction where they promote private investment, economic growth and a wider provision of services: for example, investment in electricity and mains water and sewerage supplies to rural areas and shanty towns around the major cities. Such 'basic' services are taken for granted in the developed world and have 'public good' attributes through beneficial health externalities. They are also politically and socially sensitive. Governments may feel obliged to intervene and overrule 'independent' regulators even when they formally exist, especially if services are not expanded quickly enough or price rises create social discontent. In this manner, social and political imperatives may remove the legitimacy of regulation based on economic criteria such as the marginal cost pricing rule. In particular, cross-subsidies in favour of poor households may be deemed socially necessary and even politically sacrosanct, or privatization and regulation may simply be the result of vote buying and lobbying by special interest groups and the provision of 'political payoffs'. In the cases of Uganda and Zambia, it is claimed that a number of privatizations have been used to transfer assets to senior political figures and their families (Craig, 2000; Tangri and Mwenda, 2001, cited in Craig, 2001). The privatization programme in the Philippines is said to have benefited businessmen and foreign partners and the Guyana privatization programme has apparently been a 'boon to foreigners' (Ramanadham, 1995:274).

Claessens *et al.* (1999:17) recently concluded, in a study of the East Asian economies, that 'The concentration of corporate wealth and the tight links between corporations and government many have impeded legal and regulatory development, directly or indirectly'. The losers from privatization will be those interests less favoured by competitive markets, including those vulnerable to unemployment and wage cuts and therefore usually the more lowly skilled and poorly educated. Trade unions may find it more difficult to protect working conditions where competition replaces state monopolies. An increased penetration of international capital may reinforce regressive income and wealth distribution, especially in the context of global competitive pressures. In turn, this may lead to government direction to regulators to give prominence to social over economic priorities when shaping investment programmes, further complicating regulation and increasing the scope for political discretion in the regulatory process.

Privatization and regulation policies raise issues to do with what is perceived to be a 'fair' as well as an 'efficient' distribution of gains between investors and consumers (Gomez-Ibanez, 2000). Even where higher economic efficiency results from privatization and regulation initiatives, economic efficiency is only one part of social welfare. Perceptions of social justice may clash with perceived economic efficiency, most notably in terms of what are 'equitable' as against 'efficient' prices. Under the threat of competition, tariffs may be rebalanced to reflect more closely marginal costs of supply, but rebalancing inevitably involves losers as well as gainers. The extent to which the poor are being reached or the extent of service coverage is also likely to be an area of concern as privatization evolves.

Assessing the gains and losses from the privatization of public utilities in the context of a developing economy is made particularly problematic by the existing distribution of services and modes of service delivery. For example, attitudes to disconnections vary, with some countries seemingly encouraging, or at least ignoring, non-payment and unofficial connections. In some developing countries the theft of power from power lines and other forms of non-payment are commonplace, for example. Non-payers and those 'unofficially connected' may be insensitive to price changes and new service initiatives, although they will be sensitive to changes in policy on bad debts and supply policing. Similarly, price rises for mains water and sewerage to fund new investments may not adversely affect the poor as much as might have been expected. It is estimated that between 20 per cent and 30 per cent of urban dwellers in developing countries buy their water from licensees of standpipes owned by businessmen or from traditional water carriers, and therefore may be unaffected by the pricing of mains supplies. Currently, these alternative suppliers are often at best ignored or at worst discriminated against by government regulations (Baker and Trémolet, 2000:23). Where privatization leads to lower prices, this may disproportionately benefit the better off rather than the poor because they are the larger consumers of services such as electricity, water and telecommunications. By contrast, where reductions in subsidies to network industries occur, this may actually benefit the poor if the tax funds are diverted to better social uses. In other words, regulatory impact assessment is complicated in developing countries by underdeveloped private markets and the degree of price distortion and other side-effects of existing state ownership.

One particular bone of contention when introducing privatization in network industries is likely to be the universal service obligation (USO). The

USO is enshrined in legislation covering public utilities, whether publicly or privately owned, in developed economies, where all or almost all of the population even in the remotest of areas is guaranteed connection to the supply system and at a regulated charge. The same conditions do not exist in developing economies. Regulation policies may therefore be introduced to meet national targets, for example on extending electricity and mains water supplies to rural areas, while taking a position on the future of cross-subsidies between consumers. Cross-subsidies are at risk when competition is introduced after privatization because new entrants attract or 'cream skim' the most profitable consumers, removing the incumbent's ability to subsidize high-cost users. In principle, the USO and cross-subsidization can be protected by building appropriate provisions into the regulatory rules, but in practice regulatory information asymmetries may intervene; for example, the cost of extending services to some parts of the country may be unknown or, where known, may well be prohibitive. Also competition may be stymied by the continuation of cross-subsidies. More generally, there will tend to be inherent conflicts between protecting poor consumers from price rises and the need in developing economies to create a profit-making environment conducive to attracting the necessary domestic private and foreign capital to achieve service improvements. Where the aim is to protect poorer consumers from less affordable supplies, possible solutions such as 'lifeline tariffs' may be needed: lifeline pricing involves subsidies for the first (deemed essential) block of supply, with market prices for the remainder. However, such tariffs perpetuate allocative inefficiency and can interfere with the creation of a truly competitive market populated by commercial enterprises.

Much of this discussion must by its nature remain speculative because so little is known about the nature and impact of privatization, market liberalization and state regulation in developing countries. For example, where block or lifeline tariffs have been implemented to promote supplies to the poor, there appears to have been little or no study of their longer-term results. The purpose of future research should be to explore the precise effects of competition and regulation policies, through both theoretical developments and country case studies. The aim should also be to develop a coherent methodology for undertaking competition and regulatory impact assessments (ex ante and ex post) in developing countries.[3]

Conclusions

This chapter is exploratory and conceptual. It is intended to highlight issues that are likely to be important in understanding and assessing the outcomes in developing countries of privatization with state regulation of public utilities. To date, most privatization and regulation research has been concerned with developed economies, but it is not self-evident that the lessons from these economies are readily transferable to developing nations, which have their own particularly acute economic problems and social and political constraints (see, for example, Chapter 15). Although some guidance exists, as set out above, regarding the appropriate framework for obtaining regulatory legitimacy, there is a need for each developing country to construct the form of regulation that best meets its needs, after taking into account its own specific institutional context.

At the same time, effective regulatory laws need to be established at the time of privatization if investment is to be attracted into the public utilities. A sensitive balancing act is inherent in all state regulation, involving weighing the interests of consumers, investors and taxpayers. The competitive and regulatory system needs to be devised, therefore, so as to ensure an equitable as well as an economically efficient distribution of gains between different interest groups, while avoiding, as far as possible, regulatory capture. Where this is not achieved, perhaps because of the lack of a strong and effective administrative tradition within government and an independent judiciary, privatization with state regulation may at best be ineffective and at worst inefficient and inequitable in its effects.

State regulation occurs because of market failure and, more specifically, in the case of public utilities, natural monopoly in the production technology, which rules out or limits competition. But 'state failure' also exists, leading to allocative and productive inefficiencies. When considering the nature of competition and regulatory interventions by government in developing countries, it is appropriate to remember Alfred Marshall's reply when asked whether government intervention was required to solve a particular economic problem: 'Do you mean government, all wise, all just, all powerful, or government as it now is?' (cited in Blundell and Robinson, 2000:4). Discussion of competition and regulation policy in developing economies needs to be especially sensitive to the nature and drivers of government policies, which may not be primarily economic. In other words, the development of a methodology for privatization and regulatory impact assessment for developing countries requires a sensitive appreciation of the institutional context in which economic policies are both formulated and implemented.

Notes

1. These countries include Cyprus, Jamaica, Malawi, Malaysia, Mexico, South Africa, Taiwan, Trinidad, Uganda, Estonia, Lithuania and Russia. The author is also a member of the UK's Competition Commission and Economic Advisor to the Office of Utilities Regulation in Jamaica. The author writes in a personal capacity, however, and none of the comments in this chapter should be attributed to either the Competition Commission or the Office of Utilities Regulation. The review of the literature arises from research undertaken in the Centre on Regulation and Competition in the Institute for Development Policy and Management at the University of Manchester.

2. The main parametric techniques have involved various types of cost function analysis. The main non-parametric method used by regulators has been data envelopment analysis (DEA).
3. The author is involved in developing such a methodology at the Centre on Regulation and Competition at the University of Manchester.

References

Aharoni, Y. (1986) *The Evolution and Management of State Owned Enterprises*, Cambridge, MA: Ballinger.

Alexander, I. and T. Irwin (1996) 'Price Caps, Rate-of-Return Regulation and the Cost of Capital', *Private Sector*, September, 25–8.

Armstrong, M., S. Cowan and J. Vickers (1994) *Regulatory Reform: Economic Analysis and British Experience*, Cambridge, MA: MIT Press.

Armstrong, M., C. Doyle and J. Vickers (1996) 'The Access Pricing Problem: a Synthesis', *Journal of Industrial Economics*, 44.

Averch, H. and L.L. Johnson (1962) 'Behavior of the Firm under Regulatory Constraint', *American Economic Review*, 52, Dec., 1052–69.

Baker, B. and S. Trémolet (2000) 'Micro Infrastructure: Regulators Must Take Small Operators Seriously', *Private Sector*, September, 21–4.

Blundell, J. and C. Robinson (eds) (2000) *Regulation without the state . . . The Debate Continues*, Readings 52, London: Institute of Economic Affairs.

Boycko, M., A. Shleifer and R.W. Vishny (1996) 'A Theory of Privatisation', *Economic Journal*, 106, March, 309–19.

Burton, J. (1997) 'The Competitive Order or Ordered Competition? The "UK model" of utility regulation in theory and practice', *Public Administration*, 75(2), 157–88.

Claessens, S., S. Djankov and L.H.P. Lang (1999) 'Who Controls East Asian Corporations – and the Implications for Legal Reform', *Private Sector*, September, 17–24.

Cook, P. and C. Kirkpatrick (eds) (1988) *Privatisation in Less Developed Countries*, Brighton: Wheatsheaf.

Cook, P. and Y. Uchida (2001) 'Privatisation and Economic Growth in Developing Countries', Working Paper no. 7, Centre on Regulation and Competition, University of Manchester.

Craig, J. (2000) 'Evaluating Privatisation in Zambia: A Tale of Two Processes', *Review of African Political Economy*, 85, 357–66.

Craig, J. (2001) 'Privatisation and Indigeneous Ownership: Evidence from Africa', Working Paper no. 13, Centre on Regulation and Competition, University of Manchester.

De Laat, P. (1997) 'Research and Development Alliances: Ensuring Trust by Mutual Commitments', in M. Ebers (ed.), *The Formation of Inter-Organizational Networks*, Oxford: Oxford University Press.

DFID (2000) *DFID Enterprise Development Strategy*, 13 June, London: Department for International Development.

Eggertsson, T. (1997) 'When the State Changes Its Mind: The Puzzle of Discontinuity in Government Control of Economic Activity', in H. Giersch (ed.), *Privatization at the End of the Century*, Berlin: Springer-Verlag.

Evans, P. (1995) *Embedded Autonomy: States and Industrial Transformation*, Princeton, NJ: Princeton University Press.

Financial Times, 5 January 2001, 'ADB adds battle with poverty and profit and loss account', p. 11.

Financial Times, 11 April 2001, 'FDI inflow is good for growth', p. 15.

Foster, C.D. (1992) *Privatization, Public Ownership and the Regulation of Natural Monopoly*, Oxford: Blackwell.

Fukuyama, F. (1995) *Trust: the social virtues and the creation of prosperity*, New York: Free Press.

Gomez-Ibanez, J.A. (2000) *Privatization and Regulation of Transport* Infrastructure, Washington, DC: World Bank.

Guasch, J.L. and R.W. Hahn (1999) 'The Costs and Benefits of Regulation: Implications for Developing Countries', *World Bank Research Observer*, 14(1), 137–58.

Hanke, S.H. (ed.) (1987) *Privatization and Development*, San Francisco: ICS Press.

Hart, O. and J. Moore (1988) 'Incomplete Contracts and Renegotiation', *Econometrica*, 56, 755–85.

Haskins, C. (Lord) (2000) 'The Challenge to State Regulation', in J. Blundell and C. Robinson (eds), *Regulation without the state . . . The Debate Continues*, Readings 52, London: Institute of Economic Affairs.

High, J. (ed.) (1991) *Regulation: Economic Theory and History*, Michigan: University of Michigan Press.

Hopkins, T.D. (1995) *Federal Regulatory Burdens – An Overview*, London: European Policy Forum.

Hopkins, T.D. (1996) 'Regulatory Costs in Profile', Policy Study no. 132, Centre for the Study of American Business, New York.

Ikenberry, G.J. (1990) 'The International Spread of Privatization Policies', in E.N. Suleiman and J. Waterbury (eds), *The Political Economy of Public Sector Reform and Privatization*, Oxford: Westview.

Izaguirre, A.K. and G. Rao (2000) 'Private Infrastructure: Private Activity Fell by 30 Percent in 1999', *Private Sector*, September, 5–8.

Kahn, A.E. (1995) *The Economics of Regulation: Principles and Institutions*, Cambridge, MA: MIT Press.

Klein, D.B. (1997) 'Trust for Hire: Voluntary Remedies for Quality and Safety', *Reputation: Studies in the Voluntary Elicitation of Good Conduct*, Michigan: University of Michigan Press.

Klein, M. (1998) 'Network Industries', in D. Helm and T. Jenkinson (eds), *Competition in Regulated Industries*, Oxford: Oxford University Press.

Lapsley, I. and K. Kilpatrick (1997) *A Question of Trust: Regulators and the regulatory regime for privatised utilities*, Edinburgh: Institute of Chartered Accountants.

Leach, G. (2000) 'The Devil or the Deep Blue Sea?', in J. Blundell and C. Robinson (eds), *Regulation without the state . . . The Debate Continues*, Readings 52, London: Institute of Economic Affairs.

Lee, N. (2002) 'Developing and Applying Regulatory Impact Assessment Methodologies in Low and Middle Income Countries', mimeo, Centre on Regulation and Competition, University of Manchester.

Levy, B. and P. Spiller (eds) (1996) *Regulations, Institutions and Commitment*, Cambridge: Cambridge University Press.

Littlechild, S.C. (1983) *Regulation of British Telecommunications' Profitability*, London: HMSO.

Megginson, W.L. and J.M. Netter (2001) 'From State to Market: A Survey of Empirical Studies on Privatization', *Journal of Economic Literature*, XXXIX(2), 321–89.

Molitor, B. (1996) *Regulatory Reform: Some Approaches from a European Perspective*, Paris: OECD.

North, D.C. (1990) *Institutions, Institutional Change and Economic Performance*, Cambridge: Cambridge University Press.

North, D.C. (1991) 'Institutions', *Journal of Economic Perspectives*, 5, winter, 97–112.

Parker, D. (1997) 'Price cap regulation, profitability and returns to investors in the UK regulated industries', *Utilities Policy*, 6(4), 303–15.

Parker, D. (1999a) 'Reducing Regulatory Risk: The Case for a New Regulatory Contract with the Privatised Utilities', *Public Money & Management*, 18(4), 51–7.

Parker, D. (1999b) 'Regulating Public Utilities: What other countries can learn from the UK experience', *Public Management*, 1(1), 93–120.

Parker, D. (1999c) 'Regulation of privatised public utilities in the UK: performance and governance', *International Journal of Public Sector Management*, 12(3), 213–35.

Peltzman, S. (1976) 'Toward a More General Theory of Regulation', *Journal of Law and Economics*, 14, August, 109–48.

Posner, R.A. (1974) 'Theories of Economic Regulation', *Bell Journal of Economics and Management Science*, 5, 335–58.

Privatisation International, (2001) January, editorial, p. 1.

Ramamurti, R. (1992) 'Why are Developing Countries Privatising?', *Journal of International Business Studies*, 23(2), 225–50.

Ramanadham, V. (ed.) (1993) *Privatisation: A Global Perspective*, London: Routledge.

Ramanadham, V.V. (1995) 'The impacts of privatization on distributional equity', in V.V. Ramanadham (ed.), *Privatization and Equity*, London: Routledge.

Ricketts, M. (2000) 'Foreword' in J. Blundell and C. Robinson (eds), *Regulation without the . . . The Debate Continues*, Readings 52, London: Institute of Economics Affairs.

Saal, D, and D. Parker (2001), 'Productivity and Price Performance in the Privatized Water and Sewerage Companies of England and Wales', *Journal of Regulatory Economics*, 20(1), 61–90.

Shapiro, C. and R.D. Willig (1990) 'Economic Rationales for the Scope of Privatization', in E.N. Suleiman and J. Waterbury (eds), *The Political Economy of Public Sector Reform and Privatization*, Boulder, CO: Westview Press; also reprinted in D. Parker (ed.) (2000) *Privatisation and Corporate Performance*, Cheltenham, UK and Northampton, MA, USA: Edward Elgar.

Smith, S. (1999) 'Dear Readers', *Private Sector*, September, 1.

Souter, D. (1994) 'A Stakeholder Approach to Regulation', in D. Corry, D. Souter and M. Waterson, *Regulating our Utilities*, London: Institute for Public Policy Research.

Stein, P., T.D. Hopkins and R. Vaubel (1995) *The Hidden Costs of Regulation in Europe*, London: European Policy Forum.

Stigler, G. (1971) 'The Theory of Economic Regulation', *Bell Journal of Economics and Management*, 2, spring, 3–21.

Stigler, G. (ed.) (1988) *Chicago Studies in Political Economy*, Chicago: University of Chicago Press.

Tangri, R. and A. Mwenda (2001) 'Corruption and Cronyism in Uganda's Privatization in the 1990s', *African Affairs*, 100, 117–33.

Vass, P. (1999) 'Accounting for Regulation', in P. Vass (ed.), *Regulatory Review 1998/99*, London: Centre for the Study of Regulated Industries.

Vickers, J. and G. Yarrow (1988) *Privatization: an Economic Analysis*, Cambridge, MA: MIT Press.

Williamson, O.E. (1985) *The Economic Institutions of Capitalism: Firms, Markets and Relational Contracting*, New York: Free Press.

Winston, C. (1993) 'Economic Deregulation: Days of Reckoning for Microeconomists', *Journal of Economic Literature*, 31(3), 1263–89.

World Bank (1995) *Bureaucrats in Business: The Economics and Politics of Government Ownership*, Oxford: Oxford University Press for the World Bank.

Yilmaz, Y. (2000) 'Market-based Regulatory Mechanisms', in J. Blundell and C. Robinson (eds), *Regulation without the state . . . The Debate Continues*, Readings 52, London: Institute of Economic Affairs.

26 Restructuring, regulation and the liberalization of privatized utilities in the UK
David Saal

Introduction

A substantial proportion of the firms that have been privatized in the past 20 years had originally been nationalized because they were considered to be natural monopolies. Especially in Europe, it had been generally accepted that, because of the problem of controlling market power, the efficient operation of natural monopolies was most likely to be achieved under state ownership. Consequently, when the recent privatization and liberalization of utility industries is placed in historical perspective, it must be seen as a particularly radical departure from the previous economic consensus, a departure that not only rejected the need for state ownership, but also rejected the very idea of natural monopoly as it had been previously conceived.

This radical change occurred because the advocates of utility privatization had concluded that in many cases firms that had been previously considered a natural monopoly could in fact be broken up. Thus it was now believed to be both theoretically and practically possible to separate potentially contestable activities from the essential facility or network that was the source of the state-owned firm's natural monopoly. Moreover, it was also believed that this restructuring would result in a substantial improvement in economic efficiency, because efficiency in the new contestable market could simply be achieved through competition. Thus only the rump natural monopoly essential facility would need to be regulated. However, this result was dependent on whether a former state-owned utility could actually be successfully restructured to facilitate competition after its privatization, and restructuring to promote competition has subsequently proved to be much more difficult than was initially anticipated.

This chapter considers the history of pro-competitive restructuring in the UK, after first briefly discussing the development of economic thinking with regard to utility privatization, restructuring and liberalization. The chapter then focuses on the developments in three privatized utility industries in the UK, in order to evaluate whether the radical vision of self-regulating competitive utility markets has indeed been achieved. These utility industries are the telecommunications, gas and electricity industries, which were specifically chosen because they are generally considered to be the most successful examples of utility privatization and liberalization in the UK.[1] The chapter reveals that the introduction of competition has eventually been successful, although to varying degrees in each of these industries, and it has been far more difficult to bring about and maintain than was expected in the early days of privatization. Moreover, even when competition has been achieved after extensive and sustained restructuring efforts, a continuing and substantial need for pro-competitive regulation has remained.

Privatization and the liberalization of utilities in the UK
Since the early 1980s, the UK has privatized the majority of its natural monopoly utilities, with telecommunications (1984), gas supply (1986), water and sewerage services (1989), electricity supply (1990) and the railways (1993–6) all having been subject to privatization. The decision to privatize the utilities implied a rejection of previous arguments justifying public ownership because these industries were considered to be natural monopolies. The historic emergence of public ownership of utilities in the UK has been attributed to the difficulty of preventing the abuse of market power under private ownership without also allowing for competition that would result in the inefficient duplication of assets in industries that were characterized by large economies of scale (Pollitt, 2000). Thus the utility privatization programme implemented during the 1979–97 Conservative regime both required and nurtured a radical revision of economic thinking with regard to the efficient operation and regulation of natural monopolies (Helm, 1994).

Given the rejection of state ownership, the incentive-based $RPI - X$ price cap regulatory model, detailed by Weyman-Jones in Chapter 23, was introduced. The cost plus rate of return regulatory system popular in North America was rejected, because of that system's well-known perverse incentives, incentives which discourage cost reductions and encourage capital investments in order to expand the rate base (Averch and Johnson, 1962). In contrast, $RPI - X$ regulation was designed to mimic the incentives for cost efficiency found in competitive markets by setting a predetermined price cap. In principle, this would have the effect of transforming a price-making natural monopolist into a price-taking firm, with strong incentives to reduce costs in order to increase profitability. Given the need both to tailor the $RPI - X$ regulatory system to the special characteristics of each industry and to limit political influences on regulatory decision making, quasi-independent industry-specific regulators were given statutory regulatory powers at the time of privatization. These individual regulators were supported by newly created independent regulatory offices, including the Office of Telecommunications

(OFTEL), the Office of Gas Supply (OFGAS), the Office of Water Services (OFWAT), the Office for Electricity Regulation (OFFER) and the Office of the Rail Regulator (ORR). However, as discussed below, subsequent changes in the electricity and gas markets resulted in OFGAS and OFFER being merged to become the Office of Gas and Electricity Markets (OFGEM) under the provisions of the 2000 Utilities Act.[2]

The development of the $RPI - X$-based regulatory system was also strongly influenced by the fact that the very concept of 'natural monopoly' was also changing. This change occurred because of the growing realization that, while an essential facility or network, such as telephone lines or gas mains, may have natural monopoly characteristics, other activities carried out by the state-owned utilities did not, and were therefore potentially contestable markets in which the introduction of competition could be efficiency enhancing (see Cave, 1996; Bös, Chapter 22 above). Moreover, the development of new technologies such as digital switching in telecommunications was also expected to greatly enhance the potential for competition in what were previously considered natural monopoly industries. The proponents of utility privatization therefore believed that the introduction of competition, wherever it was possible within the former state-owned utilities, was superior to both government ownership and regulation.

As a result, UK utility privatization was not just a simple transfer of ownership from public to private hands, but also involved liberalization and structural reform of the utilities aimed at facilitating the introduction of competition. Similarly, the new regulatory system was not only designed to oversee the $RPI - X$ regulation of natural monopolies, but also placed statutory duties on the regulators to encourage competition (Markou and Waddams Price, 1999). Put most simply, the new regulatory regime rejected the assumption of monopoly as a permanent feature, and therefore imposed significant responsibilities to 'regulate for competition' on most of the industry-specific regulators (Helm, 1994). Thus $RPI - X$ regulation of natural monopolies was initially seen as only a stopgap until sufficient competition developed to allow the elimination of regulation in all or part of the regulated industries. In fact, early proponents of privatization had so much faith in the potential development of competition that they believed that the need for the regulation of British Telecom (BT) would be transitory and would wither away after only seven years (Littlechild, 1983).

Almost 20 years of subsequent experience has proved that the transition to competitive utility markets has been far more difficult to achieve than was initially expected. This is because creating and sustaining competitive markets in the previously vertically integrated natural monopoly industries requires much more regulation than the early proponents of utility privatization had believed (Helm, 2001). In particular, even in the telecommunications, gas and electricity industries, which have proved the most amenable to the introduction of competition, the creation of functioning markets has required constant regulatory pressure over many years by OFTEL, OFFER and OFGAS just to break down the dominant market position that the incumbent firms held in the potentially competitive parts of the industry (Prosser, 1999). Likewise, as competition in formerly vertically integrated natural monopolies is dependent on access to the pipe or wire network, there can be no competition without regulation to define the terms and cost of network access (common carriage) and to ensure a level playing field for all potential competitors (Helm, 2001). Similarly, detailed regulation for competition will be permanently required because such network access rules will need continuous policing and are industry-specific, thereby making general competition law insufficient to maintain competition (Prosser, 1999). Moreover, the natural monopolies associated with the pipe, wire and rail networks of the privatized utilities continue to require the regulation of prices, outputs, levels of service and quality in order to prevent the abuse of monopoly power by the privatized owners of these essential network facilities (National Audit Office, 2002).

It has therefore been necessary for policy makers to refocus their objectives, leading to a system with regulation of the non-competitive network as a natural monopoly, and the establishment and regulation of appropriate structures to facilitate competition in potentially competitive sectors (Gönenc *et al.*, 2001). Industry-specific regulation of the former state-owned natural monopoly industries has therefore remained a fundamental necessity to both promote and sustain competition and also to prevent monopoly abuse. This has led a recent commentator on UK utility privatization to argue that, while: 'regulation is [generally] a more efficient means of controlling [natural] monopoly power than is state ownership, [and] that introducing competition is [generally] superior to both . . . merely chanting . . . that all monopoly power is transitory, is to elevate hope over experience, or at a minimum to give a very generous definition to the number of years that can be included in the word "transitory"' (Stelzer, 2002:82). In other words, early hopes for the withering away of transitory regulatory regimes have been replaced by the realization that regulation to facilitate and protect competition, in even the most successfully competitive sectors within the former state-owned natural monopolies, will remain as a permanent feature. Thus, much as the faith of early Marxists, who believed that the need for the state would wither away in communist societies, was subsequently shown to be misplaced, so has the faith in the declining need for regulation in the former state-owned natural monopolies (Prosser, 1999).

Telecommunications

A particularly good example, that demonstrates how 'transitory' regulation can be in an apparently permanent state of transition, is provided by the current regulation of BT, which was the first UK utility to be privatized. Given BT's continuing effective natural monopoly position in fixed-line networks, it is unsurprising that, even 17 years after privatization, OFTEL's 2001 price review extended $RPI - X$ controls on BT's network charges until 2005 (OFTEL, 2001). More surprising, however, was the continued imposition of price controls in markets that have been viewed as potentially competitive since privatization. Thus, despite a number of early regulatory initiatives to foster competition in the industry (see Cook, 1998), including the imposition of a regulated interconnection regime that required BT to price access to its network at what has been described as the world's lowest interconnection prices (Butler, 1998) and OFTEL's efforts to impose local loop unbundling since 1999 (Michalis, 2001), OFTEL's 2001 price review extended retail domestic call rate price caps until July 2002.[3] This was because, in the regulator's opinion, while competition had been increasing, it was not yet effective enough to prevent BT's potential abuse of its market position (OFTEL, 2001).

Moreover, after a year, OFTEL further extended regulation by imposing a new four-year price cap in tandem with a new requirement on BT to market a wholesale line rental charge to its competitors (OFTEL, 2002).[4,5] Wholesale line rental was deemed necessary to promote effective competition in the retail call market because it would increase access to BT's effective monopoly network, thereby demonstrating that, even 18 years after privatization, insufficient network access was still preventing effective competition in the retail call market.[6] Thus, while the new licence conditions do offer the possibility of removing these new retail price caps before 2005 if effective competition develops, it is clear that the need to regulate BT's network access charges in order to sustain competition in the domestic calls market will not wither away; to say nothing of the continuing regulation of the rest of its natural monopoly fixed line network.[7]

The continued need for regulation of BT's domestic retail call prices is largely attributable to its operations both as the effective natural monopoly landline network operator and as a competitor in the potentially competitive domestic call market. In all such situations, the basic problem that arises is that the owner of the essential facility will have an incentive to restrict competition in the potentially competitive market by controlling the terms and conditions for access to the essential facility by rival firms (Armstrong, 1997). Moreover, even if such discriminatory practices against potential competitors did not take place, the expectation that they might occur would still deter entry into the potentially competitive market (Helm and Jenkinson, 1997). Thus the 1998 Competition Act's enforcement of access for potential suppliers to essential capital facilities (Parker, 2000) reflects UK experience. This has shown that, if networks have natural monopoly characteristics, the absence of pro-competitive regulation to ensure competitively neutral network access charges will mean the absence of competition (Helm, 2001; Gönenc *et al.*, 2001).

It is also clear that the sometimes conflicting goals of the 1979–97 Conservative regime's privatization programme have also significantly hampered the introduction of competition into several industries. Thus, in the first two utility privatizations, BT (1984) and British Gas (1986) were privatized as vertically integrated firms with no break-up of their natural monopoly elements from their potentially competitive activities, a fact which has been attributed to a greater desire to attract potential investors and maximize privatization revenues, rather than to enhance the potential for competition (Weir, 1999). Initial efforts to foster product market competition for telephone services and gas supply were therefore restricted by the competitive advantages that these firms retained in product markets because of their control of the natural monopoly networks. Thus BT's new wholesale line rental obligation should be seen as yet another manifestation of how the failure to tackle uncompetitive structural arrangements at privatization has required the movement away from the 'light-handed' regulatory systems that had been envisioned at privatization. The result is a rather tighter regime in which regulators must play the role of surrogates or even proxies for competition (Nwankwo and Richardson, 1996).

As a result of this failure at privatization, BT's market power in landline telephone networks continues to hamper competition in the retail call market, as discussed above. Moreover, a significant restructuring of BT's landline network has yet to take place. This is despite Hunt and Lynk's (1991) rather prescient argument for separation of local and long-distance operations with several local or regional networks, as in the USA.[8] This argument pointed out that BT's potential to pursue anti-competitive policies derived from its integrated operations, as well as OFTEL's potential difficulties in consistently implementing pro-competitive network access regulation. Moreover, Hunt and Lynk also provided a strong rebuttal of the continued integration of BT on natural monopoly grounds. They first suggest that, given the high income elasticity of demand for telecommunications services and the resulting rapid expansion of demand, pure scale-based justifications for BT's national network would not be justified. They also cited a previous empirical study which demonstrated that, while BT had previously exhibited scope economies between long-distance and international services, there were no scope economies between local and long-distance services (Hunt and Lynk, 1990). Moreover, while an integrated national telephone network may have been necessary because of economies of scope related to switching technologies before the digital revolution, scope economies between long-distance and local networks have subsequently been substantially reduced (Newbery, 1999). As a result, efficiency savings attributable to the joint production of local and long-distance services cannot be considered a valid argument for the continued vertical integration of BT. Thus it might have been possible to restructure BT as several regional landline networks with each above the minimum efficient scale of operation (MES).[9] Such a regional system would have retained the efficiency of having a non-duplicative natural monopoly landline network, while also providing the opportunity both to better facilitate competition for domestic calls and to better regulate the resulting regional natural monopoly networks by employing yardstick competition to spur efficiency savings (Armstrong *et al.*, 1994).

Given the failure to restructure at privatization, UK regulators have made aggressive efforts to foster competition by encouraging facilities or network-based competition to BT's network. In fact Newbery (1999:327) argues that these policies have allowed the UK to become one of the more competitive telecom markets, and that, by 1998, 'the UK telecoms market was moving through a transitional phase from dominance by a regulated incumbent to a competitive and increasingly unregulated market, where regulation is confined to bottleneck facilities, and general competition policy largely replaces detailed regulation'. Moreover, on theoretical grounds, such facilities-based competition might be a superior form of competition to the one based on an effective monopoly network with competition between the monopolist and other firms for telephone services, which has characterized fixed line telephony in the UK since privatization.[10] However, I would argue that these efforts have only been partially successful because repeated manifestations of the facilities-based strategy have not led, and probably cannot lead, to the establishment of fully effective network-based competition to BT's natural monopoly network. Moreover, this has led to difficulty in restraining BT from abusing its network monopoly in order to dominate the domestic calls market.

The duopoly policy pursued between 1984 and 1991 failed to result in Mercury Communication's network developing into an effectively competitive network, despite policies favouring Mercury, including its licensing as the sole competitor to BT. In fact, the duopoly policy, which relied heavily on the presumption of substantial economies of scale to justify the restriction of competition to two networks (Foster, 1992), has been described as having been 'detrimental to [the] development of competition, and its main beneficiary has been BT itself' (Armstrong *et al.*, 1994:240). Consequently, in 1991, the duopoly policy was abandoned and telephone call services were opened to competition, reflecting an increased awareness that competition was easier to bring about in call services than in networks.

However, facilities-based competition was still aggressively encouraged by policies that were designed to develop cable television operators as network competitors to BT. Cable operators were allowed to enter the telecoms market, but BT was restricted from entering the cable market, and firms that had made 'investments in infrastructure' were given lower regulated charges for access to BT's network than other call service providers (Michalis, 2001). Competitors to BT rapidly appeared, and by 1995 there were 150 licensed competitors, with 125 cable operators, of which 80 were actually providing phone services (Bell, 1995). Moreover, by 2002, the cable operators had extensive geographic coverage, with their networks extending to approximately 50 percent of the country. Furthermore, the introduction of competition also appears to have triggered a dramatic improvement in BT's productivity (Newbery and Pollitt, 1997), suggesting that more effective competition was created after the abandonment of the duopoly policy.

Nevertheless, it would appear that, 11 years after its introduction, this new facilities-based competition policy has still failed to create fully effective competition to BT. OFTEL concluded that BT did not face sufficient competition in network access because BT continues to provide local network services to over 80 per cent of residential and business customers. This market power allows BT to maintain domestic call prices well above those justified by its cost of capital (OFTEL, 2002). Thus, while the much heralded convergence in communications technologies has caused a significant erosion of the natural monopoly position of BT's landline telephone network in densely populated areas, this has not happened in areas that are less densely populated. This is probably because high demand, which makes the joint production of telecommunications and cable television services profitable in urban areas, is not available in less densely populated areas, thereby precluding the profitable extension of the cable networks. Consequently, this suggests that in less densely populated areas, where telephone networks may have been provided only because of BT's universal service obligations, economic efficiency requires a single natural monopoly network.[11]

Consideration of BT's new wholesale line rental obligation in the light of these arguments suggests that OFTEL has accepted that, at least in some parts of the country, BT does have a natural monopoly that will not be eroded by facilities-based competition.[12] Enforcing the availability of a regulated fixed fee line rental charge to all competitors, rather than a marginal access charge for each call, can therefore be seen as a positive policy development. It should help break down BT's ability to employ its natural monopoly in fixed line networks in order to gain competitive advantage in the domestic calls market. However, given the continuing natural monopoly characteristics of fixed telephone networks to at least 50 per cent of the UK's population, the continued abnormal profits earned by BT on calls because of its effective fixed network monopoly, and the successful divestiture of other national telephone companies into regional networks such as in the USA, it would appear that the failure to break up BT into a long-distance operator and several regional network operators continues to have a detrimental impact on development of competition even 18 years after privatization.

The gas industry
Turning to the gas industry reveals that it is similar to telecommunications, in that the introduction of effective competition in gas supply only met with limited success in the early years after privatization because of the lack of vertical restructuring of British Gas at privatization in 1986. In fact, British Gas's market power was, if anything, greater than BT's. It was given a monopoly franchise for virtually the entire gas supply market (the tariff market) except for those contract customers using in excess of 25000 therms per year, and even the subsequent 1992 reduction in the contract limit to 2500 therms still left 98.5 per cent of all customers within the monopoly franchise (Newbery, 1999). Given OFGAS's statutory obligation to promote competition in the gas industry, British Gas's extensive monopoly power caused an extremely strained relationship between British Gas and the regulator, with frequent referrals to the Monopoly and Mergers Commission (MMC) to resolve disputes. Moreover, as the British Gas privatization prospectus appears to have promised a 25 year monopoly on at least two-thirds of the UK market, a particularly troublesome problem was that British Gas had entered into a large number of long-term 'take-or-pay' contracts for gas supplies that would leave it in an uncompetitive position if competition in gas supply was further developed. Nevertheless, OFGAS's considerable efforts to promote competition did result in a significant reduction in British Gas's control of the unregulated contract market, with its market share for industrial customers falling from 91 to 29 per cent between 1991 and 1996 (Pollitt, 2000).

This particularly acrimonious regulatory period culminated in the 1993 Monopoly and Mergers Commission (MMC) recommendation to break up British Gas and the subsequent 1995 Gas Act, which corrected many of the mistakes that had been made at privatization. The Gas Act required a break-up of the gas industry into gas transport, gas shipping and gas supply, and prohibited the same firm from engaging in both the natural monopoly transport business and the potentially competitive shipping and supply businesses.[13] The Act therefore led directly to the 1997 'voluntary' break-up of British Gas. The regulated natural monopoly storage, pipeline and distribution business, Transco, and several other businesses became British Gas Plc, and the supply business became Centrica, which was allowed to continue trading as British Gas (Weir, 1999). In 2000, Transco was hived off from the remaining businesses of British Gas Plc and became the principal business of the newly listed Lattice Group.

Phased introduction of competition into the regulated tariff supply market began in April 1996 and was completed by May 1998, although British Gas was still subject to $RPI - X$ regulation of its gas supply business. However, OFGEM has now concluded that effective competition in the gas supply business exists. Thus, even though British Gas still served 67 per cent of all domestic customers, in September 2001, OFGEM concluded that the gas supply business had become fully contestable with considerable supplier switching by all types of customers. As a result, $RPI - X$ regulation of gas supply was removed (OFGEM, 2002a). It would therefore be appropriate to conclude that, despite the mistakes made at privatization, the gas industry has achieved a level of competition and liberalization that probably exceeds what had been anticipated at privatization. Moreover, this success must be attributed to the forced vertical separation of Transco's pipeline network, which facilitated the development of effective competition in gas supply and shipping at a rate which would have been previously unthinkable (Fitzgerald and Waddams Price, 2001). Given this, it is worthwhile to speculate whether full liberalization of the gas supply market could have been achieved at least a decade ago if restructuring had taken place at privatization.

The English and Welsh electricity industry
Problems related to the high degree of vertical integration in the telecommunications and gas industry, as well as an understanding of the difficulty in instituting structural change of a vertically integrated monopoly after privatization, were already apparent in the late 1980s (OECD, 2001). As a result, the need to restructure industries in order to facilitate competition became much more of a priority in later privatizations (McDaniel, 2000; Giulietti and Otero, 2002). This is particularly evident in the 1990 privatization of the electricity industry in England and Wales (E&W),[14] which resulted in the unbundling of the Central Electricity Generating Board (CEGB). The CEGB had previously operated all generation and transmission as a vertically integrated statutory monopoly, with 12 area boards acting as regional distribution and supply monopolies. The resulting privatized generating sector consisted of a duopoly of private firms (National Power and PowerGen) controlling all conventional generating capacity, and Nuclear Electric. Nuclear Electric remained in public hands until it was restructured in 1996, resulting in the privatization of its newer nuclear

power stations as British Energy and the continued public ownership of its old magnox stations by Magnox Electric. The 12 area boards became the 12 independent regional electricity companies (RECs) responsible for electricity supply and distribution, while the transmission grid became the National Grid Company (NGC). NGC was at first jointly owned by the RECs, but was later separately floated on the stock exchange, in December 1995 (Cook, 1998; McDaniel, 2000).

Initially, $RPI - X$ regulation was applied to transmission, distribution and REC supply charges, because of the natural monopoly in transmission and distribution and the initial market power of the RECs in electricity supply. The creation of 12 separate RECs owed a great deal to the previous structure of the electricity industry. However, the decision to transfer this structure was also heavily influenced by the resulting ability to employ yardstick regulation across the 12 resulting privatized firms. In contrast, all generation prices were to be determined in an unregulated Electricity Pool system or spot market, to which any licensed generator could submit bids, making generation in principle open to all. Competition in supply was also encouraged by the creation of a two-tier licence system in which the RECs held first tier Public Electricity Supply (PES) franchise licences. These first-tier licences included supply price controls as well as distribution price controls, while potential competitors in supply required a second-tier licence, which was not subject to price control. However, competition in supply was at first restricted to consumers with demand in excess of one megawatt, with other customers being supplied by one of the 12 RECs, each of which had a statutory obligation to supply any customer requesting power.

Competition was gradually extended to smaller users, with even the smallest consumers having access to potentially competitive supply markets by May 1999. Nevertheless, given the continuing dominant position of the PESs in supply, supply price caps were not yet removed. Given this, and using provisions in the 2000 Utilities Act, OFGEM has subsequently enforced a requirement that the PES supply businesses be fully managerially and operationally independent of their distribution businesses. As a result of this change, the supply and distribution activities of the PES companies are now carried out by separately licensed ex-PES supply companies and distribution network operators (DNOs), respectively. OFGEM argued that this was an essential part of introducing fully effective competition into electricity supply, as it would ensure that there was no scope for cross-subsidy or discrimination in favour of a PES supply business over its competitors (OFGEM, 2001). Thus the initial electricity privatization restructuring, which maintained links between the natural monopoly distribution network and the potentially competitive supply business, had been an obstacle to competition, much as had been the case with BT and British Gas. However, unbundling of distribution and supply appears to have rapidly eroded this barrier to competition. The ex-PES electricity supply licensees remained under supply price controls only until April 2002, when OFGEM (2002a) judged that fully effective supply competition justified the removal of price caps.[15]

The initial restructuring of the electricity industry at privatization is most often criticized for its failure to facilitate competition in the generation sector, where full competition was to have been effective from the time of privatization. This was primarily because of the market power that was transferred to the two conventional generating companies, National Power and PowerGen (McDaniel, 2000). The resulting abuse of market power within the generation sector has required the government and regulatory authorities to sanction the divestiture of generating capacity, and also forced the abandonment of the Electricity Pool (Littlechild, 2001).[16] The pool was replaced by the New Electricity Trading Arrangements (NETA) in March 2001. By 2001, there were 33 companies that were considered to be significant power generators in England and Wales, and the Herfindahl–Hirschmann index of generation concentration had declined from 2621 in 1991 to 936 in 2000. This indicates a dramatic movement to a more competitive market structure (DTI, 2001). Moreover, the NETA has been designed to weaken the power that large generators were able to exercise in the Electricity Pool. Under NETA, electricity is traded between generators and electricity suppliers through bilateral contracts and on power exchanges, with only a small volume of electricity being priced by the central balancing mechanism, through which the NGC balances output with demand (EA, 2002a).

Despite the arrival of competition, it is clear that, even though the initial electricity privatization took account of the need to restructure the privatized electricity industry in an appropriate manner to facilitate competition in generation and supply, the initial restructuring efforts must be judged a failure. Thus the English and Welsh electricity industry demonstrates the difficulties of determining an appropriate pro-competitive structure before privatization, even when privatization policy is more focused on creating competition than on maximizing privatization returns, as had been the case with the privatization of BT and British Gas. Moreover, while the forced divestiture of generating capacity and the creation of NETA appear to have successfully increased the contestability of the generation market, thereby helping to bring down electricity wholesale prices by 40 per cent since the late 1990s, it has contributed to yet another crisis. Following the reduction in wholesale prices, the privatized nuclear operator, British Energy, which provides approximately 20 per cent of the UK's electricity, cannot cover its generation costs and was on the verge of bankruptcy at the time of writing (Taylor, 2002a). This might be seen as a positive development, in the sense that British Energy's difficulties can be attributed to its inability to compete with lower-cost generation facilities such as gas turbines, meaning that competition has unleashed a beneficial process that may result in the Schumpeterian 'creative destruction' of nuclear power in the UK. At the same time, however, nuclear power provides baseload capacity, which may make it inappropriate to be subject to the same competitive rigour as other producers, who provide marginal demand. Moreover, an additional related issue is that an apparently strongly competitive generation market may hamper investments in the non-polluting and/or renewable energy projects that will be necessary in order to meet the UK government's climate change targets.[17] Thus a fully competitive generation market, which does not include appropriate pricing for negative externalities such as greenhouse emissions, may be less likely to produce improved environmental performance relative to a more regulated generation sector where the cost of environmentally positive generation techniques could be more readily passed through to consumers.[18]

It is also extremely important to note that, while the initial restructuring of electricity resulted in the unbundling of the industry, the clear vertical separation between transmission, distribution and generation that was created at privatization has not been maintained.[19] Thus, in the 1990s, most RECs took advantage of licence conditions that allowed them to develop generation facilities with a total capacity of approximately 15 per cent of their peak demand. Almost all of the resulting new capacity was in the form of combined-cycle gas turbines (CCGTs) (McDaniel, 2000). In 1996, Eastern Electricity (now TXU Europe) was allowed to buy 6000 megawatts of plant that had been divested from National Power and PowerGen, making it a significantly vertically integrated firm (Newbery, 1999) with the industry's largest generation capacity after the primary generating companies that resulted from the restructuring at privatization. Similarly, as generating capacity was divested, earlier government policies that had previously blocked PowerGen and National Power from acquiring RECs were reversed. This resulted in the acquisition of East Midlands Electricity by PowerGen in 1998 and Midland Electricity's supply business by National Power in 1999.

Moreover, following the unbundling of the supply and distribution businesses of the PESs, a dizzying amount of further reorganization has also occurred, with many of the ex-PES supply and DNO businesses for a given region coming under different ownership. Thus, in seven of the 12 regions defined by the privatized PESs, different owners now control the licensed ex-PES supply business and DNO. However, a substantial consolidation of the supply and distribution businesses has also been allowed to occur, although some of the PESs have since withdrawn from the generation business (EA, 2002a). Thus, while the 12 DNOs remain individually licensed, only eight firms now ultimately control them (see EA, 2002b). Consolidation of the ex-PES supply businesses has been even more dramatic, with only six different owners now controlling the 12 licensed ex-PES supply businesses (ibid.). It would therefore appear that a process of horizontal integration will shortly result in the consolidation of both the distribution and supply sectors to, at most, five or six firms (EA, 2002a).

Nevertheless, OFGEM's recent consultation document with regard to the now completed acquisition of SEEBOARD by London Electricity Group (LE Group) is rather sanguine with regard to the effects of this most recent merger. It cites evidence for considerable consumer switching between suppliers and the continuing existence of nine suppliers in the domestic supply market and 20 suppliers in the non-domestic supply market (OFGEM, 2002c). Moreover, this assessment does appear to be well founded, as opening up the domestic market to competition resulted in a dramatic drop of the Herfindahl–Hirschmann concentration index for domestic electricity supply from its maximum of 10000, indicating monopoly in 1997, to 924 in 1999 (DTI, 2001). Given this, there are grounds to accept the argument that the increase in co-ownership of multiple ex-PES supply businesses will only marginally increase measured supply concentration, but will create larger, more effective competitors. However, careful consideration of market share data for non-domestic supply for the 1999/2000 fiscal year indicates some cause for concern, as at that time the 12 ex-PES supply businesses had 11 unique owners and controlled 81 per cent of the over one megawatt market and 91 per cent of the 100 kilowatt to one megawatt market (ibid.). The subsequent combination of these ex-PES businesses under only six owners must have caused the concentration of both the non-domestic and domestic supply markets to increase, although not sufficiently to cause OFGEM to attempt to block the acquisition of SEEBOARD by LE Group on competition grounds.

If further consolidation of the ex-PES supply businesses under common ownership continues, there could be cause for concern. This implies that regulatory oversight to maintain competition will remain an important issue in the liberalized electricity supply market, and suggests that further mergers of the supply businesses will need to be more carefully scrutinized on competition grounds. If, as argued in Newbery (1999), both a significant degree of separation between supply and distribution and a contestable wholesale electricity market are maintained, competitive markets in both generation and electricity supply are possible even with some concentration. However, as vertical integration across generation and supply would eliminate the effectiveness of a wholesale electricity market, Newbery also warns that such vertical integration may result in an apparently unconcentrated competitive market structure, that is actually characterized by uncompetitive prices. As a result, it will be necessary for OFGEM to guard against such vertical integration if the hard-won gains of electricity generation and supply liberalization are not to be lost.

Turning to distribution, the concentration of DNO ownership raises the issue of whether OFGEM will be able to continue regulating the natural monopoly distribution business with the comparative yardstick regulation model that has been employed since privatization. This is because yardstick competition, which was originally proposed by Shleifer (1985), requires the horizontal separation of a natural monopoly essential facility in order to obtain comparative information that can be use to determine the relative efficiency of each comparator. While this separation may come at the price of reduced economies of scale or scope, the information gained can be used to set appropriate revenue restrictions on each comparator, which will create incentives to reduce costs by achieving frontier levels of efficiency (Rossi and Ruzzier, 2000). Moreover, as discussed by Sawkins (1995), the system will theoretically result in the revelation of the cost-minimizing potential of every firm, as firms will have an incentive to reveal their true efficiency levels if their resulting tariff is based on their own efficiency relative to other firms. However, if separate comparators are jointly owned by the same owner, incentives to reveal true information for a given comparator will be disrupted. This is because the owner will take into account the impact on the comparative efficiency and potential profitability of all jointly owned comparators when deciding whether to reveal the true efficiency of any given comparator. In other words, the owners of jointly owned comparators will, in principle, have both the capability and a strong incentive to manipulate the comparative efficiency measures to their benefit, thereby undermining the efficiency incentives that should obtain from yardstick competition.

Despite such concerns, OFGEM has in fact taken a relaxed policy stance with regard to the ownership of more than one DNO by the same parent company (OFGEM, 2002b). Thus OFGEM's policy appears to be that, if mergers will result in efficiency gains, they should not be blocked if those efficiency gains exceed the benefits of having an additional comparator. OFGEM therefore implicitly accepts that the benefits of the potential economies of scope and scale that may result from joint ownership of DNOs will outweigh the costs imposed because of the reduced quality of comparative efficiency measurement. However, rather than suggesting a continuing case by case cost–benefit analysis of each prospective merger, OFGEM's policy statement proposes that all efficiency savings from a proposed merger should be passed on to consumers in future distribution price reviews, and each additional merger should result in a one-off reduction in allowable revenues of £32mn for each licensed distribution company in order to compensate for the loss of comparators.[20] Moreover, OFGEM does not appear concerned with the obvious contradiction in a policy that allows mergers to occur provided that the resulting efficiency gains are passed to consumers, but also requires the merged companies to pay a penalty for undermining the very yardstick regulation system that is supposed to encourage efficiency gains. Given this, it remains to be seen whether the yardstick-based $RPI - X$ regulation of the electricity distribution system, which has been judged to have resulted in substantial past efficiency gains (National Audit Office, 2002), will continue to perform well despite OFGEM's policy of allowing firms to own more than one DNO.

A final issue which must be highlighted is the increasing interdependence of the gas and electricity markets. This interdependence led to the consolidation of OFGAS and OFFER into the Office of Gas and Electricity Markets (OFGEM) in the 2000 Utilities Act. This interdependence has come about because of factors such as the increasing use of gas in the generation of electricity, after the relaxation of EU rules forbidding this in the early 1990s, and the need to account for potential substitution between gas and electricity by final users. Gas and electricity supply businesses have converged, as for example demonstrated by the fact that the ex-PES suppliers have become major players in the gas supply business and British Gas is now a significant electricity supplier. The implication of this convergence can perhaps be best demonstrated by considering that, in the recent acquisition of SEEBOARD by LE Group, OFGEM deemed it necessary to consider the effects of the proposed acquisition on competition in gas supply, despite the fact that both firms are nominally electricity firms. In this case, the impact on gas supply competition was judged to be quite minimal as the combined group would only control 4.4 per cent of national supply and 10 suppliers would still be active in domestic gas supply after the merger (OFGEM, 2002c). However, if the gas and electricity supply firms continue their evolution into more concentrated energy supply companies, such 'cross-industry' issues will become increasingly important.

The interdependence between gas and electricity supply could be extended to the natural monopoly distribution and transmission sectors in the near future, owing to the proposed merger of National Grid and Lattice Group to form National Grid Transco.[21] This will create a single entity that would control the entire natural monopoly gas transport business as well as the electricity transmission network. This raises issues with regard to both the potential interaction and the need to ensure transparency between Transco and National Grid, given these companies' respective roles as the regulated operators of the gas distribution and electricity transmission systems. However, OFGEM believes that the retention of the current separately licensed regulatory regime will address most of these issues (OFGEM, 2002d).

A possibly more significant issue related to this merger is the need to maintain vertical separation between competitive and regulated activities, an issue which may become more difficult to resolve as the gas and electricity markets come to be increasingly controlled by a relatively small number of combined gas and electricity companies. For example, while it had been fully appropriate for National Grid to own and operate EnMo, the On-the-day Commodity Market (OCM) in gas, through which gas shippers, suppliers and Transco buy and sell gas, OFGEM has recommended the 'ring-fencing' of EnMo within the merged organization. Similarly, OFGEM has recommended new restrictions on National Grid's and Transco's licences in order to restrict their ability to buy or sell gas and electricity other than for balancing the two networks, and also has recommended the ring-fencing of the limited amount of generating capacity that is owned by Lattice Group (ibid.).

A final analysis would therefore suggest that regulatory efforts which had once been focused on maintaining vertical separation within the gas or electricity industries will now need to focus on the more difficult task of maintaining a vertically separated pro-competitive market structure in an increasingly interdependent and consolidated energy market. Moreover, given the consolidation of the DNOs under common ownership and the National Grid Transco merger, regulation of the natural monopoly elements of the gas and electricity industries will potentially become more difficult than it has been before. Thus, despite the successful introduction of competition to both the gas and the electricity markets, which can be largely attributed to past pro-competitive regulatory pressure that took place after privatization, both regulation to maintain competition and regulation of natural monopoly distribution networks will remain essential for the foreseeable future.

Conclusions

This chapter has reviewed the liberalization and restructuring of the UK's telecommunications, gas and electricity industries, which were originally nationalized on natural monopoly grounds. Its aim was to determine whether privatization had resulted in the transition to effectively competitive markets and reduced regulation, which the advocates of privatization predicted. However, it has demonstrated that, despite initially high hopes, the necessary restructuring to promote competition has subsequently proved to be much more difficult to accomplish than anticipated. Even though some of the UK's utilities have achieved substantial levels of competition, the chapter has demonstrated that the creation of functioning markets requires constant regulatory pressure over many years, including forced vertical and horizontal divestiture, just to break down the dominant market position that incumbent firms hold in the potentially competitive parts of their industries.

Much of the difficulty in introducing competition in the UK can be traced to the failure to separate essential network facilities from potentially competitive activities at privatization, as was the case with BT and British Gas. This chapter has argued that the continuing failure to address this problem is at the root of BT's continuing domestic call price regulation. Also, even though the later electricity privatization took into account that vertical restructuring was required to facilitate the development of competition, the initial restructuring that took place at privatization was not sufficient to bring about fully effective competition in either the generation or the supply of electricity. This illustrates that, while it might appear a rather trivial exercise to restructure an industry to allow for competition, the UK's experience demonstrates that it is far more difficult to implement a successful restructuring plan in practice.

Given the relatively more difficult task of restructuring industries after they are privatized, this suggests that it is perhaps appropriate that future privatizations of vertically integrated utilities should use a presumption in favour of vertical separation, with the burden of proof being on those who wish to retain a more integrated structure, as Biggar (2001) argues. However, while it has not been directly discussed in the main text of this chapter, the highly fragmented structure that was created after British Railways' recent privatization has run into difficulties that may be attributable to the loss of scope economies. It is therefore more appropriate to conclude simply that even the best designed restructuring plans are likely to require a substantial amount of post-privatization adjustment before effective competition is brought about.

The chapter has also demonstrated that, even when effective competition in potentially competitive markets is achieved, the need for a substantial regulatory system will remain. Thus, as indicated in our discussion of the electricity and gas industries, there is a constant need to monitor merger activity in the liberalized industries because of the understandable incentives of profit-maximizing firms to attempt to regain the market power that has been destroyed through the contrived vertical separation of the network from other potentially competitive activities. Likewise, as competition in formerly vertically integrated natural monopolies is dependent on access to the pipe or wire network, there can be no competition without regulation to define the terms and cost of network access and to ensure a level playing field for all potential competitors. Similarly, detailed regulation for competition will be permanently required because such network access rules will require continuous policing and are industry-specific, thereby making general competition law insufficient to maintain competition. Moreover, the natural monopolies associated with the pipe, wire and rail networks of the privatized utilities are not affected by the introduction of effective competition and will also require a permanent regulatory regime.

This chapter's review of UK experience suggests that utility privatization does not result in the withering away of the state, as early advocates of utility privatization believed. In fact, some authors argue that UK experience suggests that, while state ownership has been reduced, the increasing need for detailed regulation of the privatized utilities has meant that the state's role in the economy has not declined (Helm, 2001). Thus, while it is possible to argue that utility privatization and liberalization may bring about more efficient operation of utilities than was the case under state ownership, it is not appropriate to argue that state intervention in utility markets is itself inappropriate. If anything, the history of UK utility liberalization and privatization suggests that the continued intervention of the state through an appropriate regulatory regime will continue to remain essential.

Notes

1. I have deliberately chosen to focus on the most successful examples of utility privatization and liberalization in order to highlight the difficulties that have been encountered even when liberalization has generally been considered to be a success. Thus a discussion of British Railways, which was restructured as the natural monopoly track operator Railtrack, 25 train operating companies, three rolling stock leasing companies and approximately 70 maintenance and service companies, is not included. This restructuring, which was designed to create franchise competition for train-operating licences and competition for maintenance contracts, has resulted in a highly fragmented structure with growing concerns about safety due to a loss of accountability in the system. Moreover, following several rail crashes and the resulting disruption on the network needed to perform safety checks and maintenance, Railtrack has subsequently become insolvent and is in the process of being acquired by the not-for-profit company Network Rail, which will be backed by government guarantee.

    Another significant reason for not including railway privatization in the main text is that, despite its current difficulties, it is perhaps too early to reach robust conclusions with regard to the ultimate success of British Railways' restructuring. This is because each of the three privatizations discussed in the main text required significant changes to their initial privatization structure before liberalization was even partially successful. As British Railways' privatization was only completed in 1996, such further restructuring has not yet run its course. Nevertheless, problems associated with the fragmentation of British Railways after privatization could highlight potential problems with vertical separation when substantial economies of scope are present in a natural monopoly.

    A discussion of water privatization and restructuring has also been excluded as the industry was initially privatized in 1989 with little restructuring. This was because it was believed to have natural monopoly characteristics which would make it difficult to facilitate competition in the industry (Armstrong *et al.*, 1984). Given that it was judged to have traditional natural monopoly characteristics, the industry was and still is primarily regulated through yardstick regulation, although the regulator did make substantial and successful efforts to foster competition for activities such as maintenance and the construction of additions to the network.

    However, there have been recent suggestions that the industry could move towards a system of competitive tendering for contracts to operate water supply companies, as the management of Dwr Cymru, the Welsh water and sewerage company, has recently been contracted out (Thomas, 2000). Moreover, the 1998 Competition Act, which came into effect in 2000, has also spurred efforts to introduce stronger supply competition. Thus the introduction of common carriage on the pipeline network and competition in water supply has, in recent years, become a policy priority. In fact, competition in water supply through common carriage on the pipeline network for all customers using more than 50 millilitres of water per year has been proposed in draft legislation (DEFRA, 2002). Nevertheless, it is much too early to determine whether these efforts to introduce competition into the industry will evolve into even a moderately successful liberalized water supply market.

2. Recently, the Labour government has begun replacing the individual regulators or directors general with a commission or Regulatory Authority. Thus, for example, the 2000 Utilities Act not only merged OFGAS and OFFER into the Office of Gas and Electricity Markets (OFGEM), but also transferred all the individual regulators' powers and duties to the Gas and Electricity Market Authority (GEMA) which is made up of a group of executive and non-executive directors and a chairperson.

3. BT's international call rates were liberalized in 1996 and are no longer subject to price regulation. Given BT's lack of control of foreign networks, a thriving competitive market has developed and eliminated the need for price caps.

4. This action is consistent with the industry-specific regulators' new powers under the 1998 Competition Act to enforce access for potential suppliers to essential capital facilities unless a refusal can be justified (Parker, 2000).

5. It must be noted that, owing to the increasing level of competition in domestic call services, the rigour of this new price cap is substantially less than in previous price determinations. The new cap is RPI-RPI with current inflation rates in the range of 1.5–2.5 per cent, while the earlier price cap, which expired in 2001, had been RPI − 4.5 per cent.

6. According to OFTEL, the requirement to provide wholesale line rental to other operators on cost-based and non-discriminatory terms would allow competitors to take on the retail relationship with the customer, who could offer a 'single bill' to end users for all telecommunications services. It would also provide customers in areas not served by cable operators with a choice of access providers. In addition, OFTEL believes that service providers might introduce innovative tariffs that could change the 'balance' between line rentals and call charges (OFTEL, 2002).

7. OFTEL is empowered to prevent cross-subsidy or linked provision of licence-required and non-required BT services, to ensure that BT does not discriminate unduly or drive out competitors by price cutting and to ensure that all networks have fair and reasonable access to each other.

8. Vickers and Yarrow (1988) had previously called for a similar restructuring of BT.

9. The apparently successful operation of four competing national mobile phone networks in the UK demonstrates that, given sufficient demand, telephone networks are not necessarily natural monopolies. However, as the technology and hence the MES of mobile phone networks are substantially different from landline networks, we cannot directly interpret this as evidence that BT's landline network should be broken up.

10. This is because of the large asymmetry between the network monopolist and its competitors who must buy access to the monopolist's network (Armstrong, 1997).

11. It is interesting to note that a similar course of events appears to characterize broadband networks, where duplication of local access infrastructure, using both fixed and wireless technologies, has been concentrated in densely populated areas (Michalis, 2001). Moreover, the spread of fixed broadband services is being encouraged through the competitive resale of a wholesale broadband product provided by BT.

12. This is despite arguments that new telecommunications technologies have eroded the natural monopoly characteristics of landline networks, as for example put forward by Michalis (2001) and Newbery (1999).

13. As Newbery's (1999) discussion reveals, the Gas Act allows for transport licences for firms other than Transco. However, as 89 per cent of households were within 23 metres of British Gas mains, and a new transporter must have the approval of the incumbent transporter to gain a licence for a new main within 23 metres of another main, the scope for competition is limited. As Newbery points out, new licence holders typically extend the low-pressure system into new housing estates, which does allow competitive pressure

to be exerted on the cost of installing new mains.

14.   Privatization and regulation of electricity in England and Wales was carried out separately from Scotland and Northern Ireland, and we focus on it here, given that the English and Welsh market dominates the UK market. Significant differences do exist and, for example, the Scottish industry retained a vertically integrated structure after its privatization in 1991. Scottish Power has subsequently become a significant player in the English and Welsh market through its purchase of Manweb's supply and distribution business. Moreover, with the growth of competition and consolidation of firms, there is increasing convergence between the Scottish and English and Welsh markets and their regulation.

15.   Given the natural monopoly characteristics of the ex-PES distribution companies, the DNOs remain subject to $RPI - X$ price regulation.

16.   Given the market power of the main generators, the Electricity Pool had effectively become a daily repeated game, where the competitors had developed effective strategies to facilitate collusion (Newbery, 1999).

17.   This point is reinforced if we consider that, despite Britain's aim to produce 10 per cent of its energy from renewable sources by 2010, in the last year the proportion has actually fallen from 2.8 to 2.6 per cent (*Economist*, 2002). However, this decline may or may not be attributable to the establishment of the NETA in March 2001.

18.   The failure to price externalities properly in the UK's generation industry has contributed to British Energy's difficulties. While British Energy's high costs are largely due to the need to set aside finance for the future costs of dealing with nuclear waste, it does not contribute to climate change because nuclear power does not emit greenhouse gases. Nevertheless, nuclear power in the UK is subject to the same climate levy as generators using fossil fuels, resulting in a perverse tax on British Energy's output that amounts to £80mn per year (Taylor, 2002b).

19.   The industry has also become increasingly foreign-owned with, for example, 10 of the 12 DNOs being ultimately owned by a foreign-based parent company. Similarly, as of July 2002, PowerGen and Innnogy (National Power's successor) were respectively owned by the German firms E.ON AG and RWE AG.

20.   As the DNOs are individually licensed, DNOs coming under common ownership still must maintain a degree of separation to facilitate the comparative efficiency exercises necessary for yardstick regulation of their monopoly distribution businesses. OFGEM acknowledges that this will allow only some efficiency measures to be produced, but our discussion also suggests that the reliability of these measures may be suspect.

21.   The merger received regulatory approval and was completed in October 2002.

References

Armstrong, M. (1997) 'Competition in Telecommunications', *Oxford Review of Economic Policy*, 13(1), 64–82.

Armstrong, M., S. Cowan, and J. Vickers (1994) *Regulatory Reform: Economic Analysis and British Experience*, London: MIT Press.

Averch, H. and L. Johnson (1962) 'Behaviour of the Firm Under Regulatory Constraint', *American Economic Review*, 52(5), 1052–69.

Bell, A. (1995) 'The Telecommunications Industry, 1994–95', in P. Vass (ed.), *CRI Regulatory Review 1995*. London: CIPFA.

Biggar, D. (2001) 'When Should Regulated Companies be Vertically Separated?', in G. Amato and L.L. Laudati (eds), *The Anticompetitive Impact of Regulation*, Cheltenham, UK, and Northampton, MA, USA: Edward Elgar.

Butler, J. (1998) 'Regulating Telecommunications: Lessons from the UK', in P. Vass (ed.), *Network Industries in Europe: Preparing for Competition*,. London: CIPFA.

Cave, M. (1996) 'Recent Developments in the Regulation of Former Nationalized Industries' in G. Yarrow and P. Jasinski: (eds.), *Privatization Critical Perspectives on the World Economy*, vol. II, London: Routledge.

Cook, P. (1998) 'Privatization in the UK: Policy and Performance', in D. Parker (ed.),

Privatization in the European Union: Theory and Policy Perspectives, London: Routledge.
DEFRA (2002) *Extending Opportunities for Competition in the Water Industry in England and Wales: Consultation Document*, London: Department for Environment, Food and Rural Affairs.
DTI (2001) *UK Energy Sector Indicators 2001*, London: Department of Trade and Industry.
EA (2002a) *Electricity Industry Review*, 6, London: The Electricity Association.
EA (2002b) *Who Owns Whom in the UK Electricity Industry*, London: The Electricity Association.
Economist (2002) 'How Green is Our Tony?', 7 September, pp. 34–5.
Fitzgerald, L. and C. Waddams Price (2001) 'Gas Regulation', in P. Vass (ed.), *Regulatory Review 2000/2001: Millennium Edition*, Bath, UK: Centre for the Study of Regulated Industries.
Foster, C.D. (1992) *Privatization, Public Ownership, and the Regulation of Natural Monopoly*, Oxford: Blackwell.
Giulietti, M. and J. Otero (2002) 'The Timing of Tariff Structure Changes in Regulated Industries: Evidence from England and Wales', *Structural Change and Economic Dynamics*, 13, 71–99.
Gönenc, R., M. Maher and G. Nicoletti (2001) 'The Implementation and Effects of Regulatory Reform: Past Experience and Current Issues', *OECD Economic Studies*, 32(1), 11–98.
Helm, D. (1994) 'British Utility Regulation: Theory, Practice, and Reform', *Oxford Review of Economic Policy*, 10(3), 17–39.
Helm, D. (2001) 'Making Britain More Competitive: A Critique of Regulation and Competition Policy', *Scottish Journal of Political Economy*, 48(5), 471–87.
Helm, D. and T. Jenkinson (1997) 'The Assessment: Introducing Competition to Regulated Industries', *Oxford Review of Economic Policy*, 13(1), 1–14.
Hunt, L.C. and E.L. Lynk (1990) 'Divestiture of Telecommunications in the UK: A Time Series Analysis?', *Oxford Bulletin of Economics and Statistics*, 52, 229–52.
Hunt, L.C. and E.L. Lynk (1991) 'Competition in UK Telecommunications: Restructure BT?', *Fiscal Studies*, 12(3), 73–87.
Littlechild, S. (1983) *Regulation of British Telecommunications' Profitability*, London: HMSO.
Littlechild, S. (2001) 'Electricity Regulation', in P. Vass (ed.), *Regulatory Review 2000/2001: Millennium Edition*, Bath, UK: Centre for the Study of Regulated Industries.
Markou, E. and C. Waddams Price (1999) 'UK Utilities: Past Reform and Current Proposals', *Annals of Public and Cooperative Economics*, 70(3), 371–416.
McDaniel, T. (2000) 'Deregulation of the UK Electricity Supply Industry: 1989–98', in M. Kagami and M. Tsuji (eds), *Privatization, Deregulation and Economic Efficiency: A Comparative Analysis of Asia, Europe and the Americas*, Cheltenham, UK and Northampton, MA, USA: Edward Elgar.
Michalis, M. (2001) 'Local Competition and the Role of Regulation: The EU Debate and Britain's Experience', *Telecommunications Policy*, 25, 759–76.
National Audit Office (2002) *Pipes and Wires*, London: HM Stationery Office.
Newbery, D.M. (1999) *Privatization, Restructuring, and Regulation of Network Industries*, London: MIT Press.
Newbery, D.M. and M.G. Pollitt (1997) 'The Restructuring and Privatization of Britain's CEGB – Was it Worth It?', *Journal of Industrial Economics*, 45(3), 269–303.
Nwankwo, S. and B. Richardson (1996) 'The UK's Privatized Utilities Experience: Why the Regulators are Under Attack', *International Journal of Public Sector Management*, 9(3), 26–39.
OECD (2001) *Restructuring Public Utilities for Competition*, Paris: Organisation for Economic Cooperation and Development.
OFGEM (2001) *Annual Report 2000–2001*, London: Office of Gas and Electricity Markets.
OFGEM (2002a) *Review of Domestic Gas and Electricity Competition and Supply Price Regulation: Conclusions and Final Proposals*, London: Office of Gas and Electricity Markets.
OFGEM (2002b) *Mergers in the Electricity Distribution Sector: Policy Statement*, London:

Office of Gas and Electricity Markets.

OFGEM (2002c) *London Electricity Group plc's Proposed Acquisition of CSW Investments (the holding company of SEEBOARD Group plc): A Consultation Paper*, London: Office of Gas and Electricity Markets.

OFGEM (2002d) *Regulatory Issues Arising From the Merger of National Grid Group plc and Lattice Group plc to Create National Grid Transco plc: Initial Proposals*, London: Office of Gas and Electricity Markets.

OFTEL (2001) *Proposals for Network Charge and Retail Price Controls from 2001*, London: Office of Telecommunications.

OFTEL (2002) *Protecting Consumers by Promoting Competition: Oftel's Conclusions – 20 June 2002*, London: Office of Telecommunications.

Parker, D. (2000) 'Reforming Competition Law in the UK: The Competition Act, 1998', *Economic Issues*, 5(1), 69–85.

Pollitt, M. (2000) 'A Survey of the Liberalization of Public Enterprises in the UK Since 1979', in M. Kagami and M. Tsuji (eds), *Privatization, Deregulation and Economic Efficiency: A Comparative Analysis of Asia, Europe and the Americas*, Cheltenham, UK and Northampton, MA, USA: Edward Elgar.

Prosser, T. (1999) 'Theorising Utility Regulation', *The Modern Law Review*, 62(2), 196–217.

Rossi, M.A. and C.A. Ruzzier (2000) 'On the Regulatory Application of Efficiency Measures', *Utilities Policy*, 9, 81–92.

Sawkins, J.W. (1995) 'Yardstick Competition in the English and Welsh Water Industry', *Utilities Policy*, 5(1), 27–36.

Shleifer, A. (1985) 'A Theory of Yardstick Competition', *Rand Journal of Economics*, 16(3), 319–27.

Stelzer, I.M. (2002) 'A Review of Privatization and Regulation Experience in the UK', in C. Robinson (ed.), *Utility Regulation and Competition Policy*, Cheltenham, UK and Northampton, MA, USA: Edward Elgar.

Taylor, A. (2002a) 'Perils of Increased Competition', *Financial Times*, 6 September, p. 4.

Taylor, A. (2002b) 'Cost of Electricity at Heart of British Energy Plight', *Financial Times*, 6 September, p. 4.

Thomas, D. (2000) 'Hyder: The Rise and Fall of a Multi-Utility', *Utilities Policy*, 9, 181–92.

Vickers, J. and G. Yarrow (1988) *Privatization: An Economic Analysis*, London: MIT Press.

Weir, C. (1999) 'Regulation and the Development of Competition in the U.K. Gas Supply Industry', *Review of Industrial Organization*, 15, 135–47.

Index

A.H. Plant 181
ABB 422
Acciones Y Valores de Mexico 269
Accival brokerage house 269
accountability of regulatory agencies 525–7
accounting measures, Canada 142–6
ACSA 305
Act of Leasing of State Enterprises 1992, Ukraine 464
Act on State Enterprises 1981, Poland 405
Adam Smith Institute 62
administration costs 544–5
Administrative Conference of the United States 524
administrative law 517–18, 529, 530
Aeromexico 277
Aérospatiale Matra 106
Africa 3, 28, 87, 89, 90, 91, 93, 96, 217, 291–2, 298, 304, 305–6, 307, 539, 552
African Financial Community (CFA) 315
African National Congress (ANC) 12, 291, 294, 297, 299, 300, 307, 308
AGP 121
Agra Industries 130
agribusinesses, Ukraine 466
agricultural cooperatives, Hungary 431
agricultural land
  Hungary 431, 432
  Russia 354
agriculture sector
  China 236–9, 250–2, 256
  developing economies 209
  Hungary 429, 430–2, 435, 439
  Poland 423
  Russia 354
  sub-Saharan Africa 310, 312, 315
  Ukraine 454, 466, 469, 470
Air Canada 143–6, 147, 155

air traffic control
  Canada 131, 136
  UK 111
aircraft manufacturers, Brazil 223
airlines 262
  Australia 169
  Chile 282
  European Union 107, 108–9, 111, 116, 118
  Hungary 433, 435
  Mexico 277
  South Africa 296, 297, 305, 307, 319
  sub-Saharan Africa 311, 315
  UK 41
  Western Europe 28
airports
  Australia 182
  Canada 131–2, 156
  Czech Republic 384
  European Union 109, 111
  South Africa 305
  UK 190
  USA 154–5, 156
Airtouch-Vodafone 433
Alberta Energy 130
Alcatel-Alsthom 106
Alestra 281
Allianz 434
allocative efficiency 65–9, 489
ALUSAF 293
Amalgamated Wireless Australia 162
American Depository Receipts (ADR) 278, 370
Ameritech International Ltd 433
Amtrak 153–4
Amtrak Reform and Accountability Act 1997 154
An Accelerated Agenda towards the Restructuring of State-owned Enterprises 291–2
Anglo-American Corporation 315
Anglo-Saxon principal-agent approach 387–8
Angola 316